STILL WILD

BOOK THREE OF THE ALASKA OFF GRID SURVIVAL SERIES

MILES MARTIN

ALASKA DREAMS PUBLISHING

Still Wild
By Miles Martin

Book Three of The Alaska Off Grid Survival Series

Published by:
Alaska Dreams Publishing
www.alaskadp.com
1st ADP Edition August 2021
PRINT PAPERBACK ISBN: 978-1-956303-02-5
PRINT HARDCOVER ISBN: 978-1-956303-03-2
This book was previously published by Miles of Alaska

Visit www.milesofalaska.com to find a bio of Miles, additional photos, stories, how-to videos, handmade artwork, and raw materials for sale.

Working on snow machine on the remote homestead. If I cannot fix it I have to walk fifty miles to the village.

CONTENTS

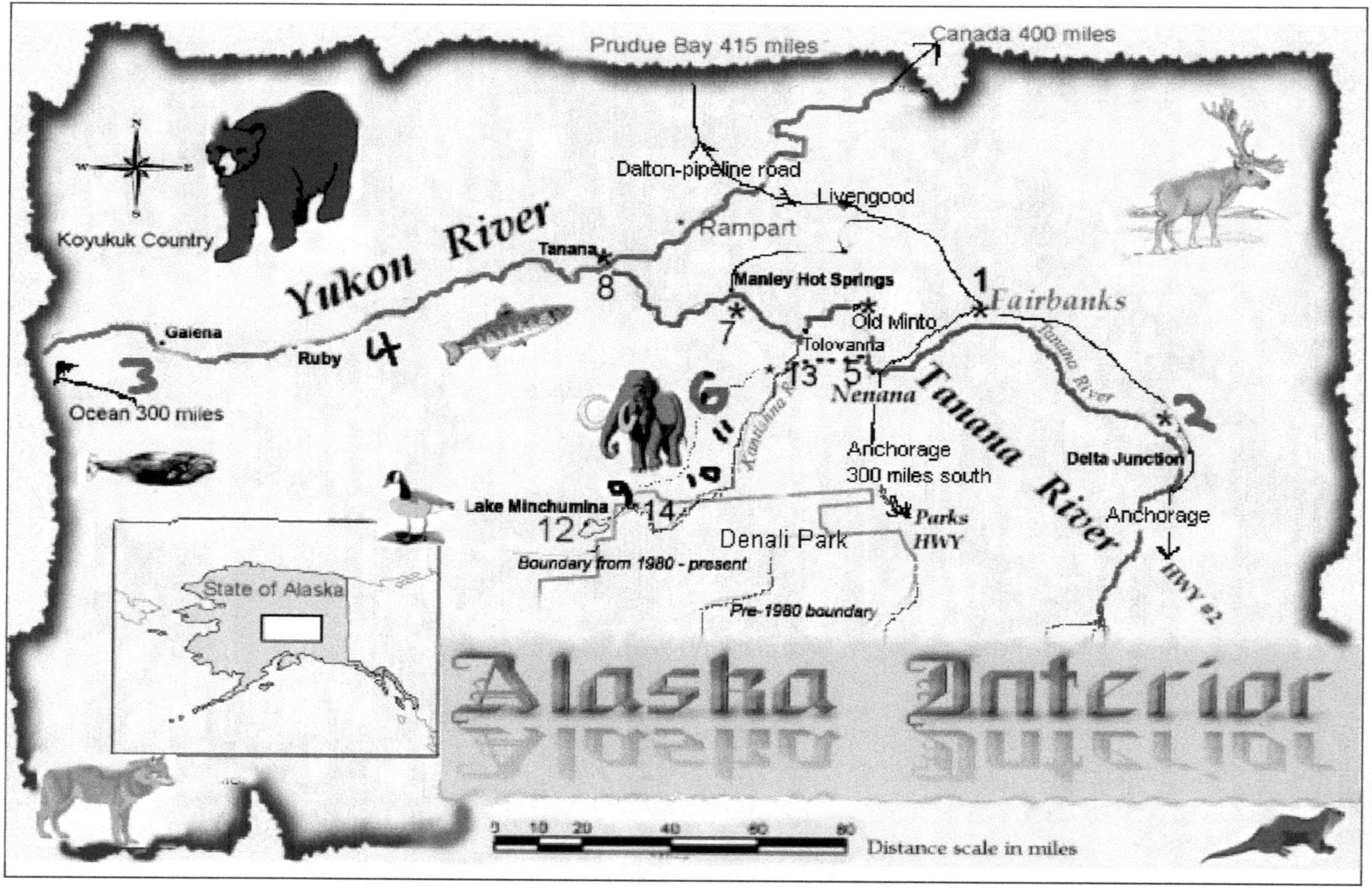
Prudue Bay 415 miles
Canada 400 miles
Dalton-pipeline road
Livengood
Rampart
Koyukuk Country
Yukon River
Tanana
8
Manley Hot Springs
1
Fairbanks
Old Minto
Galena
Ruby
4
7
Tolovanna
3
13
5
Nenana
Tanana River
Ocean 300 miles
6
11
2
Delta Junction
Anchorage
300 miles south
10
9
Lake Minchumina
14
12
Parks HWY
Denali Park
Anchorage
HWY #2
Boundary from 1980 - present
Pre-1980 boundary
State of Alaska
Alaska Interior
0 10 20 40 60 80
Distance scale in miles

The Interior of Alaska

When you step into this map, you have left civilization. This area is so different from the civilized world that it is almost like coming to another planet. In an area that covers 400,000 square miles, the largest community is Fairbanks—40,000 people. There are more communities on this map with under 100 people, then over 100 people.

There are more bears than people on this map. More Salmon run upstream to spawn in a one-month period, then the number of tourists the entire state gets in ten years. If you got lost and lived long enough, it would be possible to spend the next twenty years walking and never see another human. This is a world where if you arrive without bug dope in the summer or mukluks in winter it might cost you your life. This is a world where if you get in trouble you don't dial 911... and the laws of nature, not man, rules supreme.

I have given numbers to the places various things happened that will be referred to throughout the book. You can come back to the map to see where that is.

#1 Is **Fairbanks,** the hub of the interior. A city of about 40,000. Where I get supplies, sell my art, fly in and out of the state, sell furs, and where all the government offices are that need visiting for permits, going to court, etc. Note the map insert lower left to show what part of the state this map covers.

#2 Big Delta, where the houseboat was built (book one.)

#3 Galena, Native hub of interior Yukon River, no road to outside world, furthest I ever boated and spent a winter.

#4 Yukon River, a hot spot for finding fossils locals call 'the bone yard,' but now off limits as a Federal preserve

#5 Nenana, the village of 300 people along the Tanana River where my houseboat gets permanently parked, my friend Josh lives, and I end up buying a house.

#6 My trapline, is the dotted line between #5 Nenana and #12 Lake Minchumina with a loop close to the Kantishna river. Also acquire a Federal homesite here I call 'The Federal place.' More important in previous book.

#7 Manley Hot Springs, a village of eighty people at the end of a road and along a slough connected to the Tanana River. I pass this village going downriver, spent a winter hear in the houseboat have many friends here get gas here sometimes.

#8 Tanana, a village of 300 people on the Yukon River, at the mouth of the Tanana River. No road to the outside world. I often get gas here, have friends here, and stop on river trips.

#9 Park boundary, Back side of Denali park unmarked. My trapline crosses into the new park boundary, but I am grandfathered in to be able to continue to trap. I assume. This never became an issue but could have.

#10 Hansen Lake, My first time on the Kantishna after leaving Lake Minchumina I live on my houseboat here and have my first sled dog experiences. I have a trail here going up the hind leg of the mammoth that passes through two map lake and connects to the trapline through one of my remote camps and Wien lake where there are other trappers. I struggle with the trails in the area, rough ground.

#11 Bearpaw homestead, furthest upriver interest I struggle to get supplies in here, hard to afford the gas, big plans to live more remote here that never panned out.

#12 Lake Minchumina, largest lake in the interior at eight miles across, community of twenty people on the park boundary. Beautiful at the base of Mt McKinley. I spent time here on the houseboat, got my mail here for a while, more relevant in previous books. A few people I met here are friends who are mentioned in this book. I'm a little vague because many friends do not wish to be identified. In a community of twenty people there is a "Well Da! Guess who this is!"

INTRODUCTION

This is the third book in a series. When I first wrote this, I was twenty-five years old, 'writing as it happens'. Fresh and raw. However, at sixty-nine years old, I see a lot of edit issues I want to fix! I was so smart at twenty-five! The older I get, the less I know, sigh. So here we are with an updated 'fix'. The stories are the same, still mine in my words, but figured out the difference between to and too, coarse and course.

Though it is not absolutely necessary to have read the first two, the intent is to have a series read in order. The series follows chronologically, my dream, then reality of real life as an Alaskan wilderness trapper mountain man. The dream evolves. I become more of just a homesteader than mountain-man.

In book one, I pay a pilot to drop me off in the Alaska wilderness. I was raised in the city, middle class, a product of the 60s. A baby boomer. Some of my peers thought of living in communes, I wanted to do it alone. I felt qualified to be a mountain man because I had watched every Walt Disney movie ever made. I watched the Davy Crockett show on TV every week, so of course, know what I talking about! I made no arrangements to get picked up. I planned to walk out of the wilderness in a year. Bets were placed on how many days I'd survive. I have my diary and memories, so write about it as I go, and begin book one as I live it, starting the book in 1972. I need to build a cabin, learn how to shoot a rifle, and trap. I deal with bears, get lost, fall through the ice. I make my own soap, my own leather, all talked about in the book. I saw sixty below zero, and survived the first winter, then walked out, as I said I would.

The second year did not go as well. Not enough money for supplies, much got stolen, maybe overconfident now. I do not make it through the winter and am starving to death. I try to snowshoe out at fifty below zero, but do not make it. My rescue makes international headlines. I decide to build a houseboat, so I do not have to build cabins. Cabin building takes all summer, the best time of the year. I also do not want to worry about whose land I am on. I can travel around, check out other areas to see where I might wish to settle. The Yukon River is too big I think. I want a creek no one goes on, where I can be more alone. Book one ends.

In book two 'Gone Wild' I am no longer 'going' but have arrived. Life on the houseboat and what that is like. I live on it in winter and trap. There are more bear stories, moose hunting stories, survival stories of all kinds. My only transportation is a boat in summer, and sled dogs in winter. No driver's license, no ID, no bills, rent, and no alarm clock. I do some art and describe well, a basic subsistence life-style, living with the land, at one with nature. Again as in book one, based on my diary and written as I live it. My life is rated 'R.' Not for the squeamish, or faint of heart. It's a Bambi story, all the various ways Bambi might be served, with potatoes or rice. Yes, it is a book about how to get along and take care of the planet and keep it healthy as well, focus in 'Reality'.

This book, the third in the series "Still Wild" is more than, 'I have arrived.' I not only survive, but prosper. I cut 200 hundred miles of trapline and acquire four homesteads. My art is selling well. I have some part time seasonal work as a wilderness land surveyor. I'm working with a friend surveying homesteads and Indian lands. It reads much like book two, still calling the house-boat home. I do begin to have issues with the legal aspect of my lifestyle. Hinted at in the previous books, but getting more serious in book three. I'm accused of taking a moose out of season, doing artwork on an illegal bear claw, and murder. This becomes maybe an interesting read, as two cultures and lifestyles collide. Many issues come up! Gun rights, conservation, wolf management, Indian rights, land use, subsistence issues, etc. I am forced to buy a snow machine and give up sled dogs. I get married, have a child, then lose it all. I'm restless, unsure what to do next. Lived my wilderness dream, had all the challenges. The dream I had as a child has been realized, and as I grow, and mature, the dream and goals change. Book three ends.

This could be called a biography, except I want the freedom to move events around to make it more readable. As I said in a previous book, I killed seven bears in five days once; it makes better reading to spread that out. In real life there are hundreds of people who I know, and who affect my life. I change the names, and attribute some conversations and events to the main 'characters', to keep the number down to forty-two which is already a lot of people for a reader to remember!

With a wolverine off the trapline.

CHAPTER ONE

LIFE ON THE HOUSEBOAT. SLED DOGS ON THE BOAT. ANSWER MAIL I HAVE RECEIVED AFTER FOUR MONTHS IN THE WILD

I am sitting in my houseboat on the Tanana River pulled over for the night with the sled dogs tied up on the riverbank, at least fifty miles from the nearest village or road. It's a day like most others 'except.' Except I got a copy of the Geo magazine with my article in it. The Alaska special. GEO in Europe I gather, is the equivalent of the US National Geographic. I see the picture of the Alaska Husky on the cover. Dated December 1987. I'm seeing it for the first time in summer because this is the first I have picked up my mail in six months. Thumbing through it I see I am near the middle, a big double page color picture of me with a frozen moose hind quarter, Marten fur hat on, snow in the background. Another huge color picture of my Kantishna River cabin. *Ah, yes the picture of me ice fishing and the one of the tent set up in the wild.* The photographer was right; he could edit out the garden fence. I smile to myself. *"If people only knew the truth behind the news and the stories they read and believe!"* The visit and the events took place in 1983, four years ago. I cannot read it because it is written in German, but do note its eight full pages about me.

The photographer, Jean Eric Pasquier is one of the best in the world, and had just won the world press photo award for his pictures of the Pope. Jean spent over a week living with me alone in the wilds getting pictures. I remember his words:

"Yes Miles, I was John Lennon's photographer for a while. I mean what I say when I tell you I am not sent out on dead end stories. GEO does not send a photographer to do uninteresting stories about unworthy people. John asked the same things as you, why me? What is the big deal? What is the fuss about? It is all a sham.

You Miles, like John Lennon, are one of the best in the world at what you do, and that's why I'm here to record it." Impressive words. However, words are cheap.

"Who knows what the truth really is." My unconscious runs in the background, superimposed on what Jean is telling me, like subtitles to an old fashion film. "A woman we loved and trusted asked us to notice how 'everyone' who admires us is in the bleachers. No one close to me who knows me, truly respects me. I am a joke." It is not relevant to anyone. I am a King of what? Nothing. A bunch of useless trees. Dad is honestly puzzled. So I think, "How can your parents, and the woman of your life be wrong? And some reporter here on a job be right? That doesn't make sense." I explain to Jean. I am all excited to show the world 'the truth' about the wild. Pictures taken on the trapline 100 miles down the trail recording my life, the life of a subsistence trapper modern day mountain man. Recorded by a world famous photographer. This is my chance for a quiet reply to my woman and my relatives, this lifestyle is not just about me tooting my horn. "You want to know who cares? Look at this!" Someone standing up for me, so that I may keep my mouth shut. Also, a way to show the flip side of the Walt Disney, Bambi version of the wilderness. The truth. Therefore, this is important to me, a chance to be part of reality, real pictures. Jean is in front of my log cabin and says:

"This will do." In puzzlement I ask:

"What will do?" I remember it clear as if it were today. Jean tells me all the pictures he needs will be taken right here near the cabin. "The batteries in the camera would fail if out in the cold long. The camera is sensitive and cannot handle the rough sled trip. Right here where we are, there are the same trees as 100 miles down the trail." It makes sense. Just not what I expected. Sort of fake, sort of a con job. Editing my fence out in the lab and all that. Isn't that sort of what those close to me say I am doing? Editing my life to make it appealing to others? A con job, misrepresenting my life and myself. Leading to conversations with Jean about 'truth,' 'reality,' what sells, what the public wants, what is legal, etc. Thinking back, these conversations were a turning point in my life. Many things began to make more sense. I do not have the reputation of taking advice well, nor caring what others have to say. So many who offer advice are speaking from what position? A bar stool? Someone from the bleachers of life? It is rare that I am in the presence of an expert at anything. The best in the world at what he does. Jean says:

"Reality does not sell papers, dreams do. If I took the truth back to my boss it would not get printed."

"Doesn't that bother you? Aren't you an ethical person who wants the truth?" He laughed because I am so naïve. Also, sadly because he wants to record the truth, as much as I do!

"The truth is what we make it. The truth is what we say it is. The truth is all in everyone's head along with reality." I am puzzled. Jean goes on, "We must spoon feed the truth to the public. If we can manage to get one spoonful of truth and reality into an article, we have done our part and done a good job." Jean and I had such discussions in the dark Alaska wilderness. He was honestly interested in my views, and how I survive. I have answers others want to hear about. He wants to understand, in order to capture me on film.

His secret to success and greatness he tells me, is blending in, becoming the environment he finds himself in. I agree. I do the same thing in a way.

"When learning to follow the river channel I used to ask myself what would I do if I were water? I became the water and knew where to go." It sounds stupid to say, but he understood.

The best photographer in the world is explaining the meaning of life. Or maybe wants to talk to me, and we are understanding each other. Almost like equals. It is hard to forget, as I look over now, on the houseboat, the winter pictures in the magazine.

My mind leaves the article and story behind for a moment. The seven sled dogs I have with me are hungry. I hear chains rattle on dishes, with a few whines now and then. I stick my head out the houseboat door. All the dogs faces stop and stare. I try not to change my expression, frozen, with just my head in view as the dogs study me. It is a game we play. *"What am I thinking, what am I going to do next?"* I want them to know me so well they can anticipate my next move. Read my mind. They can, and they do. Both our lives sometimes depend on it. Therefore, I teach it.

"We are what we eat!" I say to them and they all wag tails at once. From that one sentence, they know all about me right now. I am in a good mood. I know it is dinnertime. We did well today. Everyone can relax. I stick my head back in the houseboat and get ready to feed them.

I play the 'whose dish is this' routine as I often do. I mix all their cans up. They are all # 10 coffee cans, shuffled and moved with gestures imitating a great magician —man of magic- up on stage. I hold one up for inspection. *Behold! Nothing up my sleeve.* I bow to the right, bow to the left. They all stare close. The dog that can recognize his dish first, gets to eat first, but if he gets it wrong, he eats last. Each name is written on the bottom of the can so I know. Some dogs I notice over time, are really, really good at it. In fact, I suspect they recognize their food can by the sound it makes as I touch it. Not by sight. This gives me insight as to how their mind works and how to give commands.

For example; I learned to stomp on the runners when mushing, to make a sound and vibration to tell the dogs where I want them to go. They must distinguish a command stomp from a stomp just warming my feet. Each dog can identify to me their own harness as well. Important in the pitch dark when I cannot see. I ask: "Whose is this?" and only one dog barks.

Today I am trying to teach the new six-month-old puppies how to identify their dish and give them a chance to learn the game. I tap the can and hold it high and very visible. The older dogs know this in itself means it is a puppy can, not an adult can. Thus, some elders do not even look. I give other hints so the puppies can learn. "Is this your can Salt? Is this your can Pepper?" The choice is now only between two dogs that are about the size of their food can, who now have to decide whose can it is. "I think it might be Salt's can, what do you think Salt?" Salt barks. "Very good! I do believe you are correct!" Salt gets to eat first. I'm pretty sure tomorrow if I hold up Pepper's can and ask Salt if it is his, Salt will bark. I will be disappointed and feed Salt last. Thus, Salt will learn to pay closer attention and figure out, there is a difference between the two cans. He had better figure out if he wants to be served before Pepper gets served. Our life is filled with these little games. *Not games, Life lessons!*

Yes, the way the world operates. The dogs learn to watch and pay attention to every little thing I do and say. I am constantly trying to trick them, fool them, and play practical jokes on them. We live together twenty-four hours a day. Our lives depend on each other. These games teach what is yours, and what is mine, and what is your neighbors. *Our first dog ate our wallet and the only pair of shoes, remember?* My unconscious reminds me, and yes, I recall now, after the reminder. We all learn the smart come in first, pay attention to what others around you are doing, where does food come from, how do we get it, and why? Those dogs who also know where thin ice is, where we are going, can make good decisions, are higher up in the pecking order and have more group status. I reward that with more favors.

The fish net I put out is set in the river eddy overnight. The net catches five Chum Salmon at ten pounds each. Each dog gets five pounds. But only during this time of year when there are so many fish in the river. About 5:00 am I begin my day checking the net, then boiling the fish in two five-gallon buckets, old gas cans with the lid cut out and a bail put in. I cook over an open fire on the sandy beach using drift wood. Either rice is added or cornmeal, and whatever else there is at hand. Sometimes my own leftovers. Sometimes a squirrel or rabbit, or feathers and guts off a goose, or pieces of hide and fat. There are plants to pick that go in the pot, that I know the dogs will eat, and are good for the dogs. Carrot tops, outer cabbage leaves if I am at a garden, or if traveling, young willow leaves, tender roots of about anything along the river. My reason came from the bloodline of the dogs – the wild creatures that eat game. The stomach content of game is an important part of the predator diet. So what is in the tummy of creatures that wolves eat? Well, what do moose eat, and rabbits? Partly digested vegetation of all kinds. I learned this from Karen who I miss. (sigh) She knows a lot about nutrition. My first clear impression of her is her three-year-old daughter going out to pick a wild salad. Impressed, I ask what she has picked and she knows the Latin names.

"This is Equisetum." Karen also taught the subtle differences in health between the dogs, and who needed what in the diet. I had never paid attention. In the early days, if a dog could not make it, he was shot. Life in general was much harsher in those early years. It took many years to see what Karen saw, and what Josh, the famous musher saw when he says:

"Dog no good, does not have round wrists! Feel it? " 'Round' is light and strong, like an aluminum tent pole. Take away the round, make it flat, and the pole breaks. I scratch Cinnamon behind the ears. As her eyes close, I remind her she has round bones. This year's batch of pups I named after spices. The last litter was Bullet, Case, Primer, and Powder. Cinnamon tries to lick my face.

"Yulk-0! That's disgusting Cinnamon! You probably just got done licking your butt!" Everyone wags their tail and must think that's funny. "Funny is it? All of you are disgusting!" All the dogs smile, agree, and see I am laughing too. "Okay, okay, all right I guess I meant 'we' are all disgusting. After all, the sled dogs and I have more in common with each other than I have in common with the human race. Uncivilized and savaged. That is fine. I consider 'civilized' an insult. I am ashamed of what civilization is doing to the earth, and how civilized people behave. It is enough to make a savage weep. How do I come to terms with the fact I am human? Surely, the road to survival, peace, happiness is not the road of hate—resentment-embarrassment of my species. Before I can understand civilization and others, I must first understand myself. To give, I must first have. But what do I have? Well, in my own eyes, I own the world. I am a King. By civilized standards, I own what? Am what? Only one tiny step above a dumpster diver according to how I am treated by most. *"Except our fans!"* Ya, and as I was so nicely told, fans are "people who don't know me well," and do not live in Alaska, and are not close to me!

The dogs all find a place to curl up in the dust and leaves, to sleep for the night. Unconsciously I take note to see if any seem sore, in a bad mood, tired, out of sorts. As a factory boss might watch his employees punch the time clock and note who is laughing, who is tired, and who slams the door. Words from a book 'White Dawn,' I am reading again for the fourth time comes to me.

"There is one thing and one thing only. To rise. To turn your face from the dark night and greet the White Dawn. Arise!" Or, something like that. Get up and greet the day, whatever the day has to offer, lucky we are here to see it. So primitive, so savage. This is such a simple uncomplicated truth. A basic truth filled with beauty. *How could anyone 500 years ago come up with that? Why doesn't modern man get it?*

Survival is not just about killing, and hunkering down in the cold, nor is it just about the individual. For me to survive, the planet has to survive. For me to survive the human race has to survive, for neither I, nor anyone else can survive alone. So then, what is survival? Is everything connected? I am very puzzled.[1]

I have been living on the houseboat off and on, mostly 'on' for over ten years now. It is a lifestyle and a routine that does not require a lot of thought anymore.

The homestead cabin on what I call, 'the lower Kantishna place,' is sort of home, but I was living on the boat as the cabin was being built. Soon after it was built, I focused on the upper Kantishna that used to be my old stomping grounds trapping. The houseboat is moved 100 miles upriver to Hansen Lake. I built another cabin out the trapline trail, a Federal homestead, but then another homestead that was state land about thirty miles away, on the river again, requiring the houseboat as a home. The houseboat hauls all the main supplies once a year from Fairbanks, 250 miles away, 500 round trip miles. In all those miles, trips, and nights out on the river away from both the homestead and town, there are many wilderness experiences. More days away, then at any homestead, and thus, my 'home,' is the wild and open spaces between the pieces of property I have title to. In the evening, I have the time to open more mail from the pile I picked up in the village of Nenana. I reply to one.

Letter June 1st 1987

Dear Iris

No, I have not forgotten about you, just been out of touch in the wilderness, and just picked up six months of mail.

I pause in my reply. She wrote, reminding me how we met through an ad in a magazine, but I only have a vague memory of the details- about 1984. I have met and written so many women by mail I forget. It's not very real to me anymore, just ink on paper. This feeling is not something nice to write someone though, so I'm polite, and will see what develops. I get back to writing.

Thanks for the tape, looks like music? Yes, I have a battery cassette player and can listen. Yes, I had a good winter! Thanks for asking. I trapped all winter and got okay money for my furs. I sold eighty-nine Marten, my main fur I get. I averaged $75 each, so have learned to take good care of the furs as most trappers averaged ten dollars less. I cut ten more miles of trapline trail. It seems like such slow going. It takes almost a week to get to the end of the trail to start cutting. I must have 150 miles I cut now and got the twelfth trap camp built at the end. I'm trying to tie two ends of trail together. I have twenty more miles to cut. I suppose all this trapline talk is not of great interest to you, but very much on my mind.

My art is selling well enough. However, the big pipeline money is slowing down and I notice that. It takes a month to sell all my art now, when it used to take three days! Ha! Guess I was spoiled, so nothing really to complain about. I wish I could expand my art direction. I do all my work by hand, as you know, with hand tools, no electric, by kerosene or propane light. I did make an improvement with my jeweler's torch this year. I used a bike tire, patched in a hose to the torch and now have forced air to mix with the cabin light propane. I get ten minutes of torch work before I must use the bike pump to blow up the tire again. I'm trying to get away from just gluing my metals. There is only so far I can go with 'glue,' and only so much I can charge for the work! So, I am soldering and pinning the metals now, not just gluing.

I notice I am in competition with other artists who do not have the huge transportation costs I have, and those who have electric power to do in a minute what it takes me an hour to do. I am also competing with third world countries. But, not wanting to work for one dollar a day. It's a challenge to figure out how to find a niche and offer a reason to buy my work for more money. It's one reason to specialize in animal products not available in third world countries due to import, and export laws. Moreover, these animal and nature materials are not uniform, so hard to do production using this material. Selling wolf claws for example, is a limited market and I am at the source, so no one can beat my cost of materials. Still, I see a future with some stumbling blocks I will be challenged by. I need to be prepared.

Customers say they want handmade local art- but fail to say they expect it at rock-bottom prices.[2] I see a lot of discouraged artists. Still, some of the richest people in the world are in the arts! You just have to be in the top ten. Or, more like the top one in 10,000. Just to make a living! I'm lucky to be gifted artistically. I take little credit for it, it's how I was born. The main thing is, I'm happy enough and doing what I want, how I want, when I want, living my dream, and passion. Taking my ability to the limits, whatever those limits might be.

Did I file on my Bearpaw homestead when I last wrote? I'm using the houseboat to prove up on the land. I may decide to just buy it outright from the State as one of the options though. I'll have to see how the money works out. I need engine work done in the houseboat that will cost a lot. Always money huh!? I'm trying to put a tunnel hull in the boat so it draws less water and use a four-cylinder Saab car engine with a marine velvet drive transmission. The engine requires a water-cooled heat exchanger on the exhaust manifold. That is what is holding me up right now.

I had trouble lining up the holes of the metal tunnel I made from a steel drum, with the holes in the hull. I ended up using the 357 magnum pistol and shot in the holes. The wood of the boat hull shattered pretty good from the bullet! But the holes line up now. The wood is fixed with fiberglass. What else is going on? Oh, all kinds of things. Huh? Yes, guess I'm rambling, talking of things you might not know much about. It helps me gather my thoughts when I write. So writing to myself as much as to you.

So how is your Dad? Sounds like he might not be well. You are taking care of him? Yes, that must be hard. Well, take care and will get this in the mail whenever I go to town again. In a few weeks or so. Maybe time later to add more to this. Oh, I almost forgot. I am unsure what kind of duck I did a watercolor of on your envelope. All my mail gets a watercolor. But think you got the puffin, not really a duck, but an Alaska colorful bird living on the ocean.

Sunshine Wild Miles

I set the letter in my, 'outgoing mail' box. Wood is added to the stove on the houseboat. The bow rope is checked to make sure I am secure for the night. Yup, tied to a spruce tree. *Once we were tied to a birch tree. A beaver chewed the tree down in the night and turned the houseboat loose. Woke up way downstream in a logjam.* Sometimes I secure the stern as well as the bow if the weather looks windy, or the water is dropping, or rising fast, but tonight everything looks calm and stable. One last look at the dogs to make sure they are ready for the night. No one has tangled their chain. No one has rolled their food dish in another's yard which might cause an argument in the middle of the night. No sign of porcupine around. All the little things I take in a glance each evening as part of the night ritual. A couple of dogs look up. The rest are already sound asleep. The stove is ready to be shut down for the night. Willow wood smells are in the air. Not wood I'd burn in winter, but this time of year anything will do, since it is not cold out. I'm drawing two feet of water, with almost a foot freeboard above the water line. I've been loaded before, down to only an inch of freeboard. Spooky. *Definitely not recommended!* But my whole life is not recommended, so where does that leave me?

This load is foam insulation for the new cabin at Bearpaw. I call it 'Bearpaw,' but it is really twenty miles further up the Kantishna River then the Bearpaw River. I own four pieces of land now and have to keep them all straight in the diary. I check the tie downs on the foam stacked twelve feet high on the roof of the houseboat. One more day and I should be home. Yawn, call it a day. As I get in bed, I grab the pistol over the door and open the cylinder. A nightly ritual, to check that the first load to come up when I cock it will be the hot load for bears, not the squib loads, for small game. I had been negligent once, had to use three light loads on a charging bear before I dropped him with the hot load. The sound of the river current on the hull puts me to sleep along with the crackle of a turned down stove fire.

In the morning I awake to the sun coming through the window, shifting as the boat swings slightly in the current. Through the window, I see birch leaves from the trees hanging over the water, and in the distance, Bearpaw Mountain with snow still on it. It's 5:00 am, about the usual time I begin my day. The season is headed for the never setting sun times of midsummer. As I get dressed in jeans and a plaid shirt, I hear a male mallard duck give one quiet 'quack' to a female nearby. The normal sound of my breakfast calling. Not even excited, just deciding. In a minute I will step out the door and shoot breakfast.

A blade of grass from yesterday is still on the table. I stick that in my mouth—with the long fuzzy end bouncing around as I get the fire going hotter in the woodstove. A frying pan is out, flour pepper mix I keep handy for coating such meat as duck or fish is next to the pan. The sounds the duck makes, let me know it is not nervous, and is in his 'area' so will stay around, or quickly come back if leaving. There is no hurry to harvest an early breakfast.

Another letter is opened before I begin physical work. Sipping rose hip tea I dried a year ago, steeped on the woodstove in the boat. I sit at the window looking out at the thick morning fog. My hunting knife at my side comes out of its sheath without looking. A routine task needing no thought. With a yawn, I open the letter. From a Guy, not a woman. I tend to open the women's letters first. Well, just on the off chance one of the women is 'her,' and I can identify her, or she has identified me as 'the one.'

Dear Miles

I have a deep respect for the outdoors and the lifestyle you claim to live. I question what you are doing because I see inconsistencies, 'lies' to be blunt. When you first wrote me you told me you got to Alaska in 1972, but later it looks more like 1973! You told me a bear story where you were twenty feet away from the bear, later you say, 'point blank,' so which is it? Did anything even happen if you can't keep your facts straight? You have a cabin, but say you live on a houseboat? I'm disappointed, and others might be as well. Maybe you are like a football player who wants others to see him as better than he is, so talks of touchdowns that never happened, trying to be a hero, being nothing but a person with an ego problem. I don't trust what you say anymore, though I do not understand, you seem like a nice enough person, a good con artist I guess! **Later, Bud**

Hey Bud

Well, there may be 'some truth' in what you say, but it leaves out 'my side of the story.' How to explain. Some people believe there is only one truth, one way to do things, the right way. The way they have learned. Some people see me as manipulating the facts to suit myself. Playing semantics and word games. Possibly, or partly true. But, I argue there are many ways to tell the same set of facts and each way has a different impact on the reader, and each can be correct, but each leaves something out because we don't have time for every detail, of every aspect, of every fact, of every event. Every recording of an event is a bias one, because details the teller believes are relevant are quoted, while other facts are left out. Some people remember names dates times and numbers well, so record them accurately. Others record feelings better, considering the numbers as unimportant filler.

Since numbers are not important to me, I tend not to record them in the diary. Recorded is, "Got a big fish today!" The average reader wants to know "well just how big is big?"

This is one reason I call what I write an entertaining story, not trying to prove anything at all. I say I have my place and purpose. It is the place of Jack London, Robert Service, Hemingway, Picasso, the Beatles, Edison, or Einstein. Street wise people without degrees, who are gifted artistically, are those I model myself after, and hold up as heroes. Even Einstein in my view – the greatest bean counter of them all, was more of an artist than a scientist. His theories were based on the beauty of time and space. He says so himself. His equations are as the writings of great music. Pointing with his stick on the chalkboard like an orchestra conductor. With grace, feeling, love of nature. It was ten years before anyone believed him and his crazy theories, about splitting atoms, the secret energy held within, about time being a relative measurement of motion and decay. He was a librarian! Imagine! Not among the great educated scientists of the time. Am I like these people? Who knows, probably not, but the point is valid.

I say this because it is difficult to explain the world I discovered and live in within the rules of civilization. My entire point of 'why I write' gets lost in dry facts, names, distances, numbers, order, rules, equations, and instructions. At some point it is much like stepping off the edge of a flat earth and discovering it is round. Then discovering we are going in circles talking round, and in fact we are traveling at the speed of light through the universe. Maybe even a different dimension superimposed on us made up of dark matter.

Or, maybe you expect an 1800s story of a mountain man, while I'm trying to tell a Star Wars story about another dimension. So, we are not understanding each other. You want the earth described as you know it. My talk is like telling you I saw a live mammoth, a unicorn. And, I'm saying yes, in fact it is much like that. The things I have seen are that out of sync with civilization, as a unicorn.

Any bean counter can keep some facts straight, do research, look stuff up, and write consistently the same set of information each time, that holds up to scrutiny. Lots of people can do that. Millions. Is it exciting, readable words, that is best seller material?

Many people can take a stick of dynamite, measure it, weigh it, write a paper on what it does. But, Wild Miles is the one who takes it out of the scientist's hands, and lights it. With a grin saying, "Put this in your notebook." We learn in about ten seconds that which cannot be learned in a lifetime of studies. That is my point. Passion. Loving what you do. Going for risk, and the big bang theory.

Anyhow, and whatever. I smile. Sorry I disappoint you. Oh well! I guess I can coldly add, "Next!" Meaning there are a lot of people in the world. No use arguing and defending myself. Been there and done that. **Sunshine Miles**

I sigh and think of my upbringing, trying so hard for so many years to be what I am not, trying to defend myself, prove I am sane, prove I can survive, "I can do it, see! Watch me! I can make a pitcher of juice correctly! I really can!" Only proving to everyone—mostly family, correct, no matter how hard I try, I can't do it. I can't follow the directions. I can't remember. I'm an outcast. They will love me, stand by me, as parents love the ugly duckling, the Quasimodo, the freak, the handicapped, the schizoid, the mentally challenged. If I hadn't left the planet, I'd be dead now. If that's insanity, then insanity is what was survival for me. Civilization is sane? How odd to think so.

"Give me liberty, or give me death." A caged wild thing withers away and dies on a diet of civilization. All this seems 'obvious' to me. Apparently, it is not obvious to everyone.

The male mallard duck gives another quiet quack. He doesn't know where his mate is, and for now is only curious where she is. Maybe her head is underwater, feeding, so she can't hear. If she does not answer soon, his next quack will be filled with more concern. He may even leave to go look for her, if he thinks she is cheating on him. *I better put him out of his misery*. Ha! 😁 :)

There is a new shotgun in my life that I get to try out. I gave up on the black powder shotgun, or more, a customer wanted to buy it after me telling a good story about shooting a moose with it from the canoe. I got another black powder shotgun kit at a garage sale. I can always put it together if times get hard. And I need to make my own powder and shot, which I have done. Some money from the shotgun sale got me a new longer range, more reliable Marlin long Tom twelve-gauge three-inch magnum with a foot of choke on it. With #2 shot it should reach out to eighty yards or more on geese. Impossible with black powder. I also get three shots instead of just one chance. Guns are my life, so experimenting, figuring out the perfect tool for the job is fun, and just part of what's on my mind a lot. Like knives, fish nets, saws, boat engines, and such.

The long tom is grabbed by the front door. I recall my own reloads are in here, with a full two ounces of #2 shot. Much more than I need for the little duck. *Dang*. As I step out the door, the duck flies up about fifty feet in front of me. If I wait a bit, the duck will be flying over dry ground, and will not be so full of pellets as my shot pattern spreads. I watch as the duck flap flap flap—heads for safety. Still, I wait. When the duck is seventy yards out, I pull the trigger.

I had loaded my shells hot, so there is a mighty kick, and even more mighty 'boom!' followed by the duck falling, dogs getting all excited at the sound of the new shotgun they are not familiar with, all at the same exciting, wonderful time. Nothing else in the world is like it. The smell of powder, smell of summer sedge grass, the chill of early fog. It all 'imprints' in a split second as familiar- safe- peaceful. Connected to something deep in the brain mankind has done for thousands of years. Getting food off the land.

Cinnamon had spent the night on the houseboat chained in the back as a 'problem dog' needing close supervision. She sees the duck crash land in the willow trees across the water. She dives into the river to get it. Being young, she has no clue what events will unfold. She comes to the end of her chain. The chain breaks. She hits the ice cold water with the loose chain still tied to her collar, pulling her under water. In shock and disbelief, I see all this. Cinnamon is on the upstream side of the boat, so the current pulls her under the boat. She's gone in a flash and will not be able to come back up again.

I have about three seconds to make up my mind to do something, or let her die. Without conscious thought, but with unconscious fast forward, I determine I can probably survive the icy water and current, if I have a rope to hang on to. A loose rope at my side is tied quickly to a chain with a drag on it that belongs to a trap, sometimes set to protect food in the boat from wild animals. The 'S' shaped drag is pushed into the boat gunnels so it will hold, as I dive overboard.

The cold stops my breath and cramps my muscles. Silt in the river immediately fills my clothes, pulls me underwater, and under the boat. Luckily, I am able to hang on to the rope and the drag holds at the boat edge. I assume I will follow the current in the same path as the puppy took. I can barley move, barely hang on to the rope, as I only wish myself to feel around for Cinnamon, but can't. Can't even think, it's so cold.

My legs feel a loose chain. Cold trembling legs move enough to twist the chain in a tentative grip around my leg, maybe. I begin to pull myself back under the boat, dragging the chain and hopefully a live dog at the other end of it. My face clears the water and I can barley take a breath from the cold cramps. Adrenaline and warmer air get my hands to grab the chain on my legs, then pull to get the puppy some air too.

As the puppy comes to the surface gasping and sneezing, I continue to lift, and sling her half into the boat. It's all I can do, get her half in. She seems to be gasping for air, at least, alive. Now, how do I get myself in the boat?! My feet can feel the bottom of the river a little, so I am able to give a tiny push with my feet, enough to help me use my hands on the rope to get some lift. Dripping wet, I am half in the boat, then fall the rest of the way in. On hands and knees I crawl into the cabin of the boat, and lay on the floor near the glowing wood stove. The puppy shivers next to me.

Eventually I get changed into dry clothes. I warm up, get the runabout boat to the other side, and fetch the stupid duck. This adventure took enough out of me, I don't feel like doing much the rest of the day. No one is expecting me anyplace, no appointments, and no obligations. I could spend a week here if I like. There are fish in the river for the dogs and myself. Game all over to eat, wild plants to harvest, a month's worth of supplies on board the boat. One unromantic side is, if anything happens, no one will come looking for me, I'm on my own.

There is a reminder of this, re-reading my father's letter before replying. May as well get caught up on my forty-five letters that arrived for me while I was in the wilderness.

Dear Miles

I have not heard from you in a while and hope you are okay. I thought I might hear from you when I got back from my trip to Egypt. The joint venture between Egypt, Russia, and my business dealing with shipments of steel I invested in is making progress. There are some politics still to deal with. Teaching is going well. This year the University will give me Tenure. There is a new direction to go with teaching I want to try out, but was concerned about getting support. Now it is not as important, and I can experiment more with new teaching concepts. I went on a sailboat trip across lake Champlain and was reminded of our sailing trip. Do you still have your boat? Do you drive yet? Let me know how you are.

Love, Dad

Dear Dad

Glad you are okay and teaching is going well. I wish you luck on the joint venture. Doing big business between other countries sounds exciting. Yes, I'm fine, just got my mail the other day, so have been out of touch for a while. Winter went well. I sold enough fur to make it through another season, well if I also sell my usual amount of art. Yes, the boat is fine. Not much like the ocean boat we sailed in, but some things are similar. Nope, don't drive yet, have no plans to, no need to, as I have explained before. No roads where I live. I'm hauling supplies to a new homestead and trying to use the short summer to get settled in. This is the Bearpaw River area I told you about last time I wrote. I haven't heard from Eileen in over a year. Have you gotten a letter from her? Take Care.

Sunshine, Miles

A letter from one of my best friends Will, who I have known since almost the first day I got to Alaska. I reply.

Hey Will!

Glad to hear from you. Once again we ran into each other when I came to town. Pretty weird, huh! Thanks for running me around town getting supplies. It's always good to get caught up on what you have been doing. Your ideas on how to cool the houseboat engine sounds like it will work. The rudder you made for me fits, but might be too heavy, but as you say 'sturdy.' I'm unsure if the tunnel I built will work. From reading more, it sounds like mine isn't long enough for efficiency. Also, I read all the water sucked up into the tunnel above the waterline is the equivalent of payload in the boat which might be fifty gallons, or 400 pounds. There are a lot of unknowns with a lot of time, and financial investment. If this is an experiment, and not a sure thing, can I afford that? Tying a twenty-four-foot runabout boat alongside and using it as a push boat for the houseboat seems to work okay. As I told you though, I own more stuff these days and can no longer fit everything on the boat! Ha! It means everywhere I go now I have to backtrack to the last spot to get the rest of my gear. That's costly and slow. I may park the boat somewhere for a while, like on the Bearpaw property, and just live on it as a land home. Unsure. So, this has had me slow to do the new engine tunnel work. I added five more feet to the length of the boat though, for more floatation and ability to haul more.

You were a big help teaching me about engines on that trip we made to Lake Minchumina! I'm not big on trips with others in general. Sorry to hear you could not afford the upkeep and gas for that boat you won in the raffle. So, will you get another boat? Hate to see you give up on the river life! What would you do with the Dugan land on the river? Your get-away place. Sounds like you can make a living with the car restoration business. Wish you enjoyed it more though. The laws do seem to be going against you and as you say, favoring the big business and putting the small time people out. Having a registration and papers on all the individual parts seems hard to do—sometimes impossible! Like you showed me, sometimes you have twenty different cars incorporated in one finished one. Seems like the days are gone when you can just buy junk cars over the radio ads—fix 'em up and sell 'em. That moose hunting six wheel rig you designed and built looked fine, and you should be able to sell that to some weekend warrior. I'd think you could move in that direction with your work.

I heard after seeing you, that Prim got killed in a knife fight on a visit to New York. A drug deal or something. That group we knew when we first came up here seems to be disappearing. Others you told me about are dead too. You think you and I were different? One thing, we never got into the drugs or crime! Those who made all the pipeline money seem to be worse off now than before they got all the money! You notice that? Some did okay though, like my friends the Underhill's from Alaskaland. That Bill used his money to go to medical school. Anyhow, got to run. Shot a duck today with that new shotgun I told you about.

Watch yer top knot, **Miles.** :)

Will and I always talk mountain man talk—that 'top knot' jargon, and 'watch which way your stick floats.' Stuff like that. Like me, Will dreams of one day being a mountain man, free trapper type. We have known each other since the early 70s. A devoted friend now. He got stuck in town, sort of never 'escaped.' Family obligations, parents, brothers, sisters, etc., are more of a priority. Will had to go to his best friend's wedding back in Iowa, so spent all his savings to go. He's got family and loved ones, while I have freedom. Is one of us richer I wonder? *Just different lives, different rewards.*

Looking through the box of unopened letters, I see some from mail order women I have met in years past, I still write to some now and then. Mostly I understand they want to dream, want a vicarious experience, want to read about something exciting and make it personal, but not actually experience. Okay for them, but not what interests me. I'm living the life, not talking or reading about it, and am sort of, tentatively off and on, looking for something real and tangible beyond ink on paper. I tend not to be as excited about writing them, as they are about being my pen pal.

Dear Wild Miles

Your Jane is restless again for her Tarzan. The city and pollution gets me depressed. I have no time these days to play my guitar. I still think we shall meet one day when the stars line up right. Tell me some stories, they always cheer me up. (Bla bla etc.)

Your Wild Woman

I'll wait to reply later to my Wild Woman- who waits for stars to line up. As for me, I am cause over my life. If the stars need to be aligned, I make them line up, or believe they are already perfectly aligned "Next!"

Dearest Wild Miles

Here is a picture in case you don't remember me. I changed jobs and moved to Washington a year ago. Work here is better and I have room for a garden. There are deer in the yard I feed. You'd like it here if you ever wanted to come visit. There are some art shows most weekends with a lot of free thinking hippie type artists. You'd fit right in. **All my Love—Janet**

"Next!"

My Dear precious friend

What have you been up to? I worry that I have not heard from you. Did you fall through the ice, get eaten by a bear? Let me know you are still alive. Yes, I am fine. Still alive and well. I can't tell you how much our friendship means to me. You are a life raft in a sea of chaos. I keep your precious watercolor paintings you do on all your envelopes, on the refrigerator where I can see them every day, and a day does not go by I don't think of you. **Dottie.**

No, I'm not sure who she is. But, I must be writing her as she is correct, I watercolor on all my envelopes, even my bills. I eventfully answer everyone who writes. Offer what I can, which may not be much. Or, not as much as these women think. For surely I have nothing of theirs I keep, nor is there anything they contribute to a relationship besides flattery. Their stories do not interest me, inspire me, nor do I feel like we have shared something valuable. There is a feeling of guilt for not remembering them more, or caring more. Now and then I get briefly infatuated by a picture, chemicals churn, but when does it amount to more than words? So, "humph," I say.

These women seem lonely, maybe? Seek something in their life they don't have? That they expect me to offer? But, can anyone make anyone else happy? Maybe we are happy people or not and need to take responsibility for our own lives? I'm not sure. Wanting to share a life is fine, and there is the practical aspect of life going better with two.

I think of the old days with farmers, with all the work to be done, planting, harvesting, that takes ten hours a day of back-breaking work. I can't imagine conversations beginning, "Do you love me?" Or identity crisis, or being bored, not enough time to play a guitar issues. There is dinner talk of planting the upper forty tomorrow, husking corn, a content smile at a good crop. I find that 'romantic' in the way Jack London stories are. He describes a life as living it, so busy they do not ask questions about 'who am I?' 'Romantic,' is a way of life, every minute, every step. Love is the same—not about moods, or insecurity, or hormones. Love is the shadow of two people working side by side as it disappears in the valley each and every night. Working as one, without really having to discuss a lot. Sharing a workload that is called 'life.' *We know nothing about farming.* A minor detail. The point would be, love is in doing, it's not words. *Does this have anything to do with our childhood?*

Keep on dreaming. Some sort of soul mate thing, maybe recognizing my other half when we meet. Or, she recognizes me. Karen was close to the ideal dream. We worked together doing chores in a complimentary way. We made the household work. Love to me is like happiness, if you have to ask what it is, you don't have it. We parted, Karen and I. Not sure I feel 'lost,' but re-evaluating what relationships are, what they mean, why we have them, what purpose relationships serve. My own messages are mixed because I myself am confused. 'Confused' makes women move in for the kill. Humph. It's better to tell stories, be funny, not serious, not remember much and most of all, not be confused.

Sometimes I feel like the dispenser of that which people need. Like a job, like a purpose, like a shaman or something, or a spiritual person. Folks come to me for something, answers, unsure what. Sucking of my energy. Sometimes I like it, and put myself in that position. Other times, sad, resentful, discouraged or guilty. There are a dozen letters from women. I begin answering.

Hello Wild Woman

You asked if I am getting mail from lots of women. I suppose. It's all relative. It can seem like a lot at the time, but it's a year's worth of mail all at once. Sort of feast and famine!.(I tell her the story of saving the puppy) Anyhow that is what's new here!

Sunshine Miles :)

Several hours are spent getting caught up on water coloring, about fifty envelopes, so I have plenty for the next year. While doing the painting, I admire the view outside the window. The view changes as the boat swings in the current and wind. I never fail to be impressed, in awe of the scenery around me. The happy constant gurgle of the river, adds to the input on my senses. Nothing different from usual. Just birch and spruce trees behind short willows. A bright sun coming through the leaves, then through my window like light through a sapphire. Soft, blue, breathtaking, surrealistic.

Sled dogs sleep in dry grass, glad for a day free of the cramped boat. Some are on their backs; one twitches in his sleep from a dream of running. I hear a sound out of place, that my unconscious focuses on. One of the sled dogs jumps up and woofs, sniffing the air. I already know without looking, a bear is approaching.

The rifle is grabbed up, as I open the door to see what the situation is. *Maybe the bear is a mother with cubs and will go ballistic seeing the dogs as a threat, or a bear who arrived smelling the fish and expecting a meal.* Yes, there is the bear as expected. Looks like a male, maybe two years old, just left its mother. Not sure what to do, nervous. Dogs making noise. Bear pauses and looks around, indecisive. Guessing he is looking for Momma who always bails him out of trouble and tells him what to do.

I take a chance on reading him right. My guess is, he is only confused, not aggressive, not a threat, not hungry. I greet him with my usual salutation.

"Greetings from the most dangerous, destructive species ever to inhabit the planet." The young bear does not appear to be impressed. I add, "You may pass in peace." The bear just looks around, irritated by the barking, turns around, and goes back into the birch trees from whence he came. Since I am leaving this spot soon, there is no need to be concerned he might be back later. There will be no close encounters of the third kind, every time I see a bear. Seeing bears is common. However, Spike the sled dog leader looks at me, looks down the path the bear took, and seems to be asking where the big boom is, and the bear scraps in his food dish.

"What's wrong with salmon Spike? Be happy with what you have. We'll leave the poor bear alone...this time." Spike sighs and picks up his dish hopefully. "You already ate Spike, did you forget?" Or, does he think I forgot? Who knows the mind of a dog? "I am OZ, the great and powerful! Do not pay attention to the man behind the curtain!" Most of the dogs go "oooo." Only the grouchy, now getting old, Map looks like he thinks, "Yea right, you are really one of the munchkins." So I do a magic trick for Map. "Which hand is it in?" I hold each fist out for him to sniff. "Wrong! It's in my pocket!" Mostly to show him who is smarter, and exactly what part of the food chain he fits in.

THE BOAT IS LOADED with sled dogs. We take off down the yellow brick river, seeking courage, a heart, a home, being put to the test, or being the tester. Humming, "If ever a whiz there was!" What will we run into today? Flying monkeys? What shall we find? The ruby slippers of the witch of the West? Indiana Jones and the Holy Grail? Dudgeon of Doom? I smile, for in the artwork I do is expressed magic, a window to another world. Something like Jean and I spoke of. The secret to bullshit? Is to believe what you live, do, say, with all your heart, as the truth. Beyond ordinary people's comprehension. My life is a movie. All our lives are. The universe parts ahead of me as I pass, and closes behind me, forever altered where I have been. Everything is done in a sacred way.

In this way I am in awe of everything around me and am not lonely, bored, or afraid. The boat is going two miles an hour, loaded down against the current. It takes days and days to get anyplace relevant. Am I Don Quixote fighting windmills as dragons? *Not if you ask Don.* The meaning of life? It's all in how you view it, a cup half empty or half full, notice the horse, or notice the crap. Is it all punishment or a test?

My mind drifts off into neutral, like an engine running but not going anyplace. The fifty-horse mercury pushes my flotilla. Burning five gallons an hour—two gallons a mile. With 300 gallons on board. Ordinary people might weep, fall asleep at the wheel, give up, think this is nuts, boring, expensive.

"But we are not made of ordinary stuff! Are we!" The dogs look up and ahead to see if I am telling them anything important about what is ahead, like I spotted something new- different. But no, they determine it is the same old same old. An endless river, an endless gurgle, an endless rampart of spruce trees, driftwood, day after day, without a human sign anywhere. Just wild things, bears, geese, moose, fish, forever.

This sign is hilarious, but makes an Alaskan point. Making fun of civilization, where everything is dangerous, the whole world, and we need to be told all about it. Watch your step! Wet paint! Do not slip! Duck! Caution! No one wants to get sued. In Alaska there is an assumption you are not stupid and have figured out how to take care of yourself. An assumption that when you get to the river and the bridge is washed out, you can see that, and know enough not to drive off the edge. If you do, it is no one's fault but yours.

CHAPTER TWO

REVIEW WHO MY FRIENDS ARE. TRADING SLED DOGS WITH NORMAN VAUGHN. MEET SALLY. FIRST WILDERNESS SURVEY JOB

Eventually I get to the Bearpaw homestead in the houseboat, hauling the new building materials, a twelve-foot-tall stack of insulation. The garden is planted for the summer, fish are dried for dog food. Enough art has been made to bring more in to the shops in Fairbanks. I had a rewarding experience selling art, by going on a long road trip with my buddy Crafty, who owns an art shop. We have known each other a bunch of years now. I have learned a lot about marketing, selling, the tourist industry, what shops expect, and related subjects.

There have always been aspects to how Crafty does business that I like to think I can improve on. But the proof is in the dollars, and Crafty knows how to make money. In his, or 'our' line of work, he is probably the best in the state, grossing as much as a million a season. I am therefore not in a position to comment on how it could be done better. Anyhow, I have some product to take to town. I have mail going out. *"We sure do have a lot more people to write these days huh?"* Yes, I agree with myself, as time passes there are a lot more people to write. There had been an ad in some magazine I had picked up on the table while visiting my grandmother last year. Maybe the National inquirer or some such. The ad had read:

"Seeking outdoor forest ranger type."

I had responded

"Heck yes, I range the forest!"

Ya, there had been women writing me from my own ads over the years, but nothing 'promising,' in terms of someone I might reasonably expect to show up. Pen pals are all right, but I keep looking, or now and then dream, maybe I could find a partner. Other times give up. Accept the fact I am alone and always will be. Something's wrong with me, or my life is just too far out in left field. Nice to read about 'Love,' another matter to join in on. It is hard to know at what point I believe I have some true friends. There are a few people I have known ten years or more now. Will especially. We shared the Alaska wilderness dream together living in a hobo camp – tents, and his car. The days of living under a bridge. He's never let me down. There is still a lot we do not agree on, or that I feel we do not share. He's not a very intellectual person. Yet, one of the truest friends anyone can have, worth more than gold, looks, and intelligence combined.

There are the Underhill's, Bill and Nora who took me in after I was rescued, and staying at the Salvation Army with a frozen foot- toe turning black. They encouraged me to write, and gave me a lot of insight into the ways of the world from a positive viewpoint. Almost like parents to me. But their life is so far above mine economically. Bill worked for the pipeline. Made big bucks, and got sent to medical school. Totally different then my life.

There are the Parr's who run Alaska House where I sell my art. They put on shows for me and respect my art and lifestyle. Charlie is a State Senator. Karen runs the gallery. They are movers and shakers, among those who don't just talk. Not exactly my peers, but way above me. There is Crafty who is my rep selling art, who gives me a place to stay when in town. We spend hours talking about all sorts of things. Yet, Crafty seems rigid in his ideas, and is not an outdoor person, so we mostly connect on the art part of my life, not the subsistence part. Crafty loves used stuff, garage sales, and storytelling, so we have all that in common too. He's a showman, an actor. This too bonds us.

Karen and I lived together for four years, with her two kids on the Kantishna River, was an influence, but our personalities clashed. Who among all these would be at my side in an emergency? Who is there when there is trouble? Who would stand up for me when Fish and Game is harassing me? Who would lend me money if I were broke? Who even knows me – all sides of me? Most know one side, and we relate on the level I know them at. As for all the fans? The fans are the first ones to slit your throat when you fail. Often it seems, fans are unhappy with their own lives, and live vicariously through mine. Fans all have an unrealistic view of what my life is like. Sort of like believing bears- wolves, should be protected- hugged- and kissed, or the opposite. Large wild creatures are scary, dangerous, vicious wild beasts, that need killing so the world can be safe. Few people see a compromise. Sometimes you kill them, sometimes you hug them. *Ya, first we kill them- then we hug them, after they are tanned and made into coats that is, ha!* Very funny, but you know what I mean. We trap, but at the same time we love wildlife, and want animals to be in the environment to see. Farmers butcher animals, but are capable of taking good care of the animals, like and enjoy them, want them to live a good life and prosper. Killing them is not necessarily an 'enjoyment,' it is simply how life is. There are not a lot of ways to make a living out remote. This is where our knowledge is, trapping. It's what we know and do. It's what our ancestors have done for thousands of years. Who shares this thought? This is a serious issue when seeking a mate.

But, this gal Sally responded when I answered her ad, and seems serious. She asks what I think about children in a first correspondence, which seems odd. But, I suppose women focus on that more than guys. I'm at least willing to talk about the subject, but most important is, will she and I get along? Before discussing children. She is thirty, worried about her age, not got a mate yet, etc. Seems interested in my lifestyle, even if it's not exactly what she was looking for. Nice enough looking. From California. Never been camping, but dreams of a life in Montana or someplace, 'living off the grid,' as she puts it. Not talking about 'when the stars line up right,' or 'things to take care of here first.' That I heard so much in replies to my own ads. That talk often goes on forever, people scared, can't decide. Sally just lost a job after twelve years as a checker at Safeway. All they give her was a $12 pin. This tends to wake a person up as to what they are doing with their life. Wants to start over, a totally different life. *Have I got a deal for her!* She cares most that I do not drink. Most else in her view can be worked out.

Future flash[1]

The year is 2009. I review notes letters, diaries, and memories, piecing 1984-to 1987 together. I lost a lot of information when my cabin was burned and Gene was murdered in 1992. Much got lost when my Kantishna homestead burned in a forest fire about 2001. More got wet and unreadable when Nenana flooded, and my home had three feet of water in it in 2008. My memory is not so bad if I get it jogged by a diary entry or reminder, like a letter or document. The memory itself has no time line with it, not to the nearest ten years. There are increased complications as more people enter my life. The early years were 90% about only me. No events connected with a time frame that is important, like dates, except articles that get published. As I acquire friends, women, people who were there, and are part of the story, there is an increase in having to clear it with them, unable to tell it like I want, or see it. I get a, "Oh leave me out!" a lot. I'm amazed how many people look panicked. "You aren't going to mention us are you?" In book two 'Gone Wild,' Karen was the only one who I needed to look after and smooth 'all that' out with. Along the way I actually get married, have a son, and have more dealings with more people that intertwine and affect my life, or are part of my life. There is a murder accusation I have to tip toe through, coming up in 1990. An entire year's worth of 1986 diaries are 'missing,' 1987 is only partial, as I kept two different diaries in two unusual places, but only saved one, the one kept on the houseboat.

One of the ladies I am writing off and on about this time, I am now living with, in 2009! Not the one I married! Life can be complicated, and not always turns out as we think or plan. At fifty-eight years old I can now get away with saying "Huh?" When the woman of my life asks me questions like "Do I remember?" . "I'm hard of hearing Honey – did you just ask if it's raining out?"

A lot happens in these years, so it's not like I can just skip over it!

My diary is on a calendar square where I write things like, 'Got a bear.' But which bear is this? The one I shot, and it got up and ran away as I was about to skin it? The one in the snare? The one killed with the gun set? When I started land surveying with Seymour there were no diary entries, as it seemed unimportant at the time. He was no one to me. It's often a three day job offer. Big deal. Then another three days. Okay so what. Then a week, then a year goes by, and it is 'years' before I bother to mention 'surveying,' as a real job I have, part of my life, making me significant money, and 'Seymour' as a friend in my life. There are memories- but just when was that? There are Fish and Game cases that come and go, and I forget now which time that was. When all I have in the diary is 'court case today,' and short little, 'fell through the ice again,' and 'got a moose,' (later 'took a picture of a moose'- in case the swat team comes busting in looking for evidence of a crime of a moose killed out of season). There are whole series of events summed up. "Ran dogs fifty miles, ran dogs thirty miles, cut trail, came home, ran dogs fifty miles, stuck in storm, ran dogs ten miles, finished cabin, ran dogs thirty miles, fifty below zero, ran dogs fifty miles," all in a week. All just normal stuff not worth any details. And I don't even remember which cabin, which litter of pups was that, what time was that I fell through the ice?

So! Moving right along with events as best I recall.....

Future flash ends

I'm in my homestead cabin with a salmon frying on the wood stove, going over paperwork. I review my various land agreements with the State. One is called a Remote Parcel, with ADL # 403524 as the identifier, and see my address listed as 'Manley Hot Springs.' Where I was getting my mail in 1981. When I staked the homestead. I didn't have an address. 'Mobile houseboat along the river systems of Alaska.' Would be the truth of my physical address. It is common to be unable to fill out forms legally, have a legal contract of any kind. I have to 'lie' or improvise, to fill in the standard blanks that do not apply. More and more the forms go into a computer. As computers get used, there is much more standardization, with no room for human understanding of those living off the grid. I cannot always put 'no phone' on the line that says, 'phone number.' I'm asked for digits, not letters. The entire document is rejected with the notice "Please correct" and in red, 'phone number' and 'invalid phone number.' So, I am forced to make up a phone number just so I can file the form. There is no option to get in touch with a human to straighten this lie out. There is no option called 'other,' as there once was. Nor a place to put down "Is there any comment, anything to explain we need to know about?' At the bottom is always, "Do you swear all the above is the truth?"

But the truth can't be entered! And there is no line that lets me write, "It's all made up, but it's the best I can do." Only 'yes' or 'no'- because no human will review it beyond entering it into a rigid system. So, I smile once again at phone number – address- income etc. I have to make it all up. But, also resentful I am made to be a liar, and at any time any agreement can be made null and void because I lied.

Another land agreement is reviewed, because this year is the deadline for finalizing the deal – either proving up or doing a purchase from the State. *It's easier to pay the $800 then try to prove this has been my home the past five years.* 'Proving up,' means I have to live on the land as a method of acquiring it, following specific guidelines. There might be an argument with the proving up method, due to the houseboat time. The cabin on this land has tools and evidence of permanent use. The bottom line is probably, that I do not find the government trustable. I have already acquired a Bearpaw State lease. This is land near my old Hansen Lake stomping grounds. I refer to this sometimes as, 'my upper Kantishna land.' I review the lower Kantishna land lease and review the description, to verify it is correct.

'Commencing at the Alaska Division of Lands survey control monument TASK 953-S, located within section twenty-eight. Township four South, Range thirteen West, Fairbanks Meridian… containing five acres, more or less, according to the attached plat."

There is a pencil sketch on record I made of the Kantishna River, an island, the creek, and where on the creek the land is located. Maybe no one but a surveyor would know what all that means, but any land office would be able to pull up the right map and there I'd be. Amazing. There's all this legal language about the contract, filling four pages. It's my understanding most of my heroes, the mountain men of the 1800's, never did end up with any land, as the folks in town who understood the legal language tripped them up, and got the land. The fine print the mountain man never understood. This is one reason I just want to buy it, and be done with it. I read:

"During the term of the lease, the following specific interests, which shall be in addition to and not in derogation of any general reservations to the Lessor which are required by law, or which may be stated elsewhere in this Lease."

Huh? What's a derogation? (frown) But it sounds like I am responsible for stuff not even written here, I am supposed to know. Humph. Certainly when I sell stuff, the receipt I hand out doesn't look anything like this! The longer I am in Alaska, 'doing,' 'acquiring,' the more plugged in and complicated life gets. The simple basic life with no home, no address, no responsibility, no paperwork, no bills is ending. This is reflected upon as I try to understand my choices.

Many homesteaders and wild folks I talk to, do not agree with me and feel that 'Yes!' followed by, "We can be left alone and live that basic simple life we left civilization to get away from." Oliver is a good example. He used to live with Karen ages ago before she and I were together. He tuned in and dropped out, so to speak. Off into the pucker brush, never to be heard of again. Only a handful of people know where he is. He seems to be left alone. I agree, he is left alone. But, I look at his life, and it is not what I can live.

He has cut no trails, does not trap, does not hunt, does not run sled dogs. I assume Oliver spends his life sitting in his world, the cabin, and a few hundred feet around it. He writes, but not 'published,' does nothing for income, has no bills. Eats wild plants, has someone else get his meager supplies, who flies it out to him, *paid for by whom?* I don't know, social security? Bet he lives on a few hundred dollars a year. He gets left alone. No one cares what he does. He's never been in the news, never had an impact on anything. He is not cause over his life in my opinion. If his land is wanted for any reason, timber, fish, oil, he will be told to move, and he moves. No rights whatever. Last time I visited him, he served me sled dog meat for dinner. Oliver told me the census people could not find him. I knew myself; thousands of dollars were spent looking for him, with questions asked in the village, personal insulting questions, wondering if he is a terrorist, or hiding from something.

Others are similar to Oliver I know, who grow a little pot, and spend their life sitting in a cabin zonked out. They get left alone. I'm in the limelight much more. That's one thing Karen never liked. I might impact a lot of people in a positive way, but it comes with a price. More is expected of me. There is a focus on what I do, and how I do it. I'm a player in the game of life, so to speak. So here I am with paper work, land agreements, and leases.

A must if I want a garden, a 'spread,' a presence, a shop, and 'stuff.' Tools of my art trade, a place to build dog sleds, work on the radio, work on the boat, have solar panels, etc. etc. I look over my new Bearpaw lease, so I don't confuse the agreements with the different pieces of land like the Federal home site. Which is on the trapline above Hansen Lake – my old original stomping grounds. A week goes by. I have boated to the upper homestead.

It's raining out, so I am in the houseboat at the Bearpaw land, going over the paperwork, looking at my maps of the trapline, and coming up with a plan. From a legal standpoint, a trapline has no status. The land is public land. I am 'allowed' to cut trail and trap, but this is a public access to the wild, not a personal trail. Any cabins I build are public cabins. Not how it is in practice, but 'technically' this is the law. Sometimes scary. Sometimes a problem. The law however recognized 'right of way' used to access legal pieces of property like homesteads.

I have some vague plan of acquiring homesteads as a form of retirement. The trails I use to access them will also be traplines that have a semblance of legal rights. No timber outfit, no oil company, no native claims, can cut that trail off if it is my only, and traditionally used, access to my land. It may not work, it's just an idea. So I seek pieces of land available along the route I am cutting, and want a trapline trail that forms a huge 200 mile loop. One hundred or more miles is already done. There is a total of almost 200 miles of trail available on my trapline, if I take into account the side trails. On my map I have marked where other trappers are likely to expand. Who claims what, the status of each area. One tentative plan would be to offer long distance dog trips. I cannot lease out trails! I can however, charge for the use of my homesteads. I could provide a map, keep the trail open, leave wood, propane, dog feed at the cabins along the 200 miles route. This is not being a guide, which requires a permit and insurance.

In many ways I was not originally this ambitious, to carve out 200 miles of country. I fell in love with one area, Hansen Lake, before I was able to own any land. Homesteading opened up way downstream. I hated to leave the Hansen area, part with this area I love. I got the crazy idea I might not have to give it up! I could connect the homestead I can own, with the area I am in love with.

Various interests are now looking at the land that was just no man's land in the long ago times. There is a proposed timber sale in the area I trap. Oil and gas exploration was already done near my lower Kantishna home, and trapping area. Some land is being looked at as having agriculture potential someday. Various native tribes are looking at areas where I am trapping, with possible acquisition from the Federal Government in mind as part of a land transfer agreement, in recognition of aboriginal rights. Nothing final or serious yet, but why not do what I can to protect whatever interests I might wish to keep. It's a lot of time and work I've invested, to lose with a stroke of a pen, with no compensation.

I HAVE the houseboat to use as a place to stay while building. Without this use of the houseboat, I might consider not using the houseboat much! With the price of gas going up and a shortage of gas, it is harder to travel with everything I own. Indeed I can't anymore. I am tied to the land with homesteads, and 'stuff' now. For another aspect of my personality is being a pack rat, lover of old stuff, garage sales, and piles of goods that someday might be useful. A lifetime supply of necessaries in case they are hard to get! Stoves, matches, propane, candles, sleeping bags, batteries, garden seeds, hand tools of all kinds, and on and on. I buy whenever I see them on a deal. Stuff that can be sold or traded if times get hard. Thus, the homesteads make good places to stash stuff safely away from the masses of humanity. *Why not be smart? Have sub- plans within master plans.* I also do not want society to have to take care of me, because I had made no plans to take care of myself! Nothing is going into social security except a little form my survey work.

So this rainy day is spent reviewing, looking at maps, contracts, and when I get tired of this?

"Yup, okay, okay I hear you. Time to eat!" The sled dogs are restless. There is one new dog, 'Poncho' from Norman Vaughn. Norman went to the South Pole with Admiral Byrd, and is a famous explorer. I met him through also famous Josh, a winner of the 1000 mile Iditarod dog sled race across the state. Josh and Norman are good friends. Josh kind of travels with, and looks out for Norman during the race, only 'sort of' as winning comes first, but Josh tells a lot of 'rescuing Norman,' stories. The two love to trade and talk dogs. I listen in, but don't know much. I'm in learning mode compared to these guys! Norman looks very 'English.' All gray hair, beard, big blue eyes, a hawk nose. He's written a book, "Dare to Fail." Basically about going for your dream, even if you don't make it. His early years were spent as a dog musher hauling the mail for the government. It was his ability with sled dogs that got Admiral Byrd interested in him on the Antarctic expedition. There is a Mt. Vaughn named after Norman at the south pole. He is always optimistic and encouraging when he talks to people.

I have fish nets to check. I shut the engine off and coast up to the net, as I run from the engine to the front of the boat, lean over the blow, and grab the net topline just as the boat stops. I know I have a lot of fish because they are flopping near the floats on top as I grab the line and jar the net. One end goes in one side, the net goes off the other side. I'm stopping to get the fish out. The day is cold, raining, windy, and not a lot of fun to be out. I have no choice. I'm happy because the salmon run is strong. I have over a thousand fish total so far for winter sled dog feed.

The sixty-foot net gets pulled because a beaver swam through it, making a big hole as he chewed his way out. I have net twine to splice in a new section. I must remember the right knot to use in creating net mesh. I have no way to tell time. I work as I need to, eat when hungry, sleep when tired. I am sitting on a log, a little cold, but there is no room for the net in the houseboat to fix it, so I need to do this outdoors. I look up from my work to see a moose come out of the brush. The moose does not see me. He stops, looks to the left, to the right, decides all is well in his world, so steps out into the open. I just happened to be here in the right place at the right time. I shoot the moose without incident. Just a normal event hardly worth mentioning.

I'm glad to make a good shot through the heart. I'm also glad the moose never moved, and sags down across a log that helps me do the skinning. I can get the whole skinning-cutting up job done in two hours now that I am efficient at knowing how. I am glad to get inside the houseboat with the woodstove going. Water is hauled into the boat so I can wash all the blood off. I decide to bring my clothes with me to Nenana to wash in the public laundromat. I will take the riverboat in tomorrow, do laundry, check mail, buy propane, take care of a few things.

"Huh?" 😁 :)

"Miles, I asked if you heard how I pulled Norman out of the snow bank in the last race?" I'm not sure, and know Josh is going to tell me anyhow. He is in the mood to tell this one, so I smile and nod for him to continue. I am visiting while my laundry is in the drier. I decided I do not need to get to Fairbanks, just a trip into Nenana.

"Yea, we were coming down a steep embankment. I think soon after the Roan burn, wasn't it Norm?" Norman nods, but he is not as excited about the story, as it is at Norman's expense. "Yea, and Norman was ahead of me going slow, so I told him to move over to let me by. His dogs speeded up when I approached, and Norman was not quite ready. Out of control and screaming 'Joooosssshhhh,' Norman heads down the icy twisty slope.

At the bottom I ran over him, and had a heck of a time getting my own dogs stopped to help. I looked around and could not even see Norman. Till I saw just his feet sticking up out of the snow. Wiggling feet. I had to pull him out feet first. You need to lose some weight Norman!"

We all politely laugh. Josh tends to tell jokes at other people's expense, but we forgive him, as Josh ends up a kind enough person, with some odd quirks. All of us in the room are known for having odd quirks, so what can any of us really say? None dares cast the first stone. Story telling in general seems to bond people.

One good side of all this, is Norman wants me to look after his sled dogs all summer, and will pay for dog feed, plus a little cash. He does not need his dogs till it's time for heavy race training in January. The Iditarod race is in March. He likes the idea of me trapping with them to get them strong and sled wise. Norman has money, so can buy the best of sled dogs. Dogs I can't afford to buy, worth $1000 and more each. Poncho is one of several I have that belong to Norman, worth $5000. Josh likes me to report on how the dogs are doing, and takes interest in any I might think are exceptional. Josh might work a deal out with me and Norman, if I come up with such a dog out of the untested, but good blooded dogs I get. So as a team, Josh is the expert who can spot good potential young dogs. Norman is the money man, and I'm the one who puts the time in working with the pups and the young till they are ready to race.

Poncho might be one such dog of interest. "Never likes to wait Josh." He has one speed, fast. Will not trot, wants to 'run' all out. And seems to have the stamina to do it. *Not a great trapline dog, but a perfect race dog!* I'd like to trade him for Char, one of Josh's dogs that is a little too big for racing, but perfect for the trapline. Char is short for 'Charcoal,' an all-black Belgium sheep dog. Norman leased my leader 'Spike' for $700 last year, and wants him again this season. Spike stops if you fall off the sled, then turns the team around, and comes back to you with the team. Pretty handy for Norman who is eighty years old, and not as agile as his competitors. Over the years I learn things, listening to race strategy being discussed. No, I don't want to race myself. I don't drive, don't want a vet, don't want to do all that training that is not related to trapping, or my lifestyle.

I laugh that the Iditarod winner breaks even, and everyone else loses! Not quite true. Josh tells me the race makes a profit up to about seventh place. It takes $30,000 a year to be competitive the way Josh plays the game. Still pretty serious money to gamble with on a one or two week race! I don't want to race, that makes it easier for the two competitors to deal with me. Since I get asked questions about the dogs in my care, I have to pay attention to certain things.

At one time I considered starting a race dog rehab facility. It is common for race dogs to get injured, so require months of recovery. Some just get mentally burned out. Some pull a muscle. Some need discipline, or need to learn to drink water, or need to learn other good trail habits. Trapping turns out to be an ideal set up for such a dog. A change of pace. Slower. Stopping often to check traps, but being tough, pulling heavy loads. A good way to build back up. I thought racers might pay for this service, and a dog gets returned, healed, good attitude, ready for fast training. It is hard to fit an injured dog into a hot team. It requires putting them in a slow team. *How? If you do not own slow dogs?* Thus, I offer the service!

But no. There is so far little interest. I never thought it out fully. What happens if I hurt their $5000 dog? Or, do a breeding behind their back. It works for friends like Josh and Norman, but who else? Yet, I am optimistic, believing any day now, some big name high roller musher will hire me. I do know Rick Swenson, Susan Butcher, The Redington's, the Makey's, Cotter, the biggest names in racing.

A story I hear causes me to sigh. Swenson I think it was, had an injured dog he left with a friend- fellow dog mushers care. The dog sitter told Swenson the dog is not healed up quite yet. Swenson later is watching TV, some big dog race in Minnesota. The Bear Grease race, wherever that is. Swenson sees his dog running in lead in the winning team. The sitter had leased the sled dog out without permission.

It is beyond my comprehension anyone would do such a thing. *Wow. But maybe I can put my art ability to use in connection with dog racing though!*

One art piece I have done is for the Yukon Quest race. I've gotten to know other top racers, and those in the loop, who run the race organizations. I negotiate a deal to make a trophy for the winner. One of my pieces of mixed art metal, showing sled dogs, the sled and winter camp all in many metals, on a trophy that gets passed from winner to winner each year, with the new year's name added. This is finished now, so needs to be shown to the board of directors.

"I'm out of here Josh!" he smiles, "Things to do places to go right?" As he waves me off. I do not have a heavy load this time, and travel on step, so save on gas, and going three times the speed as when plowing water. This is fall but before the water drops. I left the sled dogs at home, so am in one day spend a day in Nenana, heading home to Bearpaw the 3rd day. I have left enough dry fish in front of each dog. and five gallons of water so the dogs should be fine. I have 150 miles to go. All through the wilderness with no roads. I pass four homesteads, but do not expect to see anyone.

There are five people at Old Minto, just one boat. No one waves, even though just one boat a day can be expected to pass by. I do not slow down, and perhaps these people recognize me as local. I keep this place in mind if there is ever an emergency like breaking down. Weather is nice, I am making good time. The Minto Athabaskan's have fish nets out downstream that I pass. I see one fish-rack with thousands of fish hanging half dried. They chose a nice spot with breeze on a sandbar. It is tradition to just pick out a nice place, anywhere you wish, to set up fish racks or a temporary tent camp for the fishing season. I see no sled dogs staked out but know there are at least two serious dog racers in Minto. Josh was born and raised in Minto; I keep forgetting since I associate him with Nenana.

The mouth of the Kantishna River is an important mark for me, because from here on I am going upstream, so slower and a different water that reads different then the Tanana. I decide I am tired, so take a nap on the front of the boat for half an hour. A balk Eagle sits on a dead branch across Rock Creek, and stares at me as I nod off. I am about a third of the way home.

I AM BACK at the Bearpaw homestead after a fifteen-hour day. I have clean laundry now. I smile at my lifestyle. Life in my houseboat on a homestead in remote interior Alaska. Doing art when I want, how I want, out in the wilds on this Mobil home. I bring art to town when I am coming in along with other orders, and consignment pieces. I collect money from previous art left, while I drop off the new. No bills, just checks waiting! Life is good!

My eyes are on Poncho as I feed sled dogs in late fall, Salmon on racks, dry behind me as winter feed for these dogs. "Poncho, would you like to run fast and race? I might trade you to Josh for Char, who would rather trap then race!" I have a team that can travel fifty miles a day in deep snow, sometimes as much as 100 miles in a day. Dogs that can run at fifty below zero, know how to get across rivers, find camp, find traps in the snow. Not like most free dogs from the pound that I began with. I am spoiled now with the best from Norman and Josh. A team capable of winning the Iditarod, or so I, Josh, and Norman believe, even if others argue that Josh and Norman are behind the times, not keeping up with technology. We still discuss the old-style collars and harness, and old style three-inch-wide runners.

About everyone else is turning to the new 'Atla' style equipment since he is winning the sprint races, so is the latest word in racing. Atla, an Athabascan from the village of Huslia, has made history, and is the subject of a movie 'Spirit of the Wind,' showing his ability, and latest ideas. Josh has the nick name, "The Fox." His reputation is that he is not the fastest team, but the toughest driver with the toughest dogs. The tougher the race, the better for Josh. Temperatures dropping to sixty below zero, winds of eighty miles an hour, deep snow, open water, are all to Josh's advantage. If Josh is out front in deep snow, he needs three-inch-wide runners. But, if the trail is good, the extra width becomes drag.

I think of this, as I eat my moose meat steak, and put up a lot in jars, because I have no electricity for refrigeration. I make some jerky as well. This was not a big moose, and am glad for this. I can handle this amount of meat without any waste. Wolves have been howling recently in the area, and getting in closer over the past week. This time of year, wolves are in family groups, not packs. They get together in packs in winter so they can better bring moose down. A family group of five has a den three miles away. They came in to clean up the gut-pile from the moose I shot, and have been hanging around close. I have not been bothered by them, and consider the wolf family part of my normal environment I love. *'Love,' is not the right word 'accept' and 'find normal.'* I do smile a reply, "No, we are not about to hug and kiss them!" Me and I smile. I feel at peace hearing the wolves howl. The sled dogs listen as well, so I comment to them. "Sounds like their pups are getting better with their harmony!" I take note the dogs are nervous, more so than usual, and I wonder why.

In the middle of the night, I wake up to the dogs barking, and one of the sled dogs screaming in pain. I am certain the wolves moved in and are trying to snaffle a dog off the chain and run off with it to eat. I know what route they used to come in. The homestead is a quarter of a mile up a clear salmon spawning creek. The water level is low now, so there is a beach. The wolves have their den upstream at a mountain with a bluff I call Fossil Mountain, where I once found a mammoth bone. In this bluff, I have seen holes used for wolf dens. From here, the wolves would have open travel along the Kantishna River, and up the sandbar on my creek.

Inside the houseboat I can hear the sounds, interpreted to be wolves killing a dog and running off with it down the sandbar. Knowing this, I can take a shortcut to the river and beat the wolves there, and get a shot at them, maybe get my dog back. *Or dog's body.* One big issue is, this is pre-dawn, late fall, and not light enough to see well. I grab a flashlight and my 357 Blackhawk pistol. I would have grabbed the rifle, but in a quick decision, feel the rifle would get tangled in the brush in the dark while running. If I get to the river in time, everything narrows down, I should have a close shot, if I get there in time. There is not enough light to see by for any long shot.

The wolves know I am after them, and can see the light as I run, so know exactly where I am. I know this as well. As I run down my path I have to the river, I can hear the wolves off to the side running their own trail. They are smart enough to know to stay off my trail, I might have a trap in it and I can defend myself better on my own trail. My trail is shorter.

I hear half the wolf family peel off and circles back to intercept, maybe surround me. I am aware of the hunting technique of the wolf, having seen them bring down moose. They are in hopes I will panic, drop my light, run, maybe trip and fall. They do not want me to think, and get my back up to the brush where they cannot surround me. I know this because they are not being silent as they know how to be. They are making a lot of unnecessary noise. I have used this method myself to get my own prey, so understand the game they play well. Because I understand, I am not afraid. Because I understand, I know I can best them, since I know the game.

Also, I and my black-hawk, are bonded as one. An extension of my arm. I trust the pistol and what it is capable of. I am not bragging to myself with inflated ego issues, because I just as readily admit how inept I am in a civilized environment with phones and what-not. I am in my element. I am angry about their attack on my sled dogs who are my family, who I will defend to the death. Angry, but not filled with hate. They are just wolves being wolves, and I trap and kill them in winter. I am not going to have double standards here. We both know the rules. I know as well; the wolves do not hate me. *It is just business.* In fact, I think the wolves are having fun, enjoying this. This thought only makes me more determined and less afraid. *I will clean their clock.* I get into my 'Clint Eastwood' role. Zero fear. High tuned instincts kick in.

I beat the pack to the meeting point we both understand is critical. Two are in front of me, but one is holding one of my sled dogs in its mouth, or part of the dog, and not being slowed up much. I see the two in the beam of the flashlight. I hear three coming up behind me. I have time to deal with them later. Well, just seconds later. But in this heightened state of mind, parts of a second become a very long time. I cannot explain it beyond, *A Zen place, a state of grace.* Something spiritual. The ability to juggle ten events simultaneously, and run a timeline, I would say a fraction of a second into the future. Even though this is impossible. Fine tuned instincts. Two shots in front of me, spin, one shot behind me. Two more shots left in the gun. Hammer back. Wait. Access the situation. See the effects of my move, before deciding the next step in this ballet. During the pause, the intermission lasting a very long two seconds, in the background in my head, Beethoven music. Go figure. An insane man, who could be here, at my side, with a smile on his face. Totally in charge. One of my heroes. At one with the universe.

I have wounded one wolf in front. The half a dog has been dropped. Three behind me have scattered. I am not going to panic and run, trip and fall, so I may be torn apart. The wolf plan is aborted. They all disappear into quietness. I stand there, hammer back, two shots ready in case of a new plan. I had not had time to grab spare bullets. If I had taken the time I would not have been here for my appointment with destiny.

I am heartbroken over the loss of Cinnamon, a valued sled dog, part of my family and loved ones. His collar and some body parts are still with the collar and chain in the dog-yard. In the dawns early light, I access what has taken place. All the remaining six sled dogs are silent in fear. It had only taken seconds for the wolves to attack and run off with the dog. I think with a plan, knowing about chains and the need to work fast, come in, get the dog, then out of here. They know I sleep in the boat and understand guns. This is a hungry year for wolves. There are plenty of fish, but this is not the staple for wolves. It is a low rabbit cycle, few grouse, small game is more scarce than usual. Plenty of moose, but without the larger pack, moose know how to defend themselves.

If I had been gone on a mail trip, the wolves could have killed and eaten all the dogs! In a way I am lucky. I think the wolves did not get much of a meal, so in this way the attack was not successful. Also, one is wounded. This is 'normal,' because attacking large game like moose is risky, so it is common to have serious wounds because of an attack. Wolves are not afraid of wounds. Even though they can be shy and wary, they are brave, and able to take risk once making a decision.

I go back to the ambush spot to see what happened to the wounded wolf, if I can get him, and to retrieve parts of my Cinnamon to bury. I see some blood, further along the trail, more spots of blood. However, the tracks are not faltering, so think this wolf survives and is not fatally hit. My shot had been in the dark at a moving target, even though it had been from a mere fifty feet. Tracks show the three wolves behind me were less than a hundred feet when I fired. I had never seen them but fired at the sound. Either the sound, or bullets flying by close, ran them off.

My feelings towards wolves are not changed. I feel no shame, remorse, guilt for trapping wolves. At the same time, do not trap wolves in order to hurt, punish.

Trapping is not out of hate or revenge. It is just survival money. I am good at it, take pride in it, even enjoy trapping, as part of the whole lifestyle. I suspect wolves feel the same towards me. I will still enjoy just watching wolves at play, as I think wolves enjoy observing me at my daily chores.

I sometimes see such events in my life as 'lessons,' a preparation for 'things yet to come.' Maybe I am not even in charge. Yet if I am not, then who is? Am I simply looking for meaning, or is there a master plan in random events?

I AM IN NENANA AGAIN, maybe my last trip in before winter. I do not think the wolves will attack again, but feel concern, because they might.

"Yes Miles, you are right about sticking to the wide runners. One problem two years ago in the race was that no one else uses wide runners. So, when I need parts, like quick change plastic, I cannot get it in the villages along the way. It is an advantage to have what everyone else has so I can get the quick change plastic!" I think about this. But seem distracted. "Miles?"

"Yea, well I had wolves kill one of my sled dogs not long ago, it's on my mind." Josh snorts, "Get over it Miles, it happens a lot in your lifestyle. You better be able to handle it!" I smile. I know. Josh has told me many a story from his lifetime in the village. I focus on the subject at hand…

"So, the standard is one and a half inches? So, go with the three-inch wide, and run a double set of quick-change side by side." Josh turns to Norman:

"Miles's father is a Dean of a college with three Ph.D.'s, did I ever tell you that Norman? Can't you tell? A chip off the old block." I'm not sure if it is subtle sarcasm as Josh calls such people, 'Educated Idiots' sometimes. Book learning, without a lot of experience in the ring with the bull. Okay. I'm learning social skills. I can put an opinion out there. If it will not work, I can be man enough to back down and accept that as, 'not going to work.' We move on. Later I notice a sled of Josh's with three-inch-wide runners and a double set of quick-change plastic.

The white or black is universal for any conditions, though the black is softer for snow and no gravel. The yellow is for wet warm weather. There may be other colors. It's high tech knowledge. A pair of pliers pulls the thin plastic off the bottom of a runner in a few seconds, and a new set can be slid on an aluminum V rail. 😀 :)

There is something exciting about the Iditarod, and long-distance dog work as advertised and promoted. When the race got started, it was village teams coming in off the trapline, with folks proud of, and bragging about, their team. Then putting the team in a race to see whose team is really hot, and what musher knows his stuff! This can be important knowledge when your life depends on dogs! How do your dog's stack up? What is possible? What would it take to improve your team? People talk, but a race sorts the talk out. Racing, prizes, gambling, could be extra money and entertainment for a remote lifestyle.

The original Iditarod was based on a famous diphtheria serum run; I forget what year. The days there was a train, but no plane traffic yet. Eskimos were dying in Nome Alaska, so needed the vaccine in a hurry. A pandemic! The train got the serum as far as the village of Nenana, as far north as the train goes. Dog teams relayed the serum all the way, 600 miles further to Nome. One trapper passing packets of serum off on another, until it got to Nome in record time, saving lives.

Joey Redington Senior, whose son I know in Manley Hot Springs, was the founder who had the idea to reenact this event in a race. 'Iditarod' is the name of one of the villages along the way, and name of a section of the trail. I may not have all the details exact, but this is how I recall it, and believe it. So, I know Joey, I know Emit Peters in Ruby when he won, and Josh when he won. So feel close to the race. Norman was once a dog sled mail carrier for the post office in his youth. His work with dogs was much like I am doing trapping.

Now the race seems to be going 'pro,' like horse racing, and other types or racing, far removed from its exciting origins. The Iditarod is getting more and more like a series of sprint races. Those who win now, seem to have their own vet, lots of money, lots of dogs, as in over 200, trainers, handlers, scientific stuff in sled designs using graphite composite runners- not hand split local birch as Josh uses. They can switch out sleds during the race. Yet, all the advertising shows mushers like Josh being tough, out there alone, man against the elements, using the old primitive stuff that looks good in pictures.

Josh talks about various ways of cheating he observes, and is against. Switching dogs in the wilds along the trail, with a plane flying in new fresh dogs. Dogs being given sports drugs. Even competitors dogs being made sick on purpose. Hard to know myself what the exact truth is. I'm just listening without an opinion. Before I met Josh, he was banned from the race for a few years for 'cruelty to dogs,' charges. I sympathize somewhat. Some issues are cultural, village ways to raise dogs, wild ways I understood from my own early experiences.

Society cannot have its cake and eat it too. The ability to take pain is associated with the ability to dish it out. 'Tough,' and 'violent,' are related. There is a reason why the best football players, prize fighters, hockey players, bull riders, might end up arrested for violent related crimes. Why is the public shocked? This is a world of the tough and the dead. If you can cut it, you get rewarded. If you fall behind, you get beaten. If you can't do it, you get shot. There is something deep down in the core of Josh that is kind and caring. He is the first one to stop in the race to help a rookie out, or if anyone makes a mistake. But, kind does not give you fame, or make money, or win points. Josh wants recognition. He is also a survivor.

I look at his childhood and he is lucky to be alive. He has a past of extreme neglect. He has childhood memories of being on his hands and knees fighting with the dogs in the village over scraps of raw fish on the beach to eat and sleeping with the dogs in dog houses in winter to stay warm enough to live. His perspective on life and death is different than most civilized people's. He's a runt of a litter who survived by being feisty. Even more then feisty. The word might be tweaked or warped. I admire 'over-comers.' Those who can take what others refer to as a fault, and turn it into an asset, something positive.

"Wow Miles, I thought my childhood was harsh. But at least I remember what happened! You told me you have no memory of most of your childhood." So while I am tempted to feel sorry for Josh, he feels sorry for me! Go figure! I do not feel sorry for myself, nor seek pity. I'm sure Josh feels the same.

A trend beginning in the animal rights groups develops. Many people consider it cruel just to race dogs. Making a dog do something it does not want to do, maybe cannot do, for Man's selfish greed. Now and then dogs fall over dead from the ordeal. *But so do people.* It's supposed to be a race of endurance and toughness. If that's not what the race is about, then what is it about? As in any race of any kind, if we focus on how hard it is for the loser, instead of the winners, where are we at? Anyone who has sled dogs and races, knows the worse punishment you can give a sled dog is not let him run, and leave him behind. Josh himself would rather be dead then not race. He'll race till he falls over dead on the trail. He wants, and has dogs, who feel the same way. He asks nothing of his dogs, that he does not ask of himself. Other mushers and those in the know say Josh is just Josh. Partly paranoid, has a grudge. Few take him seriously when he starts talking negative stuff. Josh tends to go off on a tangent concerning cheating in the race and feels competitors are poisoning his dogs.

I don't know all the details of the charges against Josh, of abuse and cruelty. Don't want to know. He's my friend and that's that. I have never seen him be what I would call abusive. The dogs do not cower, nor seem afraid of him. They all obviously love and respect him. Josh cannot put down a dog he cannot keep, and has to ask me to do it for him. I only hear rumors, but am told there are race winners who win by playing kissy-poo and lovey dovey with the dogs. I have never actually met any, or seen the results. Though my homestead neighbors the Forests, might fit this description. I never heard of them winning a race. Well the relationship between dog driver and his team is much like a team coach and his football team. If the coach talks in a high pitch squeaky voice- gives his players sweet names, hugs them all for just being so darn cute, makes them beg for treats, well it is just hard to imagine a winning team. Part of winning is perhaps knowing what will happen if you screw up. Obviously, winners come from within. It is a personality and physical type. Spotting these self-made winners is a huge job of a coach as well as an Iditarod winner.

I'm known as a hard man myself. I prefer to think, "Hard but fair." I strangled Scorpion with my bare hands in front of all the sled dogs for calling a sit-down strike on me. I had a dog fall through the ice and watched her die, and simply pressed on with my trip. No 'trying to help her,' no 'poor dog,' no burial, no crying, no 'what can I do to prevent this.' We live, we die. There's hardly any nice ways in the wild to die. It hurts, it's a cold cruel world, where the tough survive and the weak get eaten. I feel like Josh, agree with him. The day I can't keep up, take me out back and shoot me. The toughest race in the world is not going to be made up of pussy coward personalities. They are not always nice people. You don't get in their way, you don't try to stop them. I find it an honor and a privilege to know the best there is at what they do like Norman, Josh, the Redington family, and the likes of them. Even Rick Swenson and Susan Butcher, Lord help me if I praised them to Josh though. 😁 :)

How different are my friends now compared to 70's, and before? I knew a lot of drug addicts, those on welfare, street people, rejects. It was okay, exciting when young. The difference between light and day in contrast to people I know now. Well, I always knew and have been affected by, good people, just was not paying attention. My best friend Will, the Underhill's, and the Parr's who sell my art, and even Crafty, are okay people I can trust. Even though Crafty is crafty? He'd be the first one to bail me out of trouble, no questions asked. He'd give me a job, a place to stay, loan me money. I don't forget that. Josh too, for all his cruelty, would be and has been, the first one to come look for me, no questions, no money, just honest concern. It was Josh who boated downriver forty miles once when I was late showing up with the houseboat. I forget that sometimes. I can be a little like Josh, maybe.

So, on this first snowy day I also review the changes going on. It seems if we stay the same, we go backwards. I like to stay challenged, to learn, to grow, to control my destiny as much as I can with correct decisions. This must be part of survival, and happiness.

There is a bear I shot in the head in the yard. I hope to be able to keep the meat for winter. A challenge without electric that offers refrigeration. Hate to make bear jerky, because bear meat should be cooked, not just dried. There are plenty of canning jars however, as a second choice to drying. But caning is getting more expensive!

"Do you think a company like Dole bought out Ball caning equipment, so that it costs as much to can something as it does to just go buy the canned foods? As a way to collect the money, even if you want to bypass Dole? A way to have a monopoly? " Josh gives a, "You got that right!" reply. Not much would surprise me. One year the price suddenly goes more than double on canning lids to where it is not economical, but a hobby for the rich. Now I dry food, instead of can. If I put up 300 jars of something. The lids alone now cost $50, that is a substantial amount of money to me. If I go to the dented cans and damaged goods section, outdated stuff, or over ripe fruits section of the store, that same $50 buys me more product then I am canning. Did some company think of that and smile, 'check mate' to the public?

If my name was Dole Pineapple, and someone pointed out that a lot of business is lost because people are canning their own food they grow themselves. I might say, "Buy out the canning jar industry and triple the price of lids. Buy out the garden seed companies, fix the seeds so they can't be saved, so seeds from the plants are not viable, and charge enough that we make as much money off gardeners as we do the finished produce! Tie up the loose ends." Not legal? Not happening? Yea right. If I'm smart enough to figure out how to do it, for sure others are too. Pay people off, change the title and papers so many times, it's a nightmare to straighten out. If I was that sort of person. The whole country is probably mafia run anyhow. Stickers, permits and promises are empty from my perspective. The entire world's economic system is rigged. Nothing happens without money and economics. My father has a PHD on the subject, teaches it. As a child I heard the details of one world government and money system. How to design it, implement it, sell it to the public. How to be among the ones running things.

ANYHOW, bear meat, a hide, and what am I going to do with these claws? Hate to toss 'em out! They go in the box to be made into jewelry. I've learned a secret process for cleaning claws with a series of three boiling steps. One step uses caustic soda to get tendon and fat off. This is not something to read about. I experiment, have failures, but eventually have a process no one else knows, and begins to get me into a new line of work, over a very long period of time. I understand this as a market that cannot be controlled by China.

A NEW BOAT has not been tried out much. That's on my mind as well. I explain it best in a letter to my buddy Will.

Hey Will!

What's up with you? Still in the car building business? Has the job on the military base worked out driving heavy equipment? That boat I picked up seems to be okay, maybe not perfect. The price was right of course. I agree with you, it is probably one of the first Compeau boats to hit the market. Sure looks nice, all fiberglass, long twenty-six feet, with big engine and low sides. The car seat and windshield make it a luxury for me. Wipers even! Also, the roll up canopy for bad weather. The external keel cooler seems to help the control engine temperature. Pulling in river water as the coolant has its problems, as we both knew. Silt tends to plug up the system, or any filter put in. Running straight without a filter seems best so far. Sounds nice when it runs, but dang, she burns fuel! The jet does help it run in shallow water when up on step, but a single stage pump is inefficiently crude. Bet I burn fifteen gallons an hour with a load in step. Sixty gallons one way to the homestead. About the same as the houseboat, just three times faster. As we predicted, the low sides make it dangerous in tight turns. I took on water in one turn.

We sank it when we first launched it, so those low sides are for sure a problem. But what was it I paid? Five hundred dollars? If it even lasts a season or two it is worth the money, that's what just one fly in trip costs. Unsure how many long trips I want to take with this boat. Keep it near town, or maybe near the homestead. The old twenty-four-foot wood boat I got in Galena, and tow with me, runs fine with the fifty horse that pushes the houseboat when tied alongside. Wish there was a perfect solution for travel. As we both noticed, the weekend warriors have the best boats, and they only use them a few times a year. Costs way more than the likes of what you and I can pay. Those who need such a boat never seem to get one. Thirty grand is beyond our means.

As you say yourself, you had to part with the jet boat you won in the drawing! Couldn't even afford to run it! Ya, BOAT stands for a in hole in the water you pour money into. But I heard another one. BOAT stands for Break Out Another Thousand! Oh, you mentioned my letters always smelling like wood smoke? I think because I have had the paper a long time since I got a deal on a huge pack way back years ago, and I keep it on a shelf over the wood stove! One gal I used to write told me my letters and envelopes drives her cat nuts like catnip! Ha! I guess the fish odors, touching the paper, and envelope with moose blood on my hands and stuff like that, leaves something on the paper.

Later, Miles

Ya, without Will, how would I have ever gotten the engine fixed when it sank on launching? But, over the years I pay attention to what he does, and have learned some basics on engine work. Wondering if the tunnel in the houseboat hull will ever work out. So many complications without money or tools. Just like way back wanting to run the houseboat with steam and a paddle. Nice dream, but not going to happen on my budget. I feel bad these days I ever made fun of Will. He's twice as big as I am, with arms the size of my whole body. Iowa farm boy. Thinks about ten times slower than me. I would tell him something just to watch him shift from neutral, to reply, then ten seconds later he would answer, real slow. With a farmers drawl, and beginning with "Welllllll." Saw Will lift an engine out of a truck, then set it on the work bench with his bare hands. Easily 300 pounds. Maybe 400 pounds. He could ask me to lift something, and find it funny watching me try. But he never did.

A kinder friend to me then I am to him. Though now and then if I get good leverage, I can muscle a barrel of gas off the ground and into a boat, 350 pounds. Or, once did. Doubt I could anymore. Maybe I just don't want to anymore. *"Let the tool do the work,"* I answer myself with a grin, "You got it!" Smart is saving your back.

There is a trapline chatter message. Each day at the same time, about a half hour is set aside to read messages that come into the station by letter, or called in. There is an unexpected message from Will, that this Sally gal I have been writing is due to arrive in Fairbanks.

Diary

June tenth, 1987 Sally due 5:30 pm.

June eleventh Sally arrives.

June thirteenth Will, Sally, and I bring engine to Nenana.

June fourteenth Cook dog food play with engine. Work on houseboat.

June fifteenth Wash clothes, visit with Josh.

June sixteenth Money arrives, two checks $4000.

June seventeenth Buy gas and transplants for garden.

June eighteenth Leave for homestead, eight hours, thirty-five gallons gas, 1800 pounds.

June nineteenth Bear in snare – shoot two more bears at fish rack. Work on fish cache.

June twentieth Can bear meat. Take a bath.

The diary is then blank. With a note on the bottom, "June, July, August, on another calendar in Nenana." Huh. Not much said about this new Sally gal. *Ya! We recorded the important stuff! Think it has anything to do with her being discontent? Huh huh huh?* Ya, well I don't remember any of that. I remember how it was all her fault, don't you? *But, ya we seemed to get along okay for a spell. I guess. I mean what do I have it to compare to?* What do I know about love? She didn't complain much. That was a change, not getting yelled at. Different personality then I had seen before.[2]

So Sally and I brought an engine for the houseboat. I had towed the houseboat with the twenty-four-foot runabout, and fifty horse outboard. New engine for the tunnel hull on board. One of Will's engines – four cylinder Volvo. His recommendation. Sally and I live on the boat in Nenana at what we call 'tenth street,' where I first met Josh, and now park my boat when in town. Sort of like home away from home. There are plans to move the houseboat once the engine is in and tunnel tested.

Sally is quite beautiful. Blondish hair down to her waist. Trim, fit looking. Lithuanian, I think. Pleasant smile, and wistful look. Soft spoken, maybe husky voice, but soft and sexy, with a quick laugh. Only a little taller than I am.

"So Sally, it is rent free, water frontage property, no taxes." I assume she likes the location well enough here on the slough of the Nenana River at tenth street. Josh and I had pulled the houseboat out of the river with his truck during high water, direct onto the high bank using steel drums as rollers. The new Compeau boat will be our transportation while I fix the houseboat with new engine, which might take a while, like off and on all summer, even a year or more. She is not that all excited by the houseboat, but I knew ahead of time. No woman would be. It's enough she will even stay here. No electric, and no running water. We drink the slough water. We have a crude outhouse I built. All normal for me. I happily assume she will like it too! 😀 :) 🩶

I'm used to time spent here at the boat landing, and know most of the boaters who launch boats. It is common to chat, help back someone's trailer into the river, hold the bow rope and discuss the weather, guns, and exchange hunting stories. I don't always catch their names, but often recognize their faces. One I will get to know better is Gene Gram, who just staked land up the Teklanika River, a tributary of the Nenana River. There's Bearfoot, one of Genes neighbors, but I also knew Bearfoot from the Kantishna River. He got his nick name from an incident I'm told of, where Bear came running into the village in winter in just his socks, as he had burned his boots in the camp fire trying to warm them. Edmond told the story, and he's a real story teller, so when Bear says the story is highly exaggerated and an untruth? Probably so. But so what?

My nickname 'Wild Miles,' is based on a bar joke I never understood, about a cross between a man and a buffalo, thinking the joke has to do with making fun of my short size. Those who laughed at me, and gave me the name, found it even more hilarious that I don't get it, when I happily, proudly introduce myself. "Hi my name is Wild Miles." Said proudly as if you should have heard of me, much like Jonny Cash when he gets up on stage. "Hello my name is Cash." I turned a joke into a driving force to reckon with.

Gene is one who thinks I'm a bit touched. Thinks I'm full of dog doo.

"Hey Miles, I see you pack a 270 in the boat. My wife likes that caliber!" He is trying to be insulting, referring to the fact that the 270 caliber is sometimes referred to as a 'ladies gun.' Less kick than most heavy macho firearms. He adds, holding up his own firearm. "So how come you never chose the aught six?" The numbers used when speaking guns usually refer to the diameter of the bullet it shoots. The 270 is .270 inches. The 30/06 Gene refers to is a thirty caliber or .30 of an inch, and the '/06' refers to the year of its invention 1906, because there are so many thirty caliber cartridges. I reply to Gene:

"I agree, the 30/06 is probably a better all-around choice of firearm. More choices in projectiles, cheaper to buy, with ammo sold in every village. But, I did not know that at the time I grabbed up my first firearm. I got used to my 270, and am familiar with it. Sometimes the best choice is the one you know, understand, and feel comfortable with."

The most common argument is the difference between .270 of an inch and .30 of an inch. The 270 is considered by many to be weak, not powerful enough for Alaska game. Suitable for deer, not moose, certainly not bears. These people forget how the caliber became so well known. A famous hunter 'Conner' killed more elephants in his life than anyone in history. All he used was the 270. It's the flattest shooting caliber there is, till you get into modern magnum guns. Extremely accurate. But yes, a lot of modern guns now outperform it. It could be an outdated cartridge if a person had to make a decision based on performance. Gene probably knows all this as much as I do, so there is no point in denying it, because I'd lose the argument. I find it a little irritating that Gene is trying to bait me, get my goat, start an argument, debate, create a challenge, or a fight, insult me. He can assume this is a way to hit my buttons, because I am a short five ft four inches, so would be expected to have a 'size, problem. I get out of it by acknowledging I chose a pussy caliber, "oh well."

Gene chuckles that I back down, and thus, loose status in his eyes. I'm being unwilling to defend myself. Now he thinks he has found a weak person he can prey on. He fails to see I am amused. There are a lot of personalities to deal with in the wild, perhaps anyplace. The bully, the macho guy is common. Gene is an okay person, all in all. I'm willing to talk to him. He is smart and handy out in the woods, so gets my respect. Gene invented a lot of cool stuff. His system for heating water for a shower is ingenious for example. He's good at getting hold of free equipment, and having it running the next day. I can respect that. He's older then I am, tall, walks with a bent back. Long gray beard and wild unkempt hair. Eyes that stand out as a little crazy looking. Intense, that stare at you and make most people feel uncomfortable., in a Charles Manson sort of way. Maybe because his tone is serious, loud, and gets in your personal space to make his point. He has recently pulled in a raft to the mouth of the slough where my houseboat is parked, and Gene has set up some sort of shelter on the raft.

Gene wanted more water depth in the slough, so got hold of a bulldozer and blocked the slough off with a damn so he has water to float in. But he blocked the slough off, so it is hard for others to get a boat in and out. True, there are only three or four of us who ever use the slough, but still, you cannot just go bulldoze and block off a waterway! It's not legal, not that anyone cares about the law in these parts. *What is he thinking?* Just daring anyone to say anything, or challenge him. Josh is upset because Josh has been keeping his sled dogs on the island, and now Gene doesn't want Josh messing with the dam, or some such argument they are into. It would not take a lot for either Gene or Josh to get violent. Josh has a temper, and if you mess with him, he'll kill you. He and I get along okay because I give him what he wants most, respect.

Sally does not like Gene much, thinks he's insane and scary. She's not sure of Josh either. But he's my friend, so that's fine then. Sally and Josh's wife Martha get along fine. The issues are on the back burner as Sally and I deal with a transportation problem. She is used to driving, so needs something to get around.

Will sells us a truck cheap, that runs, for $300. "It has a lot of miles on it, does not look great, but it always starts and will not let you down Miles!" I do not drive, but Sally does. We can get to town for supplies once in a while. Sally cannot comprehend a life without wheels. So okay, now we have wheels. We plan to boat to the homestead to check it out, and haul in winter supplies. The assumption is, this is where we will be, as it takes all summer to get ready for winter, and there is no choice. This is where supplies are being hauled. She wanted a big change, so is just taking it all in as a new experiences without a strong opinion, yet. Or, this is my understanding of the situation. I had once before thought I understood the situation with Palace, much like this with Sally. Palace had freaked out. So, I'm in hopes Sally will hold up and enjoy it. She seems to like the concept of doing for ourselves. Grow our own food, get a moose, all that good stuff.

"You'll see Sally! It's a great life!" 😀 :)

WE ARE EXCITED about the garden. The new transplants will go in the garden. Plant these, weed the garden, collect some fish for the dogs, do a few things. and come back to work on the houseboat in Nenana. A net can go in the slough here in Nenana to catch salmon for the dogs, if there is no problem with Gene. This short visit to homestead life should show her something about it, with a stint in Nenana to think about it, and adjust to Alaska, and me.

Sally loves the view, the scenery, the excitement, and the trip goes okay, I assume. Eight hours is a long time to sit in a boat and see no human sign as we get further and further into the wild. "Like the head waters of the Amazon," I like to compare it to. Sally does not seem to get as starry eyed as I do at that thought. The weather is great, nice and hot, clear sky. We have to sit close to be able to talk over the scream of the engine.

"Sally, see the owl in the tree ahead?"

"What?"

"The Great Gray Owl, on the left in the cotton wood tree." I must explain quick what cotton wood is.

"I don't see it yet. How do you know at this distance it is a Great Gray Owl?"

She sounds like she doubts I see anything at all, much less an owl, much less a certain type of owl, and am only saying so to impress her?

"Well a Hawk Owl is smaller, prefers the open, dead black spruce trees, and would tend to be moving more, looking around, flitting its tail. It would not pick such a place to sit still and sleep. A Great Horned Owl could be here, but prefers to be where there are rabbits to look down upon. This is not rabbit country. The Great Gray prefers the shadows, never in the sun, so would select a branch halfway up a tree over the water in the thick canopy, exactly where I see an owl. It's just their habit. Those would be the only owls to expect here." Finally, she sees it.

"Miles, how did you ever see that from so far off!?" I never thought about it. I'm not used to traveling with others.

"Well I guess this is my world. I understand it as you would your world. Just as if I was visiting you in San Diego, I'd look foolish and maybe incompetent. I don't drive, don't use phones well, and can't read the environment around me. I don't see street signs, and can't figure out what others are about to do, or what stuff means. There's a road sign that says, 'No stopping any time,' and just ahead of it a street light. If the light is red and you stop, will you get in trouble-disobeying the sign that says 'no stopping any time?' I don't spot the pan handler as he looks just like the shopper next to him. I guess it's like that." I'm not bragging about what I know of the wilds, or trying to look better or smarter. A while later after we leave the Tanana River and are on the smaller Kantishna, I point out:

"See the King Fisher on the right sitting still. If you keep an eye out, it will leave and go to the next branch exactly fifty feet further, and land exactly twenty feet off the water, and chatter." Sally does not spot it right off till it moves. This Kingfisher does just what I said it would do. I add, "Eighty more miles, about half way to home." She asks now and then where we are, and I can't tell her. I can only say:

When we get close to the homestead, I see the fish rack across the river where the sun shines more. So I hang fish to dry there across the river.

"Sally do you see the bear there at the fish rack?" I reach for the rifle calmly and assume she knows what to look for, how can one miss seeing a bear, big, black, nothing else around looks like it. Sally is not on my mind as I focus on the bear, and connect to the target. This is routine for me, not excitement. *Just routine.* As the city person goes to the super market. How much explaining is there to do? *Much like "I'll find a parking spot, meet you in the meat department."*

Boom!

Only after the shot, does Sally even see the bear, as it drops. Perhaps it had not been moving. Perhaps, if it is not moving, the outline is hard to decipher without a practiced eye that seems so obvious to me. Just a bear.

Quite a shocking introduction to the homestead life she tells me later. I never considered that. I try hard to imagine life without bears in it. I can't. Sort of like me not being able to spot salesman in the store—so obvious to civilized people. Or, spotting people who are not going to stop at the street light. *Or, knowing a Tanning Salon is not a place to tan furs, as happened in book one.* I try hard to imagine, and think of an analogy so I understand.

I happily, and with enthusiasm, show her how to skin a bear. "The cabin is up a creek. First, we must park in the pond behind the island, then get the canoe on the other side of the beaver dam and canoe up the creek a bit." And, and, and, "Look!! "

Then, there's the cabin! "See!?" 😀 :)

I'm unsure what she thinks. She does not say much. For this and various reasons I say:

"Maybe this should be like a visit between us and you can think about it after you see this cabin, and get back to town before we decide if a relationship will really work out between us." I think she remembers it different, and it was me who was not in 'let's wait and see' mode. People's memories don't always match. Or, we define things different. I am thinking, *Lets sleep together, and along the way see if we get along and can be friends or more! Commitment? What does that have to do with anything at this stage?* But it has to do with her wanting a child and family. Her priority is a child, and my priority is a wife. The two ideas are not incompatible, we just each have to believe we will get what we want if we are patient, and can get along. I keep changing the subject.

"Looks like a bear has been here at the cabin. I think it's not the same bear I just shot. Guessing there is another bear around. It probably does not know we are here yet. This is the best time to catch it by surprise.

I set a snare along the water on a path I think the bear will follow if it comes to re-visit the cabin. Sally is once again curious how I know where the bear will come from, and how a snare even works. I'm happy to explain. But Sally feels a bit like a three year old out here for her lack of knowledge of even the basics. But she can learn. She just has to want to. Or, hmm. *This is how it was for me, and if I managed with no help, surely, she can with help, right?*

"Miles, what's this on the calendar 'Seymour survey at Donnas' in a few days." Oh yes, I had forgot to mention. I explain how there is a homestead about ten miles downriver owned by Joe and Donna. Joe died in a plane crash up north in a private plane. Now just Donna owns it, and does not come out, but the land is in her name. The place needs to be surveyed, so she can get title to it. Seymour is the guy who surveyed my Bearpaw land, and now wants me to work for him sometimes when he has remote parcels to survey. He is boating up to meet me at Donnas, maybe one or two days of work. I get wages plus boat rental.

"How much?" I am flustered, not used to having my income questioned, at the same time, understanding a woman expects to know and we have to be open with each other. She is not the IRS!

"Well, I get $18 an hour plus room and board, and $100 a day for my boat, he buys the gas." We both know minimum wage is $4.00 an hour. The most Sally ever earned after twelve years of working was $10 an hour.

"So, you could work for this Seymour guy, and make pretty good money, why not do that, and not be so poor?" First off, I do not consider myself 'poor,' as I explained about choices we make. But, it's like the more I try to prove I am rich, the more I prove what an idiot I am, and how poor I am. So I feel guilty, selfish, bad for how I live, but only in society. I reply with insecure hesitation:

"Maybe, sure. I guess. I'm not sure how much work Seymour has for me. I think he does not want to make a full time commitment to me, or be responsible for supporting me with work. He's a one family business, just him and his wife." One employee he regularly hires lives in Manly Hot Springs. Anyhow, it has been a choice I have made. This—how I'm living is what I want. If I wanted money, I would have, could have, worked for the pipeline and been monetarily rich. I was offered $30 an hour. I got out of the Navy as a machinist mate at nineteen years old, trained with pipe. I was wanted on the pipeline. Most of the people I stood in the unemployment line with that one day got jobs, have swimming pools, fancy cars and money now. "Couple hundred grand a year minimum. Most also have high blood pressure, a drug habit, and have been married and divorced, mostly over money issues. So no, I have no regrets."

I wanted to be a trapper, and here I am. Sort of a mountain man lifestyle, or subsistence person. "One of the best there is at what I do." This is worth more to me then money, respect. This is a normal reply I hear, and yes, she says as well! "Get real!" Followed by, "Just how much money can I expect to be living on?" I do not suppose I mind. Or more like it is to be expected. I do realize when getting along, two people must be on the same page financially.

Sally does not reply, so I do not know if she understands or not. My hope is, *it is just a new concept to her. She needs to see how it works and focus on the good side.* Hopefully agree, and enjoy it because sometimes she understands, at least in theory. But she may think I'm just good with words, and talking people into stuff. She's not yelling or getting mad – guess that's a good sign. I too am trying to look at the good side. I don't want to be alone. We'll work it out somehow.

I pick flowers for her, get her interested in pressing flowers and making crafts from them, and having an interest in photography. (?!) I point out, this is a hobby that she can get paid for too, if she is so worried about money. We see all kinds of cool stuff worth a photo! In winter we can set up a darkroom to develop our own pictures! The time when there is no light anyhow! "Cool huh?" The number of things we can do seems limitless to me. So many choices and options, not much like how it is with ordinary people. *Imagine being ordinary, how sad.* But she expresses a fear or concern, and maybe a inner need to be just ordinary, even though she feels she is not. Ordinary is safe, being among the protected, in the folds of the herd, one of the sheep the shepherd looks after. She gently points out my various 'issues' that seem to never end, resulting from, being 'odd,' and not one of the sheep. All the legal stuff with Fish and Game for example. Getting deported from Canada and 'all that.' Not much I can say in response.

SEYMOUR, the survey friend understands my life goals somewhat.

"I once had a booming survey business in Fairbanks, bringing in big bucks during the pipeline days. But it was stressful. I had five crews out on five different jobs sometimes. When what I really loved was being out in the field doing the actual surveying. So, I sold my house, and moved to a remote village where I can run sled dogs, have a small but meaningful business." It's not easy to get business in a small village! So he specializes in remote wilderness surveys, homesteads, native land, and that is his niche market. He understands perfectly well how I want to just be the saw man, not be a surveyor or run any crews. Quite a change for me in a way. When I first arrived in Alaska I hated chain saws! Gave up on them! Used a bow saw only, for years! Now look! Getting paid for my knowledge of saws and ability with one!

Well Sally and I have conversations about some sort of life together. How it should not necessarily be all about me and my life, how I live, with her making all the changes. It only makes part sense to me. She says that for now she does not know my life, and will go along with the program, and do it my way, and see how it fits. But ultimately, we need to both compromise.

My view is, she wanted the major change in life. I am honest about how I live, and expect to live. I'm not leaving Alaska. Probably not the wilderness. I see my role, what I offer, is the material goods we both need. I supply the home, furniture, transportation, and income. If a couple starts off young and on equal footing they can grow together and acquire 'all that' together. She is bringing to the table, what? The willingness to change and accept what I have.

Like with the animals I know, birds and stuff. The male builds the nest and sings. Trying to attract a mate. If she likes what he built and the location she says yes. This is not her opportunity to say, "Actually would you take the nest apart, and rebuild something different over here someplace else in the forest?" *No. That is not one of the options.* Because what the female really means is, I want someone else, who chose a different location and other house materials.

I don't ask anyone to share it with me who does not want to. I honestly state this is where life will be if anyone is with me. If that is selfish, uncompromising, rude, etc. well it's honest. Say so now. Tell me to stuff it. I understand. "Next!" Or—I live alone. I am not stepping down from being a King of the forest, to be a slave to the system.

If there was some high paying respectable sort of job I could expect, I might think about it. I'm a trapper, a small time artist, as long as I live subsistence and don't need to earn a lot of money. I'm the one who is happy with my life. She is the one who is not happy with hers. Put the other way around, if the shoe was on the other foot, If I moved in with a woman who had a job, a home, transportation-everything we needed for the both of us, and all I brought was my underwear, I would not expect to be able to suggest we move, live another way. I'd consider that a lot of audacity. It's her house, her job her money her 'stuff.' I'd be appreciative she is willing to share it all with me. Because I have done nothing to earn half of it, or have a vote. Maybe later after I have contributed something.

I'm not sure we are in agreement here. Sally is being somewhat quiet till the subject comes up again and I see, no we do not have a good understanding. *Well, give it time.* She needs time to adjust. It's a shock—I'll try to understand that. (?) Not just the world I live in, but 'me,' I'm a shock. I'm shy or embarrassed, or not totally optimistic. So I don't get close, easily or fast. A sense my mind does not work like other peoples' minds. Like reading the river without knowing where I am. Opening locks without knowing the combination. I mix up my phone number with my social security number. Forget how old I am, my birthday. That's not normal. So, to cover for it, I am alone a lot, make jokes, do not get close, or do things with people. I live in a world of my own making. It is hard to share it, to show anyone this world. I'm used to the looks of disbelief. The pity. The lack of respect, lack of being able to form a connection. Sally asks me details about my life, like income. I'm honest.

"Well I don't know what I make. I work for myself. I don't keep records. Instead of figuring out what I want, then figuring out how to pay for it? I see what I have, then decide what I can afford to buy."

"How does that work exactly? How can one budget, buy groceries, pay bills, when you do not know how much you will have from week to week, month to month?" I have no answers. I'm never out of food, hungry, or without a place to stay. I feel rich. I have no bills. There are no regular services I receive. No electric, phone, rent, water, sewer, garbage pickup, no credit card, no fees, and no dues. I've never had a bill in my life. I only get checks and income in the mail.

"Look at all the stuff I have!" :)

"But it's not worth anything Miles." She's trying to be kind. Telling it from her perspective. It's all used garage sale stuff, rusty broken hardly working junk. It takes three chain saws to keep one running. I'm defensive about what I have. I don't want to hear how poor I am. According to who? We'll talk, we'll work it out. That $4000 that arrived on the same trip as she did, was nice to show her. How many people get to see that kind of cash in the hand. Untraceable, unreported, cold hard tax free dollars. And no bills to pay with it. But she is used to regular jobs, regular paychecks, and a budget. Most people are. Most will understand her, before they understand me. And do. For most of the talk is about Miles, finally settling down and changing, getting domesticated, tamed, civilized, clean, looking for an honest job finally, maybe, etc. etc. The wild horse gets a harness and a plow. I certainly would not call that love.

Sally understands. Her family. Her father who paid the bills without complaint and was so unhappy. So she'll try to fit in. I guess we like each other. What do I know? I wouldn't know what 'getting along' was if it bit me. Maybe not her either. Both sort of dysfunctional families.

ANYHOW, bears all over. Overnight the snare gets the bear. Odd to me in that, we never heard a thing just outside the cabin door. Interesting in that the snare was tied to a small willow, and it is a fox snare, not for bears. I had used it in hopes of giving a bear a chance, get caught, get away, small snare a nuisance, teaching a lesson to stay away from here. The bear is dead. Wrapped himself around all the small willows and got tangled. Not what I wanted. But we will save the hide, the claws, the skull, and all the meat.

I show Sally the small cabin Karen's child built when ten years old. I had told Sally how Karen and I, and her two kids had lived here a few years. For some reason it has a great effect on Sally. Her feeling that a ten year old has done something she could never do in a million years. Sort of like she sees the personality type, and knows it is not her. So, I am unsure what exactly **is** Sally's type. What is it she dreams about, and loves to do? She doesn't know. How odd. Too not know what makes you happy. Well. Guess we shall discover together?

But not a great situation for me, in that I know what makes me happy. I am thus not on an exploring trip with her. It is not two people discovering life together. I need to determine if life as I know it, is her cup of tea. This is one difficulty as we get older, compared to two young people starting off from scratch together as equals.

"So, Sally, the hope is to get the houseboat back in the water and get it on up to the Bearpaw property further upriver another eighty miles. It's pretty country up there, with Denali so close. Trapping is good. The hope would be to tie the trails together I have put in. There will then be more money from the trapping further out near Bearpaw." I'm reviewing with her the trapline, homesteads, and 'business' part of life. *She wants to understand the money stuff.*

"Miles, tell me again how many homesteads you have. I can't keep them straight!"

"Well there is the Quartz Lake land I first bought outright. I made payments on and is now paid off, that's where the houseboat was built in Delta Junction. That's water frontage, maybe two acres. Then there is this place I got next, called the lower Kantishna, where we are now. State remote lottery land with five acres. Then I got the 'Federal land,' I call it, up on the trapline, really remote, about three acres at the base of Roosevelt Mountain. I'm working now on the State Bearpaw property about ten acres. Still need to pay for that, or decide to prove up on it. Thinking now with you, probably not prove up but spend time at the lower Kantishna closer to town till you get used to it. Also, probably not get the houseboat in the river with a new engine, and tunnel hull this year as I had hoped in spring. We'd have to live there full time to get the work done, and not much room for two of us full time on the boat! Ha!"

I considered this 'compromising,' considering her wishes. She may not have thought eighty miles further up, or 'here' as any different. Big difference in what it costs to go back and forth, and how long it takes though. Not being here at the lower Kantishna land could mean less income, as there seems to be more fur at Bearpaw. But oh well, I'm not so worried. Is she? My wealth is not in money, and I explained this up front as I do with everyone interested in me. My 'wealth' is in land, health, freedom, knowledge of how to take care of myself without depending on the government, and such things. *I feel like a broken record repeating myself over and over.* Part of me believes if I have to explain it, you'll never get it.

My gut feeling is that Sally just needs to adjust and get used to subsistence, where you provide your needs and not buy them. She likes the concept at least. I keep saying that, huh?

With my friend Norman Vaughn. Quite an inspiration, still running the Iditarod 1,000 mile dog sled race in his 90's. Went to the South Pole with Admiral Byrd. Mt. Vaughn named after him. Wrote a book "Dare to Fail.' I leased my sled dogs to him and he supplied me with top quality sled dogs I could not afford to buy.

CHAPTER THREE

SALLY ADJUSTS –RUNS PUPS. RELATIONSHIP-PREGNANT. TOGETHER ON THE HOMESTEAD. FORCED MARCH OUT TO CIVILIZATION. JURY SUMMONS. TRAPLINE WAR WITH RIVAL TRAPPER

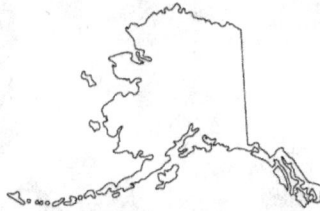

"Miles, I ran the puppies today as you showed me, and it sure is fun. The pups are just so cute!" It is Sally's job to work with the puppies and get them used to people, the harness, and getting them in shape. They probably will not be team dogs till a year from now. I have worked dogs as young as six months old, but it is like making a teenager become an adult and pull the load. In the big picture, you can sour them on the idea. We have ten dogs because of Norman and Josh. I might have gotten the team size down, but the hope is that Sally will have an interest and run a small team, maybe while I am out trapping. Maybe she can fetch firewood I cut down, or just to get out and have fun. It's easy to like dog mushing. She asks:

"Did you catch any animals?" I've been on the trapline trail for a week, sleeping in the dog sled at night. It's nice to come home to a warm cabin and partner who hopes you had a good trip. She looks with interest in the sled and at the frozen Marten. "Not very big, are they?" That had been my thought the first time I caught one, after all the whoop and holler about 'trapping' the toothed and tusked wild things of the forest.

There is an ermine living under our cabin. This little white hunter has gotten bold. Mr. Ermine now runs up to the sled with us standing here and jumps in to inspect what I brought home. Usually, I let him take some bait, an old grouse wing or something, just because it is fun to watch. Dashing across the snow with a pile of feathers bigger than he is and trying to get it under the cabin through his little entrance hole is a hoot. Though ermine is a trappable animal, they are only worth three or four dollars, and their value as vole catchers around the cabin outweighs the small fur value. Sally seems to always have some new ermine stories.

"You should have seen him try to get in the bird feeder!" We have some dry fish for the woodpeckers who like fat. The dry fish is tied to a string from the rafters. "The ermine climbed up in the rafters and tried to pull the string to get the fish, but the fish would not fit through the poles." We hold hands and chuckle together as she tells me, "So he climbed back down and looked, then studied from below on how to get the fish. I could watch as the fish is only six inches from the window. Fist over fist he pulls the string again and closes his eye and gives it all he has. He has to let it fall, and just sits there huffing and puffing, exhausted because he can't fit it through the rafter slots."

It's easy to see what he wants, see how he goes about it, why, and the logic behind it. It all makes sense. Here is the ermine again. We put our arms around each other and watch in silence. Snow all around. The only disturbance is us wild things. No snow machine this year, just sled dogs. Very peaceful. 😀 :)

"Miles, when can we get to town for mail and supplies?" I'd never thought about it till she asked.

"I don't know. When the weather says we can, I guess. Everything has to freeze more, and the sled dogs need to be in better shape." It's a two-day trip usually, with a stop at what we call 'the airport,' about twenty-five miles out. A bulldozer headed this way from Nenana in a straight line, and seismic blasting was done for oil and gas exploration. The bulldozed trail is now the access trail to this part of the Kantishna shared by the Forest couple, and a few others who come out now and then to see their land. There are three or four more families with cabins that have been built along the river in the past five years. I'm usually the first one on the trail, and last one out in spring. I'm the one who does 75% of the trail work.

There is a shack that was drug in with a bulldozer and used for a few days by the bulldozer crew as they cut out a runway. A big plane landed only a few times to drop off fuel and supplies. The runway has grown in some, but the shack got left behind, and locals laughingly call it 'the airport.' I put a stove in it and insulated it better so it can be an overnight stopping place. I had explained to Sally how Josh trains his race dogs out this way, and stops at the shack to broth his dogs, give them a snack and let them rest, maybe himself too. His race team can make the round trip in a day, eighty miles.

He does not start these long runs till after I come in and have a trail for him to run on. A few people wait for me to do the work, come to think of it. Oh well. I like being the first one out on the trail, seeing things no one else has seen since last year. New wolf dens, recent places bears go, where moose hang out, where trees fell down, and things like this that interest me. I like to feel alone in the wild, safe. No one else around. But Sally may have gotten the wrong impression, thinking we and our dogs can easily go back and forth fast whenever we wish, listening to how Josh does it. "He also spends thirty grand a year on his dogs, and 'dogs' are his whole life."

"Miles, this is not a free life then! You tell me we are at the whim of the weather and our dogs? That is not freedom Miles!" Well, I just never thought of it from this perspective before. I guess freedom and slavery are in the eyes of the beholder. We have had this discussion before, how when fish run, we catch them. When berries are ripe we pick them. We can't pick berries in spring if they ripen in the fall, and we can't have fresh salmon before they get here from the ocean. In civilization, you can have fresh berries and fish any time you want without thought, at the store, or a restaurant. That is a type of freedom I suppose I never considered. And there is a type of slavery to nature, having to wait for God to deliver the goods. So now Sally is in sort of panic mode.

"What do you mean we can't get in, there is no way?" She is not feeling great and tells me she thinks she might be pregnant.

"Dang!" No, I'm not pleased, because Sally and I might work out a relationship, but we might not. We have a lot of issues to compromise on, or get past, or work out, or whatever. 'Baggage' as some call it. If she can't live in the wild, and I can't live in the city, then what? I say to her:

"Anyhow, you told me you are taking the pills, so what's up that you are pregnant?"

"I forgot to take them." *How can one 'forget' such an important thing. Forget? Or, on purpose.* She did want a child as a first priority, and she was not happy with how our discussions were going on the subject. But, yes I suppose I should have taken a more active part on protecting my interests. Making sure we don't have a child. I tend to believe people, take them at their word, and the pill seemed an easy solution she was willing to deal with. I left it up to her. It's her body. I assumed having a child or not is 75% a woman's choice. It seems absurd to me that in this day and age of freedom and choices and such, if you don't want a child it is easy enough not to. Just take the pills. I confess I don't know much about the subject. I made a lot of assumptions. Lots of women now- a -day's want kids without a man around. In this day and age women don't need men. Women can do it all. If they can't, society steps in and pays them, and helps them. The traditional man's role in the family seems lost.

Sue, one woman in my life, is a good example. She is a woman who feels like she is never going to find a man to live with. She wants her freedom, but also wants a child, more than anything else in the whole world. Maternal instinct without a matching family instinct. I've met quite a few single Mom's with kids, on welfare, food stamps, living a pretty good life. Fewer are working and doing okay. Many tell me:

"Who needs a man, just another kid to have around!" How do I answer that one? **"Next!"** But, those standing in line for interviews to be with me are getting fewer. Huh. I miss the old thinking, where both parents are vital to a family, about unthinkable without. Men and women needed each other in the older days. So! Here we are, Sally and I out in the pucker brush. She thinks she's pregnant, and wants to go to town as in 'right now.' She had asked not long ago:

"How do I wash my hair? How do I get hot water?" I explained :

"Here's the five gallon kettle. Go to the creek, cut a hole in the ice with an ax, scoop water in the kettle and bring it up to the cabin. Set the kettle on the wood stove for a few hours, and it's warm water!" I have my expression, showing that I still find the whole concept 'awesome.' *Water we don't have to pay for! All we want! Right there, just as God created it! No chemicals, no chlorine. Like pioneers. Like people have done for 10,000 years. Almost spiritual in its awesomeness. A sacred act. Is there anything more cool or meaningful?* That's what the expression on my face said. She seems not to feel the same way.

"I don't need all this work to be happy!" How do I reply? How? I guess to some people I describe an easy life. But life is always easy when you enjoy your work. It's not work. I explain how I see it:

"Well, there are two choices. We have a regular job in order to make more and steady money.. We can then afford to pay for stuff like hot water, right out of the faucet, lights that come on with a flip of a switch, heat with the turn of a knob. Another choice!

You can provide your own water, heat, food, without a boss. Meaning you can't get fired. Meaning you can take a day off, and you might be without water, but not out of a career. "It means you can do it your way, when you want, how you want, and others may laugh, but can't fire you. Can't take away your water, source of heat, or food." We had talked about this often. Even when we wrote back and forth before we met. Doing so much for yourself occupies your time, so you are not working a regular job with a boss for wages.

The truth is, it's different strokes for different folks. Nothing is free, there is a price for all choices. Also, one thing that has bothered me all along about 'relationships,' is so often, the guys who face the music. The woman turns on the faucet and expects hot water, turns the knob and expects the heat to go up. If it does not, she turns to the man with a frown and says, "Hey!?!" Meaning fix it, where's my hot water? In this way, does a woman really understand the advantages of doing it yourself? Maybe it's a guys reward, not a women's reward? Even Karen, who loved the life told me once :

"Hard physical labor builds a man up, but it tears a woman down."

We can have whatever we want here in the wild, pretty much. It's only a matter of money. People can have hot water, easy heat, and electric. Everything town has, it just 'costs.' I explain to most women who are interested, exactly what this life means, that one advantage is, I can be around more, not off all day long on a job, meeting at breakfast and dinner, and that's it. I'm usually just out in the yard, around the corner if I'm needed, or she can come talk to me, or work next to me if she wishes. Usually impossible when the provider has a regular job and a boss. Though it can be feast and famine, I'm around all the time, then I'm gone for a week on the trapline. It suits some personalities. Not all. Possibly there is no way to know till it is tried.

Past Flash

I think her name was Sheekum. Maybe my first female sled dog I ever owned. I noticed one day she is not pulling! Not doing her share! I frown, and watch closer as we travel. Sure enough she is looking like she is leaning into the harness, bends her head down, and mimics all the looks of a working dog. But in the dips the sled goes in, I see her line bounce slack. The other dogs have a strain on the line, have a taught line, even in the dips.

Any of the dogs alone can easily pull me with an empty sled. So I hook Sheekum up by herself and give the command "Hike!" She leaps forward, feels the load, and stops. She looks back at me asking, "Come on here, give me some help." She will not pull me. Any of the males would do so eagerly. Maybe momentarily it would cross their mind to wonder why they were pulling me by themselves, pause and look back with a question. All it would take to fix that attitude was a stern "hey!" of displeasure, and that would be the end of that. Males understand dogs that don't pull get shot. Perhaps the female is smarter, understands if I know she is not pulling she gets shot, but if she can fool me and not do the work, but I think she is, she has a good life of getting all the rewards for nothing.

This attitude from Sheekum is new to me, and I have never seen it before. I try to encourage her kindly. Maybe she is shy. Maybe she is sick, not feeling good. Okay, I understand. Back in the team, same thing each trip, Sheekum not pulling, but eager to get fed the same amount as a working dog. Eager to get scratched behind the ears. Even demanding affection and attention. Eagerly licking my face like she loves me. But, the whole time being a con artist. I get angry one day and have had it with her. I stop the team and go up to smack her a good one! When I get up to her, she smiles and rolls over on her back like a puppy. I can only stand over her and scowl. How can you hit a dog that smiles and looks like a puppy on their back? So I just yell, "You straighten out or else!" She wag's her tail and wants to lick my face. I assume she understands? I go back to the runners and say "Hike!" and Sheekum does the same thing, pretends to pull. Looking like:

"See boss, see how hard I work! Aren't I good!" At the end of each day same old, "Wow we sure worked hard today huh?" and I think, *"What's this 'we' stuff Sheekum?"* She cries if the snow gets deep. Cries if her feet get wet. Cries if she gets slapped in the face with a branch. Wants reassurance. Needs a hug. All Greek to me. Male dogs are not in the least like this. A male like Clipper gets smacked in the face by a branch I joke, "Got a problem up there Clipper?" he gives a "Screw you!" look, and we all laugh. It's enough that I notice. He'd be mortified if the whole team got held up and came to a grinding halt because he got slapped in the face with a branch. What are we going to do about it? Nothing.

That's the life we choose. At best, at the end of the day I might walk up to Clipper and turn his head so I can see his eye. See if it got injured. At best, I can put something on it, if it's cut. At best, ask gruffly if he is okay. Scratch him behind the ear and tell him he did good today. But, it's not expected, demanded, or required. Of course, he did good today. So did I, and I don't look for daily recognition anyplace. I don't do this because I have to. I do this because this is my soul, as it is with the sled dogs. If I was not around, this is what the dogs would be doing with their life on their own, by choice. Running fifty miles a day as a pack living off the land.

If a male refuses to do something I say, or takes on an attitude, I go to cuff him over the head. He might growl a little and challenge me. I smack him and he backs down and acknowledges I'm the boss, and everything is fine. If it happens again I smack him much harder, with a stick. And if he still has an attitude, I shoot him, and get another dog. Exactly as the pack without me would do. Those who grumble about the leader disappear, usually publicly in disgrace as a lesson to any other who thinks they want to be the leader.

Yes, much like people in the bar. Or politics. Butting heads to see who is in charge, all males of all species. Sometimes they hurt each other. Friends tomorrow. I do not take this same outlook to the world of people. It's different in the same species. I'm not interested in the option of shooting anyone and saying, "Next!" it's not politically correct, and frowned on.

The world of females in the herd, or pack is different. Females do not get involved in power disputes, do not respond to challenges of the pack, nor team effort. As far as Sheekum is concerned as a female, the males should pull her and she should ride in the sled. So, here is Sheekum. What can I do? Pretty much 'nothing.' In this way she is the boss. She gets to eat, gets attention, a place to stay, protection, and doesn't have to pay for it, doesn't have to pull her share of the load. Pretends she loves me. Pretends none of this is happening. Pretends I don't notice. Pretends it is not so. Argues that yes she is pulling, and how can I accuse her of not! "How can I!" Sniffle sniffle.

I do not hate her, and realized it is not her fault. She does not like this lifestyle. She'd be better off as a pet, not a working dog. Someone who would put her up on a pedestal and take care of her, and all she has to do is look nice, lick someone's face and wag her tail. Some (sucker) who replies, "Oh yes! I love you so much! You are just so cute!" Well. I don't need 'cute.' We work each day till we drop, and love it. We get up in the morning and we do it again, and still love it. Of course, it is cold! Da! Of course, our feet hurt, and got wet, and we all got slapped in the face. It's all supposed to be 'free'? Does anyone think we can be among the privileged to be here, for free? Can we be the only living things on top of the snow in the center of everything for free? How absurd to think so! We are as Gods, owning all we see, in every direction. Controlling an empire the size of the state of Rhode Island. Free? I think not! There is no free ride, no free lunch out here. So I shoot her.

My past flash jumps around- memories of the past, of now, of the future.

I had other female sled dogs since, that understood and loved the lifestyle. That also taught me about other sides of the female of any species. No. You cannot 'make' a female do anything she does not want to do. But if she wants to, and is not just giving lip service, she is an asset, she can be better than the male. Or, a good combination with some males. Males listen to her. There is less fighting. The team is more complete. A good female tends to be the leader. Often smarter. Sometimes tougher. Has more compassion, sometimes a requirement in survival. A whole team of nothing but males tends to end up a fiasco. Or explained as....the male cares about his position in relation to the other males. If it is time to goof off, all the males goof off together. Females tend to not participate, be much more responsible to a higher goal. If there is a prank to be pulled, you can depend on the fact a male is behind it. If a fight breaks out, you can count on all the males having a big smile with cut up faces, and all the females untouched, disgusted. I see a lot of similarities with people.

Flashes from the past and from the future leap into my mind. Not to mention any names. Situations where women are saying to me, "See how hard I worked today?" And I think, "I worked ten hours and you worked two hours. You want me to notice, thank, and reward you as having done your fair share. How strange." Images of women in my life expecting to ride in the sled while I pull. Women crying a mosquito bit them, they got their feet wet, they are cold, they got a splinter, an ouch, want me to kiss it and make it go away. Women that look helpless when weights to lift exceed ten pounds, as I lift with a smile, 100 pounds. Women who seem helpless, or incompetent, or afraid of most everything. Bears, the dark, electricity, noises, height, deep water, storms, just about everything. Women who want to pout, look cute, whose purpose in life is to roll over, look like a puppy, and expect to get fed, kept safe, and warm.

If I say, "Here's an ax, go cut a hole in the ice and get some water, 'please,' thanks. We need water." I would absolutely never hear the end of it. "You make me do this, you make me do that, I'm not your slave...." Bla bla. I politely nod smile, pretend it's a valid point. But point out:

"I'm not asking you to do anything I can't, would not, or could not do. I'll cut the hole in the ice and fetch the water. I'm not lazy. I know how to cook. I know how to clean. I know how to sew. I know how to garden. There is simply a long list of things that need to get done. Of the things on the list that needs to be done, what can you do, or want to do?" Most women I have known can only do about one fifth of the things on the list, so what she can contribute is limited. At the same time most women I know speak of needing a break. I cook now and then, clean now and then and that is ok. Do I get a break?

"You run the trapline this trip Dear, I'm burned out on it, tired today." That is not an option, she does not know how, and could not if her life depended on it. Nor could she build a cabin, use the chain saw, skin furs, build a dog sled, fix the boat engine, or give me much of a break. The difference is, I never say nor feel I am overworked, and or need a break. I sometimes simply run out of time. My day begins at 5:00 am and ends at 10:00 pm. Seven days a week. Including Christmas, Thanksgiving etc.

I'm even willing to do it all, including the cooking cleaning hauling water. "Just be happy." "Let me do my job without complaining." Of course if you do not do anything to help, then you do not have much of a vote when it comes to decision making. Likewise the quality of both our lives drops, because there are only so many hour in a day I can work. "There may not be much time for you."

Turned around, if a woman supported me, provided all the food, the home the transportation, the furniture, all the bills paid, my income is zero, and I showed up with nothing but my toothbrush, I would be grateful. I would not expect to have the right to ask her to move, to accommodate me, do anything at all my way. This 'right,' arrives with having contributed something. *What an odd view, is this why we are alone?*

Past Flash ends

THE SLED DOGS have made runs of up to ten miles, and been run a total of fifty miles this season. Usually they have made thirty mile trips, and have several hundred miles on them when I try for a town trip of forty miles, usually a month from this date. I tell Sally:

"We can make it, and will not die, but it will be hard." She wants to go for it. She is not someone who would understand the word, "No!" *It could kill the dogs.* There is three inches of snow, and the lakes are sort of frozen. It's the first week of October. The fall leaf colors have faded to uniform browns. Only a few leaves remain on trees. We will have the Kantishna River to cross, then ten miles of swamp flats, till we get to rolling hills. In some ways the hills will be easier, certainly safer, but there are always fallen trees to cut out of the way. Uphill stretches are hard on the sled dogs. The airport is a little closer to this end then the town end, but probably we will have to stop there for the night. There will be another ten miles of flats at the other end, when we drop out of the hills to the Nenana River, which needs to be crossed. Crossing this river can be a serious problem. The Nenana often freezes later then the Kantishna River does, and could still be open. I have made the trip in the past, and gotten within sight of the village and had to turn around and come home, because the Nenana River was running ice. Neither a boat or sled dogs could cross. I keep in mind the statistic that ninety percent of all fatalities with dogs and snow machines in winter involves water and ice.

Sally asks about the snow machine I had written her about. "I thought you had a snow machine here." It is hard to explain, and may add to a sense of me as a teller of tall tales. I have come to the conclusion that sometimes the old ways work better than the new ways. Progress is going backwards. But only for some situations and lifestyles. I do have a snow machine, but it is wore out now and unreliable. I thought I could fix it and get it going good again. But no, I was over optimistic. I explain to Sally:

"Sled dogs are at their worse when you first get them usually, and are better with time, as you find dogs that suit your needs, and as you and they get used to each other. They rarely totally let you down. Maybe at first when you don't know their limitations. Usually however, one or two dogs could get hurt, or sick, or fail you, but I'm always able to limp home. It's possible to begin dog mushing on a shoe string budget and have sort of reliable transportation that improves without outflow of money, as you have puppies and make your own sled and gear."

I'm not sure she is listening. It sounds like a song and dance. But I continue, "Snow machines are at their best the day you buy them, and it's all downhill from there. Good reliable ones cost a year's wages. The average one needs replacing in about 5,000 miles. In my lifestyle it's closer to 3,000 miles. This represents miles I can put on in one year. They can unexpectedly fail at any time, even when new. Dogs do not arrive with a warranty, but what good is a warranty on a snow machine that fails a 100 miles in the wilderness? If you are stranded, what good is it, that the shop you bought it at would say :

"You are correct, the part you point at is covered by warranty and should not have failed, let me go in the back and grab you another one at no cost to you!" A five dollar part. That costs hours of walking, costs a trip to town, and three days of time. When traveling alone by machine, to be safe, you should never go further then you can walk. Snow machines get stuck, dogs rarely do. Travel conditions are more critical for machines. If snow gets too deep in a storm, a machine cannot go. Dogs might be slowed to a crawl, but I have never seen where dogs cannot get through in about 10,000 miles of wilderness travel I have had with sled dogs."

This is not something most people will understand. It's not what's advertised. It's not in any reference book I ever saw. *Our lifestyle comes with no instructions, degrees, courses to take.* "Anyhow, there is not enough snow for the snow machine, and I think I need a new one, even though the Élan snow machine is only two years old, I wore it out." I didn't tell her it folded in half from too much use in the tundra with no snow. I'd had it welded, but there are other issues, and probably an Élan cannot pull two people through the hills. I'm reluctant to admit even to myself, it was a mistake to buy a snow machine. I'm reluctant to admit I was talked into it, forced and intimidated into it. I feel almost brainwashed into believing in the industrial revolution, the jet age, now the space age, all within my lifetime.

I was stopped from fishing for my sled dogs by Fish and Game, so I got the snow machine to haul dog food for the dogs. So far I have used the dogs more, to haul gas for the snow machine. It's a sore subject, maybe it's a guy thing a woman does not understand. Like men = engines, women = cute fuzzy puppies. Engines do not compute. Women like engines when they work, are quiet and comfortable. When they break or fail they ask a man 'why?' In a tone of puzzlement. Stuff like your carbs, track tension, kill switches, is another language to most women. "Did ya check yer filter?" Gets a puzzled, "Huh? Filter for what?" Sigh, and oh well. I guess it's like when a guy is asked how the good meal got cooked. Loves to eat it. But if he makes dinner, and is asked if he used a sifter he goes, "Huh?" Cooking is worth about five minutes of my time, and I suppose that's how women feel about engines. How a man can spend all day fiddling happily with one is as incomprehensible as a woman spending all day long getting super ready. Though I suppose in this day and age, most women toss something in the microwave and calls it 'home cooked,' and most men take the machine to the shop for a spark plug change.

"So Miles, are we ready to go or what! Are you day dreaming again?!" I smile. I guess I don't come across to her like I am the dependable type. *What's this 'we' stuff woman? Rest assured I am ready and will make it. It's you I worry about.* But I say nothing about that. Probably she will not die. The trip however might have more in common with 'Donnor Pass' then 'Lassie.' Saying so would get a 'humph! Men!" I believe in on the job training. She is right, "Talk is cheap, show me!"

The dogs are eager to go, weather is an okay zero degrees. We will travel light with three days of supplies. We will hook up all the dogs to one sled, rather than run two sleds. Ten dogs can easily pull Sally in the sled basket. I have pulled this weight with only four dogs on the trapline before. I can see the dogs are too fat, and too eager to go. Mean and lean would be better. I'm the only one here who knows what's going on.

I look over the load in the hand built sled. Made from mostly local wood I cut myself. I steamed the three inch wide runners, and bent them in my own jig. Modern special plastic is screwed to the bottom for less friction. Very crude by modern standard. I sigh. Today, mushers use quick change plastic and can change the plastic to suit the exact conditions of the trail. Still, not long ago runners were steel, very hard pulling in the cold, very good on wet snow.

We take off like a bullet from a rifle. Sally seems pleased. But like that bullet, when we hit roughness there will be a collapse, a mushroom, a folding up, a slowing way down. Even a stop. Starting slow, like a steam roller, would be better. I watch the dogs and see the older ones will make it, and are already trying to slow the pace. The pups are young and resilient. But, after this trip they will not be pups anymore.

"Easy!" I yell. Spike, my dependable rock solid leader hears me and does his best to slow up the team. *Thin ice ahead.* We need to negotiate this, not go full steam ahead. "Thin ice," I whisper to the dogs. I doubt the dogs know what this means, but I say it every time, the same way, same tone, so there is at least a chance some of the dogs connect the dots from one experience when I said that, to the next time I said the same thing. Or, I hope they understand my tone, if not the words. Or, simply pay attention more because I'm talking, and I don't talk without a reason. There is sometimes an uncanny communication going on, however it happens. "You might try the right Spike, but you are closer, it's up to you." Spike looks to the right first, as I suggest, then left, and chooses to go straight. Our very life is probably not in his paws. That would be an exaggeration. But we could go through the ice, get wet, get delayed, have a miserable time, if Spike screws this up. I'd have to stop, build a fire, sort things out, and it could cost us a day. We'd be wet, and a day without food. *Been there. Done that.*

I discovered, so far, out of maybe fifty times breaking through the ice, that either the dogs go in, or the sled goes in. But never both. So far. A break through ice is usually the size of a dog. The team is thirty feet long. If one dog goes in, the other dogs pull him out, or we come to a stop and I can figure out how to get the dog, or dogs out. If the dogs get across, but the sled falls through, the ice is at least strong enough to hold the dogs. The dogs can usually yank the sled out. One reason is the front of the sled rarely breaks through if the dogs made it, because the front of the sled is light and 'floats' as the term might be, so it can steer. The weight is in the back, so the back runners usually break through. I can often dive over the sled handle bar into the basket and shift the weight balance point, and or work my way to the front with the dogs to pull the sled out with them. Or, choose to dive right, left, or behind me, to good ice. So far. Or, the dogs hear us breaking through and give a yank, run faster so the ice is breaking behind us. We are staying ahead of the break. Never mind, it's complicated. No use even mentioning it to Sally. *She'll roll her eyes up, just more of Miles being dramatic!*

I am aware however, of the number of people who go through the ice and don't make it. I have no statistics on the number, who, like me, break through and keep going. Kind of like comparing the number of people in cars who have fender benders or accidents and live, but never turn in a report. Compared to the number who get in accidents and die. Is the ratio ten to one, 1,000 to one, 10,000 to one, a million to one? Is it worth coming unglued every time you back up into a telephone pole, or fire hydrant? Or, do you just think 'rats!' and get on with the day?

"Miles, see the fox watching us over there?" I had not spotted it. Sally is in the sled basket sitting on a pillow, warm and comfortable. Enjoying the ride. *This is how it is. The man makes things comfortable for the woman, and when she is not comfortable, it is the man's fault.*

"Yes, sometimes fox see the sled dogs and might wonder briefly if they are related, stop, look, and take a step closer to get a better look. Even wolves have done this." We are seeing lots of wolf tracks on the ice. The red morning winter sun is cresting over the hills ahead, far off beyond the frozen lakes we are crossing. Hundreds of lakes with no name, no roads, no connection to anything human. I answer, "No, none of these hills, lakes, or mountains have been named."

Here is a frozen swan in the ice. Sally looks at me with a question. I reply: "Probably a young one not big enough to fly south with the rest." I have seen this with the big birds, mostly swans and eagles. "It is common for them not to have enough time in our short summer to mature enough to make the trip south." They become food for fox and other predators. Sally wants to stop and keep some feathers. I mention it's not legal. Not that it matters, but just letting her know, because we talk sometimes about laws. She talks sternly about how we need to be law abiding citizens. Like I am a criminal, and she is not. Fine when talking about someone else, about subjects of no interest to the legal beagle. Now she thinks it's 'absurd' you can't salvage feathers in the woods off birds that die naturally. Wants to know 'why'?! I know why, but it's too complicated to get into right now. We gather a few feathers, but now we are partners in crime. How easy it is to be a criminal. My mind wanders on the subject as we travel in silence. Just the soft sound of dog feet on the ice, an occasional squeak of cord lashings against wood. Viewed from Gods perspective, a tiny moving dot on still white canvas, red and immaculate, the sun in its chariot rides the sky.

Maximum twenty years in prison- depending what kind of feather you pick up off the ground. Sally would probably get off. I'd get the max. Because she'd give off the sought of attitude. "Yes masta, yes masta, sorry masta." Eyes on the ground, ready to go sit at the back of the bus. Roll over and be a puppy- big innocent eyes. I'd look 'em in the eye with my, "What a bunch of crap," attitude. A government of the people, by the people, and for the people. Those arresting me should be ashamed! Isn't there something better to do then give people a hard time who found a feather on the ice off a dead bird? Aren't jails full enough already? But no. The answer is no. There is always room in jail for people like me with the lights on. I'm sure they'd explain it different, "Kid. We don't like your kind," like in Alice's Restaurant. with two part harmony.

As I guessed, in about ten miles- as we get to the hills across the flats, the dogs slow way down to walking speed. From ten miles an hour, to eight miles an hour, (about average speed on the trapline) down to four miles an hour. I get off the runners and walk behind, going up the hills at a snail's pace. I do feel better now that we made it through the most dangerous part, the swamps and thin ice. No way a snow machine could have done it. We had gone over logs as high as a chair, barely slowing down. Gone over ice floating on water, and ice as thin as half an inch. The hills might be slow, but they will be safe. We leave behind the trail of ice fog that hung in the damp Kantishna River drainage. In the hills the temperature is ten degrees warmer, so a pleasant fifteen degrees. The view changes. Now a whiter line against black, the trail through the dark spruce forest. Sun dapples ,flits and flirts with us through the trees, running ahead of us, dancing and laughing. Daring us to catch it. But I know better. *No one can catch the sun!* But I did once shoot a hole in the sun with my rifle.

There are fresh moose tracks, wolf tracks, lynx tracks, to see in the snow. Squirrels chatter at us, and a few grouse fly off with a whirr and fairy dust of snow, to land in the forty foot spruce trees all around us. *And a partridge in a pear tree!* Shorter bushy trees have enough snow on them to be bent over. In some places this forms a tunnel we run though.

The first twenty-five miles of our journey is okay. An adventure. We are warm, dogs are excited to be out. We get to the airport in four hours, so about six miles an hour as our average. Not great, but not bad. When smart people go on a long drive in a car they have a spot they stop, like a gas station where they look at the tires, check the oil, look for leaks, stretch their legs, and buy a snack. It's the same in the wilds with the dog team.

"Are you warm enough Sally? Ready for a break. I know the dogs are!" I had thought to maybe spend a night here. But only four hours into the trip seems a bit early. Still, I know the dogs have had a hard run when they are only used to ten miles.

"Didn't you go fifteen miles once Miles?" Oh yes, I forgot, once we went fifteen miles out. "Miles, it's not even noon yet. Let's just keep going!" If it were up to me alone, probably I'd stay here, relax, let the dogs sleep, feed them good and press on tomorrow. I want the woman to be pleased, but get outvoted. She's adamant. There is some wisdom in pressing on. We are limited on supplies, and if we rest too much we could run out of food, like if we come up against lots of downed trees needing cutting that slows us up, or sloughs full of water, or the Nenana River at the other end we can't cross. We'd be in trouble to have to turn around, and make the trip back on three days' worth of food. Asking the dogs to run ninety miles in three or four days, when they are used to ten miles a day!

"Anyhow Miles, this is not much of a place to stay! I'm not sure I can get any sleep here!" From her perspective, it is small and pretty ratty looking. From my perspective, it is better than being dead. Or worse, having the trip go bonkers, ending up eating the dogs, and walking ourselves alone. That's possible.

A porcupine has eaten much of the wood, and left droppings on the bed and floor. The 'bed' is just a few planks laid on logs. There is broken glass from a window a bear got to. We'd have to make a board for the window, cut firewood, and spend several hours getting camp ready here. If we press on, there is at least a good possibility we can make Nenana 'today.' After all, we have seven hours left till dark, and are almost half way there. We'd only have to average four miles an hour. We can walk that fast probably. Anyhow, I can see Sally is anxious to be back in civilization. I can also see she is right, probably she cannot sleep in this place. Weather is good enough we could sleep outdoors if we must. I do it all the time. But still. We would not even be making such a risky trip if it were not for Sally. We'd be 'home' living the good life, out on the trapline. Only fools are out this time of year making such a long journey. But I want to please Sally. Show her I care how she feels, and want to give her what she wants to the best of my ability. Is that my weakness? Should I say the heck with that? But, she'd think I am being controlling. Not wanting her to leave. Telling some scary story about what would happen if she tried to leave.

"Well, we need to rest the dogs an hour here. You can stretch your legs." We have some soup in a thermos to eat that is still hot. I melted a little snow for the dogs on the stove in the airport cabin, and add some snack to the water so the dogs will be encouraged to drink. I check to verify my stash of emergency supplies I left here at the airport is secure. The bear got in the cabin, but was unable to get in my barrel of supplies. The bulldozer that cut out the runway left a few fifty-five gallon drums. I had taken a cold chisel and cut the top out of one. A battery drill put holes in for a hinge at one side of the cut out lid, with a hasp for a lock on the other side. When set and locked, the cut out lid drops below the rim and is impossible for a bear to grab with a claw.

After an hour of rest, the dogs are sort of eager to run again. Less enthusiasm then this morning. Some of the older dogs know where we are going, but indicate they are eager to go for it.

I point out a trap here by the shack I set for Marten each year on a log. The trap is kept here wired to a tree. A Great Gray Owl hoots above us, looking for mice, or small game we might scare up out of the snow covered grass. Nutmeg and Pepper are two pups that jump up and down barking to go. Cinnamon was part of this same litter and should be with us. I get a stab of pain, missing her, but must dismiss this, so the living may survive.

I feel a little better every time I pass the airport. 'Halfway' is the worse place to have any problems, as it is the maximum distance to travel either ahead or back. If I get in trouble before the airport I can go back, but not as desirable as being able to get to town, because I am going to town for a reason. That reason is not fulfilled if I turn back. And 'trouble' usually means I need something. Parts, knowledge, something town usually offers. After the airport, I'm closing in on town, and could walk this far if I had to. Well on a good trail anyhow, or with little snow like now.

Within an hour we are going slow, very slow. The dogs are wore out. Within another hour the dogs will not, cannot pull Sally in the sled. She now has to get out and walk with me. I'm unsure how far she can walk. But if we walk for an hour or so, the dogs might get energy back. Or, we can decide to make camp. Fifteen more miles to go. Then ten more miles to go ... but we have spent two hours going five miles. We drop off of ten mile hills into the flats. In the distance we can see Nenana hill, with lights on the antenna, seen on the hill as the sun begins to set. Our first sign of civilization in several months. It's hard to decide to spend a night when we can practically hear civilization. *Surely we can go ten miles!* It would be about as much effort to make camp then to just press on. I'm aware, that to the civilized used to driving, ten miles left to go is being there, the blink of an eye. In my lifestyle ten miles is commonly a days travel, and in poor conditions, a miles more can be forever. I once made a trip, when all I could cover in ten hours was a few hundred feet.

There are about two hours of sunset light left. Possibly we can get to the Nenana River and across before total darkness. The dogs can pull Sally in the sled on the ice here, so she gets a break. But not for long. Soon we know we must walk the whole rest of the way and the dogs have trouble just walking. I know we will not die. We will make it, it will just be hard, just like I said when we left.

Even so, I get the impression Sally blames me. Why is any of this my fault? I'm not the one who wants to get to town, as if it's an emergency. She's pregnant. I'm the provider, and this is what I provide?? And this is okay? Well, as we walk I think, and my mind spins as we eat up every foot we work for.

It's all relative. It all has a perspective. This is how man lived for 10,000 years up till 200 years ago. This is how man lives in third world countries, the majority of mankind! It is only the civilized world that is appalled by reality. This is how the animals we love, and wish to be like, live. A world where the strong survive, and the weak fall over and get eaten by wolves. I didn't make the rules. We want to deal ourselves in the game of life in the wild? We must accept the rules. We can't think it's only about the good times. I can't promise only good times. I can't provide only good times. I told her exactly how it would be, so why is she glaring at me? But oh yes, I can see the headlines, "Trapper Arrested for Negligence- Goes to Jail!" The whole 'pregnant' story. I'm not the one who accidentally on purpose forgot to take my pills, knowing I am in the wilderness. No, it's all my fault. I should have just laughed when any civilized woman or person tells me they wish to walk in my shoes, live as I do. Tell them they are nuts, and do not know what they are talking about. Yet, here I am. I started out just like her, as any civilized person, did it cold turkey, no help, no advice.

Surely, with my help and experience it would be easier then I had it? Surely, if I can do it, so can others? I am not that special. I cannot tell others, 'No it can't be done!' I believe in going for our dreams. But still, I suppose I talked Sally into this, as it was not her dream to begin with. Her dream is to have a child. Her dream was to find a game warden type. With a regular job in the woods. A life where you get to buy, and can afford, solar panels, and if the panels don't work, take them back under warranty. Be a Yuppie. Have some chickens you buy as chicks, and go to the store to buy chemically- steroid laced chicken feed and call it, 'living off the land, being natural.'

Walking through this snow covered deep dry sedge grass makes a hissing sound. The frost falls off, and sparkles in the setting sun at our feet. I'm tired, but okay. Happy enough. This is not much different then what is routine on my trapline most of the winter. Walking in front of the dogs till I drop, cutting things out of the way. I feel honored, special, just like 'Clan of the Cave Bear,' only reality! I suppose I tend to take everything to its limit. Myself, my dogs, God, my women. I see Sally has pluck, because she has not told me she can't go any further. She has determination all right. She is not in panic mode, or crying. She'll make it, so I have new respect for her. Perhaps she will be less angry, and this will be just an adventure when it is over. I recognize the first slough of the river ahead.

"Five more miles Sally." She only nods. The dogs know too, and must hear or smell the village ahead. There are still not tracks or evidence anyone else has been out here this winter yet. It often seems odd to me that I come in forty or fifty miles, and am the first tracks in the snow a mile from the village. *What do these village people do?* Yes, some live like me. Dim Burke gets out early 'sometimes.' A couple of the other natives. The Ketzlers, maybe Percy. But they are getting old, and the young ones are not taking over the lifestyle. My mind wanders about the various villagers I know who get out into the wild still, to live the life of a trapper. Though I am making more money with my art these days, and beginning to make some money working with Seymour as a surveyor. *Not that I ever want to be a surveyor as an occupation!*

Sally is not cold. Weather is still 'nice,' no wind, no deep snow, no chilling cold. It is colder in the flats then in the hills though. The temperature drops fast as the sun sets. I look over and make sure Sally is not sweating. I see she has her coat zipper open. This way she should not sweat. If she needs to stop and rest she can zip up and be warm. *The only real issue now is if the Nenana River is frozen or not!* Once my friend Josh came to the river on the other side to check on it, just as I arrived to open water, viewing him from the other side. He was able to get a boat, and pole across to fetch me and the dogs. A little dangerous with ice chunks spinning down the river.

Well the first slough of the river is frozen with 'overflow' on it, also frozen, so this tells me the main river is probably frozen. There is a first freezing, when the slough ice freezes and forms black ice. When the river itself freezes, the water under the ice is under pressure and squeezes up the sloughs as far as several miles. Usually there has been a snow on top of the slough black ice and the main river overflow mixes with this snow and forms easy to see 'overflow.' Overflow tends to be rough and lumpy. You can also see in higher spots where the overflow ice hits snow piles and frozen. The ice looks like Styrofoam. No snow is on top of this new freezing. I explain to Sally how this is a good sign. Snow can act as insulation on new ice and cause the warmer water under the cold ice to melt the ice, and we cannot see open water under this snow. Very dangerous. I tell her, "Always good to see the ice and know what shape it is in as we walk." As we get closer, the trail is getting more familiar. I have come out this far form Nenana getting firewood over the years. I come out this far from the houseboat parked in Nenana, just having fun, taking the sled dogs out on a jog, keeping us I shape.

We get to the main river, the Nenana, and pause. I take a long look out across the ice to see if there is steam coming up from any open water leads, or black strips indicating open water. The sun has set, but the moon is out to see by. Ideally, I would tie up the dogs and walk across first and come back. The dogs would follow the same way I walked. But we are tired, and if the dogs lay down now, they might not get back up again, and think we are camping here and give up.

Spike has his nose down sniffing, and leads us across perfectly sound ice. The place to tie up the dogs is just on the other side, not far from where Josh keeps his sled dogs. I have the houseboat pulled out here, ready for us. While we are unhooking dogs and feeding them, Josh comes down to feed his dogs, and is able to give us a ride, and offers us a place to stay. It has been a tradition that I have a place to stay with Josh when I come to Nenana, just as Crafty at his Craft gift shop is my place to stay in Fairbanks. Martha, Josh's wife feeds us and fusses over Sally as Josh and I sit up talking 'dogs.'

Josh has won the Iditarod 1000 miles dog race and plans to win again. He's been training with the wheeled cart, and is just now getting ready to use the sled.

"Glad you and Sally broke a trail for me! How's the slough crossing?" When Josh takes off with a hot team he can't have any trees across the trail, and he can't stop to cut them. Race dogs are not trained to stop. Or, it's bad for their training anyhow. So, Josh now knows the trail is open. He will not run into problems at twenty miles an hour. I tell him about the two slough crossings.

"Yes Josh, I think you can come straight down the first one and straight across. On the second one, stay to the left a little, there is a straight drop off the bank where the trail used to be last year." Josh likes to dive straight off. "The second slough you might want to go out ahead first and get some snow to make a ramp." Sally and I had made it up and down, but slow. It was rough. A snow shovel will level it all off. We both know the routine. Branches down first, then snow on top, let it set up overnight.

The next morning I go down to the dogs with Josh to feed our dogs and check on them. Josh has his thirty dogs nearby, and he shows me good points and bad points about the various dogs, and how you can tell.

"Miles, that Pepper is not going to make it. Her chest is not deep enough, and she is not tall enough in the front shoulders. A sled dog needs good lung capacity and strength in the front. They come down in their front end when running, so need that upper shoulder strength." He points out one of Normans dogs, Clipper, and thinks it will not be a good one, even though Norman thinks Clipper will be good. "Tail curls up!" Some of what Josh tells me I think might be like old wives tales that mean nothing, some native taboo of some kind – meaningless. I ask why a curled up tail would affect a dogs ability to work.

"A curled up tail indicates the way the spine is built. The dog can't wind and unwind his back as good with this shaped spine." Well at least he has a logical reason if it is true. I will keep it in mind. Josh tells me white dogs and blue eye dogs are no good either. I take it with a grain of salt. Discrimination. Still Josh knows ten times what I will ever know about sled dogs, and deserves my respect. But, I'm a slow learner. I often need to see it for myself. Josh goes on:

"I ordered worm medicine and shots for your dogs. You owe me $20." He got a deal ordering in quantity. Some shots require a business license to be able to order, or get a discount on. I ask why my dogs need any shots, they look fine! "Miles, you are like a child. Someone has to look out for you!" Josh talks this way a lot. I say nothing, though it is an irritating way to talk to anyone. I ask:

"So where are my dogs going to get worms? I'm not near other dogs. I cook the food they eat." Josh explains dogs sometimes catch mice in the yard and eat them. They eat each other's poop, lick their feet, eat grass. Any of these things can transfer worms. And it is true, it only takes one time of not thoroughly cooking a rabbit, or squirrel, or fish, when feeding them. The dogs don't care, and would as soon eat it half cooked, so it is easy to get careless, not have time, or have the cooker fire go out and not pay attention enough. I wonder then how life was in the old days before worm medicine! Josh tells me I need to worm the dogs at least once a year if I think they need it or not. I reluctantly decide to do this. *Money. It always costs money to do things right. Geez.* But we talk about the old days and how the natives got by.

"Miles, the sled dogs just ran lose all summer. In late fall the villagers who needed dogs to pull something just grabbed up the loose dogs and used them. Many dogs died and no one cared a lot. The dogs ran loose and ate scraps – dead fish on the beach and refuse from the village. It helped keep the village clean. The dogs were breed to be tough!" Josh describes life even when he was a child, as he remembers life in the village of Minto during the depression. "Villagers did not go so far as we do today, and we need to remember this. There was more game to eat. Hunters were better at finding the game then today. Going out ten or twenty miles was plenty far. Sometimes there was a visit between villages, and long distances were traveled, but not so many miles per day, just lots of time. They lived off the land, fed dogs fish, moose, caribou, whatever was on the land. There were certain times of the year villagers knew it was easier to travel."

There is sometimes a travel time in late fall before winter. About this time of year. Not much snow, easy to walk, yet ice. Mild sort of predictable Indian summer weather. Bull moose may be still in rut, so not so hard to find, when they are not wary. Game easy to see with leaves gone. Rabbits fur not white yet, but with white snow on the ground it is easy to spot rabbits, *well technically 'hare,'* there are no rabbits in Alaska. It was this time of year the natives would walk from the village of Telida to Lake Minchumina on the frozen swamps. I heard of this in Minchumina. I think it was done even the year I was there. I recall a family showing up In Minchumina how just walked sixty miles, with children. "Just a way of life Miles."

I understand well, what Josh says, as it has been my own experience. The perfect time to get out and cut trail for trapline, and build trapline cabins is this time of year. Another time though is when the salmon are running, when it is easy to get food as you travel along the rivers. Dogs could pull loads, or pull boats using lines. Families traveled, maybe spend a month getting someplace to trade with another village, or the Eskimos up north. Josh remembers:

"Miles, we used to get the mail by dog sled. One of my relatives ran a road house where the mail haulers dogs would get kept." I have seen pictures of Josh in the early days when he piloted a paddle steam boat on the river, and before there was a bridge over the Tanana River on the road between Fairbanks and Anchorage, he ran the ferry. We are on this line of talk because of the trip I just made, just like how it was when he was a child. Not odd or dangerous. Just a way of life. A lifestyle one chooses or not. *I do not need to be filled with guilt!*

"You do okay for a white man!" Josh often gives me this line. A compliment. White people are so stupid in general. We all laugh at them, falling out of their boats, crying, getting lost, needing to be rescued, can't read the river, or a map. Have no clue how to stay alive in a world teaming with opportunity. I only partly agree, because it hits too close to home. I was raised in such a world as locals laugh about. I too was once one of them. Sally is one of them. We must be more kind and forgiving. I cannot say "You should have seen her! What a hoot!"

I try hard to remember that old life. A world where Josh would look stupid. A world where if Josh fluffed up his feathers and proudly announced "I won the Iditarod!" People would burst out laughing. A world where sled dogs have no place or meaning. Josh thinks it is because of prejudice. I think it is as much because of cultural differences. No different from when he – we- laugh at rich people with degrees who cannot feed themselves here, or do what any five year old here can do. I remember how it was. I remember that little Indian kid in Ruby along the Yukon River telling me what was wrong with my engine. "It's yer carbs!" He told me. Sort of like a five year old in the city explaining why you got hit by the car by saying, "Red light!" Pointing at the light, can't go till it's green, what an idiot you are- don't know that? Anyhow, Josh teaches me about the old ways, how problems of survival were solved. How to dress, how to eat, how to travel. Sally may think I'm just bull-shitting when she and I have things we need to do. Will I ever figure out women? You'd think among all my fans there would be someone who would take to all this like a duck to water. You'd think.

It's puzzling how so many people can dream about something and then balk at the reality of what they dream of. I don't get it. But am reminded of the adage, 'Be careful what you wish for, you might get it.' Josh gets it even less, as a Native America, he cannot understanding the white culture well. We head for the post office to get mail. Josh gives me a ride in his truck. Sally is resting up at the house. I have the houseboat here, but it seems small and cold in the winter for the two of us. *Maybe in a couple of days we will move in.*

There is an outdated jury summons in the mail from a long time ago. In the post office we run into Mick the local lawyer.

"Miles, was wondering when I'd see you! There is a warrant out for your arrest, you need to get to Fairbanks and explain!"

"Explain what Mick?" "You did not respond to a fishing violation ticket. You have to either send in the fine, or contest it within a time limit. A warrant for your arrest has been issued because you did not respond. If you want me to be your lawyer and help straighten it out, we can go to town." I see here in the mail a communication from Fish and Game. It is mixed in the assortment of fifty pieces of mail, ranging from ads for credit cards, to letters from strangers wanting information on homesteading. I often have difficulty sorting between business, personal, and what's important.

"But Mick, how come these sorts of communications aren't sent by certified mail? That is how it used to be, that I recall and assumed was required, to prove I got it! How can I be held liable for something I never got? What if it gets lost in the mail? Why is there an assumption, that because it was sent, it was received?" Mick is big on showing people how the government has gone amuck, and without a lawyer we are screwed. How he can fix things. As a favor because he likes you. For a small fee of course. I buy into it. I'm behind a rock and a hard place, because I do not drive. Without help, I have no way to get to Fairbanks to respond, and if I do not I can be carted off in handcuffs. I am concerned it is then a legal requirement to drive and have a car? There is no public transportation in Nenana. A cab from Fairbanks is over $200, beyond my means.

In earlier times, everything required took place in your community. If there were legal problems, you got called into your village sheriff's office, at worse the local jail. If you did not wish to go to the big city, there was no legal reason you had to. No one could make you.

"What do I do Mick? A warrant for my arrest? Good grief! I can be picked up on the street, handcuffed and carted off to jail?"

Some people think I am a little paranoid due to my experience in Canada, losing my home and all I owned. At that time I had been handcuffed and taken to jail barefoot without a jacket wallet, or ID. I had considered the situation annoying, a small misunderstanding worth a ten dollar fine, or something. Even the cop picking me up had chuckled, and told me it must be a misunderstanding and I'd be back home tomorrow. I'm not a criminal. I never saw my home or belongings again.

I've had some bad experiences with Fish and Game over moose hunting and fishing as part of a lifestyle, trying to follow sport laws. Problems doing art with byproducts off animals I ate, so as not to be wasteful. *What kind of problem can that be?* Who would have ever guessed it's worth twenty years in prison, same as murder? Many laws seem to not make sense to me. It's the same to me as, well eating cheese on Thursday instead of Friday, and getting carted off from your home screaming. Yes, like being a Jew in the days of Hitler. Anything is possible. Getting shot because you are black. "So what do I do Mick!?!" Mick is Jewish. He makes money when people panic.

"No problem, calm down. I can file a *habious corpse justificationust.*" Or some such lawyer talk. The bottom line being he can fix things, stall the handcuffs temporarily till I, pardon me 'we' can get to town, explain ourselves to a judge. With a lawyers help I might get out of this alive with only a small lawyers fee, if I do what he says. Maybe as little as $700! 😁 :)

Wow! Thanks Mick! The missed jury duty issue is solved just by explaining at the courthouse in Nenana. Still, there had been a vague threat that if I am summoned and do not respond, I am in violation of the law. The Fish and Game issue requires going to Fairbanks to resolve. I do not drive. My buddy Josh shows up and joins us, after listening in as I thank Mick.

Josh agrees it is a good thing we have a lawyer who cares. Josh tells me, "Yes, Mick was our lawyer when my son got arrested." Josh thinks Mick did okay. I do not know the details. Josh's son, Guy, is in prison for thirty-five years to life, for murder. There was never a trial. I've lived in the civilized world enough to understand a few basics of how it works. It seems strange to get life in a plea bargain, with no trial. Doesn't seem like much of a deal to me. What could be worse? But not going to talk about it overly much with Josh. It's a sore subject. Josh loves his son, and is sure his son is innocent and got framed! "When it is proven, and the facts come out, Guy will be free. Certain people need to step forward and tell what they know. It's all over drugs, and people who are scared to talk." Conspiracy, deceptions, pay offs, drug lords, a crooked society, and prejudice against natives and other minorities. It makes my problems seem small. I remembered Guy as an okay kid. I like him. Now eighteen years old, and in prison for life, over a woman beaten to death with a tire iron and dragged into the woods. Anyhow. "Welcome back to town Miles!"

Sally rolls her eyes up at all this. Again, I'm not coming across as very competent. With friends like this, with events in my life like this. It's not what she imagined life in the wilderness to be like. She is more street wise then I am, and understands civilization better. Much of my problems are not normal to her. "No, not everyone has such issues Miles!" People who live normal lives don't get arrested for nothing. Don't have friends whose sons are murderers. Don't get deported and lose everything. It's all about my attitude and what not. I don't understand what she is saying. Beyond something is obviously wrong with me. Except when I'm alone in the wilds.

"Mick, you ready to go?" He has an office in the village of 300 people. He's Jewish, with hooked nose and wild black hair, feisty, cocky, ready to fight. Mick is obviously intelligent, but eccentric. In many ways 'gifted.' He's won a lot of hard cases. *So he tells me*. I had forgot till he reminds me, he is the one who offered to help in the past over the illegal moose issue I faced, ready to go to fight the State for me. For $30,000 .

He likes to specialize in the issues of the wilderness people, "Because I'm like you Miles! I have sled dogs and fish for them. I like to hunt moose and live a simple life. It's not right how we are treated, taken advantage of by the law, by people who don't have a clue how we live!" I nod my head in agreement. *What a nice guy, standing up for underdogs like this.* We drive the fifty-five miles to the courthouse in Mick's beat up truck. There is not a lot I remember or understand. No one is speaking English. *It must be Latin or something?* I leave it up to my lawyer. All I remember out of it all, is the judge asking me something and I explain:

"Well I never got the notice. It was not sent registered. I only get my mail every few months. I can get a statement from the post office if needed. All this happened while I was in the wilderness. I have come in to straighten it out as soon as I heard." The judge looks at me annoyed and replies :

"That is the sorriest excuse I have ever heard. You can't come up with something better than that?" The judge obviously has no concept of how I live, nor is he interested in hearing about it, or investigating if I am telling the truth or not. He has made up his mind, I am guilty. That seems scary to me. A judge who has no compassion, no sense of getting to the truth. Lives in Alaska and has no clue how much of the State lives, and seems to feel I and, all who live like me, belong in town, in civilization, and what a bunch of nonsense to live any other way. This attitude is controlling my life, what I can do and can't do. This is an eye opening experience. It's not much like the movies, or what I am told – taught in school, taught by society, about how the system we live in works. Innocent till proven guilty, the chance to be heard, judged by our peers.

Also affected is my sense of who I am. My worth to society, the lifestyle I am so proud of is affected. My heroes are the founders of our country. Probably I get on my soap box way too often, and anyone who knows me has heard it all far too many times.

"Those who trekked across the wilderness as hunters- trappers. Daniel Boone. Jim Bridger, even Lewis and Clark. Hundreds of great men I read about, who opened the wild west, conquered a savage land so civilization could follow later. The very spirit it might take to be the first into space, clearing the way on other planets – facing hardships so civilization might one day follow. Why am I treated like a criminal? How absurd. How very odd. How puzzling. How sad. How narrow minded."

Mick of course, supports these ideas and agrees. That's why he's my lawyer and friend, and giving me such a good deal on his fee. Mick got me off with no fine and no record. The case was dismissed because the laws concerning subsistence have not been defined. The court cannot show I am not a subsistence person, if subsistence has not been defined.

It is difficult to see, to understand, the line between paranoia and realty –truth. The line between that which is reasonable to expect, and that which is unreasonable. Facts from rumors. It is so easy to take a few facts and blow them up, exaggerate, and go off the deep end. To not be believed. This is scary in itself, to not know the line where truth ends. Not know if I am sane, or not. The fear of being locked up if I am not sane, like my sister was. Strait jackets. A lobotomy. 'One Flew Over the Cuckoo Nest' stuff. I am not afraid of civilization. I'm terrified. Thank goodness there are caring lawyers like Mick who understand what is going on.

But of course I understand, saving someone's life is costly! I give him the $700, but still, this is several months wages to me. Not a good time to be having such a bill with a new woman who is pregnant and – well. Oh well, *lucky to still be alive I guess.*

That judge looked at me like a piece of dirt, and did not care if I lived or not. I suppose my raggedy hair, torn dirty clothes and such did not help any. It is the best I have. I look like my heroes, good enough for me!

BACK IN NENANA SALLY asks me, "Well, I'm thinking I need to move back to California where I am from. I'm not sure what to do here Miles. Obviously, we can't go back to your homestead," I'm listening. But puzzled by this term 'obviously.' What is so obvious to her about not able to return? We had a hard time getting in, just as I said we would. We made it. We just need to wait for a little more snow, and the dogs to rest up some. Feed the dogs, good for a week, and a trip home would be much easier. But no. She is pregnant. Well we can stay in the houseboat. Look for work. Or, I can go back to the homestead and trap and make us some money.

"Sally, this is not a good time of year to look for work. Summer in Alaska is when money is made. We got a place to stay, enough food to live on, food for the dogs, no bills to speak of, and we can hunker down, and wait till spring for work."

"What about doctor bills Miles!" Among other things she thought she had 'beaver fever' from the homestead water. I'd never had it, never met anyone who had it. Never even heard of it till about a year ago. It's suddenly the rage. But, it is the talk of the civilized world about things to be careful of when going in the woods. How the woods is not a safe place to live. How we should not attempt to go there. I'm pretty sure she is fine, and she is pretty sure she is not. We don't have the money for doctors. One of the first conversations I had with a Native about life out in the wild when I asked about doctors and what do we do! He was a healthy happy elder who said :

"When we get sick, we die." I said, "Oh." That was simple and easy, and uncomplicated. I've never been sick. There are days I don't feel as good as other days, and it's called a off day. It's not called being sick. Anyhow, anyhow and anyhow, time seems to just pass. I will get out to trap, Sally stays partly at the Craft shop, with Josh and Maggie, or the houseboat. She feels abandoned. I feel the bills need to get paid somehow, and the best way is for me to ply my trade. Again, it is winter and there are no job offers this time of year.

The problem Sally worries about is partly resolved when we go to town and I have my art with me. We see a private home baby delivery business and they love my art. We will trade an art piece for all the bills of having a child. Sally is in favor of having some sort of home delivery. There will be the opportunity to get to the hospital if anything goes wrong. Anyhow, being poor is not always romantic. Anyhow, I don't feel poor in the wild, just in civilization. There is a new homestead program we are told about among folks in Nenana, just twenty miles up the Nenana River. A few people have already staked.

"So Sally, maybe we could get a piece of land in your name only twenty miles out of town, within walking distance on a good trail. With neighbors who might help out." She might not feel so alone and isolated then, have others to talk to besides me, maybe other women. In this way it would be a compromise. I will still have a little of my old life, and she will have a little of civilization. "Bearfoot has already staked up there with his wife."

"Who?"

"You already met him. He's the guy who came running into Nenana long ago in his socks, because he burned his boots up trying to dry them in a camp fire." She remembers now. Gene is also up there someplace. Kind of a eccentric nut, but very knowledgeable about the wilds. Spring is coming and it is time to form a plan we can agree on. She thinks maybe she can handle my lifestyle closer into civilization. Maybe there is work this coming summer. Seymour needs me for surveying, but not full time. There is not much hope of any other kind of work besides my trapping and my art for this winter. Mostly what we need is money to pay bills. I explain how I feel to Sally:

" I can't be of much help staying in town adding to high bills and no work to speak of. All the supplies are at 'home,' and home to me is the Kantishna homestead. Food is there, work is there, no bills."

"Well, I can't go back there Miles!" Yes, I can see that well enough. We came out before we should have. Ideally I would be concentrating efforts on getting traps set and making a living, as my part in a relationship. Providing food, shelter, and such. How can I do that in town? It's frustrating. Where would I keep my dog team? What would I feed my dog team? I have a winters worth of fish for the dogs at the homestead. No, I can't bring everything back into town.

Crafty said Sally could stay there at the Craft Shop in 'my room' upstairs. The room he keeps for me when I'm in town. Possibly he'd have a little work for her as well. But Crafty has a couple already living there as employees in the building – Kathleen and Tom. Kathleen and Sally seem to get along okay. They look forward to spending time together. Sally can feel safe there, in an environment closer to what she is used to. Room and board in trade for some part time work.

"Maybe I can find a real job Miles." *While I do what I do best, trap and do my art.* I don't see a lot of options. I feel guilty – annoyed – hurt- angry all at the same time. I made it clear, this is how I live. I made it clear, I have no intentions of making major life changes. If she can't live my lifestyle, I'm not interested in any other lifestyle. Or, the love of my lifestyle is greater than my love for her. Or heck, we have not been together that long, so what is love? Something scary, that's what. That can cause a man to give up all he believes in, a job, a home, a way of life, he has learned and worked hard for in his lifetime. All traded off for what? Why? Someone he meets and does not know. Something based on a week's time. A person who suddenly owns him. Has him doing dangerous things he should not be doing, for no thanks. Worse than slavery. At least slaves have a value.

It would be different to live with someone a while. Love them. Love based on having done things together, based on trust and respect. Then find out you have to move to town like for that loved ones health. Then you do what you need to do. I would have settled down a long time ago with someone if I was willing to leave the wild! I don't want to be forced out of the wild! Am I being defensive? I feel badly leaving Sally by herself at the Craft Shop. Once I leave her there and am assured she will be fine and leave for Nenana, reality sets in. To survive in this world you have to be hard. I didn't make the rules. I don't like the rules. But I'm a survivor.

One thing I had not talked to Sally about is the fact the Kantishna land opened back up again for another homestead program right in the area I live, and call my stomping grounds. I'm going to have to share the country. I know I must share, and understand I can't be greedy, understand I have had it good all these years to have it to myself. There are at least two new homesteaders within a mile of my cabin.

One is a guy who borrowed my canoe when I was gone, and staked land almost across from me on the slough. He has not built a cabin yet, but has showed up, and intends to trap. If I am not there this winter he may well take over all my trails, and claim them as his trapline. This is how he is talking. Apparently he talked to the Trappers Association, who told him he could set traps and see if anyone says anything. It is hard to believe this is the Association's stand, but that would be legal to do. The law concerning trapping rights is about nonexistent. There are no laws. It's public land. Any trails cut, work done, cabins built, all belong to the people, technically. Or, put another way, if someone moves into a trapline cabin, runs a trapline trail, or even puts traps on a trapline trail someone else cuts and is trapping, there is no legal recourse.

It's understood this is not wise, and is a good way to get shot. In general, trappers do a good job of regulating themselves. We need to try to get along, and 90% of the time do. In general, we try to stay out of each other's way, or work out private deals. The trappers themselves expressed through the Association is that, no we don't want legalization. The downside is registered traplines like in Canada. Ending up paying taxes, keeping records to turn in, and getting regulated. In Canada, I hear trappers are told by the government what to catch, how much to catch, as if you are working for the government, helping as game managers! The government is your boss who can fire you! You are allowed to trap and stay, as long as you fill the quota. So many beaver etc. If not, someone else is brought in. None of us here in Alaska want that kind of situation to even be possible. We basically have no limits here.

I have friends with 500 mile traplines. There is no bag limit. So there is something to be gained, the dream and potential of great riches. But something to be lost in a world of no rules. There is no one to go crying to if you are wronged. You fix it yourself or move over. Trappers themselves tend to shrug their shoulder and don't get involved in disputes others are having. Only curious what the outcome is. If a rival trapper mysteriously disappears, there is not a lot of shock or investigation. The problem got solved and life goes on.

Over the years I have heard of a few trappers who got killed by rivals who took over the trapline. It's considered 'dangerous' to seriously mess with a trapper. That's why it's not done very often. That's why I am concerned this guy seems willing to take it to the limit. It's already upsetting he has 'stolen' my canoe to stake land across from me. That takes a lot of gall. His reply on the subject was a happy:

"Well we both run dogs and trap! We have a lot in common and will get along great!" It's hard to put a bullet into such a happy face. Sigh. Get along, according to who? To whose benefit? He wants to share, learn from me, profit from my hard work. Offering what in return? He has nothing I want. I want peace, quiet, no neighbors. That's why we all come 100 miles into the wild, right? If I wanted a neighbor I'd stay in town, right? So, what's his angle? I feel like an old timer who expects respect. Grandfathered in. He can have sloppy seconds. I was here first. He needs to pay his dues. I said :

"Look, I can't stop you from trapping. There is plenty of country available for both of us if you take the other side of the river." He says :

"There's no trails over there!" Well da! What does he think was here when I got here? In winter he will be able to use the trail I pioneered and cut to get here to his homestead. He could be grateful. Without the trail I cut, it is possible he could not even find his way here in winter. I explain:

" I cut my own trapping trails, and you need to cut your own trails. I'm a professional trapper who makes my living trapping. I spent a lot of years cutting trails and it's a marginal living. If you trap on these trails I can't make a living. It is not fair to me, for you to benefit from my hard work and I lose out. There is less fur for you too! Across the river you can be free, lots of fur, untapped country. It's open south all the way to the Toklat River- fifty miles away. You can go east another fifty miles. It would take a lifetime to claim it all." He does not see my point. Or does, but is afraid of the wilderness and wants my protection. His point is :

"The law says I can run your trail, it's legal. There's nothing you can do about it." My reply last I saw him was:

"I'm sorry you feel that way." That was last year, and I have been pondering what to do. Not the sort of thing to bring Sally in on. It's a wilderness issue. I'm expecting him to be back. I forget his name, he told me, but I forget. It's not important. I don't remember the walking dead. Yet pause. Sigh. *Yea, he reminds us to much of how it was when we got started. He's a greenhorn who just doesn't get it. When we arrived into the country, Indians took our supplies and left us to die. There was the big rescue that made national headlines.*

Yes, I recall. I am only now understanding a little about my role in the responsibility of my part in 'the problem' from the perspective of the Indians. The country seemed so vast to me. It was beyond my comprehension it could be crowded. Beyond belief anyone had been here in the past twenty years. Trapping rights were spoken of that were a generation old! I was being asked to respect that someone had been here fifty years ago. How absurd! I wished I could lay claim to land my ancestors inhabited that long ago.

When I arrived this was the old way. Land rights could last for generations. Your children could come back a generation later and expect no changes- to plug right in. I could not understand respecting something fifty years outdated. I could only focus on my rights as I saw them, and what it was I wanted. I was even scared a little, with no other options to choose. Here I was. No ability to move, to leave, to go someplace else. I did not know how to run a boat. I did not know how to run dogs, or a snow machine, or snowshoe. All my other options were gone, no other door to open. No other road to take. I'm here and must make my stand. There were other issues, racial issues, land use issues, new laws – lots going on I was not aware of.

I think what was done was wrong to take all my supplies and leave me. But still, I do understand, and only sigh. I'm no longer angry. Not that I'd apologize, but if I had it to do over, I could have probably worked something out if my own attitude had been different. If I had promised to leave next year when I could. Promise to leave. Ask permission. Acknowledge with respect, their ancestors. My culture I notice does not respect it's ancestors as the native culture does. I don't give a hoot where my ancestors are buried. Nor what is being done to the land 100 years later. It's not sacred ground. It's a cemetery. But that's important to some people. I did not know that at the time. Anyhow. This bozo kid can create problems I don't need. Probably thinks like I did when I first arrived. Will probably be treated the same way as a result.

And *oh oh, here comes more trouble*! I'm hooking up my sled dogs getting ready to cross the Nenana River to head back home to the Kantishna homestead and trapline.

"Hey Lynus! Haven't seen you in a while. Looks like you are headed out the trail too?" We had met off and on, here and there, I forget when, where. He dresses like a 1800's mountain man, and lives that life as close as he can. The biggest difference between him and I, is that I am not born in the wrong century. I am not stuck in time, or in the past. If modern new stuff works, is practical, and I can afford it, I use it. Lynus is a purest. His clothes, dogs, sled, his hair style, are all 1800's.

His hair is long, braided and smells of some kind of 'stuff' he says ancient mountain men made, and put in their hair. Made of bear grease and oils of some kind. He has leather clothes on, and a 'possible' bag made of a beaver skin, with rifle scabbard of otter hide. His dog sled is the old style toboggan made of rawhide. His dogs are all big 'old style,' as Josh puts it. Slow, but strong. Sounds good, even looks good, but I am not impressed. Because...

Well, because Lynus seems to always need help, or be in trouble. Some say that describes me as well. But, I'm not depending on others much. Lynus has twice now, had to make an emergency stop at my place and stay, rest up, consume my supplies. He's honest, always offers to pay or trade.

"Just like in the old days Miles. Cabins were open to travelers, we all helped each other out, not like today!" I do not quite agree. But do not want to argue. In my opinion the old line about the days cabins were open to everyone to just go in and help themselves with no locks is not correct. Yes, people helped each other out. Shared. You were always welcome 'if.' If it was not an obligation, and you could take care of yourself. No one was obligated to take care of you. If you were green and needed to learn, there was tolerance till you learned. But if trouble and problems was your way of life, the door was closed. No one wanted a nuisance. Lynus is not quite a nuisance. But close. For he tells me when he stops it's an emergency. But his whole life every trip is an emergency, and has been for a decade. His dogs are out of shape, not the right kind, and the sled is too heavy, too hard pulling for the distances he is going, and he can't see it.

"Hey Miles, yea I'm getting a late start this year. You know how it is for the likes of us. Never enough money or time. I had to grab up some free dogs at the pound to fill in the dog team. They'll get in shape on the trip just like the old days!" Two of the dogs already have bloody feet, and he's only gone a few miles. His sled looks overloaded to me, and already going slow and just getting started. He expects to run the fifty miles to my place, stay a while and rest up, then press on my trapline trail and connect to his trapline, another fifty miles further. He will not be back till spring with his furs. Or, that's the plan as he tells me.

He didn't ask if he could stay at my place, I never offered, and when he does stay, I am not home. He has in the past eaten my best most expensive valued foods. I have mentioned it, but it is my fault. Probably I do not mention it in strong terms. It's only a suggestion. That he can have all the rice and beans he wants. But not my dried fruit, and honey, and stuff I ration close and put high value on, and am unwilling to share. I can't replace it. *Why should it be me eating nothing but rice and beans, while he gets the good food?* And. Well, it's slightly irritating he runs my trails as a rival trapper, and assumes he is welcome to do so and such.

I get nervous when anyone sees my exact life filled with details. I'm not used to it. There are legal issues for example. I begin trapping before the legal season. I use sets to catch fur that are not approved. I might experiment with poison or fish hooks, or build old style deadfalls. Or, use spears and trip snares or, who knows? Stuff I don't want talked about. Or, get laughed at, or criticized, or discussed around camp fires. The planet I live on is a private world I don't share. I'm extremely unconventional. What I use for bait, how I make my sets, all of it I feel protective of. Not that I don't want to share ideas. I don't want to be criticized or laughed at, or told how to do it right etc. When I come out of the wild I want only one version of the story. Mine. People rarely report positive events that make others look good. I'm not sure Lynus understands. Nor is there any way to explain. So as I do so often, I inwardly sigh, smile, and be everyone's friend.

"Good to see ya Lynus. Looking good. Not many of us left. So how long do you think it will take for you to get to my place?" I'm wondering when to expect him and hope I am home.

"Hard to know with these new dogs and the heavy load. Load will get lighter as I travel, and dogs will get in better shape. I'll stop at the airport for sure." This is another example of a place that would not exist if I had not fixed it up, put bed in, left a saw and wood, new door, window. He is not thanking me or asking. It is his right. He thinks two days maybe. And that's the problem as I see it. I'll be home long before he even gets to the airport. You cannot in fact travel forever with dogs. Yes, in the very old days. But in those very old days you stopped, killed a moose, and fed that to the dogs. In the old days you were not a professional trapper doing this. When traveling in modern times we are on a time frame. We have limited supplies that dwindle. It is extremely difficult to improve your strength or the dogs while out on the trail in the wild. Distance travel only 'takes,' not adds. Keeping warm is hard on the body and takes a lot of calories. Dogs pulling takes a lot out of them.

When sled dogs get pulled under it takes a week for them to recover. Josh has taught me this. As part of Iditarod training he deliberately pulls them under till they quit eating. Similar to the stress the trapline can do, or what Lynus is about to do. After this, the dogs need rest, warmth, hot quality food, and sleep. Not obtainable out on the trail. Even on the Iditarod, the racers are not depending on what they start with, to be in the sled when they finish. They have food drops along the way, and other supplies. A whole support network is in place.

But it's an opinion, not a fact, and what's the use of saying much to Lynus? I look at him, at the dogs, at the load, and my opinion is, he'll be lucky to get to where he is going alive. Not possible without stopping to recover at my place. Now I'm obligated to help him out, or he'll die. When his 'problems' are preventable.

But heck, isn't the same said about me? I recall the conversation with the pilot who turned me in, because he thought I was killing lots of moose and feeding them to my sled dogs. How folks don't always like to trade with me. I have no money, so they feel sorry for me, or obligated, and feel they will never get paid, so they take my art crap and smile. How my whole life is an emergency and it should not be societies burden to give me, and those like me, special privileges. Even Seymour my survey boss and friend says this.

Seymour resents many homesteaders who are poor and disrespect the life and the land leaving junk all over, abuse dogs, get welfare, and food stamps. Free this, free that. And talk about being self-sufficient. My mind goes to these thoughts as I hook up my own dogs in harness and lash the load, get ready for the trail as Lynus and I visit. In my own defense, or justifications, I cut trail around Bettes. I asked. I showed respect. I gave a toll fee to Starrs, jars of honey, by way of a payment for passing through their territory.

Did ya forget about the knock out women that hang around Lynus? I knew my unconscious would remind me. Geez. Okay, ya, maybe I feel a little jealous. He has had at least two knock out fall over gorgeous women when I have seen Lynus in town. Hanging on him with love and adoration. He's tall, handsome, dressed cool. It's a real woman fetch. How does he do it? Men alone tend to be more hormone unbalanced, moody temperamental, aggressive, willing to fight, and well, part of their life is missing and it shows. Men are only half what they could be with the right woman. So, I struggle with being nice. It's not easy. What's easy is to be selfish, and look out for myself without considering others. The difficulty increases when a childhood did not address kindness and understanding. Only the quick and the dead. I notice Lynus is not offering to fix up the airport, know he will not cut his own wood. He will eat my food there, and burn wood I cut to keep warm.

"Miles, how was fishing this year? It's been getting tough where I am with the emergency closures cutting us off just when we need the fish the most." So he is affected to. I thought I might be the only one. After all, how many still depend on sled dogs as their major transportation, and do not even have a driver's license?

"Yes Lynus, I was especially hurting last year. I had all my supplies in for the winter. A plane lands on the river while I am checking fish nets and it's Fish and Game announcing the season is closed. I could be arrested, but they will be nice and not arrest me. Yet I must stop fishing right now. Didn't I hear the news on the radio?" Lynus laughs, and I do too. At the absurdity of us having electricity, a radio, caring about the news back in civilization. After all, we came out here to the wild to get away from TV, radio, and all its doom and gloom. Now it's a legal requirement to have a radio and listen to it? "Anyhow Lynus, I had to stop fishing with about half the fish I needed to feed the dogs." I don't need to explain. Lynus knows the water level is too low to make another trip to town and buy dog feed. He knows how it is. We spent all our money on supplies, and expect to come back to civilization in a few months with furs to get more supplies, after we have fur. I can't afford dog feed now, nor the gas to make a round trip, and possibly could not make the trip with a load at low water that time of year.

"Yea Miles, pretty much the same with me. I had to shoot half my dogs."

"I'm pretty upset with Fish and Game, when the biggest fish problem is not originating at our end, but out on the ocean. Yet, Fish and Game believes, and is convincing the public, that it is trappers, mushers, and subsistence people who are killing off the fish."

"I agree, there is a deliberate attempt to make us scapegoats." I have no time to ask what he knows about commercial methods of catching on the ocean, and if he knows what 'by catch' is, mile long ocean fishing nets with no restrictions. The number of fish we are talking about that's being protected and not made public.

"So Lynus, this year was a little better. I got fishing done earlier, being suspicious of an early closure again. I got my 2,000 fish put up. But because it was too early I have a pile of them frozen in my metal boat, and it's been hard getting them out! Won't do that again!"

"I fished early too and dug a hole in the ground, and cribbed the fish. The usual old time style." "Yes, I have seen this done, but noticed how the voles and animals move in to feed, and there tends to be a lot of loss and damage. I thought the boat might contain the fish better and stop animals from getting in more. There is no easy way except to fish late and freeze dry the fish on poles, and then stack them frozen someplace. So much easier." I pause and look over my load.

"Well I'm ready to go." My sled is slightly out of style compared to modern, but not 100 years out of style. Josh and I discuss the various merits of designs. I like the three inch wide runners compared to modern one and a half inch. If I travel a lot where there is no snow machine track, the three inch width makes a track in the snow a dog can run in. The width also hides my foot so branches do not swipe my foot off the runner, or stab me in the ankle quite as often on a rough trail. Though Josh taught me to keep my feet unnaturally towed in on the runners. Few modern mushers see the rough trails I do, or trails with no previous travel. Thus, they can get away with narrow less friction on the sled width. I also need the floatation of three inches as well. One and a half inches just bottoms out to much all the way to the ground.

Lynus has a sled that drags like sandpaper. I have a towed in bow and runners by a full three inches, low handle bars, tapered handle, Petex plastic bed, with supports up high. All part of a design for my exact needs. A short tow line for the dogs keeps a short team for tight turns. I sacrifice speed for maneuverability. Various racers told me the dogs will not pull like this or get used to this. But they do.

The team leaps forward and I'm off at about fifteen miles an hour. I'll slow to a steady eight miles an hour in a few miles. Lynus takes off at five miles an hour following me, and will slow to two miles an hour in a few miles. There is more snow now then when I had come in with Sally. The dogs feel good and had a nice rest. Like me, they are anxious to get out of Dodge and back to the trapline. I stop briefly at the airport, the halfway point in three hours. Here is where I begin my trapline.

Dim and I are having a minor dispute here, but I backed off in respect for his dream of this section being a connection to another loop he has someplace else. He does not get here as often as he says he does or wants to, but maybe he will, and that's okay, that he can feel good it will be clear for him when he gets here. It's how I'd want to be treated, that's my guideline. He uses a snow machine and can cover ground faster than I can with sled dogs. So, giving up five miles is a big deal, and means an hour lost time out of my business each time I come by here. But from the airport on, it's my trapline. I set the trap at the airport for lynx. The next set is a pole set for Marten. Nice to see some tracks of a big male here at the set, so am pretty sure I will have this fur when I come back.

There is not a lot of bait to use, because my bait is at home. Though Josh gave me some rotten fish he feeds his dogs. A small jar of my special scent lure was brought with me from home. Salmon oil is mixed in to stop the lure from freezing. Actually it takes three jars. One for Marten, one for cats, one for wolf. I only have the Marten lure with me. I mix berry juice, poop from Marten scat in the trail, urine from bladders off trapped Marten, and sometimes other secrets in my sauce. Not the sort of bottle I want to have break in my pocket. It's a smell that makes town dogs bark like crazy when I come down the street. Ha!

It helps the sled dogs a lot to be stopping every half a mile, while I set a trap. This is not like race training! It takes under five minutes a set to bait and set the traps I leave hanging here year round. Some are cubby sets, while some pole sets. Each has its reason and purpose. When I make a pole set for Marten I hang a snare under the pole for lynx or fox. It could catch an otter or wolverine as well, but probably not a wolf. Wolf trapping require special care and thought. Packs containing ten to twenty wolves come through my trapline. I'm lucky to catch one wolf a year. I keep hoping I will get more, but usually not.

There are a lot of things packed in my sled load for the homestead. The snow machine I bought last year has quit on me, and unsure what is needed, but have new rings for it that I am guessing will fix it. I'll need to overhaul it on the trail in the snow. There is fiberglass insulation for my Twin Lakes trap camp about seventy-five miles out from the homestead that will be warmer once I get this in. It's a tree house, a new idea I have. I will not have to build it as strong to protect it from bears and other wildlife during the year. It serves as both a cache and a shelter. My unconscious kicks in talking like Yogi Bear the cartoon character's line *"Hey hey hey, smarter than the average bear!"*

It will take some doing to get the trail open the seventy-five miles and setting over 100 traps along the way. I really want to get much further than this. Last winter I had mushed out another trappers trail. Had paid him for permission to cross his country so I could get to the Bearpaw property. I made sure the homestead was staked right, and left some supplies there. I need to be able to mush there from here on the trapline. I'm out 150 miles, and need fifty more trail miles to get there. Hansen Lake, my old stomping grounds is on the way.

This plan was before I met up with Sally. My hope had been that with a woman in my life, there would be some help, so able to accomplish more, able to trap more, and make more money. My dreams were about a woman who took care of the home front, maybe. Bring wood in, melt snow for water, or keep the water hole in the creek open, feed dogs, cook, tend the woodstove, wash, repair stuff. Mend a dog harness, or snowshoes, or sled tarp, stuff like this. Stuff that frees up my time to do my thing, my part of the chores that need doing. Share all that so it's easier on both of us. I do the heavy and dangerous stuff. But there is this talk so often of, "I am not your slave!" I'm puzzled and wonder what the point being made is. Because I'm not anyone's slave either. I'm puzzled and think of this as I run the dogs, that 'in theory,' being with someone else should cost less, and be easier than two people with two separate households. I have never had this work. It always cost more, and I always have less time. I would not mind if the work I suggest is as slave labor. Fine, maybe you also have an occupation? Like Liller, make fur hats, or I imagine a photographer, writer maybe. "I'll do the labor then, and you make more money than me and help with the bills, I'll free up your time." First, you need to be able to make more money than me.

At any rate, here I am a month behind on making a living trapping, and the woman has her hand out wanting money put into it. I can't do that as things are – so she's looking for work, going to take care of herself, and quit depending on me. As bills will mount faster than money to pay them comes in. Now. How hard have I worked – planned- learned- sacrificed in order to set up the kind of life that avoids all that?

I snap my finger in a jump trap as I set it, not paying enough attention. "Ouch!" Shake my hand and hit the trap with a stick to teach it a lesson. *"Stupid trap!"* Setting it more carefully this time. The dogs jump up and are still alert and eager to pull. I glance back to make sure the snare is hanging the right height, as I saw lynx tracks earlier. This is good rabbit country, the food lynx live on. We drop off the bluff into, 'Chicago,' the windy city. There is always a wind here coming off the bluff, and about always cold, as in twenty degrees colder at the bottom of the bluff. It's sometimes a good place to rest the dogs as I make sure my snow suit is zipped up. I adjust my Marten fur hat and otter mittens. Cold and desolate, the flats lure me off the bluff.

Tom and his wife, my neighbors six miles away, have asked me to move my Marten set up on top here. They also rest their sled dogs here, and don't want the dogs getting off the trail and into my trap. So I have to be mindful of how sets are made, so the puppies running loose behind Tom's team do not get caught. They do not trap and are, well, I hate to say it but, 'bunny hugger' types. Though they eat moose and fish. We get along I think. I guess. Seem to anyhow. I'm never sure if it is just polite tolerance in a situation they can't do anything about or not. But we have good conversations, and certainly are not fighting. As for myself, I like and trust them.

This year I gave them some moose meat. It's a tradition. The first to get a moose gives a front leg to the one who has not gotten a moose yet. Thus, we are all assured of at least some meat. I consider them good neighbors. They have been here since I myself staked, guess it's been five years now. Seems longer....

"Tighten up there Kansas- pay attention!" Kansas is one of Norman Vaughn's dogs he wants me to train up. This litter is all States, so I have Texas as well. Both are pretty big seventy pound, and tall dogs. Naturally deep in the chest, round boned with straight wrists, as is required for a good sled dog. The two are a little tired and must have less miles on them then my own dogs. But I'm not concerned, as we only have ten more miles to go. This last home stretch is along twisting creeks and swamps. The same stretch I was concerned about, coming the other direction with Sally, with the possibility of falling into the water. It's all frozen solid now, with an otter hole showing now and then. I don't bother making any otter sets this trip in. Otter are not worth a lot, are hard to catch, and take longer to skin then the Marten. *Maybe next trip I'll stop for otter sets.* Otter will not like rotten fish for bait, or respond to the lure I have anyhow. I really need a flashy piece of tin to appeal to their curiosity.

We pass the huge beaver house where I caught the otter that my mittens are made from. This time I stop for a while to make a good wolf set on top of the house. Wolves like to get up on a high spot to overlook the flat country. I make a blind set. This is a trap with no bait, no lure, no evidence of anything. On the assumption the wolf will get on top of this house to look around. I pretend I am a wolf for a moment, looking through wolf eyes. He will face into the prevailing wind to smell. This is also with the sun behind him, so there is no glare. Most animals are 'right footed' as people are. So the assumption is that, after standing still with both feet together, a wolf will make his first step forward, with the right foot. A trap set slightly to the right of center is the best gamble. I observe through the wolf eye. Far off across the lake, half a mile away are some spruce trees. Not of great interest. To the left, tall willows, with the sun on them. This is where moose will be, getting warm, munching the tender willow tips. This will be the probable direction the wolf will step towards to go investigate. Not further left, where the country is open towards the next lake. This is otter country, not of much interest to a wolf.

Sometimes where I set my traps, and how elaborate the set is, gets determined by the sled dogs. For no other reason than the dogs need a rest here. Not necessarily because it is the best place to make the set. There are places I want to set a trap, or would be a good place to catch an animal, but I can't easily stop here, so do not. It is hard to stop when going downhill for example. The dogs are on a roll, hard to control downhill. Good sled dogs in physical shape tend to be feisty. Don't want to stop and rest. They love to run, go fast, and work till they drop. Like me.

Well no, I didn't like fast dogs at first. Too much work, too hard to stay on the runners, too much maintenance taking care of a hot team. Much like cars, a good simple work truck can be preferred over a hot one that likes to run fast. But? Maybe once a musher has good dogs and gains some knowledge, it is hard to look back. Hard to settle for slow dogs ever again. Some mushers never in their life get to run the best. Like Lynus.

Because of Norman and Josh, I have a team here that might be capable of being in the top ten in the Iditarod race. Meaning capable, if trained to do so, to run 100 miles a day for ten days in a row. Norman had offered me $3,000 for my leader Spike. I think about this as I mush along. *But hey, I bet everyone on the runners behind a team thinks they have one heck of a hot team huh?* "As it should be!" I answer myself. We both laugh, me and I.

In some stretches I have to pay attention as we jump logs, slide into turns, go airborne over low spots, drop down onto creeks from six foot high banks. Not all trips are like this of course, because so often I am overloaded, or the snow is very deep. I do not have enough dogs in the team, or the dogs have not been fed top food. The dogs have not had all their shots in a while and have worms, or the dog flu. Anyhow, the sled seems to be working good. Yes, it needs constant care. This life is hard on equipment. I'm constantly side swiping trees and cracking a station. Even cracking a runner and needing to glue it, lash it, reinforce it. The job seems to never end.

The dogs know we are near home, so pick up speed. In six hours after leaving Nenana, I'm home. About forty-five miles, seven miles an hour average. *But don't forget all the stops to set traps, and the long rest at the airport!* I could be traveling as fast as ten miles an hour. Josh came to visit last year and made the round trip in eight hours! Dang! But with some of these dogs. So in theory, I could reach my goal of running a 200 mile trapline one day. Cover it once a week. More knowledge, better equipment, what else? No time to think on it, I'm home! Get a fire going, unhook the dogs, get the feed for them started, warm up, unload the sled. All routine. All familiar to me. A sense of peace and well-being. No stress, no worries. I'm not tired. It was not a long or hard day. A lifestyle that has worked for 10,000 years. No concerns over gas shortages, the other rat race concerns when living life in the fast lane. As I relax, I think about different people I know, choices we all make and notice.

We notice that so often, if someone is not happy in one world they might not be happy anyplace. We cannot escape ourselves no matter where we go. It might even be the same characteristics that help a person survive and be happy in town, that also works and in the wild! Interesting thought, that there might be universal secrets that apply no matter where you live. I wonder about this, because some of my friends, or those I am getting to know and respect in town, admire me and I admire them as we seem to have many of the same qualities. Likewise, many I know who are discontent and badmouth society, are angry people, move to the wild, yet not much changes. Problems are always someone else's fault. There is still an 'only if' aspect to what they talk. It will all work out 'when.' But 'When' never seems to arrive. I yawn, blow out the kerosene light. And go to bed. Life is good.

On the trapline I live in a tent while I build a shelter cabin in five days. I have a shelter up every ten miles. I am in the transition period between sled dogs sometimes, snow machine other times. Right now, it is dogs!

One of my friends living subsistence along the river system

CHAPTER FOUR

TRAPLINE RIVAL ALMOST DIES. ILLEGAL MOOSE PROBLEMS. CONSIDER MOVING WITH SALLY. MORE FISH GAME ISSUES. SELLING MY ART THROUGH CRAFTY. A CHILD IS BORN, TRADE THE COSTS FOR ART- THROUGH A MIDWIFE. NEW HOMESTEAD. NEIGHBOR ISSUES. ADJUSTING TO CIVILIZATION ISSUES. ANOTHER TRAPPING SEASON OUT ALONE

Lynus shows up two days later. He's in good enough spirit, but his dogs look drained. Some have bloody feet. Some of the things Josh has been teaching me kick in. I can't help but notice some of the dogs here do not have deep chests, or the right legs for being good sled dogs. These are dogs from the pound, free dogs. But guess Lynus will manage. I've learned enough about getting along with others to know most people do not want advice unless they ask for it. In this case, there is no reasons I should know any more about sled dogs then Lynus. He has had as many years and as many miles experience as I have had. Our goals were once the same, to be mountain men. I now enjoy the thought of easily covering 200 miles with sled dogs, not possible by Lynus. I want the possibility of providing for the woman I love, requiring getting close to a civilized income. I am less interested in studying old ways and copying them. I appear to be an inventor, innovator, leader, and not a follower.

"How was your trip Lynus?"

"Oh I guess okay. Getting low on a few things, so will be glad to get to the trapline." We get my dog food cooker going. I give his dogs some of my salmon I have for my own dogs. I have a beaver carcass from a beaver I snared in the pond out back. Lynus and I both know nothing is better for dogs then beaver meat. Lynus offers me an antique lantern from the 1800's as payment and thanks. I smile and accept it, but really have no use for it and it's not my thing, collecting old stuff I can't use. I vaguely wonder why Lynus is carrying a useless antique on his sled. He's overloaded with things he needs. But whatever, and the shape of his dogs, whatever. What can I say. Been there, done that.

The Collins twins at Lake Minchumina had told me I could be arrested for the shape my dogs were in on my first long trip with sled dogs. I was surprised! Had no clue! It's a tough cruel world, and everything looked lean and mean to me. Everyone belonged in jail, everything was illegal. Everybody's crap stank. But by the grace of God, it could be you, or me, being carted off in chains. What else is new? It took time to learn about worms, nutrition, paying attention to health.

Next morning Lynus is off, down my trail to the end, into the wild white yonder, beyond. He has seventy more miles to go, and it will take him a week. Even now, I could do this in two days. It will be a year or more I suppose, before I ever see him again. I'm anxious myself to head out the trapline. Before I go, I better look at the snow machine and see if it can be fixed with the new rings, or the machine will be buried in snow and not get fixed! Not a job to look forward to. With only the most basic tools, a crescent wrench, a screwdriver and pliers, I am going to pull the head and change the rings out on the trail in the dark and cold. The machine is five miles out the trapline. I only hook up four dogs and head for the machine.

Luckily I remembered to bring the snow shovel! It takes half an hour to dig the snow machine free enough to get at the engine. No book on the machine is in my possession. There is only my basic knowledge of how an engine works. It's in general, pretty straight forward. Fuel, fire, and compression, followed by mechanical parts that take that power and convert it into 'go' energy. The first thing to determine is what part of this is the problem?

Fire is easiest to check for. Short out the plug, pull the starter cord, and look for sparkle. Okay, we got sparkle. Next? Fuel is the next easy to check. Pull er over and see if the plug gets wet or fires. She be wet? We got 'em gas. Unless it's bad gas or water? So we smell the plug. Yuppers—we got gas chock full of vitamins. Compression. That's more tricky. A finger can be stuck over the hole, and if I can pull hard enough with a finger over the hole I get some idea if there is compression, at least guess if there is enough to make it run. It takes a minimum of fifty pounds to get an engine to run. And, well here is where I frown. Just a tiny 'ffft' not a sharp pop. I'd seen my buddy Will do all this often enough on my boat engine that needed constant pampering. *Like when he and I took that long trip with the houseboat to*

Minchumina. He's the one who taught me the basics. Not what the book says, but what it takes to survive. Stuck in the snow with a pair of pliers.

I could probably reuse the head gasket, but not if I tear it getting it off, so I had bought a new head gasket along with the rings. I have to remember where all the stuff goes that I have to take off to get the head off. Carburetor linkage, throttle cable, plug wire, muffler springs, bolts, and brake wire. Everything is laid out on a cloth in the order I took it off so I can reverse the process.

The machine is on its side filled with snow. There is nothing to sit on, so I am squatting in the snow at twenty below zero, in the dark with a flashlight in my teeth, so both hands can be free. Fingers are numb. The crescent wrench is not the correct tool for head bolts, and it is hard not to strip the square and make it round. With patience the head comes off. With patience the old rings come off, the new go on. An old tin can has been cut to put around the piston, and rings, and compress the rings so they slide down in the cylinder. There is good news that the cylinders seem okay, and the rings seem only wore out. They should not be. So maybe there is some other problem, lack of oil, some abrasive in the cylinder? There has been no filter over the air intake. It looked like the machine had been run where there was a lot of river silt in the air. So my best and hopeful guess, is that the problem is river silt, and all I need is new rings and an air filter. *"For $50 do you pick door number..."* " Um uh er gee I don't know!" My unconscious is ready to ding the bell and say *"It is your lucky day you get the prize!"* Or "Ding." *"I'm sorry, gee if you had only picked door number three, you could have won a trip to Hawaii with this lovely bikini clad, gorgeous, but dumb, big tits blonde!"* So what's it gonna be huh?

We both roll the machine back down in its skis after another two hours of getting everything back on it. If it does not run, I might be able to roll it into the dog sled and haul it home. Anyhow, sigh. But then what? Use it for a fish net anchor? My one $1,000 piece of crap? *Let the show begin.*

Pull, pull, no bang. Pull, pull, cough. Hope—hold breath—push choke in, pull harder this time—Bang! Cough cough smoke- cough and 'rrrrrrrrrrrrrrrrrr' the sound of a running engine. We have ignition. We have lift off. I stand up and grin skyward at God who has been watching with interest. *"Am I the man or what, huh?"* Jackie Gleason, *"How sweet it is!"* God does not reply, but my unconscious pipes up, *"You the man!"* Heck yes. I bow to the right I bow to the left. Accepting praise all around. The snowy branches wave. *"Were you all paying attention? Did you take notes? Did you notice the analytical mind- the superb perseverance against all odds, total confidence? The high intelligence exhibited?"* One of us mentions words like egotistical, exaggerated self-worth, and stuff like that, and I think it was my unconscious. I ask, "And your point might be? Let He who is without sin cast the first stone!" There is silence. The dogs have to follow behind me as I ride the machine home.

The snow machine runs, but the excitement is short lived. In truth you can't overhaul a snow machine with a crescent wrench and duck tape, and expect to do more than bang a few revolutions. It runs but lacks Umpa- like it has the flu- coughs a lot. *But I'll figure it out.* Meanwhile back at the ranch—are the dogs.

Diary Oct twenty-fourth 1987 – Head for #1 tent camp. 25th Set #2 camp up. 26th Six hours to come back from #2 camp. Twenty-four Marten.

I'm working on a cabin at #two camp by Twin Lakes. Well actually it's 'hang a left lake' not named on the map, but that's close to Twin Lakes. The cabin is made of unpeeled poplar trees. The sled dogs move the logs for me, so the project goes fast. The hardest is just getting goods hauled in, like the stove, a bed, tin for the roof, and such. It takes about five days to build a small cabin from start to finish. Tents for a tent camp cost $200 to $300 and do not last long, like maybe two seasons. Cabins allow me to have shelves, places to hang things, and hold the heat better, so can burn less wood. Also, they can stay year round and allow me to leave goods here, without having to haul it all home at the end of the trapping season. I had tried stashing tent camps on the spot, but never had it work successfully. In the late spring, after a winter of being up, the canvas is damp. No way to dry it on the trail. Thus, no way to pack it away rolled up in a cache without it rotting over the summer.

If I cut the 200 miles I want, there will be ten line cabins. One every twenty miles. I can usually travel at least that far, but on an okay trail I can cover two camps in six hours, like today. If conditions are at their worse I am never more than ten miles from a cabin. I've never seen the weather get so bad I can't get ten miles. In this way I can travel safe, if each cabin has supplies for a few days. This is the plan. I think. Sort of. I'm not sure with a woman maybe in my life. If she's in my life.

I spend early December cutting out my Christmas linoleum block and printing cards. I have my usual eighty people on my list. Relatives, friends, and fans. The trail gets cut as far as Hansen Creek, which runs to Hansen Lake, but my dog sled needs repairing again. I need to get the cards in the mail, and I could use some supplies, and I should check in and see how Sally is doing. Or, let her know I am doing okay.

Diary Dec thirteenth 1987 Head for town.

I arrive without incident, picking up another pile of furs—a lynx, a wolverine and two otter. I stay with Josh and call Sally who is staying with Crafty. She tells me:

"Yes things are okay. I got a job working at Woolworths, till spring anyhow."

She seems only a little interested in how things are going with me. But at least she seems to plan on staying in Alaska, and is willing to try the homestead life close to the village. It seems curious to me though that she worked as a checker at Safeway and swore to never have such a job like that again! A checker at Woolworths seems about the same to me. If I get the snow machine going good it will not be so hard to commute between the homestead and civilization! The trapline begins only twenty miles out from where we would live. (!) Sally is not as thrilled as I am. The income from the furs is not as exciting for her as for me. I stop in and sell my furs to my friend Don. I enjoy visiting, trust him, we have mutual respect for each other now.

"Miles I have 5,000 marten to grade in the back." We go in the back to continue our conversation. He is grading while we talk. I pick up a Marten and comment, "This is the nicest one in the whole room." He pauses, turns it over to see his tag and markings. He is impressed. "Yes, the best of the best, but it took me a long time deciding, how did you know in a glance?" I give my usual reply with a grin, "I'm the man!" In truth, what kind of answer can one give? Beyond, "It's the prettiest one in the room." How do I know? I know marten. I could be a fur buyer myself if I wanted a life in town. But even Don says, "I envy you, I would rather be out trapping then stuck indoors here." I get paid $9,000 in cash.

"MILES, I can make more money working minimum wages." I open my mouth to reply and shut it back up again. I have a cabin, the equivalent of 'rent paid for the winter,' saving how much? I have 'heat' paid for the entire winter, with all the firewood. What's a winters worth of heat worth? I have transportation all paid for the winter. What's transportation worth? I have all the food needed for winter. What's a winters worth of food worth? So- all this 'money,' Sally makes, goes to pay for what? Rent- food- heat- transportation. There is nothing left over. How is this financially better off than I am? I am puzzled as well, at five dollars an hour, how many hours is this to bring in $9,000 profit, after taxes? But for me, not just after taxes, but after all the necessities are covered. The equivalent, in my mind, of her bringing in twenty grand. How long then would that take to earn? A year?

It does not matter who is right, or who wins this argument. What matters is, we are each happy with what we are doing, and the two outlooks on life are equally valid, but not compatible.

I head back to the trapline the fourteenth. I have materials for the dog sled, and can work at the homestead. Wind has come up. The trail home is blown with snow, so it is more of a struggle getting home then it was coming in. I have a heavy load. Dogs are a little tired, but not worn out. I see already I will be low on fish as I was stopped from fishing early, as I said to Lynus. Part of my sled load is commercial dog feed to supplement the fish. Not exactly living off the land as expected. Part of my load is gas for the snow machine *Hey! Wasn't the plan to use the snow machine to haul the dog feed?*

BACK ON THE TRAPLINE, it is another struggle in the deep snow to get to the hang a left lake camp. At this camp I now have an outdoor cooker for cooking a fast hot meal for the sled dogs. An extra chain saw is brought, so I always have a way to get wood for the stove and cooking dog fish. I have been acquiring cheap saws at garage sales, or pawn shops, and have a pile of Homelite XL saws that cost about $80 new. They only last a season or so of hard use, but I prefer having a lot of saws left at my various camps, over just one, that I have to carry with me everyplace.

The sled dogs are used to the routine at camp. I arrive about dark at 5:00 pm. The dog harnesses come off, and are hung by the wood stove in the camp so they will be dry by morning. The dogs get chained to a gangline tie out. They do not mind so much, as they are tired and want to sleep, so the lack of room they have is not a huge consideration.

Spruce bows are cut from the nearby trees and laid down for each dog to sleep on. It is not necessary, but if the dogs sleep better, it is good for me, and if the dogs do not have to melt a hole in the snow when they lay down, they do not need as many calories. The five gallons of dog food water is started. Snow is melted. It takes a lot of snow to make five gallons of water, so I need an early start on it.

Once the five gallon gas can pail is over the fire on a tripod melting snow, I can relax more, and take time to look to my own supplies. The dog sled is unloaded of whatever I am carrying to the camp. My own damp outer clothes are hung by the stove near the dog harnesses, and I put on a dry warm sweater or coat left at the cabin. In this way I will not get cold, and I will be assured of dry warm clothes in the morning, as I can wait all night for everything to dry well. There are certain tasks I want to get done before I lose daylight. If I am low on wood I sometimes see to the wood pile first, so I am not wandering around far off in the dark looking for wood.

A lantern is lit, or sometimes a propane light, depending on the luxury level of the camp. Usually it is a wick kerosene lamp, but never kerosene, as I can't afford that, so use diesel fuel. The lamp burns about a cup in twenty-four hours. The amount of light might equal a five watt bulb- like a refrigerator light, or a nightlight. Sometimes I add about a quarter cup of gasoline to a gallon of diesel to raise the octane and get twice the light. Too much creates an explosion.

A good fire is started in the stove, usually after all the earlier chores which takes about half an hour. Sometimes it takes a while to get the stove going right, so I want time to be inside to tend to it. It is easy to get the stove going, leave the damper and draft open and forget about it. However if I get distracted, the fire can take off. I then risk the shelter burning down. All the shelters are small, low roofed and about six x eight ft. A stove, a bed, a small table, a chair, and enough room to turn around, and I'm happy.

On the table are a box of matches, outdated magazines, papers for fire starter, and the lantern. One plate, a mug, and a fork are on a shelf. Metal cans with lids have duct tape on them with magic marker 'rice,' 'sugar,' 'dry vegetables.' The cans keep the mice out. There are several mouse traps on the floor. Usually they need emptying each trip to the cabin. Outside the cabin door is a cooler I keep frozen food in. Usually chunks of moose meat, and chunks of frozen cooked beans. Bears are hibernating, and nothing else can easily get in a cooler. Well a wolverine, but only had this happen once.

Beans are cooked at the home base and scooped out, sometimes directly into the cold snow to freeze, but other times in Tupperware containers. Hot water releases frozen meals from the container. The clumps are put in a plastic bag in the cooler. Ketchup and peanut butter are condiments. Local honey is in a jar for pancakes in the morning.

A book to read in the evening is a must, so I have five or six unread books at each camp. In this way if I have to hole up, I do not get stir crazy. It is a reward for me at the end of a long hard cold day of physical work to be able to sit down about 7:00 pm and read till bedtime, about 8:00 pm.

The sled dogs get fed about 6:30 in the dark. For at least half an hour I go over gear, fix things, write in my diary, and call it a day. I read, go to bed in a sleeping bag on a thin foam mat on a pole bed frame. I never use an alarm to wake up. Don't even own one, never have in my life, never will. Oddly, I always wake up when I want. Even when working surveying with Seymour, he tells me what time to wake him and I wake up at that time 6:00 am, 7:00 am, whatever he says. On the trapline I usually want to wake at 5:00 am, and do. I have no problems sleeping. I lay down and am asleep in less than five minutes, and don't wake till it's time to get up. I'm not a worrier or restless sleeper.

I wake up this morning and for a moment, forget where I am. This is common. In the dark I slowly feel around me. If the wall is on the left and has cloth over it, I am at home base. If spruce bark, I am at camp one. If plastic and insulation, I am at the tree house camp. If the wall is on the right, I am at Hansen Creek. I am then oriented, and it all comes back to me.

I rarely lay in bed long. I'm up and at it, wide awake and working within five minutes of waking. There is the lantern on the table close enough to reach and light with matches next to it while lying in bed so I can see to get up. The stove is always designed to be within reach of the bed so I can lean out of bed, grab the laid out kindling, set it in the stove, pour some diesel in, lay larger sticks on, and light it.

Shut the wood stove door, then lay back in bed a moment. Usually within five minutes there is warmth in the small shelter, enough to get up and get dressed. These rituals are somewhat important and necessary. If I have to get out of bed to start a fire for example, I might get up in a twenty below zero cabin, and already be cold before getting out of bed. If I need to get up for any reason in the dark, I must know by feel where everything is. I may have to get up to pee, or take care of a situation with the sled dogs, or deal with a grizzly bear or moose. Everything outdoors must be where I can find it in case there is a snow storm and everything is buried. For these reasons I try to repeat the same ritual exactly the same each time.

There is always a piece of screen in a frame over the stove at the ceiling to catch the heat off the stove. This is the drying rack for mitts, socks, and such. In this way the socks are hot when I put them on my cold feet. That warmth is usually enough to get the circulation going and maintain the heat till my body takes over. Usually I have a pair of slippers or shoes to wear in the cabin so I don't have to wear the outdoor boots. These boots would get sweaty in the cabin and then freeze me in the day time. Keeping dry is the main secret to staying warm.

The dogs hear me get up, and know the routine. I hear a chain rattle. A dog yawn, a dish ting as it falls over. I've taught the dogs to be quiet. There is no barking or carrying on. No whine, no crying, no yelling. As the dog broth is warming in the morning on the indoor woodstove, and the pancakes are sizzling, I might read a little more. Among my books are the Louis L'amour series, Zane Gray series, Tarzan series. I've read them all at least once. I've read all the mountain man books ever written at least once. So moved on to the best sellers, or murder—spy stuff. Or true adventure, or how someone overcame something and achieved a great goal, a story of someone famous and exciting. Arctic exploration books are of interest. Clan of the Cave Bear is my latest read.

I'm averaging a book every five days. Seventy five books a year. Seven hundred fifty books in ten years. All this reading has me thinking how I want my own writing to be. I take note of styles I enjoy. Mark Twain for example, always has chapter headings with a brief sentence telling what to expect ahead in the upcoming chapter. Book one is being worked on, but I'm still struggling. There is a manual typewriter with a ribbon in it at the main cabin I use. But have had to start 200 pages all over from scratch four times already. Sometimes I get ideas on the trapline, which I hand write as notes that go in my pocket. These notes later get transferred into the manuscript. Reminders, 'how to' notes, ideas, descriptions, quotes I want to record are all kept.

This 5:00 am morning, the northern lights are out and flashing with greens and reds. It's a normal twenty-two below zero as the dog broth warms. Today the broth has three mice, some moldy oatmeal, half a fish, potato peelings, and the water I washed the frying pan in. As part of the morning feed ritual I look over each dog to see if they are okay, alert, healthy, happy, ready to go. Sometimes how far I plan to go, and how the day is planned out, depends on the condition the dogs are in. If they only look up at me and do not get up and are slow to drink, or only look at the water without drinking, I can decide to stay at camp and skin furs we have, or mend snowshoes, fix the sled, or keep busy in some way as a change in plans. The dogs need rest.

My unconscious is the butler today as is common. *"Will that be the moose and pancakes for breakfast, or the pancakes and moose ma lord?"* I pretend it is as big debate. I say out-loud, "Let's have the moose and pancakes for a change James." It's what we always have. I can consume ten pounds of moose meat a day.

I'm not expecting the dogs to be out of sorts, or tired today. As expected, they are up and eager to see me, drink, and get the day started. They watch me load the sled and sometimes know where we are going, or what kind of day it will be by what goes in the sled. At home, if the mail bag goes in, they know we are headed for town. If the saw goes in, they know we are only going to get wood. If traps go in they know where we are headed. Today we are headed back home. I rarely tell them what trail to take, or what direction to go. I expect them to know. If I say, "Hey!" The leader goes, "Whoops!" and takes the other trail. Usually the leader knows, but tries to pull a fast one, thinking I might not be paying attention.

Today I'm expecting to cover the fifty-three miles before dark. I feel like one of the characters in Clan of the Cave Bear I am reading. But in my mind it is not the past. It is the future. Mankind has wiped himself out. If anyone else is alive, they are doing so by living much like me. Sometimes this dream is strong enough to get mixed in with the truth and reality as I know it. Planet Of The Apes comes to mind. In the beginning scene a bone is tossed in the air by an ape, and as it spins it turns into a satellite in space.

In such a world there are no days of the week. Nor are there any rules or laws beyond God's and mine. This world I created far from the maddening crowd is safe, normal, unchanged for 10,000 years. It's understandable, simple, even if tough and hard. There is no sound of a plane. No beer cans. No human trails, no engines, no smog, no smells, no sights that God did not make. Just us wild things, just us savages. Stepping out the door of my cave, harnessing the sled dogs is savored. One hundred fifty miles in the wilds is sanity. In this dream I vividly see the city when I get to it, deserted of people who wiped themselves out. Sitting on the parking meters are grouse roosting. *Already nature is taking the city back.* World War three came and went and I missed it. Or in another version, I get to town, and find a Russian or Chinese running the store. Undaunted, I pull out furs to trade, and point to a bag of rice. I have no enemies and am not an enemy to anyone. In these dreams all governments are the same, want the same thing. In real life I do not think the US will remain a super power forever. We think we can be a service based culture instead of a manufacturing and raw materials based culture. I think we are fools. He who controls the necessities controls everything else. But anyhow... things to contemplate as I travel...

Headed towards the main cabin on the trail I cut out with a machete is a good feeling in the silence of predawn 7:00 am. I cannot see well enough to know where I am to travel. It is the dogs who can see. I depend on them to know where we are. We come out into a clearing of some sort. It seems to be a lake I'd recognize in daylight, but now I am not sure what lake or clearing. Unsure if the trail goes across, right, or left. The dogs stay to the right edge, so think this is 'Foraker View,' a long marsh, that when coming the other direction I can see Mt. Foraker next to Mt. McKinley. It's about a mile long, with gradual curve toward the rising sun. There is a wolf killed moose at the other end we are headed for, and I am interested to know if any of my snares I set caught one of the returning wolves. Often the wolves do not return. They just kill another moose, if there are enough moose.

This trip, there are lots of wolf tracks! But they have not returned to the old kill, and looks like a fresh moose kill on another part of the lake. All I catch at the moose kill set is a fox worth at best $20. How he got his head in a wolf snare and got the snare tight is a mystery. *He must have tried hard to get caught huh?* Yes, sometimes animals seem to want to get caught.

The warm twenty below weather, relative to the forty and fifty below weather we had, has the fur moving around, finding new feeding spots. Every thicket of new woods in the flats has Marten tracks. A few new sets are made in places I have never set a trap before. Usually I set in the same place year after year. As long as I do not over trap there is as much game each season back again. Nature has a balance where there is a surplus of young born for each species. Some percent of the young are not expected to live forever. They are expected to be food for other creatures, or have accidents, get sick etc. There is a healthy sustainable number the environment can support depending on feed, weather, and other factors that varies and is in flux. Populations have natural high and low cycles. Plucking five percent of the population when the population is healthy seems to have little effect in the big picture. There is a recovery, and the loss is absorbed with a higher survival rate for the remaining population.

It's more theory then fact, and as much opinion as anything else. So I pull a few traps on this trip because I have seen fewer tracks then I'm happy with, and want the population to build up here. My concern for the population is greater than my desire for more money. If I want more money, I will have to work harder, cover more miles. Other stretches of trapline get traps set, as I see more tracks then expected of large male marten. Marten live in small family groups. In a healthy population the male does most of hunting, bringing food back to the family, living under the deep snow. If the males cannot get enough food the females come out to hunt more, then the young. Knowing this, I can judge the health of the population but the size and sex of my catches.

The next set has a big frozen male marten. He died curled up sleeping on the trap. Tracks show a lynx came by and sniffed the dead marten, but did not touch him. Curious why he was here I suppose. If the lynx comes back, a new set has been made for lynx. The usual dried grouse wing is hung from a string so it can move a little in the breeze. Lure is put on the wing to carry scent through the woods. No bait is used. Lynx prefer to catch their own food, and do not respond well to rotten scents, or things already dead and frozen. They like hot meals. With this in mind, one way I catch them is to get them to think there is a hot meal nearby. I make it look like something might be nearby wounded! *Yummy!* I carry a bottle of rabbit (Hare) blood that has been mixed with salt or a natural preservative so it will not freeze in the dog sled, or in my pocket.

A hole is dug with my foot in the snow that looks like it might have been made by a wounded rabbit. Blood and fur is scattered around leading to the hole. The lynx is supposed to think a rabbit got away, and dove into the hole to recover. An easy meal to stick a paw in there and scoop dinner out. *Click! A trap instead.* This sometimes works. I like it because it is simple, fast, easy, and inexpensive.

Managing my trapping area only works if I am the only one around. If there are rival trappers all around, they all want to get the most fur first, before the others do. Often none have the ability to wipe the fur out, but still, the pressure takes its toll. The luck of 100 idiots can equal the intelligence of one good trapper. Anyhow – such thoughts as I travel along.

The sun rises, purple and majestic, above the teeth of pointy dark spruce trees on the horizon, as it yellows, like a melon above the teeth of a saw. I can almost hear the squeak of the chariot wheels the sun rides in. The dogs breath hangs in the air behind us above the trail. Over a log, around a bend, down in a creek. I know we are near Two map lake. Named because the lake is annoyingly on the dividing line between two maps. We stop at a beaver house. I let the dogs rest a little as I go to sip Labrador tea from the thermos. Some jerky is chewed on from last year's moose. The dog sled makes a good resting spot to sit. I have to brush ice off my mustache and beard to get the thermos to my lips. My eyelashes are heavy with ice balls. I brush them with the thumb of my otter mitt. Vaguely my eyes go to the beaver house to see how active it is, and if I want to set a trap for beaver. No, looks like a house full of young ones. The cuttings on all the small trees nearby are low to the ground. Large beaver chew higher up the tree.

One of Norman's dogs is on her back waving her feet to get her back scratched on the rough ice. I'm ready to go, so stand up. All the dogs come to their feet. As I walk by I scratch the dogs back.

"Your harness fit okay there Kansas?" She just blinks her eyes a few times. I take a moment to wipe the frost off each dogs face and out of their eyes. "Hike!" and the sled leaps forward again. There is warmth to the sun now, or so it seems, probably not, but the spirit of the sun is heartwarming anyhow. As we eat up the miles the sun begins to set. Red. Just like the sunrise. Gobbled by the rows of saw-teeth of waiting dark spruce tree tops. Almost home after ten hours on the trail.

But here in my trail are the tracks of a snow machine! "What the...?" Then I understand it is that dingbat kid who wants to share my trapline with me. Here is a trap he set. Fifty feet from a trap I set. He had told me last time he would stay off my trail, 'maybe,' but that he has his rights. And there is nothing I can do about it. Creative thought has to be given to what I can do about it. "These things have to be handled delicately," *says the wicked witch of the west- from OZ.*

When I get home I hear the kid cutting firewood across the slough at his homestead. Should we go talk to him? *Naw. That didn't work before.* We tried three times already. What's the use of threats and having your bluff called? Why show your hand. Let him think I'm scared and backing down, letting him take my trapline and just wait. Let him weave his own rope used as the noose to hang himself.

I do not have to wait long. Next morning he goes up the slough and out my trapline trail. He does not know I am home. Firewood is needed, and today is firewood gathering day. So, I head out the trapline trail the idiot went out. While cutting firewood I happen to drop 200 trees across the trail behind me as I head home. The kid has a snow machine and the woods are thick. He depends on my trail. If my trail is not available he is screwed. I put the trail in. I can take the trail out. I am not obligated to keep a trail useable. I am 'shocked' if it turns out the kid is on the wrong side of the trail. Truly shocked and concerned. One needs to be careful out here in the wild. *I was out cutting firewood and gosh golly was he out there?* I answer myself a few times, practicing my expression. "I hope he is okay." It might take- wow- three or four maybe five days to cut the trail open and get through? Think a person might die in that amount of time? Quite possibly. Guess we will find out huh? We practice what we will say in court if there is a problem that reaches civilization.

If he lives, I hope he understands what 'can't do anything about it' means. He might try to kill us. Maybe. But according to the Territorial Imperative—the one whose on his home turf wins 90% of the time. The kid is out of his element, new here, young enough to make other choices, knows he's in the wrong, wants to follow the law. Wants the easy way out. Lazy. Not someone ready to risk his life for this. He doesn't want to call my bluff. Next time I'm not going to be so nice.  :)

Might be a good time to head for town though, huh? Give the kid a few days to cool off. *As in 'frozen' cool off?* Naw, he'll be okay, but could be highly pissed. Till he calms down and sees the light. We do put a lock on the door and pick the valuables up out of the yard. Batten down the fort for war. The kid thought it was checkmate-game over. He's used to city people. Civilized suit and tie people who stutter at the first sign of problems and call 911. People wanting someone else to do their dirty work, they haven't got the guts to take care of personally. The kid thinks it's funny, *there is no one to call for help!* Thinks I'm a helpless victim. *"Well put this in your pipe and smoke it kid."*

As I mush to civilization I think about it. Reminds me of the way criminals view the world. They break into your home and you are at their mercy. They say :

"Ha! I have the gun, you do not, criminals are armed, honest citizens are not allowed to be. Ha! It's like picking strawberries." Women say:

"Yes, yes take anything you want, please just don't kill me!" And the criminal says, "Don't mind if I do, thank you kindly Mam." He takes whatever he wants. With what consequences? Do tell. The court gives him a lawyer if he can't afford one. If he is ever caught. How much effort is made to find him? Fill out a report days later. Just another robbery, one of a dozen last night. No money, no time. Ha ha and ha again. Live like that? I think not. I'll tell you how it would be for me.

Some low life breaks into my home to rob me? He has no rights. Zonked out on drugs, his reflexes are ten times slower than mine. I'll bank my life on it. Faster than he can blink I'll have a gun to his head.

"Cool, wow, am I ever glad you broke in! I was wondering if this new load in my 357 would come out the back, and what size hole it might make. Now I get to see! Oh! Hold on, you are armed aren't you? No? Oh, okay, here, hold this kitchen knife!" Put kitchen knife in his hand. "Oh wait! I don't want blood on the rug. You don't mind standing over here on the linoleum do you? Mind handing me a towel behind you? Let me see. I need to make sure all the details are covered. Man breaks into house goes for the kitchen knife in the open drawer…." (I go open the drawer- wait! His fingerprints….) "You don't mind terribly much reaching over and opening this drawer do you?- Thanks I really appreciate it. Can't be too careful you know, it has to look right when the Gestapo arrives. I can't tell you how much this means to me. Thanks. This is exciting." Pause, "Wait! I'd like to try a wad cutter bullet instead of the hydro shock. Let me change bullets, stay right there."

Victim? Victim? I'll tell you who the victim is! It's the low life thief. But I'd realize there might be a glitch. Some detail I forgot. I absolutely and for sure have no rights. I for sure cannot shoot a thief in my house and get away with it. I'd never hear the end of it. Lawyers, trial, bla bla. So, I'm going to look out for myself and make sure I don't get robbed. Whatever society does for itself, society is on its own. I can't save the world. So I'd pull the hammer back, wave the end near his balls, and his knee cap. His heart as I ponder. As he ponders. I'd say:

"Only kidding, get out of here. Go. Don't let me catch you around here again, understand? Go rob someone else- some unarmed helpless civilized person. Maybe a vegan. " If he himself goes to the Gestapo? To say what?

"I went to rob this house and this crazy guy…." Yea right. If so I'd say:

"Are you nuts? Guy comes to rob me and I do what? Does that make sense? I'd call 911 and let the authorities deal with the situation! Am I armed? Oh goodness, I have a hunting rifle I keep out in the woods where it belongs." *Keeping in mind no firearm I own is registered. Trust civilization, the police, the system, to protect me! Not on your life. Been there, done that.* I dream. I wish. I hope. I constantly look for signs there can be trust. That the system can and does work. But anyhow—the trail miles are eaten up. I get to Nenana, and get a ride to Fairbanks with Josh.

"Hey Crafty, how's business? Good to see you."

"Miles! Isn't it, "Good to see you" first, then "How is business?" We both laugh because we both know business comes first with Crafty. "But yes Miles, business has been good. Not like summer of course, but I have been ordering for the summer and getting some good prices from Indian Crafts, who has given me a deal because I'm spending $50,000. And the Eskimos have been coming in regular to sell their carvings at deals I can't refuse." Yes I know how that goes. *The Indian and the Eskimo need money to get drunk and comes to see Crafty. Perfectly legal as Crafty points out.* I just feel sorry for the natives.

Crafty has pointed out in the past how I will never do good business if I am such a push over. There was an incident in the past that stands out that Crafty and I have talked about often. Shy Eskimo comes in with a paper bag clutched in his hands. His winters worth of carvings. Crafty pretends he is busy, pretends he doesn't have time. It's all part of the bait and hook. I was standing there watching. Crafty was not in fact busy, and he did indeed need ivory badly, and we had just talked about how it would be nice if someone came in with some carvings today.

Crafty is pretty much showing me how it's done as we had just been talking about how to buy and sell.

"C-Crafty. Y-you buy?" The shy Eskimo holds out his paper bag of carvings. Crafty and I look in the bag. Walrus ivory carvings maybe ten pounds, maybe twelve pieces, all exquisite, one of a kind museum quality done by a true artist. Crafty sighs, looks away at his paperwork for the day, like he's busy and can't be bothered but 'okay, if you insist, and need the money, maybe I can help you out' look. The Eskimo looks grateful. It is possible he has been elsewhere and not sold anything. Some local galleries prefer to deal with agents, white people who know English and how to do business. Like it's beneath them to stoop to deal with an uneducated native.

But oh yes! They will proudly tell the native story as a sales pitch to the tourist! Oh yes, they will gladly show pictures of the primitive man in his kayak in the great alone on the sea. Pronounce his out of this world name like Niuk-puck. Explain how talented he is…

"Well I'm low on cash right now but how about $50?" I'm guessing easily $1,000 worth of carvings. But the Eskimo is grateful, thankful, bows as Crafty hands him his $50 so he can go drinking. Crafty faces me after the door is closed with a big grin and wink, to show me that's how it's done, and proceeds to tell me how much money he can turn this into. I'm both sad and disgusted. But hold the emotions in, try to talk about good business—making money in the long haul, ethics and such, and how being fair works. But I can't win the argument. In fact, I am more of an example of the proof Crafty is correct.

Money talks and bullshit walks. Talk is cheap. What position am I speaking from? By what authority does my opinion count? If I were to reach a position of being Crafty's equal financially, he might ask me how I do it, and listen. Till then, he knows more than I do. Anyhow. Sigh. My Buddy Crafty. Anyhow, we all have our good side and stuff about us others might not agree with, right?

"So Miles, I heard Sally say something about another moose court case coming up? What's that all about, have you been being naughty again?" Yes, well I have been avoiding the subject even in my mind, not wanting to think about it or deal with it, talk about it, or record it. It's a sore spot as Crafty does not agree with my views, and I think he does not understand the entire situation and does not want to. It's all about black and white. Something is legal or it's not. Ethics is for suckers. Or no, he has ethics. Just his own version, just as I do. We each have a set of rules we live by that works for us that the majority don't agree with.

Crafty is a scientologist. Not just an ordinary one, but high up on the food chain on the scientology chart road to being clear. I have in fact read one of the books, "Science of Survival,' and taken a couple of the classes Crafty offers. Crafty takes it serious, helper of humanity. My position is to be puzzled, and feel I need to study on this, gather more information to figure out what it is that makes Crafty tic. What he believes seems to be working for him and getting him what he wants. I'm mostly curious. Like what will the big picture turn out to look like. Anyhow ya.

'Ya Crafty, more Fish and Game issues."

"Miles, when will you learn! Just be legal, save a lot of headache!" Someone must have turned me in for getting my usual winter moose. But who and why? Like before, who have I seen or talked to? No one. Geez. I might have said something to Josh, but that's it. Certainly Josh has no interest in Fish and Game and it's rules. I'm not going to talk about this again with Crafty, he's trying to bait me. The bottom line being my crap stinks, but his does not. Nothing is going to change his perspective or mine. We can still be friends. Maybe that is what being friends means, to not agree and still get along. Ha! But a new issue comes up about fishing, and the laws.

"Just like you fishing for your dog's Miles. That's out dated. Who does that anymore. You can't give a valuable resource to sled dogs Miles!"

But no, I want to make a point right now about the fishing. Crafty has all the facts as presented to the public through the news media. He parrots the words being fed to him through the news media.

"Miles, the biologists have done studies, counted fish, spent money to get facts, and tell us there are not as many fish as in the past, and we need to do something about it, so there are restrictions. How can you ignore these facts Miles?"

"Crafty, if there is a fish shortage, then how come the commercial fisherman on the ocean are not seeing restrictions imposed on them? No restrictions on gear use for example, when subsistence and sport gear is highly restricted. The gear commercial fisherman use catches everything – every kind of fish and animal, mile long nets. If there is a shortage of the resource, shouldn't the burden of responsibility be shared? Especially when, legally, subsistence needs is supposed to have the priority on that human harvest aspect of the resource?" I pause to see if Crafty is taking this in, understands, has any knowledge of the subject at hand. Few people know the laws or know terms like, 'by catch,' or how 'subsistence' is legally defined, and even more, who cares? Yet he asks for an example, and has a like he will listen, but with a look on his face like, whatever I say will be an excuse or a lie. It is true, there is little proof to offer up. I offer up an example.

"Crafty, long ago, there were lots of fish on the Kantishna river, in the days before civilization knew." I explain how Natives and early trappers like myself fished all we wanted, with no regulations, and there was no fish population problem in the past 200 years or spoken local history. Crafty nods, "Yes, well, whatever, there were a lot fewer fisherman back then." I go on. "It was me, at a Fish and Game meeting, who informed the board there is a strong salmon run, very late in the season, that they did not know about. I was trying to prove here are plenty of fish." No one on the board even knew where the Kantishna was, and had to refer to a map to find it! They had never regulated it. Had no idea who was fishing it, or how many fish hey caught. Those of us fishing kept our mouth shut. It was me who trusted the board to manage properly.

Now that the board knows, they figure out when this run leaves the ocean, and informed the commercial fisherman at the mouth of the Yukon, and these fisherman targeted the Kantishna fish run. "Crafty, just five years later the fish runs were only a third of what they had been the previous 200 years."

I pause. "Commercial fisherman," I explain, "have got the ear of the politicians." Senators Stevens, Murkowski, Don Young, and 'the good ole boys' group that run the state, have made money from, and came from, fishing backgrounds. Commercial fishing is a big multimillion dollar concern."

"Sure Miles, so what's your point? Fishing is big business and the politicians are involved. So what." I can tell from Crafty's expression he is not interested. He is bored. This is so much 'nonsense.' I have no proof, have no way to obtain proof. Honestly, I'm not interested in proof. I'm not stupid. I'm not going to fight the government and accuse the leaders of corruption, incompetence, violation of Federal law etc. *Me and who else!?!* I'd have to give up my lifestyle and spend my life in court. And win what? Who cares? I'd be a nut case, end up in jail, or made to disappear.

But still, it is what I believe. I can't trust my government. The laws have little or nothing to do with 'biology,' and everything to do with politics and money. Because of this, I am less likely to follow such laws, especially when it hurts me to do so. I'd feel differently if I were convinced the government numbers were accurate, or the officials have the best interest of the fish at heart. I would be willing to do my part and make a sacrifice. But not if I believe I am being played for a sucker and used as a scapegoat. I cannot forgive myself for being the one to point out the most wonderful fish run they did not know about till I told them. This will not happen again.

In truth Crafty does not care. He does not eat lots of salmon. So, it's none of his business. As with most people. It's complicated. What I point out is not in the news, and who is affected anyhow? Who? A handful of people like myself? So what. The numbers of fish I catch for sled dogs to the public sounds like an amazing big number, to people like Crafty, when I say I need 2,000 fish! Wow! But many I get are taken after they spawn and done their job, and are going to die anyhow. Salmon cannot survive in fresh water after coming upstream from the ocean. The trip is hard on them. Their one job is to get to the spawning grounds and spawn. Their biological purpose is then over.

As much as half the salmon I get are already spawned out, no eggs. Eggs already laid. Fish dying, swim the slack water back downstream as they can no longer fight the current, and drift into my nets. Others I get are the very weak that might not make it to the spawning bed, all tore up, missing fins, missing eyes, often with rot on them. Great for dogs- not for human consumption. Consumers would not want the sick and smelly fish. Only about one in fifty chum salmon I get is suitable for human consumption, and is why we call them here locally 'dog salmon' – suitable only for dog food.

Over the years, the quality of fish is noticeably more poor, and the fish are smaller. Pollution in the ocean? Global warming? Some say this is the effect of ranch raised fish being turned loose. It is hard to see how subsistence fisherman way upriver are causing much of this.

I use a net, set in the slack eddy of the river where the weak go to rest. The strong are missing the net, dashing fast upstream past me. Sure, there is some effect on the population from my fishing. How can I deny that. But heck! If I feed my dogs the equivalent of commercial dog food, what is that made of? Fish! Only difference? I have paid the commercial fisherman for the same fish, and all the factories and distributors, instead of doing it myself. I know because some of the commercial fisherman are running, operations to sell fish meal to dog food companies. Our local Kobuk feed company buys and sells our fish, as fishmeal to Purina and other dog chow companies. Dog-mushers, pet owners, are not limited, or being asked to be frugal when buying this product.

"So don't have dogs at all? Okay, but then what?" I use gas instead, like everyone else? Doesn't gas use have its own issues as well? Why then is switching over to dependence on gas instead of fish such a wonderful problem free solution? "It's not an environmentally friendly solution. But it's a commercial interest solution. It's the politically correct solution chosen by who? That the public buys into!"

"Miles, you are obviously far to wound up about all this. I'm not the one you need to convince. If you are correct then get the laws changed!" He gives a smug look, folding his arms. We both know, anyone who gets emotional , raises their voice, gets on a soapbox and lectures has lost the argument and is nothing but an extremist nut -case. I understand this about myself , so know I am not the one who can help get anything changed. This not just not what I am good at. I am not level headed enough. That does not make me 'wrong.' I say with a cunning smile:

"Well that is easy for you to say Crafty. Wasn't it you who got busted at the Fair, and had to shut down because you had been warned not to sell knives to kids, and you did it again anyhow, because there is too much money in it?"

"That was different. They were a bunch of jerks! None of my knives was ever used in a knifing at the fair- that was someone else!" Now it's Crafty's turn to get all worked up about how the laws are, wants to explain himself. Doesn't want to hear the solution is to get the stupid laws changed. I try to be patient and listen, *Oh do tell Crafty, explain how different that is, and how you are a victim of the fair officials personal vendetta, because you make so much money and everyone is jealous.* "Why are you smiling Miles, it's not funny!"

"Of course it's not funny Crafty! I understand perfectly!" I have learned, this is a downside of a democratic form of government. It's all about what the majority wants. The rights of the individual are in fact not protected.

One of the Craft shops customers calls Crafty over, and I listen in. She is an excitable gal from the University, apparently doing a study on Athabascan Alaska Indian culture. She is about to fly to the village of Fort Yukon on the Yukon river in a chartered plane to do some interviews with elders about their culture.

"Crafty, can I use your phone, I have a calling card. I forgot, and need to call the village to ask if there is anything I can bring, since I am arriving light on a charter plane, and bet there are important supplies I might be able to haul in!" Crafty shows her where the phone is, and we hear her call as she gets hold of the Native Council there in the remote village.

"Yes hello, I'm flying to your village in a few hours to study Athabascan culture. Is there anything I can bring to the village?" It sounds like she is put on hold. She tells us while on hold, that the chief is asking some locals what might be needed. She is thinking of things like fish nets, salt to preserve with, bullets, tanning solution, stuff hard to ship through the mail. The plane is big enough to haul even a snow machine or new dog sled! Big stuff like that! She holds her hand up and puts the phone to her ear. We know she has the chief back on line. We hear her repeat:

"You want twelve big Macs with French fries?" Crafty and I look at each other. "Some study on Indian culture huh?" Nice to have a lighthearted interruption.

SALLY HAS BEEN AT WORK, and not off yet. I've been chatting with Crafty, waiting for her to return. Crafty tells me her job at Woolworths is going good. She has a car now. I look forward to seeing her. Hear how she is, share with her what has gone on in my life, the good news of a healthy fur catch- progress at the camps on the trail, and ideas I have that might help us share a life.

Her first words are :

"Miles, these furs are gorgeous! I didn't know how beautiful they'd be!" She wants to feel them. I have not sold them all to Don. I know a hat maker that will pay a little more. I've learned Don seeks certain furs, has certain connections, but other fur dealers have their specialties as well. Anyhow, yes I already know how beautiful fur is. Guess most people can't afford the good fur, so are only familiar with seconds, or rabbit and fox, or ranch raised fur. I chuckle to her:

"Yea, fur is still the warmest material in the world for cold climates." It's a line trappers use to argue in favor of trapping. But sure, most of the fur goes to those not trying to keep warm! In climates not like Alaska! In truth that is not the huge market! But yes, we do see a lot of old time Alaskans wearing their furs to keep warm. Sally wants a fur hat and mittens. Maybe some mukluks- fur boots.

"Sure, next time I have an extra $1,000 I'll set you up!"

"That's what an outfit cost??" That's only if you know someone and have connections. She agrees she'd rather have the $1,000! "It would take a lot of hours working at Woolworths to make $1,000!" Yes, the rich who don't really need the furs to keep warm are the ones who end up with the coats, hats, and mitts.

"Such is life!" said with a grin. I add, "Whatever. I don't care. I mean it's their connection to the land, and an expression of that appreciation in the only way they know how to relate. It's a symbol, while I have the real thing. So who is richer?"

"What makes you so wise Dr. Miles?" She hugs me and comfortably rests her head on my shoulders. The 'Dr.' bit is in reference to the fact my father has three Ph.D. doctorate degrees, while I'm the unsuccessful black sheep of the family, and I'm hurt by that, have a chip on my shoulder over it. Sometimes she thinks I'm my father's equal, just in a different way. I do see that my father and I have more in common then he wants to admit to. Well in that we both did something radical, broke from our family, and became, after much struggling, very good at our chosen field- while not being well understood by others.

Neither of us has good people skills, beyond selling abstract ideas. Yes, I sell art that is 'real,' but art is an interpretation, abstraction in itself. I'm in the business of selling dreams, and know it. My father packages formal education with ribbons, and markets gold stars the same as gold bullion.

We are in our room upstairs at the Craft shop. It's small, filled with Crafty's junk, old and musty, but Crafty is letting us stay here, so we feel grateful. Paint on the walls peels, and is gray with dust and cobwebs. A window overlooks the town and some birch trees out front.

"Miles, on the land thing, how do we prove I have been here long enough? I have to have been here a year to qualify." I reply to Sally:

"Well it will be about a year by the time we file and stake and all that. It's hard to prove or disprove. Who met you when you first got here? How much of a big issue can it be?" The purpose of the rule is to show intent. The state wants people who will stay, and not just acquire the land for financial investment by out of state interests. I'm not a good 'time,' or date person anyhow. Ya, it will be a year give or take a week or two. So Sally is reassured and thinks this is a good plan. The truth is, we did not introduce ourselves to many people when she first arrived.

Meanwhile we agree she will work here in Fairbanks to support herself, and I'll get back to the trapline so I can save some money for us. Because we will need to build a cabin, and have other costs coming up! The baby and all that. No, I don't really want to think about it, but for sure we need money. *If I focus on that, isn't that best for now?* She still wants a midwife and home delivery. We have a trade worked out with the midwives whose office is just two blocks away from where we are staying.

"Well Sally, I wish I could stay longer, but I have the dogs to take care of, and the trail needs kept open, traps to check, so need to head back!" Sally gives me a ride back to Nenana in her used fuel efficient car. It's just an hour drive away. Josh has fed the sled dogs that are tied up near his along the river at tenth street.

"Professor Martin!" Josh greets me loudly. "The man with the Golden Pen!" I never really know if he is complimenting me, trying to bait me, or being snide and sarcastic. He's often slightly upset when he greets me like this. My guess is he is tired of watching my dogs. But I have watched his, and given him sled dogs to race with at no charge, so in my mind I am not using him.

It is time to read my mail and get caught up. There is a letter from my father who I have not heard from in a year. He almost always asks me:

"Are you driving yet?" The world begins and ends with driving. But sure he means well, and worries about me. Oh yes. I suppose it is a handicap that I do not drive, that I live with and compensate for it. Still, in my mind it is not a huge big deal. Many homesteaders who own cars and trucks have lots of major problems over that. There is no safe place to park them while at home in the wilds, because they can't afford two pieces of land. One in town, and one in the wilds. Without owning a place to park, the options are what? We have no place to pay for parking or storage. Some try leaving trucks parked for months at the lot at tenth street. Often they get vandalized. Often the old tires go flat. Often they will not start because they have been sitting so long. Or, dead battery, will not start in the extreme cold, when needed the most. Most people who drive in the cold have a home to keep the car where they can plug in the block and oil heater. Civilization is not geared for dealing with- catering to- homesteaders, so the rules are messed up for such people. It is hard to justify paying for insurance when a vehicle is not moved for four months at a time. So many drive without it. It's illegal, and if ever in an accident, a serious problem. I would not always want to be in their shoes. It might be cheaper and better to just pay for rides the few times I need them. I have said this sort of thing many times to my father who nods like he understands. So I stop saying much, and like him, nod and smile like I understand. I write a reply

Dear Dad

I got your letter a few days ago and am glad to hear from you! I tried to call you during the few days I was in town, but could not get through. Goodness, it sounds like a lot has been going on with you. You can share the bad times with me as well as the good. You know I don't like so much time going by and not hearing from you. It has me thinking I have done something wrong.

Funds for Community Methods got cut? Yes, I know you were counting on those funds for the program. It must be hard to offer courses for your students now. Russia? India? Sounds like I need to send you with some of my art work to promote! 😁 :)

Sell some of my work around the world! You seem to go to these places often. Sorry to hear you and Kate are not getting along so well. Seems like it would be good to get along and stay with someone, but am sure it is not easy. I write some about what I am up to on the trapline, goals, scenery etc. Yes, I still watercolor all my envelopes and am glad you like them. Wood smoke? Yes, probably everything I have including envelopes and paper smell like wood smoke! The feather in the letter? I forget now. I save all the shiny feathers off duck wings and include them in my letters- a little message from the wild I guess.

Sunshine Miles

Furs are caught, the trapline wrapped up, time to see about my art business!

There is a need to go make the rounds of the shops. I have art up on consignment. More than just 'the need' to go to these shops, the visits are enjoyable. The

Parrs at Alaska House have been good to me for a lot of years now. Honest, fair, kind, and just all around good people. Good examples of 'what works' to model after, and contemplate how they do it. Very respected and happy. Charlie, who owns Alaska House Gallery with his wife Karen is not the State Senator anymore, but still involved in politics and is very wise in the ways of politics. Because of him and a few others like him, I know not all politicians are categorically evil and up to no good! I deal with Karen a lot more though. She greets me:

"So ready for another show Miles? We can do a two day show announcing you are back in town!" I laugh back :

"No not this time. My life is changing, not as much time as I once had. Or, maybe just a different approach, doing more bazaars and craft shows and events these days." She knows, because we have talked before about this, but just letting me know she would do a show for me. I think Alaska House is seeing harder times with the pipeline money gone now, and the economy not what it once was. Not as much fine art being bought these days. All the clerks know me and greet me. I almost feel like family. My art is still in a prime spot by the cash register under glass. Karen goes and finds my file as we chat, and when she returns, we go over the records of what I am owed for. A dozen pieces in the $50 price range, and one larger art piece.

"It was the mirror with the whale baleen handle in the ivory stand I think." All she has is the store code number. We check, and yes that is the one that sold for $550. Out of the 1,000 dollars owed, she takes out the third for the store percentage. So she gets $50 and I get $470 on just one art piece. It's the best deal an artist can get. The usual split is 50/50. My work is popular, so Alaska House wants my best, so encourages me to bring the good stuff.

I drop off some more work, another dozen pieces to replace what sold.

"Karen, I'd like to try a custom knife with you. I know a gallery is not usually a place for such a thing, but this is a chef knife to be used in the kitchen, and would make an unusual gift item that I think might sell here." So, she takes that as the things I suggest to sell, so she trusts my judgment. It's the only knife in the gallery, and probably the only one they ever offered.

"Miles, this combination of your three metals, baleen and wood is something I have never seen you do. I also see your finished work is improving, since you are pinning the metals, and not just gluing. Very nice!" I only nod. The prices are up a little to reflect the improved quality, but it seems to me, the public wants cheaper, pay less, so what is the answer? The gallery does not know either. I smile, as it was Karen who had to convince me people actually turn the art over and look at the back. I need to sand the back. I found that shocking. By hand with sandpaper? That's another hours work.

I have a letter from a craft business in Kentucky.

Travis Handcrafted Rings and Things

Dear Mr. Martin

Good to hear from you… I often thought I would like living in Alaska. About two years ago I was ready to go, but ran into problems when I started checking into the job market. Every place I checked was painted with such gloomy pictures I changed my mind. I've married now and don't guess I will ever get to see the last frontier…I do not stock any jewelry that is not my own work—but would like to know if you sell the small animal cut outs you make. I can always use raw materials like bear claws, especially grizzly claws or teeth. If you have any extra please let me know what you want for them. I have a very limited budget and just getting started in the business. Do you ever come across gold nuggets large enough to use in jewelry? Do you ever find any green jade? …. I'm not in the jewelry business like a lot of people to make a fast buck. I do not believe you are either.

Your friend Travis

Jinx, at New Horizons Gallery, is only a few blocks away, so I stop and see her to drop art off there. She used to own the Paint Pot ages ago, and now moved up to a full gallery, not just paint and craft supplies! Everyone working there knows me as well, greeting me with affection. "Miles, you are back in, good to see you!" Could be just part of their job, but it seems sincere to me. I'm owed $500 here, and drop off more work. I'm learning to avoid the smaller shops that just opened, eager to get inventory at a low percentage cut. The sorts of places that go out of business and space out my stuff. There was a time when as much as half my art would be left on consignment and 'lost' or stolen, or at least never seen again, or paid for.

Alaska Land is the next major stop. It's on the edge of town and holds a lot of memories for me as the place I lived on my houseboat when in town, and my houseboat docking spot for so many years. The amusement park atmosphere, and the old historical log cabins are unique to this section of town. The shop owners still dress up in the old gold rush clothes, and give off the era of the 1800's they promote. I of course fit right in. The dirty scruffy looking trapper wearing a hunting knife, long hair, mountain man hat, blade of grass in my mouth, tanned skin and, 'all that.'

The little train toots as I arrive. I know the conductor who waves, so all the tourists on the train wave as well. I stop at the ice cream stand first, and of course the gal remembers me, still working there! Geez! I get a big hug and, "Remember how you used to pick berries and bring them to me, ask me to spin them up in a shake for you?" Oh yes, a fond memory, but need to get going. I back pedal a little, find a reason to move along. She's getting a little too friendly and making eyes at me, and well, I have Sally to think of.

Ken owes me $100, and the leather guy owes me $175. But it is the Underhill's, Bill and Nora I really want to see the most. Longtime friends I used to hang out with, and the ones who took me into their home after my rescue when I had frozen toes and was half starved. I can never repay their kindness, for at that time in my life I had nothing to offer. No job, no money, no connections, no nothing. They cared anyway. They fed me and got me back to health again. It was Bill and Nora who talked me into writing for the first time. My first article for Alaska Magazine was about my rescue called 'Survive.' The story that made international headlines.

The Underhill's do tell me though, that they have been kind to others and been used and abused in return, and appreciate that I made something of myself, and are thankful for the help they gave me.

"Hey Bill! Hi Nora! How is the Diamond Willow shop doing?" We exchange hugs and warm greetings.

"Doing good Miles. You know us, we just love to talk to the tourists and sit out here and carve the willow wood." They may have to give it up sometime though as it seems, Nora is allergic to the willow sawdust. Bill does most of the carving and she does most of the selling. She is dressed in frills from the gold rush, and Bill has on a suit reminiscent of the saloon keepers, with gold pocket watch and western hat. The cabin they sell from is log, with a low ceiling, and used to belong to Robert Service. So they can tell all the Robert Service stories, quote his poems, as they offer post cards, Gold Rush books, handmade diamond willow lamps and :

"Of course original work by the famous Wild Miles!" They do tell the tourists a lot of stories from the wild about me to help sell the art I do. Sadly though, I don't see the flow of customers in and out, and the Willow Shop does not owe me much money. I don't say much about it, but my thought is they are not very aggressive, but did not get a great location. They tend to enjoy the tourist, tell them stories, but do not convert that into dollars well. Which is fine I suppose. I mean, they are happy and the tourist for sure get tired of everyone trying to suck them dry of every dime they have! Bill and Nora are a breath of fresh air I'm sure. I'm told I'm a lot like that as well! Especially by Crafty. I prefer to tell stories, be nice, and not get paid! I suppose there needs to be a balance. Sometimes the Underhill's and I talk about such things. One thing that changed though, Bill tells me:

"Alaska Land is changing Miles. It's more commercial now than it used to be. Have you been to the Salmon Bake?" I'm guessing this Salmon Bake has to do with the conversation. I have only been over there once, over by the pond and sluice box where you go to pan gold. This area used to be an out of the way section, not frequented as much as the other sections. I thought the prices were higher than I can afford. I sense there is more action going on over there these days, so nod my head for Bill to go on, that yes I know the place. My blade of grass bobs in my mouth. I shift it and get a new bite on it, as Bill goes on.

"Well there is a bus that brings the tourists from downtown over here to Alaska Land. But the bus brings them only to the Salmon Bake. This is all that is promoted."

Ah yes. I can understand now. But Bill is not upset. Takes it in stride, stating it only as a fact, not any opinion on the subject offered. But the rest of Alaska Land is beginning to go belly up. I know as well, there are sort of strict rules the shop owners must follow, that shop owners elsewhere do not need to adhere to, and might interfere with business rules, that have to do with entertaining the tourist. Stuff about what your store front can look like, the kind of signage you can use, or not use, how you dress and such. This can cost the store owner money, and the rent is especially high, as if this is prime real-estate. I'm sure though it costs a lot to maintain this land as a park.

Ken, the leather man, had commented earlier, why he did not buy as much from me. He usually likes my teeth and claws. The kids just love the wolf claws, set out in a bowl to pick from for three dollars. Free to me from the trappers who have no use for them. I have to boil, sort, dry, and grade them. But if I can do 100 in a day, there is little cost and maybe $200 to $300 profit eventually when they sell, depending on the sizes sold. I talk business with Bill and Nora:

"So I have to grade the claws and only the small are retailing for three dollars, the biggest might go as high as $15. Then of course the ones I cap and make a necklace out of might sell as high as $75. My investment is negligible. There is little I have to order. I can cap with what cost me five cents worth of ivory, and make a loop on top from electrical wire that's free." They like the fact I recycle, and use things from the land in an honorable way. Much of what I do acquire is from the local Indians that helps them out in their meager basic lifestyle. We all laugh because sometimes I make art from old bones the dogs are done chewing on. Or, teeth the dogs spit out of skulls, that trappers toss them, like beaver, and I find laying in the dog yard.

"Like this beaver tooth necklace! This is one I got from the dog yard." I show them the flower I put in it out of my metals. " This silver band all the way around it, I learned from experience, stops the tooth from cracking. In order for the tooth to crack it has to expand. If it can't expand it does not crack!" Little useful bits of information like this interest Bill, as he does a few crafts and is interested in woods lore, Indian ways, simple lifestyles and such. I think as a spiritual aspect of life. Bill is part Cherokee.

"Miles, how is the book coming?" Since it was Bill and Nora who got me started writing and getting paid for it, they want to know how that is progressing.

"I've had some stumbling blocks. Unsure what to do. I set it aside and then get back to it when a solution presents itself, so now the book is on the back burner." They already know that the very first hold up was that I had intended my writings to be about a Mountain Man, first person present time, never been done before to my knowledge. Told in my own words without editing. Problem was, I was not making much progress I could see in terms of living up to my heroes. I was making all these mistakes. How can I write about that. If I ignore that, how can I call it a true story? Who wants to read about a loser? Needed to be rescued, took months to catch my first fur when learning to trap. Pretty sad stuff. Next issue was the fact I live alone, so there are few characters or conversations. How can I find a style of writing that works? It seemed obvious I can't write, 'I saw, I did, I went, I- I- I' all the time! "But now it's the technical, how to print it problem." The book is basically 'done,' but it needs review by someone else – some simple edit work for misspellings. Each time I go over it I find aspects to change, and have to write in the margins on an only copy, typed on a manual typewriter. There are enough changes and desires to move things around, that four times I have had to start all over from scratch. That gets old. I've had three different people I know try to edit it for me, and each time they rewrite the work into their own words, and add their own mistakes. Someone explained it to me. Often editors are frustrated wanna be writers. "I guess I can't afford a professional that charges ten dollars a page. Times 400 pages. I can't hardly count that high."

I don't like people to think I am just lazy and making up excuses. Most think that. Another aspect of the book hold up is, well, it is hard to sit still long enough, since I am such an outdoor person! *I can write more when I retire, and have time to sit when I cannot live my lifestyle anymore.* Meanwhile, I'd rather live it then write about it! It is a common reply to hear, "Oh ya, me too! I'm going to write a book someday." They tell me some hold up as to why it's not being done or finished. "When I find time," or "When I figure out the best way to tell my good story." "When I get the money and the time off." "When I retire some day and have free time." The bottom line being, how many people ever write a book and have it published? So I get tired of talking about it. The proof will be in the pudding. Keep my mouth shut till I can drop a book in their hand. Bill and Nora understand this well. They too have struggles in their life. Had hardships, setbacks to overcome. Possibly anyone who accomplishes anything, had to work for it and struggled at some point. Such people I admire went beyond what ordinary people do. When ordinary people give up, those who know success, stand out by pressing on, despite obstacles, and do not come up with endless reasons why it didn't get done! All the biographies I read about successful people seem to have this in common.

"Bill, it's like, how I see people in a bar drinking. How common it is to hear why they are an alcoholic. The endless stories of would have, could have, should have, but did not, because of some reason that's perfectly understandable. We can identify with, understand, and have sympathy for this person, enough to buy them another drink, and tell our own pathetic story. Maybe someone will buy us a drink. We might well say, "Yes! What else could you do?" Okay, there is a reason. But it is a reason to what? To waste a life away? No one can fault us? Still the loss is ours, also the worlds- societies loss. One more person who needs to be supported, a burden on society. Welfare, food stamps, out of work, no help to the kids, the relatives. And society understands and will hand it out! The wife left, there was a fire, got fired, got injured, the stories are endless. "But in the end I ponder what the point is!" I pause to think on what that point might be. "The point is that life is a struggle! The difference between those who succeed and those who fail is in how we handle the same situations. Is the glass half full or half empty? Do we look at the bright side or see only the gloom? Do we hunker down and wait out the pain and loss and make recovery plans after, or do we cave in? Do we see a lesson in everything that happens, or do we believe only bad happens to us? Do we give up on God, or trust in God? Successful people have created their own luck. Have been ready when there is a chance to make a move in a good direction, ready to take advantage of it and leap forward, and when a setback occurs, let it wash over them, doing the least damage as possible." We exchange examples of what this is about, and agree that this is so.

Bill himself is a good example. He got a pipeline job back in the 70's when so many found good work. Most people I know saw it as a gravy train, make the big bucks and had a good time! Ended up with homes, with swimming pools they can't afford to pay the taxes on now. Broke, no skills, no job, no future. A flash in the pan. Bill saw it as an opportunity, a stepping stone. He used the money to get an education, to set up a business. He did not think it was time to retire because he had a wad of money in his hands. It was not 'luck' that he got his business or his education. Any average person who made the sacrifice he did, would end up where he is.

"I say that about myself too Bill! There are those who buy my art at shows who want my autograph and envy me, admire me, look up to me, wish they were like me, who think I am lucky, who want to trade places with me. I'm not 'special' any more than the average person is. Anyone who walked in my shoes would have what I have, the freedoms and adventures I have. They'd have to pay the same price I pay is all. It's not free, handed on a silver platter, no life is free! Freedom is not free! So yes, I have spoken!" I can get off my soap box now and discuss all the reasons there is no book out! We all laugh good naturedly. "I do think I have a solution in the big picture though. One of these new-fangled computers would help a great deal. I hear they have a way to check spelling and allow you to move words, paragraphs, and whole pages around at will! You can't see the old version underneath the changes! But I'm not sure how I will ever have one of those. First I need electricity. I'm not going to worry about it. Have lots of irons in the fire and move in the direction of openings that appear. Like chess, we can't force one strategy or move, we have to have some options and see how the game develops. The game of life."

Eventually I head back to Nenana with supplies and more money then I arrived with.

Gene and Bear have been talking. Gene comes up to me:

"Miles, we are not happy you are moving up to the Tek land. Some of us want to trap and you are a professional trapper. There will be no room for us!" Seems like worrying about something farfetched to me. Wondering how many is 'we,' or is it just him, and intimidating others into nodding in agreement maybe?

"Gene, I have my own trapline, more than I can handle up on the Kantishna. I'm not interested in trapping in an area so full of people, so close to town, with so little fur to fight over." He seems satisfied with the answer. But I suppose I have a reputation as a hard aggressive man. I consider it a hard aggressive life among hard people in a lawless land. Where the fast and the tough survive. If you can't cut it, step aside and make room for someone who can. Not because this is how I wish it was, or want it to be, but because this is reality, and it sucks. To give and to share, first you must 'have.' "Walk softly but carry a big stick," as the quote goes.

Bear hears I want to move in up there on the Tek and asks me if I will partner up with him.

"Miles, you can help me build my cabin! And when it's done I can help you build yours!" I'm shocked at the proposal. Speechless. I have my own problems. I don't need to be involved in anyone else's. I'm not asking anyone to solve my problems, and I don't want to be part of anyone else's. Bear and I don't do things the same way. We are not friends, and hardly know each other. I explain it to Sally:

"Bear and I were building dog sleds in Josh's garage, because neither of us had a heated place to work. I see Bear is a perfectionist. I am not. I have a sled started, finished and on the trail trapping with it in five days. Bear spent over a month on his sled." I tell the story of how Bear would come over and try to give me advice on how I was building my sled wrong. I was polite and did not listen. It's my sled. I'll make it how I want. Bear does not know any more than I do about dog sled building. I probably know more. I don't go and say anything negative about how I think Bear should be building his sled. We have different goals. We get along well enough, no 'problems,' and even enjoy each other's company while building.

I am not seeking a museum piece, a nice looking sled. I want a sled 'now' to go out and make money trapping with, a sled that will hold up. I don't care if my lashings are different colors. Or overlap. I don't care if my wood is not matched, with one stanchion being hickory and another being ash wood. I use what I have, scrap wood that did not cost me much. Ten dollars' worth of wood, $20 worth of plastic, and I have a sled.

Bear has done a good job, something to be proud of and show off. He will mush around the village, and cares what people think and say about his craftsmanship. I'm sure it cost at least $300 in materials.

Bear hit a tree with his, and it broke. He never fixed it or used it again, and stopped using sled dogs. It is hard to comprehend, us working together on a project when we approach life so differently. I explain further to Sally:

"I'm not being critical. It's only that we do not have the same way of doing things, and it is not a matter of who is right or wrong." I give a frustrated pause as I suspect Sally is more in agreement with Bears' plans then mine. "Bear will build a cabin that looks good. He will spend years building it. I will build a cabin that will not look good, but will be up and finished for next winter, warm enough to live in, and functional, on an amount of money we can afford. I'm not interested in helping Bear for years on his cabin, while he helps me for weeks on mine."

Sally interrupts with her thoughts. "If a job is worth doing Miles, isn't it worth doing right?" Valid point. Hard to refute. I too was raised with these values by my father. *Maybe no, maybe not all jobs are worth doing right*. I never before thought of this. I mean, how can I defy what all of society tells all of us is a basic truth we are all taught from the day we can first do a task? There are a great many tasks that need to get done to support life as we desire it. Shelter- food- fire- transportation- communication are all necessities. How much of all that gets our full undivided attention at every step of the way? How much can we expect to get done if every task needs perfection? Should we choose our priorities? Some tasks receive less attention?

Sometimes I see a choice between doing something so it works, or not getting it done at all. Yes, the best thing of all is a wonderful sled that is a work of art that has $300 worth of the best materials in it, and took a month to build, worth $1,000 when done. Of course that would be my first choice! Reality sets in. I don't have a month to give, nor $300 I want to spend on a sled, nor the $1,000 to pay someone else to do it. I could sigh, and moan, and dream, and wish, and do without, or save.

Or, I can look at what I do have, what I can afford, and make it happen! Or, put another way. I have seen in my life, time and time again where people tell me they have a dream! But they are waiting! Waiting till something is right, till they have the money, the skills, the time. Because they want to do a good job, get it done right, and give it their best. So often the dream simply never comes together. The stars never do line up perfect, so they miss out on their dreams. I often laugh:

"I don't wait for stars to line up! Ha! It's the other way around! I do something, then the stars line up! I lead, the stars follow! Ha!" I say we work with what we have, get started, and see how far we get. If we can't finish, it is not the end of the world, we gave it a try. Not everything has to be done well, it just has to be done. This is one way to learn. It is not the end of everything to make a mistake, change our mind, discover a better way later. We can still enjoy the journey. Every meal does not have to be Thanksgiving, it just has to go down and stay there. Every shelter we live in does not have to be a mansion, it just has to keep us warm. Our transportation does not have to be a Rolls Royce, it can be an old beater. Meanwhile, back at the ranch, there is a life to live. Also I wonder how you ever think it has to be perfect, at a point when you have little knowledge to make it perfect. In doing something, but it's not right, you learn, make progress, live life, make a living as you move ahead, with less than ideal products.

It's a problem. Bear is upset I am not willing to help him. There are hard feelings on his part. Another upset for Bear is, I figure out how to stake a bend in the river he wants. It is not legal to stake, according to the staking instructions. This river bend has too much water frontage.

I talked to the state. Showed them the map, asked for a waiver on water frontage. It makes sense to stake the land as I propose. There is no room to make two parcels here out of this bend. "Why let it go to waste, un-staked?" Being a land surveyor, I know how to lay it out and present my case to the state. The state agrees and approved. I am able to stake 1,000 feet of water frontage, sharing a property line with Bear. He wanted that land, and is upset I was able to get it. Possibly he thinks I paid someone off, or had connections. Partly true! Democracy does not support individual rights. What supports the individual in a democracy, is having connections that bypass the system.

I also think Bearfoot is a little scared, and lacks confidence, needs someone to hold his hand, suck off my courage. Or even someone to blame if his project fails. "If only I hadn't partnered up with that incompetent Miles everything would have worked out!" Hang out at the bar exchanging dumb Miles stories. No thanks.

Sally does not know much about what is required in a good piece of ground, so leaves the selection of ground up to me. She is not particular, and much about the selection is more about what I want. It is access to town she wants. So, I picked ground closest to town, not the upper end of the staking area. Sally is more, 'going along with the program,' then actually being excited and happy. The man is the provider, so she is waiting dubiously to see what it is I plan to provide. I'm still in hopes the life will grow on her as she adjusts. She's making an effort to give me a chance, to see if I can meet some minimum requirement she has.

This will be the fifth piece of land I call 'homestead land,' and I know I am spreading myself thin. This is not really what I want to be doing. I have not thought it all out. Like how will I be able to commute and trap fifty miles away from here? If I don't trap, what else will I be able to do for a living? What would I be happy at? Somehow things will work out. I'd rather do something, even do it wrong, then not do anything at all. For in doing things wrong we learn.

These are the things I think about as I mush back to the trapline. This, and the moose harvest violation case I also came to town for. Once again my lawyer Mick gets me off. But once again it cost me. Luckily I have a good lawyer. Once again I got off only because the state has been unable (or unwilling) to adequately define substance to the Federal governments satisfaction. So all cases are dismissed. However, the state is livid because those involved feel I am thwarting the law, taking advantage of a loophole to get off. Throwing it in their face. Laughing at them.

They do in fact have some reason to feel this way! (grin) As when I am upset and angry I push their buttons. I also tell others sometimes what I think about the government, the state, and politicians when I feel wronged. It is possible one of, or some of these people I rant and rave at are undercover agents, or sympathetic and report me. I however always remember we live in a country where we can say how we feel. It's not perfect but, I'm not anti-American. I just want us to live up to who we say we are! Have workable laws, that we can follow. Right now the Federal government wants more control over the state. The state has representatives in power who hate the Federal government, and wish to retain the powers given to states, and are not just rolling over for the Feds. Our state gets away with more than other states because we have so many valuable resources we can count on for funding to where we do not depend on Federal handouts. The Federal government does not like to be told to stuff it! Alaska has the reputation of being a rebel state. This reputation attracts rebel people. Seek and ye shall find.

This leads me to thoughts about the kid trying to take over my trapline, and if I need to be armed on the trail, if he might try to bushwhack me as an accepted way to acquire my trapline. Like that 'what's his name,' Conner guy at Wien Lake. He's telling locals how he dumped a body through the ice, and no one can prove it. That's how he got his trapline. Yea, and I thought he was my friend, saying he was looking forward to me cutting a trail into Wien Lake. I talked to him a little on the CB radio. Finally it was someone else on that lake listening in that straightened me out.

I'm at the airport and have a lynx in the trap. I rest the dog team half an hour here, and I use the wood stove to fix lunch. There are a few drifted snow places, along with a few spots of open water along the trail, but that's normal. Ice fog covers the flats. Frost covers the dwarf birch and stunted spruce trees. There is a Jimmy Hendrix purple haze clouding the mind. Reality, not drugs. It's the way the sun hits the ice crystals all around me.

I'm in a sharp turn, go into a slide on some ice. "Blam!" I side-swipe a tree stump. *Dang, a broken stanchion! I'm glad we did not build this as an art-piece!* I smile. My conscious is referring to the difference in views between me and Bear. I wonder how many miles he has on sled dogs? I can splice in a new station in an hour, once I get home.

I'm home in three hours from the airport. The next day I'm off on the trapline, new stanchion in the sled. This is a different trail then the one I dropped trees across. My buddy hasn't opened it up for me yet. He must still be on the other side trying desperately to get in. Or dead. The trail I take is a trail May originally cut. The child who was with Karen when we lived together. May worked on this trail when she was twelve years old. It's full of twists and hard to run the sled dogs on, but is passable. It's only ten miles, but ends at an old cabin built during the gold rush days from things off the land.

May was excited when she discovered the cabin. It is now a shelter we fixed up and can spend a night in. There are basic supplies I have left here, stored in a barrel when gone, so animals can't get at the food or sleeping bag. The evening is spent here skinning furs and cooking for the dogs. The old cabin has a sod roof, and one tree growing in the sod on the roof is six inches in diameter, and ready to cave the roof in. The roof supports are split poles covered with birch bark shingles. It's still waterproof after more than fifty years.

The shelter is so small, I can't believe it. On the outside of the cabin is a wooden box attached to the wall. Weird. When I first saw this box, I had to go inside and see if I could figure out on the inside what the box is for! I thought some sort of refrigerator box. But it is insulated with moss, and it is an extension of the bed! The cabin is not six feet long, so 'someone' who was tall cut a hole in the wall, and put a box in so they could stretch their feet out! The shelter is 6 x 5 ft. I hauled in a tin stove and a lantern. I skin fur by the light of this lantern. It looks like the old fashion kerosene railroad lantern. When I step out the door to check on the dogs and feed them at 6:00 pm, it is pitch dark and the stars are all out. The light out this tiny window and the tree growing on the roof silhouetted in the stars is magical. Though not as romantic as when I was young, I have a feeling of beauty around me, safety, warmth and security. Over a 100 miles from civilization. No one can find me, no one can bother me. I'm safe. I'm happy. No matter what happens I can always come to a place like this to get my sanity back. To re-adjust my priorities in life. Yes, like a scene from hundreds, even thousands of years ago. But again, maybe a scene from a 100 years in the future, after the collapse of civilization, another dark ages, an ending, much like the Roman empire. Or, those biblical places and times. When civilization lost its way, too busy in the bathhouses sipping wine, getting fat. Sodom and Gomorra stories.

I'm glad I have my get- away place. Closer to God. I later set my book down and fall asleep to the crackle of the fire in the tin stove. Once again in the morning I have to feel around for the wall and figure out where I am.

"Oh yes, The Dry Creek camp."

This is the darkest coldest time of the season, with only three hours of sunrise fading into sunset. Dark by 3:00 pm. Trapping usually slows way down in dead of winter. Fur does not move much, but hunkers down till light comes back. Experience tells me I have made the most money trapping for the season, and may as well back off. It's not going to financially pay to keep coming out the trail and keeping up with worn out gear, wearing the sled dogs out.

This ten miles of trail is an alternate trapline that can be used when the other sections need to be rested up, to let the game build back up. It takes a lot of country to manage a trapline wisely. Two or three trappers out of the interiors population are hitting the animal population hard, making the news and giving everyone else a bad reputation. Yet this is so in any business and industry. There is the oil and gas industry, where big money talks and sometimes corrupts.

THAT STUPID SNOW machine is worked on once again. Always fiddling with something on it. No garage to work in. No good tools to speak of. No good way to get it to the shop in town. There is a dream to one day own the tools, to afford them, to have a shop or place to work on the machines in my life. If I'm going to be forced out of using sled dogs, how is this accomplished? The machine is not working. The machine is not easily replacing the dogs. The answer Fish and Game offers eagerly with sympathy and paperwork ready for me to sign is:

"Oh we have programs if you are having a hardship problem." *Welfare and food stamps is how subsistence is being defined now.* They want me on welfare. Do tax payers want their tax dollars used to support me? Is this about subsistence fisherman in competition with commercial interests, and subsistence harvest of game of all kinds in conflict with the desires of rich sport hunters? Is this the angle I need to be seeing? Anyhow, it is not the lawmakers or politicians or companies dime is it? It's your dime, the taxpayers.

Not that I pay a lot of taxes...But neither do I ask for anything free, or ask to be supported. I give little. I take little. I used to look for free stuff, look for ways to avoid paying my way. Get in the Fair free by deception, stuff like that. Joke around, minor stuff. So, I keep pondering life's mysteries as I do my chores.

"Sorry Kansas, didn't mean to miss you!" I had forgotten to give her a dipper of food and had moved on to Texas. I backtrack and give Kansas an extra dipper full of fish rice soup. "You want the squirrel too Kansas?" There is a cooked squirrel still floating around on the top of the five gallon pail of food. She looks in the pail as I tilt it, but she only stares. I take the critter out by the tail and toss it to Clipper. No one seems especially jealous Clipper got the treat. "Can't feed the snow machine squirrels for go power, can I Clipper!"

Well there seems to be fewer animals around, may as well head for town. Need to check the traps in that direction anyhow, I need to pull the traps for a while. About mid-February the fur will start moving again. Haven't seen the kid around. But he got out, as the trail is open again and his outflow tracks are there, but no return tracks. It looks like he used a survival bow saw to cut his way out. Word from others is, it took him five days to get home. Maybe the war is on. He messed with me. I messed with him. Now it's his move. Who is going to back down. What are his options? What are mine?

Mid-January, 1988 I head into Nenana again. Sally and I watch the Craft store for Crafty while he is gone to Flag, the Scientology Center in Florida. Crafty will come back even more advanced. I understand. When I first met Crafty, he could barely make out a receipt. One first memory is of Crafty asking me how to spell 'receipt.' He was selling out of a truck on the sidewalk. Selling junk, used stuff. He's come a long way. I admire that. He told me himself:

"Miles, I was pushed through school. I could not read and had to fake it, but they graduated me anyway. Gave me a piece of paper that said I knew something, rather than educate me. No one cared." But someone from Scientology got hold of him, took him in, and took the time to teach him how to read and write. He was very grateful. Now they can do no wrong. Scientology helps him sort out his life. He lives a simple basic life much like mine, as most of his profits go into Scientology. He wears old clothes, drives a beat up van, has a personal life much like a street person. Socks that don't match, frizzy unkempt hair, a shop that looks like a rundown flea market. I explain some of this to Sally so she understands, or just something for us to talk about as we help run the shop.

"Ya Sally, when Crafty first got this shop here, I stayed in the basement on a mattress on the dirt floor. This was a step up over living under the bridge. So it's all relative, this single room we have, with small closet is quite a move up." The bathroom is down the hall, and the kitchen is downstairs off the shop. We both laugh at how it was in my early years in Alaska. How I put my own lock on the furnace room at an apartment complex and moved in. "No rent! Everyone assumed I was the maintenance man! A little hot and noisy, but free. I found an old abandoned refrigerator I moved in there, and a mattress, table and lamp, all from the dump. I did what I had to do to make it work." A place was needed to stay when in town sometimes, and all my money was going towards my wilderness needs. The Salvation Army sometimes took me in. It was a different sort of people I met back then in general. Street people, losers, thieves, molesters, drug addicts, mentally retarded, folks on the run. Now and then, good people down on their luck, not very bright, or those who do not think money makes the world go around.

For good reason that sort of life scares Sally. What kind of mother wants to bring a child into that? But hey, she could have thought of that when she chose me to be the father of her child. I was honest and up front I thought, about my income, choice of where and how to live. I said I was not going to give it up. She could have told me, 'Good luck!' and said, 'Next!' Anyhow, I try hard to forgive and understand. Anyhow again, I didn't have to sleep with her and trust her. I could have told her to get lost, like the other smarter guys she told me about did, as soon as she said the word 'child,' in her first communication. Anyhow again, maybe we can get passed all that. She is not an evil person, any more then I am. Just human. If we are both, 'a piece of work,' we have this in common.

The midwife is all paid off now. I traded a piece of metalwork showing a mother and baby whale. A lot of my art is brought in, even though this is too early for tourist season. I had been asked to do an art piece for the Trapper Association. I suggested it be auctioned off at the annual banquet coming up this March. I want in trade, a lifetime membership. I get the blue lynx patch with lifetime member #42 on it. They got.... Well a whale baleen piece with a trapper scene done in metals, six feet long. There are several thousand individual pieces of hand cut three different color metals fit together like a jig saw puzzle. All done without electricity, but by propane light in the wilderness.

The Yukon Quest dog race wants another trophy made, along with a piece to auction off, after seeing what I did for the Trappers. This is a new race in competition with the Iditarod. It's an international race between Fairbanks Alaska, and 1,000 miles to Whitehorse, British Columbia.

One year it starts in Canada and alternating years it starts in Alaska. Costs are shared between the countries. It's supposed to be a tougher race then the fast Iditarod, now made up of richer experts. The Quest is more for seat of the pants type mushers. Not as much glory and prize money, less of an entry fee.

"So Sally, they asked me to make a trophy that passes from one winner to the next, with each winner's name going on it. Like with a plaque attached." I show her the ivory tusk with the dog team of metal, mounted on a nice walnut plaque in the shape of a dog sled, with room for about a dozen names. The race is coming up soon. The head man in charge of fund raising is going to take care of everything, the auction and such. We will split the auction sale 50/50. Minimum bid $1,000. I'm explaining again the economics of my life to Sally, as the subject keeps coming up.

"Sally, like I said, the pipeline days are ending, along with the big oil money that used to be so easy to tap into. It's tougher now to compete with more artists in the state and less money. Even so, I seem to be finding other markets and getting better all the time with my art. There are big orders that come in sometimes for gallery type art. Crafty sells a great deal of my lower end stuff."

"But Miles, he doesn't pay you anything! So what! He's a con artist!"

"Well I would not put it that harshly. I mean for example, we get a room to stay in, a place to cook and be warm. What would that cost? It's kept for me all year round. I get glue, sandpaper, all the things I need for my art work in trade. What would that cost if I had to buy it?" Although I am beginning to realize Crafty has been telling me he only charges me in trade ten percent above wholesale. When that is misleading. He really means ten percent below retail. Trading to my true wholesale at half price. So, he makes out like a bandit, with an extra 40% he has not been honest about.

"But Sally, I don't get mail often, have unreliable connections to town. I can't easily order things by mail." Like the time that postmaster in Manley sent all my mail back to the senders because I did not pick it up within fifteen days, as the law requires for a general delivery box.

If I got a post box, where would it be? Fairbanks? Manley? Nenana? I live on the houseboat. And, well it's complicated. I order something and leave for the wild for a month. I come back to pick up what I ordered and often as not there is a question waiting.

"Did you want that in red or blue?" Or, the price went up I have an outdated catalog and I owe fifty cents more. Bottom line, it's not here. Now I tell them 'red,' and wait another four months. Meanwhile maybe, unable to make more crafts as I'm out of saw blades, glue, or copper sheet. It's complicated.

"Yea I'm sure Miles, and Crafty is good at taking advantage of that!"

"Well maybe. It's a bummer, but tell me my choices? I seem unable to deal with civilization and conduct business. In an ideal situation, maybe my other half, a woman, might be able to handle that aspect I'm not good at? I love doing the art part and can produce large amounts. Even if I get ten cents on the dollar it's no mess, no fuss, Crafty deals with all that. I get to go back to the woods with supplies. He does pay me some amount of cash too." But my being taken advantage of as she sees, it affects her life, not just mine. But Sally drives, maybe then we can go on a road selling trip and sell the art ourselves together, and cut Crafty out as the middle man who makes all the money? A baby coming and totally dependent on Crafty the con artist. But, what is the truth, the bottom line, about all artists and all relationships with sellers, buyers, agents, distributors, gift shops, and galleries? The artist is the bottom of that food chain! The galleries now want 60% consignment.

"That means Sally, I bring them my art and leave it with them and don't get paid for it. They try to sells it, and when it sells I get 40%. It may take all summer and it may not sell at all. Art agents all want 60%. If they get 60% and the gallery gets 60%, then I owe them 20%!" We both laugh. I don't know honestly how that works beyond the artists I talk to get the same ten cents on the dollar. I do worse than Crafty offers, when someone else gets involved. That's the life of an artist.

"My experience with gift shops, is they come and go. I leave stuff on consignment and come back in six months to see if anything sold, and to get paid. It is common for the shop not to exist anymore, gone, no forwarding address, no goods, no money. About a third of all items I leave on consignment I never see again, or never see the money for. That's how it is when you're seen as a street person, with no address. Shops don't have to treat you nice, who are you? What am I going to do about it? Call the police? I don't even have a phone. Tell the police what? The police assume I'm a street person, whacked out on drugs, who can't speak any sense. Gone in the wilds for four months? Yea right. I have hundreds even thousands of dollars' worth of art? A polite smile. No receipts? No records offered up as proof? Where would I keep such things, and still have it four months later? Why would that be in my pocket as I wander around Fairbanks staying at the Salvation Army, staying in a apartment furnace room?"

Yea, they all seem so nice and kind, those buyers, when they have a want. Trustworthy, honest, pillars of the community. With kind compliments on my art, filled with promises. Till they have what they want and then they don't know me anymore. Worse than Crafty. I'm a minority, treated like the natives, blacks, a person in a Ghetto, one of 'them,' not one of us." But I have to calm down. I'm rambling about this. Obviously, Sally has no clue about this, nor cares. The bottom line is all that matters. "Where's the money we need to live Miles?" All the rest is babble to yawn about, up to me to solve. A hand is out that wants money for a baby.

Not that I blame her much, because many men are the same, "Where's my dinner?" "Well Honey the bread would not rise, then I was out of this and that so had to go to the store but had trouble with the car, then..." Interrupted with, "So where is my dinner." The details are none of his business.

Crafty may in fact be trying to do the best he can. He explains to me over and over the concept of business, and what it takes to stay afloat. He wants me to understand. This 'want' he has is genuine. He tells me what business is going to last, then who is not, when we discuss various shops in town where I leave items on consignment. He tells me why, and he's usually 90% correct. At least in predicting who will go out of business. Because? He is right. Crafty is buying out their inventory. Sometimes Crafty buys my work from these people going out of business, stuff they do not own! Buying my stuff I left on consignment, for pennies on the dollar. No, there is no obligation to return it to me. My loss. My bad judgment call. My poor business decision. Crafty is in fact a good teacher. The issues are the same as a writer. Few writers make any money. The publisher does, the distributor does. The writer is lucky to get ten cents a book.

In the future, I find out the top 50,000 writers make a little money. The other million authors do not sell even one book.

This is what my father meant when he said "Fine, but what are you going to do for a living?" So why didn't he add to that statement, some facts? Some reasons he would say that?

I suppose I can understand why Sally is dubious. In some ways Crafty offers an education not seen in school, that comes with no gold star or certificate. The school of hard knocks. The school of reality. We tend to remember and pay attention when our pocket book is affected. If I were in college learning all this, that would 'cost' too, and would my situation be any better? Would I have any more money for bills then I do now? No, I'd be in debt! I know many people over fifty, who have still been unable to pay off student loans for education. Many have gotten no better jobs then if they had not had the education. In the entire state of Alaska, Crafty is probably the best there is at what he does. There is no better teacher. My own father with three Ph.D. degrees teaching economics, could not run his own business. I think, because he does not know what Crafty does. This situation is like being an apprentice, getting paid as you learn. There are advantages to this. *It beats sitting in class every day, all day!*

I WOULD BE SURPRISED, even shocked if anyone actually liked me for real. I think about it. Many of my heroes, those I admire and look up to, want to be like, had relationship problems in a major way. It's the price you pay when life is all about 'you.' I'm supposed to be related to Miles Standish off the Mayflower. There is a story about him, and some woman named Pricilla. I forget the exact details. But he loves her, yet is always gone. Miles is the military advisor for the ship. He is gone from the fort, off with the Indians. Mingling with them, trying to keep peace, trying to learn from them. Is that sort of activity good husband, father material? It's dangerous, politically incorrect, and he just may not appreciate a nice home cooked meal sitting around the table with napkin rings.

He'd rather be out there with the savages hunkered down in the mud, eating wild Turkey and squash. Pricilla didn't wait around for him to smarten up either. She married some other guy, and left Miles to the life of his choice. Almost the same exact story for Daniel Boone.

No one remembers who Pricilla was, or who the husband was. But, 'Miles Standish' stands out in American history as one of the founders of our great nation. Without him there would be no Thanksgiving. The pilgrims off the Mayflower would have all perished. There he was, abandoning the armor and military dress he arrive with, and donned more practical dress of the Indian. Imagine how the religious stiff pious pilgrims felt! Imagine how mortified Priscilla was! How utterly embarrassing! The poor dear!

Look at Hemingway, Picasso, Einstein, Poe, Van Gogh, Audubon, Hendrix, Joplin, John Lennon. Other names in history I read about and admire, who all had pretty messed up love lives. And of course all the famous mountain men who made history. How was Miles Standish treated by his society? Was he a hero during his lifetime? No. Reprimanded. An outcast. I understand! I do!

And so. It is true. I have met many women. But have never parted on harsh terms and have remained 'friends' with most, stayed in touch, and in most cases the attitude has been a warm hug and a :

"I care about you Miles and always will, but I just can't live like this." Usually figured out in a few days' time. It's not totally about the lifestyle in the wilds either. At least partly I am not around enough. Or, not needy enough. Or, not appreciative enough. I have been unwilling to change. Or, unable. How much is destiny, and how much effect do we have on destiny I wonder? We have free will, but yet. We are who we are. A bulldozer will never win the Indy 500. Why even enter. Nor will a top race car be a good off the road rig. It would be a crime to force it. It's not about choice. It's about recognizing that race car, and putting it where it belongs, unwrapping it's rpms, burning rubber on a straight-away, showing it's stuff. People who don't like speed should not own one. Is it really self-centered to keep the race car on the track and not in the hands a farmer? Or, maybe more like trying to break a wild horse? Thus, I have spoken. The final word on the subject. *And the bird is the word, bird bird bird.* My unconscious again, an old song from my youth.

So Sally sort of gets my life and how it is, and is a little impressed I made money with the furs. I have several big orders for high end art. She seems to have a certain amount of respect here, and there, blended in with societies mixed messages. But also, she might be 'going along with the program,' full of smiles, trying to bolster my injured fragile ego. Offering support as one might offer it to a loser who earned a dollar, and needs encouragement when what is needed is thousands of those dollars.

"Sally, if people wrong me, this is more a reflection on them then me. I'd rather be the sucker then the suckee." She's just trying to look out for me. I'm like a child I guess in many ways. In her eyes. Well all men are children according to many women. I need help using the phone, can't remember dates, appointments, paperwork, names, and how do I function at all???? Well I suppose I have created a world that takes advantage of my strong points and minimizes my weaknesses. Can she join in and be part of this world, or help expands my world?

"Well Miles, look at me and my life and family! I'm not exactly normal either!"

On this note it is time for me to get back to the wilds, and get the traps out again as the light comes back, and there is warmth in the air. Fur will be hungry, blinking and digging out, traveling, getting ready for mating season and such. When I come back I will have the Quest order ready, and lots of art for the various galleries I deal with. It will be time for shops to think about the upcoming tourist season. Seymour needs me for sure on one or two survey jobs involving my boat rental as well as wages, lasting a week each. Our child is due in April, but I tell Sally:

"I need to be with the river boat at break up." She is not sure what the term 'break up' means, so I explain about the time of year the ice goes out with the rising waters of spring, and the river is a mess with big ice chunks. The boat is next to the river now, but the river in spring will swell and flood, and take out the boat if I am not there. Every year I have to spend a few days either in or next to the boat to keep pulling it into the shallows and willow trees, as the ice rushes by. It's critical to Sally I'm there when our child is born. It's critical to me I am with the boat at break up. I can't lose the boat. Without a boat, there is no way to get home, either to the new Teklanika land or the Kantishna. How could I fish for the sled dogs without a boat? How could I go surveying to make money for the new family without the boat? I can't afford a new one. I could survive easier without a woman or a child then without a boat. But rightly assume, this is not the sort of revelation one passes on to a woman if one wants peace.

Boat gets left on the river ice and must be dug out and floated in spring when the ice melts or lose the boat.

CHAPTER FIVE

RIFLE STOLEN. SERIOUS NEIGHBOR PROBLEMS – DEATH THREATS. TRIP TO LOOK FOR MAMMOTH IVORY ON THE YUKON RIVER

Josh has once again been watching over the sled dogs for the past two weeks.

"The man with the Golden Pen returns!"

"Hi Josh, everything okay here?" Josh tells me he has wormed my dogs for me. Some new dog virus going around to tell me about. I thank him and pay him for the shots. "See you after break up Josh!" He just waves and knows he will see me when I come in by boat in three to four months. The dogs are hot to run and I have trouble controlling them. They don't slow down. All the way to the airport they think it's funny to get rough on me. Laughing the whole way. Bouncing me off trees at over fifteen miles an hour. Jumping logs and being airborne.

At the airport is my first trap and there is a note in it from Fish and Game. Guessing they came out by helicopter again. Something about reminding me when the season closes. Wanting me to put my name on all my traps. It's not a legal requirement to put my name at my trap sets or on the traps. If I have not done anything wrong, leave me alone.

I begin moving my trails to avoid anyplace a helicopter can land. The kid has not burned my cabin down, or tried to shoot me off the sled as I go around a corner. I feel lucky today. But when I get in the cabin I find my moose hunting rifle is missing. I assume the kid broke in. *Who else is out here?* Took my rifle so I don't snipe him? Who knows. Confront him? Unarmed? Not very smart. Still have my 357 pistol and a twenty-two rifle. Have to think about it. See if he still wants to run my trapline, and set traps next to mine.

Has he upped the ante, in the chess game of life? That he's now involved in breaking and entering, and a Federal crime involving firearms theft? Not that the law would do anything or give a hoot. I'm not among the protected. *And oops, we forgot! We can't prove we ever owed a firearm.* This is the point where his house accidentally burns down. Geez, I sure wish law and order worked. I don't want to burn his house down. I just want him to go find his own trapline, do the work, like any legitimate trapper does.

As I work on the snow machine I keep an eye out, watch my back, am armed, careful when I step out the door or into the open. Wondering if I'd feel the bullet that took me out. Or, do I take him out first? *Geez, what a way to live. It's like life in the ghetto.* But yea, like life in a rough wild west town run by thugs. Like life in the Yukon when Soapy Smith was running things. Swindlers, con artists, bush whackers and no law, except those paying for protection to the man.

I feel sorry for the weak, the faint of heart. The young, the old, those with slow reflexes. Luckily I suppose, I'm not one of those. Lock and load. Whose going to bushwhack who first.

My outboard engine needs work. I'm only running a twenty horse engine this season. All I can afford. The twenty horse will not push the houseboat. In theory, I imagine twenty horses in harness strung out in front of me. That ought to be able to pull a house, a train, or twenty boats! Heck, twenty dogs could pull the boat, why not twenty horses? *What does 'horsepower' mean anyhow?* I'm still trying Will's car engine with the tunnel drive, run through a velvet drive marine transmission. As I work on the twenty horse I think about that transmission for the houseboat.

Ya, we got it in Seattle on a layover on our last trip outside to see Dad. Stopped at a marine salvage yard. Yes! Ha!

Past flash

I locate this salvage yard and have some cash as I sell my raw furs the fur exchange in Seattle, which is commonly done. Cut out all the fur dealer middle people. So, I explain to the guy in charge about the houseboat and it's needs. He is very friendly and accommodating. *At first —explain what happens!* I chuckle. So, while explaining my needs, the guy interrupts me.

"So how are you cooling the engine? How will this water cooled exhaust manifold you ask about pass inspection?" I'm puzzled.

"Inspection? And whose inspection might that be?" I never heard of such an outrageous thing. A permit? A fee? An inspection? Good grief! How does anything get built that way? At a price anyone can afford? So, the guy suddenly changes. He thinks I'm full of hog wash, or worse.

"You never built any boat!" Apparently boats need inspection? By the Coast Guard? Huh? How odd. Why? And the fire marshal? Why? If it burns up I lose my boat. Why is that anyone else's business? I'm not in a marina. It is not a threat to anyone else's property! No, I don't have insurance! Are you nuts? Insurance is paying the mafia for protection. Insure a boat with a wood stove on it? I think not! Ha! So this guy tells me what I'm doing can't be done. 'Can't' meaning 'not legal.' I say:

"I didn't ask for your legal opinion. I asked if it would work or not?" He thinks a moment. Yea, you think about it. It is said there are only two things you have to do, pay taxes and die. And I have it narrowed down to only one thing we have to do.

"Yes. I guess. Sure why not. Innovative for sure. A different approach. But yes, it might work." I felt like it was the first time in his life he ever had to actually 'think,' and decide for himself without the rule book, or referring to what someone else did before. He is inspired. I can kind of see how he might be if he was a free man. He'd have pride in his work, and design stuff. Solve problems. He is that sort. If he was given half a chance. But no, he's been beat into submission. It is only a brief fire and light in his eyes, soon fluttering out. If he tried it he'd be arrested. Wow! And wow again! *I sure am glad I live in Alaska! You couldn't pay me enough to be that kind of slave and zombie. Give me liberty or give me death!*

So, I buy this velvet drive transmission and it weighs a good 100 pounds. But not very big. Shipping? Gosh golly, hardly possible. Shipping on 100 pounds is like going to cost as much as the transmission costs! Worse! The shipper wants all the fluid drained, and by someone certified and shipped 'haz mat' whatever that is. 'Something dangerous,' I gather. Dangerous in what way? I wonder, flammable? The box it comes in is more flammable. So Hmmm. I'm in a hurry, I'm not from here, have no transportation etc. I don't know how to get all this stuff done, or by who, or where, and all that. My plane home leaves in like two hours.

So. *So we stop at a pawnshop along the way*. Yea, *or a thrift store maybe*. Yea, *and we get a large bowling ball bag with a long strap on it!* Yea. *And we carry the transmission on the plane with us back to Alaska as 'carry on.'* A small harmless looking bag, drug by the strap because we can't lift it. Stuff it under the seat in front of us like it's a hat in a hat box. *No one could figure the sucker weighed 100 pounds, and is still full of fluids.* Yea. We both grin at the thought. Yea. I will never forget that guys face, not believing we built a houseboat without being certified, and it never being inspected by anyone for any reason, nor it even being required. We should have got his name and sent him a picture! Blown his mind completely. People who say 'can't!' It's unbelievable what Joe public thinks is impossible! Because their government convinced them so. Sheep! People lost without the shepherd telling them what they can do and can't do. Unreal. Repeat after me:

"I'm incompetent. I can't do it. If I try I'm going to burn myself, endanger others, hurt myself and be responsible. Therefore I better hire a professional." Ha, *I don't think so*. The time will come when the public thinks it can't wipe its own butt without a professional doing it for them, because they might screw it up. Evidence of this is in Anne Landers

column, a question is brought to my attention in today's paper. A man and woman are in a dispute. They want Anne to resolve for them. "Which way do you turn a light bulb to put it in, right or left? " Anne handled the question with a straight face and serious answer for the whole world to learn from, in case others also wondered. It never occurred to any of them to go look, to test it, to actually turn a bulb and find out. They must hire a professional to change light bulbs I assume, and only a professional could answer such a deep question, worthy of being published.

Not an isolated case. I see examples all around me.

My past flash ends

It is a memory of a while back that lingers as I tinker with the outboard – totally uncertified, unauthorized, voiding my limited warranty, breaking all the rules. *Life is certainly grand.* Yea, *the freedom to break stuff and being totally responsible for it!* Yea. *It must be a guy thing.* Yea. *If it's not broken, you aren't trying hard enough*! So, let's take it apart, check if we can see if anything is broken, then remember how we got it apart! *No one looking over our shoulder clucking a tongue – giving us advice, saying that's not how it goes. Telling us what idiots we are thinking we can do it ourself.* Yea, it's amazing what people can accomplish if no one is making fun of them, and doesn't assume we are all idiots. Anyhow, what's the worst possible thing that can happen? We can't fix it? *So, right where we are now, with an engine that does not run, that we can't use.* Yea, I answer myself. Unsupervised men!

So we inspect parts to see if anything looks bent, wore out, overheated etc. For surely if something failed – usually it leaves a sign of some kind. A loose wire inside under the flywheel is spotted and put back in place. Various contact points are cleaned. The magnets in the flywheel cleaned. In general we see, and try to remember, what makes it work, so if we have future problems we can imagine all the parts, and have information to base a decision on. The book and list of parts is studied. I learned to buy the $45 shop manual for every engine I own.

Over time I accumulate basic tools at garage sales. A volt meter, a torque wrench, sets of sockets, a breaker bar. Pipe cutter, torch and solder, electric connectors, Bondo, glue, epoxy, nuts, bolts, washers, compression gauge, gear puller, C clamps, pipe wrench, level, square, and just all the stuff that comes in handy when tinkering with engines, wires, pipe, things that we depend on. Paid probably $20 total for everything, one part at a time. *When women are running the garage sale!* Yes, one secret when seeking guy stuff, is to look for a women running the sale. As soon as they say:

"Well it's something or other, I'm not sure…" and trail off, *you know you are going to get it if you need it or not, because you know you can get it for a quarter.* Yea, and when ya need kitchen utensils? *Yes, you look for the garage sale with the guy running things. Like that pressure cooker for canning the garden!*

Yea. "No gauge. What good is it without a gauge huh? Darn if it only had a gauge!" Pause "No way to test it." Pause. "Only good for a dog pot if it doesn't work." I'm watching the guys reaction. *Crafty has taught us well.* Offer the guy ten dollars, and he's glad to get rid of it, *probably only good for a dog pot.* Yea. We got a five dollar gauge and it works great. Frigging $200 top of the line twenty-five quart cooker. We are quite pleased with ourselves out here in the snow working on the engine, reviewing our past victories and accomplishments, so vast in number.

It never seems to occur to us we broke the engine in the first place doing something with it we should not have. It's a stupid engine and we are going to outsmart it. The people who made it and designed it are stupid as well. *These parts should never have been made of plastic!* No wonder the parts failed in the Alaska cold! Made to last till just after the normal warranty runs out. *That's American products for you.* Next time we'll look at a Yamaha from Japan!

Always, there is hope and optimism that the next one will be new, improved, and better. Or my personal adaptations will be an improvement. Like the first thing you do with any machine is disable the kill switch. Take off all the safety stuff. Last thing I need are the many ways to stop it from running. Safe? I don't buy stuff so I can be safe. Or more, 'safe' is not being an idiot. Like this new-fangled 'safety chain' on chain saws, so you don't accidentally cut your leg off when cutting firewood. But, *if it can't cut your leg off, how's it gonna cut firewood? Da!* And first thing with anything new is cut the fuel line and put in a good gas filter. Ya, we can't count the number of times the problem was the gas, dirt in the gas. Filling cans, barrels, jugs, of unknown origin, pouring gas under adverse conditions. Dog hair, river silt, leaves, are all normal in my environment. And siphoning gas through an old used garden hose. *Did we do that?* Yea, and the hose was full of bugs and cobwebs! *But the huge see- through in line filter stopped all that right?*

Thus, I hum along thinking to myself as I work in the snow, the dark, and the bitter cold. How lucky I am and how sorry I feel for folks whose first priority in life is to be safe. As I feel the butt of the 357 magnum in my side I wonder, wonder how safe the kid feels right now? *Strange we have not seen him around.* Doesn't make sense, he steals my only rifle, then runs? The move seems to indicate he plans to stay, and wants to know what I'm going to do about it. It's our move, and we haven't done anything.

I'm not really into bluffing and playing games. I see it in bars. One guy pushes another, the other guy pushes the first guy back. First guy breaks nose – second guy breaks beer bottle and swings. Till someone calls uncle or is laying in a puddle of blood, sometimes dead. Over what? Didn't even catch the guy's name. Like rams and bull moose I suppose. Poke each other in the chest till one punches the other.

Often as not best friends the next day. Never did understand that. When I get poked in the chest and laughed at, I make a joke, shrug it off. Play dumb. It was an accident. I understand. Probably my fault. I apologize.

Slap me, I try reason, find out what the problem is. Maybe make the other look foolish. "I got no grudge, so what's your problem? Do we know each other?" Still easy going, making jokes, playing the village idiot. The clown. I don't want to hurt anyone. If that's mistaken for being chicken, okay I suck it up. I'd still rather be the chicken then the bully. If that does not work and I'm punched, knocked down? I'm not angry usually. But I take care of business. Smile, act like it's okay, *go ahead hit me again, I like it.* Watch for my opening and the first move I make is deadly. And you aren't my friend tomorrow. There may not be a tomorrow for you. We put a little Clorox in your gene pool.

So, my mind goes around and around in a closed loop. No one to talk to about it but myself. No new information or revealing thought or answer. Some thoughts have more insight, some thoughts have more paranoia. But one idea is. Well society accepts that some people don't deserve to live. Street people are nothing but trouble and help to no one, not even themselves. Suck society dry. So, a few less here and there is nothing but good news. But. But what happens when a poor person low in the pecking order begins to have things others want? Like land, art, money, skills? *What happens for example, when gold is discovered on the Indians land?*

I've expressed the thoughts before, but I'm puzzled, so keep thinking about it. How it was, and is, for my heroes, those I want to model myself after. Do I really want what they have? And exactly what is it they have? What is the price they pay-the cost, the loss, the downside? Because I am discovering and concluding that it's not like we read about. If I'm going to struggle and sacrifice and work hard for some 'goal' of some kind, I need to know what it is I'm going to have if I get there.

The mountain men, my first heroes, were the equivalent of street people today. I review the facts again for the thousandth time. The mountain man era as stories portray it, was only a ten year time period. The free trapper was rare, as most trappers could not afford the handmade traps and a horse. Handmade traps cost at that time the equivalent of a month's average wages for one trap. So, usually some fur company owned the traps and gear. A trapper basically leased it out, and owed the company store. All the trapper got for his years' work trapping was enough food and basic gear to go out and do it all over again, in debt again. Not exactly hero material or the perfect life. There were no rich trappers anywhere, not one. It was the Hudson Bay Company that got rich. Based out of England. Or, the Astor family back east.

I heard of none, or 'very few,' who ever owned any land or got paid for their traplines or cabins. Most mountain men were not even allowed to stay in their cabins, or on their land. They had to keep on moving west ahead of civilization till there was no place to go. During the romantic gold rush days of Alaska, if you could live a year, you were an old timer, a sourdough. Among the trappers and miners I read about, if you lived three years, you went down in history, and if you made it five years, you were a legend. That alone says a lot about the life expectancy. We marvel today at what they did, but it broke them. Carrying cast iron stoves over the mountains on your back takes thirty years off most people's life. Sure, what doesn't kill you makes you stronger. So there were a handful of legends. One in 10,000.

Yes, they were bushwhacked, robbed, shot at, never went to court. Preyed on by Indians, thieves, con artists, and politicians. They had no friends in civilization. No protection from society. It stands to reason, and makes sense when I think about it. What did they have to offer? Rarely had any money, or manners, or political clout. The last thing they ever wanted to see was the marshal or the judge. You seriously wrong them, you disappeared.

Everyone made money off them like they are a commodity. Families like the Astor's or Goldberg's, got rich buying pelts and making felt top hats. Much like Crafty does. Not necessarily respecting the trapper, just seeing quick easy money. The writers from back east came along, and wrote it up in dime novels that civilized bored easterners read and ate up as fact, so long as the mountain man stayed west! If one showed up on their doorstep? The police were called. Yup. Great for the circus, rodeo shows, where there is some sort of controlled reenactment like the Buffalo Bill Show with real Indians, real mountain men, and sharp shooters. But that's like going to the zoo. Best seen behind bars. You wouldn't want your daughter to marry one.

These are my heroes. Now my view of my heroes is changing. So, now who do I admire and look up to? *So much for the great role the famous mountain man played in American history!* But, I sigh and suppose it is the same if you wanted to be an Indian chief or a fireman. Is being a fireman all about that cool red truck and siren, and everyone seeing you in that cool uniform. Or, even rescuing those who need your help. Being a hero. I'm only guessing. But can imagine there might be a lot of paperwork, fund raising, rescuing stupid cats in trees, dealing with arson and insurance claims, those who are not grateful. Low pay, lots of overtime, hard and thankless. The water you spray on the burning home does as much damage as the fire. Not all it was cracked up to be. Those who stick it out have to get beyond the cool siren and freshly washed bright red truck. I'm just guessing. And thus, it might be so for any occupation! And the public goes :

"OOOH a fireman, how exciting! I wish I could do that! Can I have your autograph?" And it's cute. It's sweet. It's naïve, and not to be taken very seriously by the fireman. These people wanting your autograph are not your friends. They will not understand 'various aspects' of your job that is not the fun stuff.

So here I am, living among the unprotected, fair game for anyone who wants what I have, to just take it. And like my mountain man heroes of yesteryear, nothing I can do about it that's legal.

Some of the midwinter blues disappear as the sun gets stronger and birds begin to return. The feeder is filled with sunflower seeds, that were hauled in with sled dogs at great effort. I eat ducks and geese daily, along with green shoots of all kinds sprouting out of the ground. This is humorous, because about every living thing in this ice box world, is out on the newly exposed sandbars sucking the green shoots sprouting. Me, bears, wolves, geese, song birds, moose, me, oh, I already mentioned myself. The sound of returning waterfowl is a constant cackle and flapping of wings, day and night. As highway traffic sounds are to the city slicker. A sound like waves washing on a beach mixed with a loud 'toot!' now and then.

There is a daily trip to the river to look at the ice and the river boat. Break up- the time of year no one can travel. A good time. Safe. No one can get here to bother me- hurt or insult me. I cannot get out, but that's fine, as I can take care of myself if left alone to do so.

Lots of art gets done this time of year with natural light. I can't trap or go anyplace. Art is made from what I have laying around. Pieces of bone, antlers, hoofs, claws, and teeth. Basically, most bush people's garbage. It's like my way to honor the animal, not being wasteful, make a necklace someone will wear and be reminded of this animal, the world it lives in, and not forget. Others who see it and comment will also be reminded of the wild, and how precious it is.

I get the idea from the Indians I admire, and their way of living. Totem animals. Wearing teeth, feathers, shards of all sorts, for protection, or to remember and honor, as something sacred. A symbol of a set of beliefs.

Some functional knives are made. I have to order the steel blades, but put on my own custom bone handles. I carve the bone, add metal scenes I cut out by hand, and acid etch scenes in the steel.

The signature trademark is added that I designed when I was eight years old, my initials M W M run together to look like a mountain range – adding a rising sun above. Miles Walter Martin the 3rd. Ha! Sounds very stiff and proper doesn't it? I provide a display box and a little card. I write the story behind that piece on the card for the customer. Like today, the necklace is on a piece of shell, and has a swimming duck cut from three kinds of metal. I write:

"Been here at the homestead for a couple of months not seeing anyone, spring arrives and I see a duck. The first duck, very exciting. The shell it is on reminds me of the look of water, and the shell comes from the water the duck sits on." The stories are not always exciting and dramatic- just everyday life from a lifestyle few live, but might find interesting to hear about.

SPRING COMES AND GOES. I assume, my son is born, and the river ice goes out. I need to boat back to civilization. That other planet in another dimension. I never know what to call this other planet. For I live on earth, and what planet civilization is on, well it's not earth. My planet is not polluted. My planet is run by God, not Man.

I am going upstream with a fixed engine. There is still floating ice. I am the only one on the river. I see nothing human. Hour after hour I see flocks of ducks, sculptures in snow and ice on the Tanana River bank. A bear coming out of hibernation is still half asleep, and looks up as I go by. I zoom past within sixty feet. The bear just stares with curiosity, never seen a human or boat before in his life. I might as well be Lewis and Clark discovering one of the great rivers civilization does not know about yet. There are huge logs and entire log clusters too negotiate through. *'Safe,' is not a word Lewis would whisper as a question to Clark.* I have to back off the throttle. There is no way through the ice and floating trees. Turning around is the only option. In just a few hundred yards I see an island. The way back upstream looks clear on the backside, so loop on back and head up this shallower backwater. The sun is directly in my eyes, so I cannot see. I slow down enough so if I run over a tree, I will not capsize the boat, or break internal gears in the lower unit. A piece of black ice is hit. This is solid dark heavy ice. Sometimes such bottom ice has rocks frozen in. The weight keeps the ice just below the surface, as it floats downriver in the main channel. Whump! The boat turns a little, but I react fast enough to spin off the ice, making this just a normal expected experience. I do not know what sense I am using to avoid most of these chunks of black ice. I suspect there is something to see on the surface in how an obstacle underwater affects the shape of the top of the river. It's unconscious. *It's a high Jesus factor.* More ducks fly by me, low, not seeing me in a sharp turn. They are just above the surface of the water. Flying fast, sounding like jets. I know by the sound, these are pintail ducks. "SSSSSSSS" A swerve around me, just three feet away. I feel the wind of the flock, hissing by as a snake. So fast and intent on where they are going, they never do understand what the obstacle in the river was that they zoomed by. Much like views in movies through the windshield of Starship Enterprise. Though exciting, this is normal. The sun begins to flutter between trees as I lean into a corner headed back to the main river. The rhythm of light almost wants to create an epileptic effect on my mind, makes me dizzy. I have to close my eyes a few seconds. I know I hit the main channel by the sound of the current on the boat hull so I know to turn. There is less ice and debris now. Often these obstacles I have to get through are in patches, representing log jams that broke.

Checkpoints are passed. Tolovana, now Old Minto is next. I cannot stop at Rock Creek, all blocked with ice. I look for an alternate stopping point. I want to transfer gas, check the water filter. This is a time to focus my eyes on something else, stand up and stretch, take a pee break, sip from the thermos. I'm three hours and eighty miles into my trip. I have still not seen another human sign. There was Tolovana, but this could be as a artifact, human relic, representing a long ago time in history. As one views the pyramids. I do not necessarily register this as something human, representing civilization. This is still part of my planet. I'm not expecting to see anything human. There are no humans here. I do not look, or wonder. I am on my planet, the only human on it.

While I transfer gas I notice the river water is unusually clear here. Possibly the melting snow and ice temporarily overcomes the silt water normally encountered. In the clear water, I see a line of whitefish headed upstream, headed for the lakes they live in all summer. I assume many of these fish are spending winter in the main river, and not in the lakes. This helps explain why I often catch these fish in streams draining lakes. Headed 'in' this time of year, headed 'out' in late fall. I do not think civilization knows this habit of whitefish, this knowledge is unknown. I understand better now, the talk of how Athabascan's used to get fish with their hands. I am viewing a solid rope of fish that never ends. Perhaps millions of fish in a mass run. Such a positive thing to see, such health of the environment, without human management. I stop for a while and just stare, mesmerized. Once before, headed for Minchumina at this time of year I had come to a fish run so strong the fish were jumping as a blanket in front of my boat, trying to get out of the way. I had to slow down or run aground on a mass of whitefish. I am not going to tell civilization, or commercial fisherman will try to figure out how to make money off this, tap into a new billion dollar business. *I'm not convinced civilization has the knowledge to get to my planet.* I do not comment. I'm puzzled, always have been, by how the planet is so overpopulated, and yet so empty.

I arrive in civilization without incident, just a normal run. Another 200 miles added to the 100,000 I have run.

I SUPPOSE happy enough to come in. Furs to sell, art to get to the shops. A woman to see, people I know, unsure if I use the word 'friends,' but 'familiar to me.' Enough I'm glad to see them and they are glad to see me. Or, I usually want something and they usually want something. They want a story, and to be entertained for the most part, and I want a ride, or for them to buy my art.

WEATHER IS WARMER, so Sally and I are living on the houseboat in Nenana. Everything went well with the child birth and *—why shouldn't it?* Sally and I both agree our son seems more 'with it,' alert and more healthy then kids born in the hospital with a mother pumped full of drugs. We all might lack a certain closeness because I was not there, but more a realization in hindsight then an actuality at the time.

The houseboat is still at tenth street in Nenana, the end of the road at the river where many launch their boats. We meet and get to talk to a lot of the river people. Gene is around a lot because he has his raft there on the slough in front of the houseboat. I am reminded again, Gene is crazy looking in his features. His hair is long, frizzy, wild looking with a beard to match. There is a way about him that is loud, and aggressive. He steps into one's personal space when he talks, like right up to you, locks in eye contact with intensity. Daring you to contradict, or even question him. When he speaks, he expects to be heard, understood, and agreed with. Usually I have no reason to disagree, or to tell him I do not agree if I do not. He has an insult for almost everyone, and most people find this irritating. I do not see this irritation as bad enough I want nothing to do with him.

Gene asks me one day if I have any marten fur to make hats with. I still have twenty Marten I have not sold yet, so tell him I do! I explain that it takes three Marten to make a traditional hat. If he wants three hats, it's nine furs. The furs are worth $85 each. Gene is upset, but I explain :

"I am not going to sell my furs for less than the fur dealer will give me. He will not give me a song and dance, and hard time. He will be happy to buy my furs for $85 average. Some sold three months ago for $95 each. It's not me who needs to sell you any fur Gene. I don't care if you get them or not, I'm telling you what marten fur is worth." He asks me if I want to trade. Often I am willing to trade, yes. But with a woman, and having to move, well 'money,' is more on my mind. But, I hear Gene out when he lists things he has that he might trade me. I've about made up my mind I need cash though.

But, Gene mentions a lumber mill in his list of things he can part with. A good quality chain saw lumber mill. *This might be good to use to build the new cabin with, instead of logs. Faster, easier.* So I ask about the lumber mill.

"New they are about $800, without the saw." Normally this line is a red flag. I am not interested in what it was worth new. Anyone who has the new price on their mind is not in, 'let's make a deal,' mode.

"Okay, sure new is new, this is well used." It is common knowledge Gene has had problems with the saw part of this mill, and it has been in and out of the shop. Though the saw new was another $800, this one with problems might be worth $300 as is. Not exactly good news. But, he agrees the $800 in furs is equal to his saw mill. But we need to talk further, and I need to see the mill.

Sally sees I am making progress, and making an effort to get her a home. A tall order on my budget and time frame we have! We briefly talk about renting an apartment, or looking for a home in Nenana. But we just don't have that kind of money. At one point, we explore the fact that I never used the GI bill. The 'home loan' aspect I am still eligible for. A government loan at fixed low guaranteed interest. We spot a home along the river out of the city limits for sale for eighty grand. I find out that yes, I could use my GI loan- no problem. *But how long would it take me to pay off $80,000 on my income? Geez!* Sally and I are talking and I'm considering. There is another place next to the post office for sale, very run down, the exact center of town, so not ideal from my perspective, but 'affordable' at about $10,000.

"About the same price as a boat and motor that I have already been able to acquire!" Sally likes the nice home with a lawn on the river for $80,000. Well of course, me to, water frontage! Nothing leaps out at us as 'perfect,' and we can't make up our minds.

"And dang Sally, I mean, we have five pieces of land already!" Staying at tenth street works because we don't pay anything, do not need to own it, but cannot consider it permanent. I had mentioned earlier, but repeat to Sally:

"There is an easement along waterways. Mostly intended for the purpose of boaters being able to pull over and stop, maybe camp. The technical part states any object left in the easement needs to be portable, removable. There is no definition concerning a length of time that is reasonable to stay." I pause for the significance of that to sink in. I continue:

" It is pretty common practice for locals to camp or build a temporary structure along the river in some out of the way place, and get left alone. As long as no one complains. Josh keeps his sled dogs here, and has for the past twenty years. I keep my boat here and tie up the dogs. I'm not sure if we could actually clear some land and grow a garden. I'm not sure we could actually build a nice home. Probably someone would complain. I may not understand civilization well, but I understand a little bit about village ways and what's tolerated and not tolerated."

The exact ownership and title to this land is in limbo. There is in fact no clear title. But, there would be if there was a need, or so I feel. Technically the railroad owns it, as the tracks are not so far off. But the railroad supposedly leased it to the city of Nenana for one dollar a year ages ago. The city has never paid that one dollar a year, and there is no written contract anymore. Records were lost, and those who made the deal are gone, so the arrangement is vague. On top of that, the barge line has a vested interest as they are not so far off downstream, and now and then use this piece of ground to store a barge for the winter. Nothing has ever been contested, and all interested parties are happy with the arrangement as it is. Either the railroad, city, or the barge line could get title if they wanted to, but why bother? It's available to these people for free. I'm guessing neither the railroad or barge line wants title, and then have to pay the city taxes. The city does not want to be legally responsible for what happens on the land if anyone got hurt or drowns etc.

I cannot do anything that makes it look like I feel I have an exclusive right here. I can stay, much as a vagrant can stay under a bridge if he's not in the way, and no one complains. I could in theory stay here for years. Josh has more rights than I do because he was born locally, and is a respected musher, and is native. (It was his people's land before the white man stole it). It's politically incorrect to have all that 'Indian stuff,' come up in a court case. No one wants to go there for frivolous reasons. It's much easier to allow natives to squat on land that no one else has an immediate need for. The Indian is moved off when someone with clout has an interest. Oil, timber, gold etc.

In a way, part of my being here has at least a little to do with being under Josh's wing. I'm under his protection somewhat. Or, put another way if Josh complained, I'd be told to leave. It's all complicated maybe, if you aren't from here. But, so is life in civilization or anyplace if you are not from there. Sally replies:

"Oh yea, I know of places where the locals park in front of the fire hydrant. The mayor, the cop, the local shop owner. But, if a stranger showed up looking poor with a broken down car, it would be towed away and a ticket given! Unless you know someone!" Yes, life is like that. Like a chess game. Some players are pawns and can move one slow step at a time, but can easily be tromped on. Others can move diagonally or two steps over, one up. It's important I suppose to understand that chess board in any environment you find yourself in, and understand where you are on that board, what moves you can make.

GENE SEEMS a bit touchy and opinionated, not a good people person, tends to make others uncomfortable. Or, I should qualify that, 'makes people I like and get along with uncomfortable.' There is a group of people he gets along with all right. Those who buy drugs from him, outlaws, and aggressive personalities. He has a personality that reminded me of Joe's, the one who was caught up in the middle of all those deaths in Manley Hot Springs a few years ago. My relationship with Gene is similar to the one I had with Joe. It does not pay to get in anyone's face and make enemies. Gene likes me about as much as anyone else he knows. Gene is not someone you want to have angry at you.

It is possible to avoid such personalities by doing what they say, and agreeing with such people, minding your own business. If he mistreats or threatens someone, it's none of your concern, keep on walking and you get along fine. Or, more like there is a strongly understood rule in the wilderness. Take care of yourself, because no one is going to look out for you. This outlook attracts two kinds of personalities. One personality is someone who is able, competent, or wants to try to be, and enjoys being left alone. The other type sees this rule as an opportunity to prey on the weak, with no outside interference.

"So tell me about this mill," I say to Gene. We get to the trade deal for the furs.

He describes his mill as 'good quality,' and is a set of tracks like rail tracks that the log is locked down on. A cage on rollers holds the chain saw and runs down the track across the top of the log. A screw adjusts the depth of the cut. The mill is well used, but seems like something useful on a homestead. It is my understanding I would get an operating mill as he shows it. Together the saw and mill might be about equal to my furs of about $800. I let him pick out the nine marten he wants, high-graded from the twenty hides I have.

The hides are dry, not tanned, as they are sold to the fur dealer. Gene is going to tan them himself. 'Whatever,' no interest of mine. I assume the deal is done and we have agreed. I come by to get my mill after he gets his furs. Gene gets mad and tells me :

"The mill does not come with a saw!" We had in fact talked a few different ideas back and forth, and one idea was his interest in both a snow machine and an outboard engine lower unit I am considering parting with. He had offered me other items or cash. But, we settled, I thought, in a final agreement. Nothing in writing.

He understood I had agreed to the furs plus a snow machine. I pointed out this is not something I would have agreed to, and asked him to review the values of what we each have. His opinion is, I am scamming him in some way, cheating him, going back on my word. Gene goes nuts. I think then, *I am not going to do any more trades with him, and whatever it takes to make him happy, do it and then forget him. It's not worth his insanity*. But my view also is: *"This is how he operates, intimidation, aggression, anger, and it is easier to go along with him then to fight back, for fighting back might be a fight to the death, as this is how he comes across. 'Insane.'"* I just give him the snow machine to shut him up. This is how he gets stuff. But now I am done with him.

Gene begins the tanning process of his furs. Something must go wrong with his tanning, but I am not sure. All I know for sure is Gene comes to me and is unglued.

"Miles the fur you traded me is no good! You rotten bla bla!" Screaming at the top of his voice. I'm puzzled. He is not making himself clear and understood. Just ranting and raving. I gather from bits and pieces that the fur on the hides slipped and came off in the tanning solution. I am not sure. He is not going to show them to me. He might even be lying.

"Gene! Try to put yourself in my position. I sell furs to the fur dealer who gives me $85 each. He never comes back to me and wants his money back saying I sold him bum furs. Fur slipping is 99% the tanners problem, with the temperature of the solution to high, or not concentrated enough. That would not be my fault, as much as I sympathize with your loss." It is possible, but not likely, for fur to dry bad. But, usually if this happens, the fur slips, even on the dry skin. It usually happens with greasy hides, but marten is not a greasy hide, so rarely has problems drying. I'm 99% sure my hides were fine when Gene picked them out. One hide might have me wonder, but not all nine! I'm just too good a fur handler for that to happen. It would require gross negligence. Even my first year trapping I did not mess up hides that badly! Besides, he got the pick of twenty hides. I did not do the picking. He wants something else in trade now, my boat engine. Which of course he had wanted all along.

Gene calls my request to see the damaged furs an insult. Gene won't tolerate the implication he is lying. Gene gets even louder after the 'my sympathizing with his situation' comment. Gene is used to people being afraid and caving in. "Gene, if I examine the furs, I might know better what went wrong. If it is my fault, this could be evident if I see where the fur slipped, like the stomach or arm pits."

"I know you Miles, and don't think I do not, and everyone else does too! You are a thief and a liar and I have no use for you. You make good on those damaged furs or I'll have you arrested!" Gene wants to go to court over this, with each of us getting a lawyer. This is too much, and I will not back down. The line is drawn in the sand. He wants to make a big deal of it? It's Clint Eastwood time! "Ask yourself how lucky you feel today!"

But I give in. I'm willing to give him a lower unit off the outboard worth about $300, to shut him up, and get him out of my face. But feel I am the one being scammed. He says this is fine, okay, we have a deal. He calms down and is my friend again. As if nothing happened, as if this is normal common behavior between friends.

But it is not okay. Things are not 'fine.' As for me, I will never do business with him again, but shrug my shoulders without anger, talk to him and be civil. I have no plans to hurt him, bad mouth him, put him down to others. We simply don't agree on how to do business. *It's not his fault he is insane.* He is like a fox with the rabies. I do not hate the fox, I simply stay away from it.

This eats away at Gene, and he will not let it go. He wants a fight. He hates my guts. I assume he's being a child and will get over it when he can see reason. I do not see much of him. He is moved in now on his homestead upriver. His pile of junk at the river front by his cabin on the raft and bulldozed dam is considered an eyesore, and gets commented on by many who launch boats here. It's in the way even. There is old plywood, an old broken toilet, a torn life jacket, broken buckets, bent rusty nails in a rotten box. Stuff that seems to have little to no value. Gene may, or may not, ever move it, or use it. Now and then high water takes some of it off downriver. The damn he built in the slough in front of my houseboat is in disrepair with plastic hanging from it, and the old raft rotting. If trucks get stuck in the mud, drivers grab a chunk of his old plywood to set down under the tires. The pile looks the same, month after month. I watched a guy take an old bucket with a hole in it for his project, and another guy grabs a piece of two x four lumber with nails in it for some project or other. Like others, I once grabbed some junk plywood and built a crude outhouse with it.

One day Gene puts the word out someone has been stealing from him. He wants to know who! Something is missing from the pile and he needs it, where is it! He tells me it is a life jacket. I tell him:

"I have not seen a life jacket, but I did grab some old wood to lean up against the trees over there for an outhouse. If it has value to you, you can take it back or let me buy it. Sorry, I did not know you even wanted it, or I would have asked first." I feel a little guilty. There is a recollection of my own beginnings in Alaska. I had things turning up missing, that others felt was junk with zero value. Once some travelers were taking some old rusty cans and used visqueen from a stash I had in the woods. Much like this pile Gene has. I was so mad I wanted to shoot them as thieves. However in this case junk is not contained, and floats downriver, as well as being in the way of a public boat launch. Incidents like this become a learning experience for me. since this is so close to how it was for me. Now I can understand from a different perspective.

Gene goes ballistic. I stole valuable stuff from him and I admit to it. It is too late now to return what I took. It is stolen, he will not sell it to me, and it is not the same now as it was, and so he will not take it back. I cannot even replace it with new plywood, for a thief is a thief, and that will never change. I myself do not have the best people skills in the world. I noticed everyone else told Gene they see nothing, know nothing, and do not have a clue who has been in his pile. This is apparently how to handle such a situation, and I am clueless, trying to be honest here. One of the few who was honest, now the only one called a thief and a liar.

Our problems escalate. Gene puts up a hug eight foot sign at the boat launch that reads, "Miles is a thief," painted in two foot bright letters. Highly embarrassing. Right next to where I am living. I can only try to avoid him, and hope he cools off. It is not even worth being angry in return. He is just a nut who needs to be avoided. Gene comes across as a very unhappy person, who lives to hate and hurt people.

Gene eventually seems to calm down, and moves his anger over to someone else. I don't hear any news on the subject for a while. Sally and I are getting to meet a few people around Nenana. It takes me a while to remember people's names or consider anyone worth remembering. People come and go in my life. Out of hundreds there are only a handful I'd think of as a friend and only 'maybe,' depending on my mood.

Sometimes we go to the local café for coffee or snack, and enjoy the relaxed atmosphere of a small town. There are aspects of the life to enjoy. One such hang out is the café simply called 'Mom's.' An old woman runs the place. She also lives in the cafe. There is a wood stove, a couch, a library of books to read. Locals hang out here all day long. Locals have coffee mugs on the wall with their name on them. We just grab our mug off the hook and serve ourselves coffee. We wash our own cup in the sink. Artists hang out and paint, some native beaders do bead work, and sometimes teach the young there as an informal class. There are several tables that are for locals only. The 'tourist' tables have a table cloth and are clean. We all understand we need to keep those tables clear in case any tourists show up.

The owner does not make a lot of money off us locals. But, we pay a little for coffee and if we hang out, surely we get hungry, and eventually order a meal. It only pays because she is retired and lives there. We locals help out by washing our own dishes and sometimes cooking our own meal.

One day the old woman, Aggie, tells us locals she needs to go to town for something. She doesn't want to kick us out, so says:

"Watch the place for me, I'll be gone a few hours." I was in there and we all said, "Sure- have a good time!" A family of tourists show up, with only us locals in the place. They sit down, We all go "Hmmm." So, one of us goes over and asks if they want something to eat. Someone else gets a menu. And together we all figure out how to cook what is ordered, and figure out where all the stuff is. We take the money and put it in the register. This aspect of a small place is nice to be part of. Most small villages I have been in are like this. Galena, Manley Hot Springs, Tanana, Lake Minchumina, all have much in common, where scenes like this would be common.

One thing I like about Nenana, I keep reminding myself, is that it offers a village life with access to the wilds not far off, yet also access to Fairbanks, the hub, with lower prices and more variety then the village offers. An outlet for my art and furs is nice too. In most villages it is expensive to get to the city. I'm trying to look at the bright side of being here. Nice enough place to get mail, even hang out, wouldn't want to actually live here, get sucked into the politics, taxes, plugged in, under a communities thumb. *Like Manley Hot Springs, remember?*

Yes, I remember what my unconscious reminds me of. *How all our mail got sent back to senders at Christmas. Lost all my checks from art sold I was waiting on, lost contact with many friends including Maggie. Because? Basically the postmaster didn't like me. Had the authority to do that.* Legally he doesn't have to hold mail for more than fifteen days. A ridiculous rule in rural Alaska, ignored for everyone else – till he wants to make a point with someone. The ability to put a monkey wrench in your gears and enjoys it. *Be nice to him or else.* Yea, if we are nice to someone it is because they deserve it, not demand, intimidate, blackmail, and extort it. It's the main reason I stopped getting mail and using Manley as my hang out spot, connection to civilization, as it's actually closer to the homestead then Nenana.

Martha, Josh's wife is the Postmaster here. She may not always be nice to everyone, but she is at least fair and equal. As I sort my mail, I see a note from my buddy Will, He asks if I ever did figure out 'banks,' have a checking account yet. I have one, but never use it. I write checks to myself then cash them, when I need money. I'll have to figure out how checks work if I ever need one. I think there is no way to get around having a photo ID, which I do not have. I'll skip the subject when I reply to Will. I'm interrupted in my reading. Someone I know but never mention. I know a lot of people and have to sort out who I wish to remember.

After we part, I think about another such person, locally called 'Crazy Lawson,' who is one heck of an artist with mammoth ivory, and is one of the mammoth hunters. So far, not much of a part of my life.

We meet I suppose, for those two reasons, he is an artist, he lives in the village, he works with, and hunts for, mammoth ivory as I do. But he probably knows more than I do about finding the mammoth tusks. So far, all I have ever found is interesting bones that are good for my art work, but never a tusk. Crazy Lawson runs sled dogs, or at least owns some, and might use dogs to haul firewood. He has a small smoke house, so smokes salmon and meat for subsistence use. Lawson lives on a low budget, and has a lot of wilderness knowledge, but seems to live more on the fringe financially- survival -wise. He is here in the village, rather than out remote. Introducing him is like introducing someone running a still back in the Ozark's. I feel like talking with a Marlin Brando accent, or Sylvester Stallone, as I introduce him.

"He's fab-ly, a stand-up guy, meet Crazy Lawson." Everyone looking stern, with hands in pockets on zip guns, daring anyone to make something of it. You're supposed to reply after you spit.

"Crazy Lawson huh?" If you was ta smile and put a hand out with, "Glad to meet you!" Everyone would be in shock and stare like you farted. I'd have to pretend I didn't know ya. Got it? Ya gots to walk like me, like this…. like a sand hill crane.

Lawson is tall and skinny, has a patch over one eye. Story is, he got the crap kicked out of him when he was caught sleeping with a local guys wife. Bush justice. No one said anything or stopped the beating. Left Crazy Lawson with a bad eye and teeth missing. Looks like a hillbilly somewhat. A character out of a movie. Always telling crazy stories, with his one eye moving around and a patch over the other, a silly grin and laugh.

I mostly respect him for his gift with art. He makes exquisite jewelry boxes out of tiny pieces of ivory that have a perfect fit. Done with hand tools, barley any electricity, maybe a drill and sander, and that's it. Being that darn good he can afford to be a little crazy.

He has a heavy set wife 'Hornet.' Like Jack Sprat and his wife in the nursery rhyme. Him 100 pounds, her 300 pounds. Nice enough lady, always willing to help out and get involved, very talkative and open. Crazy Lawson and Hornet do not get along especially well. But look like they might belong together. She looks like the sort capable of casting spells, who would have the eye of a newt around someplace to add to a stew pot on the woodstove. Pretty face, long unkempt hair, flowing loose dress, purple- with moons and stars on it.

They live in the wheelhouse of an old paddleboat that got pulled ashore. Under sort of squalid conditions, sort of like it is said I do, so what can I say? Seems okay to me, but there is a petition going around. An effort to have their baby taken from them due to such poor living conditions. Thus, some respect Lawson for his work, some associate me with him as having things in common. Some want to put him in jail and take his child. Many people I know live out on the fringes of society, so this is all normal to me. Lawson sells his art at the local bar. He seems comfortable around drug dealers, thieves, and con artists, without actually being directly involved, but like me, living on the fringes puts us both in that category of people. In truth locals would say:

"Yes, heard another Wild Miles, Crazy Lawson, story today." I see a difference between is. Others do not! Sure I associate with the same sorts, but unlike Lawson, I am not at all comfortable, just see it as a necessity. I don't even step in bars unless I have to, to fetch someone. Never once sold anything to anyone drunk. But, Crazy Lawson would see a difference between the two of us as well, and say:

"Wild Miles is okay, kind of a bullshitter, not as good as he says he is in the woods, with a boat, or as an artist, but hey, whose perfect right?" Lawson is kind enough to be forgiving and include me in the fold of 'one of us,' A Wise Gus.

And, here is Hornet wanting to talk to me. I see her across the street.

"Miles, Lawson is down river mammoth hunting, been there two months by himself. I'm supposed to pick him up, but need a boat. His boat got left in Ruby. How about I pay for gas and we go down to pick up the boat, get Lawson and look for some ivory!" More of a statement then a question. *This would be a chance for me to learn from him, about the finer arts of the mammoth hunter.* There are not many to learn from. I have heard of only three people with this knowledge. Lawson finds tusks and I want to learn how to do that.

"Sure Hornet, but we need food and lots of gear, it's still cold out." The river ice has just gone out, snow still on the ground, leaves not out yet. Still freezing at night. We will be traveling 300 or 400 miles one way with my small engine. No spare power, into country where we can expect no help. Hornet points out :

"No problem. Remember it's downstream and there is Lawson's boat with a good engine, and Lawson has emergency supplies we can rely on if we break down and have to float." I'm unclear how Lawson got there in the first place in the winter. The boat would have had to have been left there last fall. Was he flown in? Does he have that kind of money to charter in? But it's none of my business, and inappropriate to ask. Mum's the word.

TRAVELING the river we hum a few bars of:

"Coming into Los Ange-leease. Bringing in a couple of keys, pleeeeaz don't bother me, Mr. Customs man!" Dylan? Arlo Guthrie? Huh? Well, what we are doing may or may not be absolutely 100% legal. But it might be. But it would be more fun if it was not. It depends on whose land Crazy Lawson is extracting fossils from. I'd be 'shocked' to hear he has no mineral rights on this land. Ignorance is bliss. Hornet implies she last heard he has quite a pile of booty to bring back home.

The weight of almost 100 gallons of gas on board for the round trip, and all our gear makes for a heavy load. We go by familiar places. The native village of Old Minto, which has been built up now into a alcohol recovery camp, and is more active each year. Over the scream of the laboring twenty horse engine Hornet comments:

"Lots more boats here then I'm used to seeing!" I reply:

"Yea, recovery camp. First society makes a lot of money selling alcohol and creating drunks, then we make a lot of money sobering them up. I can see how it's very financially lucrative!" Thinking to myself how I'm glad I don't drink, it's a suckers game. My mind wanders, Yea, supposedly there are a lot of, a majority of, responsible drinkers. Problem drinkers are such a minority. But define 'responsible' and I wonder who funds these studies and comes up with these numbers.

"Rock Creek coming up Hornet. I need to change gas tanks, let's stop here and catch some fish for later."

"Miles, I thought you didn't like fish much!"

"True! But I like to catch 'em, and I'll eat fish if that's what is available and fresh. Anyhow, fresh pike or whitefish makes good trading material, or gifts in the villages downriver." These fish are more common in the deep interior fresh streams, not as easy to come by in the silt of Yukon River. "Well sure the fish might be there, but the fish nets mesh is sized for salmon, and using a pole does not work well since the fish can't see in that water." Hornet agrees, as she and Crazy Lawson fish a lot, and smoke it to trade as part of their subsistence income.

As I transfer gas, Hornet casts the line out and the first cast fetches a big pike.

"Miles, the fishing for Lawson and I is getting tougher all the time. New regulations and more enforcement going in with permits and such. Now we are being told everyone cutting and smoking fish has to have stainless steel utensils and table to cut on! The smoke house has to reach sterilizing temperature, and most of us cold smoke. I don't think anyone has ever gotten sick in interior Alaska on smoked fish the way it's traditionally prepared."

"I know, except maybe canned fish is not done right, but not dry strips." By the time I transfer gas to the tank with a siphon hose we have four pike, about twenty-five pounds in the cooler. I already know from traveling, this is a good spot to stop and transfer gas, take a rest stop and grab some fish. Few people know of this spot, or ever stop, as it is a small creek not easily seen when traveling by here. The mouth of the Kantishna is passed, then the village of Manley Hot Springs where I spent a winter in the houseboat.

We get all the way to the Yukon by evening. Two dome tents are set up in a few minutes. I joke:

"Ya Hornet, these new style light tents are amazing. Just ten years ago there were just the expensive heavy canvas tents. A few years ago the new nylon came out, but it was spendy. Beginning to see these light tents at garage sales now and then, along with the new fiber filled sleeping bags." We reminisce comparing the old days, with the new stuff we have now. Trying to imagine having to haul buffalo robes to sleep in and such, ha! "Different days then, huh?" Fish are cooked over an open camp fire. No wolves or northern lights, but a nice sunset over the mirror calm water.

It takes two days to get to Ruby where Lawson's boat is. Hornet and I are supposed to fetch the boat. She will run their boat, and I will follow in mine to get Crazy Lawson. But Crazy and Hornet's boat has been slammed around in the river ice and very damaged. *Now what!* Hornet happily exclaims:

"Darn! Bum luck! But that's how it is out here right? You have to be able to adapt the plan and make do, and we are good at that right?" *What's this 'We' stuff white woman!* So anyhow, looks like I have the only operating transportation. Even a suspicion she knew that before we left on the trip. Going to be a slow hard trip overloaded with three people, gear, and whatever the Crazy man has found. But I make light of it, no use being a problem.

Crazy is glad to see us all right. He is low on grub and wants to know what we brought. Hornet had talked like there was plenty of food here for all of us to rely on. Hornet had paid for gas but not food, so now I'm supplying all of us with food. Crazy looks thin, but in good spirits. He's been living in a canvas wall tent, I think, for the past month. Cooking all his meals and staying warm by a camp fire. He's talking more about finding gold, then fossils. He shows me about an ounce of gold he panned near where we are looking for mammoth tusks. Next day we look for ivory and find small pieces. We go up a few cuts and are tired. I comment:

"If I were younger I'd maybe go check that cut out over there, but I'm tired and it does not look like the best place to look anyhow." Crazy wants to work the top of a cliff. Hornet wants to be dropped off to walk the river's edge. I want to idle the boat slow looking mostly at the water's edge and up the cuts. There are lots of gnats out. It occurs to me *Crazy has been here a month, hasn't he already covered the area? Isn't it time to head home.* There is a mounting amount of strangeness to this trip.

On an impulse I go a little way up the side cut I was too tired to go up earlier, and check it out. I feel some concern for the falling mud. In my own mind, I take calculated risks, but am not stupid, or suicidal, or dangerous. House size chunks of frozen cliff peel off and fall 300 feet.

I see the end of a mammoth tusk sticking up out of the mud all covered in moss. I leave it alone and go get Hornet and the crazy man, so they can see. I also need tools like a rock pick, shovel, and the camera. I know this will be easy enough to retrieve, as it is in a slide and would not be expected to be frozen. I have no idea how big or small, but know it as a gift, easy to get. Some are not so easy!

With Crazy and Hornet I walk into the cut. I find a smaller bone nearby, and then a rib bone, so I think this is more of the same animal. A jaw with a tooth in it is found five feet further up the cut. Just a few inches of bone showed. I had no idea what bone, as it looked odd, till I dig and pull. It is a jaw with the tooth weighting thirty pounds! The tusk is sixty pounds. Between these two finds I know my trip is paid for, and this is usually of some concern as the trip costs me $300 at least, and four days of time. It is 'fun,' but I want it to be part of a business, and want trips to have a purpose, as well as be an adventure. Being able to declare the boat a business expense is becoming important at tax time. We joke. Crazy Lawson pretends to be serious:

"Miles, you do report the income you make when you sell fossils you find, and when you get untraceable cash, with no receipt, don't you?"

"Absolutely!" After a pause I add, "You know me! My middle name is 'safe' and next is 'legal.' That's me, the legal beagle." Lawson passes on a few things he knows as we haul our finds to the boat. Lawson found a mammoth leg bone totally intact as big as I am, and Hornet found a predator tooth of some kind, small, but worth a lot of money. We are not sure, but it might be a saber cat.

"Miles, see the shell layer here where we are finding these fossils, the thin white layer of shells only an inch thick? Well it represents the bottom of a prehistoric pond. If you watch the layer go across the cliff- it goes up or down, and disappears and reappears. It gives the general shape of a pond, or a creek bed. It's the bottom where heavy things like tusks sank and stopped." Most important he adds, "The tusks are heavy, and will be lower than the bones, so when you find bones, look a few feet lower for ivory." I had always looked above or at the same level. Sometimes 'below' is hard, as it can be under water, or in a layer of logs. We both recognize the special smell when there are large amounts of decaying fossils around, and that flower that grows only where there is mammoth do-do. We call it the mammoth flower.

What's interesting is the scientists do not acknowledge this flower even exists. Lawson chuckles:

"Yea, I even took one plant to the University and asked what this is." He says to them, "If it does not exist, what have I got?!" There is a pause as he looks at me for a anticipation of what they said. "No one I talked to wanted to look at it close, or try to identify it. We aren't scientists, therefore how can we possibly discover anything new?" He went on with another find he took to the University and tells me, "Never again." I give him a look encouraging him to tell my why.

"I found a mammoth leg bone with a copper arrowhead in it. The bone had healed around the copper. I thought the scientists would be interested, because they are not sure man and beast were here at the same time, maybe came across the land bridge together." The science of all this is of great interest to mammoth hunters. Information helps us in our work, helps us sell items as it has a story, and we can give some credibility if we can explain it. Most of us would love to share the knowledge! As long as it is our find, and after being studied, we get it back to sell, or the museum can buy it. But no, we are expected to 'donate.' *Yea right!* So Crazy Lawson tells me what happened.

"Anyhow, they are pretty excited at the university all right! They ask me where I got it. I hesitate due to past experience and hedge a bit. But, they borrow it without a lot of questions being answered just yet. I'm told later it came from a specific volcano in Siberia, due to the unique copper composition. So the wonder is if the wounded mammoth came to Alaska across the land bridge, or did the man who hunted him come across?" Lawson explains how the scientists got hostile and threatening, and did not want to return the find They were insistent on his telling them all the details. They flat out said the area where it was found would be declared an archeological site of social interest, and only scientists would be allowed there. The area needed to be shut down for anyone else to get into. Threats are made. Declaring Lawson a criminal.

Thus, if the land Lawson was on was a legal mine claim, the miner would be kicked off his mine. If a Indian land claim, the Indian could not hunt- fish- live on his land anymore. If the land were not legal, like empty Federal lands, there would be a fence around it, maybe guards posted, and we mammoth hunters would be excluded. Lawson could go to jail. He wanted to be fair and reasonable. Share the knowledge. Let them dig and study the surroundings to gather knowledge. We agree that is smart, as it increases the value of anything we all find, if it is backed with the seal of approval of the scientific community. The University refused to give the find back. Lawson says he grabbed the find, ran out the door, never to talk to them again.

"So don't be talking to those people Miles. I heard from Tusk, the local fossil dealer in town, that this general area we are in is carbon dated to be around 40,000 years old." As we sit around a camp fire, Hornet picks up a stick to put in the fire. She comments :

"Look at this guys. Teeth marks on this stick from a prehistoric beaver, 40,000 years ago, they weighed 700 pounds. Look at the size of these teeth marks!" We all look at the inch wide marks that could not possibly be made by any modern rodent. Here we are, tossing such things in the fire to keep warm, really taking us back in time! We talk about the cool stuff we can't bring home, and has no retail value. Much is hard to save, or we are unable prove what it is. I add:

"Yea, like I find prehistoric frozen mouse nests, tiny droppings, evidence of what life was like in the swamp. But if I try to remove it, how do I prove it is old? It looks like any rodent nest when taken out of context. But a scientist could put it all together and recreate life back then, and come up with some better idea what happened to the mammoths, why they died!" We exchange ideas we have talked about over and over as to what happened. None of us believe the comet theory, 'because,' because there is no damage. No ash, no burn. Sometimes it looks like a flash flood. "Caused by a comet impact?" Maybe. But I have my own theory, that I feel matches what I see here.

"The glaciers were expanding. But in summer there is the face of the glacier exposed to the sun. A wall of ice hundreds of feet tall. Water drips from the face and reflects light. The reflected light in a dry cold climate, along with moisture would create the most lush vegetation in this cold dry climate. Creatures great and small might be expected to gather here to feed at the base of an unstable moving glacier. Heads down, not paying attention as the glacier calves, much as the ice cliffs do now, today. A huge hunk of ice the size of a house lands on a mammoth. The animal dies instantly, with food still in its mouth. Predators can't get at it under the ice. The glacier is advancing. When winter comes, the glacier moves over the top of the mammoth. All the silt and debris in the ice would settle on top of the mammoth as the glacier slowly thawed." Over time there would be slight thaw, slight freeze, over thousands of years. That is the basic theory in the raw without all the finer details, of what I'd call evidence to support it. Lawson asks in puzzlement:

"Well okay, but how come so many mammoths died here???" I add to my theory:

"One part of the comet impact single incident theory I have a problem with is, how come there are so many mammoth dead in one small area? Was it a huge herd of thousands in one place? I think not, for how could the land support so many in one spot? I'm not seeing evidence of huge forests, or plant life of this magnitude." Also, there is more than one layer of fossils, and the layers are different ages, with different levels of fossilization. Though bison were once in such huge herds, still, the evidence to me looks more like mammoth died over a long period of time here. So with my theory, if say, even one animal a year died per square mile, over a 10,000 year period that's 10,000 dead per square mile. The kind of numbers we'd need to find remains in these kinds of quantities. For we all agree, we are only finding one tiny fraction of what exists and falls in the river.

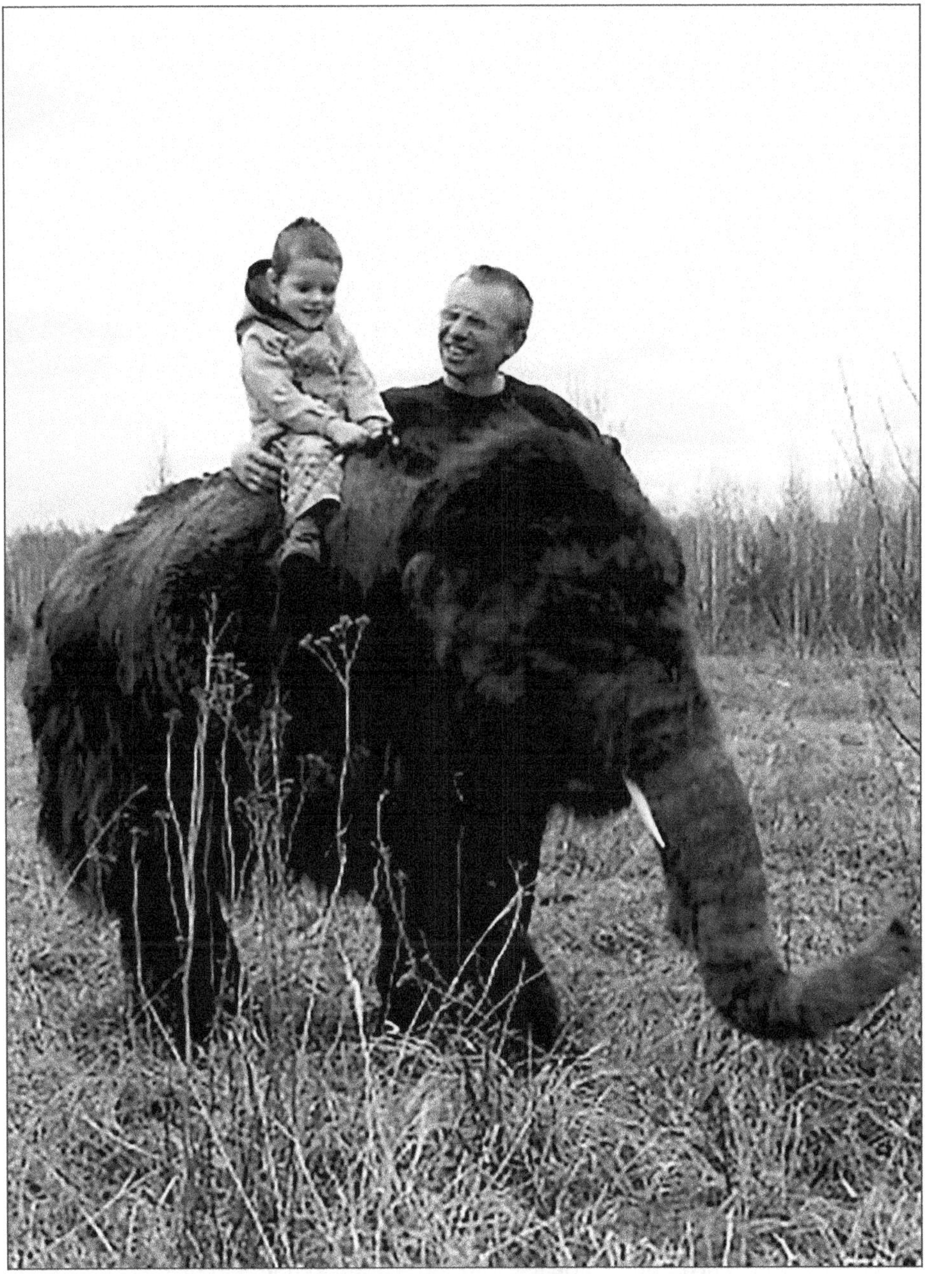

Some people think there might still be mammoth around in the most remote areas where I go to look for their remains.

CHAPTER SIX

NENANA WITH MAMMOTH TUSK. NEIGHBOR GROWING POT- PARANOID, ORDERS AL JOHN OFF THE RIVER. MORE LAND SURVEY WORK AT BEARPAW RIVER

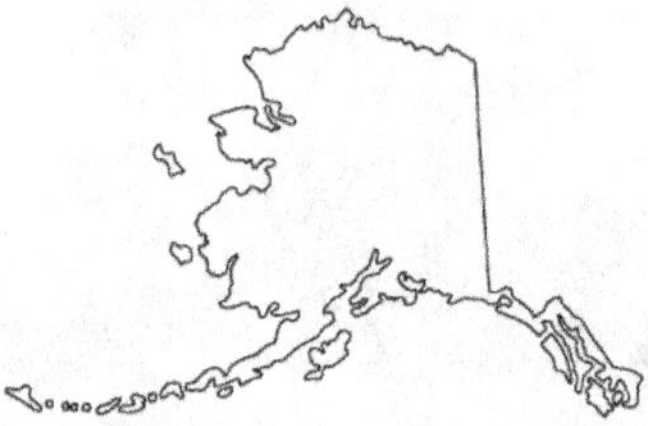

The boat engine is on my mind. The engine is our lifeline to home. Each evening I look it over, make sure the water pump is working. The fuel is clean, oil is mixed right with the gas, and steering looked at. I tilt the engine up and look at the propeller, crack the gear case screw to ensure there is oil and not water in the lower unit. Few people understand, and then accept the cost of running a boat. This is one reason I don't like to share trips in general. Most people want to split the gas cost as a fair contribution.

It was Seymour, my survey boss who got me realizing best. He does the math running a business. Seymour is a world class number cruncher. He went over the numbers with me and I had to agree with him. Bottom line is about one dollar a mile, or ten dollars an hour of the engines use. Life expectancy on a two stroke engine like I use is 1,000 hours. This engine costs me $3,000. That's three dollars an hour just in depreciation. It sounds insane, but in truth it's even worse. Few engines get the full 1,000 hours! Commercial fisherman working engines hard often plan to replace them every year. Mine last maybe three years. In terms of miles of use it's about 10,000 miles, then you can expect to need a new engine. Repairs can be expected within 1,000 miles. A dealer told me within 50 hours to begin expecting to change the water cooling pump, a $150 part. Many parts are made to last the length of the warranty in the average consumers hands. Most users are recreational. A 1,000 miles takes ten years to consume for the normal boat user. For me, it might be a year! On top of this cost, are propellers at $100 each, and figure a propeller per trip. Gas is three to five times as high in remote villages as in town, engines like this burn five gallons an hour. Lower units tend to give out before the top engine part, and costs $1,500.

Very few boaters tend to face all this. *Who wants to?* But we joke in general. "A boat? It's a hole in the water you pour money into!" Or, the latest I heard, "You know what boat stands for? B-O-A-T — break out another thousand!" I joke when I tell it to Lawson.

"Yea, I turn the engine on and I say one dollar. Count to three and go two dollars, three dollars as I run down the river." We laugh. But Lawson does not know I'm half serious, hinting at what this trip cost me. Like most who want a ride in my boat, he thinks chipping in $50 for gas is covering half the total costs. *Or he and knows, and is playing me for a sucker.*

"Yea Miles, this is working out great huh? We should plan on trips like this every year! We could do well!" *What's the 'we' stuff white man.* "Yea, and I got connections to sell everything, so don't worry about it!" Lawson adds. Yet he knows the same dealers I know. He wants and expects to split the finds 50/50. I assumed at first, he is more of an expert then I am, and would leave me in the dust with his methods and ability, as I'd been hearing about. He does know some things. I appreciate learning first hand. But, well – like the next day.

Crazy wants me to go up the cliff to the top with him, so he can show me how it's done from on top. Okay. We go up a cut, and end up on top 300 feet above the river, almost straight down. He thinks he spotted a good place to look on an outcrop of debris he swears is hung up on a tusk. Okay. Lawson has a half inch nylon boat rope with him.

"You can tie to a small tree and get away with it. You'd be amazed how much strength there in a two inch tree." It's all there is to tie off to. I believe this part, as I have had to tie my boat to such trees. *Try to pull one out! You can't!* I have had to winch the boat or winch logs pulling from such trees. So, Lawson is talking as he tosses the rope over the cliff. Before I know it, in the middle of a sentence, there goes Crazy, over the cliff, hanging on to the rope.

Dang! I get vertigo just peering off the cliff. Not wanting to get near the edge. I await the verdict from Lawson, if it's a tusk there, or not. I finally hear a:

"Hey Miles!" from way below me. So, I edge over on my hands and knees to hear better, and in case I can see anything. "Miles, I don't have enough rope to get all the way down!" There's a pause as I think, *You dumb sh+*&!* And I hear Lawson again, after another pause. "And I can't climb back up!" *So what is it I'm supposed to do?* I have nothing to go down there after him with, and no knowledge, as he has, about repelling and cliff work. I'm not the one who wants to hunt for tusks off the top.

Crazy Lawson has to let go, and take his chances landing in the Yukon River. It's eighty feet deep with strong current and undertows, enough that whole trees get sucked under and never come up. I have to climb back down to get the boat and see if I can find him. *This will take half an hour! Good grief you Crazy Lawson!* We had left Hornet at camp to clean up and fix a meal while we are out. I never expected to find Crazy alive.

But, there he is, laying in the mud at the edge of the river half a mile downstream. Happy grin on his face. Saying:

"Last time I did that I ended up unconscious in someone's fish wheel further downriver!" Said happily with pride. I ask: "And you didn't learn anything from that experience?" *God will not keep saving idiots over and over. One day God will get fed up.*

"The Ravens protect me!" What is there to say? I smile wisely, and nod that I do in fact comprehend! Hornet hears the story and adds :

"Yup, Crazy as a fox, that's My Lawson, he always knows how to get out of a jam, and he can sure tell you some raven stuff most people in the civilized world cannot comprehend, but you Miles, as a fellow bush person, understand Indian ways! One of the few who understand totem animals." This conversation gives me more insight into how the rest of the world views me, us, my kind of people. Wild Miles and Crazy Lawson. Two peas in a pod. Depending on ravens to save them. Is there any difference between Crazy Lawson and Wild Miles that anyone could point out?

"You know what your problem is Miles? You don't trust the Gods enough...." And he rambles on about the raven Gods, mammoth energy emitted from the soil, being psychic, and such things. *No wonder I do not say a word about my experiences with the unknown. What a couple of quacks!* We do both agree it's dangerous work, that not many would or could do. I reply:

"Yes, lucky for us I guess, because if it was easy, safe, 100% legal, everyone would be doing it, and there would be little value to the finds." I pause, thinking mostly about the legal aspect. I go on, "The situation as it is, makes me glad there are laws as they are. Who needs fences, big companies, no trespassing signs, and the environment ruined with dozers!" Lawson and I are not changing the land by one wit. Greed ruins so much. *If we'd all only be reasonable.*

"Yes Miles, did you hear, only this year, the University of Alaska went looking for some mammoth tusks they buried years ago?" I had heard only a little bit, but apparently Lawson knows more details. "Yea, they got so much ivory donated from miners, they don't know what to do with it, so they dig a huge pit and bury hundreds of tusks. Now they can't find where they put the pit! They forgot. It's under a parking lot or something they think, but are not sure. Ha!" It was the attitude of the Dean that got me. He was quoted in the paper, something like:

"The University is not engaged in private enterprise." Explaining this means there is no interest in selling any surplus ivory worth at the time $30 a pound, maybe $10,000 a tusk on the open market, times hundreds of tusks. While at the same time, the Dean admits the University is in financial straits.... I add:

"Yea right. Figures! Teach business, but not engage in it. And where does University money come from then? Student tuition, and donations. Why do students want to come to the University to study about fossils? And why would the public wish to donate to learn about fossils? Because people dream, they see TV fossil programs. They see fossils around in public, hear about them, are inspired by stories they hear. People buy fossils in the world out there on the open market. Found by mammoth hunters like us!" Hornet and Crazy laugh.

"So go tell the Dean how things should be run!" We laugh because of course, everyone has an opinion on how things could be so much better than they are. Spoken by people far removed from the situation. Still, hundreds of tusks worth maybe a cool million, and the university can't find them, buried them, and it doesn't matter. The university does not need a million dollars gained by private enterprise. A lot of fools donated these tusks, thinking the University put a value on them, they'd get used for educational purposes, or used to pay bills, get educational materials. People inspired by noble thoughts who could have used the money if the tusks had been sold instead.

Who couldn't use an extra ten grand for a tusk? A lot of people's precious finds come to what? Why? With no apology, no understanding of how the rest of the world operates. The public lead to believe these are so rare and need to be protected and such. But how is burying a few truckloads, and not remembering where, helping anything? It's an insult to the product, the environment, the economy, and the donors of the gift.

Our bones and ivory are stored under the bow of the boat covered in plastic to help preserve and hide the finds. Both Lawson and I know that these fossils have been frozen a long time, so should not thaw fast. Tusks should be kept damp and cool for a while so they can 'equalize,' and not crack. Keep them out of the sun. I am very tired each day from climbing, staring in the sun, and getting silt blown in my eyes. Tusks have bands, hose clamps put around them. Lawson and I exchange ideas and information we have learned on how to preserve them best.

"Miles, we used to use engine oil to coat them and stop them from cracking. That's still used over in Siberia. Mineral oil is better. I heard the carvers do not want that engine oil in the ivory."

"Well, I heard a better idea, to thin Elmer's glue with 50% water and coat the ivory and bones. It soaks in and dries, and is compatible with the moisture in the tusk. This seals the surface, so the inside dries much slower, while bonding the tiny cracks on the surface." For sure we know to cover in plastic, keep cool in the bottom of the boat out of the sun. "Yea, I already know how it is with the miners who find tusks. They are focused on gold. The tusk is incidental. A tusk comes up with the dirt in the dozer blade. If the blade did not break it, the sun does. As they toss it on the gravel heap and wait till the end of the day to pick it up. The tusk has been in the hot sun all day, so it explodes into a million splinters, often as not, and the value is down there at five dollars a pound instead of $30. I do enjoy trading knowledge, stories around the campfire. Just us crazy people.

Another night is upon us. The cliff calves like a glacier. We hear from a mile away, a huge house size or larger sections of cliff. We hear it during the night. Sleeping under the stars like cave men, the smell of decay is in the air. The chill off the ice settles as a dark coat upon us. The 'plop plop' sound of mud dripping, sounds like mammoth feet clomping by in the darkness. A flickering camp fire smells of fish bones tossed on coals. It is easy to spin back in time.

IN THE DAY TIME, only small sections of cliff seem to be falling. Instead, the mud slides like chocolate fudge mix into the river. The cliff suddenly gives way, and I spin the steering wheel. I give the engine full throttle, and we stay ahead of the falling debris. A big cloud of silt dust follows us with a hiss. We are able to stay ahead of it. I did not know how big the section was that fell, and do not know if I need to anticipate a tidal wave following behind the cloud. There was no huge wave, but there could have been. Likewise, this bluff can calf randomly anytime, anyplace, with the potential of bad luck and us being under it. This is a serious and dangerous matter as we would surely sink and drown in the extreme current and cold water.

I remind Hornet there are only a few ways to make lots of money fast. "It is possible to make good money fast, if one is extremely talented and gifted at some high paying job. I am not in that situation. Being lucky, like winning a lottery, being illegal like drugs, or being very dangerous like what we are doing. Those are the options." *What door do you choose?*

"Is it all about money," she asks? *Said by the one getting the free ride I paid for*. "Well I feel like Indiana Jones. It is about adventure and risk. Even so, Indiana Jones adventures usually involve the potential of big profits. It is the grease that spins the gears and sets all in motion. What is it we risk our life for? Nothing? It is one of the three motivators. Power, sex, or money. Pretty basic."

To report the adventure saying, "We risked our lives and then..." People do not want to hear "for nothing." One must risk for a reason, or be an idiot. To add, "because there is the potential of finding a $20,000 mammoth tusk." And or, "And then we found teeth and ivory and the trip was paid for, we made a profit, and there was the potential of…." Now suddenly it is the icing on the cake, now suddenly it all makes sense, and others can relate. We are not just idiots.

Indiana Jones did not go through the temple of doom just because he is suicidal and loves risk. No. The potential for great gain was there, and the potential was good odds, not just one in a million. One must have, and prove we have, a high Jesus factor. One must also come back with a prize. Failure is not as good a story. There must be a punch line to every joke. One must hold the prize up for anyone to get bug eyed, and want to hear the story behind it.

In my own heart I must see proof. I need to know, and see, and feel, and experience why I do this in a tangible form. I must feel okay about all this, sigh and bow my head and see God is on my side, loves me, cares, smiles upon me. If one runs a race it is not exciting to always come in last. Now and then one hopes to be in the money, even if not number one all the time. One should have a reasonable expectation of doing well to have the best feelings about what is being done. If we win a race of some kind, there is an expected prize. Oh, we can run just to feel the wind in our face, but the bills need to get paid.

We head home with our finds. Crazy Lawson wants to make a point points out at a fuel transfer stop without all the engine noise to try to hear over:

"You realize too Miles, there are only a handful of people capable of even getting where we have been. It is like heading for the Okefenokee swamp." *A place so far off and exotic we can't pronounce the place.* I laugh back that I do notice how few boats there are on the river in these parts, and few go a long way. Most 'tourists' or 'weekend warriors' buy a boat and get it stuck on the first sandbar they come across, thinking staying in the middle of the river is the way to go. I have been practicing the art of reading water. I can tell the depth of the water under the boat, by how the boat handles, and the engine sounds, and the wake we make. Almost to the nearest inch. I used to test myself with a depth finder on the houseboat. But I don't bother telling Crazy Lawson. He'd do me one better, add some account of how he asks the raven. Anyhow, it sounds crazy. How can anyone know the depth of the water if you can't see in it? How could I know? Therefore I can't. So I just do it and not say anything. If asked I make a joke, say, "Talent!"

It takes three days to get home, running fifteen hour days. But we are happy and excited. I later run the boat all the way to Fairbanks alone. Tusk is the dealer in Fairbanks who drives down to the river to make his buy. Tourists gawk at us, as it takes two people to lift a muddy tusk into the back of a van with no explanation to the crowd. The folks did not just see what they just saw because it's just so weird. Too far out of their reality.

I get $3,000 cash as my cut. *Not bad for a week's work. Beats working for a living.* Still, Sally is only a little excited and interested. Sort of like okay, I had fun. I gambled. I won, but now it's time to grow up and be responsible, that sort of attitude. I got to play in the mud like a little boy, got all dirty, sat around the fire and tell tall tales, and had my vacation. As much as a grand of this money could be 'my cost,' written off as legitimate business expense. But hey, even calling it two grand profit, isn't that worth an atta-boy?

"Luck Miles, a one-time event, You cannot repeat this month after month, enough to depend on." We get into a discussion concerning 'real jobs,' wages, money you can deposit in a bank. "I do not need banks." She snorts, meaning I am proving her point, not mine. This leads to other things civilized people have.

"What do you mean Miles, you have no photo ID!" She's in shock. Her first question" "How do you…" and before she can reply, I know what she's asking and answer, "I don't drive, remember." "What about credit, bills, bank payments…. "I do not have any bills. No rent, electric, heat, phone. No bills." I answer her expression with, "I think my situation describes the majority of the human population on the planet. All you know is civilization, not life in 3rd world countries."

I GET CAUGHT up on what has been going on in Nenana while I was gone from Josh, and the locals who hang out at the café.

It seems Gene got a license, and all he needs to run a boat charter business. He is upset he cannot get customers. My opinion is, this is because he looks like a mad man. His boat is bent up, muddy, with no 'things people expect from a charter boat,' like fire extinguisher, windshield, rain protection, spare motor etc. Gene heard the old native Al John took a boatload of people to the village of Minto. I think Al took them for free. Gene goes nuts that Al stole his customers.

"Al has no permit to do this!" The story that went around was that Gene went to Al John's house, and told Al John to take his boat out of the river and never put it in the river again, and told Al what would happen if he is found on the river. A gun was waved around. No one knows what exactly took place. I asked Al about it, as we get along, and I like him a lot.

"Yea Miles, Gene hollers outside the house and wakes me up. I look out the window and he is waving a rifle. He kicks my door in and comes charging into the cabin, and I think he is going to shoot me. So sure, I agreed to whatever he said. No, there was no understanding between us. Just an agreement with a lunatic, so I don't get shot. He ordered me to take my boat out of the water and never put it back in the river again." I know how it is with Al John, a river man like myself. Every local knows that. How can Al live without a boat in the river? How will he get his fish, how will he get to town? Like me, he doesn't drive.

There is somewhat of a racial issue here, since Al is Indian and Gene is White. The Minto Indians give Gene a hard time on the river I am told. Al is a respected elder. Gene yells at these Indians, gives the Mintonians the finger and such. *Dang!* It's a good way to get killed. The Minto people are hot angry about how a respected Indian elder got treated by a White man.

There are problems within problems within problems that all overlap and get complicated. But Gene has his hands full, and I'm off his hit list for now. It's almost as if he is unhappy and wants problems, thrives on them. Or, has a death wish.

After hearing all the news I settle into more of a routine. I have in the past, taken tourists out for hire myself, but now with Gene on the rampage, all the local river people who now and then take someone out, are nervous. As one guy at the café tells us:

"It's a small place, we can't support a professional outfit here. The typical tourist can't afford paying for insurance and the $500 a day fee. What's the big deal if a local makes a little on the side taking someone out fishing for $50?" Up till now, it has been no big deal, as part of our lifestyle we never even thought much about. More and more we hear stories in the news, and rumors of folks like us getting sued by tourists, another subject that comes up.

"Yea, if you break down and have to float for five days to Manley, and the tourist misses a flight, or gets to go hungry a few days, you'll never hear the end of it! Lose everything you own trying to help someone out!"

"Yea, for sure, but that same person is the one begging you for a real wilderness experiences you don't get on the tour bus. The one who wants to catch a fish, take a picture of a wild moose that is not a park moose." Someone else adds: "Ya, and they want to do it all as cheap as they can." Yes, it had been a habit to hang out some, and sell a little art at the café, now and then take a tourist out for an hour to catch a fish for $30. Never had any problems 'yet,' but as it's pointed out, civilization is going off the deep end fast. We don't know what to expect. It seems impossible a human being could ask me to do something, then when something goes wrong, that has little to do with me, they trip and fall, suddenly they want to sue and take everything I have. Sounds like some sort of evil monster. This only adds to the communities fear of civilization, 'they' are not human. Most of us would not treat an animal this badly. Sure, kill it to eat, but not allow it to suffer!

I'm still open to taking people out for an hour on the river, but I'm much less happy, and much more leery about it. It means a little less income associated with my lifestyle. Others feel the same, and resent Gene for this.

"Miles, it's not like anyone wants to take any business from him! Or any registered guide. If people want to pay more, go through a licensed insured guide, great. If he is running a business doing this, turn it over to him, great." I agree, adding,

"The kind of person we take out, is not a potential customer a guide gets. We get impulse decisions. A family is here checking out the area, enjoying it, and has little money. An offer to see the river, be in a boat, maybe catch a fish, get out for half an hour chatting with a local for $30 is not the person who plans ahead and orders a trip for thousands of dollars. In fact, what we do may help guides! We give someone a taste of what is possible. They do not catch a big fish but see the potential, and decide to pay for a guide and really get out! They get hooked! We are in a position to recommend a professional!" Yet I know people like Gene, if he knew I took anyone out, he would go ballistic, not agree in the least with my outlook. I am reminded of reality. I know 90% of the guides in the interior of the state. I keep cards to give to potential customers. There are guides who specialize in something, Dall sheep hunts, moose, grizzly, grayling, salmon etc., even bird watching guides. I've worked with some already.

One guide has used my remote Kantishna cabin, it's canoe, supplies, when weather stops him from taking his customer to his normal area. Now and then I hand a card out, and a guide gets a referral, a paying customer. In general we work together. Yes, a few are not interested in working with me, and see me as a threat. In the same way as is so in any business. There are artists who do not want competitive artists set up at the same art show. I and like-minded people feel more artists means bigger crowds. We do not want to set up alone!

Gene would say "Yea Miles, you are nice so long as you get your way and everyone agree with how you feel! How are you when people do not agree! I heard how you almost killed a rival trapper!"

The truth is, Gene has not had one customer. So far, no one wants to go with him, not even for free. Probably never will. "He's a nut case!" Well I don't want any problems. One thing we all like about Alaska is how tolerant we are of each other, and oddness, and one's right to be yourself, do your thing. Even put up with problems and faults, as we are made up of small communities where we all have to live together. It was ordering Al John to stay off the river at gunpoint that bothers me most. And well, putting up that huge sign at the boat landing accusing me of being a thief. Someday Gene will pull a gun on the wrong person, and someone will clean his clock. Meanwhile I have to figure out some sort of long term future plan.

At first Sally and I had planned to live together on the Kantishna homestead. But we had come out of the wilderness, and she will not go back there again. Like getting the bends from coming up for the deep too fast. I'm in a bind. I'm almost in panic mode trying to solve this problem. A new problem for me, as I am not used to being with someone else, and in a situation without a workable solution. I tend to make correct decisions that work. I am relieved when Sally reaffirms she thinks she can live in the woods, just closer to town, like maybe the Nenana homestead area, up the Teklanika River.

We have discussed how I cannot stake land there because I already have a homestead under a similar program, and I can't have two under the same program! But, Sally might be eligible, but barely. She has to be a state resident for a year. She is shy by a month, but by the time we do the paper work and such, she will be 'legal.' One problem is to prove it. When she first arrived, she did not meet my friends, or do anything to prove she was here. I remind people in the years ahead, that flying in these days does not require an ID or even using your real name. People use each other's discount miles all the time. We were not concerned with 'proof.' She came directly to the homestead, so did not collect a paper trail as one normally would. The state only asks for a statement and minor verification, so I assume, 'our word,' and maybe one witness will work, as 'intent' is the most important issue for the state. To get people who are going to live on the land, not just land speculators who hope to sell it off later.

I'M GETTING regular survey work with Seymour. *Sally and I need the money for sure!* One job we get is to survey some of the new parcels up the Nenana River that just got staked. There were five or six we got the contract for with the state. Among the parcels is Genes. One side river is referred to as 'the teck.' Short of the Native, 'Teklanika,' which White people can't pronounce.

Seymour and I of course have to walk and cut the entire boundary of the parcels in order to survey them. On the back boundary of Gene's parcel we come across a serious marijuana farm. We are impressed. It is all underground and hydroponics. Gene has an underground generator with circulating nutrients in plastic pipes. There are hundreds of plants, all in various stages of growth. Among people he sells to are many now living on the river. I am about the only one who does not smoke pot among the new homesteaders. Gene had tried to sell to me, and pulled his bully intimidation routine. I had politely said, 'No thanks.' I assumed that is not a problem, that I have a right to make my own choice and not smoke pot. Yet, it is common in my life to have to apologize for not smoking, since the majority do. I'm the odd one out. Friction over this, my being different is building, that I am not aware of.

I've already heard off and on there are a few homesteaders in the area concerned about me moving in here. Some don't want a 'Narc' in the area who might turn them in. Others, or some of the same ones, also want to be trappers. They do not want a professional trapper moving in and claiming all the country. They do not want competition that is out of their league. I tried to reassure them that I am not interested in trapping here. I have my own area already, with plenty of room, plenty of fur, and enough to keep me busy for a lifetime! But more than that. I'm just not the kind of person to do things that hurts others on purpose. I'm more considerate of others. When I had first started trapping on the Kantishna, or anywhere, I had first asked whose area it might be, got permission, worked things out, or decided I was dealing with an unreasonable person.

My honest opinion is, this area up the Nenana is way too close to town to be a productive fur area for even one trapper. If all these guys trap so close to the village, there will not be anything worth trapping in one year. They might be happy though, as they want to play at it, and if they catch one or two animals all winter they will be content. They do not depend on the money. It's just a hobby and way to get out and enjoy the land. Also this might be a good way to launder money. Grow and sell pot, claiming their income is as a great trapper of furs, since there is no legal obligation to keep fur records. Fine by me, and I want to reassure them, I have no trapping intentions here. I'm moving here only because my woman wants to. We need a place to live that is more along the lines of what I can afford and am used to. Where is the understanding and kindness the homestead lifestyle is supposed to be so famous for? Helping out thy neighbor? Helping Sally feel more at ease, welcoming her, reassuring her. It's not there.

Possibly Gene is stirring up trouble, telling neighbors I am a liar, a thief, not the sort they want in their area. I assume most of these people are reasonable, smart, and can figure out what is going on. Gene has his reputation, and I have mine. I like to think the word among those who deal with me, and know me in general, is I am fair, honest, and not a trouble maker. They will not listen to Gene, or take him seriously. So, I am not especially defending myself and buying into the game of exchanging insults. I have better things to do with my time and energy.

Sally is scared of Gene. Scared again because everyone seems to tolerate him, instead of trying to have him arrested. She's used to problems that get solved by calling 911, or involving professionals.

"Well honey, there will always be folks like Gene in any group of people. Trouble makers. If we mind our own business and be polite, fair in our dealings with others, pay our bills, keep our word, do not bother anyone, then the average person will figure out where the trouble is coming from. And it's not us. " *That did not work in Canada though, did it!*

"I don't know Miles. Maybe we should leave. He doesn't want us around. I don't want any problems." "But Sally, isn't it serious problems if we leave? Leave to where? We have a child, and no money to speak of. I feel rich, but only in my lifestyle, where we have a home we built ourselves, on land we do not owe taxes on, where we can grow our own food, and hunt for our own meat and get fish. I have a homestead with everything we need to live, but that place is not going to work out. We are starting all over from scratch here. I can afford to do that one time, maybe. But not if we keep on the run and not settling down someplace. And if this is a way of life, then we will not survive. There will always be people not happy with us, who we have to deal with."

She and I do not agree on a basic way to solve problems and survive. But, as the one in the family whose job it is to be the provider of our material needs, I have to operate by rules I understand that work for me, maybe change, but not now with a baby. Maybe a gradual change that takes a few years. I sympathize with her point. She would not care how I provide what I do for a living. Her hand is out waiting for food to get put in it, money put in it to buy things needed, and looking up for a reliable safe roof over her heard. Where is it? Nothing else matters. My intentions, my plans, how I feel is empty words. This may have something to do with my conversation with Hornet and Crazy, about ways to make money. "We do not need money! It's not about the money!" Is pretty empty when trying to raise a child. So there is some uneasiness and instability in our basic plan together.

"So Bear, my hopes are, that Sally will settle down and feel better when things work out. When a cabin is up, we have some comforts, she experiences the rewards, the beauty, peace and quiet, getting to see moose, wolves, sunsets and such."

"Well just wondering Miles. I know you already have more than one homestead, so why are you here? A land grabber? Hey, how's it working out with that mill you got from Gene?" I am using the mill I got from Gene to make lumber for a frame home on the property we staked out in Sally's name. I almost had Josh stake some land in his name for us. He said that would be no problem. When he got title I think I could trust him to turn it over to us. I felt that would not be ethical, and not the intent of the land disposal program, so did not use this method. I'm now busy and focused, not paying that much attention to everything going on around me. I take work or money opportunities if they look good when I can, since money makes it all happen. How else can I get stuff like windows, tin for the roof and insulation, stuff homes are built of?

"I guess the mill is working. Slow, and loud, needs constant attention but I'm glad I have it."

Gene has his land just a few bends upriver from us. Possibly he can hear the saw mill running. If so, it might be driving him nuts, that in his mind it is still his, and I ripped him off. He may even miss it, need it, sorry he parted with it. I do not understand the dynamics of a group of new homesteaders. If I think about it and focus on it, I see that in general, the group is scared and nervous. This is new to them. They are scared of bears. Scared of winter, the cold, getting their cabins up. They have never built before, and are unsure how long it will take, or what it will cost. They like to huddle together, visit back and forth, trade ideas, and share. Share the problems, the fears, help each other, lend support to each other, reassure each other. My attitude comes from New England. "If you need a helping hand look at the end of your other arm." Added to that, I feel, "If you can't cut it, step aside and make room for those who can." Tough love. It's how I was raised. If we trip and fall, we cannot expect anyone to pick us up. What society sows, thus it shall reap. This is what I was taught. I let neighbors everywhere I live know, I am there for them in an emergency. Emergencies, not a way of life that involves daily support. I consider 'homesteading,' an individual endeavor. "Life on your own."

I am the supposed expert who has done this before, and would have a lot to share and contribute to the group. I'm sure I'd be a big help! But ha! Why? Everyone else's hand is out with a need. Will they in turn help me? Can they pay me? Will they like me, respect me, be my friend? Or, would I just be a sucker. How can they on the one hand want something from me, ask something of me, and on the other hand want to run me off? Not welcome Sally. Do I owe anyone free help and advice? I have problems of my own right now. Generosity involves volunteering. I volunteer when I'm not in a bind and I have 'extra,' extra time, extra material goods to share. My life is in emergency mode right now. That does not happen often. Less than once a decade. I have trouble helping myself, much less anyone else right now. It would be difficult to answer Sally what I was doing all day, if I reply, "Helping everyone else build cabins and overcome their fears!"

Anyhow, connected to this, my ways are strange, ways others seem not to grasp, so when I offer a solution or help, there is dead silence, and then rumors of what a nut case I am. Stuff like I do not understand power tools, never had electricity. My nearest neighbor Bearfoot, or just 'Bear,' shares a property boundary with me. He had asked me in the past if I was interested in helping him build his log cabin, and in return he'd help me build mine. He is slow, meticulous and wants to do a good job. He measures everything twice or more so it fits. He uses the best materials and power equipment that he buys new. I use hardly any equipment. What little I do have is used. I do not measure at all, even the first time. I have a piece of string the length I want the cabin to be that I hold out on the boards. I do not know nor care how long that string is. This is about ten times faster than using a tape measure each time.

All these homesteaders want advice, but they want the advice to fit their preconceived plans. They have a dream home in their head. They want it to look nice, and want to spend the time and money that takes. However proving up to get the land should be the priority, in my opinion. What good is a nice cabin, if you don't own the land? To acquire the land, you have to live on it. To live on it, you have to have a shelter up by the first winter or your first winter does not count as your prove up time. Winter is eight months.

My advice is to work fast, have a place you can get by in the first winter. Even if this place later ends up your storage shed, shop, garage, or woodshed. You then have a safe place to store things, live and take your time to build your dream home. Most of these people, including Bear, will have to move to town for the winter and not be proving up. The money aspect of this is, if you can spend the prove up time on the homestead, you have few bills. No taxes, rent, utilities. You get a moose, fish, have a garden, and whatever money you have, can get spent on a few basic necessities, and saved to work on your dream home, not on just living expenses.

I can have a finished cabin up in the amount of time it will take Bearfoot to get his first round of logs in place. I will have a place to move into in a month. Others ask stuff like what style cabin, and "What plans are you following." Reference books put out by people selling homestead plans. Plan? Style? You mean there are styles of cabins? What is my plan? What book am I using, and what master cabin maker am I modeling after? I have no correct answer. It's the same with issues on how to catch fish, run sled dogs, fix boat engines and live life. There is only a puzzled look followed by a laugh when I try to help.

I've never even seen a table saw, much less know how to use one. I have no idea what an 'R' factor is when discussing insulation. I don't enjoy being laughed at, made fun of in return for my offer of help. So it's easier to be gruff, or vague, get out of it somehow. I have my own way of getting things done. It works for me. Go away.

I fail to recognize Bearfoot is nervous and would like to depend on me, so is put out that I am callous and not willing to be a good neighbor, and help him build. I am not meeting with the others as they all meet with each other, smoking pot, visiting, trading advice, and such. I'm a loner. Another aspect I almost forgot! I begin my work day at 5:00 am. By evening I am tires and my work-day is over. Many – I suppose 'most' people want to get together in the evening. I suspect out of habit from working a regular job, then having evenings free to do your own stuff. No one here really knows me. It's not making for good relations. *Kind of like Canada all over huh?* Good neighbors to me is, I don't bother you, and you don't bother me. I'm busy, you are busy, let's keep it that way. If you have an emergency I'm there to help, other than that, stay away. Good fences make good neighbors. If I want people to talk to and socialize with I take a trip to town. I'm not mean, unfriendly, or rude to anyone, just polite and distant. Few would admit they are scared, but the behavior indicates this. 'Scared' is not an energy I want to associate with. And, I can enjoy company, but tend to do so on my terms when I want. I go visit, usually in a public place, the café, a restaurant, a movie theater, a party, a picnic, or a potlatch. But rarely in people's homes, and more rarely in my home. And never to share work. I rarely borrow things. I do not like to lend things. *Often get suckered into lending though.*

"Miles, did you hear about that family, Karen and what's his name, with the kid? They sank the boat and almost drowned!" I had not heard. It seems Bearfoot was in his boat traveling with them, or passing them right then, and an overloaded boat swamped. The baby went under, and disappeared. Bearfoot tells it :

"I reached in the water and felt around down there and grabbed the baby and pulled her up. I have no idea how I knew where she was, it was just luck!" With incidents like this going on, why shouldn't it be seen as dangerous and scary? The mother is totally freaked! The river is cold, full of silt. Falling in the river is not a good thing. This spot is deep, swift, full of sweepers, with about a ten percent chance of survival if you go in it. This story is on my mind when out on the river near the very spot, and wow, *here is a broken down boat ahead with someone floating through the swift water.*

"Gene, oh hi! I saw a boat floating ahead and a dangerous corner coming up, so figured I'd stop to help. Your engine broke down? I can tow you in, it's not far to the boat landing." Here he is, headed for the same swift sweeper turn, and he is using a paddle with little control in a small boat. Without much talk, I stop and tie his boat to mine and give him a tow to Nenana, only five miles away. *A neighbor helping out another neighbor in an emergency, not asking for anything, but maybe a thanks.* I'd hope for the same in return if it were me broke down, and floating. No way am I wanting him to feel bad, embarrassed, like he owes me, nothing at all like that. No way am I going to talk around about how Gene needed to be rescued, or like that either.

Oddly, Gene spends the whole time badmouthing me as I tow him. I think it's funny.

"Miles, no one wants you on the river you know. You are so full of sh++*& and I know it, and I will make sure everyone knows it!"

"Gene, you know, this might not be the best time to be insulting me, can't you wait till after I've helped you out? If I'm full of do-do or not, can't it wait?" We could float here and argue back and forth, and both get caught up in the bad sweeper corner. I should just quietly turn him loose, give him the finger, and motor on to town. Let him paddle through the sweepers, or not make it, and not care if he does or not. But then he'd spread the story of how he needed help and I turned him down in an emergency, what kind of person is that? That's how he operates. Wanting me to waver with self-doubt.

He for sure is not going to say thanks. Even so, everyone deserves help. There is no one I would not stop to help in an emergency. Anyhow, we get to the boat landing with him still calling me names. I say :

"Uh-huh. Well Gene, have a good day." I'm not that confident and a little depressed as this is not the only time, or the only person there are problems with. I'm not stupid. If problems keep coming up that are similar, over and over, it can't be the rest of the world that is messed up, and I'm the only sane one left! Obviously, something is wrong with me. But! All I can do is my best. If my best is not worth much, what can I say?

I CAN MOVE the family into the cabin before winter, which is the goal. Sally is sort of okay with this. Or, at least I see her laugh and relax often. Raising the baby is going fine. Healthy, happy, not any problems I can think of. I make him a play pen out of a fish net. I make toys, and build a rocker. Life is good. We nickname our son 'Mitch,' so as not to mix him up with me when needing his attention. At his age I was addressed 'Petu' by my mother, (French I assume, some baby name) or 'Little Miles.'

I learn fascinating things about children. How he imitates me. His intensity watching me out the window as the sled dogs bark, and it is the dogs feeding time. It's easy to bond! But, I feel myself resist because his mother and I have issues, and I can't help think I was used. If so, what will that lead to? A fear she is in control – controls my relationship with our child, or can control me through him. She has it in her power to remove him from me (and later does). Maybe control our relationship, my son and I. One exchange between us comes to mind.

"It will be fun when Mitch gets older, and I can take him out on trips, go trapping together!"

"Miles! What makes you think he will want to go trapping!" Said angrily, and defiantly, with conviction. Leaving the impression if she has any say so, no child of hers will go out trapping! I wondered why she assumes he will **not** want to? Puzzled. It is not about 'control.' It's just a father and son doing something together and bonding, forming memories for later years, no matter what direction he goes. As it was with the two girls I helped raise, May and Joy. Joy one day announces she is not going to do that when she grows up. Said with such firmness and determination, I knew this to be a fact! I only chuckled and told her not a problem, she does not have to skin furs when she grows up. I'll love her anyhow, no matter what road she chooses! It is just good memories, that's all. Good only to the point we both enjoy it together.

But anyhow. I'm not going to make my son come with me trapping, nor am I going to make his mother accept it. Decisions are made, rewards and a price to pay are sorted out. But for sure knowing I will never go trapping with my son, that this is not an option, affects the bonding process. I know in my heart this woman is not going to change her mind. We sometimes know the truth when we hear it.

Somewhere along the line before he was born or right after, we got married. It's not in my diary anyplace as in, "Got married today." I..... don't have a memory of it. Poof. I'm married. Did the right thing. I assume. I mean, I assume I had a reason to get married or else I would have not gotten married, right? You'd think anyhow. I assume I was happy and optimistic and filled with love. Or, that it was for the best, all around for everyone. A simple ceremony at the Nenana courthouse. I made the rings. Anyhow....clear my throat, "Moving right along...."

THE TRAIL IS OPENED up all the way to the Kantishna River. I get out to trap there. I'm gone three days at a time, but the commute is long and hard. It's a struggle, but I am not complaining. I am in good shape. I make enough money to pay our bills, get food, and live what I consider a good life. *Maybe my wife will agree it is not so scary, and she will get into the life, maybe have some hobbies, or just like the routine of life.* I build her a flower press out of some boards and long screws with wing nuts. She presses a few flowers to do crafts. She might be interested in photography. She seems to enjoy cooking. I ask her what she likes to do. She does not know. *How can someone reach her age and not know what you like to do?* How odd. The baby pretty much occupies her time.

Gene is up to 'whatever.' I hear things. He is selling drugs of different kinds in Nenana. He has a partnership with the local drug lord. He is also selling timber off state land to a small lumber company. The lumber company sells the cut wood cheap because it is made from stolen trees. Gene wants to run a big generator and sell electricity to his neighbors. He's a real go getter, hard worker. I admire that about him. Word is, not one person has committed to getting power from him. *So if he has all these friends and is so well respected as he says, what's the problem?* If he is only selling drugs to adults who want the drugs, I do not have a serious problem with that. Or I do, but what choice is there? Do I turn in the mayor, the fire chief, half the city council at the same time as I complain about Gene?

I suspect however, many of the drugs are ending up in the hands of school kids. If the community will put up with it, this is not like I have a child in school being affected. I'm certainly not going to face a madman alone. So, I try to mind my own business and stay out of his way, and thank God I am not part of this community. If the community cared, and asked me to join in some case against him I'd stick my neck out. I do not have the social standing to be the point man, too few would rally behind me. So, I let it go, but not because I don't care.

Normally I am not the sort to stay on the sidelines or be a coward. The community seems to think of Gene and myself as one and the same, like Crazy Lawson also. Those who live on the fringes of society and suck from it, pester it, usually end up in jail, or the nut house. If I said anything about Gene- drugs etc. most people would think I had ulterior motives, like I'm a rival drug dealer. Few would even believe I'm not on drugs. Few would think I was motivated by civic duty or morality. The sacred weed gets passed to me and I just hand it to the next person. Who notices I did not take my puff?

Past Flash

Memories of drugs. A product of the 60's. The flower children. The tune in, and drop out generation. I saw my peers. First with good grades and being sane. Dropping like flies all around me as they got introduced to drugs. I did not recognize them anymore. Acid, speed, morning glory seeds, banana peels, pot, you name it. Yellow submarines, and I am the walrus, the egg man. I'm a child, okay, it's hilarious. But deep inside, scary. *What is the world going to look like when my generation takes charge?* I think at fourteen years old.

What is going to happen when these acid freak brain damaged kids grow up and are running banks? (Enron- bank issues in 2009). When these pot heads become president? ("But I didn't inhale!" said by one of our Presidents). I used to joke, "No thanks. Someday I want to be a mountain man, and when I look down the sites of my rifle, I want to see one set of sights, and one bear!" It was a joke that got me out of a bind. The bind being everyone around me is a drug addict. I'm the odd one out. I'm in trouble. "Trouble?" In the military at sixteen years old, the Navy. Nothing changed. The majority of those around me are doing drugs of some kind. (Excuse me but even alcohol is a drug). Pot, or hash is what I recall. Hilarious in that I got turned in as the one using drugs, and a search was done. It was a joke among those around me. Trying to bust the only clean person in the room. Getting set up. Getting reminded what would happen if I said anything or made problems. A jury of my peers, all whacked out on drugs. It's real, it's scary. So, I had to pretend to go along with the program as part of my survival skills.

There may have been other groups of people not doing drugs I was at the time unaware of. I can only assume later. Like the religious tribe. I did not fit in with this group. I fit in with those who are whacked out, talking nonsense. So often the main reason for people to want to go live remote is about being free to do drugs away from people. A way to make a cash income out there in the pucker brush is to grow pot, run a meth lab, sell drugs. Tune in, drop out, get rich. I learned to just nod with a 'good idea!' smile. To be thought of as a narc is not survival.

Years and years later with, the past flash being a future flash, looking back, the perspective is warped. Warped only because we all tend to see the world through our own eyes. Reality is what we see around us. The whole world does drugs because that is the world I saw. I was unaware there is another world out there. Maybe dressing different, being 'weird,' put me in the whacked out category, and a member of that tribe. Vague memories of trying to have 'descent' friends, or friends my parents approved of and picked out for me. Not being accepted. Being told: "My parents said I can't play with you anymore! Go away!" I'm strange. Not getting good grades in the early years. A problem child. Acting out in class. Odd answers to standard questions in school. Trying to introduce Einstein answers to simple math questions. Class laughing. Teacher telling me that's not going to be on the test. It's all about the test. I'm stupid, no, probably whacked out on these new drugs. Wearing a knife to school because I want to be a mountain man, but wondering, as sixty- years- old, how that must have looked from the perspective of teachers and parents of good kids. No one sat me down and explained the simple facts of life to me. Or who knows, did, but they were stupid adults.

So? Only those who were problem kids would associate with me. Only those experimenting with drugs who assumed I am too, because I act like it. Only, I can get high on my own, on life, without drugs. *What a concept! I got off on life! How odd!* But there I was, a world surrounded by the odd, the degenerate, the lost, the crazy, the drug users. It just never occurred to me there is another world filled with other people. Not till I am in my late forty's. All my heroes were 'weird!' In my mind, modeling myself after them made me eccentric but gifted, deserving respect ! **Flashes end**

Gene is making my wife more nervous. Sally is afraid of him, afraid to be alone on the Tek land when I am gone trapping because of him, who lives just a few bends, within walking distanced away. Gene is the sort, well like Joe was in Manley, who threatened the school teacher. The husband had to come home and stay with her as a result. For good reason, ten people ended up getting killed because of Joe just a year later. As in many remote areas, there is no police protection. We are expected to take care of ourselves. There is no man power or money to send anyone. Why? My opinion? We do not pay taxes into the system that supports the police. It's our choice. It's not like we deserve protection or even ask for it. We expect to take care of ourselves. So what can I do to protect my wife and child? When I ask Sally if she thinks Gene is dangerous and would do evil things. She says:

"Absolutely!" The sort who might enjoy pulling a person apart in the way a child pulls the legs off a spider. Write 'Helter Skelter with your blood on the log walls.

Gene has been trying to make problems for us all along. Some problems, even most, is just annoying and a thorn in the side. He has turned my boat loose in the river a couple of times, for example. Other stuff is more serious. Gene contacts the land office and tells them we have illegally filed on the land we are on, and Sally is not a resident yet. *Well how would he know one way or the other, what facts has he got access to??* He met her after we came out of the Kantishna area. Hardly anyone met her when she first came here. New people are not remembered, and it is hard to recall when you first met someone. Crafty honestly can't recall, and never wrote it down, why should he have? Josh would write and sign any kind of statement at all to help out. He thinks White man ways are insane anyhow. I get a letter in the mail early in spring.

"Sally, let's look at that letter again, I forget the exact details."

Miles and Sally,

Apparently some additional complaints have been filed about your new homestead entry permit application. Please call me as soon as possible. I plan to come up to the Teklanika staking area by boat on Friday 5/9 or Monday 5/19 to look at the parcel.

Pete Buist 451-2700.

I think the new complaint is from a certain neighbor who wants the land we are on, and thinks if we can get kicked off, he can stake it in his wife's name and expand. He is friends with Gene. We hardly know him. All I really know is, he lets his dogs loose, so the dogs come over to steal food from us. This neighbor thinks that's funny. He does not have to feed his dogs, I have to feed them. Yes 'hilarious.' I'm more backed off about all this then I might be on my own. My wife is very much a pacifist, and wants me to do nothing, be nice, not say anything. I'm respecting that. She's already freaked out, so no use escalating the situation. I feel helpless though, with these folks walking all over us, and us letting them. Sally says:

"Well there is an issue of when I got here, you must admit, and it is hard to verify and prove, and if it is a problem, maybe we should give the land back to the state." Yea? Well she is not the one who built the cabin, or worked for the mill, or bought the supplies, or hauled them here. She wants us to move where? On whose dime? What sacrifice on her part? I'm assuming from her position, there is no difference between life as I live it, and life working at Woolworths, and staying at Crafty's. *At least he has running water!*

From my standpoint there is every difference in the world, like night and day between owning your own place, and either renting or being given a favor. Also, a huge difference between working at Woolworths, and having the kind of occupation that lets you be free, and has room for advancement where the sky is the limit. Limited only by your own imagination. Getting paid for your work, and not having some boss get all the profits. *Some of the richest people in the world financially are among artists! No way, no how, can you get ahead as a checker at Woolworths! No matter how much you dream!*

"Free to what Miles? You call how your live free? Having to haul water, cut firewood?" I do, and learn from this, that freedom is a relative word, that means different things to different people. But Sally thinks maybe things could get better one day if she sticks it out with me. I'm guessing, 'for the sake of our child.'

Pete from the land office talks to us, and suggests an option. "This land area is opening up again for new homesteaders. You could give the parcel up, and re-file on it under this next program." We'd have to take a chance someone else might stake this same parcel, but who would even know the parcel was given up? There will be no public announcement, we are told. For sure, Sally has been here a year now, as the land office itself has records a year old. We'd lose the year time for proving up, but we'd for sure make our problems over this go away. So Sally and I do this. Give up the land, and re-file on it under a new program just a month later.

Now Gene cracks his nuts all over us again, because his plans to get rid of us have not worked. He has assumed we are now squatting, and will be evicted soon. It is spring and going into summer. I have two river boats. One, the biggest, is still up on the river bank on our Tek land, not in the water yet. This is the cool twenty six foot jet boat from the fifties. No huge amounts of supplies have to come in yet, so I use the more economical smaller boat to go back and forth to Nenana. While we are in town, Gene sinks our main big boat. I can live without it, but it is a loss. The boat was not working out that great anyhow, but could have been sold for a few thousand, and we sure could use the money. It's a monkey wrench in our gears for sure. The big inboard jet had a big car engine for power. It had been gotten through my buddy Will at a garage sale for under two grand.

"Sally, we depend on the river and boating. It is best to have back up transportation if we ever get in a bind with our boat engine." I learned in my lifestyle, to have at least two of anything our life depends on. "A backup source of heat, a backup source of light, a backup of source of transportation. In this way you don't have emergencies, only inconveniences." But now all for what, that $2,000 we could have used on the baby, or other needs.

No one particularly cares or even believes Gene sank my boat. Bearfoot has had a few problems with Gene of late, and his boat sinks, but Bearfoot retrieves it. When I visit Bearfoot, I look at the rope and point out the rope did not break. "It was cut!" Bearfoot does not want to look, does not want to see it was cut. He wants me to mind my own business.

Meanwhile there is a two or three week job surveying with Seymour at good wages.

"Seymour, I'm not sure I have a reliable boat. My boat got sunk this spring and I have only the twenty horse motor now."

"No problem Miles, I still own my boat and you can run it. You run yours to the mouth of the Kantishna and I'll meet you there with my boat. We can tie yours up and continue up river to do the parcels up near Bearpaw." At least we have a workable plan, though I miss out on the boat rental I'd get if I had my own boat. Seymour has a nice eighty-eight special outboard. I've never held the reins of this many horses before. Seymour and I meet as he suggested. I was fishing, and had been there only a couple of hours when he arrives. He had traveled fifty miles, and I have traveled eighty miles.

"Seymour, your boat sure handles different than mine!" But I'm used to a variety of styles of boat. His has a nice pointed bow for cutting waves and going out in more heavy weather. The sacrifice is, it draws a few more inches of water then mine.

We are traveling along at about twice the speed I am used to in my boat, even empty. We must be doing forty-five miles an hour.

The engine is screaming, as the boat slides into a turn in a short cut. We enjoy the scenery. The river channel is only four foot wide, and the river only twenty foot wide here. As we get into another turn, we both spot a sweeper all the way across the river. A tree has fallen, and is across the channel right above surface level. We will be lucky to survive. Lucky if all that happens is we rip the engine off the boat, maybe take the transom with it. Seymour has time to say:

"Oh no!" and without a word I slam the engine into neutral, which slows us fast enough, the bow drops and creates a wave in front of us. A half a second later, put the engine back in gear and give full throttle. Just as the wave of water the bow made crests over the log, the boat rides the wave, and the engine lower unit has enough water to miss the tree. Without barley missing a engine rpm we are up and running, over and past the tree.

Seymour is still catching his breath. He was certain he was going to lose an engine and we'd be stranded here. Oh, he doesn't blame me in the least, this is life on the river. Now and then this can happen. Going slow enough is not much of an option as we want to be there in less than a week! Seymour stutters:

"I can't believe that. How did you do that!" Being the actor I am, I deadpan.

"Do what Seymour? Oh yea, the log, no problem Seymour, stuff like this happens. I'm a river man Seymour. I know what to do." We don't run up on any sandbars. We hardly skip a beat and get all the way to Bearpaw. Seymour is the best there is at what he does. But he needs a reference place to begin on a map. He's also a numbers man beyond anything I have ever seen. Add up angels and distances by the hundreds, and never ever gets it wrong. That's mind boggling to me. Part of my job is to show him the first place that is on his map as his beginning point. Likewise he feels I am pretty darn good at what I do.

"Miles, I'm trying to read the river map here as we travel, is this bend the right place, see the mountain here on the map? And is that it over there, this creek, the one we went by a mile back?" I only glance at the map and say:

"Nope not yet. The river has changed since the map was made, that was a river slough, not a creek. We have ten more miles to go yet." I know partly because I know river miles from points to points and an estimated time of arrival based on our speed and time gone by. As Seymour knows numbers, I know bends in the river. We make a good team, or are beginning to, as we work together on more jobs.

We have a routine for setting up camp that is efficient and fast. We each pick out a spot we want our tent and begin setting it up. When we are sure we have all the tent parts and our gear is in one place, I begin getting a camp fire going while Seymour begins getting a meal ready for us. As we sit around the fire getting ready to eat, Seymour likes to review the job with me.

"Four parcels this time, ones a bitch up on a hill, so let's do that one first. The others have water frontage and will require some meanders, so keep an eye out to see if the water is dropping as we probably have to do that by boat." For the first time I get the scope of the job. Till now I don't ask much.

"Seymour, if you set up on the high spot across the river, I think you can shoot me at corners of at least two parcels so we can have solid control. Especially if you can shoot in two quarter corners, here and here." Showing him on the map, and showing him on the hill, then on the ground in the flats. In my own way, I do get to help plan out the job. Even though technically I'm hired as 'the saw man.' Seymour points out I'm the highest paid saw man in the state.

"Miles, I can show you how to run the instrument and you could end up a party chief one day. It's not that hard." But doing it as well as Seymour is hard, and an art, and I know I do not have it in me to do. I don't like to be in charge for one thing.

"Seymour, it's sort of a Peter Principal situation. I'm good at what I do and like what I do, and I'm not a numbers person. I can't even get a phone number written down right without mixing up the numbers!" he has seen examples. One of the things I do to make up for it is, to write every number down he tells me on the ribbon near where I am. I'm pretty good with a saw, but sometimes we hire someone local in a village who is better with the saw them I am, and I get discouraged. Still, I can cut a mile or more a day in thick brush. Even up to five miles. I'm good at rough country without complaining. Swamps, hills, heat, rain, bugs, tangled trees, it's all the same to me. I'm easy to work with and do not complain. I do what I'm told, with a good attitude, and I show up on time, sober. These are things Seymour points out.

"Miles, remember Dave, my old side kick?" Yea, it used to be three of us working together. This Dave guy was hard to figure, and hard to get along with, I thought. I never said much at first since Seymour hires him and he's the boss. Dave would tell me how to hold my fork. How to cut my meat at meal time. He'd grab up the biggest hunk of steak and leave seconds for Seymour and I. Stuff like that.

"Good with a saw Seymour, that much I can say about him!" He taught me a few things all right. How to guide a big tree as you cut it to control where it falls. I don't always have time to notch a tree, so usually just face cut. As we talk by the camp fire I can't help but be reminded how Seymour looks like John Lennon. Only sort of. Tall, long hair, cut well. Well-dressed usually. Very much an intellectual, but also innovative and gifted. Whatever he does, he goes at with passion, and is the best. Seymour used to be into shotguns and skeet shooting, and was once doing well in competition. He has sled dogs, and does well with them racing. He's respected, and his opinion is listened to.

Even so, he has that side of him that is a little like me. Rebellious. Enjoys certain freedoms as I do. Strong on gun rights, the constitution and such. Loves the outdoors, hunting, fishing, and boating. He does not want to live as I do however. Seymour has issues with society in general. We both have the same work ethics. Get up early, and work till we drop. No coffee breaks, and eat lunch while we work. A ten hour work day is a short day. There are no holidays. There is no sick leave. Throw up and get back to work. Neither of us thinks much of the average worker. We are among the elite. Specialists. But Seymour has issues with 'some' other surveyors who are getting into the more modern surveying with satellites, GPS, and 90% 'tweak it in the office' stuff.

Seymour began surveying at eight years old, following his father around. In those days as he tells it:

"We used real chain, a metal tape that got pulled out to measure distance. We had to know the temperature of the chain, and had to pull with a certain tension." Learning it the hard way from the beginning gave him perspective and insight. Most modern surveyors seem to forget the basics, what it's all about, what it is we are doing. Some modern ways are about playing with numbers in a computer more than giving people a piece of land they want.

"Your life is okay for you Miles, and I respect that. But money buys certain freedoms I want. I like good equipment. I like to be able to travel when I want. I have a plane, and soon we will be using it on the jobs, and I can afford to fly in fishing and hunting. I have a good retirement plan laid out with money in the bank and lots of interest to live on." He tells me how he plans to have 200 grand in the bank soon. I smile and think his ideas are great for him, and hope it works out. Many people who live my lifestyle have a bad feeling about money, put it down, insult those who have it or want it. No. Money is great, if you have it or can get it, but the secret is to not make it your God.

There are things Seymour will not do for any amount of money. First comes a certain enjoyment of life that takes priority, and level of ethics.

"Miles, doing these homestead jobs is great, but has its problems. Getting paid can be a bitch, as so many of the homestead folks are broke! There are some state jobs coming up in the years ahead I'm bidding on for more money. Same kind of work, village and remote stuff." Also, one day Seymour predicts the state will not have homesteaders go find their own surveyor. The state will hire someone to come in and do all the homesteads, and the cost will be part of the homestead acquisition costs. In anticipation of that, Seymour is gearing up and getting certain things in order. Like getting his wife licensed.

"She would be the first female in Alaska with this level of education. The state gives preference for hiring women." Also, he lets me know again how he and I have surveyed more homesteads than any other surveyor in the state, and it is our specialty. Still this is just a job to me, and I am not thinking of myself as a surveyor by trade. However, I do notice the survey work fits in well with my work and lifestyle. I meet remote people. As they know me, I get to do some trading or buying of the raw materials I use in my art. Moose antler, Dall sheep horn, even mammoth bones are brought to me and I buy them. There has been a little bit of money selling extra raw materials I have. The surplus I can never use in a lifetime, I can part with to others and make a profit. Crafty wants a lot of it in trade for silver, glue, sandpaper, stuff I'd have to buy. Some of the village people know me from long ago when I worked with the village fire fighters, checking them into rooms at the Fairbanks headquarters. Some know me from my houseboat days going by their village. As a White man, it takes a very long time to be accepted by the Natives. I'm slowly getting there, a point of being trusted. The biggest issue is, no place to store what acquire.

"Yea Seymour, it's troublesome sometimes. I keep hoping to have a big shop or bear proof cache to hold all the stuff I acquire. But as it is, I have a big pile, like a junk pile to grab stuff from. Weather gets to it, mice and bears. After a few years, whatever I have accumulated is garbage. I lose the pile to the elements faster then I get ahead." I know it is what Seymour means when he talks about having enough money to take care of stuff like this! I have felt for a lot of years now, like a train under full steam, with the emergency brake still on. Knowing if I can ever get the break off, I will scream down the tracks and get someplace.

"This spaghetti sauce Elaine makes is great Seymour!" His wife makes homemade sauce and freezes it in Tupperware. This acts as the cold source in the cooler for the other foods we bring.

"Like Beer!" Seymour chimes in. I smile. The beer is a big deal as part of the evening ritual at the end of a long hard day. I drink it because I know Seymour enjoys that social aspect. I think it tastes like piss. But I enjoy seeing Seymour happy, and we joke and talk, and that's the good part to me. I drink one beer and nurse it all evening.

Mosquitoes are always an issue, but this year the bugs are amazing. Seymour and I have a contest to see how many we can kill in one swat on our knee. I win with thirty-two in one swat. "Without spilling my beer!" The poison we douse ourselves with to control the bugs, makes me groggy after a few days use. We have to burn pic in the tents before turning in for the night. Lots of rain. We go to bed wet, get rained on all night, get dressed in wet clothes, and work all day wet. No bath, wet clothes, smell like wood smoke and bug dope. In a week I've cut down about a million zillion trees. Enough to make an environmentalist weep.

"Yea, but the same environmentalist who wants to have a survey, and buy a piece of this great country, huh Seymour?" Some of our clients are real wackos. We enjoy quoting them when times get rough. I was out on the back property line in a swamp, cutting line, when one client sneaks up behind me and taps me on the shoulder as I'm running the saw.

"You weren't going to cut that tree down were you?" It's an ordinary looking three inch in diameter birch tree out in a swamp at the back of the property. How does one answer such a question. That's my job. I cut trees. I say:

"We can survey around it if you want. You'll have to talk to my boss about the added cost based on our time, which is about $200 an hour. How many extra hours would you like to purchase? I'll pass it on to the boss." For days after, Seymour would dead pan:

"You weren't thinking of cutting that tree down were you?" Another good one liner was:

"I just love the diverse vegetation here!" As one client commented. Big happy grin, dressed in city clothes, scientist type, real dweeb. Seymour and I had just hauled our camp through the mud and bugs and heat, through the pucker brush, the tangles and soft moss. We are totally wore out, dirty, and this homosexual voice and hand wave, "Oh don't you just love…"

"Hey Seymour!" sitting around the camp fire in the evening. "Remember the squirrel guy?!" Seymour's reply is to quote the homesteader:

"We don't mind the little damage they do! Have you met our furry friends? " Seymour and I had wondered why these squirrels were so easy to shoot, and ran right up to us. The squirrels had been running off with all the insulation in the cabin. Soon there will be no insulation, and the cabin will not be possible to live in during the cold. Hard to fix, as it requires taking the walls out. Squirrels are viewed by most wilderness people, much like mice. Seymour has shot one with a forty-four magnum pistol. (A pistol typically used on bears.)

"Cool! Did you see that?" The squirrel had fallen forward instead of back! Another one I blasted right through the tree it was on, and out the other side of the eight inch tree. That was even more cool. The homesteader was not planning to be around, and gave us permission to stay in his cabin as part of the payment for the survey Seymour worked out. We were alone there, taking care of his squirrel problem. The client shows up and asks if we met his little friends yet. We froze, and stared at each other, *"Oh oh."* We simply said, "Yes, we met them!" So, for years we'd refer to the squirrels as 'our little friends.' Like now:

"Seymour! I hear one of our little friends in the tree over camp!" We both dive for our weapons, and look from tree to tree for movement, and a target. Squirrels move into our tent after we leave for the day and get into things, could even chew through the tent to get in. They can potentially raise havoc. Eat a hole in a sleeping bag, get into food, put holes in the tent and such.

Getting dressed in the rain, I'm being jabbed with rose hips as I try to get my pants on. I comment to Seymour, who is having the same problem and cussing.

"I just love the diverse vegetation, don't you?" In a homosexual voice and flutter of the hands, dancing in my undies with one leg in my pants. A squirrel chatters after stealing food from us. We are both on the alert, and Seymour says first:

"Let's go visit our little furry friends!" 😀 :)

One view is "poor innocent squirrel!" I'm not consciously aware, but shooting squirrels is important practice. This teaches us to be aware where our guns are. We do not grab, fumble, wonder which end is in our hand, where the safety is. I learn where to keep my pistol where I can grab it fast from any position I am in, sitting, swatting, spinning talking, doing chores. I adjust how to carry, based on an inability to respond in a hurry at the call of "Squirrel!" I know how to get the pistol of safety without conscious thought, at the ready. This training becomes critical when the word is, "Bear!"

Base pay is three times minimum wages at $21 an hour. Most days we put in overtime, at ten hours, and we work through the weekends. Time and a half for over eight hours, and double pay for over forty hours in a week. Eighty hour work weeks are common. One hundred twenty hours possible. It's like two months wages for some people, I make per week. Or put another way, it's more money then I usually make trapping for seven months, made per week. Put another way, I make in a week what Sally makes in several months. I'm therefore not sure what her issue is with my income or lifestyle. *I sort of get it. No matter what, if a dumpster diver found a rolls Royce for free at the transfer station it does not matter, you are still a dumpster diver.* My unconscious however, decides this bit of illuminating news is not good to remind my conscious of. We thus maintain our big grin, and have problems being humble, considering how smart and rich we are.

Diary July sixth

Finish surveying. Head for mouth of Kantishna. Five hours from Bearpaw, just one hour from the homestead to the mouth!

July seventh

Arrive Nenana 7:00 am after a sleep near Old Minto. Take care of business. Tek 2:00 pm dogs okay, plants okay. Flood conditions. Lost gas barrel, fifty-five gallons of gas.

I could have hung around my Kantishna homestead after the job, at what I call my home, which I would have done in the past. But now I have Sally, a new place being built, and anyhow, the State Fair is coming up soon. It's the best way to unload a lot of my art, and acquire dry foods, sometimes tools in trade from vendors or customers. It's also the greatest social event of my year that I've come to look forward to. There has never been a bad experience at the fair. As a result, I feel more socially confidant. Well, I'm the center of attention when selling, and a good attraction for the fair. The security people like me. The grounds crew likes me. After all, a fair is a perfect place for a character. *Much in common with the zoo. Ha!* Before the fair I want to get more work done on the Tek land.

The water table on our property is only six feet down and in sand, so it is easy to drive a Sand-point water well with just a mall. I design a hot water heater with a twenty gallon tank painted black in a small greenhouse, so in summer there is natural solar heat. In winter a hose is hooked to a smaller pot that goes on the wood stove inside, and the water circulates through the storage tank that is insulated for winter, or moved in upstairs when the upstairs gets done. The lumber mill works well, but is a lot of work. The logs feed slow and are hard to get positioned in the tracks and locked down. I'm walking on my knees running the saw in its carriage down the log. I write Will about it.

Hey Will!

You were wondering how the mill would work, and wanted an update since you might be interested in one too. It is not as good as a band saw mill, but it does the job and makes straight lumber. There is just a tremendous amount of waste of wood in sawdust and end slabs. It sure is nice to be able to build your own place on a low budget without permits, inspections, and professionals, required to do the wiring, the plumbing, and get it all approved! No, I don't always know what I'm doing, but it works ! Ha!

So are you able to keep up the car building business, or will you have to give that up due to new laws? I hope you can keep at it, as I know this is your area of knowledge. You don't seem to like it that much though, which is puzzling to me as then how did you get all the knowledge? Usually we can't remember much stuff concerning what we do not like. I'll be in for the fair again as usual. Unsure if I am staying in the tent or at Crafty's shop. I'll be set up in the usual area, but this year I have a space of my own, and not just a table in the tent! Hope to see ya. **Watch yer top knot! Miles**

My buddy Will in earlier years, us clowning around looking like wild mountain men. He has MS now, not sure if he is alive.

CHAPTER SEVEN

TANANA STATE FAIR SELLING ART. TAPE MADE FOR GEO MAGAZINE. GENE ORDERS ME TO MOVE. SALLY AFRAID FOR HER LIFE. TRIP UP THE RIVER TO KANTISHNA

Trying to work to make money, and still have time to build a cabin is not easy. Once again I notice we either have time, and no money, or money and no time. It's August, and I still have two months to finish the shelter. The money issue is hard to explain to others or grasp myself. Beyond the term 'feast and famine.' I make several thousand dollars working for Seymour in two weeks. But that is all the work he has for me. I make huge amounts finding fossils, but it's once a year, as well as the fair. My yearly income fluctuates, but might be $15,000. Not a lot, but I am only working a total of two months to earn that. Sort of. More like seventy-five percent of my income is made with five percent of my time. The rest of my time is 'saving money.' I talk about it a lot because it's hard to explain, or no, some people want to know and keep asking. "What's your income?" I explain, and they ask, "So what's your income?"

Josh gives me a ride to Fairbanks with all my displays, tables, and things to sell at the State Fair. My display is not in the best shape, as where do I keep this stuff? The tables and displays have been stored under a tarp outdoors by the houseboat. There is no easy way to wash the tables, boards, clothes, and displays. I have no running water except the silty river. This dilemma is on my mind as Josh drives.

"Miles, you look like your buddy Crafty!" Josh and I both laugh. I'll be lucky to pass minimum show requirements with electric cords that work that are not frayed. A fire extinguisher will have to be borrowed from Crafty. Clean used sheets are bought for a dollar at the Salvation Army Thrift Store to cover my piece of plywood I lay between two tables. Crafty lends me one of his ten year old tents, all tore up with falling apart missing poles.

A few of the new vendors seeing me setting up are snickering. Not because of the crudeness of my booth! But because I refuse to feel ashamed. My head is up and I am in high spirits, joking, optimistic, talking like I am 'one of us' – a vendor. "Why? Watch and behold! Be amazed! Ponder the mysteries of life! Out of ashes, see what arises." I have nothing to say to them, just a secret smile, a kind word, wishing them well. I do not look my part. I am not keeping my proper place, so some are making fun of me for not recognizing my place. On the chessboard of life, talking like I am a knight! Looking and acting like he small pawn! There was a time in life I'd have had a chip on my shoulder about it, dared anyone to insult me! Argued about my rights! Used words like 'equality,' and been defiant. Instead, with a good natured smile, I press on.

"Make lots of money!" I tell all the vendors as I go by. I love the fair. Nothing can go wrong. Like static electricity in the air. The buzz of energy. I suck it in and feed off it. This life is much like the circus life. "Step right this way for the mystery tour!" "Do not pay attention to that man behind the curtain! I am Oz!" "I just stepped through the star gate. I'm a little untidy. Step closer and let me tell of it. Behold what I have returned with!"

Every year my connections get better and I have better sources, better deals, more knowledge, a better- new product. I'm so confident I feel sorry for the competition, and it's hard to be humble. But I try. Those who know me are already coming around as I set up three days early. Secret deals with two other vendors inside the closed flaps of the tent. Like a scene from an Indiana Jones movie! The Holy Grail unveiled. This year a mammoth tusk.

"Now, who ever saw this at a fair huh?"

"Miles, this is a fair, not a museum, who will want it here? Who has that kind of money?"

"I may not sell it. But it will get a big crowd and I will tell stories and $50 items next to it will sell like hot cakes." Whoops! I forgot to be humble, so add: "That's the plan anyhow, we all have a plan right?" And chuckle like it is some silly hair brained plan. Other vendors know my items sell. I wholesale to them, so they may offer the item retail on opening day! That had been one of my plans all along.

"Keystone, half price guys." I make $1,500 the first evening before even setting up. Half the vendors here will not make this much during the entire fair. Five hundred finished pieces are laid out. All one of a kind, made by hand, without electricity. One section is just raw stuff. Skulls- bones -teeth –ivory- hoofs- horns. As well as amber, opals, fossils of every kind. I either found it all, or know who did, and I have a story connected to every single item. Ten thousand stories probably.

"Am I the Man or am I the man! Am I Oz, or one of the munchkins?" Just give me people, and I will sell. *No. I don't tell anyone this.* Why? *I'm in disguise- incognito.* Dirty jeans, socks that do not match, frizzy unkempt hair. Always walking fast with something in my hands. In a hurry to get someplace. Grass blade bouncing in my mouth. The village idiot who somehow manages to mysteriously, *well all part of a plan, done on purpose.* Not a threat to other vendors.

"Hey Dan! Good to see you again!"

"Yes Miles, go get a number in the book, we'll do our usual hamburger trade. Vision collects angels and I saw one in the booth while you were setting up."

"It's a $300 piece Dan, carved out of six pieces of opal by hand, are you sure?"

"Miles it's worth $500 in the right place. I'm proud to collect your things. If you do not run up a $300 food bill I'll cover the rest in cash." So the fair has not even started, and already my food is taken care of. Life is good. Dan runs the Patty Wagon booth, selling hamburgers, fries, and such. He's an old timer at the fair, very respected. Most of the vendors eat at his booth. He runs a tab for them. It's prestigious to have a tab with him. It means you are a trusted regular. As Dan turns to go, he asks, "Should I save the grease for the dogs again?"

I forgot to ask. Each year I get about thirty gallons of free grease from the fryer. It's set out behind his booth in five gallon plastic jugs. The grease gives the dogs energy when mixed with their regular food. Yes, there is better quality animal fats sold, but I'm not racing dogs, and this is free, and better than no grease at all! Also, well. I just do not like to see waste of any kind. The planet is in trouble, our species is a major reason. We are greedy wasteful and selfish, as a species. Fine, I'll be the garbage man then. Walk behind and clean up the mess. Turn the mess into something useful. Offer it back to people as art- as a renewable resource, as energy for transportation like, this grease. All without being in that group called 'preservationist.' *Yulk! What a bunch of pansies. What a bunch of hypocrites.* I'm not going to talk about it, or lecture, or suggest anyone else do anything, nor force them to, nor suggest my do-do doesn't stink. I'm not going to join any organization. I do not want the responsibility of setting an example. I generally do not tell anyone what I am doing, or why. I'm not sure I am clear myself. I could be nothing more than a glorified dumpster diver.

So the fair is not open yet, and I have thirty gallons of grease for the sled dogs lined up. Each year I stroll the grounds before setting up. Few understand I'm doing business. I watch. I make decisions. What goods are selling, as told by the attitude of the vendor, size of inventory, quality of his help, a changed location either down or up. If I think 'up,' I try to sell the vendor stuff, if an opportunity presents itself. If 'down,' I try to buy stuff if the opportunity arises. Out of the shadows and into the light I arrive. So much is about acting, and timing.

Often I help someone set up a tent. Go fetch a ladder, lend a light. Most important – make myself known. I've learned not to bring up what I sell unless they ask. Like fishing. Toss the fly and let it set a moment. Never yank and reel in! But no, not like that. I honestly care about at least some of these people. It is not a scam or a con. Or if it is, how do I become a better person? I do recognize I play a shell game with who I know I am. What hat I wear is real. Now you see me, now you don't. Now you think you know, and now you wonder again. No one knows the whole truth. The truth does not set us free. Who among us is ready for truth?

In the late evening I psyche up for the opening day. It's 11:00 pm. Security does not show up for the first time till tomorrow. I will sleep in my booth in a sleeping bag. It's sort of like a Zen thing, but not really. It's not like praying either. Though I could call it either or both, depending who is asking. In my mind what I do is closest to Native American beliefs. As it has been since I arrived in Alaska. In my mind. I am on the vision quest. In my half-awake -half asleep state I am dressed in buckskins. Feathers adorn me. I am up on a bluff overlooking a valley. In sort of a cave by a camp fire. It is raining and I stand erect at attention for as long as it takes. I am not praying. I am not bowing. I am not being humble. I am only waiting for a sign.

It may takes minutes, hours, or days. It does not matter in this state. Zoom in to my environment. Listening for a sign. A message. As I stand all wet in the rain, there is a burst of lightening, then thunder all around me. I slowly smile and stretch my arms up to greet the light, the sound, the static electricity. I am almost in tears. I got an answer. I review a poem I have been working on off and on.

Poem

Everyone wants to be the superstar
rarely smile at who they are.

Everyone wants to order 'Sirloin'
not neck liver or brain.
Everyone wants to be the eagle
the lone wolf and one to howl.
No one wants to be the seagull.
No one claims to be in sheep wool.

I ponder - all the chiefs, the shepherds,
but proof of the 'herd- flock'- sameness
in the talk of eagles, wolves and bears.
Few will look at the truth, into its eyes.
Yet on the one hand there are no duplicates
but on the other, the more that things--

well like an order in randomness
patterns, cards to lay down with matches

A purpose, a reason, the Queen of hearts
the King of clubs- joker in the works
and a full house of diamonds.
A card short in the full decks
with a bluff, a flourish, a pass
followed by the kiss, a promise.
Shaking my head at all this-
that life is so curious.

Over here, me.
A sinner. One of the truly screwed up.
To be counted, I step forward, straighten my jacket fringe,
step up on the stage.
I smile.
I refuse to be ashamed.
Humble will never be my middle name.
I stare into the awesome depths of my soul
at who and what I am,
and it takes my breath away...

I AM UP and about at 4:00 am with the rising sun. The fair does not open till noon. I will put in an eight hour work day before the fair even opens today. I meet the security guards who now know me. We chat :

"Was it a quiet night?" Nothing has happened the first night, so I have new knowledge that is useful. The guard remembers me from previous years, and plans to stop to buy. He knows where my booth is. I mention I have an alarm. A fish line connected to a battery operated alarm with a pull pin.

"So, if you hear it go off in the night, you know where it is coming from! Ha!" It does not hurt to be in with the security people. I consider it part of my job. I arrange my art better, count how much money I will start with today. I'm not an accountant, had no training. I have a simple system I call income and outcome. I count how much I start the day with, and how much I end the day with, and that's what I brought in, the difference, my 'gross income.' I once took good notes and discovered about half my gross income is 'my costs,' and thus, half of gross can be thought of as my profits. I write down food I got, and trades. But do not consider any of this of vital importance. Not yet. As long as I have money to buy what I want and need. When I get tired of being in the booth and restless, I take another walk to see who else is up and about. About 7:00 am , I can begin chatting with vendors over coffee with Dan.

"Did you make that cool necklace?!" One of the waitresses is staring at my seven inch cave bear fang over 40,000 years old. The necklace is worth about five grand. I enjoy the puzzled look *"How can I dress like a vagabond and be wearing a necklace worth as much as your house???"* I never reply. You must figure it out. The waitress has long hair, and I suggest she wear one of my mammoth ivory hair pieces to show it off and sell it for me, for a cut. She has never in her life worn a $800 piece of jewelry.

I pull it out of my pocket because I had exactly this situation in mind. I trust her because Dan hired her. Where would she go?

"If you sell it for me you get to keep $200." She is ecstatic. This represents several days of waitress pay. She will show it to everyone she can, and send them to my booth. I doubt very much she can sell it. I'm sure she will return it with disappointment. But happy she got to wear it! Call it an honor! Me being so famous and all. I will have sold a few items I bet, to those who got sent over. Thus, I already plan to find out what she likes from Dan. He knows what I'm up to.

"She collects crystals Miles." I will give her a crystal. I will tell her I put the special cap together just for her. As a gift. Maybe a $25 item. This is what I'm doing between 4:00 am and opening time. Fishing.

No one wants to hear the secret. Long hours, hard work. People do not come to the fair to find out it's hard work. Few want to know there are no secrets. I can't sell much saying:

"Put the time in!" That goes over like a lead balloon. A look of disappointment. Who wants to support hard work? Bummer. They can do that at their own job! They want escape! I am the man who goes fishing! The man of magic! Money just rolls in! People want to be part of that! Like following a lottery winner around. It takes a lot of energy. Maybe skill, who knows? Is it blind luck, or do I make my own luck? I only wink. I do know, I'm asked the question "How do you do it Miles!" If I reply, "Hard work, long hours!" I get only, "Oh" and no sale. When I say "Magic!" my sales go up by ten times. *And is that a lie???*

An early customer of the day is a family, mostly waiting for the rides for the kids. Sort of bored. The civilized woman is trying to get her child out of my booth that has all the dead animal stuff in it. I know this type of customer, usually. *No use changing anyone else's mind that is made up!* But they are lingering, and I have no other customers, so I want to be as polite as I can and explain as best I can. The little child is asking about the raw wolf claws in a tray in back. She also sees the nice finished wolf claw necklaces up front. I'm talking for the mother's sake as well. The little girl asks:

"What do you use these paws for, is this the same as the necklaces over there?"

"Paws? Yes, I use them in my artwork." She nods in understanding. "Sometimes I just sell the 'raw material' to those who have no way to get their own claws. A lot of the Indians want them for 'medicine,' or their own artwork. Some people believe in the 'animal energy' from the real product. So much in the world these days is 'plastic.' My own opinion is that 'the power' is in your own belief. I think of the claws as partly an educational thing, a statement." I elaborate on why I offer this. This is what the claw looks like, this is part of the wolf, and it says something real about the wolf, how big he is, and it conjures up visual images and stories, which become part of the art piece created from it. I put silver caps on metal scenes as part of my work, maybe enhance the story I see in the claw. Most of these claws are ones that would otherwise be thrown away. Few wolf coats incorporate the claws.

Local Indians bring claws to me, not knowing how to handle them or turn them into anything useful. Usually they give them to me. Who would take time to boil them on the stove, or know to use bleach sparingly, or know how long, or be willing to have the smell around, pick the fur and meat off. I do all this, and turn a waste product into something beautiful. In the 'big picture' I'm concerned with the fact that modern man has lost his roots, his ties to the land. There is little time, interest, knowledge anymore about the land we used to depend on so much. Some of the restlessness we feel as a society comes from this lack of 'something we lost.' Or, so I feel (it may not be true). So my art has 'things from the land' in it, to remind us, stir up memories, of how it was, where we came from. Not that we need to go back! Just to remember, to smile, to understand, and not feel ashamed, or disgusted, or whatever.

Anyway! What the paw boiling is all about is not a simple question to answer! I send these 'messages' I think, as a way to say:

"This is what I'm doing today, what are you doing? Yes, what I'm doing is likely very different from what you are doing, and people all over the world are doing all sorts of things we would think quite odd, or different, but they have their life, their reason to do as they do, and maybe love doing it very much, and are filled with a sense of purpose in the doing it. Something to ponder as we go about our day."

The mother is unaffected. I'm a con man, running a line on her. The little girl looks puzzled and inspects one of the claw necklaces.

"I like the turquoise on top!" As Mom drags her off. This is one reason the raw animal stuff is way in the back, and you have to know, or ask, or come specifically to look for it. The secret stuff under the counter I can pull out. Most customers who get squeamish about animal parts simply don't go to the back to look. The subject is discreetly ignored. I put on another hat.

I have some good environmental stories to tell. But, one thing I note to write down in my diary for next year? *Kids might be good customers*! Also, I can distract kids with some dollar cheap stuff, and free stuff, up front so the kids are occupied, as I make sales with the parents- adults. I can get necklaces at garage sales, the Salvation Army, Thrift Store. Just shiny stuff for kids, to sell for a dollar!

It's not as much the dollar that matters, it's occupying the kids while I engage the adults. I try that. Some parents seem relieved to give kids something to do while the adults look around.

"Hey kids! Anything in this tray is only a dollar! Look at the shark teeth, crystals, chains, and cool stones!" I show $300 necklaces to relieved mothers.

"Hello Heidi! Where is Geneva? Usually you two are together!" I have known Heidi from the fair for a few years now. I try to get her free tickets each year for her and her children I explain, "The fair assumes I will have helpers, so gives me tickets for three people each day. I only need one ticket! I never leave the grounds, so do not need any of my tickets!" They are vendor tickets, so she has to tell them at the gate she is working for me. She stops by throughout the day and watches the booth for me if I need a break. Usually to go make a deal with another vendor, but sometimes if things are slow I go look around the fair and enjoy it. Heidi often leaves her children at the booth with me and I watch them. She's a single Mom trying to make ends meet. Yes, sometimes a problem as I am trying to make money, not be a baby sitter, but sometimes her children try to sell the dollar items to the other kids for me, or straighten out tangled chains in trade for a one dollar gift.

Without doing the math or thinking hard on it, over time I know a whole lot of people. My guess is out of the 70,000 people in Fairbanks, 20,000 know me by name. I've been doing various shows during the summer over the years. It's hard because I don't drive. There were hopes my wife who drives, would do that part, and we'd do shows together. I imagine her cleaning up displays so they are presentable, keeping track of the money, driving, answering mail, ordering supplies and such. While I do the creating and the selling. Equal partners. But she appears to rather work at Woolworths for minimum wage. I am not understanding her reasoning.

"It's a sure thing," seems to be the message. Regular paycheck. So she is not here helping me. I try not to be bummed out. I'm making $50 an hour, while she is making $5 an hour. If she were here, I think we might together bring in $70 an hour. I know I am losing money working six tables by myself.

In the evening I doubt any of this that I'm learning could be learned in school through a formal education. In the final analysis we all have to find our niche market and style. My way may not apply to anyone else. Thus, I have no answers that are tangible to pass on. The subject is on my mind because a great regret in Sally's life is, she never got a formal education. Already she talks about Mitch our son going to college. So much so, Josh refers to him as 'Doc.' He's supposed to be bright and gifted. Sally prefers to compare him to my father, the part of my blood line she values. Sally always had to do menial labor for a living. There is a possibility she views the things I do as menial labor, low class – what you do because you have to, because we have to make a living. Okay, I can understand how someone might feel that way. But what do you do when you marry someone like that? It's going to be difficult coming to terms with our vastly different outlooks on life. But not impossible. In time she will see the bills get paid, there is a home and food, the basics. The standard of living economically is probably better then the life one would expect working at Woolworths as a single Mom like Heidi for example. Where probably you could never expect to own your own land and home.

The fair gets rained on a little today. The ground is damp, so will be uncomfortable to sleep on. It's important I sleep well and am alert when I sell. When the fair shuts down I wander over to see Crafty. I help him wrap up his booth for the night. He has ten times the inventory I do.

"Crafty, you headed over to the Craft Shop for the night?"

"Yes, you want to get a ride over? I'll bring you back in the morning." So we ride over in the 'mole.' Crafty's van with 'Mole' written on it. My room is there as it has always been all these years whenever I need a place to stay. Sally has an apartment across town now. At 11:00 pm I'm not going to try and go wake her up or stay there with no ride. I'm just too tired anyhow. Selfishly I need good energy to do the fair, ride on a high. Nothing can bum me out that interferes with my relationship with customers. Crafty understands. Being a one man show at the fair is very draining.

Next day is pouring rain. Crafty reminds me:

"Typical fair weather huh!" Yes, rain seems to follow the fair all right. There will be water damage to merchandise, with a foot of water in low places. It's one of our gripes that the fair knows it rains at fair time and they don't fill in the low spots, or figure out some drainage. My spot is not the worse, so I do not feel so bad.

"It's get in free if you bring cans of food day. The El-cheapo day Crafty." *Maybe some of my regulars will stop by.* But it might be a good day to take off and go around checking out the fair myself. "Maybe do my trades with other vendors today. They might be more discouraged and interested in deals."

"You're learning well from the master Miles!" We laugh. Crafty is often reminding me how much I learn from him.

"Tina, over at Mermaids said earlier she got me some gem stones in Tibet when she was there. She gets me cracked stones, and stones that were cut over or under size, so selling as rejects. Sometimes really high quality stones, rubies, sapphires, and aquamarine." I buy them by the pound, and it ends up being about ten cents a stone. I high grade, keep what I want, and offer the rest to the public. Some of the lower end is in a bowl for kids for one dollar. I can usually recover my costs in a day or two. Crafty asks me if I still have any of my cassette tapes. "Only a dozen maybe Crafty. You bought them all. Are they selling good?"

"Sold out Miles. I could use some more." *Yea right!* "Not at the price you paid.

What do you take me for a sucker!" I say with a laugh and Crafty is not upset. One of my customers overheard the short exchange.

"What's that all about Miles? You made a tape?" The tape.

"Well to understand you need to know about an earlier tape that got made."

There had been an earlier tape I made for GEO magazine. It was to be transcribed into an article about my wilderness life. GEO is a magazine like National Geographic over in Europe. Prestigious, huge circulation. GEO had wanted to do a special edition on Alaska. I was chosen to represent the mountain man-hermit living alone in the wild off the land. I only made the tape because if I wrote the story out, it would have to be transcribed into German, so why not have them transcribe my spoken words from a tape? It makes it easier for me to just talk. They had said, "sure!" I used a ten dollar battery recorder, sat down and told my story. Inadvertently, there is the creaking of the rocking chair here and there, and crackling of the wood fire.

GEO contacts me after receiving the tape, asking if they can use excerpts from the tape to promote the magazine article. They had been nice and friendly to me, so why not? I gave them permission. I never heard from them again on the subject except to get paid a few hundred for the article transcribed from it.

Months later, a tourist from Sweden flies here all the way from Europe to see if he can meet me. I happened to be on the houseboat in Nenana. This tourist wants me to sign the tape.

"Tape?" I'm puzzled. "What tape?" He shows me, and we listen. It's my complete tape, word for word. One side is translated in German. The others side, mine, in English. Being sold all over Europe it sounds like. Maybe a cool million dollars. Hard to know. I felt betrayed. This was not the agreement. But what am I going to do about it? Poor, needing an international lawyer, and for all I know it would be hard to win any case, as maybe the permission I gave for 'excerpts' applies for the whole tape. Or, maybe they own the rights to the tape since it was transcribed into the article I got paid for. I feel the $300 I was paid was pretty much a rip off.

So, I thought about that. If GEO can market a tape that took no real thought to make, and do so well with it. What would happen if I made a planned out tape with sound effects? I have no money, and no knowledge about recording. But if I begin it, something might turn up. Maybe it can be a demo, that convinces a studio to invest in a quality remake. Maybe I will have the money to have it worked on in a studio. One of my customers might be in the recording business. So I simply 'begin.'

It's recorded at the Kantishna cabin. All the sounds are real and recorded out there. There is the wind, the wood stove, pouring tea, stirring the moose meat in the frying pan, as I tell my stories. All are winter stories to help the listener understand Alaska in winter, because visitors tend to come up in summer as tourists, and think they understand Alaska. They think they have experienced Alaska. I call it 'Stormbound Trapper,' and it is an hour and a half long. Tom, who works the Craft Shop for Crafty, has a brother who is heavy into music and recording. I pay him to mix some tracks and dub in some sound effects here and there. He has a six track cassette mixer. Since there is only me talking, and that gets old and boring, I talk like I have a guest. But at the end, all I have is cabin fever and I'm alone in the wilderness.

Sally enters my life about the time I am ready to have copies made to sell. I took pictures for the cover and have a company out of California that does recording. It's going to cost me two dollars each if I get 500. I hope to retail them for $12. Wholesale at six dollars. I explain it all to Sally. Crafty has been listening in, giving advice now and then. I don't have $1,000 right now to invest in this project. I have maybe $500.

"Sally, I'm not big on credit cards, but if we used your credit card for the $500, we can get these tapes made. Five hundred dollars is not an outrageous amount of money I can't come up with if the project goes belly up. But if all goes well, we might be able to go on a week selling trip and unload 400 tapes at six dollars wholesale, $2,400. Keep some tapes to retail for $12. Another $1.200." My hope, I explain as well, is to have this as like a demo and maybe some big company will be interested, and it will not just be a few thousand dollars. More like what GEO already did with a tape I did not work on as long. It could be big money. "If not- no big loss. Just not the big money I wish for, immediately, potential for later."

This line of thinking is not, 'back to the land true subsistence.' I'm trying to branch out, expand. I want to make more money than I can do by trapping. I understand the direction society is going, away from furs, so realize this will never be the big dollars it once was for the mountain men of the past, or even during the depression in the thirties, not that long ago. I had been thinking of Sally when we were writing, realizing if I want a woman I need to make more money. "I'm trying to do so by running my own business." I explain his to the customer who asks about this tape.

"So, we do this and I can tell afterwards, Sally is dubious and wants her money back fast." I don't think she believes in the tape like I thought she did at first. I even wonder if she heard a word I said. We get the tapes in the mail and Sally wants her $500, as in 'now.' I explain we can go on a road trip in our old truck and hit all the shops on the way to Anchorage. I had gone on a selling trip once with Crafty, and watched how it is done. I had even been asked to do a show along the way, and stopped two days in Portage Glazier Lodge, while Crafty went to deal with his accounts. We came home with twenty grand in a week. The tourist shops need local Alaska items, as this is what the tourists want the most. But, it has to be cheap. I'm confident the tape will sell, as fitting in the low price range, being an honest Alaska product. And with the lifestyle the tape records being one of great interest to many people. Sally seems not to be listening. Crafty overhears us and does his thing. Moves in for the kill.

"I'll give you $1,000 cash right now for all the tapes." Sally replies before I do, and is ecstatic and grateful. "Yes! Thank you Crafty!!" As if he is bailing us out of a jam we are in. Sally can get her $500 back! All she cares about.

But it's a sucker deal. Crafty offers to buy me out at my cost. I make nothing. Why would I want to do that? Only fools and idiots do that. People between a rock and a hard place who are over there head in debt, and need the immediate cash even at no profit. Sometimes Crafty can even get deals at below cost.

I decided I had made a mistake borrowing money from my wife. I shouldn't depend on anyone else. I know better. It's her money, she wants it back right now. Not in a week. Since it's her money, I'm not going to argue. Maybe someday when times are different I can have another edition of the tape done. On my dime. I do want to keep fifty tapes. I tell Crafty, "So I can retail a few, like at the fair, and shows I do along with my art." I also want to see for myself the response from the public, first hand, on the work I have done. But, now I'm sure Crafty wants more tapes at the same price, like I'm working for Crafty for nothing.

The tape is popular, as I knew it would be. Maybe Sally will end up trusting my instinct when she sees how often I am right. The customer asks,

"Miles, is your book done yet? You have been working on it for years now. What's up with it?"

"Well yes, it's about done, but it's got notes and scratched out parts, and I have started over from scratch four times now. Not really sure what to do. If I pay someone to retype it so it can be submitted for printing there are various issues." One issue had been paying someone to work on one chapter to show me what they can do in anticipation of them doing the whole book. Crafty is back and into the conversation again. "Anyhow Crafty, they rewrote the chapter, not transcribed it. Telling me things like, "You can't start a sentence with But or And. And there is no such word as 'snaffle,' so-on and so forth. Someone told me Crafty, that most editors are frustrated writers. They don't want to do what they are paid for. They want to improve it. Real editors want ten dollars a page, and even then, will most likely rewrite my style."

"Yea, well Miles you pretty much need to use the language correctly I'd think." So what can I say, he doesn't understand. I'm a street person, a poor person, an uneducated person- who became street wise on my own. I therefore wish to write the talk of the street people. I change the subject.

" What I'm seeing is these new computers. They are expensive and not very user friendly yet. But my guess Crafty, is one year soon, computers will be more user friendly and the price will come down. If so, I can put the book in the computer. Have it digitally printed. There is a company in Germany that does that."

One of my customers is becoming a friend. Helm, and his wife Anita are from Germany. Maybe not millionaires, but certainly 'well to do.' They have a vacation home in Fairbanks. They spend a great part of the year just traveling. Anyhow, Helm has a friend who owns a computer company. Printing books by computer is cutting edge technology, not in the US yet. Crafty thinks computers will never catch on, as to complicated and technical for the average person, and will always be expensive. Maybe. I'm not counting on computers, just keeping ideas on a back burner 'in case,' with lots of irons in the fire so I can be adaptable and move in the direction of least resistance.

"Crafty, just like new improvements in phones. Big battery phones are beginning to be replaced with cell phones. It could have a big effect on life in the wilderness."

Though Sally would say that is not what I do. That I tend to seek out things that are hard and complicated. That I'm always fighting and struggling. It's interesting to see different peoples perspective on the same sets of information. My mind has been wandering while Crafty is not replying. What's on his mind is:

"Miles, I've known you practically since you got here in Alaska. You have been the symbol for free thinkers who want to be out in the wild to rally behind. Now you talk about high tech above and beyond what the average person accepts! I don't get it! What happened to the mountain man I once knew!" We have talked about this off and on, and each time we talk I try to bring up another example so he may understand.

"Well Crafty, one of the things I wanted to be when growing up was a scientist. I didn't think I was doing well enough is school, and also I did not wish to compete with my father, who has the same name and has a big name in science. But, when I was young, there were scientists in and out of the house. Some of them I see now in Science Magazine." I explain to Crafty, how I was constantly overhearing talk about computers before the public knew what they were. In the days of designing the Gemini space capsule. The days of super conductors and huge rooms that had to be super cooled. Only scientists could go in, and had to be in sterile space suits. These were the first computers in the 60's. I was fascinated with Einstein, quasars, quarks, string theory, which came out later, time and space.

"So Crafty, what if I am not stuck in the past. What if I am the cutting edge of a future?" I pause after thinking, before going further. "I do like to jump time. Like with my art. I love to take the very old, and put it in a very cutting edge modern setting." I go on to explain how many of my customers view me as shaman or guru sort. An expert on animal parts. I've said it before, but repeat again. "The Indian definition of 'shaman' is 'One who lives in two worlds, but belongs in neither.'" Crafty gives me a dubious look that says, "Yea right Miles, what a con job!" Crafty knows me well, or should, because we met when we were both street people, a long time ago, and have both made progress. Dumpster divers. He thinks maybe he is the only one who rose above that. I still dress the same, and my income on the surface looks the same. My standard of living has not gone up by much. Because I'm not trying very hard to rise and join the rat race, where money is God. Much of my money has been going back into the business. The effects of that may take years to show up. I also feel it is good to be either poor or rich, but the middle class is the class not to be in, that pays for both lower and upper. The poor get life handed to them, free food, help with rent medical etc. etc. The rich avoid taxes, get to spend money, run the world to their advantage. The secret, ideally, would be to be poor, and then jump to rich.

"Well Miles, have a good day selling. Make lots of money!"

"You too Crafty." Our conversation is at a stalemate. He does not wish to argue, and it is time to begin the day! I take off to get my booth ready, and see what has gotten wet. Some of my displays are ruined, I can see right off. Some of my art is ruined. Some is just damaged and will need repair. Is Sally right in the big picture, and knows more than me, or is showing me what I refuse to see? Sure, bring in thousands of dollars, but thousands of dollars in damages to pay for when it rains!

But this is a way of life. All the vendors are dealing with it. Some are joking. Some are more discouraged. I prefer to join the jokers. If I accept defeat I lose the war, the war called 'life.' The war called survival, making a living, being happy. I amble on over to the Patty Wagon to see Dan, and the quick order cook who has my hair piece. But on the way over I see the Mad Hatter, Daniel, and he tells me he saw a fossil shark tooth buckle I have, he'd like if we can trade. I go back and fetch the buckle, and meet with Daniel at his booth. I spot a cool Australian outback rain slicker, *like worn by Clint Eastwood*. A coat you walk in, head down as you hear the Jews harp play. Just before bullets fly. A costume befitting the outlaw I am. So, we trade and now I have a way to keep the rain off better. It's a down to the ankle flasher type coat. I amble out of the shadow, head down as I approach the Patty Wagon. Just when everyone eyes are on me, wondering who I am, and if I am here to order food or not….. I open my coat full and lift my head. Blade of grass bobs in the air as I flash… nothing. I got all my clothes on. It lightens up the mood, and we all laugh.

"So Miles, how are you doing, have you broken even yet?" For the average vendor that is a big turning point, when you have broken even on your costs to do the fair. The point at which you are now making profits. Some vendors never do, the whole fair! The booth costs for ten days is $350. I made that my first hour showing up, even before I set up the booth. I've made enough that the $350 is 'nothing,' a drop in the bucket. So I can look at the bright side. There is an effort to have better social skills. It is noticed over time, most people do not like to be told how well you are doing in detail, trying to look better than them, or out do them, seen as putting them down. I answer only:

"Yes, I'm happy." I am jokingly asked if I need a receipt for the meal. "If the IRS has any questions, I'll send them over here to be straightened out." We get into a brief unrepeatable discussion on the IRS. As I amble back to my booth, I stop and flash a few people I know. Chat with others, ask how they are doing, and work my way to my booth where Heidi has been watching in trade for tickets. No one has stopped by while I was gone. Just pouring rain.

It rains the rest of the fair till Friday night. Saturday, the last day turns out to make up for all the rainy days. I recite one of my usual lines to the vendor next to me.

"I figured out the secret to sleeping good at the fair!" I pause and go on. "The first few days are rough. But I learned if I stuff the hundred dollar bills into the pillow case, I sleep better. As the week goes by and the pillow case swells, I get more sleep. The other bills can just go in the mattress. Have you discovered this to be true too?" Said with a dead pan serious face.

"I'll have to try that." We both laugh as we take our booth down on Sunday. Dan will bring my grease to me in Nenana as he goes by on his way to the Palmer Fair coming up next in two weeks, and he passes right through Nenana. I can load my booth and goods too, he has extra room. Dan also sells his left over potatoes to me, 100 pounds for ten dollars. I give him a good deal on some extra art to use as presents for helping me out.

The helper returns my hair piece with disappointment. She did not sell it.

"Really Sorry Miles! I sure tried hard!" I know she tried.

"Well I made you this crystal necklace as a thank you. I did get some business from people you sent, so don't feel too bad!" She is ecstatic over this touching gift. Words about treasuring it forever. I return with my practiced, 'Yes, I'm such a great guy huh?' look.

In the big picture a problem is thickening, like tapioca. I have no room to keep what I need to run my business, in a way to run it efficiently and make the most money. If I haul all the booth, tables, and display stuff, back to the Kantishna homestead where there is room, it cost me $300. In the old days, such a trip would have been part of a routine, where I'd go out at the end for the fair and stay till I came out with sled dogs in November. The $300 cost is not such a big deal then. But it's still $300 to bring it all back out again next fair time, a total $600 costs, and occupies several days' time. I can stash fair goods by the houseboat in a pile? Yes, but the weather is hard on it. Mice get in, squirrels, and rain. It's a lot of damage. People might get in it. I don't own the land. So I don't have many rights here. Theft taking place on land you don't own, that you stash stuff on, is not viewed as a priory problem. Rising above bum-dumb (as opposed to a king-dom), takes more money than I have, and seems to be a slow process. There is no room on the Tek land either. The cabin is built as a minimum requirement for a small family. Sally feels this land and cabin, is all about me and what I want. It's not hers or ours. Truth is, on my own I'd have never considered acquiring this land. I have no need for a homestead so close to town. It's twenty minutes out. I could just go camping. The houseboat works fine in Nenana. My expansion on my own was moving further out to the Bearpaw land I just acquired, and now am not doing anything with. In that lifestyle, further out I need less money, and doing the fair in a big way, is not as important or needed. Moving fair stuff to the new cabin would only prove to Sally it's all about me, my stuff, my junk. Turning her nice view into a humiliating junk-yard.

I buy the fair tent off Crafty, acquire new tables and lights with some of my fair profits. Where will I keep them? Already tenth street is being called a junkyard, with all the stashes almost all homesteaders leave here till they can get it upriver. Gene has the biggest pile, and we already had a run in about that! It would take a week to mill up enough lumber for a small building to store everything. September is knocking, and winter will be here. I'm on a time limit here. I need to be focused. I don't need extra 'problems.' But, back at tenth street unloading things, here comes trouble with Gene's name on it. I'd hoped my being gone a bit would calm him down, and he'd just focus his hate someplace else.

"Miles, if you move and leave the area I'll leave you alone. This is your last warning. I'm tired of being nice. We don't need your kind around here." How does one respond to such a statement?

"Move Gene? And why would I want to do that? This is my home. We don't have to get along. You mind your business, and I mind mine. We don't have to visit, or be friends, or share anything. As for me, we don't get along. So what. I'll smile, wave, and help you out in an emergency, without being your friend. But I'm not leaving Gene, that's a pretty wild demand."

I've dealt off and on in the wilds with this personality type. People come to the wilderness for all sorts of reasons. I explain it over and over to those who ask. Only some come to sniff the posies and kiss the bunnies. Only some arrive with kindness in their hearts. A very high percentage are antisocial in some way. Sometimes mild and understandable, and no big deal. Merely happy eccentrics. Other times the wilds hide psychopaths. I've mentioned before, that some anti-social types hope to survive by getting away from people. They know when they are around people they get in trouble. But then they go nuts when they end up with neighbors to deal with. Gene is a control freak. In truth, bunny huggers tend not to be motivated enough to tough it out in this lifestyle. Few are among the last standing.

Sally re-affirms she is scared of him. She and I talk a little at the Craft Shop. I have been thinking of winter and stockpiling food. Will and I went to the, I call it 'used a bit' food place. The names and locations seem to change by the year. It's outdated food, dented cans, case lots of fruits and vegetables and such. At, 'we got to get rid of this stuff fast' prices. I'm pretty ecstatic. I just got a whole case of fresh peaches for five dollars!

"Can you believe that Sally! Awesome huh!" She seems happy enough. "But they are getting real ripe, so we have to can them, like in the next day or two!" We have a Coleman stove, a five gallon pot, and a bunch of jars and lids at the Craft Shop. The plan is to do the whole operation in Crafty's parking lot. Maybe three or four hours work. I'm waiting for Sally to take charge, or be part of the decision making, or suggest a good time that would work for her to cook peaches. *She probably doesn't want to be told what to do.* But who can understand women?

After three days of not wanting to come across 'bossy,' I tell her we got to do this, the peaches are getting moldy, and I'm not going to lose them. I'd sure like to eat peaches this winter. My grocery bill is still in at about $300 a year, under a dollar a day. More hen this though, I consider 'waste' a huge crime, especially of food. Sally won't be part of the work putting up peaches. I do not know why. I am being overly bossy? She is ashamed to put up outdated peaches to live off of during the winter? But if so, I'm puzzled because what was her lifestyle? What is she used to? Wasn't she poor? So what's the big deal? She won't tell me. My concern is, if I wait, she will say:

"Oh gee, wow bummer, the peaches are rotten now, how did that happen, too bad. Guess we can't can them now huh, have to toss them out. Too bad!" Does she want real food you buy at high prices like everyone else? Is she too lazy? Does she not know how to can food? I shift into emergency mode. Out of my way. I'm going to make this happen without anyone's help. I do this sort of thing by myself all the time. No big deal to me. It's easier than trying to motivate someone else.

But, will I be inclined to want to share the peaches over the winter? Who knows. Will she thank me later? Because I have the foresight to can the peaches now, so we eat them in the dark, and cold of winter? At prices we can afford. Besides, the quality just can't be beat. Hardly any sugar, just pure fresh ripe fruit. Not the usual canned stuff that is picked green, then dyed and sweetened. Sally treats me like I'm off my rocker taking care of this. Will she ever accept this lifestyle? Can I adjust in any way to her lifestyle? This is forgotten. We don't talk about it, and I get the case of jars full of canned peaches I did myself to the Tek land.

I GET my usual moose for the winter! This is a big thing to take care of. Doing without is not so fun. Good meat adds to good meals. Sally agrees, and thinks 500 pounds of meat is pretty cool all right. Some of us new homesteaders in this area have sled dogs, and wonder if there are salmon running up here to be had. We find out "yes," and there are about three of us who are serious, and get nets out. We all get along, and do not interfere with where we each choose to fish. There is plenty of room. I do well because I have been netting salmon now for over ten years. It's nice to know we have a way to feed the sled dogs all winter. Things are looking up. The cabin is done enough to move into. Sally's seasonal Woolworths job ends, so no more work for her. The timing works out well.

Sally seems a hard enough worker when she's motivated. She helps me hang fish and feed dogs. Life is pretty laid back.

"Yes Sally, summer can be hectic, having to make money and get ready for winter. But once we are settled in for winter it's little stress." She feels better, seeing how close this is to town. If she had to, she could walk out. Another cute ermine moves in, sort of like on the Kantishna River. She enjoys watching him out the window. If we had to, we could live like this till next May, seven months, without making another cent. So, without pressure I work on my book, and do art work, building up inventory for next year. I'd sort of like to head out to the Kantishna cabin and trap some. Maybe only because this is what I do, and this is what I love, and has been my work for so many years. I explain that a rival trapper is trying to take over the trapline. It could get nasty. Sally wants me to give the trapline to him if he wants it so bad.

"It's not worth the problems Miles, not worth your life." I think maybe Sally never had anything in her life worth fighting for. She wants us to leave this land if Gene wants us to. His karma will catch up to him. Let him sell his drugs, sell illegal timber off state land and whatever else he is up to. Eventually it will catch up to him. I agree about this part. So leave him alone and let him hang himself. But move? I think again, *It's not Sally who put the time in building, or any money into this land.* I answer myself, wondering if Sally is the sort, if a man is going to rape her, she rolls over and doesn't want any trouble.

We don't really have any neighbors we are close to in terms of being best buddies with. There is Bearfoot next door who shares a property boundary. He's polite and standoffish. I suspect 'cool and distant' because I didn't help him build his cabin, he's not done yet and I am. He'd be happiest if we gave to him more then he gives to us. But he's not especially mad at us, so that's fine. However, he is not going to be able to spend a winter here, so has to go rent in Nenana. Another neighbor on the other side of us is not full of hate or anything, but I point out:

"Sally, he is the one who tried to file on our land and get it when he heard we were having problems." The state would not let him file on it because he would not give up his existing piece of land in exchange. He can only have one parcel under one program. But he tried, and so is not our friend. He also has dogs he lets run loose. Dogs that come to steal fish from our property. Fish we need to feed our own sled dogs. When confronted, he laughs and thinks this is funny. That it's my problem, not his. On my own, without Sally, I'd just shoot his dogs when they came on my property and stole fish. I may or may not tell him I know anything about it. Depending if I think he'll go ballistic or not. I keep my dogs tied up. If my dogs left my property and bothered anyone, I consider that my business and my problem to solve. If a dog of mine got loose and stole from someone and the owner shot my dog, I'd understand. I'd even consider it proper to apologize that my dog created a problem. The same as if my child robbed someone and that person called the police, resulting in my child going to jail, or short as an intruder. I'm responsible for my kids and my dogs. You should be responsible for yours. That's what makes good neighbors.

"Miles, I don't understand. Is this an unusual situation? I always heard homesteaders are nice to each other, depend on each other, are good neighbors and friends!" I assume she imagined borrowing and lending cups of sugar back and forth. Inviting each other over for dinner. Helping each other build cabins.

"Well Sally, I suppose, yes, sometimes. You can get along or not get along, just as life anywhere else. I think most common here, is like most common anyplace, a polite distance where everyone minds their business, unless there is an emergency, then we all chip in and help. After all, if folks wanted neighbors they'd live in town. As far as I'm concerned, there is no such thing as a good neighbor." I'm not quite sure what it is Sally envisions as working. Mostly single guys out here. Is she going to cook for them and bring them a hot dinner? Want them to stop by and check up on her when I'm gone? To do what? Sit with her in the dark because she's afraid? Cut firewood for her? If so, what exactly is my role, and how will she pay them? Get together with the few wives that are out here? I can see that, but so far there aren't any wives out here except Gene's.

That's fine with me. But Gene is selling drugs, and many are using those same drugs. How close do I want to be with that? How much do we all want to know about each other? If there is trouble, how much is good to know? I don't want to wonder who turned me in. I don't want my neighbors wondering if it was me who turned them in. That is why I like the 'live and let live' policy. I'm trying hard to get Sally interested in something that can become her passion. Art- photography- writing, are what come to mind. But even totally engaged in being a mother, so long as she is happy.

A fish netting is sewed to build a crib so little Mitch can romp around without getting in trouble, like falling against the wood stove. My art work area is just beneath his play pen up high above the bed. As I work, Mitch drools on me. Quiet, staring at what I am doing. Till I feel drool dripping on my head. I scream! He screams! We both think it is hilarious. Mitch loves the sled dogs, and being in the dog sled while they run. Feeding time with all the dogs, the dogs going nuts, is a big attention getter. Some of the good times to remember. Sally shares the rewards of our babies first steps, first words and such things. He called himself 'Kiki the horse boy' for some odd reason. Where did he ever come up with that? He told us, and insisted this is his name. A story he hears that we read to him? Not that we recall.

Sometime in November, the river and swamps are frozen enough to make a trip to the Kantishna, and get to the trapline. We have not seen or heard anything about Gene. I assume he is hunkered down for winter with enough on his mind for now. A few neighbors are trapping locally and catching one or two pieces of fur, and being excited. I have not trapped locally as promised, and plan to get to my own area. It's fifty miles by sled dogs. I might make it in one day if the sled dogs are in shape. Otherwise I tell Sally:

"I'll camp at the airport." She remembers where that is.

"Are the dogs ready for such a long trip Miles?" She recalls the hard trip we made running the same route I'm planning.

"I'm guessing so. We have made a dozen runs to town fifteen miles and back, thirty miles in a day. I can see how the dogs feel at the airport twenty-five miles out. I'll rest them there for sure, an hour or so. You'll be okay while I'm gone? I have plenty of firewood cut and you know the routine now." Sally knows how to pump water from the well, cook with propane, and keep the wood stove going. "I'll be back in less than a week." I pause. "I forgot. Josh and Martha invited us over for Thanksgiving. I've been going there for a lot of years now, so almost a tradition to have Thanksgiving over there. Maybe you can make some of that good bread in the oven to bring over?" Sally makes a great loaf of sourdough bread from scratch using wheat flour.

The dog sled I built is loaded for a week with fish for dogs, bait for trapping. I have a sleeping bag, some survival food for myself, a book to read, and all the essentials. The six foot sled has about 150 pounds in it. Running seven dogs. They know we are headed out to the trapline because of how I load the sled, so they are all excited and eager to get back to the life we all love. Sled dogs seem to want to be part of a team, and doing something useful. In the wild, wolves hunt for food together in packs, and work as a team. Trapping is related to this enough the sled dogs understand the job.

The temperature is ideal. A nice five degrees above zero- blue sky, calm day. There is six inches of snow on the ground. That is enough to slide on well, and cover the dips and branches on the ground, but not so deep the dogs are struggling in it. There will be some windblown stretches I expect after years of running this trail. A few places might have open water in the swamps to be careful of, but these dogs know about this and can handle themselves. I see no one has been out the Kantishna direction yet and I am the first, *As usual!* Yes as usual. Others wait for me to cut the windblown trees out of the way, brush the trail and break it open so it is easy to run.

Sometimes Dim gets out ahead of me with his snow machine, but not this year.

Sometimes the Forests get in ahead of me. I assume they are frozen in on the Kantishna, and are waiting to come to Nenana. My special design dog sled is made for just this type trail.

Spike the leader, knows what pace to set for the team by knowing all the dogs and their ability. I put a young dog next to an elder dog so the elder can teach. I see right off, the elders reprimanding the young who are trying to go to fast, but will tire out early if they try to keep up this pace. I say nothing, and leave the teaching to the leaders. The first two creeks are frozen. We drop down, and back up the banks on the other side. These first two creeks can be tricky if newly frozen, so pleased so far with travel conditions. This is a good sign of fine traveling ahead. The swamps come up next before we get to eight mile hill.

There are several moose out in the flats we can see in the distance. Mt. McKinley, as I still call Denali, stands out in the rising sun. This stretch can be brutal. *Yea, especially coming from the other direction at the end of a long day, when it's windy and dark!* Yes, sometimes hard to see the trail in the dark. Snow-drifts, with the wind will be right in my face, usually. Today calm and no drifts, fast travel. The beaver house at five miles is active with lots of new trees hauled by beaver for their winter food. It might be worth an otter set here at the beaver house. But no, I do not want to take the time to stop here and make a set. Also, Dim sort of claims this spot, but has never set a trap here in fifteen years. He doesn't want me to put my first trap out till I'm twenty-five miles out. Oh well. I will honor that. His family has been trapping around here for several generations now. It was less of a big deal when I lived out remote on the Kantishna, and only came all the way into Nenana a couple of times all winter.

But now that I have the home base in the Nenana area, I will be coming back and forth much more. Maybe I can ask Dim again – explain the change, point out he has not set traps here. Or offer him a percentage of my take, or something. Thinking about this as I travel. Eight miles hill comes up and dogs are still hot to trot. We leave the flats and go up into the different country now. Tall spruce trees with willows and alders along the edge is a new terrain. Now there are rabbits, lynx and wolves. Less moose, otter, beaver, and mink. The local pack of wolves has been through here I note. *Looks like about twenty wolves*. I stop to give the dogs a breather. They put their nose to the snow in the wolf tracks. They know wolf is one of the animals we hunt. "Nope not here guys, need to wait till we get out of Dim's area." Dogs understand territory.

The rolling hills are more of a challenge on the dogs pulling. I have to get off and help push on the steeper hills. Here and there a fallen tree has to be cut out of the way. This gives the dogs a chance to rest a little. Some of the willows are growing fast along the edge of the trail, as the reach for the sun, getting tall. Each year it is a little worse, and each year I think I will have time to stop and do more serious brushing. Instead I just cut the worse stretches and fight the rest all winter.

We reach the airport in three hours. Not bad travel time for new snow, first trip, and 150 pounds. I stop here for a while. This is where I can set the first trap. The stove in the shed is stoked up. I melt water in a five gallon can I keep here for this purpose. There is a lantern, a bed, and locked up in the fifty-five gallon drum is my sleeping bag, some spare food, and survival gear. There are extra socks and boots in case I have gotten wet along the way. There are matches, first aid, fire starter, extra rope, an extra dog harness, bail wire, in case the sled or gear needs repairing. The small 6 x 8 size makes it easy to heat up in an emergency. The stop is long enough for me to take off my hat, mitts, coat, and hang them by the stove to get them dry. They are not wet, but I have been sweating, and there is a slight dampness I may as well get rid of. The sled dogs lay in the snow and take a nap. This is an indication of being more tired then I'd like to see them. We are halfway to the homestead. Not even noon yet. Give them an hour rest. Allow four hours for the second half of the trip, still home before dark by five or six. Hate to hang out here at the airport a whole day unless we must. It is a disadvantage to head out of the hills and drop into the Kantishna drainage and swamps, having the dogs a little tired and running late. If we run into problems, like open water, or snow drifts, it makes for a rough end of the day. The temperature is always twenty degrees or more colder in the flats at Chicago, then the hills, where I am now. But at worse, I can just stop and make a camp for the night. Sleep in the sled as I do on the trapline anyhow.

"Let's go guys." They know by this command it is time to think about waking up, stretching, and getting ready for the next command of 'Hike.' They have a few minutes warning as I tighten up the sled ropes and get my warmed up coat and mitts back on.

"Hike!" We leap forward in silence, and head on through the hills. The big change is, we are now on our trapline with traps to set. Traps get left out all year. All I have to do is set them, and put bait on the wire provided. Only sometimes I move a set, or decide this spot is not producing, so give up on it. Usually, once a trapper knows his territory, he knows where the furs will be at from year to year. I set my usual lynx snare under each Marten pole set. I never know when lynx following the trail will step over to take a look at the Marten set, even though it is in general, of not much interest to a lynx. Sometimes lynx are only curious. Lynx usually like to catch their own food, and want it fresh. Rotten things are of little interest. Marten, fox, wolf, will go for smelly rotten meat. I try to average a trap per mile. This allows for animal population to remain stable and high without over trapping. If I cover 100 miles, and have 100 traps out and each one catches one thing, I have 100 pieces of fur. A descent amount I'm happy with. Nothing that will stand out, get me famous or rich or known as a good trapper. But it creates a sustainable lifelong living, without affecting the animal population by much. This thought occupies some time as I travel, because I notice I am seeing as many animal tracks as I have noticed for all the years I have trapped here.

The sled dogs slow down at the top of the drop, as usual. It's an amazing trip down. Still called 'the drop.' I'm not as inclined to fix it as my neighbors the Forests are. I appreciate the drop. It's like the star gate. Those who can't manage it, can stay on the civilized side. It's about a 200 foot of drop in elevation, with fifty feet of forward distance. It's not straight. I have to negotiate a curve. As we drop and go faster, usually the sled ends up going faster than the dogs. Most dogs learn to jump the same side, the right, as the sled passes them and drags them down the hill. We are probably doing thirty miles an hour by the time we max out near the bottom. We shake ourselves, and ask everyone else if everyone is okay. I have to line the dogs back out and untangle them in front of the sled. We all laugh.

There is the same snow machine to see, that got down, but could not get back up again. It has been here a few years now. Hopefully the one who owned it was traveling with someone and got a ride back, riding double on one machine. But if they had to walk, that is fine too. Probably they will not be back. I once lost a sled dog at the drop. One did not jump to the right and tried going to the left. He got sucked under the sled and not much I could do about it. I have to ride the break in a controlled stall. The dog got hung up in the brake – drug over some rocks and trees. This trip we all jump up, shake, wag tails, look at each other, and press on.

As I excepted, the temperature here in Chicago, is twenty degrees colder with an ice fog hugging the valley, making the weather damp. This dampness freezes in the dogs fur, and freezes my hat to my head, and my beard to my coat. Very interesting country here though. Lots of game hangs out. Wolves love the high ridge that overlooks the flats so they can plan a strategy on the moose below. The swamps and creeks are full of otter and beaver. Many predators eat beaver, if they can catch one. Perhaps in hopes they do catch one, they like to hang out at the beaver houses. Traps are set at every beaver house along the creeks we follow. The lake has no name beyond my calling it 'Chicago Lake,' drawn on my map. Clear glare ice, with no visible trail. The place I leave the lake is in thick willows, I intentionally do not cut this section well, so it is hard to see. We travel fast over the glare ice. The creeks beyond are often snow free as well.

One swamp here hardly ever freezes solid, so I know to stay far to the right in the grass. There is a hot spot, which is common enough, and who knows what causes it! An underground springs maybe? This is the spot I had a dog fall through and had trouble getting the dog back up. This is the area I fall through with the snow machine so often. We have one log to go around where there is open water at the end of the log, but we jump the open spot. Once past this bad stretch we are home free. Oh. Except we have to cross the Kantishna River yet. I assume the river will be frozen.

There is one place I have learned to cross each year that I feel is the safest spot, even with open water below and above. It is hard to see in the ice fog, but the dogs have been here and know the crossing, so I trust them to take me right to it. A slight glitch in 'perfect,' is that the usual crossing has ice hummocks standing up, that are hard to negotiate around, but we manage. I'm home about the time expected, 6:00 pm as the sun sets. I still call Kantishna 'home' I notice.

I have a long list of things to accomplish. This is where I am set up to reload ammunition for my guns. So I have a list of bullets I need to reload to be used the rest of the year to moose hunt, duck hunt, rabbit hunt, when in the Nenana area. The dogs are unhooked. Each knows his spot, and has a house I built ages ago for each dog. I cut fresh grass in front of the cabin to go in each dog house. The fire in the cabin is started as I tend the chores. Snow is gathered in the five gallon enamel pot to make water. Dogs will need water as well as myself, so five gallons is the goal. There is hot soup still in my thermos from this morning, so I can finish that up, and eat a main meal after the dogs are fed. There is plenty of corn meal for the sled dogs that gets added to the salmon fish soup. Five gallons of the fat from Dan at the Patty Wagon at the fair is in the sled. Much of what I brought is to be left for future needs during the rest of the winter. Each dog gets a piece of fat the size of an egg.

Some of what I bring is for 'stockpiling' that is added to 'things I need to survive in an emergency.' I want a lifetime supply of certain things such as matches, stovepipe, oil for the lantern, certain foods that keep well. Among the goods I already have, are many cases of food in cans, sealed in nitrogen, good for twenty years. I think these were produced during the days society was worried about a nuclear war, and bomb shelters were outfitted with these supplies. The cases were traded for at the state fair one year. There are fifty pounds of dry beans. A lifetime supply of gun reloading goods, like forty pounds of lead shot for goose hunting.

In the late evening I get to some mail I have not replied to, and brought with me, anticipating free evening time to read and write. My buddy Will has written. Talking about the very subject that is on my mind this evening!

Hey Miles!

So how is it going? I sort of have work snow plowing for the winter, so sitting pretty good. Except the goods I stock piled were stolen, so that sets me back. Hard to find a secure place to store stuff when you are poor! Hey, I wanted to give you an update on the restrictions on the use of lead shot! We talked about it, and both agree this will not apply to Alaska for a long time, but still! There is beginning to be a shortage of lead shot on the market. Manufactures are not selling as much. Production down, price up, supply limited, shipping restrictive. I notice it is hard to find lead in

Fairbanks anyplace! So when you can find it, be sure to stockpile some! I tried some of that steel shot ordered by the government to use as a replacement. It really sucks Miles. It has no energy. You have to be half as close to the game. The steel requires a new shotgun, just for steel. I'm noticing a lot more wounded birds out in the field now too. Well, if you reload any lead, let me know and I can trade or something. I need some 12 gauge, three inch magnum with number 4 or #2 shot. It's only legal on fox in the lower states. Not geese. So, who is coming up with these rules? The rules are based on what kind of study? Can we believe our government? Is it all about control? I'm reading articles stating that no, the ducks are not ingesting lead off the bottom of ponds and dying of lead poisoning as stated by the government. So what's that all about!? Also, I hear soon we will not be able to get our propane tanks filled. We will have to buy new tanks, with new style safety values. So, all those bottles you stock piled you can't get filled. I sure wish I had taken off to the wilds when you did Miles. It's getting pretty crazy in the city! Thanks for the feather in the letter, reminds me of hunting ducks last fall. I notice you still address your envelopes upside down! **Watch your top knot! Will**

I reply to Will and just ramble about things on my mind. Covering these subjects.

Hey Will!

Remember how we used to look for supplies we thought we needed, and tried to stockpile them in caches in the woods? We'd get such good deals at garage sales and the thrift stores, but as fast as we acquired goods, they were stolen! What a life that was huh? But life has gotten better for both of us since I think, despite changes we do not like. Trying to keep on the bright side here. I'm still figuring out what it is I need, and what it is I just want as a luxury, and getting stuff at an okay price that lasts, and in general solving life's issues.

So it is well to be prepared with everything I need. My source of light- heat- food – clothing- travel etc., needs to be kept secure. So there are cases of candles, batteries, sleeping bags- sewing needles -first aid items- and on and on, that are simply 'stored' against hard times, or restrictions in the future. Life in the wilds appears to be legally a game, a sport, a hobby, not a lifestyle. You told me once, hunters in the lower states have to wear red vests with numbers on them in order to legally hunt. How can that be true? Who would put up with that? Can the government really tell me how to dress? Order me to buy a uniform? Arrest us if we do not dress like a dandy? That seems impossible. It's hard to sort fact from fiction.

I think I have solved some basic electric needs. Big four foot solar panels were bought at Battery Bob's where we used to go. A control panel, with deep cycle golf cart batteries costs me half a year's income. It should be a lifetime investment. Just to run a radio! I cross my fingers, and have tiny twelve watt like refrigerator bulbs for light. But no, there seems to be always some issue, and I think I have it solved, but not yet.

One problem might be I may have mixed good batteries with old ones, and I read now that old batteries drain the whole system down and ruin the good batteries. So, I need to invest in only good ones, and toss out what I have. Or, can I buy a load tester, and will that tell me the condition of the batteries? The little floating balls in the suck up syringe seem to not tell me all I need to know. There is something else called a 'surface charge' that needs to be understood. Somehow I need to overcome the surface charge and run serious power into the battery, like with a generator now and then. I'd think my total of eight amps of power the panels produce should be enough. Or maybe the wire I run is too thin, and I need to buy all new wire from the panel to the batteries. Except if I am getting eight amps at the controller, that is what it is I'd think? Maybe better wire would increase the amps and volts, but the meter shows what arrives at the battery, and what I have should be fine. Is there something else besides amps and volts that measure electricity I need to understand? But obviously something is wrong, as I can't hardly even run the radio, much less a small bulb. I've spent over $1,000 trying to light a light bulb. It's hard not to be discouraged.

So, here I am working by propane and kerosene as I always have. Not sure if you have dealt with much of this, as you live a simple life, but on the grid. More and more I think we should not have anything we do not understand and cannot fix ourselves. Hope to see ya when I get to town again then, **Sunshine Miles**

Will and I are close enough to the same age to have shared memories of our childhood. The president Kennedy years. We discussed atomic bomb drills we used to have in school. There were bomb shelters all over. As children we were taught what to do. We looked inside these shelters. Got told about the canned water and food stored in nitrogen gas that will last a lifetime. Will and I both wondered how that would look in reality. Knowing the dirty bombs of the time, where recovery of the land is measured in thousands of years. We look at this one room shelter. I wonder where the bathroom is and my bedroom. I try to picture forty people this room is designed for, trying to stay alive for 'years,' living on limited canned water and dried foods. I thus can understand why an entire generation tuned in and dropped out into drug land. The news in general is doom and gloom. Hole in the Ozone, global warming, asteroids on a collision course, people climbing tours shooting us down, poison slipped in medicine in the stores, drive by shootings, corrupt government, corporations, sport figures. There is a reason to not want electricity, radios or news. I even explained to Will how it was when living with Karen and the girls out remote.

The elder girl May, was thirteen when she was angry and yells at me, "So why should I want to live in a world your generation ruined!" I had no answer. I agree. I did understand better why she is so angry. There are choices we all have to make. To give up and just die? Put ourselves out of our misery with drugs? Life is still much worse in other countries!

One answer is to live in the wilds alone. Another answer might be to try to do some good, help others. Try to change what is possible to change. Accept what cannot be changed. Try to be part of a solution, instead of adding to a problem. Set an example. May ended up owning a remote lodge, and teaching dog mushing for a living. As her personal solution. Here Will and I are, still wondering what the answer is. In the 60's I did not think civilization would last more than another ten years. How could it? We were told daily Russia is about to blow up the planet. Yet it was the US who is the only country to use the nuclear bomb in a war. Is reality, is it Russia that has more to fear from us? Martin Luther got shot, Kennedy assassinated, probably by our own government, Kent state riots. And it only gets worse. At any rate, it makes sense to Will and I to keep life simple enough to be able to depend on your own knowledge to fix what you own, so we are prepared for hard times to come. For there is little good news coming out of civilization.

Photo Section

Supplies headed down river by barge . There are no more roads.

This is the shed I use as emergency shelter headed for the homestead. During gas exploration days a runway was cut out here with a bulldozer so fuel and supplies could be landed.

A view of Fairbanks coming in by boat on the Chena River.

My best dog , Spike I leased to Norman Vaughn for the Iditarod Race.

I install solar power at the homestead.

Survey boss owns his own plane, sometimes flying us and supplies to remote homestead jobs.

Mammoth tusks I found. I forget exactly where, when, if, or who sold to. I do recall where I did not find them. Matched set like this worth $20,000.

Instrument man on remote survey job. I'm the saw man.

CHAPTER EIGHT

LIFE WITH SLED DOGS ON THE TRAPLINE. SKI PLANE VISIT ON THE TRAPLINE BY MY DENTIST

I decide to rest up the dogs the next day, rather than tackle the trapline. I can walk a little way, and make sure the trail is clear, maybe set a few traps on my creek. I need to focus on the good stuff. I can't let civilization bring me down. All the rules, restrictions, loss of freedoms etc. Well it all seems far enough away. *Yes! Where is the law now? Who is going to enforce anything?* But yea. 'problems' I have no time for. Changes Will speaks of? I suppose. But look around, what has really changed? It's the same trees all around me, that have looked like this for 50,000 years since the last glacier period. It's the same water that gurgles with the same happy noise. It's the same blue sky with the same sun in it. The same God hauls this same sun in the same chariot since the beginning of time. I can inhale, and the air is the same as it was a million years ago. There are critters leaving footprints, making noises in the woods, scurry sounds, screeches. All the sounds that have been here for millions of years. Look around, what is really changed?

The wind has blown the snow off the lakes and swamps out back. In the past I have put on ice-skates and gone out across the lakes exploring. This is a good time to try this again. The conditions happen only a few days a year, sometimes not at all. Ice skates are fast, easy travel, when there is no snow. I am able to travel for many miles. This allows me to see what kind of critters are around and in high population this season. A twenty-two rifle is brought along. I shoot two rabbits and three grouse. The feathers of the grouse and skin of the rabbits are used as bait for trapping. Wolves killed a moose less than a week ago on the first lake out back. There is a big cleared area where the moose tore down some willows in the fight. It looks like the moose had its intestines torn out by the wolves and ran a ways dragging his guts. I had heard of this as a common method for wolves to kill moose, but never seen it before. Certainly here is lots of blood around, along a trail half a mile long. The spot where the moose fell for the last time is found. Some snares are set for the wolves, as surely they will come back, with so much meat left here to still eat. If I am lucky, the wolves do not know I am around yet. If they are less wary, I might have a better chance of getting them. I do know it is common for wolves to kill a moose, take one meal, and not eat off this moose again, leaving 90% behind. When hungry again, they are more likely to kill another moose for a hot meal, not a frozen meal. However I also notice other wildlife depends on this surplus moose meat created by wolves. This is great for fox, scavengers of all kinds. Nothing appears to be wasted.

Ice skates make only a slight sound on the ice as I move along faster than I could run, with no effort. Under overhang willows with snow, up a creek with grass as tall as I am, three feet on either side of me and on to the next lake and the next swamp. No human signs. No tracks in the snow on the edges except wild creatures. Mink and otter mostly, but a few lynx mixed in with the rabbit tracks. I do not set any traps this direction because it is a dead end when running the sled dogs. I'd have to come all the way in this dead end and turn around. I'd rather run the loop I am still working on. About 100 miles. It usually takes four days to complete the loop. Unsure how that would work if I am also getting to Nenana regularly. Maybe I will run a fifty mile loop this year. A day or two out, a day or two back. Into Nenana once a week. Thinking of this as I ice skate miles from home base. Here is a spot where a swan froze in the ice, and fox have been feeding. I often notice, swan signets do not survive to make it south. I think they do not mature enough to make the trip. They are big birds, and the season is short. Unable to fly, they freeze into the ice. White feathers all over the ice with fox tracks. I pause. Stop. Bend over to look closer. *Reminds me of the trip with Sally and her retrieving the feathers.* Through the clear ice I see a fish, a pike hovering near a log, knowing I am above, but thinks unseen. I am of the air, he is of the water. *We are of the universe so I know the reason why, he is lonely, and he wants to die. From the Beatles song!* Smaller fish come to peck at the remains of the swan under the ice. The pike pecks at the nibblers. I smile. I could shoot the pike through the ice if I wanted to-for dog feed, but no, there is enough food. I like the expression on the pike. Fat with a big smile, luminous eyes. Little fins fanning away, at peace with the world. I get up. Skate over the top of him, while he thinks I never saw him.

The next day is a little colder, at twenty-five below zero, but still comfortable, and we are all eager to get out on the trapline. The dogs seem stronger from the days rest. Enough for a week is packed in the sled, and off we go. There are lakes, creeks, hills, and trails going over yonder and beyond. The dogs know the routine and where to go. I don't have to say much. Every mile we set a trap. There are lots of tracks. So I am excited. We get to camp one, but it is so early in the day I treat it as I did the airport. Broth the dogs, let them rest an hour, dry out my clothing, rest a little myself, and we are on our way. I doubt we will get to camp two by dark, so understand we will camp out in the trail, which is done about half the time.

There is a spot I have camped before, out of the wind, with dry wood, and a level spot for the sled. I will sleep in the sled. There are good trees to tie the sled dogs to. About 4:00 pm I stop for the day. It will be dark in an hour anyhow, and I can use that hour of dusk to get camp ready. First I want to secure my wood for the night as a number one priority. I cut and pile enough to last a night, while the weak fire is built up to a bigger fire, with some warmth and the ability to cook our food. By the light of the fire I unload the sled and prepare camp. Now I do not have to go outside the light of the fire the rest of the evening. I made the fire using fire starter. This is strips of rubber bike inner tubes I cut. The rubber will burn hot and can be lit if wet or cold, and is not affected by much that stops it from burning hot. Dry branches can always be found at the base of a big spruce tree with lots of overhang branches that catch the snow and rain. There is light moss on the branches that burns well. I look for some birch bark nearby. A bow saw in the sled never fails, and cuts enough for the night very fast. As water melts in the five gallon can for the dogs, I unload the sled and make a pile nearby on spruce branches. Other long soft spruce branches go in the bottom of the sled as my mattress. My snowsuit will be my pillow. The sled tarp drapes over the sled rail and acts as a mini tent in case there is snow overnight. The dog harnesses are set on branches nearby to see if they will dry out at all overnight. This is the same process repeated whenever I stop. An owl hoots at the disturbance of his world. The moon is full this night.

Dogs are fed. I'm fed. I lay in the sleeping bag with a good book relaxing in my sleeping bag by the fire. Within reach is my container of matches, some kindling for a morning fire. My boots are upside down so if there is snow in the night my boots will not get filled. A pot for making tea and pot for cooking soup is within reach. In the morning I can get a fire going, drink hot tea, have breakfast, all before I even get out of the sleeping bag. *Talk about luxury!* This is more than just for comfort. If for some reason I cannot sleep well or get cold, hot tea and broth can warm me enough to be able to get out of the sleeping bag and get dressed, then stand close to a fire already started, already warm to face whatever emergency there might be.

It seems almost a requirement to have a 'relax' time to unwind before bed time and sleep. I'm in bed and reading by 7:00 pm. I read two hours before falling asleep by 8-9:00 pm. Sometimes, I get cold, and roll another log into the fire. But the sleeping bag is good and warm. I rarely feel cold unless the temperature drops to sixty below. I can survive that, but it is just hard to be actually comfortable. I could live with this twenty-five below every day all winter and be fine. Except the sleeping bag builds up frost! Every few days we have to get inside a cabin someplace to dry it out! *Yes, I'm unsure what old timers did about this frost.* Supposedly, caribou fur can be shaken out and not build up frost. It seems so heavy though. I would not want to carry such a sleeping bag. I bet such a bag is fifty pounds. The one I have is four pounds. Sweet. Yawn. and the book gets put down.

There are minor northern lights out, with lots of stars. The hoot of the same great horned owl nearby lulls me as I fall asleep. In the morning the routine is normal. A fire is started while I am still in the sleeping bag. When the fire is hot- warm and bright, I get up, get dressed, and get the dog pot over the flame melting snow. God is still waking up, and loading the sun in the chariot before hauling it across the sky. I take the time to stop, look, and wave. While snow is melting, I cut a little wood I had drug over near the fire pit the evening before. This wood has some ice on it so I have to spend more time making sure it does not put the fire out. Supplies are sorted, checked, and things that need drying are put near the fire, or only turned around. The dog harnesses are always near the fire. I eat oatmeal with powdered milk, and half a can of peaches. The dogs are checked. After brothing, I harness them up. They all stare ahead up the trail, as eager as I am to see what is there.

We are off on the trapline headed further out. There are trees to cut that blew down over the trail. Traps need digging out that got buried. I get twenty miles, and to one of the line cabins for the night. Next day we head further out. I camp in the sled again. Now it is time to begin the trip back to home base. It has been three days since I was on this trail, so there is fur in some of the traps I can collect on the return trip. A night on the way home will be spent at twenty mile cabin I built. At this cabin, I hear a plane, so step to out to look up.

The plane circles low upon seeing me, and searches for a place to land. My trail passes through a meadow. A long stretch of short grassy dried up slough. Perfect for a ski plane to land. It allows the pilot to walk the dog trail to the cabin just ahead. I see who it is, this is my dentist friend Dave!

"Dave how are you! I thought you might be Fish and Game!" He laughs as he puts his hand out to shake mine. We have talked before about governments, rules, and such topics, the ability or inability of man to govern himself without a stick.

"Miles, I was pulling teeth this morning, and wanted a break, so flew out to see if you are around. I saw your trail and followed it." Dave has been my dentist for a lot of years now, and has become a friend. We trade my art work for his dental work. I get my teeth cleaned once a year. He looks my teeth over, and lets me know if I have any upcoming problems with my teeth I need to know about. It amazes me that he can run my trapline looking for me. A trip that takes me four to five days with dogs, that takes him under an hour with a plane. It is amazing he can be pulling teeth, afterwards, on a lunch break, fly from Fairbanks out here to visit and get away. He has told me in the past, it is a nice break to sit in a cabin by kerosene light watching me skin furs and talk about other things then teeth, then get back to work for the afternoon. "So Miles, how is the trapping going this season?"

"Looks good so far Dave." He looks in my sled and sees the six marten and a lynx. The dogs are tied up, a fire is quickly built in the little cabin. A little cramped for two people though. I have been to Dave's home for dinner and know his wife and children. Dave admires my life choice, and can see the rewards it offers. He sighs as he often does, as he unwinds.

"Yea Miles, if I was not a dentist I might choose a life like this. I once tried to have sled dogs, but never had time to run them and had to give them up. While you have Fish and Game to deal with, I have other government agencies to contend with. They all seem the same. And insurance companies, strong arm tactics pushing new drugs, and equipment on us to offer to the public. Dentists do not always have choices, nor are we free to just do our job. It bothers me to have to needlessly charge so much when people depend on and have to have dental work."

He is forced to throw away equipment that works just fine, based on laws requiring updates. He is forced to fly a specialist in from the lower states to do root canals for some reason I do not understand, but have sympathy for. "Miles, before I forget, I brought you some used dental tools for cleaning your own teeth. I showed you before how to use them. And here is some pain killer you asked me about. I thought about it, and think this is something you might need in an emergency in your lifestyle." Another example of 'something illegal,' because there are people who would abuse pain killers, so therefore no one can have them. We all suffer because of the actions of a few. Why? Why can't responsible people have access to 'whatever' as long as it is to be used wisely.

I had in fact been concerned in general about what to do out remote if I have a medical issue of some kind. What have I got that can take care of the various things that can come up? There are things that need much more than a band aid and antiseptic! I had showed a book to Dave once, called 'Mountaineering Medicine,' that is a serious book about serious problems. There are instructions for how to take out your own appendix for example. Good information, explaining what you must accomplish before you pass out, when you can relax more, how to cut an artery and clamp it. The sorts of things that can save your life. Like if I had to cut my foot off! Like that one trapper did when he got his foot caught in the track of the snowmachine and the machine quit, and held his foot. 'How to cut your foot off with a Swiss army knife and live,' is useful stuff to know. So Dave, being a doctor, might be someone to talk to. He understands my point, and provides me with certain basics. Like serious pain killer.

"Thanks Dave, hopefully I'll never need it!" There are instructions on how much to take based on body weight. It might allow me to get to civilization if I broke a leg or something. Help me be functional if there was a lot of pain involved. "Yes Dave, in my lifestyle I need all sorts of varied knowledge to survive. Or even to just have a higher level of existence. Like knowing how to fix a radio- weld, make soap, fix engines and a whole variety of topics. It makes life challenging and interesting."

" Miles, few lifestyles allow for such a diverse set of knowledge as yours. Few of us can branch out so much with our experiences. Most have a job, maybe a couple of hobbies, and that's it. They are clueless about how their TV works, or how to make a pair of shoes, unless it is one of their few hobbies. Not much time even to learn about much. Well, it is always interesting to talk to you Miles. I better get going, teeth to pull, an appointment at three, meeting at four. The plane allows me my freedom, glad I have that!" I tell him we need to work out a system so I know it is not Fish and Game coming! I see him off, and all is quiet again. It is hard to believe I just had a visitor. *Had I only imagined it?*

The furs are skinned at this line cabin into the evening, since I stopped early so I could be at a cabin. This will save weight going on home and the animal carcasses can provide bait out on the trapline, so I need not haul as much bait out this far. Thus, nothing is wasted. The lynx hind quarters are put in the pot with rice for my own food. Lynx is good meat. The rest of the lynx goes in the dog pot. Marten could go in too, but the dogs like that less, and it is better for trapping bait.

The furs are rolled up into balls with the skin side out and frozen. This protects the fur. The frozen balls can be put together in a burlap bag I have in the cabin, and tossed in the sled.

Back at the Kantishna homestead I see no sign of 'the kid' who has been trying to take over my trapline, and staked land almost across from me. Still, this is on my mind. I still look and wonder when he will be back, and how it will go between us. Someone has stolen fifty-five gallons of gas from the river bank by the homestead. This has a high value way out here, and I depend on it being here. Had it been the kid? Or a moose hunter low on gas? Someone I know? Problems out here are on the increase. Tom and his wife, my dog racing neighbors have had things stolen off and on in recent years as well. We think it is outside moose hunters, as this area gets more popular for hunting. We have a few record size bull moose along the river that trophy hunters want. Tom tells me he heard from one of the hunters, Fish and Game is sending people this direction as a suggestion for getting their moose, putting increased pressure on this river drainage. He thinks this has to do with upcoming fights over the land that has oil under it. "Clear the game out, get subsistence people out of here" It's an old topic.

I had allowed one of my guide friends in, Dell, from Caribou Loan. Dell owns the pawn shop where I get my guns and used goods. He was in a bind, and could not fly a client into the Brooks Range up north, due to bad weather. He needed to get his hunter out someplace to hunt. I told him he could use my cabin and canoe for a few days. He paid me and all had gone well. They had taken a big bull moose out of the area. But word gets around, and others show up, and then it is not a quiet secret spot anymore. Anyhow. On my mind as I mush on to Nenana and the Tek land to see what Sally has been up to. I have been gone a week.

Sally is fine, for the most part. She has been listening to the radio, taking care of the baby, the usual cooking, pumping water and keeping the place clean.

"But I need a shower!" She tells me right off. We need to go to Nenana and use the public shower at the Laundromat. While in Nenana we run into Josh.

"Miles, I need someone to handle dogs for me at the Iditarod race in Anchorage. I'll pay for the trip, can you do it for me? Also, Norman wants to lease your dog Spike as a leader in his team in the race." Also, in return, I will have access to both Josh's dogs and Normans for breeding pups and working with the younger dogs on the trapline that are too young to race. "Miles, I am impressed with what you did with Char!" Josh had given me a dog named Char a few years ago. Josh told me the dog was to slow and not good for racing. I had told Josh I did not agree, that I thought maybe he was just maturing late. I ran Char on the trapline and got his confidence built up, and toughened him up. Josh had always felt the trapline would slow a dog up for racing. But after a few years, I told Josh I thought Char was one tough dog, and might be able to be trained for speed in a faster team then I have.

Josh took Char back, just to try out. It took a few runs to get Char faster, but he is one awesome race sled dog. There have been a couple of other dogs.

"Miles remember Poncho? Sort of sick, and you fixed him up. He was too fast for your team!" Josh took him back and sold Poncho to another racer for $2,500. Me taking on dogs, fixing them and getting them back to Josh, and Josh doing well with them was okay with me 'because' like with Norman, I have the use of dogs worth several thousand each that I cannot afford. I am learning a lot in a hurry about dogs, dog breeding, gear, and health care, all invaluable to me. The sort of stuff no one gets for free, or told about unless you are trusted and like family with a good musher. Anyhow, I could not possibly get the kind of prices for dogs Josh gets, no matter how good, because I have no name, and no one will pay me that kind of money. You are mostly paying for the name behind the dog. Everything seems sort of okay with Sally about this. I'd be gone just a few days. Sally is good about not wanting to interfere with my way of life, and how I want to do things. Except maybe when it comes to the child. But, I guess it is a mother instinct thing to think first of the baby, and everything is for the baby and what not.

Josh loads up his truck with the dog box. This is a big box that bolts into the bed of the truck with compartments in it for the sled dogs. Room for fifteen dogs. We get a hotel room in Anchorage. It has been a five hour drive. The climate is different here on the coast. Snow is melting a little. The city will put snow down on the main street so the dogs can run the street in front of a crowd.

"Sort of a joke really Miles," Josh tells me, "It's a false start. We stop, collect the teams, and restart further up the trail in Wasilla, where there is snow, no road crossings, and access to the trail all the way to Nome, 1,400 miles away." I already know the race is based on the serum run when there was a diphtheria outbreak in Nome, and no way to get the serum there. It was the days before planes. The serum was brought by train to Nenana, then trappers did relays and hauled the serum all the way to Nome.

I repeat the story a lot, it's pretty exciting.

We run into Norman, now 80 years old this year. He has had Spike for only two weeks. The three of us go around and mingle with the racers. Josh introduces me to many of the winners of the race. The big names. I'm not introduced as a handler, but as a friend. We eat at a big banquet. All the past race winners give a talk. There are seventy-two mushers this year in the race. The news media follows Norman around.

This race is a big deal to Josh. His entire years income is based on this one race. He is trying to win it by running straight-without drugs. There is controversy. Josh feels most of the winners have been giving their dogs illegal drugs. Other racers tell me Josh is just Josh, paranoid and coming up with excuses for why he is not the winner again- because someone else was cheating. I am not in a position to know one way or the other. But some of Josh's stories do sound convincing, actual evidence and things he has seen himself. I try to avoid the negative talk, and want to think good things, have a good time, enjoy the race, the mushers, and the dogs.

I remembered to bring some of my art work. I figured a dog theme would sell, so have some buckles and bolo ties with sled dogs on them, I cut out by hand with my metals. I make $400 at the banquet selling my art to mushers I already know. A lot of business cards are handed out.

JOSH IS in the lineup and will be taking off in twenty minutes. He tells me he is short some gang line he must have forgot to bring. He cannot hook up all his dogs. I am in a rush running to the nearest hardware store to buy rope, then busy as heck braiding a section of gang line with backline and neckline. I have help, and we get it all done in time for Josh to get to the start line.

The sled dogs are eager to go and cannot be easily contained, so it takes six people holding the line to keep the dogs from taking off. We all walk the dogs to the start line to the cheers of a crowd and in front of the TV cameras. Once a racer takes off, he cannot receive any outside help except at designated check points along the trail. So, it is important we see he has all his gear, and that all is in order.

Josh has to cook for the dogs on the trail, and has a cool set up. A roll of toilet paper goes in a #10 can. Alcohol is poured over the paper in the can. This burns hot, long, and cooks a five gallon container of food. Josh gets off okay. His wife, Bearfoot, and I, head for the pickup point, where we collect Josh and do the restart.

Anchorage is all about the TV, the crowd, pleasing the sponsors with their name on sleds in front of the news media. The real race is alone out there on the trail over the next ten days. I recognize there is no race without the money from sponsors, so it is very important to keep the sponsors happy.

Josh has the nick name, 'The Fox' in the news media. He is known for his tricks. My favorite story is how Josh was out front, but a little concerned he could not keep up the pace. A few others were pressing hard right behind him as darkness approached. None would stop unless Josh did, for fear of losing too much distance between them. So Josh pulls into a good camp spot, calling it a day. His competitors are glad, and set up camp nearby just like Josh. His motions look like settling in for the night. But instead it is only the motions. When the others are settled in for the night, Josh quietly gets on his sled and takes off again.

As the race progresses, Norman has to scratch with many others in the first 300 miles. There is a place called 'the burn,' lots of tundra that gets windblown and hard when it is a low snow year like this year. Sleds get broken, and racers lose teams here. I'm unsure exactly what happens, but am glad enough my leader Spike will not be run to death, and has had only a short run, and I will get paid. No one really expected Norman to be competitive anyhow. It is amazing he can run the race at all, considering his age. The race officials had considered having an age limit. They did not want the expense and bad publicity if anyone old dying on the race. On the other hand, Norman does a lot to promote, and bring publicity to, the race. Norman has a book he tells me he is working on called, 'Dare to Fail,' about following a dream, taking a chance, with risk and failure, as a possibility.

Norman got into sled dogs as a mail carrier by dogs, in the days before any motorized transportation. He told me a lot of stories of those days, and his life as an explorer to the South Pole with Admiral Byrd. It is easy to feel inspired, and see why Norman is successful at what he does.

BACK IN NENANA, and on the Tek homestead with Sally, I follow the race on the radio. "All the racers will fly back from Nome to wherever they are headed Sally." There are of course no roads to Nome. "No roads anywhere on the entire ten day race." This is beyond comprehension to Sally. She has a different perspective on our friend Josh, who has 'oddities.' "Sally, do you think such a life, such a race, is won by normal people?" The radio reports Josh is down to nine dogs, in tenth place and holding.

JOSH TELLS me later that the last 100 miles of the race had his fastest time in the race. Meaning he did not work the dogs hard enough early on. "Miles, I have young dogs this year. I did not want to burn them up." Also, the charges of abuse may have been on his mind, and so he held back, least he have problems again.

'Well Josh, tenth place is not bad. You told me before, it more than pays your years' worth of dog expenses. You run without a sponsor, without a vet, without handlers and trainers, with the smallest dog lot of any other competitive racer. It's amazing you do as well as you do!" Josh has other things on his mind as well, and I know him well enough to know what that is. His son. His son 'Guy' is in prison for a brutal murder when he was only eighteen. He got thirty years. No one knows for absolute certainty what actually happened, because there was no trial! There was a plea bargain of some sort, but it seems odd to me to plea bargain, and get life. If he had not plea bargained what would he have gotten?

Josh feels his son got a bum rap. Railroaded for being native. There is even a small possibility he did not do it. Even though Guy knew where the body was, out hidden in the tundra. Supposedly he woke up to find a bloody tire iron in his hand, and a body. He had been out partying with his buddies. Where were his buddies he had been with? Why was he alone when he woke up? Talk was, drugs are involved. Guy had joined the military, and had just gotten out of boot camp. He may have quit drugs and wanted the local 'drug lord' to stop dealing. One story on the street was that Guy wanted to sell on his own, and the drug dealer got upset. Guy may have got a new source among new friends in the military.

If the local drug lord wanted Guy 'eliminated,' and a message sent out to all the other dealers who might want to break away? Well, one good way might be to set Guy up. Send him out with 'friends,' get him high and out of it. Kill the girl. She supposedly owed a lot of money for drugs to the lord, and might have become a liability. Supposedly, she did have a lot of money on her at the time she was murdered, and the money never turned up. Who has it? Implying Guy was not the only one involved. But, the murder weapon could be left in his hand, and Guy left at the scene to wake up and think he did it. Just a possibility, but no one will ever know. There are other various rumors and speculations of different sorts, some with merit, some off the wall. Even rumors of Gene being involved. Needless to say it was a horrible thing for the family to go through. A son in prison thirty years is devastating to the parents.

"Miles I don't think Mick did a great job as a lawyer."

"Our good buddy Mick? The one who gets me out of all my Fish and Game jams?" I'm being sarcastic, as I already know I got set up at least once. I'm trying to get Josh to chuckle, as he has a lot on his mind all right. Josh was also banned from running all local races in Nenana years ago, before I arrived, for abuse to a dog. During a race, he hung a dog by a chain from a tree on the side of the trail. I do not know the details. Like if the dog was dead, still alive, or what this was all about. But think all the other mushers had to go by it, and that must have been not very cool.

Josh has a kind generous streak in him. Maybe just a lot of baggage. A lot of demons. There are stories he tells of his childhood. Raising himself in the village of Minto. Competing with loose sled dogs for fish eggs on the beach. I have this image of a child on all fours pushing dogs away to eat rotten raw fish. He's lucky to be alive at all. To rise to be a top dog racer is astounding. If that comes with a price, or certain oddities, I sigh, and try to understand.

I myself have never seen Josh be cruel to a dog. Seen nothing but taking good care of them. It is easy to see the dogs love him, and are not afraid of him. Some of what I do see, is a culture clash. It has not been the events, the deeds, that seemed so awful, but the way Josh handled it.

"Josh, you cannot tell officials you broke up a dog fight with a metal snow hook!" Which resulted in one of the dogs having a broken tooth. I explained, you have to say, "Oh my gosh I hope my dogs are okay, someone get a Vet. The dogs got in a fight, and I think one has a broken tooth!" Turn to the TV camera and make a statement about how everything is being done to take care of the dog, and you are considering scratching."

"Miles , I cannot lie!"

"Josh, that is not a lie. It's just not telling the whole story! It's saving your bacon. It's what the public expects, and the Iditarod can cover for you if you take on the right attitude." I have seen enough of other racers, and mushers in general. Josh has not done anything others do not do. The only difference is, he is singled out because of how he handles it. I find that sad. That others silently look on, knowing they do the same thing and keep their mouth shut, let Josh burn.

One example is our friend Norman. He and I had been talking about barking dogs one day.

"Norman, I notice your dogs do not bark much. Is that part of breeding of the dogs, or is that training?"

"Miles, my dogs do not bark. Maybe they bark once. If they bark I shoot them." He told me this is how it was as a mail carrier. I think dogs were supplied to him as part of the job. If he did not like them, he shot them. Josh told me Norman is getting older now and forgetful, and forgets the name of his dogs, and how many he has. Josh went to visit him at Trapper Creek once, and Norman had forgot he had five dogs moved to a new spot. Josh found them starved to death, and frozen to the ground, covered in snow, forgotten in the back yard, still on their chains.

Josh is resentful, it seems to me, that no one is going to point a finger at the great Col. Norman Vaughn. The white man with good breeding, who knows how to con the news media and public.

"It's not a con as such Josh. It's about passing on certain sets of information, and just not bothering to mention other bits of information."

"The man with the golden pen!" is how Josh refers to me. But, I am trying to help him understand, and have his life be better.

The public does not want the truth! The public wants glory, flags waving, a hero, a winner, sponsors want their name seen, everyone wants money to flow. Who wants all the gory details of anything? Ha! Name me a sport, a money maker of any kind that has not got a dark side that no one wants to make public. Except enemies, competitors, and those who have an ulterior motive to try to bring down the sport or the specific hero!

My honest opinion is, there is energy put in the direction against Natives being in the race. Against the race being seen as the old style race between village dogs. Possibly however, I have been listening to Josh too much. The Iditarod, it looks to me like, wants the image of a high end race that attracts high dollar sponsors. Josh stands for 'let's bring in the trapline team and have a race.' No, it needs to be about the vets, the special dog foods, the new style sleds, and plastics on the market. Money flowing. Money does not flow when racers have no sponsors, have no vet, no employees, are independent, stand alone, need no one and race in the old way, with no new products used. Many of the old time and native mushers are getting left by the wayside. Is it only because they cannot compete? This is what the top white racers tell me. That high tech is wining out, and the natives can't keep up. From my viewpoint, nothing is better than knowledge and experience. In a race between wisdom and technology, wisdom wins. Those who know dogs, who know how to camp out, who know how to read the weather, will do better than those who are green, but have the best equipment. These green White racers are learning fast though, and gaining that experience needed.

A new race is starting up called the Yukon Quest. In competition with the Iditarod, same distance, but more of the old style Iditarod, for those who do not want to race high tech. But it's got a smaller purse, and is not as popular.

Way back in 1975 I met Emmitt Peters, and did a special order art piece for him when I went by Ruby on my houseboat. We had talked about various issues concerning the race. Emmitt had won the Iditarod the year before I met him. Also, I notice, I myself live 'the old way' to some extent. I notice certain trends, patterns of behavior. I began my time in the wilds, looking up to, and admiring those, who founded our country, who were brave, tough, and went through hardships so our country can be what it is today. Much like people admire the Iditarod race. The symbol of tough men with tough dogs, who traveled across a wild hostile land and survived, who cared about each other. "Such people got things done!" The old way worked when it came to saving those in Nome. It's a noble story, much like the stories I read about mountain men, who prepared the ground for the next wave, the homesteader, farmer, miner, by putting in and marking trails.

Well, I assumed our country was proud of the pioneers I admired, because the proof was in all the books on the subject, Walt Disney movies, and TV programs. Much like the Iditarod race as part of the Robert Service poems, and Jack London stories. People performing incredible feats, surviving against all odds. Heroes.

I come in out of the woods with my stories, life, right out of Jack London. The man on the street is impressed. Shakes my hand. Wants a story. But is that so with all segments of society? I have a vivid memory of looking for a job. A hotel restaurant decked out from the gold rush trapper days. Old snowshoes on the wall, dog sled on the roof, old time pictures of people who look just like me! My thought was to basically say:

"How would you like the real thing here! Not just pictures, but someone with the real story to tell! Your customers would go nuts!" I envisioned a response of:

"Wow, how cool is this! A real trapper. A real mountain man. We'd be honored to have you on board. The rest is just trim, and you are the real product!" Maybe get hired to mingle and tell stories to guests. *What did happen?* I was tossed out the door on my ears by disgusted people in suits and ties. Treated like a bum, low life. Like a dumpster diver going in the Ritz. I was shocked and puzzled. To a lesser degree, maybe Josh has similar stories. "What does this look like Miles?" "Most of this trim is just that, trim. Looks, not reality, and it's about money and image, and is much like the false storefront of the west, where a building was made to look like two stories with a false wall on the roof. It's all about looks. A marketing study is done, a committee reviews the proposals, and one is that the old time look will sell."

The trapper miner days is turned into a tourist attraction, a money maker. Tell the visitor a line of crap, give them a meal you name 'Sourdough Jacks Omelet,' offer a room with a brass bed and fake kerosene lamp, charge double the price. The big tourist organizations that are taking over tourism in the state, are more and more selling hand crafted in Alaska items made overseas. Bought cheap that might fall apart. Bought for fifty cents and sold for $50 as 'made by Alaska Indians.' Tour guides are not people like myself, nor are people like me desired. Young vibrant outsiders are hired for minimum wage, who do not know a thing. Hired cheap, and given a two hour orientation. Now qualified to talk to tourists about the wonders of Alaska. Seeing this, why would I think the general public wants reality and the truth? It's all about money. The customer wants it cheap, not genuine, and the business wants the most profit. Hired college kids with summers off are often happy just to be in Alaska.

The Iditarod might fit into this story somewhat. Owned, managed by those who do not own dogs, never raced, who wear suits and ties, and manage the money. It's about image. Getting sponsors. Way down the list someplace is pleasing the fans, and giving the fans an honest product. In some ways the public says it admires what the race stands for, admire folks like Josh. But give the public 'Josh' and what does the public have to say about it?? If there is only a picture on a cover of a magazine, and a quote in the paper, the public cheers. But see what happens when Josh talks to sponsors, does TV interviews, and greets the world in the name of the Iditarod. Partly a culture clash. Partly just not being business savvy nor caring about the big bucks being made by sponsors. Telling it from his perspective, with honesty.

"Ya, I culled some dogs the other day – shot them and dumped them in the river. I don't want anything to do with bum dogs." Or, "How did Rick Swenson and Susan Butcher win four times? By cheating and using drugs." The truth might be, our heroes who are rough and tough who win, who are independent characters, tend to be antisocial, or have social issues. There are those I see who can put a suit and tie on, and address the public on TV, who are well spoken, know how to smooze the sponsors, and who the public can identify with. But who are not winners in the race.

This reminds me a little of a true story of a top bull rider who is famous. I pass the story on the Josh. "This bull rider rested a lot, and took a helicopter from event to event, while others had to do the long drive that wore them out more. He played the percentages." Carefully chose the events that might gather the most points and publicity. Chose events that would least likely get him hurt. Planned around image, not about being a tough bull rider.

Yes, all this is somewhat important in understanding the dynamics as seen by Josh and myself, and why we are friends. Possibly I'm wrong, or it's not quite to the extent I see it, but I have just observed too much to not think there is something in it. So, I respect Josh as being the truth about what the Iditarod stands for and is all about. The one everyone else is trying to imitate and pretend they are like. Oh yes, sure, most earn their place. Anyone who wins deserves that credit. Still, Josh tells me details like how 'someone' in the top three turned trail markers around to indicate the wrong trail, on purpose, so competitors will get lost and lose time. Again about points and winning, not about who has the toughest dogs, or won fair and square. It is hard to think Josh made it up, because he was not one of the ones who took the wrong turn, so is not using it as an excuse for not being in a better position. He is telling me how he felt bad for those who made the wrong turn. "Miles, you mean like your own book? Not passing on the fake dream?" There is nothing to say.

Josh cares about being honorable. He will stop and help another racer in trouble, even if he loses time. He encourages the new racers. Cares about the sport. Might even care about the dogs, more them most. As for cruelty....

Oh yes, there will be a few bleeding hearts, a few kissy pooh dog people who think withholding a treat is cruel. But get real people. It's the Iditarod, advertised as the toughest race on earth. Anyhow, I stand by Josh. Maybe he has social issues and

I do as well. Saying the wrong things, at the wrong time, to the wrong people. Being the best at something, and that having a price.

I even consider that a high percent of those who are the best, are driven by strong feelings, maybe even a level of insanity, or how would it be put, 'obsessive personality?' That causes them to not be normal. I see many football heroes, boxers, movie stars, artists who are, well, amazingly strange human beings when the truth comes out. I ponder at the mysteries of life.

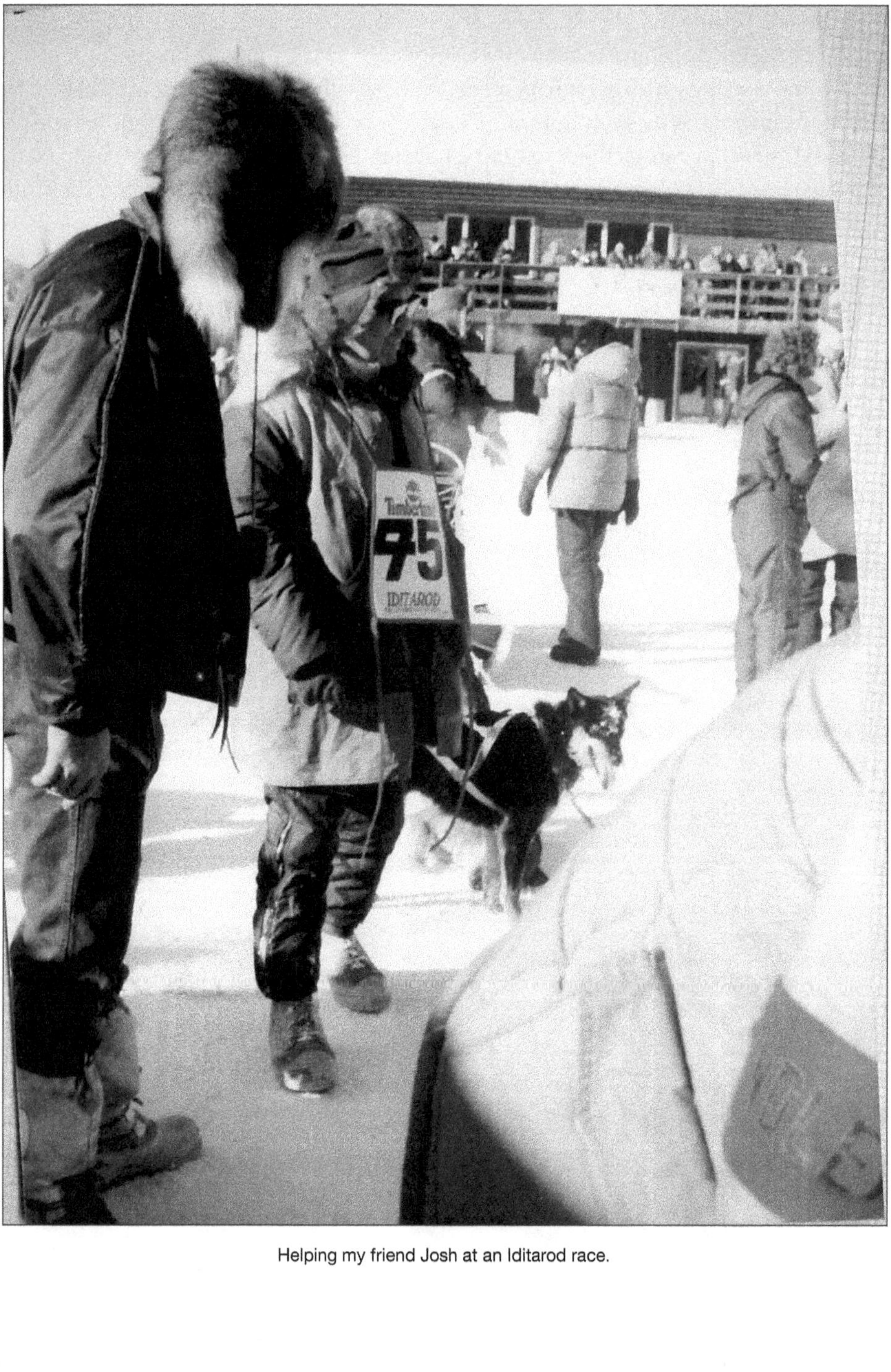

Helping my friend Josh at an Iditarod race.

CHAPTER NINE

HELPING OUT YOUNG TRAPPER GOES WRONG. MORE SURVEY WORK. SET UP AT NENANA TRIPOD DAYS SELLING ART. STRANDED WITH MOOSE HUNTER

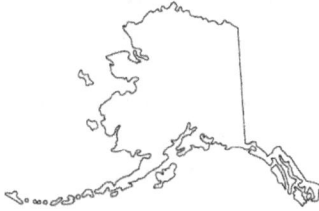

Two years pass by fast. Life has been much the same as the last ten. I'm trapping, doing the state fair, seeing my various friends off and on during the year. Every Thanksgiving is with Josh and Martha. I'm cutting trails, working on the boat, working on the homesteads. Most of the details are repetitive. Much I do not recall the time line on, especially things not going well, that I prefer not to focus on.

THE RELATIONSHIP with Sally is falling apart, but not all at once. In hindsight there is a progression downward. We get married sometime, I forget when. A small event by the local Nenana magistrate. It means a lot at the time. Sally tells me I am the one she wants to spend the rest of her life with. I guess that is as good as it gets. The word 'Love' was not used. I never thought of that. It's not a word in my vocabulary anyhow. It's not a nice word. *"Love is a sword in the heart you cannot remove" That is what I learned about Love from a young age.* We get divorced, I forget when. Not long after. Sally is in California with her mother living on welfare. "The government can take better care of me then you can Miles!" I'm tired of trying to prove different. That's her reality.

We visit my father sometime, I forget. Our child, 'Mitch' we call him, goes along with us, I guess. I forget, but it must be so. Sally wants to live like that! Wow, live like my father. *Who would not want to?* Anyone would be nuts not to want two cars, a nice home on Lake Champlain, a gazebo, a sailboat on your own dock, in a neighborhood of the elite class. A perfect environment for raising a child. No one, not one single person indicates they understand why I do not think it is so perfect. Everyone has sympathy for Sally and our child, tells me I need to change, that I can't raise a child in the wilds! Or, expect a woman to live where I do! "Good grief Miles, smarten up!" I am absolutely totally alone. In my life, I have gone through a lot of effort to live on the opposite end of the country, to get away from my parents and upbringing. To escape various influence and controls. I am not keeping notes. This is all stuff not suitable for a book. *Personal stuff involving people who do not wish to be written about. Sooooo, there is a big confusing gap.*

In my opinion, a true friend should at least acknowledge understanding my side, even if they do not agree. There is no such person. Therefore, I have no friends, as I'd define the word. That's the bottom line. Anyone can be your buddy when it's good times telling stories. The test of friendship is when it is under stress. Everyone thinks the world of Sally. My father sends money to her, paid for her to visit him without my knowledge. I called at Christmas to wish Dad happy holidays, and my 'X' answers the phone as if she lived there.

I have the love of the trail, homesteading, the lifestyle thrills. But, am I 'happy' deep inside? Am I getting out of life what I want? I mean beyond the laughs, jokes, stories I tell, autograph signing I do, shows I am asked to do, and exciting adventures I am having.

IT IS JANUARY OF 1991. A younger guy who pumps gas at the A frame gas station has been talking to me excitedly about trapping, and wanting to be a trapper, "Where can I trap?" He has been talking for months, asking for advice and my help, wanting to know if I can help him. Trapping is a one man operation in my mind, and I had received the advice long ago from more than one trapper not to take on a partner. Even Don the fur buyer had a story. Think told to me by someone else. How Don had a partner one year. They got into an argument over who would skin fur and who would cut firewood. Don shot his partner in the leg with a rifle.

On the other hand, I need to be nicer, work better with others. I need to give sympathy, and understand how it was for me when no one would help trying to get a trapline. How much harder my life was then it had to be. This Franko person has a snow machine, and is telling me how we can work together, me with dogs, him with machine, and how he can help me out. That might be true. Like during the problems I had with 'the kid,' who ran circles around me with his snow machine, and might have taken my trapline from me. That kid left and never came back. Had problems proving up on the homestead and lost it, like most do. Now others with fast snow machines zoom out and run circles around me. I cannot keep up.

A partner with a machine might maintain the trails better as 'our trapline.' So, Franko and I talk details about splitting the furs, and how it might work. We have been at this a few trips. I have shown him how to get to my place on the Kantishna, allowed him to stay and use my traps. In return, I get half the furs he catches. It has been a learning process for him, and he has no furs to share. He is still learning. Meanwhile this partnership is costing me time and energy.

It is a help having the trail broken open with a snow machine so the dogs can run better, and Franko cuts wood and does some chores that saves me time, so guess it is okay, but not as I envisioned. I'm at the cabin with Franko.

"So Franko, I need to take a trip back east to see my father. You know the routine now. You can run the whole line, and check all the traps, keep half the furs and I'll be back in two weeks." He is okay with that.

I COME BACK from my trip and Franko tells me, "Bummer Miles, all we caught the whole time you were gone is owls!" This seems mighty strange to me. I have caught an owl now and then that is going after the mice, that are going after the bait. It happens. If Franko told me he got two, I'd think it was interesting. Three, and that would be amazing! *But, all the traps is impossible*. There of course is no value in owls. So, he is telling me we made no money, and caught no fur. Not in 100 miles of trail in two weeks. Impossible. But, what can I say beyond "Amazing!" Still I am learning about this Franko kid, and see signs of a con artist, lair, and insincerity. Oh, he wants to trap, and has had that dream, and this dream is real all right. But, maybe he is in it for the money, and is unhappy with how long it is taking to learn the ropes. Combined with the desire to find an easy way out. He also might b taking advantage of the fact I'm vulnerable, having just lost my wife and son, and told I am worthless and selfish. I am thus motivated to help others right now. Find a friend. A like-minded person who loves the outdoors. Maybe I can be a mentor for this kid who is so full of energy.

When I get to the fur dealer next, I mention having a partner. I am seeing Dean this time not Don. I ask:

"So has my partner by any chance been in here with any furs?" Dean tells me yes, he does recall :

"Let me get out my receipts, it was not that long ago. Oh yes, here it is, $2,000." So Franko has ripped me off to the tune of $2,000. I get back to Franko at the homestead.

"So the fur dealer tells me you sold $2,000 worth of furs, so you owe me $1,000. I doubt if you have it, so I'll take it out in trade. You come up with stuff I need. Like I will take that barrel of gas you brought here, and any gear you have here I want. You need to leave, and we are no longer partners."

"Miles, you hurt my feelings! I forgot to tell you I got a friend who traps who asked me to bring his furs in to sell for him! Just a misunderstanding!"

"Franko, I do not care. We did not catch fifty owls in traps in two weeks. I can't prove it, and cannot prove you sold my furs. But I think you are full of crap. I cannot trust you, and this is the price of the parting of our ways. Consider it a lesson in life." Franko is not pleased, tells me it is me ripping him off. How part of this is his trapline now. "I worked for it, and deserve it, and will take it if I have to."

Tom and Forest, my long time neighbors, who I assume are friends out here, come to me upset that I have brought someone out here who does not belong here. "This Franko kid has been tearing up the dog trails we train on with his snow machine, and we think breaking in and stealing supplies from us!" So it is not just a problem for me, but my decision has now caused my friends misery. I feel bad for this. Yet I cannot stop Franko easily. He knows the trail and how to get here. It is a public trail. I am not here enough to stop him, as I am often away on the trail at the other end, or at the Tek land.

I am not sure of the exact feelings Tom and his wife have. Mostly we seem to get along, but they were also upset when my guide friend brought his clients into the country. They feel this has increased hunting pressure, and they partly blame me for this increased hunting. Sometimes I'm just trying to be a nice person, helping someone out, never dreaming these people would do anything to hurt me, or the land I love. After all, these people tell me how they admire the land, respect my lifestyle, and how we share the love of the land and its resources. It is not logical to then screw over the one you claim to admire. This is very strange. Life just seemed so much better when I was not in the position to know anyone, and make such friendly offers.

I put a lock on my remote cabin for the first time in my life, so Franko cannot get in without breaking in. I lay claim to all his gas and supplies, and secure them so he cannot take them back. He tells me he will call the police, and I tell him to go for it. Let us each tell our story. Not that I think anyone cares or wants to be bothered. The police are not coming out here to investigate who owns a barrel of gas.

"What barrel of gas?" I reply. Franko is pretty upset. But not long after his problems with me, he gets caught robbing the safe of the gas station where he works, and has more to worry about then me.

There is another fellow named 'Hans' from Switzerland, who I met as a tourist, and through my GEO article. He wants very much to see what Alaska is like in winter, and is paying me to be his personal guide. He will spend a month with me at the Kantishna cabin, and I pick him up soon. It is the first of February. I have done this sort of thing before, but not recorded it in my diary, so forget when and how often. Certainly never for a month! Usually it is someone I meet at the Nenana Cafe who wants to go out on the river for just a few hours. It reminds me of a village on the Amazon.

Imagine a tourist showing up, who wants to hire some local with a dugout to go see the river. See things from a locals viewpoint, take a few pictures. It's absurd to think in terms of contracts, receipts, insurance, and permits. Just an enterprising off the grid local, trying to give a tourist a good time, and make a few bucks for a meal or something, at the edge of the world. It's not exactly big money.

Now and then someone I meet has money, and wants to come back and do something more serious. See a rare bird. Hunt a bear. Run a dog team. Sometimes it goes well, and other times I'm sorry I offered. Now and then it is the highlight of someone's entire life, and I hear about it for decades. But after the Franko fiasco, I am leery of having any more visitors, but am committed now, so hope this Hans is a decent person!

He is about twenty-five, medium build, curly black hair, and has lots of enthusiasm. We dog mush out to the homestead without incident. Hans is thrilled by the whole experience. He runs the sled dogs about ten miles on his own, three days after he arrives. He wants to see what checking the trapline alone is like.

I have a snow machine running now, so I head for Nenana for supplies. Mostly Hans supplies. It's fifty below out, and the snow machine is hard to run. Steel crystallizes and can become brittle like glass. Sometimes bolts break on the ski, or other parts that get a lot of jolts. On the way back to the Kantishna, I get stuck on a hill and cannot get up. I have to unload the sled, turn the machine around, go back down, get the sled down, and get another run at the hill. All difficult, at these frigid cold temperatures, when it is hard to work with heavy mittens on.

I get within twenty-five miles of home – near the Chicago drop and get stuck in snow drifts. I have to unhook the sled and come home without the load. The drop at Chicago is more mild. Tom came and made a new way down that is more gentle. So at least my snow machine can get up it.

Hans and I go back with the dogs to fetch the load left behind. Weather warms up to plus ten, so we are comfortable now at least. Hans makes a big deal about the northern lights he has dreamed of for so long, now seeing it for real! We get along. He is funny. He has problems with English, so uses his hands a lot. Some of his literal translations are cute or funny, or teach me about my language. He tries to explain to me how he wants to build an igloo as a longtime dream he has had.

I try to explain to him how the igloo is a shelter of the north, in Eskimo country. Where the snow is the right consistency, all windblown, so bricks can be made of it.

"Our snow is interior, Alaska snow, deep and fluffy and no good for making bricks." But Hans shows me an article he cut out of a magazine. Saved with diagrams showing what an igloo looks like, and how to make the snow bench inside, with the entry way, and all this. He seems to see 'snow' out the window, thinks it is all the same, one word 'snow.' *The Eskimo has I hear twenty-six words for all the differences in kinds of snow.* But I do get an idea, and am curious myself if it might work. We can use snowshoes to trample down the snow, then let it set up overnight and become stiff. Possibly we could get bricks from it, thick enough for an igloo brick, maybe two feet thick.

I'm unsure if Hans understands, but we each have snowshoes on, tramping down an area where the snow gets deep on the creek. Next day we go out to see if we can make snow blocks. I know enough to understand we need a 'snow knife' to cut bricks. I use a machete, but make something longer and serrated out of wood for Hans. I point to the picture of a snow knife in the article he has, and put this tool in his hand and he understands.

We begin sort of okay, but it is easy to start an igloo. The first layer is bad looking, and rises a foot above the surrounding snow. Blocks can be lopsided and mismatched till we get to the 'leaning in' part halfway up the wall, to where eventually, we have it totally leaning in. There is a final brick that holds it all together. I have never done this, and am not sure here what to do. If it were me, depending on a shelter, I would maybe make such bricks, build a wall in a square or circle a few feet tall then lay spruce branches across the top and cover that with snow, or some solution like this. But, as I understand, Hans wants a traditional igloo, looking like the picture in his article. Okay. We get a first leaning row sort of, to begin the lean inward.

But the second row of leaner's is turning out to be a disaster, and I know the reason. We do not have the right snow, and the bricks are too soft and imperfect. But Hans insists this is not the problem.

"Bricks fine! Bricks fine!" In his heavy German accent, he keeps repeating this. They fall down and we try again. Hans stops me, "It is necessary to handle the bricks gently with great force!" He keeps saying this and I sigh, am frustrated, and once again try to explain with my hands- because obviously there is a language misunderstanding.

"Gently," I say, as I hold my left arm way out and shake it so he sees gently. I say "Great force," and hold my right hand far away saying "No meet." Trying to tell him again that 'gentle' and 'great force' are two concepts that do not meet. We can be gentle, we can use great force, we cannot do both. We argue and he swears, yes we can do both. Finally he tries explaining another way saying:

"You know, gentle, with great force, like you handle women!" Ah yes, now I understand. Somehow, we do in fact get the bricks to work, gently with great force. We laugh pretending we are dealing with a woman.

"It's all right honey, everything will be just fine." I say jokingly, as we push the block against the wall so it can't move. Eventually it stops struggling. To my amazement we actually end up with an igloo we can stand up in. Hans reviews the instructions on making the entry way so it does not let much cold air in. The sleep platform is exactly the right height with piled up snow. Hans shows me a picture of the seal oil lamp that heats such a structure. I get out the kerosene lantern, and show him how it is similar, and burns oil with a flame, just like the seal oil lamp. Possibly about the same size fire. For I have seen real heating seal oil lamps in museums, and there is a wick platform to put moss on, and I imagine a flame about like my lamp. Not a huge change in 50,000 years.

Hans and I both seem to share the basic wonder of the igloo. He wants to see how people lived in them, to have such an experience. So the plan as I understand it, is he is going to light this lamp and spend a night in here. He is not listening to the fact it is fifty below zero out, and there is no way this dinky wick light is going to heat this place enough to notice. That he is going to freeze his ears off.

But I get him a sleeping pad and sleeping bag. He lights the lantern and settles in for the night. It does bring up the question of just how did the Eskimo survive? One possibility is, there were big families, and there were lots of people in an igloo. That's like lots of heat given off. Also, maybe it was windy, but not cold temperatures, just cold wind chills. It rarely, if ever, gets to fifty below in igloo country. Maybe if the igloo is build on sea ice, there is some sort of sea ice warmth like thirty-two degree water under it, not fifty below ground. Hard to know without experiencing it. I'm just 100% certain there will be no warmth is this igloo.

In the morning I go to check on Hans, who has had hardly any sleep, and is shivering in the sleeping bag. But he is in a good mood and happy. But says to me:

"There is a hole in my pleasure!" *I love his translations from German to English.* I reply:

"Yes, and the cold air is coming in through this hole!" We both have a good laugh. It is very complicated getting Hans and all his things back out to civilization. He has a good time. An example of a decent human being, who it is a pleasure to be around. *Giving hope for the rest of the human race.* "Or more hope for me" I answer myself. I just need to somehow do better at spotting sane, nice, people, and associating with them.

Often times I think good, sane, kind, people see me, and understand I wish to be alone. So they leave me alone. Those who do not leave me alone might be the ones up to something, who want something, and are not looking out for my best interest. So, I am trying to make an attempt at not putting out, that I want to be totally alone. That it might be nice to have friends. *But we are as we are.* "Damaged," I answer.

Truth is, I tend not to remember your name till I have seen you around for a year or more, met you 100 times or so. You are an acquaintance in about five years. I sort of know you in about eight years. Maybe a friend, just 'maybe' after twenty years.

That's just me. Even if I greet you with honest enthusiasm, and am glad to see you. But I'm just as glad to see Bob or Bill or a tourist or a stranger. I act like I want social contact without commitment. The truth is almost the opposite.

TRIPOD DAYS in Nenana is coming up, and I have plans to set up at the bazaar to sell my art. This is early in February each year. A tripod is put out on the ice with a rope hooked to a stop clock. When the ice moves the tripod 100 feet at break up, the clock stops. People bet on the day, hour, and minute the clock will stop. Worth about 300 grand. Tickets are two dollars each. So, this is the day the tripod gets set on the ice. There is a big celebration for the event with dog races, dog weight pulls, contests of all kinds. There is a lot for kids like pie eating, and a dirty car-hart contest. Vendors set up in the Civic Center, paying a table fee to sell fur hats, homemade foods of all sorts, quilts, and other crafts. My 'usual table' is reserved for me by the door. It costs ten dollars. I'm staying on the houseboat that is parked in Nenana now again at tenth street on the Nenana River bank, near where Josh keeps his sled dogs. This is an event that allows me to get known, and I have people I see over and over, and begin to recognize over time.

Some consider me a friend, but I just smile and nod and only know them. Some I might go so far as remember their name. It all takes time. Lots of things just take time. It is enjoyable to do the shows though. It's a good experience for me, positive. People are in a good mood, making money, getting compliments and such. For years it was mostly the Tanana State Fair I did.

"Miles, good to see you here. Where are you living now?" I'm not sure who this is so I reply:

"Good to see you too! Well I have the houseboat here in Nenana. But spend some time on a new homestead up the Nenana River, and time on the Kantishna land. But guess Nenana is my home for now!"

"How is the art selling? You got it in New Horizons? Thought I recognized your work there."

"Yes, probably my work. I'm at Alaska House, New Horizons, the Artworks, and the Craft Shop with Crafty. I think that's it. I have more shops with my work on consignment. I'm unsure how I feel about it. A good half of my product on consignment I never see again, or get paid for. I repeat this often, but seem to forget. Shops go out of business, lose stuff, lose receipts, ownership changes, all sorts of excuses. So I have been trying to retail it myself as much as I can, doing more events during the year than in the past." We chat and whoever it is nods and moves on.

The train has brought tourists from Fairbanks to Nenana. So we have an unusual number of outside customers this year. The Tripod Days lasts two days, and I make

$600. Not bad for a ten dollar table! I chuckle and think in terms of a ten dollar investment, and two days wages making $300 a day.

IN APRIL the temperature is above fifty, so snow melts. I spend time at the Tek property getting the saw mill running. The sled dogs are used for hauling logs to the mill. From slab wood, I build a little greenhouse and have twenty-two plants that go in it that I have had started and growing on the window sill in the house. Siding is still going up on the house. I had plastic and insulation on the second floor, but am now doing the siding on the second floor. I am not sure why. This place holds no meaning for me. It was for my wife and son. They are gone.

In May after the ice breaks up, I boat into Nenana and hang out at the houseboat. Work needs to be done on it. The stove pipe is moved to exit out the side, because the roof leaks no matter what I do when the pipe exits out the roof. *Finally, I put an end to that!* There is a bicycle I bought for ten dollars that needs some adjusting. After it is fixed up, I have good transportation between tenth street and downtown Nenana.

It is time to prepare for summer. Seymour is called about summer survey work.

"Miles, good to hear from you! Looks like a big job in June by boat up the Kantishna again. Will you be available?"

"Sounds good Seymour. Whose homestead?"

"Well we have two or three, but the main one is Steve Sparks."

"Yes, I know him. Nice wife. Met him on the river once when he broke down on the way in for supplies. Anyhow, I'll call closer to the job date to see if there have been any changes, and get details on what to bring- how much gas, where and how to meet you, etc." *So looks like at least a little survey work for the summer.* At the post office I run into Martha, Josh's wife. She's still the postmaster.

"Miles, what do you hear from Sally?" I'm slightly miffed she asks about Sally before saying hi to me and asking how I am, or saying good to see me, or how was river break up for me.

"I got one letter before I went up the Tek for break up, guess she is fine, Mitch is fine."

"Yes, such a nice woman. I like her."

"Uh huh." I head on over to see what Josh is up to after Martha tells me he's in the house. The post office is just a few blocks from their home.

"Hi Miles, what do you hear from Doc?" Josh refers to Mitch as 'Doc' because he is convinced Mitch is a smart kid, and Sally has convinced Josh that Mitch is going to end up with Doctorate degrees like my father. Follow in my father's footsteps.

God forbid he follow in mine. I tell Josh pretty much what I told his wife. "Yup everything is just honky dory." Josh has company and introduces me.

"This is Miles, his father is head of a college back east! Wouldn't know it looking at Miles huh? Ha ha." I smile, nod. *Yes, what went wrong huh?* Josh admires my father more than he does me. But 'whatever' he's entitled to an opinion, and not much I can say about that, but suck it up. I do not mention that my father plans to help Sally put Mitch through private school. A school that has no art program, nor outdoor activity like sports, nor anything to do with working with your hands, just strictly academic. Now he can amount to something. My opinion as the father is not sought after. I'm told how it will be.

I decide I am not going to go to court and fight. It is the child in such cases that suffers, the lawyers who get rich, and it rarely seems to make anything better. Sally wanted a child more than anything in the whole world. I care about her. So let her have that which she wants so much. I cannot find it in my heart to deny it to her. To fight a lot about it. I feel I am stronger then she is. Mitch is her whole world, and she would fall apart to lose him, or to not have her chance to be the best mother she can be. I will take the pain because she cannot. Also, I know Sally will do her best and will be a good mother, and so our child is in good hands.

Anyhow, who am I to complain, to want things different then everyone else? Selfish of me. If I did go to court I'd lose. My family and friends would be on Sally's side. My father would pay for her lawyer. I'd stand alone broke, with no defense. I do not want to go through that. To declare war. Sometimes I fall apart. But, I explain to Sally that it is not anyone's fault. I am not angry at her. I am just 'hurt' by life, by reality, and when we hurt, who cares why, or who is at fault? There is a sword in our heart, and all we know is pain, and we want it removed. We know nothing else. Does it matter how the sword got there, or who put it there, Even if I stuck it in my own heart? But this is only sometimes. Other times I enjoy the life I have chosen.

It is hard not to enjoy spring time in Alaska. The geese and ducks fly in. I harvest two geese that are cooked in the woodstove on the houseboat. *Gosh, I sure love roasted goose*. Stuffed with cooked rice and apples with sage, basil and parsley dried from what I grow.

A new boating season is always exciting. Engine problems already though, and I sure better have a running engine when it is time to survey with Seymour! It's a never ending job keeping an engine running. Honda has just come out with a new four stroke engine, the first of its kind. If I can afford one someday, maybe this is the way to go. There is a fifty horse four stroke, equal to about a seventy horse two stroke. Four stroke means no mixing oil with the gas. It has a crankcase with oil under pressure like a car has. Heavy, but more reliable, and expected engine life is three times longer. For now, have to keep a fifty horse mercury two stroke running.

STILL WILD

In early June I meet Seymour at the mouth of the Kantishna. I get there first, make a fire, and start lunch. There is a creek nearby to catch fish, so I have something to do till Seymour arrives. When he arrives he explains the plan again.

"My boat will not haul everything we need to the job. There is not much point running two boats when yours can haul everything. So we can tie mine up and leave it here near the mouth of the Kantishna till we get back in a week." His load is transferred to my boat. "Oh yea, I brought my spare twenty horse to put in your boat in case we break down. You told me your spare horse is not working?"

"Yea Seymour, still problems with it. It runs but something is wrong. I think I will haul it to the homestead and leave it as a possible spare, or work on it there if I have idle time, sometime." We plan to leave some gas for the return trip home at my homestead which we pass along the way. Travel is much slower now as I have doubled my load, and we are going upstream instead of downstream. We have the boat maxed out at almost 2,000 pounds and going twelve miles an hour. I get paid by the hour as a boat operator, but want to see Seymour make money, and feel bad for the slow speed.

There is no time to go up to my cabin. We drop gas and my twenty horse off at the river bank on the main river, and do not canoe up the slough to the cabin. It is a record hot day, so it is good to be out on the water at least. About thirty miles upriver from my homestead near the Toklat River, Seymour spots what he thinks is a wolf out on the sandbar.

"See Miles, up on the left on the point in front of the drift wood?" It is strange for a wolf to hear an engine and stay out in the open like this. Stranger as well, to see a wolf alone this time of year. They should be part of a family unit. But here is a wolf staring at us, and even taking a step closer as we approach in the wide open with a screaming engine. In early June it might still have prime winter fur. Even though on this exact day is record heat, still the fur is prime based on a date of the year, more than anything else, in tune with daylight hours. I decide I will try to shoot it and save the fur since this is so easy, a gift almost.

I shut the engine off and wait till the boat is still for a good shot. I fire my 270 rifle I am familiar with, and am good with. The big wolf drops in its tracks. So I get the engine going again and idle up to the sandbar, pull up, and tie the boat to a driftwood snag. *Looks like a nice black wolf.* We think it might have wandered out of the park down the Toklat River, and never heard an engine, or seen a human in its life. This is still pretty wild country.

"Wow Miles, that was a good shot!" I rarely have a witness to a shot made, so do not think much about a good shot or not. It's just a normal shot for me. But I shoot a lot, and so it might be something I am okay at. I jump forward to fetch the dead wolf. Tail in my hands, I struggle to move him. He's big and heavy. As I begin to move him, the wolf's head comes up! So I drag faster, to get him to the boat, so we can thump him over the head or something.

Seymour begins laughing. It is hard to turn around and look. I have both arms on the tail over my shoulder pulling. The wolf is coming back to life, and trying to bite me on the butt.

"Shoot him Seymour!" But Seymour is laughing too hard. Somehow we manage to dispatch the wolf and get him in the boat. "Dang Seymour!" We have had our adventure for the day. The fur of the wolf is in bad shape. We now think the wolf was sickly, so it is as well I shot it. I will keep the fur, but probably the skull will be worth more.

It is dark before we arrive at Ketzler slough where our job begins. We are always nervous about how a job will pan out till we see it firsthand. It is especially hard on Seymour, who has bid on the job based on gut feeling as much as anything. Seymour has amazed me in the past with his ability to know almost to the nearest hour, how long a week job will take! But, much depends on our ability to get around.

"Miles, do you think we can get all the way up the slough to the Sparks property?"

"Pretty sure Seymour, looks like extra high water here, also, if Steve gets in here with supplies as the access to his land, we can get in too." But we run into an unexpected problem that can take up a lot of our time. We need to tie the homestead mathematically, to an existing monument someplace. We are expecting to tie it to another homestead near the mouth of the slough we have already done in the past. But it is up high on a bluff. How do we get off the bluff with our survey, up the slough, and up the bluff again to Sparks parcel? We end up having to set Seymour up in a piece of plywood in three feet of water. Worse, Seymour has to do a solar to fix our position. This requires sitting still and viewing the very edge of the sun twice, knowing the exact time and doing a triangulation. It is not done often, but sometimes is the only option we have.

There are a record number of hornet nests this season. We get stung a few times. My concern as saw man, is that I will be in thick brush sawing, and drop branches all around me. I might get into a nest and be unable to get out, or trip and fall. I used to be allergic to bees when a child, and have not had a reaction since. But, it indicates I have a low tolerance to stings, so might not be able to take many multiple bites. I'm not 'scared,' but it is just so much nicer when there are not so many nests around!

Camp is across the river at another parcel we will be surveying. The homesteader has got a wood platform to set a tent up on, and outdoor shelving to set a stove and gear on that we can use. We play the usual, 'who can kill the most mosquitoes with one swat' game, by swatting our knee and counting how many we got.

"Not as many as a few years ago when you got twenty-five, but eighteen is not bad!" In the evening I sharpen the saw while Rick cooks a pot of spaghetti with his wife's famous sauce. Seymour usually needs quiet time to do some calculations from today's work, to get us going for the next day. Later we sometimes review how we will approach the next stage. I have about 1,000 feet of line a day to cut, plus we survey the lines. Usually I only go 500 feet at a time. It's interesting work. Very physical. Cutting, climbing, hauling gear on our backs, eating lunch on the go. There are usually bears around. Sometimes grizzly.

A bear has been to the Sparks homestead since they were last here.

"Doesn't look like they got in the cabin Seymour, but tore up the snow machine, the dog sled, all the cans and buckets." Food and gear is scattered all over the property. Fresh bear scat is in the trail. We have to keep an eye out since the bears are nearby. One of the cabin walls is just off the property line! "Geez!" We talk a lot about how so often, homesteaders crowd a line and rarely build in the middle of their land. Out here, who will care? But some day it might be a problem if there are ever any neighbors.

Just as Seymour predicted, in exactly seven days we are done surveying. We stop long enough at my homestead on the lower river for me to get my twenty horse engine up in the woods better, and verify my canoe is still safe on the beaver damn. The trip down is much faster. We have left all the monuments and markers lath, eaten most of the food, and burned most of the gas.

A bear got into Seymour's boat, but seems to not have done any damage. "There might be another job in the fall Miles." Seymour will let me know.

Sally has a friend who has dreamed of coming to Alaska all his life. She asks me for a favor. "Take him out on a moose hunt please? It would mean the world to him." He is willing to pay for the trip. He wants to come this season, early in September. This can work out good for me because I need to make a trip to the homestead, and can't afford the gas. This also gives me a chance to get my own moose, or share the moose this Dave friend might get. He is sort of looking for a trophy more than the meat.

I'm not excited about taking a trophy hunter out. My hunting is strictly about eating. I care about Sally, and I don't want to look like a schmuck. This guy would be really happy, and it's not a hard thing to offer. So Dave writes and introduces himself, telling me how excited he is. He is a policeman, and has been hunting all over the world, even though he does not have a lot of money. This is how he spends it. He has hunted big game in Africa. He knows all about the wilds, taking care of himself in the woods, and will be no problem to me. He has a lot of courage facing game. So he tells me. I got it.

It does not register, but it seemed just a little odd to mention all that. It never occurred to me he might not be brave enough, or capable enough in the woods, or unable to shoot something. All that sort of stuff you just deal with as you go along. But anyhow, I advise him what to bring for clothing, how much money I need and all that. Legally I can only ask for expenses. In truth I do not get more than that. Money is not my God. It matters more to me that someone have a great experience.

I have told Sally many times I still probably will never be rich with money, and one reason is because that is not my goal. For too many people, 'money' is the objective. We tend to get what we seek. If we do not seek something, it is unlikely we will get it. But anyhow, this Dave Guy arrives and once again is pretty excited to go out on a hunt.

He's a big man. Easy to see how he is a cop. Muscular, kind of leans forward like he is off balance, like a practiced look of intimidation maybe, or 'presence.' *Showing off his size?* But charming enough. Full of compliments on Alaska, of me, of my lifestyle, and how he admires it, and he wants to be 'one of us.' Part of the same tribe. An exclusive group of those who understand each other. The sort who sits around the campfire telling hunting stories while sharpening knives and cleaning guns. I simply find this interesting, and do not comment much.

Without being aware of it, Dave is assuming we sing from the same sheet of music and are comrades, that I am someone who can be trusted. I only think of it as being polite. I'm not really interested in being friends, or being from the same tribe. I want him to have a good wilderness experience and hunt, not be my friend.

"Wow Miles, this is really wild out here all right!" I only smile and nod. We are not even to Old Minto yet, thirty-five miles out. But we have seen a few geese, a lone swan. Maybe it is more what we have not seen that impresses Dave.

"No road, no plane, no noise, no footprints, no cabins, no cement, no beer cans, no old tires." I guess it has been a while since I thought about that, and I think back to the days I had the same impression. Now the surprise would be to see human sign. I point out Old Minto as we go by and explain it has no road access, just the river. New Minto, much further away has a road and runway, but the only way here to this village is by river, or dogs- snow machine in winter.

"Miles when can we expect to see a moose?"

"Well it's legal to hunt anyplace from where we left to where we are going, and moose get shot all up and down the river. But, the hunting pressure is the easy access, like where we are now. It would take luck to have a moose show itself on the main river. That sort of stupidity gets culled from the gene pool fast. The big moose live to be old by staying off the main river. Our chances increase as we get further away." Dave asks about bears, and he got his bear tags, and can hunt bear too. "Yes, there might be a bear at the cabin. That would be the most likely place to get one."

"Bears at the cabin? Geez Miles, how do you deal with that!" He talks as if this is brave. Never thought in those terms. *Bears are just part of my world*. Why should I be afraid? I can shoot them if I think they represent a threat. *Fear is all about people!* But I do not bother to say anything. Dave thinks I'm bragging and trying to impress him. He tries to one up me by telling me harrowing big game experiences he has been involved in.

"There was this Cape buffalo once in a swamp I had trouble putting down." I'm only partly listening as I watch the river. It is hard to hear over the scream of the engine anyhow. All about his 458. *Now it's time to talk guns*. I just nod that I heard and understand. *He would not be impressed with my 270*. He'd call that a small deer gun. With talking guns, the bigger the number, the bigger the gun, pretty much. Usually the number designates the caliber measured in parts of an inch or in millimeters. The projectile for my 270 for example is .270 inches in diameter. Just shy if a 30 caliber, at .30 of an inch across. .458 does not sound like much difference, from .3. A tenth of an inch or so. But represents maybe three times the horsepower.

I notice Dave seems nervous or something, the further in the wild we get. Sort of like he is talking to himself more than he is to me. Like he's scared or something. *But that can't be. What is there to be scared of?* So I dismiss the thought. But he's sweating, looking around a lot, and talking faster. I am not paying much attention. There is a dark rain cloud forming off to the side of us in the distance. Probably not coming our way, but amazingly dark, black, with streaks of gray rain pouring down. It almost looks like a tornado. It can't be of course, but when we get around a bend in the river it is straight ahead. When we make a turn it is off to my left. I slow the boat a little and turn the boat so I can see it as this massive black wall builds.

"Ma- Miles! Is everything okay with the engine?" Dave is mightily nervous for some reason.

"Sure, sorry. Isn't that cloud over their amazing!" I'm in awe, want to see it a minute and take it in. A freak of nature. It's beautiful. I assumed someone else from my tribe who loves the wild would feel the kinship. I expected him to smile, nod in the affirmative, that it's beautiful and awesome. *Seymour would understood slowing up to watch.* Anyhow, we get to the homestead in the usual six hours I expected, almost to the minute.

Dave is excited to be here where we hope to hunt.

"Miles look at these monster tracks!" There are tracks in the river silt where we are parking the boat. I do not want to hurt his feelings or insult his abilities but point out.

"Pretty big for a cow all right. Maybe the bull is nearby!" The tracks were in fact ordinary, and probably made in spring, months ago, because nearby are tiny calf tracks that look to me to be associated with the cow tracks. And a calf leaving tracks that small would be only a few weeks old. Dating the tracks at mid-May. But, also meaning this cow is not coming into season this year, so will not be attracting the bulls we want. A cow moose has a calf and keeps it for a season, so does not come into heat the next year. The calf gets kicked out at two years old and the cow is ready to breed again. So what we want to see in September is a set of cow tracks with no calf tracks nearby.

If the calf is a bull – he might be nearby and stupid, being new on his own. Such a moose will stand there and look at you with the innocence of a teen. An easy target. The mulligan moose. But Dave here would not be as interested. He wants the big one. I try to explain some of this, but Dave keeps interrupting with his own hunting stories. Talking loud. I assume he thinks I'm trying to make him look bad, or brag about my knowledge, and I'm not. I just keep quiet now, and let him think what he wants, hunt how he wants, but in fact cutting his chances of getting what he wants in half.

"So Miles, where is the tree stand?"

" Dave, that is one way to hunt, especially in more populated areas. But this is not the most effective way out in this area in my opinion. A month ago the moose were living in a pattern of habit, following the same trail at the same time. But in September the habits begin to change as the rut begins. The bulls we want are less predictable in their habits. They are changing territory, moving around, figuring out where the eligible cows are. We cannot predict ahead of time where these cows are. Because of this, a tree stand might work if we are lucky and there is a cow in season here. Or, overlooking a long stretch where random bulls might be expected to pass by." But Dave is not very interested in what I have to say.

"On all the hunts I have been on we use stands and beaters!" Said firmly, as if giving orders. I do not know what to say. We have no slaves around to do the driving of the game. I have no stands I built that I hunt from. Dave assumed there would be wild Indians around who would do our biding? I'm not sure what he is thinking. Dave also wants to sleep in late, then hunt in the warmth of bright sun at mid-day. This is the worse time to hunt moose. Moose are creatures of the night. Or at least sunset, and sunrise are the good times to hunt. Good rifle scopes that gather light that give an extra half hour of hunting time at dusk can be very productive.

But, if Dave wants to hunt at noon? What's it to me? *"We shall hunt at noon Sir!"* He wants to be the boss. The one in charge. Everyone else is stupid. Okay. Whatever. I just think it is humorous. He's still a likeable person, and I enjoy talking to him. We have about ten days to hunt, or this is the time he allowed. So on day two I set Dave on a high spot I know of, overlooking a lake and grassy area that is as likely a spot as any to find a moose at noon.

Not surprisingly, when I pick him up at the end of the day and he tells me he saw no moose of any kind, but lots of tracks. I smile and nod and look concerned. Dave is in good spirits though, as he saw a beaver, an otter and a bald eagle. But I want him to get a moose and have the experience he came for.

"I have the canoe here Dave. I think it might work well to drift one of the long sloughs no one can get a regular boat through." We have heard a few other hunters go by as moose season gets going. I can drop Dave off upstream with the canoe and his lunch. He can drift slow all day, stop here and there to look in on grassy places, and end up at the end of the day at the mouth of the slough where I can meet him. "This is at least more interesting than sitting in one place all day long staring at the same grass!" he chuckles and agrees.

On the way to the long slough I have in mind, we go by a shortcut I duck into, where there is an old cabin from years ago. A trail there goes to a lake, but it is not great hunting because the lake is too far to haul a moose if we get one. But, I just want to look in and see what the area looks like. I tell Dave: "There has been someone coming by here every year killing a cow moose each year. And here is a gut pile and evidence someone has just killed a cow moose in the past week. Dang. Dave, taking a cow now and then is understandable if you are hungry. But to come here as a hunter from outside the area, and kill a cow in the same spot year after year hurts the moose population in the area, and it happens to be an area I depend on and live in." I have never seen anyone here, so do not know who it is.

At the end of day three Dave has seen only tracks and is frustrated. *Of course! The moose are all around, but they are sleeping when you have chosen to do your hunting against my advice.* But I do not say anything, nor have an, 'I told you so' attitude. I nod with sympathy, and wish him better luck tomorrow. While he is hunting, I am working on the cabin. Cleaning up, fixing the cache, cutting the tall grass, and just the chores that need doing. If I run out of things to do, I can always cut firewood and leave it for when I come here exhausted, and have no time to go look for wood. In the evening Dave loosens up and tells me about his life.

"Yea, we are alike Miles. You understand. You also love to hunt and kill things. It's in the blood." I'm thinking yea well for sure I like to hunt, but the killing is not the enjoyment, it is the sad necessity. Or maybe no, but at least just one part of a long process filled with many memories. But I do not know Dave well enough to discuss such things. I just let him ramble.

"As a cop I get to engage in the greatest hunt of all." He pauses to see if I catch his meaning. He goes on, "There is a list of people, call it a hit list. People who do not deserve to live, or who no one cares about. Unproductive people, chronic criminals that there is basically open season on." Another significant pause, to see if I get what he is talking about. He's expecting I think a, 'Wow, this sounds interesting and fun!' But I play dumb. He goes on, "No one cares overly much if the scum is weeded out." I am listening, and taking this in, it's interesting. "So my friends and I go hunt them down. Chase them through the streets." I'm curious about this list. Who is on it, how those on it get there. I'm curious how common this is. Here is a cop out of the blue who says he has other like-minded cops who declare open season on human beings, chase them down and kill them. He's not saying, but guessing most of the hunted are black.

If I said I was being chased by cops who were out to kill me, hunting me down like an animal, I'd be called crazy, deluded, paranoid, and locked up as insane. I only nod to Dave like I understand. I do reply:

'Well we aren't all created equal that's for sure." My meaning, I am sure he is not picking up on, is what a low life he is.

"You got that right buddy!" If this guy and my X are good friends, I have more insight now into where she is coming from, and how she feels about lower class people like me. I have a vivid image of a human being running the streets screaming for help, but worse. The police able to track him. If he goes to the bank, an ATM, he is on camera. His address is known, as well as the address of his parents, all his friends, where he works. There is nowhere to hide. It's great practice for the police. They let him run, reel him in, let him run again. Play with him for a month. When Dave gets tired, catch this guy someplace and torture him before killing him. "He was armed, we were afraid for our lives!" *Get a medal for it.*

The next day I tell Dave I want to work on the boat engine. "You can use the canoe today, maybe up and down this creek."

"Is the engine okay Miles, maybe we should go to town!" The water pump has been getting weak. I have not had the money to buy a new one. I think it will hold up for the rest of this season, but it might be at least part of the problem. I can look at the water pump and make sure all the fins are still on the rubber impeller, and there is no metal of the housing peeled off cutting the impeller. If so, I might be able to tweak the pump and get more out of it.

"Well Dave, for sure we do not need to go to town. I want to tweak the water pump, it's running a little hot. Not serious, but want to do some prevention here. No big deal."

"If the engine is not right. that's a big deal, I'd think. We need to go to town for parts, or haul it in to be fixed by someone who knows what they are doing!" Dave appears to be moving into panic mode. He is someone who feels 'safe' in civilization. If anything at all looks even slightly wobbly, it's 'rush back to town to safety,' time. The wilderness is not his home, and is not his friend. "So Miles, why not use the spare twenty horse to get us to town?"

"Dave, the spare is needing work too, and might make it and might not." "Nothing is reliable then Miles, that you have for transportation! Is that what you are telling me!" I try to point out the facts of the matter.

"Dave, if worse comes to worse, we can float to Manley Hot Springs. It might be four days getting there, but floating is a good way to hunt. It's safe, we are not pressed for time. We'd get to Manley, and there is a mail plane you can fly to Fairbanks on, and head on out. I have friends there who could help me out." I'm explaining the worst case. "If the engine looks like it is going to give us trouble, probably I'd keep hunting and keep an eye out for someone I know who is headed back to town, who is out here hunting now. Maybe have them bring a message to someone in Nenana to try to bring me a part out when they come up here hunting. Or, have the local bush pilot we all fly with fly the part in." *I doubt very much it would come to that.* I'm pretty sure I can improve the engine by working on it. Maybe it will not be new again, but it will work for the rest of the season.

I figure it's more my business then his, it's not his engine. I can get him home, that's all that should matter. But again, I pick up on what he is used to. He likes being in control. He is controlling his temper as he knows if he messes with me and starts a serious fight, I might leave him out here. Probably I would not, no matter what, but he does not know that. He knows what he would do in my shoes. *Tell the son of a bitch to walk.*

But now Dave can't stop talking about the engine, and is not talking about hunting. He can't hardly sleep. He thinks we are in deep trouble. I think about it and sigh. It's not that big a deal to head home with Dave. He is not going to get a moose the way he is hunting anyhow. Go back early. Maybe pretend to hunt on the way home. There is a slim chance of getting a moose along with everyone else running the river. But not in the day time, but heck, all I can do is my best.

"So Dave, let's head for Nenana. The main fifty horse runs, and the twenty probably runs, so we'll just go for it and I can fix everything up in town. We can hunt on the way in." Dave practically jumps for joy. He gobbles down breakfast, dashes to the canoe with his sleeping bag and gear and waits for me to follow. I can see well enough there is no use trying to hunt, he's had his fill. I only inwardly sigh because this is not a good plan.

I am leaving without having torn down the engine to look at the water pump as I want. I am therefore not totally trusting the engine. Sort of a cross my fingers and hope situation. Get this guy back to civilization and get on with my life. *Take a chance on this trip, because this fellow is freaking out.* As I explained to Dave, if I tore into the water pump and saw disaster, I'd wait for a boat headed downriver and send a note to civilization. Someone like Josh would make arrangements, know who is headed up this way hunting in the next week or two. Bring me a new water pump, or whatever. Wait here at the cabin enjoying life in relax mode till the parts arrive. Maybe even get a moose with the canoe while waiting. Not even an emergency, just normal life here.

As BAD LUCK would have it, we are not thirty miles and the main fifty horse overheats, so I shut it down. I am sure now all I need is a water pump. The engine has not seized up, but we cannot run it. The pump probably pulled in some sand and burned it up, melted the rubber fins in the pump. I should have had a spare, and used to have a spare water pump. Instead I have the spare twenty horse, so did not keep up as much with all the spare this and that for the big engine. It's not life threatening, so financial priorities went elsewhere.

Dave is in stuttering mode as I hook up the spare engine Seymour and I had just hauled out here. And dang, wouldn't you know how bad luck runs in streaks. The twenty horse goes belly up on us after a couple of hours running. I only sigh. It means a three day float from here, maybe only two days, to Manley Hot Springs. I could actually enjoy the float. The peace and quiet without the scream of an engine. Weather is Indian summer perfect, calm blue sky, seventy degrees. We have a week's worth of food on board. We have all we need for a comfortable camp.

"Well Dave," I say into the silent void, "It's a good way to hunt. Quiet. I do not hear any other boats around. I'll sit on the bow with the paddle and steer us. We'll be going about six miles an hour. We'll be in Manley in two days. Probably only one overnight in the tents. It's just another adventure. I have friends who can drive you, or us from there to Fairbanks, or you can fly!" I have a no big deal attitude. I'm trying hard not to instill panic in an unstable man.

"What do you mean Miles, 'float.' We can't float! We need help! We need to be rescued!" He is scared to spend a night in a tent on the bank with bears around, and thinks someone needs to stay up all night taking turns being bear guard. Dave comes unglued when I transfer gas.

"Geez Miles, you are going to blow us up! Don't you have a transfer pump!" I am pouring a five gallon can of gas into the fuel tank as we drift, just for a chore to take care of. There is no open flame, and there is not even an engine running. But yes, we can smell gas and see the gas. Yes, a few splashes goober out and spangle on the outside of the tank. Oh yes, I suppose it could be more than a thimble full, and as much as a few tablespoons. It might be as much as a cup. *And? Your point is? A transfer pump? What planet is he from?* The fumes will blow away in a minute, and all evaporate in a short enough time. Ignite by what means? Unless he pulls a lighter out.

"I've transferred gas like this for almost twenty years, and so has everyone I know. I never even heard of anyone who blew themselves up doing it. I wouldn't have begun the pouring if I knew it would bother you. Sorry." He acts like I am messing with him on purpose. *But hark? Don't I hear a boat engine coming towards us coming from yonder bend?*

"Miles! Miles! I hear a boat engine! we can get rescued!" Before I can comment, he takes his shirt off, then his white undershirt off, and ties it to the boat pole, and begins waving it in the air. Even before we see a boat. Finally, a boat slowly comes into view loaded for moose hunting further upriver.

I recognize the family. This is Hank Ketzler, from Ketzler slough where Seymour and I surveyed. Hank comes within talking distance, and slows up at the site of the white flag and yelling. Hank looks both concerned and puzzled. He addresses me.

"Is everything okay?" It is hard for us to hear each other over the yells of:

"Save us take us back to Nenana, help!" I calmly and politely reply:

"Yup, fine. Some engine trouble, no big deal. We have food and are hunting by floating. We'll be in Manley tomorrow." Hank nods, he understands, and simply says:

"Have a nice hunt. See you around. Bye." Because all of us river people have had this happen, float to Manley. Dang. As long as we remembered to have enough food and have a tent and basic supplies and weather is warm, it's just a normal event. Something we forget a few months later saying:

"Oh yea, and I floated to Manley, forgot to mention." But here is this Dave outsider.

"Help! Help! Please! You have to turn around. We are broke down." Hank looks concerned that this person is bonkers. Hank politely replies:

" No. We are going hunting, and see no need to turn around and give up our moose hunt. Miles knows what he is doing. Have a nice float," and revs up his engine and takes off. Dave is almost ready to jump in the river to try to get in the boat with a running engine. It dawns on me again, this is Sally's friend. *I wonder if everyone from California is like this, or if like-minded people hang together?* It's just a brief thought as I flash on Sally's expression, and it was a lot like Dave's.

I flash on the conversation they will have when next they see each other. Dave saying:

"And then both engines broke. And I trusted him, but enough is enough! Then, can you believe it, he pulls out a crescent wrench and screwdriver and he thinks he's going to fix it!" her saying, "Oh yes, I believe it all right." "Then he almost blows us up! I'm lucky to still be alive, I tell you! Too proud to accept a rescue. He can die if he wants, but dang if I want him taking me with him!" Yes, I can imagine the conversation. Proving that the more I try to look good, the more I prove how messed up I am – in the eyes of people who are non-believers.

I wonder now if Dave will pull out his rifle and order Hank to turn around, or even begin shooting. He's pretty disappointed and in shock. He's used to a world where, when he talks, people jump.

Not long after Hank goes by, we hear a rifle shot! My first thought is, *Someone just got a moose!* I know this floating is a good way to hunt, and I have my rifle within reach, and eye out for a moose on the river bank as I steer with the paddle. This is getting to the time of day the bulls might be expected to be waking up and beginning to come down to the water for a drink *and brush their teeth.*

Around the next bend we see a boat. I recognize it as Seymour's, my survey boss! We pull in and Seymour is just coming out with the gear he needs to butcher a moose. He greets us, and is glad to have help skinning and hauling. Dave is excited I think, and interested in seeing the moose, and being part of the butchering. He has seen a big bull now, and knows they do exist out here after all. It's not a dream or illusion. It takes a few hours to butcher the moose as the day ends. We all make camp here with a big communal fire, tents all around it. The bull has to be hauled out of a grassy swamp in pieces on a tarp. Seymour tells us:

"Yes, I had to go in and look. I did not see him from the boat. I saw a clearing through the trees, and thought I'd stop and investigate. At first I only saw a cow! But the bull showed itself when I banged on the brush." Around an evening fire we exchange hunting tales.

In the morning Dave wants his picture holding the moose rack. Seymour whispers to me:

"How much you want to bet he says he killed it and has this picture on his desk!" Seymour explains that yes he can haul up both to Manley. I assume then, that Dave has secretly asked for a ride. It means I have to tie up my boat and get a ride back here to the boat somehow. It complicates my life a great deal. I will need a way back to my boat now. It is easy to get Dave to Manley. But I will deal with it as I must later. First thing is to rescue Dave. Or more, be part of Seymour's rescue.

Dave has not made any offer to chip in for gas, or help in any way. He has mostly only watched us butcher the moose. Claiming he did not know how. Seymour did not seem to care for him much. As such, he assigned Dave the seat furthest back near the noisy engine, and offered me the seat closer to the front and steering so he and I could talk. Beggars can't be choosers. The back seat has a little bit of spray blowing in the boat coming off the side as we are very loaded, and throwing up quite a wake.

"Hey guys, how about some consideration back here, it's wet!" Dave expected a more privileged seat. He wanted me to sit where he is and get wet. Someone had to be there. Dave has a raincoat, so should not be getting wet, it just was like a mist, like a light rain. Seymour asked him if he wanted to walk. It's like hitch hiking, and then complaining about the ride.

So, we get to Manley in a few hours instead of a long day if we floated. It is a sixty mile ride. Maybe a ten hour float.

A ride to Fairbanks is lined up. I am expected to pay for the gas, not Dave, because it is me who got us into this mess. I'm lucky I do not get sued! In Fairbanks, Dave is in civilization, so knows what to do, and takes off on his own. I do not recall a thank you, or good luck with the boat engine. He's looking out for number one.

I stay with Crafty at his Craft shop in the room he keeps for me. I am able to use the phone for local calls. My dentist friend is in need of getting away and will be glad to fly me to my boat with his float plane if I buy the gas. About $40. Dave pays me nothing, so this 'fiasco,' is costing me big time.

My friend Will helps me get to the boat shop, where I buy a water pump, $150. I'm flown out, and the dentist needs to get back, so just drops me off with his float plane, at the tied off boat on the river, and wishes me luck and is gone. The weather is getting a little colder. I have to stand in a foot of water to work on the back of the engine. It is time consuming with a screwdriver and crescent wrench to take the lower unit off and get the old water pump off.

I get the new pump out of the box. I frown. It is not the right size. The worker at the boat shop had handed out the wrong water pump. He will tell me it is no big deal, apologize, and hand me the right one, or give me my money back. Meanwhile, *now what?* When I look at the new water pump, I see the impeller has the right diameter shaft hole, so it will fit on my shaft. The housing of the old pump is not in terrible shape and could be used. But, the impeller is not going to fit right. I'd have to file a flat spot for a key that matches the flat spot on the shaft. And some other small alterations. There are not enough tools with me to do the alterations. But back at the homestead are the right tools.

I can walk thirty miles home, and use the canoe to come back with the tools. It would be faster and cheaper then floating to Manley and then trying to fix it there, and trying to boat back to Nenana. There is one part I need that I have at the homestead off an old engine I once had that is like this one. So I begin the walk, carrying a back pack with some food, sleeping bag and basic survival gear. I'm guessing I can be home in ten hours. The distance walking will be less than running the river, I can walk some shortcuts across bends in the river.

After five hours of walking I hear a boat engine coming from downstream headed up my direction. With excitement I scramble down the river bank and make my way to an open sandbar. *It is Tom my neighbor!* Cool, a ride the rest of the way, how slick is that! Talk about good luck!

As he comes around the corner I see him plainly. I am in the open, and I am sure he sees me just as plain, but I wave to get his attention anyway. He slows down and I wait. But then he passes me! He had only slowed up to get through a narrow spot in the river. I realize now, the sun must have been in his eyes as he looked in my direction and was concentrating on running the channel, and never saw me!

My 357 magnum pistol comes out and I fire three times in the air to get his attention. Tom looks back at his engine, then ahead and on around the bend. *He must have heard the shots but thought it was some sound coming from his engine.* Dang! It is disheartening. But, oh well. I am not tired, and I had planned to walk the whole way to begin with. I am in shape from walking, and cutting, carrying gear while surveying all day long. There are creeks to cross and a slough to wade across waist deep. But not a huge big deal, as this is normal as well when surveying. Working wet all day is normal.

I will not get home by dark, but guessed I might not. I am near Tom's place, and walk on in to spend a night with Tom and Forest. I simply say hi with a smile, and a matter of fact tell them I'm walking home. My boat broke down. Tom is sorry, says he never saw me. No big deal. I appreciate being able to spend a night here. I have six miles to walk in the morning. Tom would give me a ride, but they are on a deadline and have to get things done, as a plane is coming and they have to get the boat out of the water first. I do not expect a ride, and am happy to walk. I have walked twenty-five miles so far, so what's another six miles? I actually prefer this kind of neighbor and consider these two good neighbors. I don't appreciate neighbors who come around a lot wanting to borrow stuff, expecting help, favors, and my time.

I am home in a couple of hours. I rest up a little and grab up the tools and parts needed. Dave had been asked to shut off the battery power as we left, and he insisted he had done so. But the power was left on, there was a drain from someplace that made the batteries totally dead. The solar panel switch to charge is off. Probably Dave had flipped the wrong switch by accident. My own fault for not checking, but still it cost me a good $100 in damage to the batteries. It had been Dave who insisted on running the battery lights till way in the morning when it was time to go, and not wanted me to shut down as my normal routine dictates.

Also, the tools I need are here, were here before we left. My pilot friend could have landed right here with the part. My hunting friends who stopped would have come but here and I could have got a message out through them. Meaning without my guest with me, none of this would be happening.

The same day I arrive, I take off in the canoe. Before dark I am back at the boat. The parts and the impeller are adapted. New bolts I brought will fit. I file the slot like I know needs doing. The key holds the impeller in place as it should. In theory, as good as new. The lower unit is put on, and it is pitch dark.

There is a tent and everything I need with me, so I spend a pleasant night up on the river bank. No sense being nervous, in a hurry, or stressed out. A feeling of being 'home' where I belong. Even a feeling of missing this life. Not looking forward to boating to Nenana. But no trepidation, just acceptance.

The canoe is loaded in the boat. The fixed engine runs fine. Without Dave and his gear I can afford the weight and space of the canoe. I'm back in Nenana, I suppose about the same time I was expected back. Gene is at the boat landing as I pull in, and makes some rude comment I cannot hear over my engine. Something about fishing this fall for salmon up the Nenana River, we will not be able to, and how it is my fault. I pay him no mind.

But Bear tells me in a more sane language. A Fish and Game officer has put the word out to all of us that it is illegal to fish with nets on the Nenana River, because it is a spawning river for salmon. The law clearly states no netting in spawning streams! I was the one catching the most fish and had the bigger dog team to feed. Feeding sled dogs salmon is a controversial subject with the public and Fish and Game. I think because sled dogs is a big factor in the definition of 'subsistence.' Which by law is supposed to have priority over human consumption of the resource, which is in conflict with financially lucrative commercial interests. Fish and Game might like subsistence to quietly disappear and become a non-issue.

Bearfoot is not very interested in politics, or 'why' we are being told to stop. A few others aren't interested either. It's simpler to listen to Gene, easier to focus anger at Miles. Again I am in hopes smart people will figure it out, and not buy into Genes world. But, meanwhile a crimp is put in my life. A kink in the hose. *How am I going to support a dog team now?* How can I live my subsistence life?

Without Sally around I have little use for the Tek land. Sally has told me to just give it back to the state! She does not want to talk about it, or have anything to do with it. The land is legally in her name. This is frustrating to me. She sees zero value in this land, the cabin, or the work we did. But no, I mean 'I' did. Maybe that is what it all comes down to. None of her money got invested in anything. It was me who built the cabin, ran the mill and paid with blood and sweat. It was my time involved. She invested nothing. Thus, it is easy for her to say "Give it back."

Give up your home you built? For why? Let the state sell it off and keep a surveyed piece of land and home? I think not! Sally and I have different opinions, and ways of dealing with life and problems. It is my belief this piece of land and cabin probably will be the most valuable thing Sally ever owns in her life. She is now living a life on welfare, and probably will be renting all her life. What's wrong with fighting for what's ours, and keeping it, even as an investment? I add:

"For Mitch!" Someday it could be his home or the sale of it could put him through college! "River frontage property will be in demand and go up in value. One day homesteading will stop and the only practical wild property to be had will be original homesteads like this." Sally never says she agrees, understands, or believes me, but latches on to 'Someday Mitch might get money.' What's it to her anyhow, if I want to keep making payments! Go for it! But she wants nothing to do with it, yet it's hers, not mine, and she is insistent she is not turning it over to me. She'd rather let the state have it then me. What's that all about? Spite? The option to prove up on this land is lost now because the owner is not living on the land. Two years of proving up is lost as 'nothing.'

Forced now to buy it from the state as one of the options to acquire it. This is aggravating, because the whole concept of how my lifestyle works, is that I have things like land, without paying money, like offering my time to prove up instead of using cash.

"Miles, realistically we just can't afford what would suit both of us!" She does not want me to live that kind of life in misery stuck in debt. This situation reminds her to much of the situation her own parents were in staying together for the sake of the kids. Dads nose was to the grindstone till he died of overwork in misery. This part of her thinking I understand.

We looked at a few places we could maybe afford, but places I could not use the GI bill on because these pieces of land we looked at could not be insured and would be owner financed and such. Run down shacks that are hard to heat and leak when it rains. No big deal to me, but maybe reminds Sally of poverty or something. But 'hello!' we are in fact financially poor.

I am not used to that. Gosh. I never saw myself as poor. Geez, when I am not around people, I own the world. I'm king of all I see as far as the eye goes. I'm the richest man on the planet. I envy no one. I bow to no one. All I want, I have. So Sally speaks of is new to me kind of, or it is all brought to a head. 'This' is what my father sees, trying to make ends meet in some ho-dunk run down town in a shanty. This is what everyone is telling me a good education avoids. I have no answers for the family.

So much of this stuff is on my mind as I ponder where to live and how to live. Changes are going on. I can't live my subsistence life that I know, understand, and can survive well living at. On the Tek land, I can't fish, there are too many neighbors, it is too close to civilization, and all of us are expected to live by civilized rules.

I might move back to the Kantishna lower river homestead where I lived when I met Sally? Maybe go back to my original plans and expand out to my Bearpaw property, and the old Hansen Lake area I love so much? It is hard to ever go backwards once we move forward, 'back' is never the same again. There have been slow changes over a ten year period.

The Kantishna homestead.

CHAPTER TEN

STOLEN RIFLE STORY ENDS. HOMESTEAD PAPERWORK ISSUES. MORE GENE PROBLEMS. TRAPPING AGAIN WITH THE DOGS. MOOSE HUNT WITH THE SLED DOGS

The pipeline days of the 70's and early 80's is over. The big Alaska money is not around as it once was. I keep mentioning that, but it becomes more evident with each passing year. Thus, the whole Alaska economy feels it. It is harder selling the art fast. I need to do shows, bazaars, and push my work now. With my art, there is much more competition with third world country products. There are more Alaskan artists competing, driving the over-all price down. I actually get less dollars now than I did ten years ago, and ten years ago the dollar was worth almost twice as much! That is a huge change! In the past, inefficiency was absorbed in the high profits. It did not matter that I had a high transportation cost getting my goods to civilization. The cost of my materials was insignificant. How long it took to create an item was not a huge factor. Thus, making items by hand without electricity was not an insurmountable obstacle- in terms of how much longer it takes to make it by hand.

Fur prices are steadily going down, while trapper population goes up. Like with art, there are fewer professionals, with many more hobbyists. Trapping for fun or selling crafts for fun, not caring if they make a profit drives prices down. In competition with those who do care. Traplines are not as big, catches are down some, and prices are down some. Animal rights is affecting trapping and hunting issues. So far, ranching and meat eating, is not affected, but suspect a day will come the issue will be about all animals, even farmed ones, pets, zoos. Inflation is going up, higher prices on everything. Snow machines cost twice as much, things to support the dog team go up. The cost of maintaining a boat engine goes up, along with the price of gas. Food costs more. It is harder to find places that sell bulk cheap foods to the public. Laws change, so it is harder to live remote and be legal. I need to get bears tagged now, some furs I sell need tags and permits, fishing laws changed. Various costs, permits, insurance, license, to do almost anything. This began as a way to control to many people in civilization, but slowly spreads to include even remote people, told they must also abide by the laws of the land.

Subsistence is gradually becoming an 'Indian only' life, with my rights as a white man getting lost. I feel hit from all sides. I can overcome one or two obstacles, but not all this! Most important is that 'respect,' is a major goal I wish to arrive at. Perhaps ignorance was bliss, but now I realize, my present path is not going to bring me respect. If not, what good is any of it? If I had a partner at my side, much could be faced. Losing a wife and son is the hardest. I do not believe in divorce. I believe in forever. Within weeks, my hair turns grey. (I'm 70 years old working on an edit, I have never taken my wedding ring off.) I do not always verbally express how I feel.

Sally said she is going to leave me. I replied, "OK.' I suspect she wanted a different reaction. She had told me long ago, of a childhood traumatic experience. "I told my parents I am leaving home!" She tells me in tears, "My father said, "Fine, don't let the door slam you on the way out!" I'm waiting for the punchline. *So what's the problem? You want to leave, you are allowed to. The problem would be if the reply was to get tied up, beaten, punished, told you cannot leave.*

What should my response be to be being told I am being left? Try to convince her she does not feel what she feels? That's an insult. Fight, argue? Why? She knows what she wants, I respect this. She is not asking me a question. This is not up for discussion. She makes a statement, informs me of something. Do I not understand what she said? I do! I expect her reply to be, "Thanks for understanding and not getting mad."

I DEPEND MORE on my survey work with Seymour. I'm wore down. Money does in fact make the world go around, as my X proved. Respect is all about money. To work or Seymour, I am expected to be able to be contacted. At first Seymour could tell me in early spring, what kind of work we have, and when. But his own work is changing. Now he does not know himself what work there is till it shows up, and off we go! To really and truly work, I'd need an ID, have to drive, be in the system – an entirely different lifestyle.

I have not given up. I am just more challenged to come up with some solution.

Many people are not making it! Many people are not figuring out what to do as life gets tougher. Still, I do feel lucky as I watch others around me not doing as well.

I'm kind of stumbling along with no long term objective firm in my mind. Going where life takes me, the path of least resistance. Open to new opportunities as they may present themselves. Some options would work well, but I feel I would not be as happy. Art is selling wherever I go. I am confident I could travel anywhere I want, as in anywhere in the world. Pay for my trip and make a profit off selling my art. If I wanted a life of travel. Also, I could possibly do a lecture tour.

More and more people in a position to make the offer, tell me I could show up and get paid to 'talk' about subsistence, teach survival class, and work with kids. I could work at wilderness retreats. Again, if I wanted a life of travel. What path do I want? Much like the days I could have worked for the pipeline and got rich, but turned high pay down because I wanted to be a trapper.

In my rambling and wanderings I stop to see various people in Nenana off and on who I am getting to know better. Jenny is a woman I met, or sort of knew but spend more time talking to these days. She is running a small gift shop at the local gas station. She is all excited and full of energy and ideas. Jenny likes my art a lot, and thinks she can sell a lot for me. But also we talk about life and issues that face us.

"Miles, I don't know what to do about my boyfriend!" She tells me more then I tell her maybe. Women in general I notice seem to be able, or feel comfortable, talking to me. As long as we do not get close. I am not sure what to tell Jenny. It's common knowledge except to her, that her boyfriend has just been looking for a short term fun type situation. He is from Germany. He is a dog handler for one of the Iditarod racers. His visa permit expires, and he is headed home soon. Word has it, he has a serious girlfriend, is even engaged, back in Germany! He takes this dog racing serious. He is here to learn to compete and get back home to train dogs for the Iditarod. He does not sound like someone who wants to change his goals for Jenny at this point. She apparently is taking the relationship seriously.

I try my best to explain 'men' in general, how we think different then women.

"Jenny, I think men and women are equal, but different. If I ask for an orange I do not want to be given an apple, even if I like them both the same. You cannot just replace one with another. There is a reason this is so. Men are not worse, are not better, just different. It would be good for men and women to see the difference, understand and accept. So yes, I suppose men are like children sometimes, not as responsible as women all the time. At least at a young age. Men have what women call 'toys' they spend a lot of money on, and have a deep interest in." She laughs and tells me the things her boyfriend likes as his toys. I help her get in a better mood chatting there in her shop.

"So Jenny, you got one of these new computers on the market? What are they, how do they work?" She explains a little. She is just figuring it out, but has plans to put a catalog together of my art work! I think a catalog is not going to work well. As much as I wish and hope. "Because Jenny, my work is all one of a kind, so how do we offer it? Once an item is sold, it is gone, not to be repeated again. As soon as a catalog is printed it is already outdated!" I wonder how I can promise something in the catalog, offer it as still available? But she thinks we can just keep it updated with the computer and printer.

"Do small runs you replace once a month!" This is a new age where we can do this, a new concept! In the past, printing costs were high. We had to have hundreds-even thousands printed at a time to get a decent price, with lots of lead time, slow turn over. Printings get done in the tourist industry as in once a year, not once a month, as proposed now. So all this is going on with Jenny.

I stop to see Judy who often needs my help. She is an elder woman who I know through our selling side by side at various events. She sells balloons and toys to kids. She is a willowy built, long straight hair, always in a flower dress and sun bonnet, 60's hippie-ditzy-chickie-type. She has a Buda carving on the porch, wind chimes, sun catchers, and birds all around. Judy lives in a hobbit looking house built in 1916. She has little income, and often needs snow shoveled, a stuck door fixed, a plugged drain cleared, and such things as happen that men tend to take care of. Except she has no man.

I have helped her in the past, but came to realize over time, she can't pay me, and often makes excuses about when she might be able to pay me. I finally told her not to tell me about it. "I'll just donate my time now and then as long as you appreciated it, and there is no obligation." On my own, I am figuring out a 'play it forward,' view.

I recall people in my life who helped me out for no reason other than, 'they could.' I had no way to pay, no way to even thank them properly. Possibly not even been appreciative enough. They helped me anyway. My payback is to pass this on.

So, I stop by. She has heavy flower planters she is moving out of the greenhouse at the end of the season. I carry the heavy planters of dirt.

The local café is always filled with locals I know and I am considered a local now. There are homesteaders I know, Mick the lawyer, Josh sometimes, some of the Natives like Dim and his brother Pat. Old Al John. They all like me well enough. So even though Gene is giving me a hard time, not everyone is. Sometimes I just forget.

I'm not out in the wilderness, no plans, just hanging out in Nenana. I have no reason to go into the wilds.

Gene has been saying once again that he wants me to leave, that I should move. He does not want me around. I sigh. I get out and review a letter Gene wrote me when Sally was still around.

Miles

I contemplated not even answering your letter for a long time and decided I probably should just so you can keep your lies straight. You f&*%ked me on the fur trade for my mill. And to raise a baby in the conditions you live in is despicable. I am not the only person who thinks you are a slime ball. I could not get one person on the Kantishna who you know to testify against you, reason they want rid of you—told me they know you well and hope you leave. Said you were a lying thieving bastard. You are a bold faced liar and fraud, just like you told me about, you write (quote: "Tell them what they want to hear, it doesn't need to be the truth"). The real reason other than the above listed I don't like you is because you claim to be human. I have nothing against Sally, but if I have to go after her to get rid of you I will. She is the one who sleeps with and is the cause of your filthy stinking a*&s being my neighbor. I am prepared to go all the way to the State Supreme Court to get rid of you. By the way, fraud to the ADL carries jail time. So you just carry on a&^*hole, and I will get every f&*^king one of you. I will not quit till you are out of my neighborhood. Maybe Josh has a spare dog house you could live in.

Gene

So this sums up seven pages of the letter. Gene's income, lifestyle, level of cleanliness etc. is no different than mine. I think his income is even less than mine. Thus all these words seems so outrageous I do not know whether to feel sorry for him, because he lives with so much anger and hatred, or to consider him dangerous. But till he actually does something and gets caught at it, there is not much to be done. He has been fairly annoying. My boat has been turned loose a few times and found downriver. A box of tools was tossed out of the houseboat and into the river. Mostly harassment more than crimes to pursue seriously. There is a reference to 'ADL' and jail time. This refers to the Alaska Division of Lands, and was the time period Sally and I first staked the state parcel and had problems proving how long Sally had been in Alaska. This issue got resolved. We turned the parcel back in to the state, and re-staked the same land a month later. Just a pain, nothing serious. Gene may not know how we took care of it.

I can think of maybe one person on the Kantishna who does not like me much. Some of the younger natives who try to follow after their industrious parents do not think any white people at all should be on the whole river, that they feel is traditionally Indian land, to be used only by Indians. One Native in particular has issues with me because he lost a good rifle off his snow machine sled out on the trail, and believes I found it because I was the next person out on the trail. I never saw it. There was a snow storm going on, and assume the rifle got buried, but also may have bounced completely off the trail and landed in the deep snow. But this Indian is sure I have his rifle and hates me. Gene probably ran into him at the bar when he was drunk and in a bad mood.

I think about the 'it doesn't need to be the truth' quote he says is a direct quote of mine, that is misleading. I had been questioning just what 'truth' is. *Different things to different people.* We were talking about advertising, the topic at hand, him offering boat trips. He has zero customers. The quote is taken out of context and slightly altered. Maybe not on purpose, for Gene may well honestly feel his interpretation is what I feel. I said, "Tell them what they want to hear, it sadly doesn't need to be the truth." Meaning I am not happy about what I am discovering. I want to tell the truth about everything, wish we all could! But, some people- maybe most- can't take it, don't want it. So. "Oh well! Give as much as they can handle and accept that." The subject was offering his boat trips on the river. I meant it needs to sound romantic, fun, exciting. Sentences ending with exclamation marks. Sort of an adaption from what Jean Pasquier had told me doing the story for the New York Times.

Yes, come to think of it, Gene had in fact come unglued. At the time I suspected Gene is someone to who there is no gray area. Everything is black and white, either right or wrong either legal or not legal. There are no 'extenuating circumstances,' or situation ethics. It's about 'order.' A place for everything, and everything in its place. I was not stating anything in concrete, just tossing out a concept I thought interesting. Looking for an opinion. That truth and reality might be relative. Gene being a prime example, of holding dear, a set of information deemed to be correct and factual. Then coming up with a set of logical reactions based on this miss information, without going back to question the basic premise. I think Gene has a set of irrefutable concrete set- in- stone facts that are not universal facts as held by others.

Anyhow, no, Gene has not gone away, or forgotten his issues with me. Though others come and go, on and off his list, I seem to always be there.

There are other issues on my mind right now. There is little choice it seems to me, but to move up to the Kantishna River at least for the fall, and fish there for the sled dogs. Otherwise, I will not have food for the dogs this winter. This is a big change in plans, as I had been fishing the Tek area and assumed I could again, and stay here for freeze up. Fish and Game ordered us to stop fishing.

There are issues even on the Kantishna. For several years, while on the Kantishna, fishing for the sled dogs, subsistence fishing, has been shut down by emergency order. The board of fisheries has been declaring a lack of escapement for spawning fish as a reason for the emergency. Only subsistence fisherman at the headwaters are being shut down while commercial fishing continues without restrictions.[1] The closure has always been at a bad time, right when I am settled in and getting ready for winter, unable to leave till I come back out in winter. I am the only one in the area, as in 600 miles, who has dogs who will die if I cannot fish. This is the true definition of 'subsistence.' It is true, there is no such thing anymore of true subsistence.

I cannot trust and depend on being able to fish. Just about all the other fisherman on the river have been forced out of a lifestyle, and are no longer fishing except Tom and Forest, who can buy commercial feed if they must. They are not subsistence people. Both have good jobs in Denali Park in summer. In winter they freight with sled dogs for the Denali mountain climbers. They have an exclusive contract with the park, which does not allow motorized transportation. They haul freight much of the winter to leave at base camps for the climbers. They can use fish for the sled dogs, but it is not a necessity as it is for me. For those who truly depend on the fish, who are true subsistence, the closures three years in a row are devastating. Most of us do not believe there has been a shortage of salmon, or at least the salmon we target.

Fish and Game found out there is a very large and strong run of healthy silver salmon they did not know existed, that locals had been harvesting for years. A run no commercial interests had tapped into because it is so late in the season, ice is beginning to form. But once Fish and Game found out about this exciting late run, the lower Yukon River was opened to commercial fishing to target this run. The upper river subsistence fisherman are now seeing devastating results. Or, for sure will 'soon.' I feel badly because I think it was my sharing this information with Fish and Game that speeded up the disaster.

It takes about seven years for the results, for the salmon to return that were hatched seven years earlier. My heart is broken over what I am seeing. Over the insights I am getting a glimpse of. The thrill of catching fish for the dogs is lost now. It is exciting to tap into a strong healthy population unaffected by my activity. Just as it is exciting to get into good fur country and harvest the surplus, or take a few geese out of the thousands that fly overhead, or pick a bucket of berries and still see buckets left behind. It is not the same at all to shoot the last moose, pick the last berry off a dry wilted plant, shoot a goose when seeing only three, or to get a net of fish when I recall fish so thick in the river, when in the past, I could almost walk across the fish to the other side.

I am not going to argue and fight over the last salmon. But like much of my life now, it is what I know, and what else am I going to do now? Well maybe somehow this will be a good fishing season. *Maybe we will not get shut down.* So I head up to the Kantishna, mostly just to fish for the sled dogs. *This is my life, what else is there to do?* I have homesteads, a trapline, that all revolve around a lifestyle. Jenny points out:

"Miles, you could fish someplace on the Tanana River couldn't you?" Yes, probably legally. But it seems crowded, with lots of competition and jealousies over fishing spots. I do not want 'problems.' Some fisherman telling me I am in his spot.

Nor do I want some inferior end of the line fishing spot that will not get me enough fish. I understand my spots on the Kantishna. I'm alone there. Left in peace, accept if Fish and Game comes to inform me it's over. From Fish and Game's standpoint, it is easier to watch and regulate activity if everyone is in one place where they can keep an eye on us.

This does not agree well with the whole concept of 'subsistence' the government claims to be protecting, and giving priority to. Subsistence people need to fish near their home. Near the sled dogs, the garden, their moose hunting- berry picking area etc. Subsistence requires small groups out remote and alone, spread out so as to have the least impact on the environment, and keep the resources sustainable. Everyone grabbing the resources from one designated area is not biologically sound.

Tom and his wife tell me there are some new laws coming along restricting gear we can use to subsistence fish. It will be a legal requirement next year to use a fish wheel and not a net. The wheel is a huge contraption you have to build with store bought stuff that is hard to build, time consuming, expensive, difficult to move and manage without a big boat. I cannot imagine using one. The wheel was never traditional subsistence gear, but designed for commercial harvest of fish. The wheel can be seen from an airplane easier than a net, so easier to keep track of what we are all up to. For sure we need to put our name on nets now, with our permit number. So far I have refused. If I wanted to be assigned a number, I'd move to town. It's like going to the headwaters of the Amazon, as I often compare, and asking the locals to fill out paperwork, have a permit and keep records and such.

This is 150 miles into the wilderness, go away! Go ruin your world, leave mine alone. I know as well the polite line given to us is, "Not a big deal, a $5 permit easy to get, painless, it helps up get a handle on who is fishing where what they are catching so we can help the fish population." However, this is usually just a beginning. Once a permit is required, it can be denied. There can be penalties assigned for not complying, as getting this permit gets more costly and involved. Acceptance begins with being easy. Control comes in stages. I keep repeating, this is all about lack of trust.

But of course, it is not possible to talk to an officer like that. We have to bow and go to the back of the bus saying "Yes masta, yes masta." So the best thing is to never see an officer. However, there is one officer who has shown up, who I respect. A native guy named Gary Folger from Tanana. He seems to understand how life is. He tries to leave people alone as much as he can. Concentrate on the real crimes. I think one reason is he is not a desk person, but works a lot in the field traveling around by boat, and has a love of the wilderness, and not a love of the politics. So I do not have a hatred and fear of all government people. I want to remain open to the few I think are moral and ethical, as well as legal.

So Gary and I talk sometimes when I see him on the river.

"Miles, you wouldn't be up to anything illegal would you?" Said with a kind smile.

"No sir! But wait. I don't know. What's not legal today?" He chuckles as he knows I refer to the fact that laws change practically by the day. The state and federal government can't keep it straight or be in agreement, or understand each other's laws and fight over what exactly the laws mean. Thus, if the highest courts in the land cannot figure it out or agree, where does that leave the poor schmuck in the field?

In truth I have a duck locked up under the bow of my boat I shot with lead shot instead of steel, and shot from a moving boat. I do not know anyone who is using legal steel shot, nor waits till the boat is no longer moving before shooting a duck. Gary is smart, and no one is pulling the wool over his eyes. But am I a criminal?

If I had killed fifty ducks, that might be of interest. Maybe. But it is to the officers advantage to be on speaking terms with the locals. We can help out a lot when it comes to serious crimes.

"Miles, seen anything I need to know about lately?"

"Nothing that can be taken to court as evidence. But yea, a couple of things to be aware of maybe." I tell him about someone showing up, it looks like a few days before opening moose season and killing cow moose in the same spot every year. Maybe he can keep an eye out if he boats by at that time of year, or watch out from a plane if he flies over. I'm honest with him.

"I have a vested interest. I live here, this is my home. I hunt here, trap here. I depend on the moose population around here. Hunting cows year after year on the same lake is hurting me." He nods he understands. "Rumor upriver is there is a regular guide flying in and out of here who uses the plane to spot moose, then directs the hunters to the moose with the plane." By law a hunter cannot hunt the same day they fly. A plane cannot be used to spot or drive the game. This is a pretty serious offense, because it gives such hunters so much advantage, and about every hunter who engages in this can get a moose, devastating the population. If you own or can pay for plane back up, you obviously do not need the meat, you are most likely trophy hunting. Trophy hunters have a reputation of taking the antlers and leaving the meat behind to get wasted. Gary says:

"Yea, I heard the same from someone else. We have not found out who yet." I nod.

"I saw the plane once, and it is green with white stripes but could not get the number off it. I heard the plane land, soon after a gun shot, and a few hours later take off again." This kind of hunting bothers me. I do not have as much of a problem with someone who needs the meat as part of a lifestyle, especially someone local. Sometimes hunters bend the law a trifle.

Often guides communicate with the locals. If a trophy hunter wants a huge moose rack, the guide makes sure the locals are given the meat. At least the meat gets put to use. But, this guide I speak of is not talking to the locals. Rumor has it, taking the big rack and leaving the meat behind in the woods.

"Well the information helps anyhow. Sometimes we have to piece a lot of little bits of information together to make a case. Let me know if you can get a plane number or a picture. Here's my card." I would not help out just any Fish and Game officer. But this Gary officer has earned my trust. It is hard to sort in my mind, the 'how I feel' part. Some officers would treat me like I am an informant. Defined as one criminal giving evidence against another criminal in return for favors. Viewed as 'a criminal' not trusted, not treated like a friend, or a citizen, or a human being. It's the necessity of having to deal with low life to catch bigger low life. I see that attitude reflected in how some officers treat 'us,' locals who try to be descent people and who care, but some of the laws are simply not workable and were made by desk people or politicians. Some laws that may not even make biological sense. But anyhow. It is easy to see Gary as a human being. It is easy to see he views most of us locals as human beings.

I would not want to get on his bad side. I think he would cut me no slack, and give me no favors. Hope to never give him cause to come after me. I assume our conversation is over, but Gary hesitates, then says:

"Miles, Fish and Game has a rifle of yours, taken from your cabin," I'm shocked.

"What? How? Why? I mean I assumed my rifle was stolen by a rival trapper, not Fish and Game!" Gary asks:

"Why didn't you report it as stolen?" Obviously there are things Gary does not understand, but he seems to be honestly trying to see my view. *It seems so obvious to me! How can I explain to him, that when you are poor the law is not your friend?* No matter what I say or do, it will be my fault.

"Gary, the law does not have time or resources to come investigate the complaints of a trapper out in the wilds, so why even bother. We take care of ourselves out here. Filling out reports, singing papers, showing up for various reason at your office, is just another punishment. I do not know one person on the river the legal system ever helped."

"Well I was curious because that rifle had previously been reported stolen at the time you had it." I'm puzzled as I review how I acquired it. Oh yes, "Gary I got that rifle at a pawn shop in Fairbanks. Friends run the place. A legitimate honest pawn shop. If I bought a stolen rifle, I'm pretty sure the pawn shop does not know it." I pause and try to think this through. "But hold on Gary. I don't get it. I have lots of questions. Why was Fish and Game in my home without a warrant? If the rifle is stolen, how did the officer know at the time he grabbed it? If it is stolen, how come I was not charged with possession of a stolen firearm?" All the confusion in my mind. All these questions leap out. "And how come there was no notice left, a receipt for the rifle confiscated? I mean geez Gary, are you telling me it is legal to go into someone's home, take something, and leave, without saying anything, no receipt or paperwork, take something without making either a charge or returning what was taken? Even with a warrant?"

Gary admits he was with someone else, and it was he, and someone else, who confiscated the rifle.

"We got a complaint we responded to Miles. You were not home. We saw wanton waste- you had Marten hanging outdoors not being taken care of, rotting." I'm thinking this is just an excuse for 'probable cause.' But who knows? It is common for me to hang furs on the roof rafters outside to air out. I recall these three Marten that I could not sell. They had been heavily damaged in the trap. Voles had chewed the fur on one, and the fur on another was not prime. It was the last Marten caught as I was pulling traps at the end of the season when the weather is getting too warm to keep fur prime. I was not wasting them. They are under my care. I later kept them for myself. I tanned them for my own use, since they could not be sold. Part of 'subsistence' is using everything, even the damaged and rotten. Like a personal need for warm clothing like a hat, made of fur. So of course I'm going to select the damaged pelts, if possible. These were three marten out of 150 caught. They were damaged and rotten before I acquired them.

"But Gary! Didn't I deserve a chance to defend myself, to explain myself? How is it I am made out to be a criminal with no charges filed?" I pause in shock. "Isn't this why we have a court system and trials, so we are not made into criminals without the chance to defend ourselves?" *It is only third world countries where strong arm government officials show up confiscating without due process.*

So Fish and Game apparently had been waiting to see if I would report a rifle stolen or not, and if I do not, this is proof of a crime. They think I cannot make the report, because I know it is a stolen rifle? I see the logic, but the logic is based on a lot of assumptions. That I trust the law, and use the law. When in fact I think the legal system and government is as full of criminals as any other segment of the population. The difference being, the government and legal system carry guns and can use them on people more readily than the general public criminal can. Thus, citizens must be especially careful what sort of officer they are dealing with, for the damage of dealing with a criminal officer is great, even life threatening, and sometimes not worth taking the chance on. The situation might be much like a Jew, being asked to do business with the SS. The less paperwork they have on you, the better.

In a situation such as this, if I had known Fish and Game took my rifle without leaving me notice of any kind, and I assume, without a warrant, and assume without probable cause. (my viewpoint based on logic and the information I have) I am going to assume I'm dealing with some crooked officers. There is no way I'm going to say, "Hey, why did you break into my home and steal my rifle!" This is how to end up dead. I watch TV, I know! I try to explain it all to Gary, but do not know how much of it he believes, understands, or thinks is reasonable thinking. Nor do I want to get on his bad side. Nor assume at this point he is honest. People in the wilds can be made to disappear. Rather than get caught stealing, a crooked officer can bury me out here. He says:

"Anyhow Miles, the rifle is in the evidence locker. The statute of limitations is going to run out. If you want it, you need to go to the police station and claim it." I'm thinking *"Excuse me- but if it is mine and you took it, it needs to be returned to me at my home where it was taken from!"* I cannot easily get to Fairbanks, and once there, I cannot easily get to the police station. This will occupy a full day of my time. What if I took something that belongs to Gary in Fairbanks. His wallet. And tell him if he wants it back he can come to the Kantishna River to claim it. Anyone would say "Yea right!" But anyhow.

"Well thanks for letting me know at least. I appreciate it. First I will go to the pawn shop and discuss the rifle with my friends and find out from them, if it is likely a stolen firearm or not. Look at the pawn receipt. If it's stolen, maybe they will replace it. If not, then yes I need to get my rifle back." It's still a very puzzling story. I miss that rifle. I need it. I cannot afford another one as good. It is my moose rifle I depend on, is accurate, and I understand how it shoots. Plus, I have done a lot of silver inlay work on it, and it is drop- dead gorgeous. Silver swans, copper moose, brass trees. All inlaid flush with the wood, magnificent curly birds eye walnut. Wood we can't find anymore. Hand rubbed oil finish.

Gary leaves. I get back to my life. Begin fishing for the sled dogs. I have two eighty foot nets set. I get pike, whitefish, and enough salmon that I am happy with this compromise in mesh size of five inches. There is one river eddy that I have used many times, that always produces fish. The other net I usually put in different places and move around. Temporary racks are built from poles out on the open sandbar, left when the water drops for the fall and winter. These temporary racks get washed out each spring at high water. The sandbars are traditionally ideal spots to dry fish because they are out in the sun, and along the river where there is always a breeze.

There seems to me to be plenty of salmon this season. There is a concern there will be another emergency closure, I will be stopped, or will be arrested if I do not know the season got closed. There were threats in the past that if I fish illegally, my boat can be confiscated, as part of the equipment used in illegal activity. I have heard of such happenings. Even planes get confiscated and sold off at auctions. Some people at Fish and Game would be pleased to see me unable to live on the river without a boat, forced to give up dogs, forced to live in town, forced to be on welfare. There would be some back slapping, and a "finally got him good huh!" Even the well-meaning act like it would be good to turn a non-productive low life into a meaningful taxpaying, consumptive citizen. So I live in fear.

There is an old sailboat I bought off Dim a while ago. *Maybe the boat can work as a river boat if I go slow.* It is not worth much. So, I put a rundown five horse engine on it. If there will be a boat confiscation it can be this one, that I can live without.

It's a little hard checking nets with this sailboat, and it is slow, but I do what I have to do. There are thirty to forty fish a day on the average. Not the most I have ever seen, but a fine run of fish. Certainly there is no shortage. I think the lack of catch has more to do with the mesh change requirement being not as efficient.

The sled dogs are with me and tied out on the river bank where they can get the sun. I cook on the beach for them. They get all the fish guts while I am cutting and hanging fish. Once weather gets cold, like about now, I hang the fish whole and it freeze dries before rotting.

Taking care of the fish consumes half of my day, every day. But if all goes well, getting all I need for a year is only two weeks of fishing. From this work I have feed for my transportation for the rest of the year till fishing season again. I'm feeling better, less stress, getting back into the wilderness lifestyle I love so much. 'Town' life is okay, rewarding in its way. I do love selling art, chatting with friends at the café, but it is stressful. This life here seems so sane. I chuckle because it only takes three days or so, for me to forget what time it is, even what day it is, or how many days I have been here. No news from civilization, so no negative events to hear about. Just the sound of birds, the wind, the lapping water on the boat, the smell of fish. All stuff mankind has smelled, heard, sensed, for 100,000 years. There is something almost sacred about it.

Sometimes out here I do feel guilty for the thought, *I hope civilization destroys itself, and I discover I am out here alone. How wonderful life would be.* I have almost enough fish to last a year, and will be ready to stop fishing within a few days when I hear a boat, and it is Gary the warden again, but this time with another officer. They are here to check up on who is fishing and what is going on.

"No there has been no closure yet," I give a sigh of relief. The officers come up the bank and inspect my fish that I have hanging. They then decide they want to check my fish net I have set nearby. They are not used to checking fish nets, and mess up the procedure a little bit, breaking the net loose from the tree it is tied to on shore, so they have to haul the net into the boat while drifting downriver. Partly too big a boat to be doing this with. The officer I do not know, gets out a ticket book and tells me:

"Going to have to write you up. There are two fish in the net that are illegal. You are supposed to be fishing for Silver salmon and you have two chum." I do not know what to say. *How can I control what kind of fish I catch?* But I know the answer in the regulations. I am supposed to be staying with my nets, pulling the nets when I have fish, and turning the ones loose while still alive that I am not supposed to have. Well who came up with such a hair brained notion as that? The whole 'point' of net fishing is to be able to set the net and walk away to do other things. No one has time or resources to go back and forth between nets all day long saving fish, and pulling the nets at night because you cannot turn fish loose. I could catch as many fish with a fishing pole. An ocean fisherman can set a mile of net. His incidental catch of other non-target fish is called 'bycatch.' Acknowledging it is impossible to catch just one kind of fish.

Anyhow, by the officers own words, it is two fish out of how many? About 1,500? And that is not an acceptable 'by catch'? No use arguing. The one officer I do not know wants to confiscate my boat and engine. But Gary talks him out of it. They do however confiscate my nets as evidence, so I cannot fish anymore this season, and I do not have enough fish to make it through the winter. My court date is set for the middle of winter when it might be hard to get into town from here, depending on what kind of winter we have.

If I do not show up in court there will be a warrant out for my arrest, and they can come out with a helicopter and haul me off in handcuffs. Now all my plans have to change. I do not have enough fish for the sled dogs. There is no use staying here now, because I cannot fish without my net. I will have to buy commercial dog feed. I will have to base out of Nenana, or the Tek probably, to make sure I can get to court, and to make sure I can feed the dogs. Also, if I make the trip into Nenana now, I probably will not be able to boat back again. The weather is getting colder, boating season is quickly coming to an end. Also, I am unsure if I can afford another boat trip at $200 a trip. A set back as well is, I have much of my winter food and supplies hauled here to base out of the Kantishna homestead. So this is a huge monkey wrench in my gears. All over two fish.

I am also not convinced we can save a fish so it survives, after it gets caught in a net. The net usually grabs a fish near the gills, a sensitive part on a fish. There is enough damage to the fish, it seems to me, that they would have a slim chance of surviving. For all the huge effort it would take to try to save two fish, it might not be possible. The rule is unworkable except on paper. Biologists who catch and turn loose, say nets do not work, it usually kills the fish.

The trip back to Nenana is rough. Water levels are low on both the Kantishna River and the Tanana. The temperature is below freezing. Wash on the boat freezes, and builds up thick ice. I have to stop and chip it off.

Moonshine- a soon to be famous dog racer, is at his camp fishing and getting ready for winter. Like me, he traps and lives a simple life with sled dogs. He also had fish and nets confiscated and will have to go to court. He and I are the only two subsistence people fishing this year in this area. Tom and Forest had no issues, so assume either got lucky and had not caught any chum salmon, or been able to turn them loose. Moonshine and I both suspect Tom has connections at Fish and Game. Moonshine tells me about his new fish wheel.

"I was getting lots of fish all right! Good fish run! I was wondering why I did not see other wheels turning when I passed them on the river though. Turns out I had the day's backwards! I had the wheels running on Wednesday and Friday. I was supposed to have them off on Wednesday and Friday? Dang!"

"Explain that one to a jury in court Moonshine!" We both laugh. City people would not believe anyone can lose track of what day it is. There is a fire going in the wood stove in the small log cabin. We are sitting on gas cans for chairs. The late fall colors are bright yellow and red, seen through a soot covered window with fly paper strips hanging in front.

After a lunch of moose soup with Moonshine, I feel warmer and head upstream for Nenana. My boat engine is at least holding up well with the switched out parts in the water pump. There is still some concern, because the ice in the river gets sucked into the engine cooling system, and might plug the water cooling intake. There are no gauges with this engine to indicate engine temperature. It is good to get to Nenana and have a fire going in the wood stove on the houseboat. Too tired to cook for the dogs. I just give them dry fish and water.

"Miles, what you doing here this time of year, thought you were freezing in on the Kantishna to trap!" Josh greets me in the morning when he comes down to water his dogs that are staked out nearby. I explain what is going on. "Sounds like you need to talk to Mick the lawyer. Come on by to visit. You can use a shower! What are your plans for Thanksgiving? We're expecting you!" Thanksgiving is still a ways away, but Josh gets my attention on something positive. Martha puts on quite a spread that is remembered the whole rest of the year. I've been over for Thanksgiving quite a few years now, almost like part of the family.

I ride my bike into the village and see Jenny, to see if any of my art has sold. To see if by chance there is some extra money to be had anyplace. If I lose my fish case I might have a big fine to pay.

"No Miles, sorry! Well, wait, I think two smaller items sold, but it is not the tourist season, so I don't expect much to be happening." She shows me the catalog of my art she has been working on.

"Well Jenny, it is kind of exciting. Wow huh!" It's not huge, just twenty-five pages, but all in color, with nice descriptions and order numbers. I had made up a code to use for order numbers. Fwi/p/45 for example, tells me this is a fossil walrus ivory pendant for $45. I trade her some of the art she wants for the work she has done, and I get twenty-five copies of the catalog to get into the hands of my regular customers, maybe big shops.

"Jenny I went once with Crafty on a wholesale trip, and once for the Anchorage wholesale gift show. This is where the big buyers shop, the gallery owners from all over the state. It might be worth going with the catalogs!"

"Or, the big one in Seattle Miles?" Yes, I'd heard of a big show there as well. Seattle is a stop on the way to all points south – about anywhere in the US I go, I stop in Seattle it seems like. I'd had a good experience three years ago selling enough to pay for my round trip in a few hours at Pikes Market, kind of a waterfront row of fish shops and vendors set up with a festive atmosphere. "Jenny. I hear there have been changes and in order to fly I will need an ID!" She does not answer.

"Jenny what are you upset about. You seem depressed today?"

"The usual I guess Miles. But my boyfriend has already left for Germany. I'm thinking of following him and staying over there for a while." But she had never talked before of any interest or opportunities in Germany, and only about this gas station and shop, with goals concerning this area. *What would she do in Germany? Goodness!* I see the future of that. *Dismal!* She asks me if I'll write her while she is gone.

It occurs to me she will be seeing hard times, and might welcome news from Nenana. She will need cheering up. No use saying any of that to her though. But how can it go, the man is engaged to be married back in Germany. He had his Alaska fling. He will not be pleased to see her. I shiver at how blind love is. I sigh inwardly and reply:

"Sure Jenny, you know me, love to write!" I make light of it. She and I have talked about my 'book one,' and how to get it printed or published. She has been telling me about computers. Sure I see how the computer will be the way to go, but geez hers costs $5,000 and takes skill to use, knowing computer language and all. She had to go to college to learn how. I have still never actually seen a personal computer, just talked about them. No use even seeing something I can't afford.

"It's the wave of the future though Miles. Companies and stores are beginning to do bookwork on them now." I have been to such stores, but it is not impressive. I saw no one understanding the computer, and longer waits in line as employees struggle to get the computer to work. All I hear is grumbling about how the boss is making everyone use a computer, and how it is slowing everything up. Still I agree with Jenny. I also have childhood memories from the late 50's early 60's, as my father is helping to design computer language. I'd overhear conversations between him and other mathematicians, discussing the future, discussing the complications needing to be overcome.

"Imagine Jenny, if I could put my book in a computer. I have started all over from scratch four times using the manual typewriter. Every time I want to make a change, I have to toss out pages and whole chapters of work. There is no way to move things around without hand writing notations in the margins for when I retype again. I'm sorting through pictures to use for illustration though, and the book could be done soon if I didn't have to keep retyping it!"

"You are persistent Miles, and I am sure one day it will all get done!" I thank her for the catalog. But now she will not be around to keep it updated. Still it will have a lot of uses, like just to show examples of the kind of work I can do. There are some good color pictures. Like one of my art pieces is a shadow box using a thin piece of jade as a sort of window with a light behind it, inside a handmade wood frame just two inches deep to hide the light and batteries. On the front are fire weed flowers of copper and silver, and a humming bird of three metals. The light shines through the green jade and metal lacework. This makes it look like an early morning sun in a garden.

Another piece is a long six foot piece of whale baleen, black, with bears on it. There are tree stumps, grass, and little birds on branches in the trees overhead. Six feet of scenery done with thousands of tiny pieces of hand cut filigree metals. There are ivory boxes with intricate lids of mammoth ivory I found, with carvings for lid handles. I got the basic concept from Crazy Lawsen who does such incredible boxes of fossil ivory. I do metalwork all around the round box. Like ring or watch boxes meant to go on a night stand when a woman takes her jewelry off at night, and wants it nearby to put it on in the morning.

I have twenty of my custom knives. Mammoth ivory handles, walrus ivory handles, moose antler, and wild sheep horn. Mostly hunting knives, but a couple of chef knives and paring knives for the kitchen. Everything with a order number, description, price, and personal story that goes with it. Mostly high end goods because of the costs of keeping track of it, and having a color picture in a catalog.

I'm always trying out something new, some idea that might work. If the idea does not work out, I'm excited by the next idea, and leaving the old idea on hold. I joke with Jenny.

"Yes, dozens, maybe hundreds of ideas fail all right! But, it only takes one to make up for all the loss!" I give my favorite come back line about failure. "Thomas Edison had thousands of light bulbs that never lit up, before one finally did, and all we hear about is the one that lit up." I laughingly tell Jenny, "But I bet in his day – going through all the thousands of failures, there were a lot of people who called him an idiot, made fun of him, were ashamed to know him. I bet he had little respect. Maybe even called a con artist, because who was supporting him while he was engaged in this ridiculous project thinking the 'stuff' he put together might be a source of light!"

"Well, I don't know much about Edison's early life, or how it all came about beyond what everyone knows Miles."

"Me neither, just guessing. The one who made the first match instead of flint and steel, or the one who designed the first electric guitar may have had the same experience." I pause. "Not that I have or will invent anything earth shattering when referring to 'me' in the context of the conversation. But everything I do, I change. I rarely accept things as they are. I redesigned the dog sled so the one I use works well on the trapline. I designed an arrow that shoots out of a shotgun. I've altered all my traps that I trap with. My art technique does not even have a name. I read a term once called 'married metals,' that simply has a nice sound to it. Sort of like what I do, so use that to describe it, but not really. Who else combines rocks, wood, fossils, antlers, and adds intricate metalwork scenery as an art form?"

"Well Miles, I think it is very recognizable as your style, even to people who do not know much about art. I see your art all over now. Not just in Alaska. I saw two pieces of yours in one trip, in two different states at airports, did I tell you?"

"Yes you did, and others tell me the same thing. Someone told me they went to a meeting in the Netherlands. They met a woman there who was wearing one of my necklaces, and had actually bought it from Alaska House. For some reason the Germans love my work. I think because my work, to some people, is big and gaudy and showy. But Germans as a people love 'things that stand out and make a statement. "I add "Maybe you can make some extra money over there in Germany by bringing some of my work over with you to sell?" I'm always looking for angles and selling opportunities. But no, she expects to be too busy, and have a lot in her mind, and does not want to be responsible for the care of my art. Rats!

I am creating and accumulating art faster than I can sell it these days. I have 500 finished pieces at any given time. Oh, mostly in the $35 to $55 range, but still, it's a lot of inventory to be sitting on.

"Geez Miles, what other artist has that kind of inventory? All the artists I know can barely come up with enough to do a small bazaar!"

"Yes, I suppose whatever it is I do in life, I go after it with a vengeance and passion." Jenny needs to sort and pack now so I wish her a good trip. I need to see Mick soon, to find out if there is anything I can do about my rifle, and this fish case.

Mick has his bird 'So -Sue -Me,' in a cage in his office. The place is a mess. But Mick comes out from a room in the back when I holler. He seems to live here as well as use the place for his office. He asks me questions about the rifle, and I explain I went to the pawn shop.

"Marcy at the pawn shop is a longtime friend. She told me this whole situation seems highly irregular. The police never came to find out who pawned the rifle, which is normal protocol. She has the ticket and showed me. There is also a process, that if followed legally, prevents stolen firearms from getting put out for sale." I go on with some interruptions, explaining how the serial number is called in. If the rifle is on the stolen list, she gets told, before the rifle even gets put out for sale! "And anyhow Mick, she told me if I can show it was stolen, she will give me another rifle to replace it. This shows me her sincerity, that she is not involved in this rifle being a stolen one." I explain all the inlay work I did on the rifle, increasing the value. I explain how I went to the police station and the evidence room, and asked for proof this rifle was stolen. I want it back. I'm told to come back in a week.

When I return I'm told it has been returned to its rightful owner. I assume in the past week. After holding it for four years? That seems odd. I cannot be told who the owner is. I never saw the rifle and have no way of knowing if it was ever here at all, and if there was a previous owner or not. Without 'proof' the pawn shop will not give me a new rifle. They feel the rifle is not a stolen rifle. "So what can I do Mick?"

"Well Miles, it looks to me like the officer saw it, liked it, took it, and kept it."

"How can they do that? How can they get away with that?"

"Happens all the time Miles, and they know there is not much that can get done about it. It's hard to go after, or sue the government. We have to go after an individual and that's hard. I'd need about $30,00 just to get started. They know you do not have that kind of money, and will not be able to take it to court, so they get away with it." If it was a rival trapper, an ordinary person who stole my rifle, I might have a chance of getting it back, but not when the thief is an officer. I'm puzzled why Gary said anything to me at all. As if he wanted me to know, or wanted me to get to the bottom of this. Perhaps it was the partner he was with who took the rifle. Gary did not stop him, but at least he said something to me about it. I'm guessing the partner said:

"If Miles doesn't report it missing- stolen- then the heck with him!" Possibly believing a poor subsistence person living in such filth did not have a right to such a fine rifle, or could not afford one, so it must be stolen. Not realizing it is I, Miles, who did that artwork! One reason I think this is possibility, and likely is that it is a common reaction customers have.

" I can't believe it! You do this work? I don't get it! Why are you so poor? You should be famous! You are so gifted! You need to enter contests!" Along with thoughts expressed wondering how I – so unsophisticated, could produce the cutting edge of finery. I smile. For in fact the whole package is part of my communication and message. "Behold! All is not as it seems! Be slower to make assumptions in life!" A sort of secret or mystery. Perks interest. It's a new slant on life to see. Beauty where you least expect it. The flower that pushed up through the sidewalk in a slums. Why? How? The infinite mystery. On purpose, I take pictures of beauty beyond compare, held in the hands that created it, that show in the picture – dirty, broken un-kept nails, tattered shirt sleeve. Extremes, or life from one end to the other. Or, living for the art, letting the art speak for me in my place. I, merely the unworthy humble tool. Not caring about much else but my trade. But anyhow. No. Not everyone believes what is in front of them. That I created this. Art that some tell me they feel is in the top five in the state, or even the country. Some art done in my style in fact no one has ever seen, and who knows if anyone else could do it, even if they tried? *The best there is at what I do in the world.* This is how a few customers feel, who collect my work.

It might be easy to understand how a policeman who believes in black and white, right and wrong, with no gray area and no unknowns, might see this rifle, worth more than the cabin and the land it is on, carelessly leaning against the wall, believing it must be stolen. Treated as ' a fact,' and if there is no report on it, well then the owner does not know it is missing, or never filled out a report. Thus, it is up for grabs, so to speak. There is no clear title and ownership. I explain to Mick the lawyer my theory.

"Sort of like how there are a lot of cops, who would enter a home and see a stash of money on the table and no one around. 'Obviously' this money does not belong to whoever owns this dive! It must be drug money." It's not reported stolen or missing. So the cop pockets it, justifying this because the junkie who owns this dive does not deserve this much money. He might return it if a report of it missing is filed. He doubts such a report will be filed, proving it is stolen. Like that. Thus, in his mind he is not a thief! He is being part of someone's karma. What goes around comes around. Like the attitude of the cop I took on the moose hunt, what's his name, the friend of Sally. A list of people, a type, who open season is declared on. People who have no rights. Mick thinks I am paranoid, so I make light of it. Change the subject.

"Gary will be a witness for the prosecution in my fish case coming up soon." Mick wants to know the details of what they might have on me for evidence, what I said, the evidence they have. "They took the fish and I'm told it will be frozen and brought in for evidence." Mick is not sure the fish is illegal, and can't find any new regulations on the subject. Mick also feels this is part of the whole subsistence issue that is not clearly defined. Even so, I see a serious effort to put a monkey wrench in my gears and I'm scared. The government is all powerful. If they can't get me legally, they might plant or alter evidence.

"Miles! Come on! Who are you? What is the big deal? You flatter yourself! Why would the government be so interested in you to go through so much effort!" I have no answer, so I must be delusional. Now I question my own sanity. But maybe Mick buys into the look of things. How can I, who looks as I do 'matter?' Miles the dumpster diver. *How could anything I do matter?* Yes, quite a puzzle all right.

I flash on Gene and the thought that maybe this is his bottom line issue with me. I'm a dumpster diver. There is an image of what that is and means in his head. If it walks like a duck, and quacks like a duck, it's a duck. Only one in millions might not be a duck. So I'm a liar. I can't possibly write. I can't possibly know anything. All my stories must be crap. It would be like, I suppose, a dumpster diver street person—Red Skelton as Kidittlehopper on the park bench, sitting up and wiping off the snow saying:

"Actually I have a Ph.D." We all laugh, as long as it's a joke.

My own view of myself is the admission right up front, "Yes, I am damaged goods. Tweaked. Scars, with limitations on some levels, social levels." But when I am done with "Alas to bad, sigh," I smile and add, "But gifted," with a sly wink. My ace in the hole. That brings everything else into balance, changes everything. I actually have a very high IQ, and as a matter of fact graduated from high school with 3.5, grade point, B+, not the top, but not the bottom, and I could have done better. I did not try very hard. I remind Mick, "I came out of military school in the top ten of my class."

So we go to court, this Mick, self-professed 'gifted' high fluted lawyer and I, to fight for my life. To play games with words like 'subsistence.' Get me off on a technicality. It might not work. Gary is going to nail me to the cross. Mick and I get to look at the prosecution's evidence. Here is the ticket written. Mick wants to inspect it because he thinks the fish they confiscated was actually legal. We both see the ticket has been altered! The original copy the court has, does not match my carbon copy that I signed. The species of fish had been scratched out.

"Mick, how can that be legal? I read and signed the ticket as understanding and agreeing to what was written down. How can my signature be valid in this context, if my copy does not match the original other altered ticket signed?" Mick agrees, and we may have a chance to bring that up, but it might not be necessary.

"But Mick, what if it is altered because the fish confiscated were legal, and the officers had no right to confiscate my nets, stop me from fishing, writing me up, causing me to have to hire a lawyer and come to town to go to court. What if the ticket was altered as a tampering with evidence thing, to lie about the actual evidence."

"Miles calm down. We can deal with that later if we need to." Gary the fish cop gets on the stand, and I assume it is all over for me. But as his story unfolds he says:

" We drug the net while hauling the fish into the boat. I think we may have killed the fish. It may have been alive at the time we drug the net." And, "We accidentally mixed up the fish we confiscated that day. I cannot swear the fish we have as evidence is the same fish that was in Mr. Martins net." This is a highly unexpected answer. Obviously, Gary's boss is upset. This is not good for the prosecution. This statement makes Gary look incompetent, almost like saving my bacon at his own expense. Helping me, making himself look bad. There are few human beings in any walk of life willing to do this. Or more, this is not at all how I expect a member of the Gestapo to behave. He acts like a human being. This is very strange and unexpected. Though I was thinking I liked Gary even long ago, still he was there when my rifle was confiscated and was an accomplice.

The case is dismissed. I had wanted the chance to point out the discrepancy between the citation tickets.

"Your honor the fish confiscated from me does not match the species listed on the ticket and you can see how the ticket was altered, because what I caught was legal." I expected the judge to say something like:

"This is highly irregular, are you sure? Let me look. I will not tolerate the tampering of evidence in my court," or something along that line. Like on TV, Perry Mason, Iron Sides, CSI, Miami vice . But no. The judge replies:

"And what is your point young man. You won your case and are free to go, the case is over. If you wish to file charges of misconduct, that is a separate issue to take up with your lawyer," said down his nose, with distain, for wasting his time. For knowing so little about the law. For demanding justice when he is sure I am a criminal who looks forward to the chess game of life and seeing me again when I will not get away, and he has the pleasure of a checkmate. When he can lecture me on the evils of my way, as he delivers a just sentence befitting who I am. That is his tone. That too, surprised me. I assumed from the movies that all I had been taught that judges were impartial. Honorable. That's why we call them "Your Honor."

Mick, my lawyer tells me not to let it bother me. I never even got to talk, or present my case. More an effort to clear things up and stop getting harassed. Which is how I viewed what is going on. The papers are in my hand:

Letter – Evidence – Exhibit A

In the spring of 1990 I received a notice in the mail from Russell Holder, management biologist dated March 5th 1990 (Exhibit B), which states salmon fishing in my area – the lower Kantishna, has been closed to salmon fishing. Some Kantishna River fisherman were unclear as to the wording- interpretation of this notice. I for one believed all fishing of any kind was closed. There was certainly no mention of a Coho opening, or any helpful information as to what we Subsistence fisherman were to do.

This notice came as a shock to me. I had attended an emergency meeting of the Board of Fisheries on 5/28-31/1988, and a meeting of Interior Regional Council May 20th 1988. I had addressed questions during the public comment portion of the meeting, and answered questions directed at me concerning subsistence rights and fishing on the Kantishna River.

At these meetings, information came out relevant to this Kantishna closing, such as the fact biologists admitted their fish counts for Kantishna, Toklat Rivers may have been off by 100,000 to 200,000 fish, or about 100% inaccurate. There were no accurate statistics on how many fish were coming, going, or being harvested. It was stated there is a big communication problem between subsistence fisherman, commercial fisherman, and Fish and Game. There were up until this time no restrictions whatever on the Kantishna subsistence fisherman neither a time limit, catch limit, nor a need for a permit or reporting catches. The boards philosophy was stated : "To impose as few restrictions as possible in areas and on fisherman who are subsistence only, like the Kantishna." One reason given was we are few in number and wide spread.

I brought up the question of emergency closure possibilities, which had cost me such a loss the preceding year. I was told there were no foreseeable problem on the Kantishna. Thus, receiving a notice of a complete closure of all fishing for all time left me with many questions. Where did the new statistic come from in the past two years? Reported catches by who? if it is not a requirement to report catches?

Officer Foldger informed me I could catch subsistence fish, but needed a permit from Fairbanks. At great expense and lost time, I went to Fairbanks and was told I would not be issued such a permit for a closed area where I am. I had been told at the Board meeting any future permit would be for biological count purposes only, not for regulation or enforcement. The subject was extensively discussed by fisherman up and down the river who were concerned, torn between the need for fish to survive, and what the consequences of doing so might be or not be.

Ending with…. The point being, I am concerned and wish to abide by the law. What is the law, and who knows it? The law officer? The Board? The judge? Subsistence is not being defined. Why? I desperately need fish, and am trying my best to harvest wisely and legally. If I am in error I am merely mistaken about what I understood to be the law. Not a criminal! ……If I do have the right to live a subsistence lifestyle, I'd like to be left alone to do so, unless **I am in violation of the law.**

Mick is not interested in my statement, or evidence, or who said what, and what promises were made. None of it is relevant. As I saw.

"Public comment means what then Mick?! The word of an officer, of a board of game, means what?" I have in my possession, eight cassette tapes, the recording of the board meeting with the statements made by everyone, so I have proof and exact quotes. All meaningless. I'm quite puzzled. Even the board meeting was confusing. All the local subsistence fisherman who attended were polite, and truthfully answered questions directed at us. The board acted interested, asking us how we drift net fish for salmon. In shock we informed the board, "No! We do not drift net! Impossible! We use set nets or use wheels!" 'Shocked' that this board is running our lives, and does not even know how we fish? At one point I was addressed specifically by the chair of the board.

"I do not understand why you subsistence fisherman are not angry about the current laws?"

I blew up. Lost it. We had all been trying to be polite, state our case rationally with facts and reason. He wants emotion does he? I jump up and began foaming at the mouth screaming my head off. I had to be handcuffed and escorted screaming out of the room. It's all on tape. Locals forever after referred to this as, "The day Miles socked it to (The Harper Valley PTA) Fish and Feathers." I did not really want to side with the local illegal commercial fisherman, but it seemed preferable to the hypocrisy of those so far away, and out of touch. The board will be long gone and unreachable. The locals are forever. One way or other I need to come to terms with the locals, as a first priority. One way or other, we must learn to stick together. Sigh.

Shuffling through a manila envelopes full of letters, permits, requests, denials, case numbers quotes, etc., I glance at one from the department of Fish and Game. When I did get the required subsistence permit, after a great deal of effort. I got this notice.

Notice

On May 21st of 1990 you were issued a Subsistence Salmon permit, number SA-31-90, for fishing in sub district 6-A which includes the Kantishna River. **The issuing officer was in error when she specified on your permit that only Coho salmon may be taken after August 16th.** ...... it is up to the individual to abide by the regulations that apply to the specific location being fished. I will, by this letter, amend your permit to 2,000 chum or Coho salmon.... I apologize for any inconvenience this may cause. **Keith Schultz, Area Biologist**

I turn to my lawyer. "He apologizes and is sorry? What happens when I make a mistake Mick? There is a financial consequence! The 'error' on the departments fault cost me thousands of dollars in loss. 'Sorry,' doesn't cut it!"

"This is the real world Miles. Get used to it. Don't take it so personal. You got off, just be glad. It seems silly to question the method." Rumor has it Mick specializes in getting guilty people off so to speak. The local drug dealers in Nenana turn to Mick in their time of need.

"Miles I don't ask if my clients are guilty or not, that's none of my business. I get hired to do a job and I do it." Yes, well whatever. What do I know. I don't have a clue how the law is supposed to work. Obviously, I'm in the dark here. I thought it was all about morals, and right and wrong. I assumed that's why people want to become lawyers.

"That was pretty amazing of Gary to cover for me Mick." Trying to change the subject into something more positive.

"That's not my take on it Miles. My guess is Fish and Game did not expect you to show up with a lawyer. It's just a citation, a violation, same level as a traffic ticket. Even if it can comes with a $1,000 fine, it's low level. Once Fish and Game knew you were going to fight it, they had to cover the snow job they thought they could pull off. They had to have the case dismissed before the evidence of their illegal activity came out." I never thought it might be like that. Good thing I have a lawyer as a friend.

"So Miles, what's going on with the rifle confiscation?" I explain what has gone on since we last talked about it. "Let's go to the police station together and see what they say."

At the evidence locker, the officer behind the desk looks overworked, tired, and not very friendly. I have a case number written on a piece of paper to refer to.

"Case 82-9188." The clerk goes in a file and looks it up.

" A note here says the rifle was returned to its rightful owner. So, sorry, we don't have it." Mick wants to know how the rightful ownership was determined. Where is the paper trail. Who is this owner? "That information is not public information." I interrupt:

"But it's my rifle!" The clerk shrugs like who cares and it's none of his business. I'm taking to the wrong person.

"Did you report it stolen?" I turn to Mick:

"So if I don't report it stolen it wasn't really stolen? I'm not really missing a rifle? It's all an illusion!?!" But of course this line of talk is not going to get me anyplace. Oh yes, Mick might get to the bottom of this! For a fee! For more than the price of a new rifle! So I calm down and ask the clerk.

" Is there anything you can offer me as proof that you ever had a rifle, like a serial number, or statement of confiscation connected with it that I can take to the pawn shop where I purchased the rifle. The pawn shop told me if I could prove the rifle was a stolen firearm they would replace it." No they have nothing. I am not convinced the rifle ever made it as far as the evidence locker. Mick agrees after we leave.

"Pretty common Miles. Cops confiscate stuff all the time and just keep it. Money, drugs, guns, all sorts of stuff. Not much you can do about it. Unless you're Serpico - *the story of the cop who busted all the other cops for corruption*. Cop enters your home without a warrant, sees something he likes, and takes it. It's the wilderness, who is there to question what he did? What witnesses are there? So he waits a period of time to see if it gets reported stolen. If it got reported stolen he'd step forward with some cock and bull story about evidence, or he thought it matched a serial number off a stolen firearm list he has, and is mistaken. The rifle would get returned. But he is pretty sure you will not report the rifle missing. He may assume you bought it used. Maybe even stole it. He knows you can't afford such a rifle new." "You told me this already!" "Well apparently it has not sunk in, or you would not be asking stupid questions!" I'm not sure what to believe. But figure I may as well cut my losses and pain. I'm not getting it back. I got screwed, robbed by those sworn to uphold the law. And here is Mick, my lawyer, laughing, thinking it is funny I am so naive saying:

"Happens all the time Miles, bend over, take it like a man!" And people wonder why I do not trust my government, and wish to look out for myself without the government's protection.

At least it is fair time again! Always in a good mood. Such a festive air. Associated with so many rewards. (!)

 :)

History repeats itself this time each year. I'm making money and having a good time. One of my female fans – customer who collects my necklace art, stops in, looking for this year's addition to her collection.

"Miles so many nice new pieces! What inspires you! Is there an artist you look up to?" The truth is, "not really." There are some artists I suppose I might mention so reply:

"Audubon is special to me. One of the first wildlife artists. He represents an interesting time in history. The days before animal photography. He represented…" and before I can continue, this excited female interrupts…

"Yes! I know Miles. I too admire Audubon. In fact I am a member of the Audubon Society! I did not know you were a preservationist Miles! I donate money to ensure no one harms animals or the environment!" I'm now unsure where this conversation will go. If she looked around, I sell animal body parts. This is partly what I mean when I say we all live in our own world with our own interpretations of what we do, and events around us. What then is 'truth?' There a recent special on TV I happened to catch at Josh's. Audubon was quoted in his notes, "Any day I do not kill at least 100 birds is a wasted day." I understood him to be a hunter who killed birds – propped them up on sticks, did sketches and walked away and left them. He lived off the land and ate game. I mention Audubon a lot because as an artist, he is one of my heroes who affected my ideals and life a lot. It was he, who in my opinion, started an interest in wildlife art as we know it today, with the emotion of the wild animal. Aside from this, he was a mountain man. He was a story teller. He was a braggart. He was in the limelight, the hit of parties, and in the news media, a ladies man. Many did not like him, while others did. He had personal issues. He was more famous than rich. He was a romantic. His last words were "Let us go shoot some ducks!" At sixty-five. He struggled. He had vision, passion, imagination. For all his faults the end result is a very positive influence on our country, on art, on history. I find it to be an inspiration. How to I convey all this to my customer? I do not, and reply:

"Yes indeed. I think wildlife is worth saving. I try to do scenes from nature to show the beauty and remind us to be responsible for the preservation of nature. Like this pendant on amber, with two flying geese. The amber represents the ancient past. See the ant trapped in the amber? Reminding us of wildlife having been here millions of years ago before we even got here! The geese are animals of the sky, giving a welcoming greeting to the word as the new sun rises each day!" And so on and so forth…I stand there waiting as I turn the piece to catch the light, as the lure attracts the fish. Jiggle jibble She bites.

"Oh this is breathtaking Miles, and such a sweet story! I have to have this one!" Crafty would be proud. I quote a nice high price appropriate for such a noble piece.

"It's one of a kind, hand done, and this is the only one you know, a never repeated idea." I carefully gift wrap it and nobly give her a free velvet box to put it in. "I usually charge an extra five dollars for such a box, but I want you to have it, it will help protect your art piece," $350. *Nice. Just yesterday I tried to sell it for $195, and could not close the deal.* The Wizard of Oz does it again. The noble savage passes himself off as civilized. I could hum, "Bringing in the sheep…" but that might not be a good idea.

The very next customer is a kid who I have seen before, hanging around eyeing a wolf claw. "So kid, how much money ya got?" He reaches in his picket to show me the pile of nickels and dimes. No bills. "Huh! Not much!"

"No and I need to get lunch with it, but I wish I had more. I sure like the wolf claws even though I can never afford one!" He has been eyeing a necklace for $75. He wishes he could even afford a five dollar raw small one. I sort of know his parents. Homesteaders without a lot of funds. Honest hard working sorts. I take the necklace off the stand so he can try it on even though he can't buy it. He looks in the mirror like he has died and gone to heaven.

"Well kid, guess you can have it. Looks like it belongs on your neck. Now you wear it and don't be going and selling it on me!"

"Wow, you are just going to give it to me? For nothing? I'll wear it forever!" He goes dashing off jumping hopping to tell his parents. Doubt if the kid can even count to seventy-five, much less have a clue how much $75 is. The parents come by, concerned, making sure their kid did not steal it. Want to know why I gave it to him. I trail off vaguely.

"Oh… well… I guess I have a hundred of them. Anyhow. Maybe he will come back in twenty years when he has money and buy something. It's like an investment in the future." In truth the kid tells his friends and a few come buy and spend a total of $25. That approaches about my cost breaking even on the necklace. Not that I really care. I bring in a couple of hundred extra dollars on one piece, and give away a $75 piece. That's how I am. There is my usual trade with Dan for food, I had made an angel just for his wife, knowing she collects them. I did another, "If you sell this, your cut is $100" The enthusiastic teen did not sell the necklace, but she sent a gazillion people my way. As Dan tells it, "She leans out my window points down my aisle, telling people they can't miss it, how Wild Miles has a sign out, and you'd see the mammoth tusk."

The fair ends, and it was basically just the usual fair that blends in with one of many. I make a little more money each fair, not enough the fact leaps out at me. I gross fifteen thousand in ten days.

I SEND out another letter to Jenny. I have been writing her in Germany. Not got a reply yet, and may not. But suspect things are not great with her, chasing after this dog musher she is in love with, who is marrying someone else. What a mess. Poor gal. I began just chatting the local news. But expanded to filling my own need for, 'someone to confide in," who will not be judgmental etc., and 'no reply' is okay. Or, it is better than writing to the stove as I had been doing.

Dear Jenny

So yes. Anarchy. A selfish thought. I'm convinced I'd do just fine. I know how to take care of myself. I know how to keep what's mine. I know how to get back what's mine. If it's one on one. Or even a gang. I'm smart. I could probably bushwhack ten ordinary people before they knew what happened to get back what was stolen. Even a gang, or The Mob. But no, I can't bushwhack the entire government. Ha! .....

And I was talking about my friend Mick. But that is sarcasm. He's okay, met worse, but no he is not my friend. But in my position what do I do? When you can't afford a lawyer? Go to court without one? I once thought I could! Give me a jury of my peers. Ordinary human beings. Take away all the weird language no one can understand. Just tell it like it is in plain English. I'll usually win because I am right, or 'moral,' or interested in the intent of the law, not the fine print. But? Well when I lived with Karen? Yea well- we had a custody issue with her kids. The husband arguing we are unfit parents and our lifestyle is unsuited for the raising of children. We had to go to court. Had social services come pay us a visit. That we had to pay for no less! Fly them in, fly them out. Anyhow. When we first got the notice in the mail we were in panic mode. We had no money for a lawyer! Good grief! We barley could afford to come to town to respond! Karen was freaked out and in tears. The possibility of losing our kids. The husband wanted full custody, declare her an unfit parent. There was a phone number and we called it. It must have been the fathers lawyer. I did not know.

"So what's this? What's going on? What are we supposed to do?" The lawyer-guy says:

"Don't talk to me! You need a lawyer! Have your lawyer call me!" He refused to talk to us. He only talks to other lawyers. Nothing gets done without a lawyer. I heard of people representing themselves, but they must know something. We did not even know who to call. There was just this one phone number. Even when I calmly said we did not have money for a lawyer, and we saw nothing wrong with telling our story in our own words, and we should be able to defend ourselves as we have done nothing wrong. It's just discrimination by lifestyle. He did not want to hear it and hung up on me. I found out about life in general. The last things you want to do is get anywhere near the legal system. Unless you are among the protected. So ya. Mick is all I got. And he knows it and plays on it. But what would you do in my place?

I learned some things from a book from Crafty. He's a Scientologist. I got one of his books 'The Science of Survival.' The title intrigued me. I'm into survival. One concept leapt out at me. It has to do with right and wrong and good and bad, and truth. The line, "The most good for the most number of people," as a guideline. What that means to me is- sometimes telling the truth is not the right thing to do. Like what good comes of telling someone you think they are a fat slob? Even if it's the truth. Sometimes people hide behind telling the truth. "For your own good." It's the truth. But sometimes people focus only on negative truths and the purpose of telling the truth is to hurt people, use people, weaken people, cause despair etc. I guess I always knew that, but it was not made conscious until I read that. How you can't argue with the truth. But can smile and nod and see and understand what they are about. Bringers of bad news. Negative energy swirls around some people. So I'm a little concerned. What kind of energy do I attract? Why? How? Do good things happen where I go? Or, is something happening I do not recognize? I do know all this 'stuff' in my life does not happen to everyone. There are people who will never have a rifle stolen out of their home by the police. Never have child care people come to try to take the kids. Never lose their home and everything they own to a community that set them up. Never have these experiences I have had. Logic tells me the problem is not mankind, but me. Still trying to figure out .... But if I ask anyone they laugh "What do you expect?" Maybe I have disowned society and so society has disowned me. Or, we get out of anything what you put into it. I'm not contributing much. ....

So like Gary. I do not think I am that bad a judgment of character. My gut feeling is that he is a human being, an okay person. I think he got me out of a jam he thought was frivolous, or out of line, or a waste of everyone's time. He was not going along with the program. Also? Well. If I examine everyone involved in the rifle issue and their behavior? How do things look? Marcy at the pawn shop was friendly, willing to talk, showed sympathy and was eager to make things right if she had made a mistake. The behavior of an honest person. The police- the judge?

All gave me the run around with scowling faces. None volunteered information, told me where to go for help, or seemed to care. The behavior of people up to something. Mick? Mostly it's the money that is his God. He did not get me off, Gary did. But Mick collects his money, much like the moose case that was dismissed and would have been, even without Mick. Beyond that, I have been hearing around that it was Mick who turned me in on the moose issue, because he needed the money representing me. There is sometimes a side to him, that honesty matters. A side that wants to right the wrongs of the world. But maybe somehow got caught up in the garbage he finds all around him. Got discouraged. Disappointed, angry. If you can't beat them, join them. Survival as he sees it.

I saw a tee shirt at Crafty's I thought of getting for Gary, but was not sure he'd smile. It said, "Catch and Release," a pro fishing shirt with a picture of a fisherman holding up a big fish. The shirt next to it I almost got for myself, "Work is for people who don't know how to fish," ha! So I got my fish nets back way after the fish season. Big deal. I lost half a year's wages. How would you feel loosing half a year's wages over a traffic ticket that got dismissed? No. No one cared. Probably even glad. Except as I say. Gary.

Yes Mick tried to get me all riled up I think. Riled enough to want to fight, riled enough to come up with the money to pay him. The thirty grand he says it takes to get started to make a point – to make a difference- to change things- to take a stand- to clean their clock. Make them back off. All that. But sometimes you have to back down. Choose another time and place and method. Sometimes I find, time solves a lot. Time is the great leveler. In time, we all pay for, or are rewarded for, choices we made. The lawyers, the banks, the government, big corporations, are all in fat city right now. But maybe not forever. People are not happy. And in the big picture it all revolves around people. Cooperation, trust. When that is gone, all there is, is dust, a Ponzi scheme. Fabric without the weave. Printing money with nothing behind it. But anyhow. Tired. Gotta go. **Sunshine Miles**

Sometimes I write very long letters thirty pages, fifty pages to Jenny. I told her how I used to write 500 page letters to Maggie, when I was a teen. I'm slipping, these now are short! Ha! But no reply. Unsure if she is even getting my letters, all the way in Germany. None have been returned though. *It helps me sort out my own thoughts- writing it down.* I put my usual bird feather in with the letter. I pick the iridescent feather off the wing of a widgeon. The envelope is water colored, as all my envelopes are. A swan flying over a marsh in the sunrise. Faint cattails in the misty mist of morning sleep. I sniff the paper. It's true, all my letters smell like wood smoke as many recipients comment. Well. I usually get paper on sale in huge amounts and it sits on the houseboat, or in the cabin for years before being used. Sometimes I spill stuff on the stack of paper. Usually there are fingerprints on all the pages. I write by hand, and there are no margins to see. The words go to the edge and disappear off the paper. *Obviously, someone who has boundary issues.* Said with pride. I do not even try to write in the margins, keep fingerprints off the paper. I smile. *"Look! I am human. I have a personality! See who I am? Isn't it great we are all different? This is me, who are you? I mean you know, when we take away all the trappings and restraints."* Is Jenny someone who will chuckle and smile? Think "Why I never!" I do not know.

Gene is on my mind on this subject. I am reminded by my not writing in the margins, following rules well. There had been a few of us locals in the café, and the subject at hand was how to get water out of gas. What do we add, and how much, that will get the water and snow out of gasoline. In summer we all have condensation in the gas issues with boats, or a little rain getting in, and in winter sometimes snow drops in the fuel tank of the snow machine when we take the cap off. We used to use the stuff in the yellow can, till we heard later that, no- this is the stuff that can dissolve the gaskets in the carburetor! Bad news! So we learned we need the stuff in the red can!

Gene is trying to explain the technical names of each. I can see, not everyone is going to remember. Or care. So I put in my two cents worth on the subject.

"The one I use is the 'icy-opal' (isopropyl alcohol) and the other is 'icy pro-ball,' but since I don't play ball I don't need it. Before anyone could chuckle Gene screams and comes unglued foaming at the mouth.

"Call it what it is you idiot! You can't go around making up names for things!" My first reaction is "And who is going to stop me, you?" but no I never told the truth or how I felt. He's just a lunatic. I had no reason to piss him off. Over what?

"You're right Gene I'm stupid. I just can't remember to keep it straight. The bottom line I guess is, I put the right thing in, and do not hurt my engine, using a method of remembering that works for me."

"Yea, well to bad what you do messes up what everyone else is doing!" What an odd conversation. I'm curious why what anyone else does, should affect what he thinks and does so much. I think though that he was trying to have a serious conversation and he saw me as making a joke of it. I had no intention of making fun of him, just loosening up the conversation. I thought everyone was getting tense. I now have more insight into 'why.' But there I go, seeing again in my life, the consequences of being a round peg in a world of squares. Like the painted bird, that gets all its feathers plucked out by the flock. It's not a good time for me right now.

All the food that on the Kantishna – enough for the entire winter has to stay there. No money to get it out, no way to get the boat back there again. It is all frozen now. Much will have to get tossed out when I can arrive again – probably next spring. I now have to replace much of that food so I can eat this winter. Most of the money I make at the fair is spoken for. There is little money. Normal for this time of year, as I have spent it all getting ready for winter and usually come out with furs that get me back into the money again. But I will not be able to trap as much this winter. It is not workable to trap from this end. I have fifty miles to go to get to my good trapping area. That is too far to go back and forth once a week. This would also wear the dogs out, and double the amount of food they need. I will run out of feed and have no money to buy more.

The fish for the dogs that I do have is on the Kantishna River. How do I get at it? Animals will get it, and it will not be there by spring if I wait to boat in then. I could spend all winter accomplishing nothing but trying to save everything on the Kantishna. Josh tells me:

"Well I have extra fish Miles. The commercial fish plant dumped fish for me in a pile by the dog yard. It's frozen and hard to separate the fish but it's there, more than I can ever use." Yes, the commercial fish plant looks for ways to get rid of or use the female salmon after the eggs are removed. It is the eggs worth ten dollars a fish that is saved, while the stripped fish is worth less than a dollar, so hardly worth dealing with. The same fish I am hanging and taking care of for my dogs someplace else. So much for a shortage, and so much for concerns about the fish population.

It's a pile several truckloads big. Josh guesses, 8,000 fish. All frozen in a pile. Ravens eat off it, loose dogs eat off it, and Josh chisels some off, it as he needs it. In the spring maybe half of it will have been used, and the rest will rot and become flies. This is normal, a yearly event. It's nice of Josh to offer it and remind me it's there. It would be almost impossible to dig up enough to haul anyplace else. It's half rotten now and very stinky. Dogs love it of course! Ha! But the pile is not so far from where I tie out the dogs by the houseboat.

Luckily too, I keep the houseboat totally outfitted for emergency. There is a chain saw, sleeping bag, some extra firewood on hand, dishes, all I need to live – duplicated also at the Tek land and the Kantishna.

"So Miles, maybe you can still trap this year." Yes, I can use the fish on the Kantishna when I stay there and have this fish pile in Nenana when I am at this end. So the situation is a little brighter. Still, I am upset over 'all this' over 'nothing,' two fish that were legal and not even an apology. Just a "Free to go! You are lucky!" To me 'lucky' would be to make it to trial, bring up all that is going on, and rub their nose in it, see it stop, get compensated for the loss they deliberately, with malicious intent, caused. I'm not feeling very lucky. I will be lucky to break even financially this year- keep just ahead of poverty when I could have been ahead. Ahead to repair my boat engine, to build a shop, make new dog harnesses, get some art tools and materials, who knows, lots of things need improvement. *Maybe my X could think better of me if I managed to get ahead.* But. Oh well. Not going to get ahead in life dwelling on the negative, and coming up with excuses for why I did not get anything done.

I spend time working on my book on the houseboat with the manual typewriter. I have to wait for the river to freeze to get back to the Kantishna. It will be at least a month. I will miss the most productive time to trap, the time the lakes are frozen, with the river still open about two – three weeks of time. The time I sometimes get half my winters fur catch. The book still has stumbling blocks. Whose name can I use, and if I substitute a name but the 'characters' are recognizable? Who might care, and what liabilities do I have? If I get permission from everyone mentioned, probably they will want 'their part' altered to meet their version of events. Well, we are not writing to get even, to hurt anyone, to make me look good and them bad. Yet to tell the true story, I need to review factors that had effect on my views and behavior, or it may not be understandable! At least a few real people with real names is a way to offer up proof that some of what I say, do, am, is verifiable. "Go ask them then if you do not believe me." One can ask such a person, "Is Miles even a real person?" It is a struggle.

I'M in a café-bar at Alaskaland, minding my own business at a back table by a window. I come here sometimes to be alone, undisturbed, to watch people, sip my sarsaparilla, now and then meeting someone worth talking to for pleasant conversation.

A guy plops himself at my table without introduction, without asking, and I glance up to see there are other places to sit. I make the assumption this is someone who can't stand to be alone. I wait for him to speak first, as I slowly put my 'Going Wild' manuscript down. To begin a conversation, he comments on my wolf claw necklace.

"Did you get the wolf yourself?" I shift the blade of grass in my mouth, and tip my leather hat back as I think how to reply. I get the first impression that the guy is trying to bait me. He's an environmentalist. Is he wanting a fight, merely being curious, interested in learning, or what. I might reply with a question for him, "Did you grow the cotton your pants are made of? Did you make your own watch?" Instead I decide on the nicest, kindest, approach first.

"Yes. I'm an artist and trapper, a subsistence person. I get as much directly from the land as I can. Keep life as simple as possible. I wear the claws out of respect for the animal, and to remember this particular wolf and keep it personal, as a reminder." He replies:

"As a reminder of what—the cruelty you enjoy?" I sigh inwardly. I vaguely reach under the table to make sure my knife is handy in case this gets ugly and I need to defend myself. I'm glad I sharpened it. I chew on the grass a few times and shift it to the other side of my mouth, noticing it bothers this person. He makes a comment:

"Why do you chew that blade of grass anyhow, don't you know it's annoying! Put it down while I'm talking to you—it's very rude!"

I laugh with a smile and the guy says, "You are really beginning to piss me off!" I go "hmm,' with a amused smile. "You don't stop laughing I'll wipe it off your face. You think I won't, try me!" I reply, "Oh I'm sure you will try. I have no doubt of that. But let me tell you what I see from my perspective, since you told me how it is with you." He says, "Ya right, you don't have a perspective—you're cruel to animals. You deliberately annoy people, and you're nuts." I nod, like he has a point, and I am not denying any of it. But say:

"I was sitting here alone, minding my own business not bothering anyone. You choose to come sit here at my table when there are empty tables around. You enter my private space and insult me. You feel my crap stinks, which I admit, and you act like you don't have anything that stinks. You call me names, you threaten me, while I'm trying to be kind, understanding, be forgiving, of your faults. You want me to be afraid, but I am not, so you are angry. You are demanding my attention and my respect without earning it. Now you want to take me out back and damage me, to ensure I remember you and your opinion. I find it interesting that you feel I am cruel and dangerous, while you feel you are not." I vaguely wonder if I have the word 'kick me' on my forehead. Wondering if most people have these experiences too.

A lady at a nearby table has heard part of the conversation and comes over and pulls up a chair, like she knows me. and sits close to me. I never saw her before. She's wearing a fur coat, but not a rich gal—maybe made it herself, or got it at a pawn shop. She smiles and says, "Is this man giving you any trouble Dear?" The man frowns as I say, "No he was just leaving, sit down, let me get you a beer." The problem person gets up and leaves in a huff. I say to the girl, "Thanks." She just smiles and nods. She explains her perception as to 'why.'

"You look like a book worm. You are not drinking. You are short. That adds up to target."

THANKSGIVING IS with the Josh and his wife. Bearfoot is here with his woman, and a couple of others I know. Good conversation, good cheer with good food is always nice. I enjoy talking to Josh about his sled dogs. Many evenings are spent talking and watching movies on TV in the evening. I help Josh feed dogs and improve my knowledge about sled dog care. There are other Nenana locals I get to know better, hanging out at the café in late fall when tourists are gone and all there is are us locals.

The topic of Gene comes up sometimes, since he has been creating problems with Al John, the respected native elder, and others like myself. This reminds me of a letter I still have on the subject of Gene and the Tek land. Reminding me of that time period of trying to get the land. I'm not sure now how I got the letter, or why, or what this is all about. The first couple of pages are missing. Page three has the heading:

Jerry L Brossia

May 23rd 1989

Page 3

CV: If they lose it I would like to stake the parcel.

PB: What do you know about the history of the parcel?

JW: We know that she got the jump on the parcel by falsifying residency.

PB: You have personal knowledge that Sally wasn't a resident of Alaska when she staked the parcel?

JW: Not personal knowledge, no, Gene Graham told us that. We do know that she wasn't around here most of the winter; she was here in the fall.

PB: Is there anything you would like to add?

JW: No.

CV: I'd sure like to stake that parcel if she doesn't get it.

PB: I don't think that this problem will be completely resolved before your staking packet expires!

At approximately noon, we left Wilson's cabin and took the boat up to Gene Graham's cabin (On Joan Graham permit). I had not been instructed to interview Graham, and did not. Unprompted, Graham held forth at some length about his contempt for Miles Martin. He never at any time in the conversation referred to him or Sally by name, but rather referred to Miles as "That f---maggot."

Graham told us that he just couldn't stand having people like him around, and that he would do "anything (except shoot him) to get rid of him." If that "meant using the land laws to do it." He would force DNR to enforce them.

Graham also mentioned that Miles Martin had stolen some lifejackets from his boat, and once even stayed in his cabin without permission. He also mentioned that he had reiterated his threat to run Miles out, while Martin was helping him tow his disabled boat to town!

Page 4

Graham told us that he was also going to bring Senator Jack Corncob up river to see the problem. Graham seems convinced that a politician would be able to force DNR to "follow its own laws." At this point I mentioned to Graham that Senator Coghill was already encouraging DNR to do a special sale to accommodate a trespass south of Nenana! I thought it odd that he would then turn around and suggest that we somehow find a way to cite the Martins for a trespass only three months old.

Graham went on at length about all the 'new' people coming in and especially about military hunters using the area. He said he salvaged moose meat from their kill sites to feed his dogs.

Graham also complained that "DNR had never been in the staking area." Dave reminded him that various staff members had been there four or five times, including the initial trip when we caught him flagging out his wife's parcel the day before the staking opening!

We left the Graham cabin at 12: 55 and returned to the boat landing at Nenana…

Note: On our trip in, we stopped at the (Bearfoot) parcel (ADL 412985) just downstream from Martin's cabin. Bearfoot has a small frame shack similar to Martin's,

> but we walked back into the woods where we found a much larger cabin under construction. It appears that some of the logs are being cut on adjacent state land and being illegally skidded to the site with a chain saw winch. Gene Graham is building the cabin for Bearfoot.
>
> **PB/Br**

The letter ends.

I assume the letter is some report as a result of a complaint filed.

I have no real reason to spend much time on the Tek parcel at the cabin. I do not have money to make improvements on it. All I need to live is also here at the houseboat. There is no chance to 'prove up' on the land as a way to acquire it as the land is in Sally's name, and she is the one who has to spend the time on the land in order to acquire it. I forget the length of time. I think five years. I explain to Josh when we are talking at his place watching TV.

"No Josh, we will not lose the land. One of the options is to buy the land from the state. I'm not sure what the price will be, but has been reasonable enough on other parcels I purchased, with good payment plan at low interest. Two hundred dollars a year payments for ten years or some such." Josh wants to know why I'm not spending more time there, and I explain.

"Josh, there are not a lot of good memories from there. Not that Gene exactly ran me off, but there are no neighbors who are glad to see me there. I suppose one day there might be a use for the land when I'm older and can't make the trips out to the Kantishna. This Tek land could be the ace in the hole- the closer piece of land where life is physically easier and costs less. Or, it can go to our son. But no, I don't think Sally is interested in it as a place to live." There is a rumor going around that we lost the land and it went back to the state because neither I or Sally has been around much. Josh heard that someplace. This makes the cabin and supplies 'up for grabs' not on a legal piece of land, stuff stored by illegal squatters. No one would care if items turned up missing.

"Yes, probably from Gene." The subject comes up at the café again. For the first time I hear some talk about someone needing to clean Gene's clock.

"Yes if anyone did that kind of stuff to me I'd make him disappear." Someone else,

"I agree, I just never caught him alone."

"Maybe he'll have an accident and solve everyone's problem."

I honestly had little comment. I felt this is bringing the level down to Gene's. I feel sorry for him a lot, and even when angry, I feel I want the problems to go away, but maybe by having him locked up for some crime. Or, maybe so few will be his friend, that he will burn all his bridges and eventually leave himself. If I had any feelings to the contrary I certainly would not make them public to where it's evidence in court if he suddenly- mysteriously disappeared. If I wait, hunker down, give Gene enough rope, he'll hang himself. Stuff like his comments to the DNR on record is not very bright. I'm confident in time, he'll get himself locked up. Josh and I sometimes talk about 'ethics,' and related issues. His son is still in prison for the violent killing, and Josh is, and will always be, all shook up about it. He struggles with 'why.' Struggles with what our various options in life are, when confronted with the seemingly unsolvable.

"Yes Miles, I don't care much for Gene myself. He first dammed up the slough where we park our boats! Then he ordered me to stay off this dam as a way to get to the island!" There have been dog arguments with Gene as well. Josh has a violent temper he struggles with. The subject has to be tip toed around. Josh pulled a gun on me one time, for no other reason than he did not know who I was in the dark down at his dog yard, and assumed I was someone trying to poison his race dogs as a way to thwart his ability to win a race. His only comment had been:

"Oh, it's you," and let the hammer back down, then took the gun out of my face.

"Did you hear me Miles?"

"Oh yes, sorry Josh, got a lot on my mind."

"So you are the man with the golden pen, can you write a letter that can get my son out of prison?"

"What sort of letter Josh?"

"Well for sure he could use a job offer, some situation that looks good if he were set free. You know he is a good artist. Maybe you can offer him a job." Sure I can do that. When someone does me a kindness, befriends me, I tend to be loyal, accepting of the realities of life.

" I could say I'd help him out with a job and say I trusted him and have known him a while. I'm not sure Josh that this sort of comment would have much weight. I am not anyone important. Information on me looks like I'm a criminal as well. No regular job and such." But anything might help. So I write up something and have Josh look it over. *He is grasping at straws, thinking he can get his son free.* There are theories to listen to as to who might have really done murder, and framed his son. Maybe. I listen to the theories. Josh reminds me of the time I took his son out in the woods out to my homestead long ago. Apparently Guy still talks about his trip and how he likes the woods.

Meanwhile, it looks like the Nenana River froze last night! The Tanana, the bigger river, is still open, but I know from the past that the Kantishna freezes about the same time as the Nenana and these are the only two rivers to cross. My few traps I have here are put in one of Josh's spare sleds – along with some fish for a few days, some food for me and survival gear.

"Josh, I'll be back with your sled. I'll run two sleds tied together. Unsure when I'll be back. Might be a few weeks or more." And I'm off! It's mid-November already. Not much snow this winter, with no serious cold. The sled dogs are not in great shape, but think they are up to a fifty mile trip if I go slow and maybe take two days. I can spend a night at the airport, that halfway shack. I'm anxious to get home and see if bears got to my fish or broke into the cabin. I want to see how much damage is done with the frozen food. The potatoes for sure will be lost. Or, I can boil them frozen but it's a very inferior product, good for starving times only. The dogs of course remember the trail and are glad to be out, and are being frisky on me, and in a high energy mood.

As usual, the summer- fall winds have blown a few trees down across the trail I need to cut out with the chain saw. As usual, I am the first one across the river and on the trail. I vaguely wonder why Tom and Forest are not in yet, or if they even spent freeze up on the river. I know the trail well, and arrive at the airport without incident in four hours. This is not good travel time. The dogs are tired, and slower now. I can't assume another four hours to home, even though I am halfway. It is better to stop and rest up the dogs. I tell the happy dogs.

"Anyhow, I need to do some work on this place and brought some tin." Porcupines are eating the entire building up. It must be the glue they want in the wood. I can slow the damage up if I put tin over the holes and thin spots so at least they cannot get into the cabin itself. The sled dogs are tied to the travel cable instead of chains. It's a long twenty-five foot cable with swivels in it, and short neck lines only eight inches long. The dogs are usually so tired they only want to eat and sleep after working so hard. If they need to move around they can move the cable slack and have five feet of travel room. Spruce bows are cut for the dogs to lay down on. Dog dishes and lots of supplies are already here at the shack for emergency use. All sealed up in the drum and padlocked.

Two grouse that are hiding in a tree near the shack are shot for dinner. There is no daylight this time of year past 3:00 pm. Or, it is gray out till about… well it is pitch dark by 5:00 pm. So I have a lot I want to get done in the dim light before calling it a day. I cut some extra wood. Not for this night, but to keep here for when I stop again. I'd rather do it now than in the morning. I make sure I have a usable dry sleeping bag, some pots, and pans to cook in. Snow melting is a priority for water right now, since the dogs need five gallons and I need enough for myself as well. There is a flashlight, but it uses big C batteries. The light is dim, batteries low, and I have no spare. *At least I will have some kind of light later on if I need it. I better get an updated flashlight for here though.* The kerosene lantern is relied on as well as a candle lantern I can carry outside.

There is evidence of a bear having been around, but am sure it is a black bear and hibernating now. I do check to make sure he is not hibernating under the cabin! No hammer, but a staple gun allows me to put up the thin tin over holes and porcupine damaged areas. That keeps the main outdoor cold draft from getting in. The stove is oversize to make up for the poor construction of the building. *It's hardly an airport terminal any more. Ha!* Ages ago a bulldozer put this trail in through the wilds doing seismic blasting looking for oil. At first, only three people used the fifty miles of trail.

Another homestead program opened and more programs yet, each with different rules, different amounts of land, different prices, and these newcomers begin to also use the trail. Still, there are only six or seven people who use the trail, with weeks and months that go by with no one at all using it. It is me who maintains this shack for emergency use for any of us who might need it if in trouble. I'm the only true subsistence person out of the bunch of us, and guess it is me who needs the rest stop the most. The others use snow machines. Tom and Forest have sled dogs, but have enough dogs for two big teams, and tend to travel together so have a safer, faster trip. They take less chances, do not push the dogs, have top feed, good equipment, because they have good summer jobs. I'd think they'd stop here to broth the dogs though. But, oh well. Maybe they consider it like one of my trap cabins and respecting that, so not using it.

In the morning there is new snow that fell. The dogs are eager to greet me when I step out the door. Each shaking the new snow off their fur. We are all well rested and ready to trap. We have our home at the end of this day. There are new fresh animal tracks in the snow. I set small traps for Marten, big traps for wolves. A wolverine set, some lynx sets. A few otter sets, a mink set. I decide not to try for the beaver. No time to cut the holes in the ice and no money in beaver. Game looks plentiful, good healthy populations. *Man has not devastated the area. No oil, no timber, no roads, and no pollution.*

MORE HUNTERS SHOW UP, sort of like how Gene mentioned in his interview—how the military hunters and new homesteaders show up and kill off the moose. But, I'm not angry about it. "Oh well!" It would only be 'nice' if the hunters learned in time, to have more respect for the land and the game. It hurts the land, but lots of things hurt the land, all of civilization and our consumption hurts the land. Everything we consume comes off the land.

My mind wanders on the subject in the long empty stretches we travel. An otter sees us coming. He is on top of a beaver house, and dives into the snow bank. I assume Mr Otter has a hole in the ice someplace under the snow. A Raven overhead squawks, as if he thinks that's funny. I look up and give my raven clack. The raven lands on a tree ahead and clucks back. The dogs are used to this, and pay no attention. The raven jumps up and down yelling. I have no idea what I said. His mother wears bloomers or something. I say the same thing again, and the raven puffs up and refuses to say anything more.

A pack of wolves has been across the lake at the bottom of Chicago. Chicago, the windy city. The windy spot on my trapline. I assume the wolves are watching us, because the dogs lift up their heads all in unison, and sniff, look around. As if they heard something and smelled something. Possibly the pack will be curious, and follow us after we leave the lake. This is one advantage of using sled dogs, it attracts game much more than a snow machine. I cannot make a wolf set on the lake in the open with the wolves watching. I have to wait till we duck in behind the tree line ahead. When we get there I set five snares all around, and a tree is pulled down low behind me so the wolves have to leave the trail to get around it, and maybe into the snares. I try to make it look like I never stopped here, by working off the back of the runners, and not stepping off to leave my footprints and scent. From the number of tracks on the lake it looks like a pack of about eighteen.

There is overflow water on top of the swamp in the one spot that always seems to give me trouble. But over the years I've learned how to stay on the edge, and where to cross to the other side. There is open water just three feet to the left in one spot. The exact spot I lost a sled dog once when she fell in. The ice cracks under the sled, but we are going fast enough we slide over the half inch of ice.

The Kantishna River is open in some places when we get there. But it has certain places that tend to jam up the ice and be more solid year after year. I have cut trails through the woods that give me three choices as places to cross the river. We cannot cross at the place I thought, so turn the dogs around and run one of the trails I cut a quarter of a mile to the next choice. There is only last night's snow on the ice, so know it just froze up like 'yesterday.' Good enough for us. This life is not for the faint of heart. That was a smart move yesterday, to stop at the airport instead of pressing on. This river crossing requires some daylight and alertness.

😬 :)

When I first arrived in the wilds I had a set of beliefs based on my city upbringing. I was worried about the balance of nature. How I need to be careful trapping, least I hurt this delicate balance of nature. I learned that one on one, nature is not that all delicate, Man is. The ice makes noises as we cross, and creates what Seymour refers to as 'the pucker factor.' We have to travel a quarter of a mile at a diagonal to cross safely. The dogs have been on this route before, and know how we did if before. Sometimes if there is open water and it shows up dark in the distance against the white snow, the dogs get curious and want to run over to investigate. On the ice it is hard to stop the dogs as they run to the open water.

I have yelled at them and beaten on them for doing that in the past. Sure enough there is a thin dark line of boiling open river off to our right towards the other side. The dogs perk up and look that direction. I give my deep, "Don't even think about it!" growl. Ears come down, tails go between legs, and we stick to the task at hand with no fooling around. The homestead is just a little further. Behind the back of the island, left into a pond, over a beaver damn and drop onto the slough- creek we are on. It could be either a slough or a creek. It used to be a slough till the beaver damned it up. But during floods the river cuts through. Yet it is deep and has clear water, and drains some lakes out back so in this way it is more of a creek then connected at both ends to the river.

Home sweet home. All covered in pristine undisturbed white snow. It looks like a hobbit house in a dream story from Lord of the Rings. The sunset glitters purple on the snow covering all the trees and bushes. There are bear footprints on the cabin door where a bear tried to push the door in, but did not succeed.

"You need to pull dummy, not push! Geez!" Some fish are missing. Hard to calculate how much without counting every fish. "Good place to set a trap!" Yes, lots of tracks for sure.

In two weeks I manage to catch an otter, two lynx and several fox here. Trapping is going well. Snow conditions are about perfect. The trapline trail is broken open 100 miles in two weeks. I'm living in the dog sled, a lot like mushers during the Iditarod race. Life is about pushing myself and the sled dogs to our limits every day. Work till we drop.

It feels good to accomplish something, to feel physically healthy. It feels good to take care of myself and feel that pride. It adds to my confidence, adds to my definition of who and what I am. It gives me a sense of serenity and peace. There is nothing to prove to anyone. Where I am in the pecking order is not relevant. Once again, I feel like I am on another planet since it is so vastly different then the planet called 'civilization.' Everything is different. Different rules work here, different food. I get up, go to bed, different transportation, paying bills, getting water, method of staying warm, how I dress, how I shop, it is all different. Beyond comprehension unless someone experiences it. This is a world where I hold my head high, and even get sassy with God!

These are my thoughts on the way to home base. I've been on the trail four days, have another two days to get home. No other human sign. Not a trail, not a plane, not a footprint, no sound of an engine or people in the distance. The closest human being to me might be over 100 miles. In my mind I compare it to, and say often, the equivalent of being at the headwaters of the Amazon in its remoteness.

In the back of my mind is 'moose.' *I have not gotten a moose yet and need the meat.* It's a lean year financially due to that fish case fiasco. I lost probably half a year's wages over that. *All the money I made surveying all year is what that cost me.* I can recover, and not be crying in my beer, using it as an excuse to fail. I will overcome. But doing so requires a plan, hard work, and some idea of what needs to be done to recover. Food is one of the basic needs that has to get met as a requirement for survival. I'm eating frozen potatoes turned black because I was not around to stop them from freezing. The rice and beans are okay, but when expending the kind of calories I am doing in my lifestyle I need a good balanced diet.

I'm not in panic mode, or angry, or scared. It's just on my mind. I keep an eye out for promising signs of moose. Oddly, it is not on my mind at this exact moment as I push through deep new snow headed home. The dogs are working hard in chest deep snow. I keep quiet and let my leader set the pace as he understands best the condition of the team, knows where we are going, and what pace to set. I let them rest when they need rest. The leader lets me know when the team has had enough rest. Though usually there is rest at each trap and this is enough. We are only making two miles an hour average progress. Thirty miles to go is going to take fifteen hours. I'm guessing two days. This is what I'm thinking about and accessing the supplies in the sled. There is a trap camp fifteen miles from home we will probably stop at, I have extra food and supplies here. It's an ordinary day, and set of events. This is how I live. It's not an adventure, it's life.

We come over a small hill and are headed for the easier down slope. The dogs start going much faster so I perk up and wonder why! There is a moose sleeping in the middle of the trail, and it is just waking up as we come upon him. *Dang!* The dogs are all excited of course, so charge after this moose. We will be upon it at any moment. Again "Dang!" I carry my 357 pistol in a holster that hangs from the dog sled top rail where I can reach it in a hurry. It's a little frozen in its holster as I have not had it out in at least a week.

But, by the time I get the pistol out, the dogs are right there at the hind end of the moose. A similar situation had happened years ago. Moose tend to follow trails that already exist, rather than make their own, and a trapline trail has short willow trees on the edges that moose like to eat. Trees I try to keep trimmed back. Now and then a moose goes to sleep right in the trail. Before the dogs can try to jump on the moose and be in the way of me shooting it, I give a quick aim at the back of the head and get off one shot.

Kaboom! Into the quiet world of peace goes a spinning copper messenger of death stepping out at 2,000 feet a second, or ten feet in .002 of a second. In terms of human comprehension, zero time. The bullet probably hit before I heard the gun go off. The slap of the bullet was covered by the beginning of the boom. The moose goes stiff a moment but shakes his head, and begins to turn. Past experience tells me it is very difficult to kill such a large animal with a 357 in just one shot. I do not recall ever having done it in one shot. Usually it takes three. So I am ready.

Kaboom! In the temple. As he turns and Kaboom! Again between the eyes, as the head swing is completed. Before he can charge? Oh yes, only if I miss. All sorts of excitement would result. But, I have no reason to miss. *Why would I miss?* That would require an amazingly low Jesus factor. God is my friend. I don't freeze up in wilderness emergencies. I know by how the moose is acting that he has been mortally hit. No pain, no mess, no fuss. He was alive. And five seconds later he is not. Blood is running all over.

The dogs froze at the sound of the pistol. The sled drag is on a short rope, and gets tossed in the brush at the side of the trail. When the dogs leap forward to claim the kill and partake of the feast, they are pulled short by the drag and cannot quite reach the moose, or the leader can, but only a little fur, and he only rushes forward to sniff. He knows that even though we work together, I am the leader of the pack. Who gets to do what, like eat and when, is decided by me. As is so in any pack. I'm generous, but I'm still the King. Lord of all I see in every direction, second only to God. Man, and his laws are not relevant here. *Not that I'd express that sentiment to the game cops! Ha!*

I have one of my good custom built knives with me, razor sharp. One of the tests for my knives is, they have to be able to skin a moose out without needing to be re-sharpened. None of this is new to me. This is not an adventure. This is not thrilling. This is routine, what I do once a year and have done 'a bunch of times.' I know what to do and am prepared. I'm not puzzled or confused.

I decide we may as well spend the night here. So tie up the dogs to the travel wire, get a fire going, and cut enough wood to last the night as the first priority. I get the dog pot out of the sled, fill it with snow, and begin making water as the second priority. I will be sleeping in the sled, so empty everything in the sled, and set the supplies on spruce bows I set in the snow. Only now do I turn to the moose.

It's not the biggest I ever got, but nice size bull. I should get 400 pounds of edible meat off it. Guessing he weighs 800 pounds. Moose can get over 1,000 pounds. I think even 1,500 pounds. Almost twice the weight of this one. The snow is deep enough I decide I will not try to roll the moose over. Usually I gut the moose and roll the moose away from the gut pile as I quarter it. But each situation is different. I need to be adaptable. I decide to take half the hide off and peel it back, for something to put the meat on that I cut off. I will gut it later! The hide is peeled back and the easy front quarter is removed, and carefully laid on the hide.

Past experience tells me if I lay the meat in the clean snow, the hot meat will melt the snow and then freeze as a big bloody ice ball, hard to deal with. The hind quarter is harder to remove, and weighs twice as much as the front. This is the hams. Also, the tenderloin sirloins are back here. And rump roasts. The hind leg goes up on my shoulder so I can work under it to cut to the leg socket joint. The one and only bone in the leg here. There are only a few tough tendons that hold the leg in the socket. If I reach these tendons, removal is easy. The leg pops out of the ball and socket joint. It can be done with a pocket knife if you know how. That leg is set on the hide. I trim all the meat I can off the top of the moose exposed. This goes in a pile of its own on the hide. Once frozen it will be easier to deal with. Once this good meat is removed I cut the head off and save the neck meat.

"Where did the bullets hit, what did they do?" My unconscious asks the age old questions. I am sure enough of what happened there is little need to verify. The first slug to the back of the head was a heavy hollow point that flatted out before it broke through the skull. The aim was fine, but if the bullet had broken through the skull, the moose would have fallen over dead. A solid nose bullet would have done that. I have chosen to keep a hollow point as the first round to come up, because in an emergency the hollow point makes the biggest hole. The second temple shot killed the moose, because as he turned, he exposed the thin part of his skull, which I hit and penetrated. The third shot was not necessary, but could have killed him, but probably not, but would have stopped him from charging 'probably' as a knockout punch between the eyes. Moose have a lot of sinuous cavity and skull, so it is unlikely a shot between the eyes would reach the brain with a 357 magnum. I only take a glance between his eyes to verify what I know.

Putting life down humanely requires knowledge of ballistics. Selecting the correct tools and such. I have an equal fascination for the chain saw, and how it cuts trees. I examine the wood chips, run them through my fingers to check thickness size, from this, know if I have a sharp chain, and have selected the correct chain for the job. In the same way I check my knife steel when I make a knife, and the same way I review my art inlay work and it's tools, and the same way I check fertilizers in the garden or types of leather, and the various tanning methods. My mind wanders as I cut the tongue out as one of my favorite parts. Then I cut a hole in the ribs to have access to the heart. The heart is about the size of a three gallon jug. I cut the back strap off. The back just at the snow line. I decide not to save the ribs as I sometimes do. What I have will be a heavy load as it is for the dogs. I salvage at least a third more than is required by man's law, but still feel bad I can't salvage more. There is no way to come back for it, as within hours ravens, fox, and other critters will be feasting on it, and in so doing peeing on it and leaving spit, feathers, and hair all over the meat.

There is one glitch. Usually I roll the moose onto the hide to get at the other side of the moose. I can't because all the meat is piled here. If I gut the moose I have to roll the moose over the gut pile. Risking contamination of meat.

I cut a slot in the ribs and tie a rope. I hook up two sled dogs and tell them to tighten it up and pull slowly. The moose rolls away from the hide before it is gutted. I tie off the rope as the moose breaks free of the snow. I can now cut the hide under the moose even though it is hard working on the ground level. As I cut, I have the dogs pull, and soon I have the moose rolled over, and the other half of the meat exposed, with the entire hide laid out as a blanket. I need only half the hide to pile up the meat. The other half I cut down the middle. This half of the hide is set in the dog sled, fur side up as bedding for me to sleep on. I also know that by morning the hide and meat will all be frozen, so I need to decide how to deal with it all now, before it freezes. If I sleep on the hide, the hide will not freeze. In the morning I can flip the hide over, skin side up, transfer the frozen top layer of meat onto this skin. The meat underneath will probably not be frozen and can be piled on raw. The other half of the hide will also not be frozen as it is buried under the snow, and the hot meat is piled on top of it. This hide then goes on top of the pile- skin to the meat, and wraps the meal pile. This wraps the meat pile with all the fur around it. The pile should not freeze before I get it home.

It will of course be one big mess to have 400 pounds of meat and 100 pounds of hide frozen together, and frozen to the sled. I also do not want to find the meat frozen in the morning in one big pile that I am unable to load in the sled! Thinking ahead means a solution I can live with. I could just load all the meat in the sled now and sleep someplace else! Yet, the meat is less likely to freeze in the insulated snow then in the sled.

By the time I have the moose taken care of, the day has turned to dark. The water on the fire is boiling. I can put some guts and snow blood into the pot for the dogs. There is plenty of blood frozen in the snow I can easily transfer to the dog pot along with the kidneys and intestine fat. I save the liver for myself, even though I do not like it much. There is no pot or pan with me to cook my own dinner in. I think of tossing in a good cut of meat and let it cook in the dog pot. But notice there are some stomach contents in there. The dogs love it, but gosh, it gives a nasty taste to food by human standards! Very acidy and sort of a poop taste. So I cut a green forked stick with three branches on it to make a grill. Some green pliable sticks are weaved in to make what looks like a tennis racket to make a grill to set my meat on with some fat. By the time it is done I am drooling. Wow, is it ever good! Well, compared to black frozen potatoes and rotten fish. Civilized folk might not find it perfect only because there are no spices or side dishes to this meal. Just a five pound steak to wolf down. Some would call it a roast! As I wipe my paws on one of the dogs fur as a rag I grunt, "I suppose" with a 'who cares what is happening in civilization' tone.

ON THE WAY HOME, the dogs ears perk up. I look around to determine what they have sensed. The dogs are my eyes and ears. There are huge grizzly bear tracks in the trail. He has stopped at one of my traps to rub his back on the end of the pole I have the trap on. He is not very far off as the dogs had either smelled, or heard him. It's unusual to come across a grizzly in winter on my trapline. I recall only one other time. Usually of no real concern, but today of all days there is concern. I have a sled load of bloody meat the bear would kill for, and I am traveling very slow breaking trail so could not possibly outrun, or out maneuver a bear. If the grizzly sits by the edge of the trail and waits for us to come along, we are in big trouble. Probably the 357 pistol will be of little use.

I'm not sure, as I have no knowledge how this pistol performs on grizzly. Many and even most experts tell me the 357 is not good for what I use it for, even moose. I wonder, 'compared to what?' If compared to more modern weaponry it is very outclassed for horsepower. Possibly a third or less power than can be bought now. 'However.' Compared to the past – compared to using a rock, a stick, a club, even a spear, the 357 is magic! As in, 'excuse me, but what did mankind use, how did we survive before the days of Mr. Smith and Dr. Wesson?'

"Dr.? I never heard Wesson was a doctor!?!" Okay.

Well follow my drift here, "Let me fix what ails you! Boom!" Cured. No more pain. No more hurt finger, no more cold, no more needing leaches, no more tooth ache, no more medicines needed. *You have a sick sense of humor Sir.* I'd call it 'explosive' myself. Anyhow hey. Blast that 357 into something and take a look. It puts a hole in flesh two feet deep and six inches in diameter. I do not know for sure, but I bet even a grizzly would notice.

Anyhow, what else am I going to tell myself? Ignorance is bliss. Here I am on the trail with a grizzly on the loose, me doing two miles an hour going towards him with his favorite meal that can be smelled for ten miles. Traveling bait. Wetting my pants would be even more of an attraction. Being unable to even shoot the 357 would be even less of a survival situation then at least going for it with all the confidence I can muster! But we make it home with no more sign of the bear.

My diary for the winter of 1991 is filled with days on the trail.

Diary

Jan first Haul supplies from lake—dogS fed. Have to shoot Toolie.

Jan second Twenty below zero. Run dogs, haul wood, do art, dogs out of shape.

Jan third Break trail across river with dogs, Cut wood.

Jan fourth Run dogs four hours going about four miles towards town.

Jan fifth Stay home, dogs need rest not doing so well- discouraging.

Jan sixth Break trail almost to bluff. Dogs doing better.

Jan eight Break another four miles with dogs. Out seven hours, thirty miles out and back.

Jan tenth Thirty below zero. Head for airport hard day.

Jan eleventh Fifty below zero. Head home with dogs tired, damp clothes, cold trip.

I had left when temperature was above zero and worked up a sweat. I had no new clothes to change into at the airport, and what I had did not dry out as temperature dropped on me. I was not ready for this kind of cold.

Jan twelfth—thirteenth Three dogs in the house to get better, dogs thin.

Jan thirteenth Forty five below zero. Run dogs to the drop break. Five more miles of trail. First marten in a month of trapping.

Jan fourteenth Time has pups, but is too young and thin to keep them. Load sled for airport, maybe Nenana.

Jan fifteenth Sixty below zero. Time and Whitie in the house.

Jan seventeenth Run dogs ten miles, break trail all over due to wind.

Jan eighteenth Zero degrees. Run dogs three hours. Break five more miles of trail.

Jan nineteenth Snowshoe lake out back. Rest up dogs.

Jan twentieth Plus forty degrees! Run dogs to the drop. Break five miles of trail not hard in the soft snow. Easy run to airport.

Jan twenty-third Gain ten miles, but dogs very worn out even when I snowshoe in front.

Jan twenty-forth Decide to return home to rest dogs, deep snow towards Nenana.

Jan twenty-fifth Snow melts plus forty degrees. Dogs eat good

Jan twenty-sixth Trail a mess turn back.

Jan twenty-seventh Leave for Nenana, plus twenty-five degrees night at airport.

Jan twenty-eighth Leave airport with three days of food. Hit Dim's trail 1:00 pm – a snow machine trail. Have to jog over to commission trail. Meaning Dim had taken another route and it is easier for me to take his longer route because it is broke open. Nenana by 4:00 pm at houseboat.

Jan twenty-ninth Fetch mail and snow machine To sum it up, it took almost a month of solid work to make one trip to town.

Jan thirtieth Ride to town with Josh, thirty below zero.

Feb first Return early from Fairbanks have court stuff to tend to.

Feb second Get trail open to Tek land.

Feb third Run dogs in front of snow machine.

Feb forth Machine in from Tek to see lawyer. Retire Spike.

Feb fifth Stay at Tek land. Cut wood.

Feb sixth Snow machine to Kantishna five hours felt sick, have flu.

Feb seventh 3:00 am leave for return trip to Tek for dogs.

Feb eighth Hard trip yesterday had to leave sled halfway. Dogs loose and fought. Clipper in the house.

Feb ninth Go to Fairbanks with Josh, sell furs $1,720 , thirty-five Marten.

Feb tenth Machine to Kantishna, pull dog sled full of dog feed, but have to leave 100 pounds on the trail, only got fifty pounds home.

Feb eleventh Return to Nenana.

Feb twelfth Spend the next week making fast trips to Kantishna and back with snow machine hauling dog food, trying to stay ahead so I can move back with the dogs and finish up trapping.

Feb twentieth Machine to Kantishna hauling pups in sled, prepare to move back to the Kantishna.

Feb twenty-first Have to see lawyer on court case.

Feb twenty-second Windy, feed pups main team still at Tek.

Feb twenty-third Machine to Nenana, go to Tripod Days. See Crafty about buying art Tripod days is an art selling event for me.

Feb twenty-fifth Cannot go to Kantishna as have hearing tomorrow. Pups have been without food now a few days.

Feb twenty-sixth Nenana for hearing, but hearing has been postponed a month.

Feb twenty-seventh Run sled dogs in front of snow machine to airport three hours. Machine ahead alone to feed pups.

Feb twenty-eight Moved back to Kantishna. Machine to airport to pick up main team.

Give up on trapping. Dogs not in shape. Needed fish. Spend too much time trying to haul dog feed, and needing to go to town for trial business.

March Caught about a third less fur then I usually do. Missed a lot of fur, lots of tracks, discouraging.

Diary for March and April reads much the same as January and February.

Many trips with the snow machine, here crossing two map lake.

CHAPTER ELEVEN

GENE TRIES TO KILL ME- NO ARREST - NO POLICE HELP. COMMUNITY VIGILANTE MEETINGS. GENE KILLED. I'M #1 SUSPECT

I still have not gotten a reply from Jenny but keep writing.

Dear Jenny

So I had a chat with the Carver family. I think you know them? Rain and her husband who live up the Kantishna beyond me near the Toklat River. Homesteaders like me, who come to Nenana for mail as I do. Their life is somewhat like mine, but more of a family story. They have sled dogs and fish, or are trying to! Like me, they are having problems with the way the laws are. So it is not just me who has some personal issues. They were told years ago that the Toklat River is closed to fishing because it is a spawning river. This was not the truth. The Toklat River was open to fishing the whole time.

Someone at Fish and Game either lied or did not know correctly. So they and no one else fished the Toklat, even though there are lots of fish and it is nearby. Like me, they went to court over fishing issues involving a lifestyle and trying to support a dog team. Like me they discovered 'Subsistence' is a racially based law and for Indians only. They hired a lawyer and spend thousands of dollars in court costs, arguing discrimination by race is illegal. They won! But won what? It cost them their life savings to go to court. They could not recover from this financial loss. Like with me, Fish and Game was happy to put a monkey wrench in their gears.

It seems of little use to use terms like "I have rights!" But I know. You do not want to hear about it Jenny, and I know you would suggest I get over it, to get on with life, not dwell on that which I have no control over, and focus on the good things going on, right? Okay, but still when people ask me about this most wonderful of lifestyles, envy me, and consider quitting what they are doing to live the life of Miles- shouldn't I be honest and mention the less than perfect stuff? And if someone is calling me a friend, and thinks I am nothing but happy and everything is going perfect in life, well shouldn't I be able to mention the issues and the prices as well as the rewards? Should I simply say "never mind," and or "you wouldn't understand," or be afraid of my government and keep my mouth shut, or afraid I'd look bad. Friends is not about how we look is it? Still, yes, you are right. I need to remember the good stuff! Thanks for helping me focus.

So as I said, I got a moose and have good food now for the next year! That is such a relief and such a necessity in my diet. I saved the hide, but am unsure what I will do with it as I have so many moose hides already! I was also glad to get a moose so far off the civilized beaten path. It looks to me like the roads and rivers get so hunted, maybe over hunted, while the harder more remote areas have no hunting pressure at all. Biologically it makes sense to me to try to get a moose way out as I do, where there is so much less hunting pressure, and the animal population can better deal with the loss of the moose. Sure, it's on my mind. Sure I care about the animal population…

Yup—getting art done. Wish you were still around to work with me on a catalog. I'm unsure if that will work. How can I offer a catalog economically when I sell one of a kind never to be repeated designs that cannot be re- ordered? I need a product line, but seem to never be able to! I'm always coming up with new ideas, not sticking to proven designs that sell. Shops seem reluctant to order things they do not know about, tend to ask for stuff they know sold last year, not take a chance on new designs. How am I going to overcome that? I had that guy I told you about try to help. He spent his own money as an investment. He spent $800 just to have professional pictures taken. He meant well, but was out of his depth I think. He had inherited a pile of money he was not used to managing. He wanted to invest it, and considered me a good investment, but did not know anything about the art world. Yet, professional pictures are expensive! You are telling me about the computer and the ability to take what are called digital pictures, and the ability to edit the pictures yourself and not have to send picture out to a lab. This might be a way to go in the future as my answer? Of course it requires electricity and connections in town. Do not see how that is ever going to happen – not on my income. But something to keep in the back of my mind.

You told me as well that, I cannot expect to find companionship unless I make myself available, and so I need to hang around town longer. But can I survive town? I have Fish and Game wanting me so bad I think they are capable of planting evidence, and framing me in order to put me away. I have Gene threatening to kill me. I do not have the sorts of skills I can get paid well for in a town job that would be consistent with survival. I do not consider welfare and public assistance an option.

So with my art I make a lot less money then I should. I can wholesale to Crafty who takes care of all the stuff I am not around to do. It's not as bad as ten cents on the dollar, but it might be twenty cents on the dollar. Ha! Not a problem, just a challenge. I do not like this word, 'problem,' it translates into some situation we cannot solve causing grief and is a negative word. I'd rather think in terms of challenges with various choices as solutions to choose from. In the same way I do not like or use the term 'victim.' Victim is a rabbit sitting there with its eyes closed waiting for the killing bite of the fox, helpless. There are always choices, actions we can take to improve the odds. This fishing issue has had a big effect on the lives of us subsistence people. It cost me half a year's wages to go to court, then the date gets postponed. Put in perspective, imagine paying $30,000 (half a year's wages for you) and having the hearing postponed, and having to pay that amount again for the next hearing. 'Winning' but being out sixty grand. But anyhow……

Sunshine Miles

After feeding the sled dogs, I skin furs till I get tired. I still use propane light. I keep trying to get the solar panels to produce enough power for light. The problem I seem to have is that when there is light I am not inside needing power. When I need to run lights it is winter, dark and the sun is not producing electric. The ability to store the summer power is lacking. Golf cart deep cycle twelve volt batteries are supposed to work. The best are two volt cells hooked up in series for twelve volts. I do not have that kind of money. I give up after paying out money, then I get motivated again with some new idea I think will solve the power problem. Right now I am happy with the propane light. This light gets supplemented with a kerosene Aladdin lamp.

Furs hang all around the side of the stove from the ceiling, drying. A fleshing beam, a hide scraper, and stretcher boards, take up most of the cabin space. On the table where I eat at, chain saw parts are laid out with the tools needed to fool with the saw. Everything is simple pole made furniture. Except for the original 1800 treadle sewing machine that dominates the room by the window. This machine gets used often. Tomorrow I will sew holes torn in the sled tarp. Also, I will see if I can sew a new zipper in one of the trapline shack sleeping bags. There is always something that needs repairing. On the 'to do' list is also putting Wesson oil in the chain saw and cutting up more moose meat steaks. I only cut meat for a few days at a time so the meat does not get freezer burned. Things from town like aluminum foil, saran wrap, zip lock bags, or butcher paper are not out here. Electricity for a freezer is unheard of when I can't even keep a light bulb lit. Why bother anyhow, when the great outdoors is frozen between mid-October to the following mid-April or May.

There will be meat left over in spring. Each spring I dry it out or can it in canning jars for summer needs. Sometimes there is someone in town with a freezer, and if I offer up some of the meat, even half of the meat, I can keep my half in their freezer.

Grabbing steaks as needed. I don't mind sharing half of maybe 300 pounds left each spring. Some town people do not have time, or do not know how to hunt, or are not set up for it, but at the same time love wild game, or can use the savings over having to buy meat.

I have a hand crank meat grinder to make burger, but it plugs up every five pounds of burger, and has to be taken apart and cleaned. So I keep the burger part to a minimum, and rely on steaks and roasts. Sometimes 'stir fry.' It is possible to cut moose meat paper thin, just as it is freezing. It 'shaves' easily and I can shave up ten pounds in half an hour. Some of this information I review in my mind as I skin fur, wait for a moose steak to cook on the wood stove.

Spring is around the corner. I have to think about wrapping up the trapline, selling furs, and how to prepare for spring. Will I stay here? Or, in the houseboat in Nenana? I guess I have to be in Nenana since my boat is there. I could canoe out from the Kantishna, but really need to be with the big boat to tend to it when the ice is breaking up and water levels rise. Furs have to be sold no later than the end of March, maybe early April. Fur buyers leave after this, and take what they have to the last fur auction in either Canada or Seattle.

I have not seen anyone in a few months now. I have $1,500 worth of fur. Sounds like a fair amount, but not for three months of work and out of this comes my costs. There are always traps to replace, dye for the traps, lure ingredients, things for the dogs like harness repair, sled repairs, new plastic for the bottom of the runner each season, and such things that all add up. It will take two round trips to Nenana to get everything I need out of here, like all the moose meat. There is art work as well, and maybe if I bring more tools and raw materials I can work better at the art on the houseboat. I'm still doing all my work by hand with hand tools. The nice thing is, I can work anyplace!

The fish here is all used up anyhow.... I cannot stay any longer on the Kantishna without hauling in heavy frozen fish from Nenana. Not very productive as I can only haul two weeks of food at a time. It's rotten and all frozen together, so not practical to haul anyplace. In Nenana I will have that pile of fish Josh will share with me. It did not cost him anything, and will be a mess when spring comes, and the fish thaws if the dogs do not eat it.

Luckily my neighbor on the Kantishna, Tom, has made a trip to Nenana from here. I run into his trail fifteen miles out. I'm able to make the trip to Nenana in one day without an overnight at the airport. Several round trips get all my moose meat and supplies I need to the houseboat in Nenana. The dogs are tired, thin, so glad to stay put for a while and eat lots of rotten fish. I'm not as glad as they are to be here instead of on the Kantishna, but make the best of it. Weather has been twenty below zero, cold but normal. Much of what I go through revolves around getting stopped from fishing last fall. The price is beyond measure. I even lost a couple of good dogs. I'm sure lack of top food, not enough fish, was a contributing factor.

There is an art show in Fairbanks I go to and make some money at. My furs are sold, so I have money to exist in Nenana. I notice I make more money and have more access to financial opportunities, based out of Nenana, but the bills are also higher! Am I better off than with much less money, but so few bills on the Kantishna? 'Money's is what makes the world go round, so I try to get a handle on where I am at financially. People ask. Tax people ask. What exactly is my income? I trade, re-trade stockpile, blend work with hobbies, which blended with things I take care of myself, but need tools and time that is also business expense related or helps produce income. How do I value my time and factor in the savings?

One example is thinking of my moose antler pile. I can call it 'worth 100 grand,' being honest with myself. My logic being, I get $5 to$15 per tine, and can count 1,000 tines. Do the math, that's just the tines. Bases worth $25 to $35 each, palms by the pound at $10 a pound. An easy hundred grand. *If I could sell them all retail and have no advertising costs.* On the other hand. If I died tomorrow and the antler pile is part of my estate, reality is, my relatives would pay someone to cart the antler pile to the dump. That also is 'the truth.' So just the antler pile alone is worth anywhere from a negative number, to $100,000. The question mostly is, who am I talking to? The IRS might ask "So what did you pay for it?" Much I found myself, or got given to me. I could say "nothing," or do I count the cost of my boat and gas while I was out and about finding antlers? Define 'free.' Crafty might offer $500 for all of it. A knife maker might offer $5,000 for all of it, if I caught the right maker in the right mood. I might call it a retirement pile, selling off some amount retail a little at a time, for the rest of my life. That seems to be the million dollar question in society, "What are you worth?" That always comes down to your income. Our entire social status revolves around the answer. "I do not know, nor care," is not the right answer, not even a legal answer, but a crime, if said to the wrong people.

I go to the café and it is as if I never left. The same people in the same chairs talking the same stuff. *Do these people have a life?* But it gives a sense of belonging to a tribe when we meet at the watering hole.

"Hey Miles, Gene says you left, that he ran you off. What are you doing back?" It would be easy to get angry and make some rude comment on the subject. *Ran me off indeed!* Let it be. I reply:

"No, just been out trapping, got to make a living." But everyone has to fill me in on the latest with Gene. "He has been saying someone has been messing with his boat and he was seen up on the hill across the river with a sniper rifle. Says he'll shoot anyone that goes near his boat." The community is worried it might be an innocent person, a child, or who knows, someone even checking on the boat for

Gene to make sure it is okay, maybe bailing rain water out for him, or something. Heck of a reason to get shot. More talk about someone needs to do something. I ask:

"So has anyone involved the local cop? What's his take on this? What's being done through the legal system?" There is a, 'Yea right!' laugh throughout the group. This reminds me of how life was in Manley Hot Springs during a hostage situation at the Roadhouse.

"Gene has not committed a crime yet. Till then there is nothing to do." He has not threatened anyone in particular. There is no law against being armed. He's totally legal. The police will get involved after he shoots someone. Maybe one of us. One homesteader reminds us:

"Remember how he ordered Al John to stay off the river and get his boat out of the river? Al says Gene marched into the house with a gun and Al had to go along with the program. Al is too scared to press charges. Knows Gene would kill him. Old man like that living in fear is not right!" Someone else suggest we set Gene up and kill him, make him disappear. Solve all the problems. Considering how no one else cares. Of course there are no hands waving saying they will be the volunteer to kill him! Ha! I flash on the thought Gene must be suicidal. He can't possibly think the community will put up with this. Threaten an entire community with a gun like this.

WHEN GENE RUNS into me he is not at all pleased. He looks bad after telling everyone he ran me off and is being ribbed about me being back, so what's that all about. He says to me:

"I thought I told you to leave!" I give this some thought, and reply:

"No you did not. Not quite. You suggested I leave. And I said No thank you." He says:

"I warned you! Now you'll have to face the consequences!" I have no reply. Ask what he has in mind? I go over my options. Bow to a lunatic? Move? *There will always be a lunatic in the environment.* Running seems like it is not going to solve anything. More than that, it supports this guy. He learns that his behavior works. Gets him what he wants. Is he just a bully and full of bluff? If I ignore him, will he go yell someplace else? *I'll try not to antagonize him. Make some effort to avoid him, but not let it interfere with my life. I am not a victim.* Should I go to the law? Sniffle and point, expecting protection? Would I be a hypocrite to do so, considering I do not pay for protection?

I need to be very careful what it is I say. I wish to be someone who says what I mean, and do what I say.

I DO GO to the local cop to have a chat.

"I do not want problems with Gene, or hurt him. I do not hate him. I think he has serious problems. I feel sorry for him. He needs help. If nothing is done he is going to get hurt, or will hurt someone else. The situation seems to be escalating. Can't we do anything?" I consider it is not just my problem, but a community- social problem, since Gene is threatening just about everyone. The police reply is:

"People threaten each other around here daily Miles. You want to know how often I get calls involving what someone said? How often do you think someone does something, and someone else does something back, and who did what to who is one big mess. Who do I arrest and for what? When there is a body someone will be arrested. He complains to me about you all the time. Now you complain about him. Who do I believe? I don't really care who kills who. You work it out. Otherwise, one of you will be dead, and the other will be in prison for life." That sums up how it is. The situation might resemble repeated domestic violence in the inner city.

A MONTH or two goes by. One day I ride my bike as usual, from the village to the houseboat at the end of tenth street. I take the same route, as there is only one way. I must have a routine I am not conscious of. The day is warm. There are fox tracks in the dusty one lane dirt road. Close to the river Gene jumps out of the woods and stops me at gunpoint. I almost fall off the bike as he gets in front to stop me. Gene is dressed in camouflage. Not normal for around here. He is wearing gloves in summer. Carrying a rifle is normal, but not an assault rifle, and not pointing it at anyone.

"Head on over to the river Miles. The time for talk is over. I gave you a chance. Now I'm going to kill you and dump the rifle in the river. No one will ever know. Stand over there." He is absolutely going to do this. There is no bluffing. He is not angry. He is stone cold. He has thought it all out and has been waiting for me. This is not done on an impulse. I'm about to die. The bolt comes back on the rifle. I'm on the river bank, so I will fall in the river when shot. The rifle is pointed at my chest. Behind me is the Nenana River, 150 feet across and five feet deep, running seven miles an hour. I feel the gravel slipping under my feet. In my view is the boat launch parking lot. Just a bulldozed dirt patch, and two cars with trailers hooked up. We are half a mile from the highway. Fairly secluded. A quarter of a mile downstream is the barge landing with fuel tanks, and noises to cover evil deeds.

Just as Gene is about to pull the trigger we hear a car coming. A broken down smoking white car comes into view. The driver can see us. Gene whispers harshly:

"We'll take care of this later!" The car pulls up, and a girl asks, "Is everything okay?" She sees things do not look right here. Gene walks away and leaves. I only vaguely know this woman. About twenty-five years old, shoulder length dark hair. Dressed like she is poor. She has an interest in mushing, and keeps a few dogs near where Josh does. She comes down in the evening to feed them. I ask her what she saw, explaining Gene just tried to kill me. She is shocked and ready to take me to the cops. She suggests we go right to the courthouse and talk to the magistrate.

"Miles, I can't believe it. I never come to feed the dogs at this time of day! But this time, for some reason I felt compelled to come down early! Wow!" So we go to the courthouse and get to see the magistrate. The magistrate is interested in what the witness saw.

"So the situation looked odd, and you saw a rifle pointed at Miles?" She says, "Yes."

"Was the rifle being held in a threatening position?"

"I couldn't see much to be honest. It was maybe causally pointed in the direction of Miles as the two were talking." Based on this, there is no proof of a crime. There are no grounds to do anything. I get the same impression from the magistrate as I did earlier in the week from the cop. Tell him when there's a dead body. I do not get a sense of concern. No feeling it would be too bad if I was killed. Possibly even a 'good riddance' if either of us is killed. The world does not need our kind around.

I DAY DREAM, about my heroes and lifestyle, as the witness and magistrate talk. My personality type founded our country. It was 'me' who got on the Mayflower, headed for a new hostile world filled with promise. It was me who put a 100 pound stove on my back and headed over the mountains to make it to Alaska, looking for gold. It was my kind, who paved the way, so civilization could follow, who tamed the wild, made the trails that later became roads. Trappers, traders, living a harsh life, because it is there. Our social purpose stated well for the Star Ship Enterprise. "Find, map, explore, new worlds for the purpose of saving civilization." I come back to the situation. The witness may not have wanted to get involved. She had been more sure when she spoke to me, that I was being threatened. I'm on my own.

Word spreads among the homesteaders and the locals I know who gather at the café. There is more intense talk about someone needing to do something, the community needing to take care of itself, and how come the law will not? What do we pay them for? And such talk. We all want the community to be a safe place.

Out of the blue, one of the homesteaders who does not talk much, steps up to me. I just know him as 'Guam Joe.' I surveyed his homestead at Clear Sky. He lives a dozen miles off the highway up in the hills. No roads, just a rutted four wheeler trail.

"Miles, I'll stand guard while you sleep at night." Just like that. The concern is, the walls of the house boat are thin, and it would be easy in the middle of the night, to riddle the boat full of bullet holes and kill me. Guam sits up all night with a shotgun in case Gene comes. It's nice to be able to sleep and have someone who cares if I live or die. A stranger no less. Civilization is quite odd. Guam does not talk much, or boast, or say what he will do. He is not asking to be paid, or for any favors, or expecting me to be especially beholden to him, or anything at all. He is short like me. Stocky built. Short neck. Like a wrestler. Black hair. A little oriental looking. He'd say, "An Islander."

He used to live on Guam. Owned a sailboat and lived on it. Had more money in his life then he does now. Lived on fruit and farm stuff. There were wild pigs. He tells me a little about such a life. There were problems of some kind he does not say much about. Organized crime- maybe drugs, stuff going on that causes him to stand up for the little guy. He hopes to be a writer maybe. But has not written anything yet. Just kind of drifting.

But for how many days can he stand guard over me at night? Gene can bide his time. Wait a week, a month, till things calm down. Shoot me from a lot of places, even up on the hill with his sniper rifle, and get me about anyplace in town. There is a trooper who has a different job then the local cop. I do not understand, but guess he is state employed and wears a uniform, has a badge. The local cop is sort of like one of us, hired by the city.

THE TROOPER SEEMS to care more about my situation then the local cop. I like him well enough. He is maybe, not as caught up in the local politics. He tells me, no, we can't go arrest Gene. But is willing to help me set Gene up, get evidence against him that will put him away. I tell the trooper:

"I want him locked up or getting help someplace—not dead!" So one plan is for me to be 'wired' or have a video camera. If Gene comes for me, the words and actions can be recorded. Before I get killed, the trooper will step in and make an arrest. The trooper explained it all in different terms that are legal. But there is no money available for the use of a camera or wiretap. Maybe I can buy something we need with my own money? The trooper is not forthcoming with what I need to buy.

Meanwhile, the community members meeting at the café are talking blood. Want Gene dead. Want protection. Want to feel safe. Pissed nothing is being done. Pissed there is no money for a wiretap.

"It's not just Miles at risk. Remember when Gene was up on the hill with a sniper rifle ready to shoot whoever came near his boat?" Someone else reminds us. "Al John is my friend, and deserves to be on the river. Gene had no right to threaten him and order him off the river at gunpoint! Who might be next? Any of us!" Others had their boats turned lose, or had bad business deals with Gene they are upset about. All are afraid of him.

There is an agreement. Maybe ten people. Whoever catches Gene alone will kill him, and the others will cover. Provide alibis, whatever. Plan B. I never agreed. Well, no one did. *That would make all of us accessories to murder wouldn't it?* I was honest with the trooper and told him where things are headed without giving specific to get anyone in trouble. One way or the other, something is going to get done. It'd be nice if the trooper could come up with $50 worth of prevention in the form of a wire tap, or something. Otherwise, I'm going to end up dead, or Gene is. I wondered how practical that is! A murder trial will cost a lot more than wiretap equipment.

"Isn't that going to cost the state a lot of money if there is a killing? With trial fees, investigations, and all the people involved? How come you can't spend $50 on prevention?" I'm puzzled. Are we that worthless? Why? "What'd I ever do to anyone to deserve this?" I consider it an honest question. I'm not angry. I'm confused, puzzled, and hurt. All these people in my life, tourists, those who buy my art, who slap me on the back, who tell me they are proud to meet me, tell me what an inspiration I am. Want my autograph. What kind of mixed message is this from society? The trooper seems to sympathize with my position. But who knows. It might be just lip service. He may not care who he arrests.

I already know there will be no such thing as 'self-defense.' If Gene comes for me and I manage to stop him, and kill him, I may as well commit suicide. I'm going down. Self-defense is not an option. This is seen as a feud. I do not have societies protection, yet must abide by its laws. No. I do not understand. It is not what I was taught in school. The trooper tries to tell me I have rights. But he is not showing them to me.

I am hanging out more at the Tek property. Partly to avoid town, but also there are things I can do here to finish up the cabin. There is also survey work here, and Seymour and I can stay at the cabin while we do the three surveys in the area. Gene's is one of the parcels we will survey. Gene is not at home. We are at Genes homestead.

'Miles take a look at this!" I come over to see what Seymour is looking at. An underground entrance. We go in, and there is a generator, and huge pot farm growing operation underground. All hydroponics with pipes, pumps, water, and plants in all stages of growth, maybe hundreds of plants. At the back of the property are some plants above ground in bud, ready to be harvested. Quite a sophisticated operation. But not hugely illegal here in Alaska, only mildly so, and if anyone would 'care?' Who knows.

My guess is, if I say anything, it looks like me trying to make problems in a homestead grudge war. So it is only 'interesting.' Gene will not be happy we saw this. But may have wondered how the heck he is going to get his land surveyed without the surveyor seeing. Our reaction was mostly, 'Cool!' I do not smoke or drink, but respect that others do. I do not feel pot is any worse than alcohol. The laws for now, allow us to smoke and grow a certain amount, but not to sell it. My take, the reason is only because the government does not want income without getting taxes. But anyhow and whatever. Looks like a 100 grand or better worth of pot here. I add to the conversation with Seymour:

"Talk is, Gene is having money issues with the lumber people he deals with, and owes them, but refuses to pay. Likewise, there is talk Gene is having drug distribution disputes. This can be the kind of problems that get people killed. So maybe Gene will hang his own self if allowed to gather up enough rope?" Seymour prefers to keep our talk more on business. He does not want to badmouth his clients who are paying him. Seymour does not want to get involved. I understand, so life is better changing the subject.

Once again my survey work ends and I have a big wad of money from the work. Once again I have boat rental money as well as wages involving time and a half for over eight hour days, and over a forty hour work weeks, which is half the time. It is not hard to bring in over $1,000 in a week. My dogs are being kept and fed at the Tek land. So I continue to hang out here for a while. In the evening I still write Jenny.

Dear Jenny,

So it looks like Gene is acquiring more problems, with ever more people who want nothing to do with him. Jack Corncob, and Gene had a falling out I hear. Why Jack had anything to do with him in the first place is not understandable. As you know Jack is pretty well known and connected. He helped write the Alaska Constitution, was an original signer, and was Lt. Governor of the state. He was Mayor of Nenana for five terms in a row. I recall part of the relationship with Gene, hearing it from Gene. Gene has this concept he wants to sell to the state. It has to do with an ice railroad in winter to haul supplies downriver. A train of some kind that runs on ice. Jack promised Gene he would approach the legislature and propose the plan for Gene.

It seemed to me when I heard, it's kind of a hair brained idea. Possibly Jack thought so as well, but being a politician- gave lip service to Gene with "Ya ya, I'll get right on it I'll be in touch! Good luck!" But nothing ever got done, and at some point Gene realized Jack was full of beans. Or assumed, maybe misunderstood the conversation. Gene is not someone to trifle with. If you make him a promise, you better be serious and live up to it. Gene told me a while back he has special training in demolitions, and knows all kinds of ways to start a fire. One way mentioned is how to rig a clothes drier to overheat and burn a home down so it looks like an accident. Oddly, Jack's home just burned in exactly this manner. If Gene did this, and Jack suspects, I wonder what Jack is capable of? He has the reputation of someone you do not want to mess with. A 'connected' man.

This pot farm is interesting. There has been a connection with the local drug lord never fully understood. I thought the connection was only lumber. Or, the lord being the supplier and Gene the user, not the other way around. I know enough about the local drug lord to know he is not someone you mess with either. I'm convinced he has had people 'offed' in the past. Maybe even involved in the incident with Josh's boy. Not that I'm someone who wants to get to the bottom of all this, and come up with any proof. I'd just as soon keep it talk with no substance. We need to choose our battles, and I have enough issues to deal with huh? So anyhow the plot thickens. I also talked to someone who has been to parties where the local cop was smoking weed. Not that I care, but what if it is being supplied by Gene? It might give a personal reason to not want to rattle Gene up too much? Who else might be involved, paid off, part of the problem? People who make money off what Gene is involved in. The magistrate?

It might have to do with why no official seems to want to touch Gene. All I need to do is avoid Gene. My guess is someone will solve my problem for me. Or, I might find a way to solve the problem on my own for myself and for everyone else. **Sunshine Miles**

I leave the dogs behind and boat on into Nenana to mail letters, return books to the library, and have a good meal at the café. Several hours later someone comes running in to the cafe breathless.

"Miles! Miles!" Looking around and seeing me. "Miles your home just burned down!" At first I think my houseboat. I had a fire going in the woodstove and maybe something happened. But no, it is my main Tek land home. But? But? I'm puzzled. *How would anyone know if it burned or not?* I was just there a few hours ago and left nothing burning, there is no lightening, no electric, no fire in the stove to be a source of flame. There must be a mistake.

"The firefighters came Miles, and couldn't save the cabin, and have already gone!" I'm still puzzled. I get in my boat, going upriver the twenty-five miles, and yes, my cabin is a pile of smoldering ashes. Nothing at all remains. Even the iron stove melted. I check out the root cellar to see if my supply of canned food survived. Most jars broke, but some are okay. On the root cellar floor is a dead cat, not burned, with its neck broken. I don't own a cat. Cats do not run around the Alaska wilderness wild. Someone put that cat there. I therefore understand this to be a message from Gene, so I know it was no accident, but not anything I can prove. My poor sled dogs are totally silent and in shock. The one closest to the cabin has burned fur on her back. She had tried to dive in a hole she had dug, but could not protect her tail and back. She seems okay, but wow, what was that like for the dogs?

Gene had been the first one on the scene and told the firefighters I had been cooking dog food indoors and left with the stove burning. Totally untrue. The fire fighters had no reason to investigate further. It's a pretty sad event. To lose a home and all its belongings. I'm in shock. I slowly boat back to Nenana. *At least I have the houseboat as a place to live and am not out in the cold.* I'm not paying attention, but not one person tells me they are sorry to hear of my loss. There is no mention in the local paper the next day, a paper that has trouble finding anything of interest to report. There is room for a story about how someone found their lost puppy. No one asked me if I needed anything. No one offered me a shower to get cleaned up, or even asked what my loss is – if I have a place to stay. No one wanted to hear about it when I began with, "My house just burned down." "Ya, well bummer. Welp gotta head for town, late already bye!" is a typical reply. It's an eye opener. A house burning down is a good time to look around at who your friends are. I don't bother saying anything to the police. Why bother. They'd probably say "Good!" or at best ask me if I have any proof, or any facts. They'd tell me there is no funding to investigate. *Been there and done that.*

I notice right away I'm being followed everywhere I go. Not the police. It is the drug lords people. *Gene must be connected with them.* I'm not sure. Possibly Gene has a contract out on me, and these people are trying to set me up- catch me alone. Or, they follow me so Gene knows where I am so I can't get at him. It's unnerving to be followed everyplace. One main follower is, 'Fast Eddy.' I do not know him well, or anything about him, except I see him around the drug lord a lot. Yes, it is also interesting that the whole town knows who the drug dealers are, yet they never get arrested. Why? It adds to my suspicion the entire legal system is bought off, can't be trusted. *Except this one trooper I get along with.*

This trooper asks if we can prove the fire was deliberately set. I look close around the fire scene. One fire fighter had mentioned something that puzzled him, but he had dismissed it, but comes to me as I look. I had three different structures, and each burned without showing a connection between them. In other words, if my main cabin caught on fire, how did the fire get to the other structures? If a wind took the fire, how come there is no 'direction' that shows? Each structure has fire marks on the surrounding trees that radiate away from each structure. Showing each structure was the center of three separate fires. That evidence does not support a fire starting from a woodstove in the main cabin.

I had a five gallon can of gas out front. This can is now empty and sitting in the path away from the fire, and near the river. I never put it there. How did it get moved and empty? I know I never had a fire going in the woodstove in the house. How did Gene have any information to give, concerning me cooking and having a morning fire? How would he know what I was doing that morning, and why would he say that? It seems to me there is plenty to investigate and ask. What about the dead cat? How would a cat with a broken neck get into my root cellar on its own? I have pictures to show the trooper. The dead cat, the structures showing the burn marks on the trees.

The trooper mentions funding again. "It's a long ways off the road system. A boat is needed. Investigators have to come in all the way from Fairbanks. The legal system is already financially taxed. Fairbanks cannot even take care of Fairbanks!" But, I feel I have someone on my side and he will see what he can do.

A FEW DAYS GO BY. Gene is missing, and suspected murdered. *Oh oh!* I'm the main, and only suspect. There is evidence of a struggle on the river front just 100 feet from my houseboat. Gene's boat is missing. There is blood. The newspaper in Fairbanks is already jumping on it with headlines of "Homesteader War Results in Murder!" I of course have to account for my whereabouts between 11:00 pm and 1:00 am. It's the middle of summer when the sun never sets, so it is never dark. I reply, "It was a hot day. I usually go to bed early and would be in bed at this time. But could not sleep due to the heat. I was out on my bike."

"Can anyone verify that?"

"Yes. I ran into Judy Knott around 10:00 pm. She was doing laundry at the public laundry mat and I helped her out. We talked a couple of hours until well after midnight." Did I see anything, hear anything unusual? "I wasn't at the river front, so no." My mind is taking in a lot of things fast. Sorting out what I do know, and who is saying what about their whereabouts. Not a lot is fitting what I know as the facts.

Early that morning before there was such a ruckus about Gene missing, there were odd events. I get up at 7:00 am to the sound of someone poking around in the boat parking lot. I stroll over to see what the fuss is. The drug lord himself is looking at the dirt and kicking it up around Genes truck, bending over, picking things up. I am about to ask what he is looking for. He gruffly asks if I have seen Gene, but what does that have to do with rubbing his feet around in the dirt?

It is common knowledge, this parking lot is one of the drug money exchange points. River people meet town people to do various deals. Before I can ask, Bearfoot shows up in his truck. He is just checking on his boat tied up on the river. But he later comments to me that he saw, even from a distance, that the drug lord was acting odd. "Almost as if he was covering up footprints in the dust." Bearfoot says to me.

It is the drug lord who greets the Federal investigation crew at the boat landing.

He acts like friend, offering up theories and facts. Notes are taken. He is treated as if he is in the know, and this is their prime source of good reliable trustable information. I'm thinking:

"Wait a minute, this is one of the prime suspects! The community drug dealer." *What's this 'helpful concerned citizen' talk?* Right from the get go I think the investigators start off on the wrong foot with the locals. I am here on the scene seeing it first-hand. First thing is, the local cop and trooper are told in unkind terms, the case is out of their hands. They are not in charge, and even their assistance is not necessary. Treated like country bumpkins, very disrespectfully. Local citizens seemed to be treated the same I thought. Gruffly, with suspicion, except for the drug lord- who is treated with respect. *Wow, how odd is this!*

Various people show up during the day who have normal business here at the boat landing, who also might have information, and get asked about their whereabouts. Here is Pat Burke, Dims brother. The one who more than once put a gun in my face and told me I have no right to launch my boat here, this is Indian land. He reputedly has dealings with the drug lord and Gene. I have no direct knowledge. With a hot temper, quick to pull guns. He has a scarf around his neck, and I see a wound of some kind on his neck when the scarf moves. Investigators do not notice. Pat says he was home sleeping. I know for a fact this is a lie, because I saw him as I was headed to the road on my bike coming home at 1:00 am, out on the river in his boat.

What I honestly suspect is, Pat was out working for the drug lord delivering or picking up drugs. Apparently Gene was supposed to be bringing in a shipment for transfer at this remote boat landing. Pat probably got the mark on his neck from a woman he was with, who he was not supposed to be with, so is not being honest because of this. But who knows?

Bearfoot is supposed to answer questions. It is his turn. Bearfoot is the one whose boat was cut loose by Gene. He's going to overlook it. Oh really? I'm curious what his story will be. Bearfoot gets indignant and rude saying:

"I don't have to answer any questions, and won't without a lawyer!" I think *wow, that's pretty ballsy to talk to the Gestapo like that about your rights!* I expect the Feds to jump on that and consider him a suspect for not cooperating. But the guy in charge gives a knowing smile that says, "Smart man!" with a "Next!" How odd.

Can I say that also? Like Bearfoot? "&^%$ you, leave me alone!" Some of Gene's family shows up now. One of the Gene's children, Sam, jumps in my face screaming – right here in front of everyone.

"I'm going to kill you, you son of a bitch! I know you killed my father and I'm going to get you!" Wow! Pretty heavy duty. Right here in front of everyone. Threatening my life. *Isn't that a crime?* No it is not. The federal man in charge is comforting, and asks him politely to calm down please. How we all understand how he feels. I get the impression, if Sam jumped on me, and starts killing me, the officers would step back, and not see anything. This guy in charge says to someone else:

"Just give me half an hour with Miles, just half an hour alone. I'll get it out of him!" Once again I think, "wow!" What a learning experience all this is. This is how the law operates? He wants to be alone with me to beat something out of me? This is going to solve things? I expect this in a third world country, not in America. I catch his name now, I think McCann. He's the top guy in charge, later in the news as the best cop on the force, up for promotion to be chief, having made the most arrests of anyone on the force.

It's my turn to get asked questions, to tell my story. I open my mouth to speak, and I notice no one is ready to write anything down, like was so with the others. The local cop is in the group, and gives me a glare of pure hate and a, "You keep your mouth shut about the drugs you piece of dung!"

Bearfoot is still standing here, the drug lord is here, Pat is here, and a pile of locals and suspects. People in power locally. My first thought is another "Wow!" And *"Shouldn't these interrogations be done in private? Is it normal to interrogate all the suspects in front of each other, so they all know how to fit their stories together, know who is accusing who?"* Certainly I'm not about to tell what I know for a fact, and have evidence offered here in front of people who could have me killed. The impression I'm getting from locals is;

"You play dumb, you shut up, you cover our ass, and we'll cover yours." The ones here who had nothing to do with Gene's death assume I did. But, who here is willing to sacrifice me? Offer me up- railroad a conviction and make all this go away? It's obvious this McCann Guy thinks I'm guilty, and has no interest in anything I say except that which will convict me. So like the rest of the community, I play dumb. Know nothing, see nothing, hear nothing. It's not to my advantage to have the case solved. Whoever did kill Gene did me a favor, and I want to thank them. In no way do I want to see them convicted, or me testify against them. I do not favor the local cops on the take over the drug issues, but dislike how these outside officers are treating my community even worse. First question:

"Did you and Gene have any problems?" I may as well answer that as it can't be covered up. The whole town knows.

"Yes Gene and I had serious problems. But Gene had serious problems with a lot of people." "Were your problems with Gene serious enough to kill him over?"

"I did not kill him if that's what you mean."

"Now this is the time to tell the truth! If you killed him in self-defense say so now. If you tell me later I'll be pissed! This investigation is going to cost a lot of money and I need to know now if we can wrap it up." He implies if I did kill Gene in self-defense, maybe I can get off and a lawyer will be provided, and McCann will be on my side bla bla. I know this is a bunch of crap. Look at how I'm being treated.

Not even the courtesy of a private interrogation. I'm not going to say any of that. I hear an, "Ok" and "We'll talk to you later and don't go anyplace." Dismissal. I notice no one else was told they can't go anyplace.

Now there's the whole 'looking for a body routine.' They think the body was dumped in the river. Divers show up. The missing boat is a puzzle. Gene's boat ends up being found, down by Minto tied up. If I did it, how did I get the boat to Minto and me get back again? That's thirty-five miles downriver. If it drifted there, who tied it up and why? This brings up in my mind the Minto Indians who are still mad at Gene over how he treated Al John, the respected Native. I hear Al John's story, another lie. "Gene and I were not getting along for a while, but that was a while back and everything is fine. We worked it out and are friends now." *Yea right.* Al told me just two days ago, how the problems were escalating and why didn't I kill Gene. I had joked back "Why don't you!" His only answer was: "I have never caught him alone." Anyhow I wonder where any of these ten people are who swore they'd cover for whoever did it. What's the plan? Who did it and whose covering? Maybe the plan is, everyone lies, so nothing can get sorted out. It's a big fiasco.

Speaking of a fiasco – this is when I realize Karl is gone, or is it Kyle? I can never keep the two straight. Two guys who look alike and hate each other. A true homestead war. One of them moved into a van at tenth street here. Suddenly the van is gone, and so is he. Why? How odd to choose exactly now?

They both lived at one time near Guam and a bunch of others. Bob, Mop and bucket, and Bill Gill and all of them. They got involved in wife swapping. Who knows what all. Kyle put sugar in Karl's gas. One killed the others dog. The dog got propped up, frozen along the trail. They threaten each other, pull guns on each other, mess with each other. One of them had come to me saying:

"Hey, if you kill Kyle for me and solve my problem, I'll take care of Gene for you. You'd never be a suspect if you kill Kyle." "Yea right!" Both are a couple of bozos if you ask me. But Karl says to me the other day:

"So I took care of Gene for you, now it's your turn!" Again "Yea right!" Like I believe him? But suddenly the van is gone? How odd. Hell no, the Federales don't have a clue what's going on. Absolutely totally in the dark. Depending on force, intimidation, threats to get information. Small towns don't like that much. We are not quite as under the thumb as civilized city people. We laugh at the thought of the government coming to Alaska to disarm us for example. Ha! We think not! This is not a land known for its sheep. This is the land of wolves. Piss us off and we do not bow down and go to the back of the bus as we are told. Rules regulations, threats, is not how to handle us. Our entire state has told the Feds to go stuff it. The Feds can take their grants and stuff it. That attitude trickles down to the villages. Now I'm seeing part of what the issue is.

The diving crew looking for the body are laughing, having a beach party and making jokes. They are not 'involved' in the least. It's just all interesting event to watch.

Yellow tape is tied in the trees as crews comb the woods looking for a body. Crime scene tape is all over. During all this, I see someone out of place, walking on tenth street headed for the river and us. A beautify woman in her twenties comes right up to me, and pulls me aside. She sets her backpack down. "Miles, I read in the paper about your troubles, and figure you could use some help, so here I am. I'm Viki, we have been writing back and forth, from Kodiak, remember? " Before I can remember her, she asks, "What have you told the police so far?" I tell her. She sighs, and calmly calls me a dumb ass. I later wonder if her purpose for being here is damage control. I end up with a lot of wonders!

She is a knock-out pretty willowy tall blond, long hair, Scandinavian features. She physically resembles Goldie Hawn, from an old TV show 'Laugh In." Without the dumb blonde act. I had been writing Vicki among many others. She wrote she commercial fishes in Kodiak, Alaska. (Reputed to be one of the roughest toughest occupations on the planet).

'First, keep your mouth shut Miles. These people are not your friend." I try to use a sentence with the word 'truth' in it. She interrupts:

"Screw the truth Miles. The truth will get you life in prison." I go on:

"But I didn't…" She interrupts again.

"No one cares what you did or did not do Miles. This is not about the truth, this is about putting someone away." What she says is supported by what I'm seeing. "You listen to me or you will die, you got it?" I do not even consider protesting. She appears to know what she is talking about, has zero fear, showed up to help me. What can I say? My life is in her hands.

She sees the houseboat, and makes no comment, just nods, that we are going there. She picks up her pack. It is the things she needs for a long stay. No comment about how I live. She looks around with almost a professional eye, taking in where the windows are, the door, escape routes, access points, view from the road. I'm not paying attention. I think I am in shock over the turn of events. A murder suspect.

We are interrupted the next morning by helicopters zooming overhead—looking for a body. Vicki pulls out her Glock semi-automatic nineteen shot nine millimeter pistol, and calmly sets it down within easy reach. I notice it is chrome plated with gold inlay, and has 'champion' engraved in it.

McCann shows up for further interrogations. Vicki is here to make sure I'm not roughed over. Pistol out in plain sight so he understands there will be no rough stuff. McCann seems to simply accept the situation. McCann is going to be going up the river to investigate the Gene homestead and talk to homesteaders up there. I mention what I saw, about the underground pot farm. Right now, the only motive and line of investigation has to do with a 'homesteader feud.' *Why not at least consider a drug feud*?

He treats me like I am just trying to cover my tracks, misdirect the investigation. Heck, it is probably true. I don't want the killer caught. I just want the focus of attention to leave me. I accept I am going to be a suspect. That is reasonable. But not an only suspect. McCann is still not taking notes, not interested in anything I have to say concerning my opinion, or facts on the case I might have that do not involve me as a suspect. He's very hostile and trying to be intimidating.

"So Miles, where are your guns. I'd like to see them." Vicki answers:

" Is Miles under arrest? Do you have a warrant? No? Then we think you need to leave."

After he leaves Vicki says, "He wants to disarm you." She tells me what McCann said to her when they were alone.

"He asks me why I am with you. That you are a scumbag, and does not understand why I am sleeping with you!" I'm puzzled with what her sleeping with me has to do with anything in terms of the topic at hand. Is Vicki lying about what the cop said? What an odd thing for the head of a Federal investigation to be saying to anyone. *Why would Vicki lie?* Vickie wants to run up the river and look at the burned homestead. We will be up there at the same time as the police. She wants to make sure they do not tamper with evidence. She tells me more about herself- information explaining what makes her street wise.

"Miles, I lived for a while when younger, with a drug dealer in Florida. We were big time importers. We had body guards, a swimming pool, and a very rich life. We were always armed. There were wars with other drug dealers, and the police all the time. It was common for the police to plant evidence, lie, steal from us and sell the drugs to someone else. That sort of thing. This guy, my boyfriend was killed in a shoot out. I got away, with a new identity." She had showed me some serious wounds over her body when we were in bed. A life I do not know much about. She knows this. Believes I don't stand a chance. She feels she knows what is going on. She's seen cops like this, acting like this before. She doesn't need many facts.

WE GET to the homestead on the Tek. She can see right off, the fire was deliberately set, most anyone could see that. The dead cat is still there. As we examine the dead cat the police show up. First thing they notice is that Vicki is well armed. The cops eyes get big and round, and they split up fast. I joke:

"And this is my body guard." I show them the dead cat and how it was dead before it got here, and what is a dead cat doing in my root cellar? No one is interested. No one takes a picture. No one wants a statement. Also, at Genes, there was nothing out of the ordinary. No pot plants anyplace. I know because the local hired boat operator pulls me aside. All this is just so far out of my league it is beyond comprehension. I saw the underground operation, and it is not something you can make disappear. One of the policeman is in the boat talking on a radio.

Vicki whispers to me, "He's checking me out, seeing if I have a criminal record. Finding out if my firearm is registered or not. They will get even more excited by what they get told about me." *Wow! How does she know this? I never would have guessed.* The police are in fact in a dither, because I have no record whatever. In fact No ID. I'm not in the system. I do not exist. I have no drivers license. I have never got a permit of any kind, or been fingerprinted for any reason. I have to prove who I am, and cannot.

It is believed this is an alias, and I made it all up. Who am I, really? No one exists without a police record of some kind. I can offer up my library card. The police are not amused. I think it's hilarious. Behind my straight face. Apparently my fish and wildlife issues were violations and not recorded? Or I never lost, so were not recorded? Vicki might understand better than me.

Mick is consulted when we get back. Vicki thinks he's a piece of low life, decided at first glance. But at any rate. Mick tells me not to worry. The Feds are just shaking all the bushes to see what they can scare up. Maybe and maybe not. Mick who defends the local drug lord. Not a good idea to tell Mick very much, seeing how I think the murder might be drug related. But I explain to Vicki, if there is any paperwork required by me, Mick can supply that cheap, without having to go to Fairbanks. "You know, we might need a habitués corpse or something." Vickie is not amused, and everywhere we go she is armed, and looking around at the streets, the rooftops, the windows, and steering me behind cars, making sure we do not follow a routine. She is serious, that there are several people who want me dead. *She has been a professional body guard before?* If we go to the café, we are against the wall near a window where we can see who is coming in.

I run into Bearfoot, who tells me that yes, he knew Gene was trying to kill me. That in fact Gene had showed him the rifle with a video camera taped to it saying he was going to film the execution. Bearfoot never warned me, or told me ahead of time, or told the police. "I don't want to get involved." Meanwhile, days turn into weeks and nobody has been found. It's hard to arrest someone with no body. Another 'meanwhile back at the ranch' is, experiments are being done concerning Gene's boat, and the fact it was found way downriver by Minto. It is not possible to just turn a boat loose from where Gene was probably shot, and have it drift as far as Minto from here. Someone had to take it there. If it was me, I'd have had to have an accomplice.

Meanwhile, back at another ranch, the FBI suddenly discover their star witness is the local drug lord. As in "Da!" Any local could tell them that if they bothered to ask. But the Feds showed up 'telling' us local bumpkins how it's done, rather than asking. The local police are told again, to back down, it's not their case. Meanwhile one of the Gene kids is in jail for something, and the family is in court fighting over Gene's possessions already. It does not look as much like a innocent harmless happy family. Meanwhile, some of the locals interviewed made statements I'm hearing about. One statement is made by a sort of a ringleader in the group who suggested 'we' the community, kill Gene. When asked:

" Do you think Miles is capable of having done this?" The reply was:

"Hell yes!" When notebooks were brought out to record the further replies and damaging evidence, he is asked for more details. He says:

"Half the town wanted him dead. If I had caught him alone I'd have killed him myself." More details come out. Facts about Gene. And what is coming up about Miles? What dirt? What reputation and background? When we get away from that circle of people Gene has influenced, there is no substance. "What is it we can state as 'facts' concerning Miles?" First. I have no criminal record of any kind. Not a traffic ticket, not a drunk ticket, absolutely nothing. (All my Fish and Wildlife cases I had won- or had been dismissed). There is in fact a huge difference between Gene and I. Gene had drug charges, was a murder suspect himself at one time, had violent crime issues, war related stress issues, psychological evaluations done, domestic violence issues, firearms issues, theft charges, and I'm not sure what all, but a regular rap sheet no locals I talked to knew of.

Interestingly, even the trooper is a suspect. He tells me he is under investigation, and cannot talk to me. He had taken vacation time exactly when Gene disappeared. Just coincidence? What was he doing with his off time? Did he suspect something was coming down 'soon,' had inside knowledge and left to avoid being involved? These questions are being asked.

"So Miles, I'm not in a position to talk to you on the subject much." Was he one of the few cops not on the take, caught up in the crap and thus various people wanted him 'gone'?"

Josh may not have been such a great help. Hard to say. He himself has the reputation and a record. Saying we are best friends may not be a huge help. He offered to lend me his pistol during my problems. Someone must have said something because that pistol is confiscated and examined. He's native, there was the Al John issue, and issues between Gene and another Native, my friend Josh. There may have been a brief thought, Josh and I worked together. I was a little out of the loop for getting information as to the progress and direction of the investigation. As the main suspect, the FBI did not want to answer any questions, but maybe they told no one. I do think at some point many officers went "Whoops! Bad call on that one." Too much time went by before the police realized who they needed to be talking to more.

Vicki needs to leave.

"Miles, you can come to Kodiak to visit me you know. I'll put you up and there is a festival every spring. 'Crab Fest,' with vendors set up, tourists, and money around. You might do well selling!?" I tell her that might be a good idea, and in fact plan for such a trip next year. If I'm not in prison. I have time to think, and am puzzled, raise a finger to interrupt, but stop, shake my head, 'never mind.' How much does it matter? "Does what matter?" And she's gone, poof.

I mention this to my buddy Will.

"So Vicki shows up. But Will. We were not that close. I had never even met her before. She was one of the many I was writing off and on. If I recall, from Florida. Yet when she made her move to Alaska, did not come to meet me. She said she preferred an ocean life, so settled in someplace in Kodiak. How would she have been reading the Fairbanks paper? The paper only said, 'homesteader war.' My name was not mentioned. So how did Vicki get the news it was me? She simply shows up. With a change of clothes and a multi-thousand dollar custom Glock automatic pistol with cleaning kit." I pause to let this sink in.

"Wow Miles that is strange, come to think of it." I nod. "She came across like a professional Will. Like a body guard. It was not till later I realized I have never met this Vicki I was writing. This who I met might not even have been her. "But Miles, if it was not her, who was she, and why was she showing up?" The reasons I come up with are so farfetched and weird I dare not mention. I answer,

"Well she took over. Moved in, told me what to do in a very professional manner. With me, twenty-four hours a day, will not leave my side. Sets that Glock where she can reach it at all times." The vigilante group that agreed to back up whoever kills Gene might have paid for protection. Maybe the local drug people hired someone to keep an eye on me and make sure I kept my mouth shut. The local police. "I can only speculate." "Or you have a wild imagination Miles. Maybe Vicki knew you, figured you deserved help that she could offer, and stepped forward, on her own." Will hesitates… "You seem among the protected Miles, special. Like the pilot rescue story, like me showing up every time you need a ride, ESP stuff, or something. It's just weird Miles!" This is as weird as the theories I already proposed. Nothing I wish to talk about, so we end the conversation. The phone number and address for Vicki do not connect to her. No one in Kodiak in the fishing industry ever heard of her.

I NOTICED a lot of people did not tell the truth to the Feds. It would be impossible to sort out the truth from all that was said. So, who am I to point all this out to the

Feds, who are obviously not my friend, obviously have no interest whatever in what I have to say beyond a confession.

A COUPLE of months go by, sort of peacefully without much going on with the Gene case. I'm expected to hang around. Life in Nenana becomes a routine. Weather is nice. There are no bills for me to pay. No rent, no taxes, no phone, or electric. No insurance, no payments for anything. Life on the houseboat, doing some art, peddling my bike into the community for mail and hang out at the café. It is still common to sell crafts to the tourists who come to the café. I can probably live on ten dollars a day. I buy a little food to supplement the game I hunt and wild foods I pick. There is laundry every two weeks or so, but sometimes I wash clothes in the river. Books from the library keep me occupied for entertainment. There is a paperback exchange at the library I use a lot. Leave a book-- take a book. It is common to find me out on the river 'fooling' around. If there is a duck, I might snaffle it for dinner, but sometimes I'm just taking pictures, looking for antiques, looking for mammoth fossils, gold, or simply enjoying the day.

It's a good enough life. Not the life I want forever, as I feel like I want to accomplish more than this. It is in the big picture boring, lacking challenges, not being conscious of any future like retirement, or putting anything by for hard times. It's life hand to mouth. Unsure for now what else to do. Should I move into town and get plugged in? Could I, if I even wanted to? Do I want to go back and be alone in the wild, move further out to the Bearpaw homestead, develop it, and cut more trapline, see if I can make a better living trapping? There are advantages and disadvantages to each choice. Obstacles no matter which way I go. Right now is the easy life of no decision made. A buzz around town.

A body shows up way down river. Stuck in someone's fish wheel. It is verified by the teeth as 'Gene.' I do not know the details. If a bullet was recovered, how many times he was shot etc. It's best for me to have no knowledge. However, a rumor has it he was shot in the back. One local who was sure I killed Gene reprimands me sternly:

"He did not deserve that. You should have faced him like a man, head on!" The Gene boys have given me trouble for a long time. They mess with my stuff, threaten me etc. I know enough to understand I am among the unprotected. There is no use reporting any of this. There is talk of details of how my home was burned. *Not by Gene! But by his son- who got tired of hearing his Dad cuss Miles out, saying what should be done about it.* Trying to please his Dad, he burned my home down. I tell the police what? And Why? The FBI was there on the spot while I was there, and told me themselves, the fire was deliberately set. No interest in who, why, or caring I lost my home. So there is open season on me and my stuff. Help yourself. It's hard to get ahead when stuff is missing as fast as I acquire it. This supports what Vicki had said, that I had not believed. Supports what the X's friend, the cop told me about those who have open season declared on them.

So, the Gram boys are a thorn in my side. If I do anything about that, it only supports the theory I'm a loose cannon and evidence I killed their father. All I can do is sigh and hope I can wear them down. Some day they will just go away. A thought that this sort are the losers, and in the end destroy themselves. Twenty years from now where will they be? Where will I be? All will be known in the end, if we just wait. As soon as their father died, the boys began fighting over his belongings and selling it out from under each other. The family turned on one son and had him arrested and put in jail for a short time. There was no estate left to divide up The mother ends up destitute. I wonder then, what kind of friends they have.

Hauling moose meat off the trapline fifty miles, back to the houseboat in Nenana.

CHAPTER TWELVE

BUY HOUSE IN NENANA. SALLY GONE. BACK ON THE HOMESTEAD. KILL MOOSE WITH KNIFE. SNOW MACHINE TRAPPING. NO MORE SLED DOGS. BREAK DOWN WALK FIFTY MILES

Not everything is going bonkers in my life. I focus on the positive. I review a letter I received from GEO- the prestigious German magazine. I see from the heading they have a New York office. Josef Hurban writes from 685 Third Avenue New York, New York 2/21/1996

Dear Mr. Martin

I hope you are well and the winter is not too hard this year, or at least it is as you like it! I am sure that you are aware that German GEO Magazine once published an article about you and your harsh, but courageous life in our special issue on Alaska in August, 1987. Later in 1994 New York Times Magazine had sent a team to you, writer Ted Morgan and photographer Rex Rystedt. Now I cannot be sure whether you know that GEO bought the rights to this 'update' from them. Well, we did and they published this story in our latest Alaska Special which comes out in October, 1995.

I am writing you today, since in the wake of our publication we are getting all kinds of requests from our readers that wish to get in touch with you. However I feel, that we must ask you first, whether, and if yes, how- you wish that this should happen. I shall try to reach you also by phone in the meantime (908-324-1988) but in case the letter is more successful:

Would you be so kind to let us know, whether we can give your address to readers to direct contact, and which address this should be..(the present POB one or another?).

Or, should we rather tell them that you rather not be disturbed? I feel you have the perfect right to decide whichever pleases you.

I am enclosing one issue of our Alaska Special for your perusal. Apologies for not having done so earlier. Very much looking forward to hearing from you with best regards **Josef Hurban- Bureau Chief.**

This communication lets me know the story of my lifestyle is of interest to readers. If I wish to market my lifestyle through art and writing, this is a good thing. There is so much interest! My first book is getting into a computer with the help of Jenny here in Nenana. Yes she returns from Germany during a time there were more eventful things going on. She got all my letters. They meant a lot to her. She is grateful. "You saved my life Miles!" She is helping me with my book. A first draft looks much like a comic book format, or like the old dime novels of the wild west. Printed from a computer with each cover hand painted. It costs a lot, but this might work as an inquiry copy for review by publishers.

A young lad from Switzerland shows up in Nenana looking for me. He flew all the way here, just to meet me and shake my hand, with hopes of having a conversation with me.

"Miles, I just admire you so much! What a breath of fresh air to meet someone living the dream, and not just talking about it! You have a copy of a book you are working on? I will be going to Germany and know some people there in Hamburg who might be able to print the book, but also I can go to the office of Geo and speak for you and maybe get GEO to publish your book, since the article is so popular and they already like how you write! GEO is big! They own publishing companies in the US. They have connections with Bantam." This sounds like a break I wait for and hope happens, and need to be ready for. I know I cannot make much money with paying for the printing and advertising on my own. Any writer really needs the backing of a big outfit to move volume. It would be awesome to not have to do much but write the book. Let a publisher cover costs, marketing, printing, distribution, and all I do is collect the pay check! This can free up my time to do more art, or write the next book!

"How cool would that be Stefan!" We agree that would be awesome! And why not? I mean here is the interest right here in the letter. GEO already knows who I am! Knows I am marketable! How cool is that? Stefan leaves, and I eagerly await his next communication.

I tell friends, "Well only somewhat excited and hopeful. Not putting all my eggs in this basket and counting on it. There have been others in the past who meant well and said they could help, and tried, yet somehow it is not as easy as they think." I can write the US office myself, but will wait to see how Stefan does with his connections right in Germany. He speaks German and that might be better. I have printed four or five copies of the first book for review. It's pretty rough form, but heck GEO has editors to fix all that. "Just like Alaska Magazine did." There is also the aspect Stefan speaks of with me about maybe getting the mess fixed about how I never got paid anything on the tape that got transcribed. Sort of a 'If we straighten this out maybe we can talk more business' approach.

I do struggle with the thought that if a big company basically screws me, do I go back for more? Will they treat me any better a second time around? How bad do I need them, and how much can they help me, and how much of a chance need I take in hopes they can? Am I truly in a pickle without them, or some big outfit like them, and are they all alike? I call my German friend Helm. He is in Fairbanks now at his Alaska home.

"Yea Helm! Pretty exciting huh? You told me I am famous over there in Germany!" Helm has been collecting my art for many years. A customer has become a friend. He is very stereotype German in his looks and way of talking. I find him to be gregarious, passionate in his beliefs, and loyal to his friends.

"Miles, you should really come to Germany and stay with us. Think about this. We would be glad to have you. Bring your art! I can introduce you to my friends. There is an Indian Cowboy club that meets once a week. They would like to meet you and buy your art. Some of them have lots of money. There is a new plane with Condor Air. A direct flight from Fairbanks to Frankfurt!"

I have thought of this before. Helm sounds serious too, not just giving me a line about 'be sure to stop and visit when you are in the area.' He truly would be happy to have me come visit. Helm proudly wears one of my bear claw necklaces wherever he goes. His wife Anita is a pretty woman, good match for Helm and loves my jewelry as well. Many of my customers at shows tend to be German, or at least Scandinavian. So maybe going direct to the source is a good idea. Helm himself seems to be well off and knows a few millionaires. Helm has spoken in the past about his work, and how he got to where he is.

"Worked for Westinghouse. I was in Arabia, Afghanistan, places of political unrest keeping things going." He did not elaborate beyond, "This can require knowing interesting types of people, with a variety of talents."

"But Miles, we do not enjoy so much the cruise ships. We much prefer to be with you in small boat in open air on river, listening to your stories and sharing your life!" I have to give all this some thought. But if I could bring my art and work on book business at the same time over to Germany, it might be worth the trip? Helm has a friend who owns a printing business. Raak has up to date digital printing with the first 'print on demand.' No US company at this time can offer this. This certainly involves a different mindset and lifestyle then the one I have been living in the past! I'm the guy who never drove, can't answer the phone, and is socially inept. To say to my father when he next politely asks how I am doing and reply, "Well I'm thinking of a trip to Germany to take care of some business…" and trail off. Would certainly give him food for thought. About his loser son. Some sadness in that, I'd trade all my fans for a pat on the back from relatives who think I have done okay with my life. No matter what happens in life, nothing ever quite makes up for what your family thinks.

In some ways not much changes. Just a repeat of the many other years. Seasons come and go. I go to the Kantishna in winter to trap, come back in spring, do some survey work with Seymour. I do the Tanana State Fair in midsummer, get ready for winter in the fall, with the garden harvest and getting a moose. Some art gets sold- furs get sold. There is life on the houseboat when in Nenana. I still have my room with Crafty in Fairbanks when I need to spend time in town.

I write my son regularly, but he is still too small to read. His mother reads him the parts she wants him to know, and leaves out parts of what I write him. I'm not sure what is left out, I'm not told. The Ex has full custody, full control, and this is what she wants. I want her to be happy, so go along with that. I keep hoping there might be a change. In some ways the wind has been taken from my sails. It's hard to recover. But no, maybe it is just a different kind of wind in my sails. I am not as certain everything I do is correct and right. God may look after me, but it is nothing to be smug about. For God looks out for everyone else just as much. I've given up on my heroes I once had. I do not read all I can about mountain men any more. Clint Eastwood is not as much my hero anymore. I've seen Fist Full of Dollars, and Hang 'em High enough times now. Maybe I reached an age I just don't need heroes anymore.

Jenny returned home! Back to Nenana from her overseas adventure. I never knew if she was getting my letters, even though I wrote almost every day. I have not had much of a talk with her since she got back. I've been waiting to discuss more than just business. She told me life was not good there in Germany, and my letters saved her life. She can never thank me enough. I only dumbly nod. She tells me she will thank me later. I hold my breath. I am unsure what will transpire. If she tells me I saved her 'as a friend,' I will nod and understand. If she tells me she understands most of what I wrote, accepts it, likes who I am, and wishes to pursue this further? I suppose I will also nod dumbly.

She begins going out on dates with guys who never remembered her while she was gone. Life can be like that. She never does talk to me much, and never does thank me and as she said, how can she? Sometimes we just have to do something with no thought of any gain, because it's the right thing to do. Maybe it will come back to us some day from someone else. Or, it is only a lesson in life. One of many. A test. In my stack of mail, I have not gotten to yet, is one from a stranger, it looks like a postmaster. I can make out the postal stamp and address as someplace in Pennsylvania, but cannot make out the name of the city. Harrisburg? Is there a Harrisburg in PA? I open it to see what this might be about.

Hello Miles

Just wanted you to know how beautiful your watercolors are that we get through the post office here. I am the postmaster who has been stamping them here for years, and have always meant to take the time to thank you for the beauty you bring in the world, and smile you put on our face. **Martha**

I do not think about the watercolors in this way much. It never occurred to me others besides those I send them to, see the paintings as well. This does encourage me to keep it up. This post office must be along the route on the way to upstate New York where I write my father.

There is a Christmas letter I saved from my step mother.

Christmas Greetings 1994 Mamar/Henry

Another year of learning more about what's really important—being care giver—being a receiver—neither is easy—and staying in the moment, as our yoga guides say, because it's the only place where life happens. It's now eight years since the cancer message came along in 1986—much has happened and we're surely a long way from where we started, and maybe a bit closer to where we're going, but who can tell? Just now our big issue is Mamar losing weight—88 pounds this morning, and down from previous weigh in. Getting around also tough—a few steps of walking but mostly wheelchair to get to the bath, and 'stair lift,' to get upstairs, but mostly 'Henry power.' But on we go, learning more every day about what we really value, and where our strength is and especially the joy of friends flows over us at this refection time of year…

The Xerox portion of the card ends with a personal note.

Dear Miles

I'm the writer this morning because Mamar really isn't able to write much. One aspect of her cancer condition is it makes her the nervous system fuzzy. friends gave us the New York Times article about you- very nice!

A copy of my reply is saved.

Dear Mom

I admire your bravery- perhaps beyond anything I've done. I do not know, once you learn what I have done with my life, if you will feel proud or ashamed, especially when you see the trapper magazine cover photo of me next to a snared wolf, with a happy grin on my face. I know I took a fork in the road and went off in life at a tangent.... But it is something I had to do, things I had to learn. Yes, I still have major social problems. I've never been close to anyone, probably never will be, but like to think I've made the best of my life I could. We are all dealt a hand of cards, and the best we can do is play that hand out up to our ability.

I've learned some things probably that you have learned too. I have had scurvy, lost my hair, had my teeth loose, crawled on my hands and knees unable to walk, been unable to see, known great pain, and known what it is to struggle, just to take one more step. It teaches us about ourselves, about life, and our place in it. We share something that makes me wonder if all roads meet somewhere, that it is not so much a path we are on, so much as the lessons we learn, preparing us for what we meet in the future. So hang in there! I may put you in my last book, the one in which all roads come to the same spot. **Sunshine Miles**

I write to my buddy Will, filling him in on the latest news.

Hey Will!

So I have a house in Nenana now! Wow huh! An interesting story I guess. This is a house that is the first one I'd see when coming in off the Kantishna trapline. And the first house I'd see riding my bike into Nenana from the tenth street boat landing. I would stop and say hi to Judy when I saw her out in the yard. (Judy is the lady I was talking to at the time Gene was killed).

I knew her for a long time as the old woman who sold balloons and toys to the kids. A 60's hippie hold over. Flower child. Flower print dress, big floppy sun hat, long flowing hair, wispy build. Not especially bright, but kind, and soft voiced. Loves cats. House full of cats. Into Zen and Zither music. Incense in the house all the time, mixed with the smell of pot. Buda posters and Eastern culture all over. She grows flowers in the greenhouse on the property. It's three big lots with nine structures on it. Dominated by this little log cabin built in 1916. I'd stop and she'd fix me tea. We'd chat, and I'd usually end up getting asked if I minded fixing something. Stuff she can't, that does not take long. Like unplugging a drain, or fixing a door that sticks, or broken window. Usual every day maintenance stuff. She barely owned a hammer or screw driver, and was helpless as a fixer upper. In winter I might help her shovel her truck out of the drive. She'd promise to pay me next time, or trade me something. At first I believed that, and assumed she'd catch it next time. Soon I realize she has no money, and will never pay me. It's not so much she is using me, as that she has nowhere else to turn. No one is helping her without getting paid.

I sighed and told her it is not that big a deal, and not to think about paying me anymore. I'd just do it. No use pretending and making the situation awkward for both of us. Society in general needs to look out for its old and young. It's a small thing to me. Half an hour of my time that is a huge thing to her. So over time, several years, we became sort of friends. She has a good life. Lives in her own world with the birds and her flowers she grows and sells. Her yard is a secluded one, receiving few visitors. She is a recluse. I'm reminded of the church lady in Galena. I spoke of in book two. I had thoughtlessly trampled on her wild roses. When reprimanded I told her smelling roses is for old people, when we are young we trample them. And anyhow trampling them makes them smell and grow better. She burst out in tears. Now I at least understand how someone might lock themselves up—in a rose garden of their own making.

The place is a mess, and smells of cats. Cat fur is everywhere. Civilized people would not step in the door. She knows I like the place because we talk so much about it. She believes ghosts, spirits live here, who like peace and quiet. I have in fact heard doors quietly close, soft talking, rocking chairs creaking, when no one was around. I do not try to explain how that can be. One day I see Judy at the bar going upstairs to take a shower, where the shower is. Not her kind of place! So I ask what this is all about!

In a kind accepting soft voice she says, "My bathtub fell through the floor. I asked a carpenter if he would fix it. He told me I need a new house. There is nothing he, or anyone can do. All the supports are rotten." I'm sure it can be fixed. I have solved a great many more challenges then this in my lifestyle! I tell her I will stop by to see her later.

When I come over, she shows me 'the problem,' as she describes it. It's not a problem. Just a challenge. I use her car jack to lift up the tub. The bathtub is resting on the ground. The floor is only two feet above the ground. I take some of her firewood pile, and stack it neatly and level under the tub. I let the tub down on the firewood pile. "Not a problem!" Till I see the copper water supply line is now bent and crimped, so water will not come through it. I'm not a great plumber, and do not have tools handy, like a pipe cutter, a torch and such tools as would be required to fix this.

At the local hardware store I buy a garden hose, pipe fittings and adapters for a few dollars. The main water supply is shut off. I can figure that out. All the bent thing-ma-jiggers and do-hickies are cut out with a hacksaw. Stuff I do not know what they do. I do know it's a simple bathtub. How hard can it be to figure out how to get water in it? At one of the fittings I hook up the gadget that turns water pipe to garden hose thread. One for hot, one for cold, and run the hoses into the tub. Now there is flexible hose, not attached to the tub. The tub has some wiggle room if it settles. Even if the tub moves, or even falls back to the ground eventually, she can still step into it. She is grateful.

"Miles, I can hook my longer garden hose up to this end in the tub, and water all the house plants without lifting the heavy water buckets!" She does have an amazing number of plants everywhere, now that she mentions it. It must be hard for an old fragile woman to lift heavy water cans.

An hour job. I'm on my way. It turns out she is thinking of moving! It is getting too hard on her here. She has a daughter in Anchorage, and wants to be near the grandkids to help raise them. So she will sell out here. I only nod when I hear, and will miss her. We sip tea and look out the window at the birds at her feeder. A world without violence. A world of peace and tranquility. Hemmed in with lilac bushes you can't hardly see past with that beautiful smell and colors. Butterflies flit around. Unicorns. "Knights in white satin, writing letters, never meaning to send. Just what the truth is, I can't say anymore." It must be the Rolling Stones playing on the radio in the background, but no, that's 60's music, it's a phonograph record. She asks me if I want to buy the place!

"With what!" I say in a shocked- loud- stunned voice. "I'm like you! I have no money to speak of!" We drop the subject and I forget about it.

But, parallel to this story is another story developing. I have a step mother I lost touch with when I moved to the wild. Years and years have gone by. I was sixteen when I lost touch with her. Dad has remarried, and life goes on. She sees one of my articles in a magazine. It might have been the New York Times one. She contacts the Newspaper, asks for my address! A letter is forwarded by the magazine. Here is a letter from someone I thought was dead, from the woman I saw as my mother, after ten years have gone by with no contact. As my heart leaps forward to embrace the old memories, I read. She has cancer, is dying and has thought of me all these years. She is leaving me some money in her will, now that she knows I'm still alive. She'd like to hear from me.

With sad excitement, I write her and fill her in on all I have done. She has written that it looks like I finally grew up and am someone she is proud of. My letter arrives the exact same day she dies. She never heard my reply. But her husband I never met, writes me. He is a nuclear physicist and works on cyclotrons. They both have a lot of money. I'm not up to handling going to the funeral. But I get an inheritance of ten grand. And one of her pieces of pottery she made (which means more to me then the money).

I see Judy again soon after all this turmoil with Mom. Judy is so worried about the house and who will have it. She is scared to sell it, as she knows so few would keep the house. Most want the lot, and will bulldoze the rotting log cabin down. She's been offered thirty-five grand, but she knows the house will be gone and she cannot stand that thought. Probably as well, the greenhouse and lilac bushes, all would be bulldozed to make room for an updated modern setting. The lot not far away was cleared and a modern building put up selling for 100 grand. Just a single lot while Judy has three lots. The modern lot is all gravel with not one tree on it.

Judy and I have talked. What we like is not in style, and few want a secluded looking antique gingerbread house. We both think what she has is worth more than that modern place that just went up! Ha! She does not need the money that badly. She is used to being poor. Her health is failing. This past hard long winter was too much for her. She has no more dreams that cost money. She can no longer run the greenhouse. I see piles of flower starter pots in the path as she set them down, intending to get buckets and trays to the greenhouse, but cannot, so sets them down, never to pick them up again, still here from over a year ago. The whole property is very neglected. The bushes need trimming.

"Miles, I have the chance to be with my grandkids in Anchorage where it is warmer. I want to be an influence on them, help out the parents who are having problems with the kids." I tell her I have ten grand cash and it's all I have as down payment. I am not especially looking for a home. I have the homesteads. Yet, at the same time, there are troubling concerns building up. It is great to have the house-boat at tenth street on the edge of town. Wonderful to pay no taxes and have all the freedom I do! Still, the price of that, is to live poor. According to society. I can never build a real house where the houseboat is. I can never have a garden or electricity there, or a phone. Selling art is getting more competitive. It is hard to compete with no home, no place to store art, or place to work out of, and no phone to do business with. Nor even electric to create the art! My fair booth sits out in the weather on land that is not mine where it can be vandalized and I have no recourse. When poor, if you have anything, and it gets stolen, that is no big deal because it was acquired at the dump or a garage sale anyhow. I can replace it. If an item gets recycles again, through theft, I can file no complaint. However, now I have a few valuables I need to keep someplace. I want to work on my books. This requires a computer which requires electricity. Getting power to the homestead has not materialized. Nor has the shop I keep dreaming about to work on the snow machine and other engines repairs. This place Judy has, comes with a shop as big as the house, and actually, all the things I would want. There is a way to grow food to eat, a shop to work in, a little hobbit house of a log cabin for short people. There is a well and septic system, so no water, sewer city fee, with land tax at an affordable $200 a year.

Judy tells me she will sell it to me for twenty grand, half its actual value. Half down and the rest at $200 a month payments, with no interest. Basically a steal. How can I turn that down? With the stipulation I not tear the house down for at least five years. It's difficult to make that kind of agreement legally binding, and she knows this, but is trusting me to live up to, and honor this, as otherwise it will break her heart. This is owner financed of course. No bank. Just a piece of notebook paper we write the agreement out on and get notarized. Almost the same deal as the first home I bought in Canada, before I lost everything I owned. I am smart enough to do a title search. It turns out the house is in Jack Corncob's name! Records show the property was up for back taxes in the 1950's, and disappeared from the city records while Jack was mayor. Showing up later in the land office as owned by the city mayor. Judy never knew the land is in his name! I sure do not want that. So she straightens that out with a quit claim, and it's a done deal. She moves to An

chorage. I get left the wood stove—dishes—bed—dressers—everything I need to live, all furnished. She took with her one box. Her daughter is the wife of the lawyer Mick I told you about! Ya, he moved to Anchorage where there is more legal business for him. He took his silly bird 'So sue me' So here I am! It was a great thing to invest my step mothers inheritance in. Now I can think of her whenever I think of having a home. Mom would smile seeing the place, as she loved flowers too. It's an amazingly run down acquisition, but you can't run down ornamental trees, location, seclusion, and the single word might be 'quaint.' Or 'cute,' a polite word meaning 'little value.' Without that down payment at exactly this time, it could have never happened. Without my helping out an old woman who had no way to pay me. Well, a lot of things just seemed to come together all at once. Fate. Decisions made, affecting forever.

You probably wonder if I gave up the wilds? No, it is just not quite as it once was. Nothing is. Everything changes Will. With a home and electricity I can make more money. With more money I can do more out in the wilds. I have a boat engine that actually runs! I now have more than a 50/50 chance of getting someplace! So I cover more river miles in a summer than ever before. I still trap, but now use a snow machine, and get out to the cabin in two or three hours, instead of five or six hours. I am still re-cutting all the trails as they now have to be cut to accept a snow machine. It's a lot of work, but I'm getting it done. Watch your top knot!

Sunshine Miles

It's June, and time for the big Nenana celebration called River Daze. We celebrate the summer with events on the water front. Vendors like myself set up to sell wares. There are contests like tug of war, egg toss, a boat race. There will be a dance in the street. The street is closed and a band sets up in the road. We dance in the dusty road. I've done the event before. Mop looks forward to dancing with me again. Her husband Bucket does not like to dance, and he approves of me dancing with his wife because I do not like to drink, and can be counted on to remember she is married. Mop and Bucket belong together, in the way two peas in a pod do. They work together well. Bucket is tall, quiet, hardworking, with big bushy beard, maybe an Amish dress and look. Mop is very short, pretty red head, full of energy. We both just like to dance. Crafty is coming down to sell. That will be fun. We will set up next to each other. It costs ten dollars to set up. For that we get two six foot tables. Since I have a home and storage buildings, I have been able to accumulate displays and cloths. With electric! For the first time in my life I have some basic tools like sanders, a drill press, and good light.

I had not even seen the shop before I bought it. Judy refused to acknowledge its existence. Some 'X' boyfriend built it, and she never approved of it. The shop turns out to be worth more than the home, with cement floor, steel framing, and only ten years old. The shop does not blend in well with the Zen experience of the rest of the property. Judy had told me when we first met, "Oh you can't sit there, that's the cats place!" Indeed. I can only imagine what her boyfriend went through, what place his was. Someplace beneath the cat.

MY ART TAKES a big quantum leap forward. I'm soldering and pinning my metals instead of just gluing now. I can shape my natural materials better, like turquoise, softer stones that I had trouble with before. My work is less rustic, so this fetches more money. At River Daze, Crafty is impressed.

"So Miles, I don't see you as much these days. I taught you well. Nice displays, good set up, lots of inventory- good sales pitch!" We both have a good laugh over this. For years I'd have to borrow displays and use second hand stuff to set up at shows. It was a bit rough looking in the past. I can give Crafty a run for his money now, well almost. He's, 'The Man,' in this business. He has grown and changed some as I have. Money is still his God, but he is smoother about it these days. A good person to buy from, not as good to sell to. We are enjoying the river front. A light breeze on a hot summer day. The Nenana hill is the backdrop, 'Togetille" means "A good place to meet."

"Crafty, did you find me anything at the garage sales in town?" Crafty gets out a propane tank for the homestead, a nice rain suit for the boat, a bucket of used oil. "Ya, I can use it as fire starter in the wood stove and as bar oil in the chain saw." Total is worth $20. Crafty wants to trade. But I am ready. Yup. *He wants to trade me my wholesale to his retail.* He makes twice as much money that way. I only smile.

"Crafty! My buddy Crafty! How can you do me like this?!" We both laugh that I'm on to him.

"Okay, Okay, let me refigure things." I watch again at his routine and learn. I love how he does it. He turns his back and punches keys on the calculator so I can't see. He pauses and thinks, and punches again. He scratches his chin. He pauses again as I wait. I recall this same exact performance selling furs ages ago to Don the fur dealer. Then he says, "Tell ya what I can do for ya." Smooth. Same exact words as Don. You hold your breath to hear what the deal will be. I adapt the same style. He makes a pile of my stuff, and next to it a pile of his stuff, and says nothing. Just has me look. While looking, I notice Crafty's tee shirt that reads "For you, a special deal!" I take one item out of my pile back, and let him look at it. He sighs deeply and waits, thinking. He begins to take something of his pile back, but before he does, I put something of mine in the pile, not worth as much as what was taken, but a better deal than before. He says nothing, but begins putting my stuff in his box and I begin putting away my new stuff.

The silent language I see often, especially dealing with people in other countries, of different cultures. Partly though, I have done business with people who are not very trusting, and wonder if our deal is being recorded. Why take a chance if it is not necessary? Who would record the deal, and for what purpose? *Can you say, "Big Brother?"* Thus, deals done with no words.

We both do okay selling to the public. Lots and lots of people know me. Only one in 100 does not. I wear the same showy hat, same spendy fossil necklace at all shows, so people remember me. I have a trademark, an identity, that people associate with me and connect with, that I consciously created. I've controlled the direction my art goes, and what I will sell, what kind of customers I will have. I'm pleased with how things are going. 😁 :)

I dance till I drop, at the street dance with Mop. We have a grand time. I tell her I'm headed out to the Kantishna soon to check on the garden, hunt, hang out a while. She and Bucket have to work in Denali Park to make ends meet, while I try to spend as much time on the homestead as possible.

"Yes Mop, it is a new world out there now huh? We need to work a regular job to make ends meet. I notice as well, we get more visitors in the wild, with more people who do not understand the wilderness." There are more fancy boats these days at the river front. People with money launch at tenth street now. The parking lot has been expanded. It is not a quiet place there anymore. The fuel guy no longer brings gas to the river to fill us up. Too much liability these days. *What if he spills a drop or two?* He'd never hear the end of it. The joke is? Many times I have seen boaters try to roll a fifty-five gallon barrel of gas to siphon it into the boat, and not be able to control it, and have fifty-five gallons of gas roll into the river with the lid off. At least once a year. I've done it myself. The fuel man would not likely spill this much. We are expected to own a truck to haul fuel in. I have a small three wheeler I bought for $200, and a cart. But what would life be like if I didn't? No way to get gas to the boat! No more subsistence life on the homesteads, it's all recreational. The few first original homesteaders still around had to adapt, get jobs in town, treat the homestead as a vacation home. *It is illegal to live off the land.*

My boat now is a new Carolina Skiff with a fifty horse four stroke Honda. Very quiet, very reliable, and very fuel efficient. No more mixing oil with the gas. The boat and engine is a bit faster than the old style set up. The Carolina is a pig getting up on step, but once it planes out, it flies. It's possible to hydro plane. The old wood boat could not possibly, by design, 'hydroplane.' Hydroplane is a state of grace, where the boat leaves the water and rides on a cushion of air. At about forty miles an hour. This is like the Star Ship Enterprise switching to warp speed. The only real issue I have, is that the fifty horse has to wind out at over five grand to attain warp speed. The old wood boat sure looks nice, but was a lot of work to take care of. The wood wants to rot, gets water logged, heavy, and needs paint or oil. The Carolina is fiberglass and needs nothing. It's just ugly. Ha! It looks a lot like a bathtub. And at high speed it tends to side slip in the turns with little control. But I get used to that. I just slow down briefly, let the back corner dig in and goose it into the turns.

There are gauges for the engine now. At least rpm and trim ad temperature. Yes I have power trim! Push a button, and the engine tilts up. Trims the load as I travel. As I burn gas I can trim it out. At hydroplane I can trim the front down so I don't take off like a plane.

As I get to the halfway point on the Kantishna River, while taking a trip to the homestead, I see a moose on the river bank ahead, and slow up to watch. It is a female with a calf. There is a bear trying to take the calf from her. The bear has forced the calf in the river, and is in hopes the calf will wear out, and struggle ashore someplace where the bear can snaffle it. The mother does not know what to do. She keeps chasing the bear off, but sooner or later the calf will struggle ashore, and will not be able to follow the mother. I see a chance to help the mother. The tired baby has drifted down stream. The mother has a way to get past the bear, and over to the baby if I can distract the bear. I run the boat close, and at the bear. The bear now has to concentrate on me and what I'm up to. The mother gets around, past the bear, and on over to the baby. I hold the bear at bay till the mother has the calf out of the water and into the woods to some safer place. It's just an interesting interruption on an uneventful trip.

The homestead is okay. Not great. I notice with each trip, the homestead is a little more run down from no one living here, and needs repairs of different sorts. For sure the tall bushes need trimming back with the cycle! Rosehips get over head high. There is hardly a path from the creek to the cabin till I clear it. Still, it is always good to be here. There is an idea I have, that I got parts for. I want to install an automatic watering system for the garden. A fifty-five gallon barrel with a float switch in it to turn a twelve volt pump on. When it gets full the twitch turns on the pump to send warm water through the sprinkler- soaker hose, gravity feed with the battery operated timed value. I set all this up to see if it will work. A small one foot solar panel is used to power the battery and pump. The plan does not work.

A simpler plan does. I forget the barrel. I float the pump and solar panel in the creek on a Styrofoam block. The foam can go up and down as the water rises and falls. When the sun is out, the weather is probably hot. The sun runs the solar panel that puts out just enough power to run the water pump. When the sun goes down, I can assume the temperature cools, the garden is less likely to need any water. No sun, no power, no power, no running pump. That simple, a solar panel hooked direct to the pump with no controller of any kind.

There is a plan now to run a twelve volt drill using my main solar panel bank. This is a battery operated drill. The battery takes a charger that needs 110 electricity. Cheap efficient inverters are not available yet. There is a solution I want to try. One of my first projects is to carve a battery of wood for this drill. This is about a foot long and two inches in diameter. I make a wooden dummy of a Makita drill NiCad battery. Two grooves for wire are cut with a hand graver. A tin can is cut with tin snips for electrical contacts. These are inserted in the same spot as the battery has them.

When the wood dummy battery is inserted, the metal contacts allow the twelve volt power from the solar panel to run the drill, either direct from the panels, or off the battery bank. This is an exciting day! "For the first time we have a power tool!" This drill allows me to run a disk sander, for sanding –polishing, or a drill for making holes. Till now I have used a hand drill, and sanded with my hands. It has been getting more difficult to compete with the new third world country products entering the art trade and gift shops, even the galleries. In the beginning it was the joke, "Made in Japan." Referring to junk that falls apart- seen in dollar thrift stores. Then it was Korea, then Bali with imported cheap jewelry and carvings. Mostly in the cheaper tourist shops. Yes, more and more we see acceptance of these imported products. It's put a serious crimp in the local hand crafted market. Nothing I can't overcome, just some extra added challenges. Possibly the quality of imports has in general gone up, while quality of American made has gone down. This is a little scary. It's a bigger challenge now to compete. There are ways however to compete with motivated skilled workers overseas earning a dollar a day.

First I want to try to offer as best I can, some aspect of my product that cannot easily be mass produced- copied; or the materials are hard to get, or I am in control of the material that is limited in supply. "Way you gonna git wolf claws Mr. Bali Man huh? Make yoe move, but tink ya been check mated eh?" I must also speed up the time it takes me to create my art to get the price down. I've known for a long time customers just love to hear how it's hand done without power, or light, and how I slaved away at their personal piece of art. All for a deal. "You want a deal Dear Customer? You want a part of my soul for ten cents on the dollar?" With a straight face, "I offer you that which you so richly deserve." This twelve volt drill is a big step for me.

A cutting tool is designed that fits in the drill so I can slice and dice with electric. There will be a bigger inventory this season! Another aspect of doing business is, I see myself more as offering magic. *Reality is for engineers.* The artist is the dreamer. Creating beauty from rawness is more and more my role. One of my roles when selling then, is to determine what it is the customer seeks. Or even 'deserves.' *"Seek and ye shall find."* I try not to be upset, feel indignant when a customer expects a real diamond ring from a bubble gum machine. While unwinding in the evening I begin a letter, maybe to help sort my own thoughts. Jenny is back so I suppose I cannot write her any more. I write anyway.

Dear Jenny

So even though I got a house in town I think of it as a place to stay when in civilization, but my real home and heart is in the wild. There is electricity at the new town place. I spent a long time in awe of flipping a switch and having light! Imagine! I go into each room. 'Flip flip flip,' with a big smile- just to see it work. I spent thousands of dollars trying to get a light bulb to light up here at the homestead, and still, after ten years, not successful. It is awesome as well to turn a handle and get hot water! How cool is that!? I forgot. It is how I was raised, but I just forgot. Still, what good is all that nice stuff, easy stuff, if you don't have the money to pay for it? It's like getting a ride in a Rolls might be the experience of a lifetime! But it's not necessarily healthy to think of it as a way of life. It all costs. Where's the money going to come from? On a $2,000 to $3,000 a year income, buying a stamp and envelope to send a letter has to be budgeted. I live well enough all right, but it's a lifestyle, and some things can be made to happen in that lifestyle, and other things need to be seen as daydreaming. I also make more money then I began with, over $10,000 a year now.

So 'electric' is nice all right. But to run what? I can't afford tools and things to run that need electric. Ninety percent of what I have now I have because I built it myself, or got it very well used at a dump- garage sale or thrift store. I tell myself I have the most valuable things in the world as it is! Time, health, independence. But yes, money is the grease that makes the world go round. Anyhow, yup I'm fine, doing good, glad to be back at the homestead. Lots to do. Some bear damage again that needs fixing. I'll put fish nets out and get some salmon, pick some wild herbs and things to eat, maybe dry some for later. Hope all is well in your world.

Sunshine Miles

I THROW the letter in the stove when I am done. There is no one to send it to. It is important I wrote it. It is better actually, to send it to no one, and then I will not be disappointed.

Life seems good, back in a familiar setting where life has been a success for me. This is the world I have knowledge in and I am 'able,' as well as confident and happy. Meals are salmon, ducks, grouse, rabbits, beaver, along with wild plants like mushrooms, marsh marigold, Eskimo potato, and many berries. This gets mixed with the staples I bring from town and have stockpiled. Barley, whole grain rice, corn meal, oatmeal, are bought at the animal feed store in bulk. Corn meal is 50 pounds for $15. Sure it has some flax seed and cob parts in it, and it's on the coarse side. But I remind myself; *hey it's natural stuff, no chemicals, preservatives, salt- sugar- all that stuff that gets added to 'modern foods.'* The real bottom line though is 'cost.' This is what I can afford. There are a few dented cans from the ten cent section at the store, soups to put over rice with rabbit. My grocery bill is still under $300 a year. Even including an occasional meal out on the town. Still, time in town means bills. Time in the wild means no bills.

There is no extra gas to go anyplace or do much. But when fair time rolls around in August I am ready with lots of art to come in and make some operating cash. The trip goes well enough. I get mail in Nenana, and boat on into Fairbanks. The fairgrounds is not far from the river. As I expected, I do well selling, am almost doubling how much I make every year now. I made $200 before I had my own booth. The next year with a booth I got $400, then $800, then the next year $1,600, and this year looks like it will be about $3,000. *Not bad for two weeks work!* But of course I am only thinking of time selling, not creating, and ignore the fact that there has been so little other income this year. But, whatever, not a huge big deal. It's enough money to get my winter supplies so I'm sitting good. 😀 :)

Heidi and her kids come by, and the kids hang out at the booth as usual. Dan at the Patty Wagon trades for my food again, and leaves me five gallon containers of fat for my dogs. I probably will not have dogs, but know I can use this fat to trade with Josh who needs it. Hate to see it get tossed in the dump.

I head back to the homestead for the winter. The temperature drops and weather is unseasonably cold. Ice builds up on the side of the boat. Every ten miles I have to stop, pull over, and knock the ice off. Ice runs on the river so my engine cooling system sucks ice into the water pump. Moonshine is out on the river checking fish nets in this weather. I stop to say hi, and knock more ice off. We both laugh at the weather, and find it annoying, but part of a lifestyle we both live.

"Miles, you headed up the Kantishna to freeze in?"

"Yup, hopefully trapping will be better this winter, especially fur prices." Moonshine has trapped a little with his sled dogs as part of his dog training for racing. Trapping puts a lot of miles on the dogs.

"I heard lynx prices might come up this season, but marten should stay about the same."

"I heard the same, but who knows? I need marten to come up. I don't get many lynx on my line. I might tan fur this year and sell to the tourist market, cut out the middle people."

"Sure Miles, if you can afford to wait on your money, and you have money to invest in tanning!"

"Good point, but I have the outlet when selling my art. I get asked a lot if I have any furs. But then some bunny huggers will not shop with someone who kills cute fuzzy things for a living."

"I know what you mean. Tree kissing bunny screwers are also trying to stop the Iditarod dog race, calling it cruel and inhumane. It's harder to get sponsors now." While we chat I get out my thermos of hot soup I made this morning to have as my lunch as I travel. I hand a hot cup full to Moonshine. When we are done eating, I ask how the fishing is going. Moonshine is using a wheel instead of nets.

"Well I got 400 silver and 200 chums today." He runs the fish to Manley Hot Springs downstream and sells to the local processor there, who shows up during the short commercial season. There used to be more money in fishing, but well, various things are going on affecting profits. "You don't have dogs any more Miles ? What happened? Give it up?" It's not something I want to talk about. To many years in a row I got stopped from fishing by Fish and Game having its emergency closures in late fall. "Sure I understand Miles, civilization wiped out the buffalo for the purpose of controlling the Indian a hundred years ago. That still works." Moonshine thinks of a new topic and brightens up wanting to get some fresh news. "Hey, heard Genes body was found, any news on who did it?"

"One thing is Dough is sure I did it and reprimanded me for shooting Gene in the back, saying anyone deserves to face their executioner." "An interesting viewpoint, that there are rules to follow concerning killing people properly." "Yes, as if there is something wrong with using cheese and a trap to kill a rat, that one must face the rat and strangle it one on one, give the rat a chance, to be fair to the rat. Except I do think nothing deserves to suffer, even if killed." "Maybe Miles, but now and then suffering helps deter other people from doing the same thing." "Maybe, but I still have my view that is not going to change. A dog might have the rabies running around threatening to bite everyone, terrorizing the neighborhood. The dog should be shot, but it is sick, what good is making it suffer going to do? We just do not want the dog to bite and infect anyone." "Hey Miles, I just thought of something. I heard in the past Dough is one of the major money investors in the community drug business. Gene owed him a lot of money so would have a reason to be upset he got killed." "I suspected this, but never heard of any evidence, and you know how rumors are. Hey weren't you in Manley when that crazy guy held a few locals hostage at gun point in the lodge? Speaking of people needing to be got rid of."

Moonshine was there and explains. He was not one of the hostages but his wife was. One of the hostages manages to get access to a phone and calls 911, getting directed to the Fairbanks police. The first question is "Is anyone in particular being threatened? The second question is " Can you tell us the caliber of the gun he is using?" Not "Is everyone ok" Or even "We will be right there, hang in there!" There was a reluctance to respond. It is not Fairbanks jurisdiction. No one wanted to try to disarm a crazy man waving a gun. Moonshine and I discuss what we see.

"Moonshine, on the one hand I understand and accept what we are told." We remote villages and people are not tax payers. Like everything else, if you do not pay you do not get anything. I agree, and fair enough. We are on our own and should be expected to take care of ourselves. Personally I trust my ability to take care of myself, more then I trust some paid stranger. "I also trust locals I know personally more then I trust even a trained outsider who does not know our local customs or issues, nor cares."

Moonshine agrees and adds "We both know the problem. If civilization does not like the decisions we make in taking care of ourselves, suddenly there is all the money in the world available to straighten us out!" "Yes so we are damned if we do and damned if we do not. Told to take care of ourselves, and when we do, arrested for breaking the law." Maybe keeping people out of prison is not the objective. It's very profitable." All we really know is, we have to follow civilizations rules, face it's punishment, without civilization's protection. "Fair would be to either leave us alone, or live by the same rules as civilization, with the same protections."

"I better get going if I want to be home by dark." And I'm on my way again. The new 'made in Japan' engine beats what Americans are producing. Sigh. *It took another country to give us what we asked for, a four stroke outboard good on gas.* This is the first one on the market. Moonshine bought one too. So quiet I have to look at the cooling water discharge hole to see if the engine is running. The sound of the water on the hull is louder than the engine.

"Geese ahead!" "Yes I see them." *Geese ahead, four on a sandbar.* They see me and have not decide yet what to do about it. The boat is quiet, so sound is not spooking them. They know something is strange, but have not decided upon the word 'dangerous' yet. They bob heads, then stretch necks out long and thin and freeze. This is okay. They are about to fly, but this is okay also, because it will be too late for them, in ten, nine seven...

I have an old Marlin long tom twelve gauge goose gun, three shot bolt action. As tall as I am, with a foot of choke on it. I have three inch magnum shells with two full ounces of #2 lead I reload myself. *Probably illegal.* I think it reaches out to 100 yards, but no one believes that. I'm full of hog wash.

I fire my illegal hog wash, as the geese open wings and begin to take off. Two get away clean, and two stumble tail over tea kettle into the river silt. One is dead, but one has a broken wing. I have to run down Mr. broken wing and roll in the sand with him. *Goose dinner! All right!* No I do not get to pick my meals in this lifestyle. We eat what is served. Nor do we follow recipes often, because we serve it up with whatever is at hand. Tonight goose is served with, 'nothing.' We do not make it home and I am tired. Night is upon us. By a camp fire I hunker down with a goose on a forked stick. Sleeping bag laid out on a cushion of spruce bows that will be my bed under the stars.

During the night there is a heavy snow. A record for this time of year. This is still moose season, and the first snow is not due for another month. I sleep all right, but have four inches of snow on top of the sleeping bag in the morning. The boat is filled and heavy. An emergency folding shovel is gotten out and used to get some of the snow weight out of the boat. Some of my supplies are getting wet, but nothing I can't fix by drying out later.

The boat engine is consuming twice the expected amount of gas. I think I will run out before I get home. If so, there is a good possibility no one else is on the river in this kind of weather to bum gas from. Most likely I'd end up in Manley Hot Springs after three days of drifting. I've had to do this a time or two over the years. Gas is expected to be three times what I'd pay in Fairbanks, or Nenana. *But wait, we used to have gas stashed along the river for emergencies, did we forget?* I bet it's still there! Yes, not so far from here is a place I have kept gas stashed over the years. Not much, but five gallons, enough to get me home for sure. The extra gas needed is probably due to the engine running cold with ice, possibly causing a fouled spark plug, and or a slightly dinged up propeller running in the slush.

Behind a knoll and around a dry slough of grass I trudge, poking in the dense willows looking for my five gallon can. It is still here! So an almost disaster- adventure, is just another part of another day to be forgotten in a week. Summed up with, "Had another routine trip home."

THE SNOW DOES NOT MELT AS EXPECTED. The snow machine is at the homestead, so I decide it might be a good time to get out early with it, since there is enough snow. I'll scout around for good places to trap. I do not pay much attention to the legal seasons for hunting or trapping. I tend to simply manage my turf as if I care, sensibly. If I see little fur sign, legal or not, I will hold off trapping hard. If I see lots of fur sign, I might snaffle a few early furs while it is easy to do. In general, targeted fur will prime up about the time rabbits fur turns white. Rabbits turning I think is related to a combination of factors, like amount of sun, temperature, humidity, but seems to be a good indicator of how other fur is priming up. Prime fur is what sells. Most animals have a winter coat and a summer coat, even if the color of the fur is the same. There will be more under wool in winter, and the hide itself is thicker. An unprimed fur has a black skin when dry, more true with the water animals like mink and otter, so very easy to spot even for an amateur buyer. No use trying to sell unprimed fur. No use wasting the catch and getting a third of the money!

All this makes it important to keep an eye out on what is going on, and why I am so eager to get out and take a look around. Part of my reasoning for managing my own turf is the fact that I am so remote there are no numbers and no count, with no money for a study to be done where I am. Therefore how can game be reasonably managed by outsiders? Who knows more, and who cares more about my area then I do? Partly I am not trusting my government. I do not agree with what Moonshine says, about how white man wiped out the buffalo to control the Indian, but believe the Indian was deliberately given measles infected blankets as gifts to wipe them out. I believe the government is not happy with people who know how to live off the land and be self-sufficient. If true, the government might be willing to not care, or actually manipulate the laws to not be in my favor and force me out of a lifestyle and into dependency on civilization. It is easier to control populations that are concentrated in central areas within sight of a camera. I do not trust the game laws I read are about biology. So, I get up early and load up the snow machine sled with a day's worth of 'stuff.' Food, a thermos, a map, some survival clothes if I get wet, matches and such. *Oh yes, extra gas!* I almost forget and dash back for a five gallon can to set in the sled, with some oil to mix with it. And I'm off, into the wild white yonder!

Right off it is exciting. Marten tracks, lynx tracks, and wolf tracks. The lakes are not frozen yet so I have to skirt them. There are some late geese, but I can't get close enough. Or more, I can't convince them I am harmless, no matter how friendly my cackles. Sigh. With a smile I settle down on a log near the snow machine for a snack, and sip from the thermos. A cloud above looks like the tail of a horse. *A weather front moving in maybe.* Leaves on the trees are still green, but covered in snow. Entire trees are bent over enough to touch the ground. This has made it a struggle to get down the trails, with a lot of cutting and sweating. This snack stop is a welcome break I take.

Across a tundra clearing, near a pingo that is sticking up like an African ant hill, I see a moose step out into the open, unaware I am here. For sure I can use some moose meat for my winter food. Money is tight and I cannot get to civilization again for more fresh anything. Dry goods, and what I get off the land is all there is for me, maybe for the entire winter. I am more than mildly curious when seeing a moose. With 'Africa' still on my mind, I crouch down with the expression of a lion who has just spotted a zebra. *But darn! What do I have for a weapon?* All there is, is my 357 pistol! *Rats, and double rats!*

I have however, shot big game with this pistol, and even made shots as far at 200 yards. My eyes stay on the moose as I debate taking the shot. No. I better not try. Sigh. Not a good day for getting food. Sigh. Suddenly the moose stops and turns sideways, right out in the open. A beautify broadsided shot at a big target. *Perhaps it is a sign from God! How can I refuse??*

I go into 'Zen' mode, connecting to the target with my mind. Becoming the bullet, is the objective. When I feel the connection I torch off a round. One of my hot loads that cannot be bought in the store, with everything maxed out. Before the first round reaches its target, I fire again a foot higher, and again a foot higher than that. Three rounds in a pattern. Only then do I stop and look, wait to see what happened. So far away. I'm aiming five feet high.

The moose hunches over, *He's been hit!* He staggers towards the knoll to hide behind it. If he makes it around that knoll, I can no longer see him to get more shots. So, I fire till the pistol clicks empty. Total silence as the echoes of the gun bounce around in my head. I hope for the best, as the moose staggers around the knoll. I was so sure that if I had the height right on the hit, I'd get another hit with following shots. Logic says so, but it was not to be, or at least I am pretty sure I saw no second reaction after the recognition of the first hit. Even at the 220 yards, I thought I heard the slap of the bullet hit. But how bad hit?

It is better to sit here and wait before checking. If he is hit bad he will get out of sight and lay down. If he lays down he will get cramps or bleed out or get weaker, and in half an hour be unable to get up again. So often, other hunters I watch, go chasing after game right off. The animal gets an adrenalin rush, knows he's being chased, and makes a survival flight to hell. Over hill and dale – further than any hunter wants to carry a moose out, or falls into some horrendous thicket. It's hard to wait!

In half an hour I slowly approach the knoll with the snow machine. I'm so sure he will be laying there! He better be, because I can't seem to find any ammo to reload the pistol with, even though I usually keep spare ammo handy in the tool box at all times. Had I used it up target practicing and forgot? It seems too far to go back to the cabin for more bullets. I had so much brush in the trail, and hard going, I think I cannot make a round trip home and back before dark. I'm assuming the moose will be almost dead, and I can finish him off with—oh, the ax or something.

Around the knoll I go. Where is my laying-down-moose, that is almost dead? He is well, and alive, and still standing! Or, had gotten up when I arrived. Not a good sign. It looks like he is hit low in the leg, and just a flesh wound. The leg is stiff and he wants to use only three legs, but turns to face and fight me rather then run. Perhaps he knows he cannot move well. Assumes I can outrun him due to my fast approach on a snow machine. Now what.

When I back up and wait, he lays down. When I get closer he gets up. Maybe if I get him to go up and down enough, he will get tired and not get up as fast. I can run in and finish him off with the ax. Wolves in this situation sometimes have to wait for days for the wounded moose to wear out! For sure I do not want to just walk away. He is wounded, may not survive, and I need the meat. It is my duty to harvest him, since I put him in the situation. A deep seated feeling and a reason I don't want to wound anything. *The knife. We have that new knife we made!* We can lash that to a long pole and make a spear! As I review my weaponry with me, the knife is remembered.

The ax idea seems less appealing right now. If I dash in with the ax, the moose seems to have enough time to get up by the time I am within ax reach. *Offering what for an ax target?* I'm guessing he knows how to use his front feet as weapons, and a lowered head with big rack shows me he intends to impale me if I get close enough. It would be best with the ax to get to him before he can get up, and clobber him over the head. But the knife on the pole used as a spear and thrown, would let me stay out of the danger zone.

Some twine is found in my tool box. The knife is a hunting knife with a five inch blade that was custom made by a friend that I got in trade for some art I did. One of the lodge pole pines nearby is cut and fashioned into a ten foot spear with a minimum of work. In about five minutes I have a crude but stout spear I can throw from fifteen feet. This seems to be about the distance that is just out of affective charge range when the moose makes a defensive charge.

Spear in hand, I begin a slow circle around the moose to determine the best approach for a throw. I decide I need a heart shot, as the only affective vital spot I can expect to reach. Just behind the elbow is a place between the ribs a blade might reach the heart. As I approach from the side, the moose begins to get up. When I am within the effective fifteen feet, I toss the spear with all my might into the vital target area.

The bull finished getting up and spins, and moves a few steps. The spear is stuck in his side within the vital area. The moose does not seem to be getting weaker from the wound. There is an indication from his changed behavior that he might simply walk away from me and keep going, with my spear in tow. This would stop me from having a second chance with the spear. Snow falls from the bent over trees being hit by the spear as the bull spins. Footprints and blood now cover a twenty foot radius. The spear falls out of the moose, as the moose stands his ground, rather than walking off. He apparently does not know he can save himself by just walking away.

I am able to retrieve the spear, and decide that this experiment of tossing the spear at his heart is not going to work. The heart may be more than five inches under the rib. So, a new plan is more dangerous and requires I move in close and actually stab, and not throw. Another pole is selected, and new spear made, that is longer and will suit the purpose of stabbing from a distance. This spear will be too long and heavy to throw.

This 'plan B' is a little scary, as it means getting in there close and personal. Yet, I have always been of the opinion this is how hunting should be. Still, I am afraid, and reluctant, and hesitate. I try to sneak up from behind. Oddly, the moose seems to allow this. When I am within effective thrusting range, a three inch diameter birch tree next to me cracks loudly and begins to fall over. Several things register in my mind as one moment, not separate events with a sequence. Only seconds later do I unravel what happened. The hind leg of the moose shot out faster than a blink of the eye, and hit the tree next to me.

Anyone with experience with horses would know about a hind kick. I just never had any experience except in the movies and books. Now I remember something about, "Never come up on an angry horse from behind." And read about wolves getting kicked, coming up from behind. If the kick had been accurate, I think the hoof would have gone in one side of me and out the other. Judging from what the kick did to the tree. This is sobering, because it shows me how little I know of what I'm in for and up against. Still, how else will I learn and gain experience?

How many people are there in the world who I might know, who I can ask, "By the way, have you got any advice on how to kill a moose with a knife?" Again, I am a strong believer that if we do something, we need to be able to face the consequences of our deeds. Such as hunting. If I attack something and expect to be able to hold my head up, I have to be able to deal with the consequences. This is easy when all goes well and as excepted. As in all aspects of life. It is easy to take compliments on a job, or eat good healthy meat, or deal with dispensing death at a distance. It is another matter, and the true measure of someone, to take a reprimand or being fired, to finish any job when it gets sour, hard, or falls apart. *We need to know when to back down too! Not be foolish and stupid!* Yes, true. But I think we can do this. Our ancestors did it. We do have the advantage. The animal is wounded already.

My next attack is head on. I must step within effective bull charge antler range. A quick fake and step to the side, and the moose lunge jams his rack into the tree a foot or two to my left. I move in fast with a stab to the neck, and spin to move out of the way. This worked, as far as getting in a stab and not getting hit before it is too late. *Pay attention!* He is faking moves consistently to the right, getting us to move more into the thick willows- and him in the open ground. We want the moose to get tangled and unable to maneuver in the thick brush, not us!

The amount of blood, noise, smells and visual input is beyond describing to civilized people who have no reference point to compare to. The neck stabs I make are not effective. The hope was to find a main artery. Otherwise, the neck is just muscle, damage is not fatal and does not even weaken the moose. I end up putting his eyes out. I hang my head. I'd really not rather describe that. Once he is blind he is mine. I'm able to cut the windpipe. If I had known ahead of time. Well I might have let him go, if he survives, fine, if not, let the wolves rejoice. This 'event' is a lot to have burned into my brain.

The good news is, I will not go hungry this winter, for lack of good food to eat. It is in fact, very important to eat right, and eat more than rice and beans when expecting to work hard out in the cold all winter. There are big plans to keep cutting, and expand more trail for trapping this winter. Perhaps using the snow machine will be an advantage over the use of slower sled dogs. I am excited to find out. I am in mid-life, realizing my physical limits. I actually get tired now, without the recovery of 'back to normal' in an hour of rest.

IT HAS TAKEN a lot of work to adjust the dog trails to accept the snow machine. In some places the trail has to be made wider. Other places require the curves being be taken out. Some places the trail cannot go off a steep bank, then up another steep bank. Dogs can do this, but a snow machine cannot. The dogs could go in a different sort of risky place that a machine cannot deal with. One big condition dogs can deal with is water. A snow machine cannot deal with water very well. Some more expensive snow machines can run on top of water. But this requires skill, power, and luck. The snow machine I have is for trapline use, good economy on gas, easy to work on, but will get filled with slush and stop, then freeze.

There had been a disappointment to see how good a trail has to be for the snow machine. Dogs can go over stumps the size of a chair, logs across the trail as high as three feet. As long as the dogs are inclined to jump over, rather than go under! Ha! Re-cutting the trail has meant 150 miles of work. Anyone who thinks this life of a trapper is about being greedy, lazy, or economically motivated is just not plugged into reality. Trapping is accepting about fifty cents an hour for one of the most dangerous jobs in the world. The amount of work can be overwhelming. But finally I have cut enough trail and opened up the trapline for the snow machine enough to feel good about it. There are six line cabins up now. All six have a wood stove, a bed, a light, and a way to store supplies against bears, mice, and squirrels. All this has absorbed half of my gross income each year. Each year there has been damage to repair and replace. At least one of the six camps gets broken into by a bear, or has weather like rain damage.

This year there are two camps bears damaged. One is on Dry Creek, and think it must be the same bear every year. Somehow he got the tin off the roof and got in through the roof. This is a disappointment, as I had put plywood with nails in it by the door and windows feeling sure this would finally stop him. Eventually I will outsmart the bear, but how long and how much damage will it cost me? Darn. I do not have spare tin anyplace. It will have to go on the town list, so it might be another year before I can fix this roof. The roof is patched with screws and baling wire, enough to stop rain from getting in next summer. 'Tar' goes on my list next to 'Dry Creek.' When I am at home base I will review the list and pack roof tar in the sled. Everything else is fine, and it feels good to be here, out in the quiet under the stars.

Moose meat and other supplies are dropped off at each line cabin. Traps are set between. I'm trying to space the cabins ten miles apart. This is as far as I think I can snow shoe in a day in any condition. There would probably be a base to the trail made by the snow machine, even after a big snow storm. A record snow here is eight inches. Two inches is normal. In theory I could walk out the whole 150 to 200 miles at ten miles a day. Assuming I am not injured or sick.

It has taken years to accumulate over 200 traps. Some traps, like the wolf traps, cost $100 each. There is much to feel good about, and proud of, with a sense of accomplishment.

Diary Nov fifteenth 1997

Cut wood. Work on Christmas things. Pack for the trail.

Nov sixteenth Thirty five below zero. Machine out trapline. Three Martin, one mink, night at # two camp. Nov seventeenth Haul insulation needed for camp three stored at camp two. Forty below zero. Nov eighteenth Back to home base from camp three. six hours. Total this trip, ten Martin, one mink, two fox and a lynx. **My diary entries end for now**

In the evening by propane light, I answer a letter I have not replied to from my father who wants to know what I have been up to.

Dear Dad

So how is life with you these days? Sounds like you had a chance to enjoy yourself with that sailing trip you took. You like the new sailboat? I still remember our trip in Curlew. This new boat of yours sounds faster, lighter, easier to take care of…

You ask about my sled dogs. No I have not talked about them much. I had to give them up. It's a lot of factors. Any one or two of which I might have overcome, but not all three major truths. Most important is I can no longer depend on being able to feed them subsistence off the land with salmon I catch.

Second is the trend for more snow machines used by more people out here in the wilds. Snow machines are getting reliable, more comfortable, more powerful. New GPS navigation is being used, so basically more incompetent people can get further out in the wilds with less skills and knowledge. Some of these people find my trails, my homesteads, my traps, my cabins, and put a crimp in my lifestyle.

Third, laws in general concerning dogs are changing, it seems to me, having to do with pets.

I just decided I'm not going to fight all this anymore. There is a good side to snow machines!

It's a new challenge I am excited about.

Two big issues are presented. Being able to work on machinery requires a place to work. In winter, a heated shop, tools, and knowledge. My Tundra would not fit in the house to work on it. A problem I can solve. The ski base is to wide. So I cut a notch in the door frame with the chain saw, three inches high and six inches in. The ski now just fits through that slot in the door frame. I plug that slot with a foam wedge. Hopefully a bear will not discover this weak spot in the cabin, and rip the wall out. I installed a eye bolt in the back wall so I can hook a come along winch and pull the snow machine into the cabin when it needs to be thawed and worked on. Lots of things to change, to do, to know. Different sets of stuff to know compared to sled dogs. I had sled dogs over fifteen years and was still learning. Will it take that long to understand snow machines? Geez! I spent more miles on a dog sled then in a car. I think I averaged over 2,000 miles a year behind dogs. Yes, I need two snow machines. If one breaks down I need a way to go get it and have it in a place it can be worked on. One snow machine I had a while back sat for two years as I tried to overhaul the engine out on the trail.

Have you heard anything from Eileen? I have not heard from her in over a year and hope she is okay. We are not close, but still, she is my sister. The last I heard from her she was working as a parking garage attendant and seemed happy enough, sharing an apartment with a friend to save money, and she had some goals to bead bracelets and sell them. She asked for my advice, and I think I just encouraged her to stick with it if it is what she wants to do. It's hard to give advice to her. It is a life I do not understand…

Sunshine, Miles

I have not written my father in a while, so spend time to fill him in on what is going on, and answering his questions.

Future Flash

Years from now my father passes away from old age and I inherit his trunk of memorabilia—valuables—news clippings, high points in his life that he wanted to remember and preserve. There are many strange things to find out about my father that are puzzling, from his past and what he has been involved in. One packet I find is a string tied around dozens of my letters he collected throughout the years. Most of them were never opened. All had my watercolors on the outside. Dad is not reading my letters. I have no idea if he finds them hurtful, or embarrassing. Guessing it is one or the other or both. **Future flash ends**

I had summed up briefly, some aspects of what has been going on when writing to my father. The dog issues. I did not go into any detail. It is years before I can think or talk about it. I had hoped that somehow, some way, there would be a miracle.. [1]

In other countries people eat dogs as a staple food. Mexico for example, Vietnam, maybe other places. The quality of life we offer animals is relative, and depends where you are from. We decide this animal deserves booties and electric blankets when it gets cold and will be a pet, even a member of the family with equal rights. This other life over here gets eaten, but this one over there is sacred. The pet might be a dog, a snake or a sacred cow. That same sacred cow is served up for food in the US. There are work animals—all levels of life as assigned by the master race, us. What life has what value? Which animal has more feelings, and or is more worthy to be put on a pedestal? Who decides? Do I have that right? Does anyone? Or, if I do, maybe I need to understand there are other answers and ways and try to be tolerant. If I wish to survive, I must make my ways and behavior within the range of understanding of those in power- both the public and my government. Nothing will be won playing Rob Roy.

I smile and listen to my battery radio as I skin furs. I made my own stretcher boards that work better than what is sold. Mine have a rounded back so the fur of the Marten stands on end when dry, and fluffs up nicer. I can average five dollars more per fur because of taking good care of them. I am curious and excited to see how much better I can do with modern equipment. I'm ready to embrace the snow machine, after giving up the outdated sled dogs. *Oh brave new world that has such things in it!* I wish to pay my own bills, take care of myself, not be a burden on society. That takes money. The measure of a man is his money. Or, it is money that makes the world go round. Or, everyone wants money in exchange for anything at all, goods, services. You can't even say I love you, without money. A man without money is no one and nothing. *Just ask Jesus, hanging there on the cross, next to someone with money problems.* Yawn, time to turn the propane light off.

For the first time in many years there is no block print Christmas card to offer anyone. I do not have the money for the block. It cost ten dollars. Instead I had spent three dollars on children's water colors, and hand paint eighty watercolors to fill my Christmas list. I have to paint on scraps of paper. Mostly flowers are painted for the women and birds for the guys. Macho guys get eagles. Frail ladies get cut flowers in a garden, maybe with a lady bug, or butterfly. Then I see, I do not have money for the stamps to send them.

NEXT DAY on the packed trail I travel ninety miles. I could not expect to do this with sled dogs. *This is exciting*. If I can cover more miles and expand, it is harder to find me, harder to know where to look for me, know where I am holed up. I can be safer. I have several homesteads, the houseboat and trap cabins over a huge area. No one knows where I might be. That makes it harder to drag me out of the woods in handcuffs, as I was once dragged out of my home in Canada, never to see it again. I can randomly come into Nenana briefly, go to Fairbanks unannounced, drift here and there, randomly return, and am I still in town? Or, did I go back to the homestead, and which homestead? No one knows. Perhaps I can stay alive this way, and be happy.

I sleep well and content in an eight x eight log trapline cabin tucked in under trees that cannot be seen from a plane, out in the wilds. It is forty-five below zero. Nice. Fewer planes fly in this weather. I wish the weather would stay like this. Sixty below would be even better. Hardly anything moves. It's safe. I'm lucky. I can take it. Not everyone can. I do not contribute this to skill, just the luck of the draw, heredity. Maybe motivation, the desire to survive.

In the morning I vaguely miss the routine of the sled dogs. I miss opening the door and being greeted by soft noise and tail wags, being asked how I slept. I miss asking in return if they had a good night. Cold steel and fake plastic greets me. Transferring gas instead of dog poop is my morning ritual. Ha! In the purple of dawns early light, our furs still wave. My fifty below zero country is covered in quiet white innocence. Until I pull on the starter cord, and the wonders of gasoline shows it's magic. It's a nice enough sound I think, the purr of an engine running. It is amazing, how all those little parts work together as one. It's a miracle. *Man is so smart!* It's easy to understand why we are so smug and walk the earth as Gods.

Speaking of which, I look towards the light at the horizon. The sun will be coming up eventually. As we speak, God is loading the sun in the chariot. Probably feeding His trusty steeds. God never seems to forget, and is never late. I wave in hope God sees. With a silly grin, I point to the snow machine to show God. I imagine God laughing good naturedly along with me. God lifts up the cowling to look inside.

I proudly say, "Pretty slick huh?" Of course I imagine God knows everything! No need to lie or mince words. God knows the past, present, and future. God knows exactly what to say on every occasion. In this case, God need not say a word. We both stare, with our own private thoughts. Vroom, Vroom. I test the throttle. Let my transportation warm up. At fifty below, steel begins to crystallize and fail. Things tend to break. It is difficult to learn to be gentle in such a harsh world. If I can take it, I expect my machine to be tougher then I am. My dogs could take it, and the world laughs and tells me machines are better. Show me. Prove it. Talk is cheap. Show me why I got rid of my dogs and how much happier I will be. Show me why the world is a better place with machines in it.

In truth the machine is okay. Different. Easier then dogs. It takes less skill and time. Maybe. At least anyone can sit on the machine, turn the key and make it go. Not so easy to jump on a dog sled and steer the team. Several friends have told me a snow machine will go on the ice much like my sled dogs.

"If you can run dogs in that ice, the snow machine will go in the same place, just as safe." So I use this is my criteria. I ask myself if I could go here with the sled dogs. On the trapline is a lake ahead with thin ice. I stop and look, deciding that yes, if I had my dog team my lead dog would take us over this. 'Safe' is something you have to find out for yourself. If trappers followed all the rules, regulations, and safety bulletins, they would stay in the cabin and never get anyplace. This suggested 'wait till there is five inches of ice' is a joke. I know that for a fact. For years I have taken dogs across half an inch. The males. *Remember most of the females close their eyes and lock their legs.* The males laugh and drag them across screaming. Oh yes. I forgot.

So the little Élan is out here in the same sort of ice. The ice sags as expected, but we keep going because dogs can do this, and I am told so can snow machines. Not to panic. The ice is awfully bouncy. The machine and I keep moving. I was told you can't stop, never stop on such ice. The ice begins to crack. Suddenly there is a dropping sensation and I stop moving forward. Going down.

Water is up to my ankle before I react, as I am not believing this is happening. My reaction time would have been faster if I had considered sinking as a possibility. *This is not happening.* It takes maybe a second to realize it is happening. A second is a long time. My normal reaction time can be counted off in hundredths of a second. *The truth is whatever you believe.*

The front is sinking first. The engine is still running. I stand up, look around, and think fast as to where to leap. With the machine going down so fast, front first, I stand on the seat, spin around, and make a mad leap back the way we came. The leap is behind me, off to the side a little in case the ice was made weak by the snow machine traveling over it.

In the immediate view I am safe and well, am not going under with my machine. If my snow suit had gotten hung up on the snow machine I'd go down with it. The machine sinks fast with the engine still running and I see the headlight go under water, still on. The sled I pull is hung up for a short time, so I have time to grab a few emergency things. Luckily, I have learned to keep a bag handy, not tied in well that is easy and fast to grab.

The sled follows into the hole. Now there is nothing to see but a big black hole, Starship Enterprise sucked into the wormhole in outer space filled with stars. "Beam me up Scotty!" But there is no Star ship, no Scotty to the rescue. I am alone in the dark far—below—zero silence. Of deep space.

The first thing I do when I crawl on my belly to shore, is look myself over to see if I got wet. As I look myself over, I stomp my feet in the snow because I know my boots got wet. Snow acts as a sponge and wick. Snow sops up water fast and helps the remaining water to freeze fast, making a seal. This stops water from soaking in further. Often this ice on the outer clothing stops water from reaching the skin. The layer of ice can even act as a wind barrier and help keep me warmer! At fifty below, water will not remain water long, just a matter of seconds. There is some moisture on my sleeves and snow suit cuffs, but no water got in my boots or against my skin. My otter fur mittens stopped water from reaching my hands.

Should I build a fire first? If there is a cabin nearby, should I head for it? Try now to salvage the snow machine? First I look in the bag I grabbed to see what is in it that might help me decide what to do. For sure I have matches in my pocket and emergency fire starter. Building a fire should not be a problem if I decide this is needed.

The problem I have had in the past, choosing to build a fire, is that I am talking about two to three hours occupied getting the fire, by the time I get kindling, gather a lot of wood, and get a roaring fire that would be of any use. I expend a lot of energy doing this, maybe as much energy as I would walking ten miles. Sometimes it is less wearing to just walk ten miles. I'm out in the harsh environment, with the clock is ticking. Every hour consumes BTU's. I can go only so long without eating or sleeping, so I must use my time and energy wisely. Once dark arrives, my options become very limited.

In the bag I have some rope, some emergency food, a knife, hatchet, wire, and a trap drag. The trap drag looks like one of those pronged grappling-hook gizmos used by batman to toss up on a roof to snag the edge, and climb up the rope, or by cat burglars in Pink Panther movies. In my case, this device, when tied to a trap, snags on brush so the animal stays where it is. In a situation like I am in now, I consider this drag might be lowered in the ice hole, and snag the snow machine. This option, to retrieve the snow machine, is worth a few minutes of investigation. Coming back later for the machine after trying to walk out, presents 100 times more problems than if I can get it now.

Already I know the ice is too thin to build a tripod to lift the machine up from. If I can snag the snow machine, maybe I can cut a trench in the ice to the shore, and drag the machine along the bottom till I get to shore? The hatchet would cut such a trench in this thin ice in short order.

I lower the drag on the rope and discover the water is twelve feet deep. A sobering thought, to know it is well over my head. After only three tries I snag what I think is the snow machine ski. This is a good part to snag if I want to drag it. The rope will not reach the shore, but I have a full role of twine. Some of the rope is used to tie around a big birch tree. Twine is able to be doubled, tripled and doubled again to weave a rope. My guess is this will only hold 150 to 200 pounds of pull. The little Élan only weighs 100 pounds. I think. *At least I know I can lift it.*

There is a small rope winch in the emergency bag. I had seen this contraption in a hunting catalog. Usually sold to lift deer up into a tree to skin it out. This weighs only a few ounces, and uses what we call parachute cord. Light, strong, but thin rope. I thought this might pull my snow machine in an emergency. It is common to get into various jams needing it pulled. Like stuck under a log, in overflow water with slush on the ice, or if it rolls over into a ravine or hole. Maybe such a winch can move logs or serve other useful purposes requiring magnification of strength. *Like now!* Yes like now.

So I am not in panic mode, or overly worried. A rope is hooked to the snow machine, so I know where it is and have the means to get it back. When I put tension on the winch, the snow machine moves easily. Possibly it weighs less under water. Possibly there is air trapped in it someplace, like the gas tank, the foam seat, under the hood that helps lift it. I do not need to know why. The trench in the inch thick ice is quickly cut to shore. This trench is not as far as I first thought. Looks like thirty feet to the first hummock on the shore where the water is only a few inches deep. The machine moves along the bottom. Hopefully, there is nothing on the bottom for it to snag on, like a submerged log. The bottom of most ponds where I am will be sand, or river- silt -like soil. No rocks, no thick vegetation. Usually smooth. The whole process occupies only half an hour to an hour. Less time than getting a good fire going.

I see a ski brake the surface and the pulling gets harder. I have to grab both skis and pull with more strength. Finally I get the machine and sled out of the water. There is not much time at this temperature before the water freezes. Most of my goods are still in the sled in the tarp.

My five gallon gas can is found. I turn the snow machine upside down, with the gas cap off the tank to get the mix of water and gas out of the tank. The tank only holds two gallons in it, but half is water. I right the machine again as water keeps dripping from the seat and other parts. I pour a little of the gas back in the tank, and set the jug aside to see if the water will freeze. Then I can pour the rest of the gas in the tank. Gas and water do not mix, and the gas floats on top. I need enough gas in the tank to begin the process of seeing if I can get it to run.

The gas hose at the filter is pulled off. The filter is emptied, just to make sure if there is water in the filter it can leave before there is ice that will not let gas through. I suck on the hose to make sure it is gas I get in my mouth, not water. Now I know I have gas to the carb. I now pull the plug and use the starter rope to pull the engine over. I'm glad the engine turns over at all. Some water squirts out of the cylinder, so I keep pulling till no water or mist comes out.

A two stroke engine has no oil crank case, so if some water is in the crank case it should not stop the engine from running, or damage the engine. I cannot find a crank case drain plug, so forget that. A clean new spark plug from the tool kit is installed.

My fingers are getting cold. I have to work with my mittens on as much as I can, and this makes everything go slow. But I am aware time is critical, as I need to get this running fast, before it freezes up! I pull and pull, and in about four tries the engine coughs. The engine tries to run but will not. My guess is, the problem is not a fuel problem. I assume it is a spark problem, not mechanical because when it sank, it was mechanically sound. When I think hard, and imagine the entire electrical system and begin checking wires and such, I consider the magneto that makes the electric is at fault or something in 'there,' maybe points are wet. The power is started from a magnet in the flywheel moving across a coil of wires creating induction. But that build up of electric has to cross through the points in a spark through a capacitor. It's an amazingly simple fool proof system. Everything is visible.

I cannot get the magneto off though, and taking that off will take time. I have some starter fluid, and wonder if this can act like ban ice and get rid of moisture. I squirt some behind the magneto and try starting the Élan again. The engine coughs, catches, runs, and begins to idle and build up heat. Hands can now be warmed on the muffler. In less than three hours after losing my machine through the ice, I am back on the trail safe, warm, and back trapping.

There is one of my line cabin emergency shelters less than five miles away. I can go stop and look the machine over more, also go over my gear. If I had not been able to retrieve the snow machine, I would have probably survived all right. I have these cabins up for just such a situation, every ten miles all the way back to Nenana, 120 miles away. Twelve days of walking. Not that big a deal. That is also why I also have a spare snow machine. I can choose to walk for two or three days, and have another machine to go to town with and get parts, or explore my many more options. The five mile run warms up the snow machine and evaporates much of the internal water. I will have to pull the Élan into the house to dry it out when I get back to home base. The thermometer at the line cabin reads thirty-two below, so it has warmed up since I left this morning.

By diesel fuel light in the wick lantern, I skin furs. The lamp calls for pure clean kerosene, but I smile, "Yea right! And on whose dime will that be?" Diesel fuel works, it's just not as bright, and there is a little more smoke. As I skin fur I am upset at the advice I got about snow machines and ice. I considered the sources as professional. From those who know more than I do, and deserve respect. This incident supports my notion that I must be responsible for my own decisions. I cannot rely on books or advice from experts. Maybe take what I read and hear into consideration as an interesting possibility, but not a golden rule set in concrete.

When done skinning furs I wad the furs up, stuff them in a bag and set them outside to freeze. At home I can thaw them and put them on the stretchers to dry. No northern lights out, but the sky is clear and filled with stars. The snow crunches under foot, like I'm walking on Styrofoam. The air is cold enough to make me catch my breath. My exhaled breath sounds like bacon frying as it freezes in the air going past my ears. It is good to step back into the warmth of my little shelter.

I used to spend more time sleeping out by an open fire. I can still do this, but think it drains my energy and takes away from what I can accomplish in the daytime in the way of work. I'm not trying to prove anything. Just be happy, comfortable in a simple basic stress free life. People everywhere in all counties of all races and religion seek similar things. We all have different ways to accomplish it.

This thought has me thinking of my Ex and my son. I feel too wound up to go to sleep, so write a letter to Mitch, my son. I guess that is what he is being called. He was named after me, but think his name got changed, probably officially. That would make sense, considering the situation. No I would not be told. I understand. I seem to come unglued so easily. Every time the sword in my heart is twisted I scream. I explain to the X that it does not have to be anyone's fault. I'm not even angry. Hey, I admit I may have even put the sword in my own heart! We are all responsible for our lives, how we feel, what happens to us, to some extent anyhow. Certainly when life repeats itself. So what can I say to my son?

I suppose if I just be myself, talk of my life, what I like, be honest and open, maybe he will respond. I'm not optimistic. He's pretty close to his mother. My hope has always been, Mom finds a guy she can love and respect, who will be a father to her son. So he observes what love is, and equal parenting, so he understands his role when he himself grows up.

Hey Mitch!

So how is life with you these days? School going okay? It is hard for me to remember that far back in life. I did not always do well in school. I liked some of the teachers though, and some classes, and had some friends. Do you bring your lunch to school? I had a Disney lunch box with Pluto on it for a long time that I loved. My Mom would make me sandwiches. Sometimes I traded my lunch off to other kids for their lunch or stuff they had I wanted. Maybe I was training to be a trader huh? Maybe that was my business degree? Ha! Curious what subjects you are good in. I already know you are good at reading and writing!

I am writing this from the trapline. Not much like where you are! Cold here compared to California. No people around. I'm in a little log shelter I built myself with a wood stove and lantern for light. I love this life very much. My greatest hope for you is that you have choices when you get older, so that you may follow your dream, whatever that is.

That story you wrote me about the bus, and how you hate busses was good. The headlights as evil eyes, and how you know something will go wrong, and they hate you, and some day you will buy a bus and shove it off a cliff. Very expressive, and I know how you feel, as I feel the same about telephones. Someday when the time comes let me know! I might help you buy the bus, and help you shove it off the cliff. Tell your mother I said hi.

Love Dad

I pause and smile. Or sigh. Mitch seems to have anger in him. But my guess is, not a lot of ways to express it or anyone to talk to about it. I do not think giving him a lecture about anger management will help. He's a kid, and we are not that close. It might be better to let him talk to me as an outlet. Buying a bus for the purpose of destroying it, is not the end of the world. It is a good way maybe, to give your fears and anger substance, and a way to master it. How many times have I wanted to smash telephones with a hammer into little pieces?

He's afraid of dogs. I wish I was around to help him. He visited a short time. The dog issue came up. He was more than afraid, 'terrified' was the word. What happened? When he was a baby, and we were all together for a short time, he could not keep his eyes off of the sled dogs, and what I was doing out the window. He would even stop feeding to come stare out the window, and loved being in the dog sled. Now terrified. I suspect his mother resented that dog bonding thing he and I had, so has made sure Mitch and I will never bond over the subject of dogs. *Maybe not consciously though.*

I introduced Mitch to the wonderful world of pepper spray. "You too can be in control." We zapped a few village dogs that tried to bite us on our walks. Pretty soon, like in a few days, it was 'fun.' We actually looked for, and looked forward to, meeting stray mean dogs. Taught him we do not have a problem, it is the dog that has a problem. We'd laugh, "Make my day!" pffft! Dog's go running, yelping like little babies.

Once a dog's owner came unglued. I showed my son what to do when someone who owns a mean loose dog, who enjoys seeing his dog scare people, meets people who do not buy into that game. The dog owner is foaming at the mouth, much like his dog. Screaming, "You can't do that! My dog has the right to be free by God!"

I politely replied, "You are correct. Your dog has the right to be free. With that freedom comes a price to pay, and your dog just learned that. There is a leash law in the village. No one cares unless there is a problem. If you plan to create a problem, we can go talk to the mayor, or the cop. Are you telling me this is a problem?" The dog owner and I both understand the village law. Loose problem dogs get shot. I didn't make the rules, and I do not like that solution, but I cannot change what has been decided by the community. The dog owner agrees there is no problem.

I'm amazed at how fast children grow, learn, and change. In three short days my son went from terror to 'this is fun.'

Mitch later tells me he can't have pepper spray in California, nor carry it to school. I have no answer. I don't live there, and would not, and could not live there. I guess being afraid is a way of life. I do not understand how people live in a state of fear. I have nothing to say, behind "Listen to your mother, she should know." I also heard dogs have more rights, and are more valuable to society than people, and I have simply not embraced that yet. I suppose because we are overpopulated, so it makes sense. That was not so when I was a child his age, so I'm baffled. His mother must think I'm insane, sending him home with a can of pepper spray, and stories of how he and Dad cleaned a few clocks together. No wonder she has full custody, and me limited supervised visitation.

But, I also want to let my son know I do not hate or have resentment towards his mother. I'm sad and I do not understand, but I never bad mouth her, and always ask nicely how she is, remind him he needs to listen to her as she is his mother. I suppose I had hopes she would see a positive change in her child after being with me, and understand that maybe pepper spray is better than terror. Maybe in the long haul it will teach him something useful. My hope is, over the years he will have time to reflect on life, choices he has, and if he cannot live as I do, at least understand why I do. My guess is that will be many, many years from now. Sure, I know what solution is offered, "Call 911." Let paid professionals deal with your problems. Do not work on your own car and void the warranty. Do not grow your own garden! Who would you sue if you got sick? Do not defend yourself! Let the dog bite you, then call 911.

ON THAT LAST NOTE, I blow out the sooty dim lantern, and fall asleep under an old torn, dirty, squirrel chewed, army blanket, covered in porcupine droppings. Because this is how my heroes lived. Because I café about the condition of our planet and what humans are doing being such big consumers with many wants.

There is some concern the snow machine will not start in the morning. There could be water someplace that turns to ice and stops some part from moving, or water can short out some wire someplace. At fifty below it is hard to get any machine to start. My lantern is put under the hood next to the engine, and the blanket is put over the top to hold the heat. *Do not try this at home kids it's very dangerous.* The gas lines are all around, and they leak. But the machine needs warming, or it will not run. There is very little I do in life that is recommended. *Or legal, do not forget that part!* Yes, I suppose if I were around civilization there would be laws against about everything I do. Laws about burning diesel in a kerosene lamp. And especially that little known secret of adding high octane gasoline to diesel, to brighten up the flame! Laws about going out on ice with a machine, laws about how to preheat a machine, books, fine print, and permits to no end. I smile, glad to be a free man.

The snow machine starts and seems happy. It is time to make a trip to Nenana. There is the usual routine, almost a ritual by now, of looking at the snow machine, checking my load, making sure I have survival gear and basic tools with me. Mixing oil in the gas is sometimes a concern, did I forget? Did I get the right mix? Is the oil settling to the bottom or really mixing in the tank? A solution is found. I mixed up fifty-five gallons in a drum, by measuring, to make sure it is a perfect mix and now I will never forget! *Aren't I slick!* After gassing up I take off on a warm ten below morning. My dark snow suit has been repaired with red thread, blue thread, white thread, and patches made of old jeans and a plaid shirt. On my head is a Marten hat I made, and otter mitts from fur I caught. Beadwork on the mitt cuff is Indian made paid for by trade. *You can tell by my outfit that I am a cowboy…trapper I mean!* From a country western song stuck in our head. Trying not to be the coke-a-cola cowboy. Because, well, so many people scoff and tell me I am such a story teller, con artist scammer – likeable, just full of crap. Sigh. Life is puzzling. What does it take to earn respect?

There is some fur in traps along the way. No wolves as I hoped, but otter and marten. The halfway airport shack is stopped at. Time is spent going over the snow machine, having hot food from the thermos, getting the chill out of my bones by getting a flash fire going in the wood stove in the shack. Wood I burn is replaced with new wood I cut. Cutting this new wood warms me up more. The fire in the wood stove melts the icicles hanging in my beard, and ice balls hanging from my eye lashes, so I can see better. My mitten thumb goes to my eye and spins to knock the melting ice balls off my eye lashes. Now I can see.

Before I leave, I put the bow saw back on its nail, and give the shack a scrutiny to make sure it is ready for any emergency. The matches are moved more into plain site. The lantern is set in the middle of the table in case I arrive here in the pitch dark. Just habit.

I miss looking after the sled dogs. My normal routine would be wiping frost off them as I did myself. Giving them hot broth, interacting with them. I miss their love. The world seems a colder place now.

A family of porcupines have moved in under the floor of this shack. They have been eating the floor and walls. Over time I have used tin plates, cut pie pans and other scrap metal to staple over the holes and discourage further eating of the wood. This shack is always a turning point in my mood. I am halfway there. Either almost home, or almost to Nenana. If I break down, I will head for Nenana from here. If I am not here yet, I will turn around and head back to the homestead.

The snow machine gives a cough, then catches and idles. I'm glad I cut the main fuel line and put in a big gas filter, as I do on every engine I buy as soon as I get it. There is a little dirt and ice in the fuel filter. I put a thimble-full of icy pro-ball, the ice remover in the red bottle. No big deal with a big filter, so we are moving along now. Some of the hills are a little steep for this underpowered machine, and the Élan has to work hard to climb. Sometimes I need a run at the hill and cannot just creep up the hill in low gear. About five miles from the airport shack the Élan rpm drops and the engine locks up, just as I am climbing a steep hill. From the sound I can guess what has happened. The engine is overworked, overheated and locked up. Sure enough the engine is too hot to touch, and the rewind will not pull the engine over. *The rings have grabbed the cylinder wall.* Pieces of melted aluminum are probably in there someplace. Nothing will fix it but a major engine overhaul. There is nothing out here in the wild I can do to fix it.

I have a civilized contraption, that is nice when it works, but needs civilization to keep it maintained and to fix it when it breaks. I sigh, because dogs can be fixed out here. I rest half an hour to see if a cooled down engine will turn over, maybe after the expanded heated parts contract, they will turn loose. Sometimes this works. Well maybe once it worked. Or, maybe the real part that works is me just sitting down, calmly thinking, resting, and often some solution comes to me, or I at least arrive at the best, most rational decision, after waiting. Experience with engines tells me though, that once an engine has heated up enough to stop running, all sorts of damage has been done. Bearings will not last, gaskets give way, parts warp. So here I am in the silence of the wild with a dead transportation. I optimistically recall I do have a spare snow machine! I am not down for the count. I do wonder at what point I will see the wisdom of trading in dogs for a machine. The spare snow machine can drag this one. The spare is back at the homestead. Even though I am closer to Nenana, what I need is back at the homestead. So I decide to walk home thirty-five miles, rather than twenty miles to Nenana.

Survival gear is gotten out and looked over. Here are my snow shoes, my matches, my fire starter, my emergency food. A small back pack is in the supplies so I can walk, and carry my gear. A pair of warm fresh socks is in the gear because walking causes feet to heat and sweat, any moisture stops insulation and makes the feet cold. Sometime I will have to stop and change socks. In my food are strips of moose jerky I begin to chew on as I snowshoe.

I'm actually enjoying the walk. It is quiet, slow enough to take in the scenery. Travel with the machine involves keeping a close eye on the trail in front of the skis. A grouse flies up out of the snow, but I do not have my gun to shoot it. I have enough food for the walk home. There will be more supplies at the airport. In three hours of easy snowshoeing I am at the airport. Nice to be here. Nice to have kept this shack outfitted 'just in case,' and sure enough it is dark, and by feel I know where that lantern is. There is a sleeping bag here, and stove to cook on. A pot is found to melt snow for water. After dry jerky and walking, I have a powerful thirst. *Yes! We could do a coke-a-cola commercial!* I smile to myself, all these cool ideas for commercials we could sell and get rich and famous off of. Instead, I have a packet of crystallite, or tang, to choose from.

Lots of rice, lots of dry garden tops, like turnip, carrot, cabbage, to sprinkle into the cooking rice. Moose meat in frozen balls was brought out here in a bag and left, as it will stay here frozen for at least six months. If I do not use it, I can return it to town or the homestead. Glad to have it here. I can eat all I want, there is plenty. If I can eat good, and sleep good, I can accomplish about anything. If I cannot eat or sleep I am dead in the water. So, after a good night sleep I am sure I will be at the homestead in one day, it's twenty more miles. Guessing eight hours of snowshoeing. The equivalent of a normal days work for me. *Days fun you mean!* Yes, we have agreed we do not work. What we do, we enjoy, and we get paid to have fun. If we had a vacation, this is what we'd be doing. I am always telling people at the shows when they ask about my life.

"Figure out what you like to do! Then find a money angle!" Lots of people need breaks from work and what do they do? They go out on snowshoes! *Are we ever lucky.* We get to go out on snowshoes any time we want, go camping, and this wilderness experience others might pay big bucks to have. *Boy! When you put it that way, am I ever glad the snow machine broke down!* I frown, "Very funny!" I say out loud. Still, I am not in emergency mode. But interestingly, this distance I need to go, is about the same distance I needed to snowshoe way back when I needed to be rescued and could not do it, when I was twenty-two years old in book one. The difference might be in skill level, knowledge, equipment, maybe even in better shape. So I have much to be grateful for.

As I snowshoe, I review the snow machine failure. *Probably my fault and preventable.* The going under water and surviving did not mean no damage was done. Possibly the running engine hitting ice cold water warped the head. I should have done a compression check. I should have kept a better eye on it, working it so hard and not let it overheat. Everything that happens becomes a lesson. With each new experience comes new knowledge to file away. To be pulled out later. To be prepared for.

There is a swamp to cross near a beaver house that is often dangerous. When I travel with the snow machine, I try to go fast, and skip over any soft spots. There is one place I want to walk way around because the ice conditions do not look good to me. In fact, to be safer, I cut a long pole and put it under my arm. This is standard procedure when there is the possibility of going through the ice. The pole will catch on the edges of the hole and give me something to hang on to and use to climb out.

I do not need the pole this time. It was only a precaution. I toss the pole aside and am on my way. The thermos is in my pack. I have hot moose rice soup for lunch. Also in my pack is some 'cup of soup' I make myself from dried goods. I had examined the ingredients in the store bought cup-a-soup. I used to carry and eat this, but rarely felt satisfied. So I put dry beans through a coffee grinder, crumbled up herbs I grow, added dry carrots, turnips, and beets I grew. I added some corn meal to thicken it, and onion powder. The mix can vary depending what I have on hand. This goes in zip lock bags that hold about a cup. If the bag is not broken I can add boiling water right in the bag and eat out of it. This is light weight, has a lot of nutrition, no preservatives, no salt, no junk food. The kind of food that will sustain me when I work hard and need strength. There are several of these bags in my pack. I am not tired, stressed, or concerned. I live a life where time is my own. I have no appointments, no one is expecting me, so there is no pressure or stress. Imagine if I was needed, expected, had to get to town by an exact date for an appointment of some kind? In this lifestyle that can be an unrealistic expectation. I will now be at least a week later than anticipated getting in. I will have to tow the snow machine home, work on it, turn around and make a return trip.

A great horned owl is startled when I get close. The big bird silently flies ahead of me, lands on a tree branch within site, and glares at me from a distance. Snow sifts down off the branch he disturbs. This causes a squirrel to chatter. A jay squawks and flies up. A whole chain reaction begins from my passing through. A Raven overhead circles to see what the fuss is all about, thinking perhaps there is a meal in this someplace. All these various communications mean something and are noticed. They tell me something about the land and what is going on around me.

One marten trap has a marten that just got caught. I thump it with a stick and reset the trap, setting the marten in a tree fork nearby. *Another $50*. Yea, $50 sounds good, but it's going to take $400, maybe $500 to fix the Élan. But I do not want to focus on that now, just see the good news. Maybe I need to sell the Élan for parts and buy a bigger stronger machine. The Élan's only two years old, was brand new, now 'junk.' *So much for a lifetime investment.*

I eventually get home in the eight hours as I expected. I could look over the spare snow machine, dig it out of the snow, but decide I am too tired, and will do it tomorrow. I want to eat and go to bed. First I have to get a good wood stove fire going and make sure it will hold the night logs. The snowshoes are hung on a nail on the log wall near the stove so they can dry out. I had needed the spare socks, so two damp pair of socks are set in the wire drying rack over the stove. Life seems to revolve around the heat of the wood stove.

In the morning I feel refreshed and ready for a busy day. The spare snow machine is bigger than the Élan, but older. This is a Tundra, similar to the Élan but longer and more horses. It does not take long fooling with it to get it running. I put in plenty of gas from my barrel and take off to fetch the Élan. In only an hour I am at the airport. I do not even bother stopping. I am not pulling a load, so this trip is fast and easy. I heard from another trapper how to tow a machine successfully, and know it works. I take the skis off the one being towed, and turn them around backwards. The back of the snow machine being towed is lifted, and set on the back of the good machine, then lashed down. Now the machine being towed has no track on the ground, only the skis facing forward now. It tows easily. An easier way might work, but is harder to pull. I just unhook the drive belt off the one being towed so when the track turns it is not turning over the engine, put a pole through the skis, and pull it by the skis, forward. The track free wheel spins, and it works, but this is harder to steer and keep on the trail, if the trail is twisted with sharp turns.

I should be home in two hours. Here is my broken down snow machine up ahead. As I climb the same hill, the Tundra slows and comes to a halt and stops. It too quits on me, within 100 feet of the Élan. De ja vu, the feeling of having been here and done that. Same silence greets me, same trees, same hill. Maybe more of a discouraged feeling. This time, no back up to walk to. Two machines down for the count! *What is going on? What might be common between the two machines?* During the half hour I rest and wait to see if the machine will run after it cools, I ponder.

The gas? We mixed the oil in a 55 gallon drum. Maybe it did not mix and the oil went to the bottom? The cold made the oil settle out? My unconscious is right, it is probably a gas—oil issue. Lessons come so hard sometimes. Knowledge arrives at such a high price sometimes. This is totally discouraging. How do I get home? How do I get to town and get back and forth. How do I check my traps that are out? Where will I stay, in town, or on the homestead?

All my food and supplies are at the homestead. I can go there and live out the winter, but without transportation. And I can get out in spring by boat, but what of my snow machines that sit here? If they sit all winter and all next summer then what? When do I get them and how? How will I check or pull my traps? I can't leave them set all year! If I go to town for parts, do I walk back with parts? Can I even be sure I can overhaul an engine and drive it out? *Do I even have the money to eat and get parts and live in town?* Well first I will look over the machines and see if there is a fix it solution. Maybe I can take an engine out of the machine, and carry it out on my back in the pack. Or pull it in a hand sled I can fashion here with trees, a knife, and twine. I do have enough tools with me to tear an engine down. Maybe I can bring out only the damaged parts. Still, what a mess.

Duct tape is our friend tra la la. Duct tape is our friend.....Oh be quiet! No! Duct tape is not going to fix this and it's 'duct' tape not 'duck' tape! *For fixing ducks when they break?* Yes, that is the joke in Alaska, we use duct tape to fix everything, even broken ducks.

Upon studying the Tundra I see something amiss. The rewind cover screws are loose. The cover is coming off. When I take the cover off I see the rope rewind spring has spun all over. One end has a little hooky thing on it to hook into something, that stops it from coming unwound. The plastic thingy it hooks to is broken. The hooky thing spun all over and wound itself someplace involving the crank shaft, and stopped the crank from turning. The symptoms were exactly like an epileptic seizure. If I unwind the spring and yank it out, I can free up the crank and the machine should run. I will have to start it by wrapping a rope around this spinney thing.

Sometimes you do not have to be a rocket scientist to see what is wrong. Soon the Tundra is running, and the Élan is ready to pull using the 'flip the skis around' method. Towing the Élan backwards goes well without any problems. When I get home, the wood stove is still going, leftovers are still hot on the stove. How much different it would all be if both machines were out of commission. There is no perfect plan. Even backups for backups can fail. All is still a fragile complicated web. Ignorance is bliss. I do not need to know this right now. I only need to know I am the man. I can fix anything. I am cool, and God loves me. But still, I stop mixing fifty-five gallons of gas and oil at a time. There is a suspicion the engine getting hot contributed to the cover screws working loose, and everything in there was getting hot enough to melt the plastic spring holder.

With my art metal abilities I am able to fabricate parts for the Tundra with a saw, files, and sandpaper, to fix the part that holds the coiled rewind spring. The towed Élan needs new rings, pistons, and who knows what all. The engine has to come out and get brought to civilization. Perhaps one day I can realize my dream of having a garage—shop, with tools, and space to do my own engine work. There just never seems to be enough money, nor I suppose enough time. It seems just 'living' takes up my whole day. This is rewarding enough though, and I will just have to get the engine to town using the Tundra, and pay the money to fix it.

This becomes a complication and challenge. I would be gone a week, spend $100 just to get to Fairbanks from here and back. I'm reluctant to leave the traps set for over a week. It is not only bad for trapped animals, who usually die within hours, but other animals take them from the trap or voles and shrews pull the fur off to make nests. Trails blow in with snow, and it would take two weeks to get trails open again as the darkest, coldest time of the year sets in.

The decision is made to tow the entire broken snow machine into Nenana not just the engine. The towing had gone so well for twenty miles, I'm guessing I can as easily tow it fifty miles. In this way the fixed engine can be tested, someone who knows more than I do can put it back in, and the entire machine can be looked over. I can grease the boggiest myself, but the frame is cracking and could use some welding.

Traps are checked as far as the airport on the way to Nenana. The trip to where I broke down goes smooth. I am still the only one who has been on the trail in a month. The new breed of homesteader is not a trapper or mountain man. There are a majority of bunny kissers, weekend warriors, good weather people. The activity is early in the season and late in the season when the trip is more like a picnic. I do love the freedom of the trail in bad weather. It's nice, I suppose, but only suppose, when someone else has broken the trail. The trip goes easier. Yet, if it was an easy life I was seeking I would have done something else with my life. 'Easy' is not necessarily everyone's goal. With easy, come complications and prices. So I'm pleased I'm the only one out here. I had expected Tom and Forest to have made a trip. But think they are in civilization now, or on another part of a job.

They have been freight haulers in Mt. McKinley. Guess we are to call it 'Denali' now, the Governor or President changed its name. Tom and Forest have an exclusive contract in the park to haul freight for mountain climbers by sled dog. There are no motorized vehicles allowed in the park off the single tourist road. Thus, every climber who attempts to climb Denali, has their freight hauled by Tom and Forest to their base camp. They used to haul people and do dog tours, but they told me it is such a pain dealing with people. "Freight can't talk back, and you can dump freight off and get it later!" Forest explained their outlook to me one day.

So Tom and Forest use the Kantishna homestead as a training spot for the sled dogs, and place to fish when they are allowed to fish. The dogs can be gotten into shape for freight hauling running the swamps around the homestead, and hauling goods back and forth to and from Nenana. They live somewhat like I do, but are not subsistence off the land as I am. They are not around in summers, but both work in Denali Park full time, plus have the freight job in winter. I think they make a pretty good living, because they have been buying up property, and getting into the cabin rental business. In Healy, the next community down the road from Nenana. Tom is a good carpenter, and has been paid to build a couple of cabins for homesteaders from three sided log kits he hauls in with a boat in several trips. A barge company once brought one cabin kit.

I think about those neighbors, Tom and Forest as I snow machine along breaking trail, dragging the Élan. There are a couple of hills I cannot climb with the load, so have to stop and snowshoe up the hill to make a trail the snow machine can get up. While cresting one hill after snowshoeing, I see a dog team coming down the hill in front of me into the valley I overlook. I know it is Forest, by the hat she wears, and how she stands on the dog sled. I wait till she gets to me, rather than going out of site and starting up the snow machine. The noise of the machine would be bothersome to the dogs, maybe to her as well.

She has seen me as well, so is not surprised to have me greet her when she makes a turn in the trail at the top of the hill.

"Hi Miles! Good to see you! I hope winter has gone well with you? I've missed seeing you on the trail!" She sets the sled hook so the dogs do not take off. All the dogs wag and want to sniff at my snow suit as I walk by them. Forest gives me a big bear hug as greeting.

We have been neighbors and running into each other on the trail for, gosh…"Has it been for ten years now Forest?"

"Closer to fifteen Miles!" She smiles fondly. My inability to keep track of time, events, and names is legendary. She looks past me at the snow machine, and the fact I am towing a broken one. "So how are you taking to snow machines Miles. Tom has one for breaking trail for the dogs, but I don't like them much, always breaking down!" Forest has three puppies with her, too young to be in harness, that are learning the trade by following. They are sniffing around the snow machine investigating it. I look over to her dog team before I say anything. She is running eight dogs in tandem with a double lead. Both leaders are female. I can tell by how they behave. Two huge wheel dogs, both male are next to the sled. It would be unusual to put a female in wheel. The swing dogs are not as big as the wheels… "So Miles, do you still have any dogs?" I have not said much. Usually I'm a big talker, who jabbers away. I'm a little resentful, or sad, or simply have mixed feelings on the subject.

Tom and Forest were never overly concerned it seemed to me with the changes in fishing laws, and it's politics. If a lot of us had stuck together, backed each other up, gone to meetings, made statements, maybe we could still be fishing. I even suspect Tom would prefer no subsistence fishing be allowed, to cut down on the number of homesteaders who can survive and stay out here, giving him more privacy. Tom and Forest can haul in dog food as part of their dog training, and getting them in shape for freight hauling. They are middle class, maybe better than that, so the cost is possibly not a big deal, compared to the gain of privacy. The law changes did not put them out of business. Nor did they stand up for the rights of subsistence people to fish. Nor did they even express any concern what affect it is having on some of us.

When we all got told it was now illegal to use fish nets to catch fish and we have to build wheels, Tom seemed pleased. I thought it did not make sense, since wheels catch ten times the fish. If there is truly a fish population problem, why force wheels on us? Nets would save more fish. But 'whatever,' Tom and Forest happily built a wheel. I could not afford the parts, so spent a summer building one that only worked for a day, made out of bum materials. It takes lots of cable, wire mesh, winches, and a big boat to move one around. Yes in the old days locals built wheels from materials off the land. That takes skill and training, and is not easy. I was unable to figure out how to build a good one on my own the first time. My dogs could not wait till I learned. While I had to shoot some dogs, Forests dogs are fat and sassy, thanks to Kennel Crunch nuggets, or Pet Pride at $30 a bag, that lasts three days. Whose fault is this? I cannot blame my neighbors in any way and is no one's fault. I decide I am not resentful, just sad.

On the one hand Forest has said to me for years how she envies my lifestyle over the one she and Tom live. She wishes they could spend summers here and grow a garden, and depend on the land as I do! "It's not exciting being a park employee." She told me. I think she drives a tour bus, which involves telling stories as you escort tourists through the post card scenery. In early years we neighbors needed and depended on each other. I miss the days we brought moose meat over to help the other till they got theirs. I finally reply to Forest.

"Yea, machines break down. Ha! At least I have the spare Tundra to haul the sick one in with. Nope, no more dogs. Couldn't fish for them, now depend on gas!" I try not to sound upset about it, well in fact I'm not horribly upset, why bother? Where will that get me? It's a new challenge I am excited about.

"Tom was able to get the contract to do test fish counts with the state, so we were able to fish." Yes, someone has to count the fish for the government. Several fisherman I know got contracts to catch fish. Big signs up, 'test wheel.' Moonshine has one on the Tanana River, someone else in Nenana. I would not know who to see about such a job. People looking out for themselves and their interests in a way I am not good at. I had joked with Moonshine, "This job is like putting a fox in the henhouse isn't it?" he had chuckled indeed this is exactly correct, and he's glad to do it. Back to Forest:

"Looks like I have a trail into town and you have one headed home!" I smile at the fact we meet on a day we are both out here, and it helps us both out. I will not have to snowshoe up the hills now. "How long you going to be at the homestead Forest?"

"Just a few days. We need a few things from the homestead, so should come out Tuesday."

"Tuesday?" I ask vaguely. She can see I do not have a clue what day it is, lucky if I know what month it is. She wishes she could forget what day it is too. But doubt she would like the price paid. "Oh. While snowshoeing up the hills I used a machete and trimmed the willows on the edge of the trail." We have talked about this before, how the trail is growing in and we have to keep up with the trimming, brushing, and growth is getting ahead of us as fifty miles is a ways to trim every year. Tom and Forest talk about one time taking the time to make a special effort to get out and just trim trail, but there never seems to be time. Now there are places the trees bend overhead and form a tunnel, that collects snow, and drops the tunnel down to where we have to duck under. In some places it touches my windshield, and I have to bend my head down. It can be magical and pretty going through the tunnel.

"Well, good luck getting the machine fixed! See you again this season I hope!" I am reminded of Judy, the hippie I know in Nenana, same willow build, quiet voice, easy going personality with a constant smile. Younger, not as stuck in the 60's as Judy. A lady who does well in the wilds, likes it. She pulls the snow hook and is off, with three puppies chasing behind.

IN NENANA, Josh knows a local mechanic who can fix my snow machine, who does small engine repairs in a shop just down the road. I sort of know the guy, Mash. He can do the engine work and welding on the frame. I have this idea he says will work. To weld angle iron to beef up the frame and extend it out the back. "Put an iron plate across, so I can carry a tool box, or a can of gas on the back of the machine without the sled." He needs some moose meat, and is interested in a custom knife I made. So we can do at least a part trade. Parts for the Tundra are ordered as well, just to be on the safe side in case the parts I made do not hold up. I spend a night at Josh's.

In the morning Josh notices I do not have to be in a hurry to go take care of sled dogs as he does. "Miss the dogs Miles? I don't get it, why you gave them up, I hate machines myself!" Norman has my best dog Spike, and Josh has a couple of dogs, but has said they are not working out well. He has already shot one. There is not much to explain to Josh. Being Athabascan he does not have to abide by all the White man laws. Thus he will not understand the issues in question.

Josh thinks of something else... "Hey Miles, whatever happened with the German Guy who was going to help you get a publisher for your book and make you rich?" I am wondering myself actually. This Stefan person seems like he meant well, but is not following through, and has all these excuses, delays and what not. It might be worse. My friend Helm wants me to take legal action. I had sent an original, but not yet copyrighted version of the manuscript to Germany. Helm wonders if this kid is having it published and printed in his own name, or somehow is doing something that is not helping me. I need to get back all my stuff I sent, and make it clear it belongs to me. I am merely puzzled why nothing is being done. Nothing returned, and limited replies with vague meaningless jibber.

"Not much going on Josh. You know how it is. People talk, tell you they can help you out. Remember that one guy who was going to do so much with my art?" There had been an elderly man who got a money settlement for a car accident. He has a big wad of money now, likes my work, style, and thinks he can invest in me and my art. " Turn it into profit for both of us." He spent twenty grand, and never got anyplace. Money is not always the answer. For example, he paid $800 to a professional for a handful of 'the best' pictures taken of my finer art. Then does what with the pictures? No firm plan. No true sense of business. Thinking all it takes is tossing money at a project. He truly wanted to help, but it also takes ability or connections.

"I never did think that guy was very smart Miles."

"Well Josh, maybe this Stefan kid is the same. Meant what he said at the time, and it turns out to be more then he figured when it comes to deeds. Still Josh, it is worth being ready. One day talk will be action, and something might work out as dreamed. Good to have lots of irons in the fire and ready to move in the direction of success. Not dwell on failure. The way it is when you race Josh. You do not dwell on what anyone else is doing in the Iditarod race!" He knows he tells me that to win, he is in his own zone. As we assume all winners and very successful people are.

THE NEXT DAY I head back to the Kantishna homestead, and arrive in three easy hours. There is a memory as I arrive home safe and sound of another trip. A forced march in with the Ex, that seemed to take forever. Now the trip seems routine. The forced march seems like such a long time ago. Before my son was born.

I spend some time updating my map of trails and studying where I have gone, and what kind of future I envision. Some trails have to be given up as only suitable for sled dogs, while in other areas, I am better off out in the open country with the snow machine. Having to re-cut existing trails was not part of the original plan! Still it is a lot of trail I cut. I have the 'inch to the mile' scale maps. They cover ten feet of the ceiling. Here is school bus lake, and on through a narrow marsh over some hills to hang-a-left lake, where a cabin is up, and on through some flats to Foraker View. That has a gorgeous view of Mt. Foraker when the sun is right. There is a cabin up here. Then pressing on to the west, there are some nice lakes in a row that look like a string of pearls on the map, till I get to two map lake with another cabin up. This lake of course occupies two maps. So my eye adjusts to the new map and pen line across the next map, in a series of wobbles and jerks through some hard country. But then get into country I cut from the other end when I was at Hansen Lake with the houseboat. There is a cabin I can use built by 'Sandy,' the retired school teacher now living in Washington. He has his own plane and flies it into the lake on his vacations sometimes. It's a big cabin and hard to heat for me, but is a shelter on a lake with fish in it. After this, there is some windy open country hard to cross, till I get to my Federal land in a protected valley with a small cabin on it.

A bulldozer was run not far from this land. This cat trail is called the Brice Trail, and is used as an access to Lake Minchumina. There used to be the old dog mail trail used for years, but it has grown in a lot, and now hard to find. Just a few old timers know where it is. Now there is more traffic past my most remote property. *Well maybe one or two people a year go by.* That's a lot relative to seeing a blaze on a tree thirty years old, and wondering why the country is so crowded. *The nerve of someone being here before us thirty years ago!* A lot of history out here, as everywhere I suppose.

This country used to have some trails between the Kuskokwim River drainage and the Tanana River drainage. The Kusko country tended to be Eskimo, while Tanana was Indian. Sometimes there would be trades, sometimes wars. Now and then there is evidence I come across, or that I hear about. There was the handmade wood sled runner that got broken and leaned against a tree. Nearby, a cut tree where a new one was made. Done with a stone ax. *A few hundred years ago?* Hard to know in the dry arctic climate. As long as 1,000 years ago.

Interior Alaska is classified as a desert according to its annual precipitation. Permafrost holds the moisture from draining so plants can get at it, and ponds form on top of this frozen ground. As I study my trails, there are memories of different kinds of terrain along that 200 miles I cut by hand, and have run back and forth on and explored. There is 'Castle Rock' where the Athabascan's held up, and did battle with the Eskimo in a major war spoken of by old time Indians. Trails families used to use as trade routes to the Cosna River. There is evidence from the gold rush days, and the depression years of the 20's. In one spot on my trapline are double ruts in the tundra that used to be a horse cart trail during the gold rush days 100 years ago.

In my homestead house, I have collected old bottles, a pair of shoes I found, rusted gold pans, parts of radios with tubes, steam engine parts, and 'stuff' I find along the creeks, rivers and trails. Some found in old cabins, now with the roofs on the ground. One idea I have is to do what Tom and Forest once did, offer wilderness trips. Instead of guided tours, offer the trail cabins, supplies, and transportation. Or, offer a trip to those who have their own recreational dog teams. Begin in the park, end up in Nenana a week and 200 miles later. I haul the propane, food and other supplies. I cut firewood and provide a map of a broken trail, with shelters every ten miles. If I am not guiding, I do not need a license. I cannot get paid to have others on public land, but I can get paid for the use of my cabins on homestead land, and for services I provide.

Maybe in this way I could supplement my trapping and art income. *I can make more money with the art then I do, but it requires I spend more time then I wish to in town.* I'd have to do shows and travel to sell art. I'm just day dreaming about various options and directions I might move towards. *That's the biggest stopper for people living out here. It is how to make a living and pay the bills.* I mention it a lot. There are so many people who dream, and think they will live as I do when they retire, and live like me on retirement income. Probably the income works, but most people who have not been active much, who reach sixty, have health issues, and simply cannot do it. The life also takes more knowledge then most think it does. People like Tom and Forest have jobs to support this life, but not the time to live it as they wish, like being gone all summer and missing one of the best times to be in the woods! Those like me who try to make a living out here, seem to be between a rock and a hard place. Money makes things happen, solves a lot of problems. There are various permits and licenses, requiring not just the money, but transportation to town, and knowing what day- date it is, knowing arbitrary boundaries not marked on the ground. The way to find out is ask. Asking usually involves going to town to see someone or having communications of some kind. All that costs money. Just checking my mail can cost a few hundred dollars in transportation alone. Thus, statements like, "Just mail it in to comply!" can create financial burdens.

I sigh because it might cost me half a year's wages to get my snow machine fixed, if it needs major parts. Luckily it looks now like I can trade, but can I always count on this? Money could help me with a shop and help me with tools to do more of the work myself. This idea fits in with the self-reliance I believe in. There was a rule I once lived by. "Never own anything you do not understand and cannot fix yourself." It kept life simple. As time passes, this simple life has more complications. Many of these complications seem to be imposed upon me.

I now must have an ID card. Josh tells me it is not possible to run the Iditarod dog sled race without a credit card. Thus, if you leave a mess on the trail, or one of the check points, the cleanup cost is automatically taken from your account. A race that started out as a race in the wilds, between Indians, trappers, is managed by city slicker sponsors who call the shots. Life in general is just like that. Subsistence fishing began with the concept of folks in the bush who could not get to town, who in such a remote lifestyle, depended on the land for food and shelter. In the beginning, a primitive self-sufficient minded person could build a fish trap from sticks and roots if they needed or wanted to. Totally with and off the land.

Now subsistence fishing cost $1,000 in complicated gear. Once subsistence self-sufficient minded folks could do all their hunting with one rifle they could afford. Or even hunt with a spear. There are of course seasons for everything. It all costs. A special duck stamp, a special tag for moose or bear. Realistically, when I am hungry and need food I am out looking for anything edible that moves. I am not in the supermarket where I can order up the food I wish for. God serves me what He will. It might be a fish, duck, porcupine, grouse, rabbit, beaver, bear or moose. I cannot afford all the different permits and guns required to be legal. This legal stuff becomes quite complicated. I'm not allowed to shoot beaver at all, but can trap them. I can hunt ducks, but only with steel shot. I can hunt grouse with lead shot in a shotgun, but not a rifle. I can hunt bear with a big rifle but, not ducks. I can hunt rabbits with a twenty-two rifle, but not birds, bears, or moose. Not so long ago wilderness people hunted everything with a twenty-two. I myself did for my first few years.

The sled dog issue comes down to laws. Dogs in the cold are required by law to have booties. Unwanted dogs must be taken to the pound, for a fee. Dogs cannot live on a chain, but must be in a humane pen, cement floor, wire fencing, specific minimum standards. Dogs cannot be fed any wild game. Over five dogs requires a permit, insurance, and a vet. Selling dogs requires being in business. Using dogs to chase game is illegal. 'Humane,' is being redefined, and 'animal rights' is a coined phrase. Animals have almost the same rights as people, and this is the goal of a kinder civilization, that wishes to consider my lifestyle, an old savage way, no longer necessary or condoned. "Rise above our barbaric history."

There is an effort made to understand and comply with the laws, because I am not stupid. Big Brother carries a nasty stick. In the long term, I am not going to win against the government. My survival depends on cooperation and getting along. I thought survival might depend on simply staying out of Big Brothers way, off the grid, not noticed. Anyway, I have a handful of new pamphlets and regulations to look over.

> **Yukon Flats National Wildlife Monument**
>
> This booklet points out some of the proposed wildlife monument regulations that will affect people living in the Yukon Flats area. Please read the booklet to find out what the Fish and Wildlife Service is proposing. This booklet is a summery and is not complete. If you rely on it, you could miss important details. If you have time, read the compete regulations. Think about how the regulations will affect you and your plans for the future. If there are things you don't like, let us know about them. If there are changes needed let us know. Please send comments by September 26th. After reviewing your comments, we will write the final regulations. Whatever regulations we adopt will be enforced. Let's continue working together to make good relations.

I pause,

This is the first page. Nowhere are we told where to find the compete regulations we are responsible for knowing. I turn the page and there is a map. I read below the map.

> This map shows the boundaries....
>
> Regulations are proposed for the Federal lands and waters inside the boundaries. The regulations do not apply to state and private lands in the area. Native allotments and village selected lands, even if they are inside the boundaries of the monument, are not part of the monument and are not affected by these regulations.

I pause again.

Sounds reasonable, but the map on paper is not a marked boundary on the ground. Where are all these places, exactly, when I am on the ground? There are no signs, no ribbons, no close up map provided that shows all the land use boundaries. There is Federal land, monument land, private land, native allotment land, native selected land, state land, homesteads, all overlapping. All with different sets of rules, with nothing marked. Some of the offenses if in the wrong place by mistake, carry twenty years in prison, and or $200,000 fines. Let's assume I can figure it out, or do not get caught…I skim the next few pages to grab items of interest.

Compatibility

The key that decides if an activity will be allowed, is if the activity is in the monument or not. If an activity does not damage, or lessen scientific, or historical resources, some activities such as the continuation of traditional lifestyles are thought to increase the historic value. These types of activities are generally given priority.

I pause again,

So this is what gives the Feds the toe hold on remote lands. The 'scientific' part is how the university gets in the mix. Much can be done 'for educational purposes.' This could in theory supersede commercial interests or subsistence. There can be a scientific reason wildlife cannot be touched as it is studied. Designated monument areas can and will grow to encompass more and more wilderness. I see the word I am looking for, slow down and read more carefully:

Subsistence

Does your life depend on it?

I notice this big bold headline that stands out.

The regulations say…

…non wasteful subsistence use of fish, wildlife, and plants by local rural residents will be given priority over other consumptive uses of those resources… The regulations give the state of Alaska authority… The proposed regulations requires you to obtain a permit to do any of these things. **You may be denied a permit.** Listed activities requiring a permit are building cabins, cutting trees, trapping, fishing. ….Travel by off road vehicles like trail bikes, four wheelers, jeeps, trucks is prohibited…..Travel by snow-goes, planes, boats is okay unless…. Authorized use in specific areas or over specific routes. Anyone who legally owns or occupies lands located within or surrounded by the monument may obtain a permit to come and go along traditionally used route.

So ends the pamphlet

Well a lot to think about. Sounds like a pile of permits. Where do I get them? What might they cost? How do I renew them? This talk about ways to get denied, does not match the headlines, "Depend on." So something I depend on, some pencil pusher, is going to be in a position to say no about. With no recourse.

There are aspects of my life changing financially, besides needing three rifles, and $1,000 for a fish wheel. Years ago, 'bush folk' could own an old clunker truck and use it to go to town and get winter supplies one or two times a year. Now it is difficult to find insurance for two days out of the year. It is hard to keep it street legal. There is more effort now to register and license boats, trailers, snow machines, and ATV's. Registration means inspection, fees, time limits, expiration dates, paperwork, compliance to meet like pollution controls. There are lines to stand in, rules to follow, hoops to jump through, with the possibility of being denied, and records kept with personal data on file. A form of control. Many ways to get denied.

All this requires many trips to civilization.

One big aspect is, subsistence people understand how to make do, with used stuff, fix it themselves when it breaks. It is common to build your own trailer, design and build your own boat as I did my houseboat. I hear all the time, of bush folks working on snow machines and swapping out engines between brands, and adapting for a different gear ration, or power belt, or track underneath.

On every level, remote people are adaptable, design things, invent things, come up with innovative solutions to every issue. Hunting, getting water, staying warm, is all regulated. Heating with wood will require a special exemption permit, until it is eventually outlawed, because it causes pollution. Yet so does fuel oil, which is the replacement alternative.

I'm guessing the future is to not allow my lifestyle.

Hey Miles!

I have not seen you around since summer, how is winter going for you? Thanks for the duck feather in the last letter. Reminded me to get out hunting again. This town food is crap and making me unhealthy! I got laid off again and collecting unemployment. I still have a few old cars around to work on and sell, but like I told you, new laws put me out of business. It's all about big business. The small guy hasn't got a chance. It would be good to live more like you. You got the right idea there Miles. I should have done what you did back when I had the chance, and we were planning together in the early 70's. Those were the days huh! Let me know what you are up to, heard a rumor you got out of dogs! Must be just a rumor. Figure you'd never turn to machines! Except boats! Ha! Be nice to go back to the old pole boat days though huh? Must have been nice back in the 1800's!

My Dad has not been well lately, so I have moved in with him and taking care of him. He asked how you are and remembers when you and I would come see him on weekends, when he was working on the pipeline. We'd have those huge buffalo burgers at the Tamarack. That was how you met Steamer and got the houseboat built. Been a while ago.

Oh, not sure if I told you. I was trapping a little and joined the Trappers

Association. But then got a note with ashes in it saying, "This is what is going to happen to you if you keep trapping." It was from outside, so think they got my name through the Trappers Association. The police were not interested, and I got the idea they considered me the criminal. For sure times are changing!

Gotta go. Write and let me know how you are.

Watch yer top knot!

Will

I smile. I have known Will a lot of years now. He's a friend who thinks of me as stuck in the 1800's. Dreaming of how great life must have been back then, but not able to actually try it out himself. Yet, I stand for that dream to him, give him hope, inspire him when he's down. I admire his sense of family ties and values I lack. I write a reply:

Hey Will!

Good to hear from you. Sorry about the work situation, but glad you can get unemployment and have some projects to work on. It's one reason to work for yourself instead of someone else. You can't get fired! Ha! You told me about that moose call you designed that the sports store was interested in. That sounded like a nice idea, to make them and market them. You still think about that?........Ya, I pretty much got forced out of dogs. Maybe it is related to what you say, how big business runs things. The dog feed companies are not as powerful as the gas companies. The gas folks want us all well plugged in and dependent on oil. They make sure it happens. That reaches all the way out to where I am, and my lifestyle.

I was looking at my maps today, reviewing all the trail I have cut, and cabins I built over the years. Thinking back to when we had conversations having to do with a good place to settle and be free. I see the Kuskokwim River. There is not one road to that river. There is zero tourism. There is zero news about anything happening there. It's still true today. Therefore, my guess is a person could be left alone there. My guess is no one cares what day you catch a Marten, or what caliber gun you use on what kind of game. No one driving a car will suggest your boat engine is polluting the river, and shut you down. I bet a person could still fish for sled dogs. The area is below the radar. It has never been opened for homesteading, and is not mentioned in any regulations. I had that choice to move there at the time, when I was in Minchumina with you, and decided not to go for it. There are always choices in life we can reflect on – the 'would have, should have, but did not do' things. I do not suppose it helps much to have regrets. Would I be happier, better off there?

I remember at the time, I simply felt a bond to the interior of Alaska. I felt I needed an outlet for my art. I felt I needed better access to supplies. Folks in McGrath pay nine dollars a gallon for three dollars a gallon gas. Food of any kind is three times as much money as in Fairbanks. I thought I could see the best of both worlds. Be alone on the Kantishna 300 miles from any village, and still get to civilization once or twice a year to get good prices, to sell art, sell furs, meet with people I know and understand. One big factor is that all the villages on the Kuskokwim are Native. Hardly any white influence. I had not had a lot of good experiences being of a minority inferior race. I'd have zero rights. Must be nice to be an Indian huh? Actually I think I said once before, I am part Indian and maybe even enough to qualify for subsistence rights. Proving it would be hard. In the old days people tried hard to cover up the fact they had any Indian blood. A DNA test would show, but that costs. Plus, well, I do not believe in discrimination by race. I do not want to wave my hand and say I have special rights for no other reason than my race. Oh, I do want special rights! I just want special rights because I earned them, not just handed to me, due to the color of my skin.

Oh, wanted to tell you I am doing okay trapping this winter. A wolverine, some Marten, fox, otter, and beaver. A few thousand dollars. Sounds like a lot, but not for six months wages! Ha! It's especially not a lot of money when our lives get threatened by bunny kissing terrorists. I'm not surprised you got threatened. I hear about people wearing fur and getting spray painted. I've received a lot of hostility too. One art show would not let me set up to sell because I had furs for sale. Even though it's legal, the manager of the show told me he did not want the controversy. I decided I was not going to get anywhere by arguing with the manager about my legal rights. Has our country forgotten its roots, or is it ashamed of our past?

Anyhow looking at maps. Thinking of the changes going on in Alaska. Yup, I watch my top knot. Not going to get scalped any time soon I hope.

Sunshine, Miles

Will and I have talked over a lot of years about choices, lifestyles, and how it might have been in the past and such things. I'm not someone who seeks out problems and controversy and wants a fight. When I had the dream to be a mountain man it seemed like a legitimate noble dream. While my peers were dropping like flies whacked out on drugs, I dreamed of what I thought of as a positive, healthy, productive lifestyle. A lifestyle that made our country. I got laughed at because it was not the dream of my peers, but still, I never thought it would come to such hostility. I never thought it would come to death threats. I think of such behavior as nothing short of terrorism. Radical terrorists being supported by well-meaning folks who donate their money to Green Peace, The Audubon Society, Friends of the Animals, and other groups thinking it is all about saving the planet. All about peace. When in truth, from my perspective, it is about hate, and money. It is hard to know what percent of the population feels this way.

I think laws reflect the sentiment and morality of any democratic society. Sometimes laws lag behind. But the laws eventually catch up. If it is true, a majority of the population wants all wilderness to be a park, no hunting trapping, no oil exploration, no timber cutting, then eventually the laws will reflect this sentiment. I find that disturbing. This same population has 'wants.' We want to drive, we want to fly, we want electric, and all that takes power, and the source of that now is oil. We want nice homes and wood products, that takes timber. We consume resources.

MEANWHILE, back at the ranch... We study the map and trails and cabins. It's a very long way to get to the Hansen Lake area I love so much.

That area is sort of lost to me now. The nice cabin on the lake I had permission to use is owned by someone else who put a lock on it and tossed my things out the door. In his mind 'garbage,' but to me necessities after running 200 miles by dogs over a weeklong trip. For him an hour trip in his plane from Fairbanks. Last time I was in the cabin there was a map on the wall where he had named all the lake coves, and hills in the area, like Columbus discovering the new world. Me, a savage with no rights. He claimed the area for trapping. At first telling me I was welcome to share trapping with him, if I wished, out of the goodness of his heart. He had argued I made no improvements, thus had no claim. While he has built an air strip and put a new roof on the cabin. Speaking honestly and frankly of how he views the world. Kind and logical. Civilized. It makes sense. The same reason the savages in America had no rights when white man arrived. The savages had not devastated the land, but left it as nature gave it to us. Ownership is directly related to how much you control, alter, destroy something. If you do not subdue, change, control something, you cannot claim to own it.

I have to think about that. It is true an air strip is not 'destroying' anything by most mind sets! Who would agree with that! I feel the same when Fish and Game 'claims' to control animal population. There are numbers, charts, graphs, theories, profiles, and models done up to prove 'we are in control.' We can count them, we can harvest them, we let them live, we do not, it's all up to us. Except one tiny problem. Where do the numbers come from? Besides ink on paper, what do we manipulate? Those of us on the ground in the field living in the area being studied never see the one doing the counting. It's all done by a plane. The animal population is owned because someone flew over it. I do not buy that. So then what is ownership?

When I helped raise the girls on the homestead they had a fight over ownership of a toy. I took it and held it over my head and asked whose it is. The oldest firmly told me it is hers. I had told her to come and get it then. She could not. I asked again, "So who owns it?" She grudgingly admitted I did. We reviewed what ownership is. I explained, "This is how your little sister feels when you have the toy." I handed it back saying, "You can borrow it, treat it as yours, as long as you understand where 'stuff' comes from."

And so it is. The land, the trapline is not mine. Even if I buy land, it is only mine if I follow certain rules. I cannot do anything I wish. So I can only sigh that a guy with a plane and money simply took over. It does put a fizzle factor in my grand plan of tying two valued areas together with a trail that has taken twenty years to cut. So much for my empire, and so much for creating my own planet. Ashes to ashes and dust to dust. I have my hands full with what I bit off anyhow. There is still plenty of room. I have seen beyond my limits. The comet that once burned with a never ending fire has been sucked in by earth's gravitational pull. Is now smaller, less free.

A new concept of 'ownership' sets in. *I own my memories, the thoughts, the experiences in my head. No one can take that away. It cannot be bought or sold.* So someone thinks because they can fly into the wilds, and turn the wild into civilization, that he owns it. He thinks because he names it, he transfers ownership. But what memories does he have? What experiences? His own for sure, but not mine. This thought goes to some of my customers I sell animal parts to. More and more customers want raw materials to make their own art with. Customers who believe in 'animal energy.'

"Miles, my totem animal is the bear! I need a bear tooth or claw so I may be complete! I need bear energy! Because of how you live I'm sure you understand, so I have come to you for the connection." My materials tend to be handled naturally with few chemicals. They arrive 'direct' or at least I know the source, a friend who is an Indian, or connected to the land closely. *But no, you cannot really buy that.* When I wear a bear claw, it is a bear I killed myself. *The strength in that claw is not the claw, but the memories connected with that claw.* The memories of the experience, a time when I was able and successful, overcame fear, proved myself as strong and fast. A time God smiled upon me. Thus, when I need these feelings and wish to repeat or have a similar success in life, I can hold, or look at, the claw and be reminded.. What memories are connected with this claw if you buy it, and thus what is the energy?

Oh, I suppose some memories of stories heard, legends told, and the dream itself can offer up good thoughts. Still, the direct firsthand experience with this exact item has got to be, well, closer to the real thing. Just so, this person takes over my trapline and thinks he is like me, connected to the land, at one with nature, a mountain man, a trapper. His latest communication with me was:

> "Hey Miles, I just bought a houseboat in Fairbanks. Can I hire you to run it up the Kantishna River to Hansen Lake?"

Ah well. Few people would have much sympathy. I am claiming to control a lot of country. "The size of the state of Rhode Island." "With no one there but me." It worked for a while. It was so for a while. Very little is forever. In fact my very dream is shifting, if I look hard at it. Is living alone in the wild as a trapper my only dream? Worth 100% of my energy? The truth is, I have artistic goals, writing goals. Things I just know I can accomplish, if I put my mind and resources to it! I want my writing in print. I take that seriously, even though, after almost twenty years of talking, no one has seen a book in print. Talk is cheap. Respect is from results, not 'some manuscript' I say I have, that no one has seen. Finishing it will take electricity, and a computer. I see more and more there will be no publisher knocking on my door begging me to sell the rights to my manuscript. Only vanity press, where you pay to print, and the press gets the profits. There is something my German customer Helm tells me about called 'on demand printing.' The US does not have it yet, but Germany is on the cutting edge of this new technology. Helm has a friend who owns such a printing company. Raak, in Frankfurt Germany. Jenny had introduced me to the idea a few years ago. Now it looks like computers and on this kind of printing as coming down in price and more available.

It is common enough that the dream we have at five years old, and again as a teen, should be expected to alter somewhat as we get older. Many midlife people I know, once dreamed of being a rock star, or a fireman, policeman, or be like Daddy when we grow up. At some point, various factors come into play. We need to make a living. We need to follow our ability. We are influenced by events, and important people in our lives. We come to see our original goals in the new light of wisdom, knowledge. Reality sets in, replacing, or altering the dream. We get married and or situations affect us we never considered before.

Some of the thrill of my original grand plan is lost. The realization there is no such thing, and never was, a mountain man that matches the legends in my head. It's like dreaming of superman. The entire mountain man era romanticized in literature was a mere ten year period in American history. Even then there were only a handful of 'free trappers,' trappers who were not employees of a fur company. In general a trapper could not afford his own horse, nor the traps. Thus, most owed their soul to the company store. In debt, on credit, earning just enough to pay off last year's debt, if lucky. That is not the life I dream of.

It has been a huge accomplishment, just cutting 200 miles of trail through the Alaska wilderness. Maintaining it, continuing to running it like clockwork, keeping it open, is not insurmountable, but would occupy every ounce of my energy and time. Likewise, if it was my life's goal to get my Hansen Lake holdings back, I could. The guy bought the cabin, but no trapline came with it. I could simply show up and open trails I cut and prove I was there before he was, and maintain that. I can be there much earlier in the season then he can fly in. I can be there with traps all around the lake before he ever shows up each winter. If that was my life's goal.

If it were my life's goal, I could probably go to court and prove there was never a clear title to the property he bought to begin with, and the ownership is in question. I have some exact details on the history of this cabin. No one had a right to sell it. It should be a public cabin. *That's not what I'd argue if it was me who bought it. Ha!* But anyhow. This is a blow to my big dream. No possibility of an empire, carved out of the wilderness with my bare hands and the sweat of my brow. In the beginning I expected, even wanted, my first book to be dedicated to no one! No one helped me, no one was part of it, no one else but me deserves any credit – or blame if it is a flop. In the beginning when young, my motives were different. There were no social motives, only a personal motive. Originally I wanted to discover myself, make it on my own, not off my father's name, not follow in my father's footsteps. Partly a rebellious teen. At some point in life we grow out of that stage. Part of me back then, honesty wanted an outdoor active adventurous life, never seeing anyone, ever. I'd had some bad experiences. Not trusting my parents to look out for me, the military during the Vietnam era, being deported from Canada, arriving in Alaska to live like the Indians, then having the Indians in general not accept me and more than one, tried to kill me.

My social life is still not wonderful, but there are some good people in my life like Will, and the Underhill's from Alaskaland, Helm- my new German customer-friend, Josh, the Parrs at Alaska House. There are others, in Nenana and among my customers and fans. Guam and Vicki risked their life to save mine when my life was threatened. Socially more than money, I seek respect. I now conclude I will not have that as a trapper, mountain man, hermit. Yes, there are plenty of 'fans.' It was my X who points out, "Ha! And who are these people? What is your relationship with them, and what do they really know about either you or your lifestyle?" Dreamers. Clueless. If most knew the truth they'd lynch me, call me an imposter, not find it acceptable. It's more and more an illegal lifestyle.

Most people are law abiding. Those who are not, seem like radical outlaws and social misfits not to be trusted or respected. As I may appear to 'normal' people, an outlaw. The respect I thought I had, might be merely flattery. Or puppy love. Love based on, "Oh isn't he cute!" I wonder if he's potty trained- house broke? This is not the same as respect. Put another way, National Geographic may well do a story of a remote person in a remote part of the world and hold up their lifestyle and that person as worthy of a story! Yet their own words have to do with "No, we do not pay people we do stories about." Such a person provides free transportation for everyone, feeds the movie crew, offers a free place to stay. The kindness and generosity is recorded, of how quaint the savage is. Is this savage our equal? Will we pay him for our lodging? Would we let our daughter marry him? He is welcome at our parties as entertainment, not as an equal. I am getting it, after twenty years of seeing this. I get it.

Respect is coming more from my art. Likewise, so is more of my income these days. I set these thoughts aside for now as I go through my stack of mail. Under the pile is an old letter from when I was reviewing the laws. Way back in 1980, from a lawyer my father paid for to try to help me out, and understand the laws. I was living in Lake Minchumina at the time.

Peter Aschenbrenner
Attorney at Law
Dear Miles,

Bla bla …Oh yes here is the relevant part...

Also enclosed please find three issues of the Federal Register which describes Fish and Wildlife regulations governing… answers to specific questions you have should be found in one of the registers. I have spoken to both the U.S. Fish and Wildlife and Alaska Department of Fish and Game in an effort to find out what the present restrictions are on possession of baleen, ivory, eagle claws, bear claws, and other parts of wildlife… **It is illegal for any non-native** to possess raw, uncrafted products of seal, walrus, porpoise, whale, polar bear, bear claws, **unless such came into your possession prior to 1972**. Fish and Wildlife did inform me however that once a piece of baleen, ivory has been handcrafted by a native and sold, the purchaser is entitled to do whatever he wants with it. Though the expense may be prohibitive, you could legally cut up a scrimshawed, or carved piece of ivory, and use it in your own work…a favorable exception...from 1976-1979, jurisdiction over walrus was granted to the state.... Any subsistence user—native or non-native was allowed to hunt walrus… ivory exempt from the Federal possession restrictions. You could conceivably purchase a tusk harvested between 1976 and 1979 and use it as you wish- provided you could verify its origin. ....**Present regulations don't favor the non native artist. Sincerely bla bla etc**

Yes, I already read this, and know all this, but it is good to be reminded and review it.

My simple lifestyle is not so simple. Life, all life is complicated. But who wants to hear the exact details? First, I did not make the rules. I did not set out to make my life complicated. However I do intend to be among the survivors! I get asked "Is that legal?" I believe in honesty, and open communication as the first line of defense. When I reply "My lawyer investigated this subject and informs me…" Followed by quotes from this letter like, "Before 1972 or between 76 and 79…," Or 'if I buy it from a native and cut it up and resell it as mine." I, 90% of the time, get a negative response. "I never heard of that, that cannot be true! Because I know someone who got arrested…" Or "But what about?" with puzzled follow up questions, that do not end, and do not accomplish what I wish. No sale, no respect. I'm just finding legal loopholes for being an outlaw.

What I learned from many encounters is, "You are right, but shhh let's keep it between ourselves. Are you interested or not?" This gets followed almost always by, " Yea, screw the government, what a bunch of crap all these rules are, good for you." "I'd love the piece but am to scared, but good luck" "I know this item is hard to get. I'm amazed you know how to get away with it, paying someone off I suppose, I'd like it!" Along these lines. I suspect many have a little outlaw in them, or sense of a dare, being part of an adventure, an adrenaline rush, something secret, rare, that few are part of, making this item a treasure in their collection.

I'm sure these customers tell all their friends. "Yea it's sort of a hush hush acquisition wink wink, isn't it gorgeous?" Followed by the friends envy and "Where can I get one?" Followed by "Well you have to be quiet, and not tell anyone else, it's between us, tell Miles I sent you." Followed by " Miles, I was told you are the Man." "Yes." I like being the man. I might be mistaking that for respect. But the reputation is started, and cannot be easily stopped. I'm Indiana Jones. The secret to survival is to cover myself. I in fact have the proof and receipts in most cases, to produce if it is ever needed. I assume Fish and Wildlife will now and then do a check and send an undercover person. "Ok, so what is the problem?" I will ask. I get told what the problem is and I produce the proper pre ban 1972 papers. Or the receipt for native purchase between 1976 and 1979. I get out a quote of the law. I assume, "Problem gone."

When I acquire, trade, buy raw material I slowly develop a set of ethics I want to operate by. Some of these rules I abide by are set by native culture, some my own personal experiences, some by social consideration, some by laws covering the deal. I decide I am not very interested in record sizes, trophies, number one A grade quality, or animal mounts that involve trophy hunters. I want my acquisition and market of raw materials to be craft people, spiritual people. The rules are not set in stone, and take a while to come up with after a lot of varied experiences and deciding who and what I wish to be known for.

Back to my letters…

I can end up with 100 letters over a period of a few months. Mostly junk, but many fans write, many of the girls I met through ads still write and we are pen pals. Among the stack I missed before as junk mail is a letter from the court system. I assumed if it was important it would arrive certified. I assume it is some document, copy of court transactions. This is not a good subject, and put looking at this off. But it is time, so sigh and tear it open.

I am wanted for more questioning concerning the Gram murder.

My lawyer had told me the police have no right to detain me unless they want to arrest me. All this was 'over' long ago. Something about an appointment for DNA sample. The date has come and gone. It is not like I can show up at the whim of the court, when there are questions. On whose dime is the travel cost? It's a week's wages sometimes to come in, or the loss of a week's wages in furs if I leave the trapline to get to Nenana. I am not confident enough to tell the court to stuff it. Tell the court I am too busy. Tell the court to make me, or ask, "You and who else!" *They want me to come in, well La de da. I have wants too.*

It's everything I can do to work full time at my lifestyle to eke out a bare minimum living. I cannot do so with constant interruptions of demands on my time. Another example of the lack of respect I refer to, how society treats me, my occupation. So I pack for Nenana 'once again.' It seems I use up so much of my energy going back and forth to civilization. *Oh well!* I suppose I enjoy the trip well enough. The trip in is part of the wilderness. There is a lot to see. It is a nice trail. I'm sure I can find other things to accomplish on the trip. I cannot stress out overly much about things not in my control.

I come into Nenana and spend a night at Josh's, as has been my custom. It is nice to visit with him and Maggie. 😁 :)

"Mr. Maw-tin. So tell me what is new. Entertain me with one of your stories!" I laugh because he has as many stories, and we both know it. "How is the new machine?" He is curious because he is a dog man, and will never give them up. He races and can make money at that so is in a different situation then I am. He also has a wife who works and helps subsidize his dog interests. He swears his racing pays all the bills, but it is not hard to make his rough math look like dreaming. How many times has he told me how it cost at least $30,000 a year to be serious about entering the Iditarod race? He does not average $30,000 a year with his winnings. But, whatever. None of my business. He still deserves respect as he places 'well' about every time. Certainly in the money. Last year was fifth place, I think at $20,000. He'll make up for it this year by winning, he says. He says that every year. I respect him a lot, because the amazing part is how he does it alone! No dog handler, no partners, no sponsors, no hired vet on staff. No infrastructure the other winners have. Other winners have 200 to 300 sled dogs in the dog yard. Josh owns less than twenty, and pulls it off by the seat of his pants. That is just so amazing. Unheard of really. Often people who do unheard of things, have unheard of minds that work in quirky ways. Perhaps that is the bond between us.

Josh considers having a snow machine to open up some if his training trails, as most dog mushers do. But lacks information on type of snow machine, costs, what they can really do. So seeks information from me that might be useful.

"Josh, I didn't tell you about walking twice?" I tell him about the break downs and probable costs. I remind him, this never happens with dogs! He only laughs.

"What about the time you walked all the way in when the dogs got away from you?" Oh. I forgot about that. Josh wants to hear that story again, as we sit around his wood stove. Maggie makes tea. While it is steeping, hangs up dog harnesses to dry on a string over the wood stove, and stirs some concoction in a five gallon pot being heated for the sled dogs. There are a few wood chips on the floor near big boots drying by the stove. Josh has sled runners in the house being worked on. I hold one end of the six foot runner while he screws on a new plastic guide on the bottom.

"Well Josh, all I wanted to do was get some firewood. I was going to haul a heavy load, so hooked up all the dogs to pull 500 pounds. I hooked up a new dog from Norman that I did not know well. Put him in swing. It is a routine trip. I have depended on my leaders in the past, who know where I am going by how I load the sled. Spike is in lead, and he sees the saw go in the sled, so knows we are headed for the wood lot."

"Yea, Spike is a good dog all right. I could sure use more like him huh? I came in second using him in lead." Josh likes to reminisce about sled dogs, breeding the various good dogs he has owned, seen, or knows about. This is normal conversation with Josh. His whole world is 'dogs.'

"For sure Josh! Spike knows what it is all about, so I usually have no concerns!" I explain. I have the sled tied off so the dogs cannot take off without me. I pull the snow hook, but am careless, and slower then I should be getting on the runners and hanging on. The dogs leap forward and yank the sled out from under me. I'm only a little upset, but not concerned. I'm sure in a 100 feet or so they will stop, or get tangled, or the sled will tip over and stop them. No way they can get out of the slough and across the river and up the other river bank! At most, I might have to walk half a mile on a good trail. I'm upset my day will be cut short now by half an hour. I'll smack the dog responsible, this new dog from Norman who instigated the bolt.

I walk the slough out to the Kantishna River and see no tangled dog team! I know I will have to cross the river now, and the dogs will be up in the woods tangled. The river is crossed, then up the bank I go. No dog team. There are all kinds of obstacles along this stretch. Tight turns, trees that hang over the trail, grass tussocks and logs to jump. Any of these can turn the sled over or hang it up. If not, the dogs will tangle themselves. So I keep walking.

An hour later I am still walking, and the dogs have taken the turn off to the Tom and Forest's place. Weather is nice enough, trail is in good shape. It is spring and I am comfortable. Once I realize my day is shot, and this is all I am going to get done today, I relax and enjoy the walk. The dogs will be at Tom's. A total of a ten mile walk. I have not been on this stretch of the trail in a long time, because it is not the way to town. I see Tom has improved the trail. There are logs cut and branches cut out of the way. There is a new slough they use now to connect to the river. "You know where that is Josh, just past the tripod we put up in the flats with the ribbons on it, below Chicago."

Josh nods yes. He knows where this is, as he had not been sure which trail to follow to get to my place the first time out, and this tripod marks the fork in an open area. I go on and lead up to the best part.

"So Josh, I get to Tom's and the trail my dog leave show they went around the cabin in a loop, came back out, back onto the river and out the trail to Nenana. No one had been home at Tom's. How the heck could the dogs negotiate that?" Apparently no tangles or problems that showed in the trail they were making. I'm a little concerned for the first time. I wonder how far they can get! Surely the dogs cannot get up the bluff at Chicago! Even with the steering of a person to manage the sled, it is hard to keep the sled upright. *Dang those dogs anyhow.* I am not tired, so just keep walking. The dogs got up the river bank again, and on out the trail forty-five miles to Nenana. They cannot possibly go to Nenana. "Why would they even want to, it's a lot of work." Josh nods that indeed dogs would not want to work unless they had to. Maggie hands me the tea I forgot about, and I take a sip before continuing. Maggie has not heard the story yet. "So for sure I will not have to walk any further then the bluff at Chicago." Maggie does not know where that is, so Josh tells her.

"It's so cold in this one place with the constant wind along the bluff, we call it Chicago." Maggie nods and I go on.

"Well I get all the way to Chicago, and see no tangle or stopped dog team! All the way up that twisty bluff to the top around the sharp bends, then out onto the straight trail to Nenana. Nothing else to stop them or hold them up now." Josh says:

"Except the airport."

" True." We usually stop and do a break and snack at the airport so the dogs might be expected to know that routine and pull in. If I am lucky they will pull in to where there is no room to turn around and not be able to get back on the trail.

I am not tired, and the weather is still nice enough. The trail is hard packed. I get to the airport. No dogs here at this shack! I look forward to a rest here at least, maybe even spend a night. It is late now. I have walked twenty-five to thirty miles, considering the roundabout way to Tom's and back here. I have always made sure there is wood at the airport, with a sleeping bag, food, everything I'd need to spend a night. "I get in the cabin door and get the lantern light. There is no wood! Not one stick of wood in the shack! Worse, there is no saw I left here." Josh interrupts and tells Maggie:

"I told Miles I saw Bill Cotter on the trail. He trains out this way sometimes and began using the shack to broth his dogs. But he uses up all the firewood! Then takes the saw! That's what you can expect from those dopers!" I let that part pass about dope. Josh has this thing about most other mushers. He is set on the belief all the winners except him, drug their dogs. Josh's big goal in life is to prove it, and clean up the race. I don't even know for sure it was Bill Cotter who used up all the wood, or caused the saw to go missing. Even Tom has stopped and used wood and not cut more. There are some other homesteaders out who do not make very many trips, but when they do, seem in a hurry and do not understand bush etiquette. Almost like, if there is no cop around to stop you, you can do anything you want! Like a child left alone with the cookie jar for the first time.

"Yes, probably that no account Cotter used up all the wood and took my saw!" Maggie interrupts that thought with:

"Wasn't it Cotter who married Liller, that gal you were fond of at the mouth of the Kantishna?" Something like that, not really. Sure I always liked Liller. Nice outdoor gal. Happy in the wilds. Good looking, about my age.

"She was with Weedz Maggie, back in Manley, one of the Burke boys. The one that got killed by Silka when ten people were killed by that nut, remember? Anyhow, I always accepted she was Weedz's girl. After he died I was half interested, but yes, Cotter jumped right in. He even suggested I not stop in to see Liller anymore, he had a thing going with her. I used to stop and have tea when I was making boat trips. She stayed on for a few years there in the cabin. But the Burkes would not let her keep the cabin, even though she was Weedz's wife. Because she is White. Go figure. So she had to leave. Or maybe wanted to." I'm straying from the dog team story, want to get back on track here. "So anyhow, no wood, no saw. Too dark to go out looking for dry wood, to tired. I am able to lie down in my snow suit, pull a blanket over me and get some rest, maybe even a couple of hours of sleep." I pause here to sip tea and let that image sink in- trying to sleep in the cold, dressed in a snowsuit.

"It is still dark out when I am wide awake and worried about the dogs. I have visions of them on the trail tangled, maybe fighting, maybe hurting each other, or in some other way in trouble. For sure they would be hungry and missed a meal. Maybe a good thing though. Teach them a lesson, that life is not so great without me around. Better not to run off!" I sip more tea and ponder the next set of events.

"I think about this as I walk. I begin to get a cramp in my legs. I have walked now for forty miles. If I slow down and walk slower, the cramp goes away, so I can walk further, just learn to pace myself. I do get more mad at the dogs for taking off. It is evening when I arrive in Nenana, having walked fifty-five miles. My dogs are in the spot I always tie them up at tenth street. All lined up with straw, and a dish in front of them. Happy to see me, but well fed and comfortable!" Josh happily interrupts:

"Yea! I saw the dogs all lined out where Miles always stops. The dogs are still in harness and I assumed Miles had just left the dogs and gone into town, so I unhooked them gave them straw and fed them!" No one knew I was walking in, and the dogs came in without me. I finish up with:

"Bearfoot was there at tenth street when I walked in, and he says I looked like I had just taken a stroll, not walked fifty-five miles. I was not worn out or looking tired." I wanted to add that so I would not look so bad, some positive note to the stupid act of letting my dogs get away. This is what is remembered, the day the dogs got away from Miles. Who remembers or repeats to anyone how I once made it in with sled dogs in four hours. Fifty miles in four hours is Iditarod winning speed. Not bad for six dogs and a freight sled. But no, no one even believes it when I tell it, but they always believe how I failed once. Want to hear all about that time, and repeat it all around the neighborhood. I sigh.

"That was pretty funny huh Miles!" *Yes about as funny as how Josh got banned from the race. Who remembers the times he won? No, he goes down in history as the musher who got banned from the race.*

"Yes, that was funny all right. How the dogs went all the way and stopped, all lined out right where I always stop! So yes Josh, I forgot that time. But you are right, it reminds me, that yes, there are problems with dogs too, as well as snow machines! There is no perfect solution. If it was easy, everyone would be doing it, right?"

I review a few other things I notice that are an issue with dogs, solved when you own a snow machine, beyond the fact the snow machine will never run away on you. "My whole way of trapping can change when I use the snow machine Josh. With sled dogs there are places I see fur signs and cannot set a trap because it is not a good place to stop the dogs!"

"Yes Miles, like when coming down a hill! Or out on glare ice!" Yes, Josh knows about this as well. The snow machine can stop about anyplace and stay till I have the set finished.

"Once Josh, I jumped on the snow machine and wondered why it did not leap forward! I gave it throttle and then realized I had forgot to pull the cord and start it! Dogs of course are silent, and take off when you get on. No cord to pull. No engine to warm up. No spark plugs or complicated gadgets."

"Well Miles, I'll leave the engine stuff to you. Dogs are complicated enough for me! You can break trail for me with your snow machine when I need it." I do not answer, but think only 'maybe,' because Josh had asked me to break a trail already, and he does not understand the limitations of the snow machine. He had asked me to break a trail uphill with deep soft snow. My snow machine is not designed for that. It just sinks in the snow and stops. Josh had gotten angry, thinking it is all my fault, and would not help me dig the snow machine out of the snow when it got stuck. The experience for sure convinced him he did not want one of these machines. He never has to dig dogs out of the snow! Ha!

I was pretty mad at Josh. He'd once run my machine right into a hole in the river, plain as day, got mad at me saying, "Come on Miles help me pull this out! Why when I was your age I'd have done it alone!" No way in hell. Covered in ice and snow, with the sled under water it weighs 800 pounds. This is really bad. We could lose the entire machine under the ice and never get it back. What was Josh thinking? Maybe he is just used to sled dogs, and dogs could get through this spot. Maybe, like me, Josh had been hearing how wonderful machines are and how much better then dogs and such an improvement, to the extent he thought the snow machine would be equal to his dogs. But 'equal' does not mean 'the same.' We'd had a bad experience that took us three days of work and permanent damage to the snow machine. I had been shocked at Josh's handling of the situation. I thought Josh was wise and had a high Jesus factor. Someone made of the right stuff. With the nick name of 'The Fox,' he should know how to jump the right direction when the do do hits the fan.

Do I have a strange friend with a twisted mind? Do all of us have a strange inexplicable side when people really get to know us? Stuff the public never gets to see? There is a possibility I consider that Josh unconsciously, deliberately, wanted to destroy the snow machine, symbol of what he hates. There was no apology. It was all my fault. We are known by who we hang with. It has cost dearly to be known as Josh's friend. Josh has many fans, but few to no friends. Or, so it appears from my perspective. If I try to talk about 'what happened' to anyone it's, "Well yes, that's Josh all right, you chose to be his friend." Followed by some related Josh story….

"Miles! Are you day dreaming again?" Maggie interrupts.

"Josh, maybe Miles is tired, it's late, time for bed!" I unroll my sleeping bag I keep behind the chair, and unroll it on the carpet as Josh and Maggie turn off the lights and head for their bedroom for the night.

THE POLICE HADN'T REALLY WANTED anything. "We didn't know where you were Miles! What's up with that? Are you running from something? Our main murder suspect drops off the face of the planet. Put yourself in our shoes." Why couldn't they find me? That's not normal. That's not good. Normal is good. Abnormal is suspicious. Weird. People who are weird are guilty. If anyone did it, it is probably the weird guy. I'm following along with the logic here, nodding my head. If I jokingly say:

"Hey, I'm not weird, it is the rest of the world that is insane!" I doubt the police would laugh in agreement. I think I'd be locked up.

The houseboat permanently parked at tenth street where I keep my fair displays, where Gene was killed, and where I kept my dogs. I do not own the land, but can stay as long as I wish, as long as what I have is a temporary structure and there are no complaints. The river slough is right behind me. I am waiting for an engine for the houseboat. The project is expensive, with issues of how to make happen what I wish. There is not much room on the boat. The life is somewhat like living in a VW van.

CHAPTER THIRTEEN

OLD TIMES COMPARED TO NOW. AGGRESSIVE RIVAL TRAPPER MOVES IN. SNOW MACHINE TRAPPING DESCRIBED. PREVIEWS OF BOOK FOUR

I'm once again back at the Kantishna homestead after a routine snow machine trip in from Nenana. I had lost a week's time trapping, coming in to talk to the police for nothing. It is a marginal subsistence life I live. A weeks lost wages hurts. I'm in a good enough mood though, because the weather is perfect, and trails so good I can get a lot of new cutting done at the end of the trapline. I'm about 200 miles out from home base now, able to make the trip all the way to the Hansen cabin, my old stomping grounds before I acquired any of the homesteads, when I was based out of Lake Minchumina in the houseboat. That whole area is one of the richest in furs on the entire trapline. Bearpaw Mountain is right here, with its thick forest of spruce that supports grouse, mice, and other small game the predictors I trap feed off of. Denali Park is not far away. This is a preserve that breeds lots of game that spreads out of the park. This presents a new issue, in the news now. Years ago a friendly biologist had stopped in the see me, asking me about trapping. Just curious. Doing a study of some kind. Wants some facts.

"So how many wolves can you catch in a winter, on the average?" I had wanted to be helpful to this nice person.

"I do not get many. I see a lot though. Packs of as many as twenty come across my trapline out of the park and all the way to Minto flats." Years later I see that the information I gave him was used to help stop trapping near the park. There is concern that animals leave the park and get killed by trappers, so a 'buffer zone' is proposed and approved, based on information gathered by this biologist. This buffer zone makes it illegal for me to trap wolves on my trapline. While at the same time, the department of Fish and Game has stated there are too many wolves. The department will deploy pilots- at the tax payers expense- to go hunt them down to protect the moose population and village sled dogs.

If so, then why are tax dollars being used to thin the wolf population? It's not a little bit of tax dollars. Just two years ago a government plane was crashed and lost on a wolf hunt. A plane tax payers paid for, and will be replaced. A widow to support the rest of her life. *Why not work with the trappers? Not use tax dollars?*

This is on my mind as I am way out near the back park boundary seeing tracks from one of the wolf packs, twenty members strong. Such a pack might be killing an average of a moose a day all winter. Over 100 moose a year I'm sure. I stop on the trail to examine the tracks and determine what the pack is up to. Here is a beaver house on a pond the size of a football field. Several wolves had gone to the top of the beaver house to look around for game. One had stood here a long time facing the willows off in the distance. Looking for moose browsing, I'm guessing. The big tracks on top showed these animals had stopped a few of the younger pups from coming up on top to join the adults, and the younger had left, and gone off to play. I walk over to where the young were at play. One rolled over to scratch it's back on the rough ice, while the playmate teased him. There had been a game of tag that followed, a fun chase through the dry brown grass and onto the windblown ice where the tracks disappear.

I had seen this situation before, and know that a high spot that overlooks lots of open country is a good place for a blind trap set. This is a trap with no bait or lure. I might get as much as $400 for one of these wolves. Why let Fish and Game shoot one and leave it to rot in the woods? If biologists say there are too many for the land to support, let me make $400 helping to solve this dilemma of overpopulation? I carefully make my blind set. Looking around and thinking like the pack, I set snares around the gaps in the tall grass. If I do catch one, the pack will not return here for at least a year. If I am lucky, I might catch two, or three at once. I would not have another chance for a year. One thousand dollars. More than a month's wages to me.

So that is always the trappers dream. Much of the excitement over trapping is taken away if I will be told this is a bad dream that can never be. Even if I never catch a wolf, it is all about the dream. Now I have a reason to come back here. It is a lot of effort to get here. I'm a week's travel away from civilization. Another planet. This lifestyle, this place, is so different from civilization, I may as well be in a Star Trek time warp. The snow machine has been stopped on glare ice so there will be no tracks. I follow the glare ice so it will be less likely the wolves know I stopped at the beaver house. There is no way to fool a really alert smart wolf in this way. I can only catch wolves if they are not paying attention, are lazy and careless. There will be faint marks on the ice a wolf can see, and faint odor of gasoline and rubber on the ice. It will be easier to catch the young and foolish in the pack. The leader is the least likely to get caught. Trapping can cull the weak, slow, lazy, careless, and the stupid. Shooting from a plane has no natural selection factored in.

But no, *we can't worry what those silly civilized people are up to.* It can give us a headache. All we can do is try to live our own life in an honorable way. Too bad civilization carries such a big stick. Maybe I will get lucky, and civilization will get weak. It looks more and more like civilization is committing suicide. *My rabbit cycle theory of civilization at work.* The planet will be very happy and rejoice if man's power is taken away. I day dream what earth might be like without gasoline, satellites, cement, plastic, pollution, and sky scrapers. I dream of a recovery. Earth cleansing itself. Clean air again, gurgling drinkable water again. I dream I'd be very happy on such a planet. The days of pole boats, sled dogs pulling boats against the current from shore. Yes, those must have been wonderful days. Or the Tarzan days.

MY CUSTOMERS WANT the claws off the wolf, the bear. They seem to want the huge biggest claws. Many get upset if their treasure is delayed a day in the mail. Back in the Tarzan days, to acquire a bear claw you had to go fetch it yourself, kill a bear with a rock or a stick. A claw or fang had meaning to wear then. The days of the quick and the dead. Who among us can walk that path? Who of us today is deserving? Who of us today has the balls? Sometimes it bothers me to hand over a claw to someone in a suit and tie with lily white soft skin who would not know wolf shit from a tootsie roll. I try to be kind, understanding, forgiving, and sigh. *Maybe the claw will be part of an educational process. Or maybe I am only an enabler.*

Old time Natives tell me reality of those old days sucked. Few Natives in Alaska would want to go back to those days. Indians did not even name their babies till they were about two years old because they usually died before then. To get sick was to die. Tolerance of pain was required. Starvation was common. Old age was forty. Few lived past fifty. It is difficult to be in those shoes. Maybe it is easy to romanticize about better times. Grass is greener on the other side of the fence.

Still, even in my thirty years' experience, I have seen enough changes I think life here was better in the 70's then the 90's, and moving more towards worse times ahead, not better. Has civilization seen the best of times, peaked out, and is headed on the downslide? Maybe the 60's the 50's all the way back to the 30's was better? *I'd have thought the depression would not have been good years!* I'm curious about history, and how life was in the past compared to now, so ask a lot of questions. *Maybe we can learn from the past, and not just repeat it.*

There are piles of papers I have saved concerning changes as shown through the laws. Much more then I can talk about, or show, or offer up as evidence and 'proof' backing up my opinions. One aspect of 'subsistence' stands out, concerning the fishing part. Quoting court records

> **Ass'n VS State 628 p. 2d 897 (Alaska 1981)**
>
> "Before 1978 subsistence fishing was defined as fishing for personal use and not for sale or barter. In 1978 the Alaska State Legislature enacted Ch. 151 sla 1978 (hereafter the 1978 subsistence law). Subsistence fishing was redefined as "customary and traditional use."

I set that paper down. 'Customary' and 'Traditional, 'seems not to include an individual, such as a remote homesteader or mountain man. Of importance because the bottom line ends up, my lifestyle is becoming illegal as I live it. Also, there are no public announcements concerning these changes. To quote a magistrate friend of mine:

"There is a legal obligation for you to know what the law is, but no obligation for the law to inform you, or offer you access to these changes." He agreed the way the public finds out, is people begin getting arrested, and the word spreads. Very effective, and that is simply how it works.

I smile as I skin a wolf I caught. There is pride in knowing how to outsmart the wolf and how to properly skin one. Pride in being able to take care of myself without welfare, in a remote land with so few jobs. There is pride in running a trapline for so many years and still having it be productive. I pause and frown. Many people quote me the bible, telling me pride is the root of all evil. Having no pride is supposed to be a goal. That's hard to understand.

As the wolf goes on the stretcher and set by the woodstove to dry, I think about recent events cumulating around me on the land I love. A fellow named Horror married into one of the Indian families on the upper Kantishna River. He has been very aggressive and ambitious. The whole fishing issue on the river came about as a direct result of his blocking off the Toklat River and harvesting huge amounts of fish. If not, he certainly aggravated the situation and gave reason for law changes. It has made him a lot of money, at the expense of the fish population. He alone has been responsible for hundreds of thousands of salmon getting harvested. This has caused all of us on the river to be watched closer and having more rules made, regulating our fishing activity.

Horror has recently moved on to the trapping industry and aggressively acquired trapping country. He is working hard to make a fortune at trapping. I only hear rumors, and have only a few actual first hand facts. Talk is, he has hired others to work for him, has planes coming in and out, and is harvesting up to 500 to 700 Marten a season. The country he is in cannot support that kind of harvest. I do notice, when I get near his area, the country looks desolate and empty of game. I'm concerned, and find it hard to believe any one person can have such an impact. The fur dealer, Don told me that one trapper near the village of Minto has single handedly harvested over 600 wolves in one season. While people like this get 'trapper of the year' awards and a 'well done' slap on the back from the Trappers Association, I wonder how the country can support such a harvest without hurting the land? Geez, I feel thrilled to catch two or three wolves a year! Ha! But I will never get the trapper of the year award. These are new changes I notice. Possibly it is new modern equipment and methods that allows such huge harvests to happen, impossible in the old days.

There are new reliable fast snow machines, more satellite phones and better GPS location equipment, so wilderness trekkers do not get lost. They can find their way into remote places. There is better warm clothing, electric heaters on snow machines to keep hands and face warm, better tents, better concentrated foods, and it all adds up to more people getting out remote- able to stay out longer and easier, who do not deserve to be there.

By 'deserve' I mean having taken time to learn, and respect, which goes hand in hand with time, knowledge, and skill. Traps have come down in price and are better made. There are new snare wires and snare locks on the market, more lures that work, game calls and fancier methods of harvesting game. Irresponsible people are now capable of great devastation, that was simply not so thirty years ago. In this way, years ago might have been better times.

In the business of trapping, no degree is needed in order to practice your trade. It is possible to simply 'begin.' There are not a lot of occupations in this day and age, where you can ply a trade with no training or fee. This has always been part of the dream! Any poor person can work hard, begin with nothing, and be able to pay the bills. 'Education,' happens with time, and practice, but not college and unaffordable degrees. In the 'old days,' you had to learn how to stay warm, build a fire, use a map, build deadfalls, make a camp, and on and on. It took years! The equivalent of having attended college, just no fee or needing good grades to arrive.

Except it was the 1800's that wiped out the beaver and the buffalo. Maybe ignorance is bliss and I have just not been aware. Surely it is hard to sort out 'the truth,' concerning history. Sort out relevant facts to base decisions on. Life can be simpler believing what you are told. Life can be difficult for those who ask questions. On that note I turn off the propane light and climb into the pole bed. I have a big day ahead tomorrow.

I'm up at 5:00 am, and using a flashlight to gas up the snow machine. I load the sled for a trip to the end of the line 200 miles away. There are ten camps I have built, all outfitted with bed, stove, and survival gear. My hope is to get 100 miles today, pulling traps at the end of the season, and putting in a last effort cutting and clearing more trail. A moose steak is cooked the size of a dinner plate for breakfast.

Rice and moose with dried garden vegetables is cooked, and put in the wide mouth thermos so I have a hot lunch on the trail.

A bracket has been made on the snow machine muffler to latch down the thermos and keep it hot. A cooker is also built for the muffler. As I travel, I can cook a snack from the heat off the muffler. A spare spark plug holder is checked to make sure I have two new plugs and a belt holder is checked to see I have a spare drive belt. There is a place for folding a saw under the muffler along with a come along winch and folding shovel. All is stuffed in places under the hood. In a tool box is a spare headlight bulb, first aid kit, matches, knife, twine, and various tools to work on the machine.

Extra wide skis for the machine had to be purchased to help the machine float in the deep snow and handle overflow water better. There is overflow to deal with right off, but I skim over it fast and nothing gets wet. Some open holes in the swamp are jumped as well by going fast. The biggest secret is to not slow down. However… I read that exactly thirty miles an hour sets up a harmonic vibration that breaks ice. It is better to go either faster or slower than this. I keep that in mind. I also keep in mind statistics tell me 90% of all snow machine deaths and problems involve water. Jumping open leads alone, 100 miles in the wilderness with no communication, is not for the faint of heart.

The trail is familiar enough I barley pay attention. I know about every bump. The electric heaters in the hand grips keep my hands warm. Bumps in the trail are brutal on the back. I'm groaning as I see the sun peek over the horizon, so forget my back, turn my face to the warmth, and pause on the trail at the top of a big hill.

Good a place as any to stop for my lunch. The thermos is fetched off the hot muffler. The spoon is in the thermos so I do not lose it. There are three caribou in the distance, winding their way through the valley below. No planes, no roads, no human sign anywhere in view. Not in the valley, not on the hilltops. I can see fifty miles in every direction. Frost on the spruce needles glitters like gem stones in the morning red light. Like a scene out of 'Clan of the Cave Bear.' No. More like the sequel, 'Valley of Horses.' Books about what life may have been like back in the days of saber cats and mammoths. My thoughts go to a trap on this hill I was able to set this season. I had never been able to set here with the sled dogs! I could not get the dogs to stop on the down slope of this hill, so had to zoom by for years, with a sigh that this would be a good spot for a trap. So, one advantage of the snow machine is that I can stop anyplace I like to set a trap.

I'm reluctant to disturb the peace by starting the snow machine engine. Being practical, I am not disturbed enough to let it bother me to the extent I feel guilty. The sound of a running engine, my transportation, is a good sound, as good as the sound of silence. Silence is the sound of big trouble, ggrrrrr and the smell of gas fumes is all about getting back home alive. By the end of the day I am at the halfway point 100 miles out the trapline. Out past Twin Lakes, two map lake, and am able to spend the night at the upper Hansen Creek cabin. There is no use trying to cross the harder traveling tundra while tired, with dark approaching. This cabin is four x ten. Enough room to have a stove and a bed. There is enough room to stand and turn around. The bed is the table till I am ready to sleep and unroll the sleeping bag. For now I can sit on a tree stump chair and cook on the wood stove, as clothes dry out in a wire rack over the stove. I unwind with a book read by kerosene light. I feel safe and happy. I will be on the trail a week before seeing the village again. This is not camping or vacation time. This is how I make my living, and is my life.

This is as good a place as any to end book three.

THE END OF BOOK 3

A personal note—

Reviews help! If you enjoyed this book, please leave a review where you purchased it—it would be greatly appreciated!

Sign up for my newsletter, "Keeping Up With Miles," @ www.milesofalaska.com

Deals, new books, comments, links to YouTube. Stay updated!

The Alaska Off Grid Survival Series Summary

Book 1 - Going Wild

In 1973, I am 22 years old, and a city kid. I enlisted in the Navy and got out after the Vietnam War.

I travel to interior Alaska, a 'Cheechako' (Greenhorn) by Alaskan standards. But I have been raised on Walt Disney and feel qualified to be a mountain man!

I arranged with a pilot to drop me off in the wilds of Alaska. I do not have everything I need and have things I do not need. I learn about guns, trapping, and the loneliness of living in the vast wilderness with no other humans around.

I do not see anyone for many months, then walk out of the wilds to civilization in the spring. After working odd jobs to make supply money, I return to the wilds in the fall and have a hard time my second winter. I almost die, and need to be rescued.

I decide to build a houseboat so I can travel around without having to build another cabin. I have to accept summer work in Fairbanks to pay for the boat materials and work under a builder. The boat takes much longer to build than expected.

I live as a street person much of the time to keep expenses down.

Book 2 - Gone Wild

I have many adventures on the houseboat and acquire a dog team. There are issues with the police, a bear on my boat, and a trip to see my family who live a civilized life.

My houseboat sinks. I get lost and learn other hard lessons. I start doing artwork and end up on TV. I win a land lottery and start my first homestead.

There are mail order women, and I live with a woman and her kids. Ten people are murdered in a village we visit, and myself and the family are almost among them. Family life is more difficult than I imagined.

Fish and Game becomes a concern.

I head back into the wilderness, which leads into book 3.

Book 3 - Still Wild (This Book)

I acquire a couple more homesteads and cut more trapline.

I give up sled dogs and enter the world of snow machine adventures.

I winter in Galena and visit many native villages. There are bear encounters, and many survival situations to learn about.

I become a serious mammoth hunter and find fossils as part of my living. I work with a land surveyor specializing in homesteads and wilderness surveys, getting paid to use my boat.

My art sells well, so I do some big shows. I become more social and understand civilization better. I see the wisdom of being accepted by others. I learn. I grow. I try to change, as the world does.

The economy changes. It is less acceptable to be a trapper. I never become totally civilized as a city person defines it, but maybe I do, relative to the life I had in book one.

Book 4 - Beyond Wild

I am getting past just survival and doing well, even prospering. I own more than the houseboat can easily haul. Gas gets expensive. I need a new houseboat engine.

There is a homestead and trapline that keeps me in one place now. There are more bear stories and adventures into the wilds, including a 300-mile boat trip looking for mammoth tusks, which has disastrous consequences.

I find where I want to live on the Kantishna River. A river 300 miles long with about five people on it. I hang out in the native village of Nenana, spending a lot of time here.

I get my first computer and learn to build a website. People are looking at the pictures and buying my raw materials and art. This is a chance to make a difference.

Life is beautiful. Life is precious. I Dare to live it.

Book 5 - Back To Wild

I acquire a home in Nenana and start a web store. I am forced out of my subsistence lifestyle, partly because of changes in the laws. I do some serious mammoth hunting.

Unstable power causes a lot of computer data loss. I learn by punching keys to see what happens. It takes a long time to get good enough to create a book.

I continue the Mammoth hunts. The Tucson fossil gem show and State fair do well for me.

This period of 'being civilized' that I am trying out, has advantages, but also a price to pay—a big change from the wilderness life and being alone!

I am a suspect in a murder investigation. Another trapper tries to move in on my territory. There are neighbors and infringements on my property.

I fear I cannot change who I am. There is difficulty blending the two lives and ways of thinking. There are mail-order women coming and going, as well as the usual adventures and situations I manage to get myself into.

Book 6 - Surviving Wild

Iris is my partner. Business grows, with money coming in, but causes 'complications.' I understand why I left for the wilds in the first place.

I get better at fossil hunting and have some exciting trips getting mammoth tusks and other ancient treasures. I am viewed as an expert on a few subjects and Discovery TV and reality shows contact me several times.

The new life in town causes legal issues that have been nipping at my heels off and on throughout my time in Alaska. Fish and Wildlife ask, "Why are you alone out here where we cannot keep an eye on you? We know you are up to something. What is it you have to hide? We will find out!" This mentality is that different is bad and of concern. I end up being investigated. A SWAT team shows up at my property with a dozen cars and 20 cops.

My arrest makes headlines. I'm sentenced to Federal Prison for six months as a felon. This is a stark contrast to 'Book 1-Going Wild,' where I have as much freedom as it is possible to have.

How did I get from there to here?

Book 7 - Secretly Wild

I am a convicted felon, describing life in prison from the viewpoint of someone used to freedom and the wilderness life. The same feather in the hat I wore on the cover of Ruralite magazine in 1979, is now worth five years in prison.

What do I need to do to survive here? There are classes to take, books to read, farm work to do, and people to help. There are interesting felon stories.

I observe more crime within the prison system by the system than I am accused of committing. "The prison could not survive if we operated legally," I am told by officials. I do my time. Now what? Am I a better person? I see the error of my ways. I am saved. Society is safer now.

Book 8 - Retiring Wild

I talk about news relevant to living off the grid as an individual in the wilderness that few citizens are aware of. I adapt my business, and still have adventures, depending as much as I can on the subsistence life I love and understand that is now becoming illegal as a white man.

I ponder whether the end of my life is in agreement with the views I held dear from the beginning. I have hope that even in times of control and suppression, I can still focus on the plus side, and continue to find ways to enjoy personal freedoms and individuality.

I continue to explore choices, how to have better control of my destiny, happiness, and success. I refer to this as 'Survival.' I have few regrets, and hope my life's path as written can provide entertainment and insight.

As someone who is interested in being different, not one of the sheep, I look realistically at the rewards that choice offers, but also the price that has to be paid.

Please visit www.alaskadp.com for links to the books.

Visit www.milesofalaska.com to find a bio of Miles, additional photos, stories, how-to videos, handmade artwork, and raw materials for sale.

Magazine and News Stories

Alaska Magazine

Alaska Magazine July 77—Survive by Miles Martin two pages, Photos. By Miles about my rescue, walk out on the Yukon River, five days at 50 below zero.

Nomadic House Boater Have Cabin Will Travel January 81—by Miles. Three pages, four color photos, a map. About life living on a houseboat, trapping and selling art (photo of my art), and all the adventures I have had on the river.

Would You Make A Good Bush Homesteader? June 86—by Miles four pages, six color pictures (One shows my custom knives.) A story I wrote about what it takes to be a homesteader.

Surviving The Big Lonesome— March 98—by Jim Rearden five pages, two color photos, one double page photo of Miles. Photos by world-famous photographer Jean Erick Pasquier. Describes life in the wilderness.

GEO Magazine

GEO in Germany is like "National Geographic" in the US.

Life in The Wilderness Alaska Special—87 by Miles Martin ten pages, sixteen color photos, a map

Photos by Jean Erick, one of the best photographers in the world, I Wrote it myself, winter life in the wilderness.

Alaska Special - 95 Einer gegen den Rest der Welt

Eight pages, seven color photos, three are double page. A follow up story to the first, written by New York Times reporter Ted Morgan, with Brigitte Helbing, photos by New York Times photographer Rex Rystedt. My fight for a lifestyle.

The New York Times

New York Times Magazine an insert to the paper, April 17, 1994, section six, The Vexing Adventures of the Last Alaskan Bushrat.

Six pages, four color photos, one is a double page Written by New York Times writer and bestselling author Ted Morgan. Photos by Rex Rystedt (World-renowned photographer). Facing twenty years in jail and a $10,000 fine for putting artwork on a bear claw and selling it.

Book-- A Shovel Full of Stars 95—Published by Simon and Schuster — New York

By Ted Morgan about ten pages with Miles. About one of the last homesteaders, and the lifestyle I live, of a Subsistence person.

Ruralite Magazine

Put out by Golden Valley 180,000 circulation

Wild Miles August 79, two pages, four black and white photos, Full cover page photo of Miles doing artwork. Story and photos by Margaret Van Cleve — Mostly about my artwork, some about my lifestyle on a houseboat

Newspaper, Daily Newsminer, Fairbanks Alaska

Associated Press, date unreadable, think a Thursday, and think spring of circa 74 **'Trapper rescued by Chopper**; Vows to Return to the Bush' headline, one column, National news, about my rescue after five days walking at 50 below.

Alaska Trapper Magazine

Put out by Alaska Trappers Association, a cover photo of me with Wolf. Five-page story by Miles comparing snowmachine and snowshoe trapping Nov. 99—four pages. Over the years, another six-seven articles on various trapping and related issues. Contact organization for exact issues.

Me in 1975.

OTHER TITLES AVAILABLE FROM ALASKA DREAMS PUBLISHING

Visit www.alaskadp.com to see these titles.

Books by Miles Martin:

- Going Wild
- Gone Wild
- Still Wild
- Beyond Wild
- Back To Wild
- Surviving Wild
- Secretly Wild
- Retiring Wild

Titles by other ADP authors:

- Rookie
- Alaska Freedom Brigade
- Apache Snow
- In Search of Honor
- A Coming Storm
- Arizona Rangers Series – Blake's War
- Legend of Silene
- Inspiring Special Needs Stories
- My Life In The Wilderness
- All Over The Road
- Ghost Cave Mountain
- Inside the Circle
- The Silver Horn of Robin Hood
- Alaskan Troll Eggs
- Through My Eyes
- The Professional Ghost Investigator
- The Adventures of Jason and Bo
- Seeds Of The Pirate Rebels

FOOT NOTES

CHAPTER 1

1. The main reason I went out into the wilds in the first place was to be alone, so as not to go off the cliff with the Lemming. Did I really escape by moving to the wilds?
2. Mass importation of craft items replacing local art is new, and was not prevalent in Alaska before the mid 80's. In the beginning, imported items were seen as cheap, inferior to our better quality, and 'made in Japan,' was a joke referring to cheap junk. But in later years it seems to me, American quality goes down as our prices go up, while import quality comes up, with prices staying low. Now there is serious competition!

CHAPTER 2

1. I use the terms 'future flash' and 'past flash' to separate then, now and later. Used in the entire series of books. The idea is from 'knock out fifties of the past, golden oldies" when talking of outdated songs we remember. We hear it, and get spun back into 'that time' filled with memories
2. I got to know my mother in years ahead after not being in touch many years. She told me all her life she believed love and happiness is the absence of pain. She was in her 60s before she understood differently. How much do we pick up from our parents and upbringing? Love may even be a romantic notion many dream of, but few truly achieve.

CHAPTER 10

1. In later years more fishing including commercial fishing is restricted, but it started out at the weakest link, the minority of subsistence users closest to the spawning grounds.

CHAPTER 12

1. Fifteen years from now, Fish and Game admits the fish numbers were not affected by subsistence fishing. As proven by the fact that after many years of shutting us down, the fish count drops even faster. The real issue had to do with overharvest on the ocean and maybe pollution, or global warming changes. But the politics would not allow placing restrictions on ocean or commercial fisherman. Since the blame had to be put someplace, and something had to be done, the subsistence fisherman were wrongly targeted. Subsistence people were convinced of this from the beginning. There is a verbal apology. Which is touching, but it is not made public.

www.ingramcontent.com/pod-product-compliance
Lightning Source LLC
Chambersburg PA
CBHW070326090426
42733CB00012B/2384